HANDBOOKS

D1510238

GUATEMALA

AL ARGUETA

GUATEMALA

MEXICO

Presa
Netzahualcóyotl

Río Grijalva

MEX 190

Comitán

Presa de la
Angostura

Ciudad
Cuauhtémoc

La Mesilla

TOJCUNENCHÉN

Todos Santos
Cuchumatán

CA 1

INTERAMERICANA

Volcán Tacaná
4,093m

Volcán
Tajumulco
4,220m

MEX 200

Río Suchiate

San Marcos

ZACULEU

Huehuetenango

Nebaj

Sacapulas

Sierra de los Cuchumatanes

Río Negro
(Río Chixoy)

Playa Grande
(Cantabal)

Sierra de Chamea

Cobán

CAJYUP

Puru

Salas

UTATLÁN
(K'UMARCAAJ)

Santa Cruz
del Quiché

Sierra de Chuacús

Tapachula

El Carmen

Quetzaltenango

Chichicastenango

Totonicapán

Joyabaj

MIXCO VIEJO

Ciudad
Tecún Umán

Ciudad Hidalgo

Volcán
Santa María

Lago de
Atitlán

Sololá

Panajachel

IXIMCHÉ

KAMINALJUYÚ

Guatemala
City

TAKALIK
ABAJ

CHUITINAMIT

Santiago
Atitlán

Antigua
Guatemala

Volcán de Agua

Tilapa

Retalhuleu

CA 2

Volcán
Atitlán

Amatitlán

Champerico

EL BAÚL/BILBAO

Escuintla

Cuilapa

Río Samalá

Santa Lucía
Cotzumalguapa

LA DEMOCRACIA
(MONTE ALTO)

Chiquimulilla

CARRETERA AL PACÍFICO

Río Madre Vieja

Sipacate

Puerto
San José

Iztapa

Monterr

Las Lis

PACIFIC OCEAN

El Naranjo

EL PERÚ

Río San Pedro

PIEDRAS
NEGRAS

Río Usumacinta

Sierra del Lacandón

YAXCHILÁN

Cooperativa
Bethel

DOS PILAS

0   10 mi

0   10 km

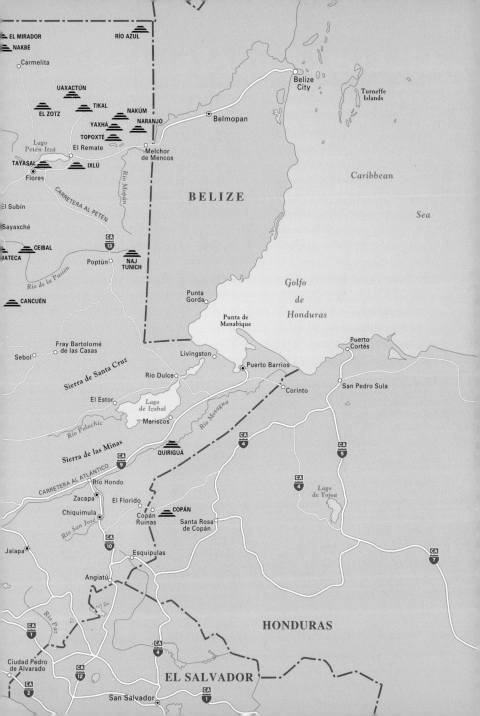

DISCOVER GUATEMALA

Guatemala has always been the stuff of legend.

For me this was evident early on. Guatemala represented an exotic land with a palpable sense of magic and the source of my family's origins – a land of rugged mountain trails, exotic jungle ruins, and fascinating Indian culture. I first visited Guatemala when I was three and was captivated by the country from the moment I set foot there. Some of my earliest memories are of mysterious Mayan Indians who giggled easily and carried baskets atop their heads while walking barefoot down dirt roads.

But there was always a dark side to the beauty, an underlying mystery to what was really happening in Guatemala. I was too young to understand what was going on, much less to conceive that Guatemala was embroiled in a full-fledged civil war.

But that's all in the past. The war ended more than 10 years ago thanks to a peace treaty, which, although not yet fully implemented, holds real potential for transforming the country. Change

villagers of San Juan Atitán in traditional costume

is in the air. This became clear to me during a recent visit. I flew into the tiny city of Flores, in northern Guatemala, on a recently added flight from Houston. My destination was exotic La Lancha, on the shores of Lake Petén Itzá, the third installment of movie director-cum-hotelier Francis Ford Coppola's brand of luxury jungle accommodations and a sure sign of northern Petén's untapped potential.

As mosquitoes busily nibbled at my ankles, my thoughts turned sympathetically to a ragtag group of renegades camping out somewhere in the Petén rainforest enduring much greater hardships for a crack at a million dollars. *Survivor* was being filmed here and I predicted that like other host locales for the popular TV show, Guatemala would soon see a tourism boom. Meanwhile, out on the tarmac, our brand-new, brightly lit Embraer jet shone like a neon sign announcing the imminent arrival of Guatemala on the international tourism scene.

keel-billed toucan

Forget everything you've ever read or heard about Guatemala, for this is a land that surprises and astounds. In his book *Guatemalan Journey*, Stephen Connelly Benz describes his own culture shock upon his return to the country in 1988 after a 10-year absence. He writes, "It was something of a shock to have made the long journey to a Third World country – one of the poorest in the hemisphere, according to the statistics I had seen – only to discover landscaped avenues and speeding BMWs." He adds, "What I learned that first weekend, or rather what I began to learn, was one of the important lessons of my sojourn: you cannot anticipate a place like Guatemala; it defies facile definition."

And that is the truth. It's hard to put your finger on the pulse of this mysterious land simply because there's so much going on here. What is clear is that there has never been a better time to discover this enchanting land of steaming lowland jungles, white-water rivers, misty mountains, coffee farms, colorful villages, black- or white-sand beaches, Mayan ruins, highland lakes, and colonial towns. From the chic cafés and high-rise hotels of Guatemala City to the mountain

Río Usumacinta

trails and quaint dirt-floor huts of the most remote Mayan village, Guatemala is a land of contrasts offering an incomparable palette of pleasures for any visitor.

One of my favorite things to do is to make the two-hour drive from Guatemala City to Lake Atitlán through the mountainous spine that crosses this part of the country. Guatemala's astounding landscape reveals itself as you wind your way through pine-studded hillsides tended by Mayan farmers much as they have been for centuries. The sense of otherworldly magic is utterly palpable. Just when you think the scenery couldn't possibly get any better, the road twists and turns sharply down a vertiginous hillside. You're quite suddenly confronted with a bird's-eye view of a shimmering sapphire-blue lake surrounded by mountains and three conical volcanoes shrouded in afternoon clouds. Rays of light peek through gaps in the clouds, painting the lake's surface with their luminescent beams. Equally inviting is indigenous Mayan culture found in the villages on the lake's shores, with their bustling markets and displays of lives lived in Technicolor.

near the village of Acul

Guatemala's allure has captivated its fair share of notable travelers. Author Aldous Huxley called Lake Atitlán "the most beautiful lake in the world." And in early 2007, President George W. Bush spent a day in the Guatemalan highlands visiting the relatively obscure villages of Santa Cruz Balanyá and Chirijuyú. Before a quick trip to the Mayan ruins of Iximché, he and the first lady were treated to a traditional Mayan dance performed by children. Bush later referred to his day trip through the Guatemalan countryside as "one of the great experiences of my presidency." It might be hard to believe that a visit to a pair of dusty Mayan villages and some centuries-old ruins might be so captivating to the leader of the free world, but I think I understand what he's talking about. Something about this place (and its people) just draws you in.

I invite you, in these pages, to discover a land that challenges you to uncover all that it has to offer. Then, take the next step and make the trip to Guatemala. My fellow Guatemalans and I welcome you with open arms.

Semuc Champey

Contents

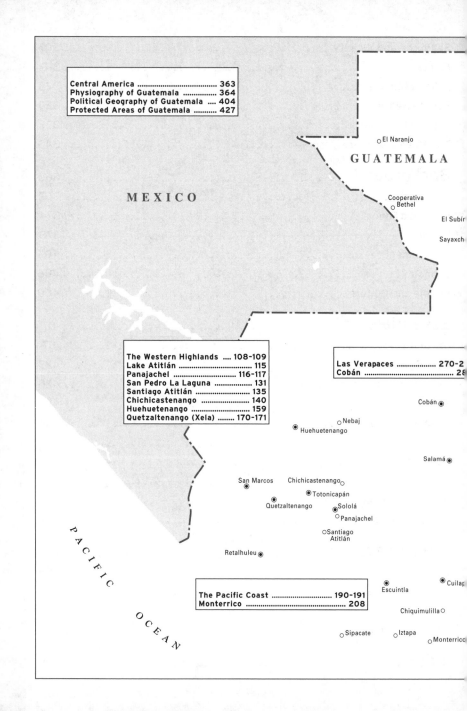

o El Naranjo

GUATEMALA

MEXICO

Cooperativa
o Bethel

El Subír

Sayaxch

Cobán ◉

o Nebaj
◉ Huehuetenango

Salamá ◉

San Marcos   Chichicastenango o
◉   ◉ Totonicapán
    ◉
Quetzaltenango ◉ Sololá
         o Panajachel

o Santiago
  Atitlán

Retalhuleu ◉

PACIFIC

◉   ◉ Cuilap
Escuintla

Chiquimulilla o

O C E A N

o Sipacate   o Iztapa
                o Monterrico

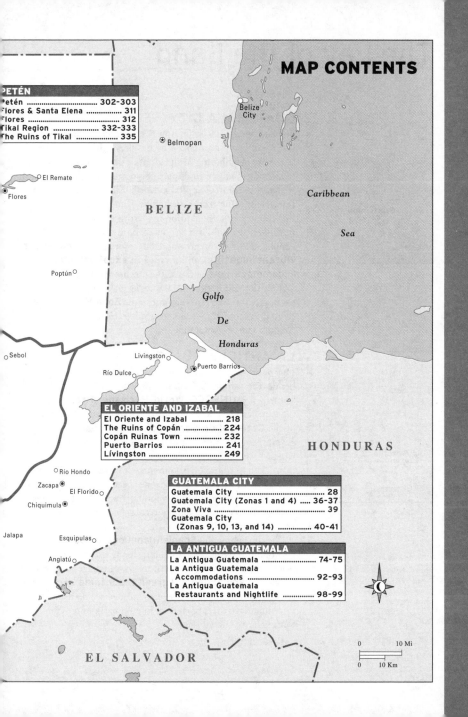

MAP CONTENTS

Belize City

⊛ Belmopan

El Remate

Flores

Caribbean

BELIZE

Sea

Poptún ○

Golfo

De

Honduras

○ Sebol

Livingston ○

Río Dulce ○

● Puerto Barrios

HONDURAS

○ Río Hondo

Zacapa ●

El Florido ○

Chiquimula ●

Jalapa

Esquipulas ○

Angiatú ○

EL SALVADOR

0   10 Mi

0   10 Km

The Lay of the Land

GUATEMALA CITY

The largest city in Central America, Guatemala City has a long history of being overlooked by travelers, who tend to make a beeline to neighboring Antigua. While other guidebooks might talk about the place in disparaging terms, my sincere opinion is that the country's capital is worth a look for the informed traveler wanting to get an honest glimpse into what makes this country tick. In addition to serving as the country's major transportation hub, it is also its economic and political center. Among its attractions are numerous recommended **museums, vibrant nightlife,** and a range of **excellent dining** and **accommodations** options. The downtown area is undergoing a promising restoration and is once again becoming a hip place to congregate. Closer to the airport, the **Zona Viva** is the place to go for nightlife, pleasant streetside cafés, and some of Latin America's finest restaurants.

LA ANTIGUA GUATEMALA

One of the former capitals of Guatemala (there have been three besides the current capital), La Antigua, as it's more commonly known, is a **UNESCO World Heritage Site.** It features Guatemala's loveliest town plaza, graced by the elegant facade of the **Catedral de Santiago** and the former colonial-era government buildings. Antigua harbors the ruins of the third-largest Latin American colonial capital, after Mexico City and Lima, with its collection of convents, churches, and monasteries. Along the city's pleasant cobblestone streets, you'll find a sublime assortment of restaurants, accommodations, and shops housed in beautiful old houses dating to colonial times and painted in an array of bright colors.

The city's numerous **Spanish-language schools** have been beckoning travelers for years and this is still one of the best places in Latin America to pick up the language. Enclosed in a valley by **volcanoes** and **green mountains** draped with coffee plantations, the city's surroundings are perfectly suited to outdoor activities, including hiking, mountain biking, and touring farms and villages.

THE WESTERN HIGHLANDS

The Western Highlands boast not only Central America's highest mountains and volcanoes, but also its most authentic and vibrant **indigenous culture.** You'll find colorful **Mayan markets,** quaint mountain villages, and gorgeous alpine scenery. Also in this region is spectacular **Lake Atitlán.** On its shores are three volcanoes and a dozen or so Mayan villages where you can take in the local culture or simply relax and unwind. From a junction near Lake Atitlán, the Pan-American Highway continues west to **Quetzaltenango,** Guatemala's second-largest city and an increasingly popular language-school destination. North of here, the department of El Quiché is home to Guatemala's most famous market at **Chichicastenango** as well as an emerging eco- and cultural tourism scene in the **Ixil Triangle.** The neighboring Huehuetenango department is crossed by the rugged **Sierra de los Cuchumatanes** with many a Mayan village and scenery that evokes the Peruvian Andes.

THE PACIFIC COAST

Guatemala's Pacific Coast has long been overlooked by travelers, though recent developments have begun reversing this trend. On the western end of the Pacific coast, the town of **Retalhuleu** has become a tourism hot spot and is home to Guatemala's single most popular tourist attraction, the twin theme parks of **Xocomil** and **Xetulul,** receiving well over a million visitors yearly. For **bird-watchers** and **nature lovers,** several private reserves in the area offer birding and hiking opportunities, including a fantastic lodge built on the ninth terrace of the Mayan site of **Takalik Abaj.** Heading east along the coast, you'll find the small village of **Sipacate,** home to Guatemala's **emerging surf scene,** and **Iztapa,** Guatemala's sailfishing capital. A road connects Iztapa to the once-sleepy fishing village of **Monterrico,** originally conceived as a turtle hatchery for endangered sea turtles but now also the Pacific coast's most popular resort town.

EL ORIENTE AND IZABAL

The dry plains of El Oriente are populated by Ladino cowboys and cattle ranchers. One of the region's main attractions lies just a few kilometers across the Honduran border to the east. At the world-class Mayan site of **Copán,** you can admire some of the Mayan world's finest stelae and one of its best on-site museums. Back on the Guatemalan side, the road continues east to Izabal and the Caribbean town of **Puerto Barrios,** the gateway for adventures into more **remote reaches** of the Guatemalan Caribbean coast, including untamed **Punta de Manabique,** the seaside Garífuna town of **Lívingston,** and the **Belize cayes.**

Across the Bahía de Amatique fronting Puerto Barrios, **Puerto Santo Tomás de Castilla** will soon house a cruise ship terminal. Across the forested mountain chain north of here, lovely **Río Dulce** connects **Lake Izabal,** the country's largest, with the Caribbean Sea.

LAS VERAPACES

Las Verapaces, comprising the departments of Alta and Baja Verapaz, are the green heartland of Guatemala. Here you'll find the country's best-preserved cloud forests in the **Sierra de las Minas Biosphere Reserve,** with excellent opportunities for getting off the beaten path. If you'd like to explore the cloud forests but aren't a hard-core naturalist, then the newly created **Cloudforest Biological Corridor** should suit you just fine. Including numerous jungle lodges and the **Biotopo Mario Dary Rivera,** the corridor runs along the road heading north to the town of **Cobán.** The latter enjoys a pleasant mountain setting amid green hills and coffee farms, making an excellent base for trips into northern Alta Verapaz. There you'll find the spectacular limestone pools of **Semuc Champey,** white-water rafting on the **Río Cahabón,** the Mayan site of **Cancuén,** the fantastic **Candelaria Caves,** and splendid **Laguna Lachuá.**

PETÉN

Petén is to Guatemala what the Amazon rainforest is to Brazil. In this **lowland jungle frontier,** you'll find the remains of several Mayan cities, with new ones being discovered via satellite imagery almost yearly. The best-known Mayan site is **Tikal,** a must-see for anyone with even a casual interest in the Mayan civilization. In addition to the impressive **temple pyramids,** Tikal is a refuge for varied wildlife in the protected forests surrounding the ruins. These extend for several miles into the larger **Maya Biosphere Reserve,** with Tikal being just one of several parks encompassing this vast protected area. Another Mayan site of note is **Yaxhá,** made famous in *Survivor Guatemala.* At the center of the department is the island city of **Flores,** on **Lake Petén Itzá,** a transportation and services hub that is now being rivaled by **El Remate,** on the shores of the same lake along the road to Tikal.

Planning Your Trip

Guatemala, the third-largest country in Central America, has an incredible variety of worthy attractions despite being roughly the size of Tennessee. You could spend months in Guatemala and not run out of options, though the average stay, according to tourism figures, is around a week. Whether you have a few days or a few weeks, there is plenty here to see and do depending on how much, or how little, you want to take in. It's easy to get around Guatemala by cheap public buses and by increasingly popular tourist shuttle minivans plying the more popular tourist routes. The main roads are in fairly decent shape, much better than roads in Costa Rica and Belize, for sure.

WHEN TO GO

Guatemala has two seasons, rainy and dry. A visit during each has its own distinct advantages. The **rainy season** usually begins at the end of May, with the summer months marking the early part of the rainy season, which is characterized by short afternoon or early evening showers that usually clear up by nighttime. By September or October, however, the weather is often socked in for days with rain and clouds. If you don't mind the rains, it makes a great time to visit, as foreign visitors are noticeably fewer during these two months and many hotels offer discounts in hopes of filling their rooms. Some parts of the country, most prominently the Caribbean coast, are rainy throughout most of the year.

The **dry season** runs from November to early May. December through February are the coldest months, with cold fronts from the north often making their way down to this neck of the woods, bringing temperatures into the mid-60s for daytime highs in mountain areas such as Antigua, Quetzaltenango, and Guatemala City. Things tend to warm up dramatically in March and April before the arrival of the first rains in mid-May. During this time, thick haze from heat, dust, and agricultural burning clouds the views of Guatemala's stunning mountain scenery, easily viewable during other months of the year.

The **high tourist season** in Guatemala runs from December to Holy Week (usually in April) with a second high season between mid-June and early September. Europeans on holiday are very much in evidence during this time, as are Salvadorans, for whom Guatemala is a favorite destination during their annual August vacations. **Language schools** in Quetzaltenango and Antigua are usually full with college students during the summer and rates go up accordingly. School lets out in Guatemala during the middle of October, with the local equivalent of summer vacation taking place until January. Families with children tend to take over many of the destinations popular with Guatemalan travelers and flights to Guatemala City are often full with the well to do (and their families) returning from a stateside shopping spree. My favorite time for a visit is between mid-May and mid-June, when the rains have usually arrived, greening up the scenery, and just before the summer high season.

WHAT TO TAKE

As a photographer, I often wish I could pack light, but I find this is usually not the case, as I invariably wind up kicking myself for not having packed some gizmo needed somewhere along the way. If you're like me, make sure you bring all your **photography supplies** to Guatemala, as it's extremely difficult to find necessary items. Professional slide film is available in only one place that I can think of in Guatemala City, though for digital shooters the city's shopping malls can probably supply most of your needs.

Getting to the basics, keep in mind that

Guatemala's huge variety of ecosystems also means you might find yourself changing clothes more often than a Milan runway model. It's a good idea to **dress in layers.** Pack a good assortment of short-sleeve T-shirts, sweaters and/or fleece, shorts, and pants. Shorts are perfectly acceptable in resort and beach towns, but not so much in Guatemala City or large urban areas, where people tend to dress up and the climate isn't really all that warm. I'm a big fan of synthetic fabrics that are quick-drying and can wick away moisture during strenuous hikes in the backcountry. Lightweight travel pants might be your new best friend, especially for trips to jungle areas where mosquitoes are usually a concern. Where mosquitoes are rampant, try sticking to lighter colors and bring lightweight shirts with long sleeves you can roll up. This will also keep you cooler under the rays of the hot tropical sun. Guatemala's mountainous areas can get downright cold, especially after it rains and the damp chill seems to permeate your very bones. Pack a light rain jacket and at least a sweater or two. Also pack plenty of sunscreen, bug spray, and don't forget a wide-brimmed hat or at least a ball cap.

If you plan on doing some **adventure hiking,** plan to bring everything you need, as rental equipment or that provided by local outfitters is usually not the greatest. These items include tents, sleeping pads, hammocks with mosquito netting, and sleeping bags. If you have one, it's always a good idea to bring along a water filter for those backcountry adventures. If you should need anything else, Guatemala City has at least one recommended outdoors shop. (See *Shopping* in that chapter for details.)

Footwear is an extremely important consideration. For serious jungle hiking, you'll want to bring high, military-style boots that you can wear in the mud and that will also protect you against snakebites. If you plan on white-water rafting or cave exploration, bring amphibious sandals with a good tread that you can wear on the boat or on slippery cave surfaces. If you plan on checking out the nightlife scene in Guatemala City, bring a good pair of dress shoes, as sneakers are verboten in the city's trendy nightclubs.

Finally, for visits to **remote highland villages** with large numbers of poor children, bring pencils, crayons, and other gifts to donate to local schools. You'll be surprised how something as simple as a writing instrument can bless a child. Packing photos of family and loved ones back home is also a great way to cross cultural barriers with friendly Guatemalans you'll meet along the way.

Explore Guatemala

THE BEST OF GUATEMALA

If you have only a few days to enjoy the best that Guatemala has to offer, the following itinerary will help you see as much as you can in a short amount of time without running you ragged. After all, it's a vacation.

Day 1

Fly in to Guatemala City around lunchtime. Take the afternoon to visit the **Archaeology Museum** or the **Museo Popol Vuh** and **Museo Ixchel** (next door to each other) for a crash course on the Mayan civilization. Enjoy dinner in one of Guatemala City's excellent restaurants.

Days 2-3

Take an early-morning flight out of Guatemala City to **Flores,** the gateway to the Mayan ruins of **Tikal,** in the northern Petén department. Tikal is the most famous of Guatemala's Mayan sites and boasts impressive temple pyramids. Spend all day exploring the ruins and enjoying the sublime jungle environment. You have the option of staying at the park and seeing the sunrise over the rainforest from the top of Temple IV or heading back south to **Lake Petén Itzá,** where you can stay at the ultrachic La Lancha. The lake, with its turquoise waters and tropical forest ecosystem, makes a good alternative to staying at the ruins. Fly back to Guatemala City on the afternoon of the second day. Upon arrival, grab a shuttle bus or taxi from the airport to **Antigua,** Guatemala's old colonial capital, and check in to any of the city's fine accommodations.

Days 4-5

Grab breakfast or coffee from any of the coffee shops along the plaza. Café Condesa makes a fine choice for breakfast. Take the suggested **walking tour** in the *Antigua* chapter, allowing you to see all of the major sights. Return to your comfortable hotel room for some chill-

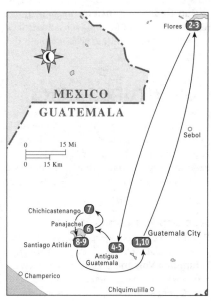

out time before heading out to dinner. On the second day, head out to **Finca Filadelfia** for breakfast and take a tour of the coffee farm. Lunch is at your leisure and you can also use the time to do some shopping. In the afternoon, head out with one of the groups making the **Pacaya Volcano climb** to see the lava light show. The trip returns late at night.

Days 6-7

Take a shuttle bus sometime around noon for **Panajachel,** on the shores of spectacular **Lake Atitlán.** You also have the option of continuing to nearby **Santa Catarina Palopó** or **Santa Cruz La Laguna** if Panajachel doesn't suit your style. The afternoon is yours to explore or simply relax. Plan on Day 7's being a Sunday or Thursday so you can grab a shuttle bus from Panajachel to Chichicastenango to see the colorful **Chichicastenango market**. Return to Panajachel in the afternoon.

Days 8-10

It's up to you. Head to the other side of the lake to **San Pedro** or **Santiago** for some more highland Mayan culture amid splendid settings or any of the other Mayan villages around the lake. You can also stay right where you are and do the other villages as day trips. This will give you time to really enjoy the lake, as the pace of your visit to Atitlán thus far will have been a bit hurried. Take a shuttle bus back to Guatemala City on the afternoon of Day 9 and check in to your hotel. Savor the culinary delights at another one of the city's excellent restaurants before packing your purchases for the flight home the next day and turning in for the night. Be sure to leave room in your carry-on for the excellent duty-free shopping at La Aurora Airport.

ADVENTURE HIKING

Guatemala's rugged mountains and jungle plains make for some extraordinary hiking opportunities for those wanting to get off the well-trodden path. Adding a human element to these hikes is the fact that many are guided by local Mayan people. You'll have the chance to stay in basic accommodations with Mayan families along the way, thus contributing directly to their economic well-being and greatly enhancing the cross-cultural experience.

Western Highlands

If you're up for the challenge of scaling Central America's highest volcano, then 4,220-meter **Tajumulco Volcano** is right up your alley. It's very close to the Mexican border and accessible from **Quetzaltenango,** where a few outfitters now make the challenging ascent with some regularity. From here it's also possible to hike east to **Lake Atitlán** via old mountain paths through cloud forests, grasslands, and river valleys, passing Mayan villages along the way. This hike requires three days and ends in the pleasant lakeside village of **San Pedro La Laguna.**

There are also several excellent treks leaving from the town of **Nebaj,** in El Quiché department's Ixil Triangle. Perhaps the most popular adventure hike from here is a three-day **Nebaj-Todos Santos trek** across the Cuchumatanes, where you'll encounter Andean scenery the likes of grassy plains strewn with rocky boulders in addition to Mam-speaking indigenous peoples herding sheep and llamas.

Other overnight hikes from Nebaj lead west to picturesque lagoons near an area known as **Las Majadas** or to the villages of **Xeo** and **Cotzal.** Many hikers favor this route for the chance to get up-close with the local culture in seldom-visited Mayan villages.

Las Verapaces

Some of the best hiking anywhere in Guatemala, and Central America for that matter, can be found in the **Sierra de las Minas Biosphere Reserve.** Several trails wind through this remote wilderness, allowing the opportunity to spot Guatemala's national bird, the quetzal, and explore its unique cloud forest habitat. Starting in the village of **San Rafael Chilascó,** hook up with the local community tourism cooperative for hikes to the nearby waterfall of **El Salto de Chilascó,** one of Central America's highest waterfalls. Longer, more challenging hikes take you up the mountain spine of **Lomo del Macho** and deep into the cloud forest to a research station at **Los Albores** and the **Peña del Ángel** rock formation.

Izabal

While plenty of folks, including cruise-ship day-trippers, check out the waterfalls of **Río Las Escobas,** the more adventurous among you can enjoy multiday treks from the adjoining **Cerro San Gil,** part of the **Montañas del Mico** chain. You'll trek deep into the heart of this forested mountain and make a steep descent to the banks of a jungle river on the other side. The trek heads across rainforest trails to the highest part of the mountain and a radio tower known as **Cumbre las Torres.** It continues to the jungle settlement of **Carboneras** before finally ending up along the **Río Dulce** on the other side of the mountain. The rainforest here is the real deal, receiving Guatemala's greatest amounts of yearly precipitation. Contact local conservation group FUNDAECO if you're up for the challenge.

Petén

There are many adventure hiking opportunities in the **Maya Biosphere Reserve,** the most hard-core being the two-day hike from the village of Carmelita to the ruins of **El Mirador** through knee-deep mud along swampy terrain surrounded by tropical forest. The rewards for the intrepid are well worth it, with the opportunity to explore the largest and highest pre-Columbian structures in the New World, the temple complexes of **El Tigre** and **La Danta,** with bases the size of three football fields. Other recommended treks include hiking from the ruins of **El Zotz to Tikal** and **Tikal to Yaxhá.** There are also good opportunities near the village of **Poptún,** in southern Petén, available through the excellent area jungle lodges. Poptún sits at a comfortably higher altitude than the rest of Petén and offers an interesting mix of ecosystems, including the mountain pine ridge (which extends into neighboring Belize). The presence of caves also characterizes this karst land area.

MAYANS PAST AND PRESENT

In Guatemala, not only can you see the ancient wonders of the Mayan civilization long before the arrival of the Spanish, but also the Postclassic highland ceremonial sites that greeted the conquistadors upon their arrival in 1524 and the modern-day villages harboring the descendants of these groups.

Preclassic and Classic Period Mayan Sites

You'll find most of the Mayan ceremonial sites that were at their cultural zenith during these time periods in the country's northern Petén region. Among the largest and most sophisticated cities from the Preclassic period is **El Mirador,** which flourished between 200 B.C. and A.D. 150. Numerous discoveries here have led archaeologists to reconsider their previous notions concerning the level of sophistication of the Preclassic Maya. No self-respecting archaeology buff would come to Guatemala without visiting the ruins of **Tikal,** at the center of a 575-square-kilometer (222-square-

mile) national park protecting the historical site and surrounding rainforest ecosystem. Farther north is the interesting astronomical observatory at **Uaxactún.** West of Tikal, after traversing dense rainforests, you'll come to the sites of **Nakum** and **Yaxhá,** the latter of *Survivor Guatemala* fame. Despite its TV celebrity, it's still possible to visit the site on a quiet afternoon and have its temple pyramids overlooking a placid lagoon all to yourself.

The island city of **Flores** makes a convenient base for these trips, particularly those heading to El Mirador, as many of the region's outfitters have their offices here. It also has grocery stores and a well-stocked outdoor market, which you'll need to hit up for supplies before heading out into the wilderness. Tikal is easily accessible via a paved road and frequent buses. From there, you can easily add a visit to Uaxactún, about 26 kilometers north along a rugged dirt road. Yaxhá and Nakum, east toward the Belize border, are best reached from the town of **El Remate,** on the shores of Lake Petén Itzá. Minivans have begun offering service to Yaxhá fairly regularly and at fair prices.

Highland Postclassic Mayan Sites

Real history buffs might want to check out the ceremonial sites found and subjugated by the Spanish at the time of the conquest, thus completing the picture of Guatemala's pre-Columbian archaeological heritage. When the Spanish arrived in Guatemala, they first secured an alliance with the Kaqchikel, who had their capital in **Iximché.** The Spanish would eventually establish their first capital on the same site. You can visit the restored ruins of Iximché, very conveniently situated just a few kilometers from the Pan-American Highway running west into the highlands and about an hour from Guatemala City.

With the submission of the Kaqchikels, the Spanish were now free to turn on the K'iche', whom they met in battle near present-day Quetzaltenango. The K'iche' invited the Spanish to their mountain fortress at **K'umarcaaj,** just outside present-day Santa Cruz del Quiché. A plan to trick the Spanish into coming into the city backfired and the K'iche' were massacred, with their rulers burned at the stake. Nowadays, you can visit the largely unrestored ruins, which are still the site of Mayan rituals and feature a noteworthy underground cave tunnel.

Near the city of Huehuetenango, the inhabitants of the Mam ceremonial site of **Zacu- leu** were done in by starvation after Pedro de Alvarado's brother laid siege to the city for two months. The ruins have been restored in a way that somewhat resembles what they might have looked like at the time of the conquest.

Northwest of Guatemala City 59 kilometers via a paved road, the ruins of **Mixco Viejo**

were once the Poqomam capital and ceremonial center, falling to Pedro de Alvarado in 1525 after a typically ruthless attack. In addition to temple pyramids, the site has two ball courts decorated with twin serpent sculptures harboring human skulls in their open mouths, a rather unusual embellishment among Postclassic highland sites and further evidence of the Toltec and Aztec influences of the times.

Modern-Day Mayan Villages

You can see the age-old customs of the Mayans' descendents in Guatemala's numerous villages. Perhaps the best introduction to Mayan culture is the K'iche' village of **Chichicastenango,** famous for its twice-weekly market on Thursdays and Sundays. Here you can also witness Mayan-Catholic syncretism in the whitewashed church or visit the idol of **Pascual Abaj,** on a hillside just outside of town where Mayans still perform religious rituals, including animal sacrifice. Chichicastenango is a popular day trip and shuttles leave from many of the main tourist towns (Antigua, Quetzaltenango, Panajachel, and Guatemala City) on market days. Continuing farther north into El Quiché department, about five hours from Guatemala City, are the splendid villages of the **Ixil Triangle:** Nebaj, Chajul, and Cotzal. Chajul in particular still conserves its traditional flavor and the weavings produced in all three villages are among Guatemala's finest. West across the Cuchumatanes chain is the traditional Mam village of **Todos Santos Cuchumatán,** famous for its annual November 1 horse races. You can hike from here to **San Juan Atitán,** another very traditional village. Todos Santos is most easily accessible from Huehuetenango via a paved road that heads up the mountain before turning into an all-season dirt road. San Juan Atitán is connected to the Pan-American Highway via a rough dirt road heading down the steep mountainside. The Huehuetenango department harbors many other traditional Mayan villages in its northern reaches, including **San Mateo Ixtatán,** with its church featuring a decidedly funky facade somewhat resembling a giant cake.

BIRD-WATCHER'S DELIGHT

Guatemala's wide diversity of ecosystems makes it a birding hot spot with more than 700 species of birds found here. You could easily center your entire Guatemala vacation around birding. Guatemala's best birding outfitter is Cayaya Birding (www.cayaya-birding.com).

Lake Atitlán and Vicinity

With its own private reserve on the southern slopes of Atitlán Volcano, **Finca Los Tarrales** harbors forests ranging in altitude from 750 to 2,500 meters (2,500 to 8,200 feet) that include broadleaf and cloud forests. Bird species are correspondingly diverse and include horned guan, long-tailed manakin, Pacific parakeet, orange-fronted parakeet, and several species of hummingbirds. West of Lake Atitlán near Retalhuleu, **Finca El Patrocinio** lies south of Santiaguito Volcano at an altitude between 750 and 850 meters. It is a good place for observing birds found in lowland and middle elevations. A substantial network of trails leads through protected patches of forest interspersed with coffee and macadamia plantations. Hawks, vultures, and falcons abound, as do parrots and woodpeckers.

Pacific Coast

On the Pacific Coast proper, the best places for birding are the vast **Manchón Guamuchal** wetlands and the canals and mangrove swamps bordering **Monterrico.** Species found in both parks include great egrets, roseate spoonbill, blue heron, and belted kingfisher.

Caribbean Coast

On the moist Caribbean coast, the **Cerro San Gil** harbors more than 350 species of birds, including the black and white hawk eagle and keel-billed motmot. More than 90 neotropical migrants, including the wood thrush and blue-winged warbler, winter in the area. Also with more than 300 bird species is the remote peninsula of **Punta de Manabique,** which is a transit and wintering area for 25 Nearctic shorebirds. Notable bird species include the yellow-headed parrot, great curassow, and several species of herons.

Cloud Forests of Las Verapaces

Birding is excellent in the **Sierra de las Minas Biosphere Reserve,** particularly if you want to see Guatemala's national symbol, the elusive quetzal. If you want to bird-watch in the cloud forest while keeping a comfortable base to come back to after a long day, consider a visit to **Chelemhá Cloud Forest Preserve,** with its wonderful **Chelemhá Cloud Forest Lodge.** The preserve lies at altitudes ranging from 2,000 to 2,500 meters (6,500 to 8,200 feet). Found within its forests are at least 14 bird species endemic to Central America's Northern Highlands. A total of 145 bird species have been recorded here to date.

Petén

In Petén, it's hard to beat **Tikal National Park.** You'll see oscillated turkeys along the forest floor as well as keel-billed toucans and Montezuma's Oropendola, among hundreds of other bird species, zipping about the forest canopy. The temple pyramids provide excellent vantage points for bird-watching. South of Tikal, on the shores of Lake Petén Itzá, **Cerro Cahuí** is also an excellent place for bird-watching with several waterbird species, including pied-billed grebe, herons, and northern jacana as well as the more typical rainforest birds such as toucans. Two trails wind their way through the forest with some excellent vantage points over the lake.

LIVING IT UP

If you're sick and tired of hotels that all pretty much look the same but like the opportunity to check out unique boutique hotels and jungle lodges near worthwhile attractions, then this itinerary is for you. If you're a movie star or just like to live like one, then this itinerary is for you. If you think zipping around the world to stay in chic hotels and then write about them is a dream job, then, again, this one's for you.

Guatemala has some of the hippest digs anywhere on the planet and I would happily fly down there just to spend a few nights at any of these properties. Equivalent accommodations elsewhere in the world would cost twice as much. You can find some of Latin America's best restaurants in Guatemala as well as shopping and museums that are quite simply fabulous. After all, Guatemala's wealthy elite need somewhere to spend their money—besides Miami.

Guatemala City

Try to fly in on one of the numerous flights getting in around lunchtime. Check in to either **Otelito** or the **Intercontinental,** two of the city's hippest haunts. George W. Bush and his entourage stayed at the Intercontinental during a visit in March 2007. Enjoy afternoon coffee at any one of the recommended Zona 10 cafés or take in one of the recommended museums showcasing elements of Mayan culture, including **Museo Ixchel** and **Museo Miraflores.** Enjoy a dinner of fusion cuisine at **Tamarindos** or **Jake's,** considered by *Travel and Leisure* magazine to be among the best restaurants in Latin America.

Spend an extra day and take a **downtown trolley tour** or go to Zona 1 on your own steam. After exploring the **Parque Central,** enjoy a drink in the newly refurbished downtown core or head to the **Cuatro Grados Norte** pedestrian thoroughfare in the up-and-coming Zona 4 warehouse district. Alternatively, you can see some more museums, shop for handicrafts, or spend the afternoon in a café. Have dinner at the fabulous **Portal del Ángel** in the hills on the outskirts of town overlooking the city; then head back to Zona 10 and enjoy a night out on the town in the **Zona Viva,** the aptly named lively part of town known for its nightlife. If you're staying at the Intercontinental, eat at least one meal at any of its excellent restaurants with elements of French and Japanese cuisine.

Antigua

Take a shuttle van or cab from Guatemala City. Check in to any of the city's fabulous boutique properties, including **Quinta Maconda** and **Casa Palopó,** a pair of elegant colonial houses converted into charming inns. Spend some time exploring the myriad shopping options, historical attractions, and excellent restaurants this town has to offer. Better yet, book a private shopping or historical tour with **Martha Hettich** or the folks at **Quinta Maconda.** If you don't want to walk, book a trolley tour. Check out Quinta Maconda's collection of Indonesian hardwood furniture, available by appointment only.

On your second day, head out to the nearby town of Jocotenango to visit **Filadelfia Coffee Resort and Spa,** a stately hotel property set on a working coffee farm. Take a coffee tour here or at the nearby all-in-one music/culture/coffee museum at **Centro Cultural La Azotea.** Back in Antigua, don't miss the wonderful museum in the ruins of the former monastery at **Casa Santo Domingo,** or better yet, spend the night there. Be sure to eat at least one meal at **Meson Panza Verde,** known for its Swiss-born chef's fantastic cooking. And if you want to come home with recipes for Guatemalan favorites that would make Emeril avocado-green with envy, check out **Antigua Cooking School.**

Lake Atitlán

Take a shuttle van from Antigua or Guatemala City to Panajachel, the largest of the dozen or so towns on the lake's shores. From there, take a cab to the quaint lakeside village of Santa Catarina Palopó, where you'll check in to fantastic **Casa Palopó** (on the cover of this book) overlooking the lake. You can also take a chopper from Guatemala City. Leave your cares behind and enjoy the excellent service, allowing plenty of time to watch the light change on the volcanoes or the wind dance across the lake throughout the day. If you've got the cash, rent out the entire **Villa Palopó,** higher up the hill, and have your private butler fetch you cocktails or anything your heart desires.

For the optional second day, book a trip across the lake to see the village(s) of your choice and get a different perspective. For a change of setting or a sudden attack of pocketbook conscience, stay at the also-lovely **Villa Sumaya,** near Santa Cruz La Laguna.

Pacific Coast

On the ninth terrace of Takalik Abaj, **Takalik Maya Lodge** gives you the option of staying in quaint jungle cottages painted with yellow and green frescoes or on a converted coffee farm house overlooking a swimming pool and a coffee-drying patio. Explore the ruins by tractor-pulled trailer from the lodge. If you want to see Guatemala's version of Disney World, check out the well-executed **Xocomil** and **Xetulul** theme parks and stay across the street in the excellent **Hostal Palajunoj,** where you can choose among African, Indonesian, Mayan, and Southeast Asian–style accommodations. Eat at **Restaurante Kapa Hapa** overlooking the swimming pools.

From here, head east to the beach at Mon-terrico and check in to the brand-new **Dos Mundos** resort, with cabanas featuring all the feel of an exclusive Mexican beach villa, or the modern but manageable **Kaimán Suites** along the road to Iztapa. Continue west to Iztapa for sportfishing based out of the **Salifish Bay Lodge** or just enjoy the atmosphere at this beautiful seaside resort.

Izabal

For the ultimate private getaway, head up the Río Tatín, a tributary of the Río Dulce, to **Rancho Corozal,** a sumptuous thatched-roof private villa beautifully furnished and decorated. Use the skiff to explore the surrounding jungle rivers or simply relax in the hammock lounge with a good book.

Petén

Fly up from Guatemala City with prior arrangements to have the friendly folks at Francis Ford Coppola's **La Lancha** pick you up. Enjoy the 45-minute ride from the airport to your lakeside resort. For activities, there are hikes to the nearby **Cerro Cahuí** forest preserve, fishing on the lake, shopping for wooden handicrafts in the village of **El Remate,** or simply lounging by the pool overlooking the turquoise lake waters and beautiful jungle. Take a day trip to **Tikal** and/or a half-day trip to **Parque Natural Ixpanpajul** to walk along a series of hanging bridges in the forest canopy. As a further option, do as Mel Gibson did and take a chopper up to the remote ruins of **El Mirador,** deep in the jungles to the north near the Mexican border. It sure beats walking through knee-deep mud for two days from the nearest village.

GUATEMALA CITY

The largest city in Central America, with an estimated metro area population of about four million, Guatemala City spreads across a large valley scarred with ravines into which it extends, fingerlike, surrounded by mountains and smoking volcanoes. For most visitors to Guatemala, this is their first glimpse of the country and it can be a very welcoming one. Flying into Guatemala City's La Aurora International Airport on a clear day is a most breathtaking experience. The airplane descends over forested green mountains as clouds part to reveal the sprawling metropolis below. It makes a sharp bank at the edge of the valley just before making its final approach, flying uncomfortably close to the rooftops of dwellings perched precariously on the edge of a deep gulley. At once, the runway rises to greet the plane from out of

nowhere. The aircraft bounces with the initial touchdown before coming to a screeching, abrupt halt on the short, high-altitude field.

Guatemala City is a city on the move. You'll find its newly remodeled airport modern and attractive, befitting of the largest urban agglomeration between Mexico City and Medellín, Colombia. As one well-heeled Guatemalan businessman pointed out to me upon arrival recently, the country has one of the highest per capita ownerships of private aircraft in the Americas. Many first-time visitors express astonishment at the city's degree of modernity, the high concentration of high-rise condominiums and late-model BMWs cruising down its tree-lined boulevards. Indeed, Guatemala is also a top importer of luxury automobiles. The city center, long avoided by locals, is also

© AL ARGUETA

HIGHLIGHTS

C Palacio Nacional de la Cultura: At the heart of downtown Guatemala City is this former presidential palace-turned-museum worth a look for a fascinating glimpse into the country's rich history (page 32).

C Zona Viva: Guatemala City's most cosmopolitan sector, while offering some of the city's best hotels, is also a fun place to eat out and enjoy a night on the town (page 39).

C Museo Ixchel: The city's finest museum is a wonderful tribute to Mayan culture and to Guatemala's famous textiles and traditional village attire (page 42).

C Museo Miraflores: This excellent museum is dedicated to the ancient Mayan site of Kaminaljuyú, which occupied the valley in which Guatemala City now stands. Several of the site's temple mounds lie nearby (page 42).

C Museo Nacional de Arqueología y Etnología: Before or after visiting Guatemala's fascinating Mayan sites, head to this museum to admire many of the original pieces once found there, including beautifully carved monuments and brilliant jade masks (page 43).

C Pacaya Volcano National Park: Get up close and personal with brilliant lava flows at this impressive active volcano over-

looking the city and nearby Lake Amatitlán (page 70).

LOOK FOR **C** TO FIND RECOMMENDED SIGHTS, ACTIVITIES, DINING, AND LODGING.

making a comeback and it is the focus of an ambitious restoration project aimed at bringing back its former glory. Hip and trendy new cafés are springing up throughout this part of town and people are starting to come back for an afternoon of fun in the downtown area, something that seemed completely implausible just a few years ago. The construction of loft apartments is also bringing a whole new demographic to a part of town once left to decay.

To make a long story short, it should be expected that a country of such great wealth (though badly distributed) should have a modern capital with all the First World comforts one would expect to find there. Like everything else in Guatemala, it all coexists side by side with some of the uglier realities. It's all there for you to see, and nowhere else in the country is this striking contrast of wealth and poverty so evident. Look at a visit to Guatemala City as a lesson in history and politics and a worthy introduction to a fascinating country of contrasts with some unexpected surprises around every corner.

PLANNING YOUR TIME

Upon international arrival into Guatemala, most travelers eager to make their way to the country's fascinating interior head straight to

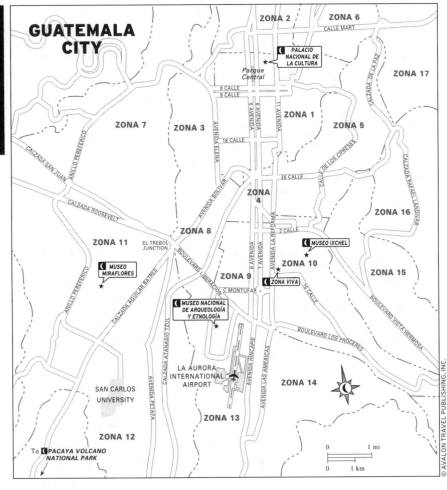

Antigua Guatemala, taking a shuttle bus from the airport and bypassing Guatemala City altogether. Whether at the beginning or end of your trip, a visit to the country's capital is crucial to understanding what makes this country tick. It is certainly worth spending some time here and it can be an extremely rewarding destination after weeks spent in the countryside, offering fine restaurants, excellent museums, and all the comforts that a modern capital city has to offer. Guatemala City is also the country's transportation and business hub, so if you are trying to get around the country or are in Guatemala on business, you will find yourself on its streets sooner or later.

Most of the major attractions can be seen in a day or two. If you have more than two days to spend in Guatemala City, you might consider staying in Antigua to make better use of your time. Exceptions to this would be those in town for business looking for things to do after hours without taking a trip out of the city. Zona

10, conveniently near the airport, has some fine hotels and is home to a number of highly recommended museums. It is also the city's most attractive commercial and financial district. A day strolling down pleasant Avenida La Reforma and sampling the Zona Viva's cafés, bars, nightclubs, and restaurants is a great way to cap off your visit to Guatemala.

HISTORY

Guatemala City is in fact the fourth capital of Guatemala, the other three having been destroyed by natural disasters, including earthquakes and mudslides, or having been replaced by the establishment of Spanish-modeled urban centers, as in the case of the first highland capital Iximché. Like Iximché, the land now occupied by the modern-day urban center was once the site of a Mayan city that exercised considerable influence over trade routes for obsidian during Classic Mayan times thanks to an alliance with the Central Mexican powerhouse of Teotihuacán. Kaminaljuyú, as the city was called, was first settled sometime around 400 B.C. The early foundational cultures preceding the Mayan city established agriculture in the valley now occupied by Guatemala City and settled much of it, mostly in the western part of the valley. As with the other Classic Mayan sites, Kaminaljuyú was just a distant memory by the time the Spanish arrived on the scene in the 16th century.

The city's modern settlement dates to 1776, in the aftermath of the 1773 earthquakes of Santa Marta, which rocked the previous capital, now known as La Antigua Guatemala (The Old Guatemala, or "La Antigua" for short). Debate over whether or not to rebuild La Antigua raged on for a few years, but in the end it was decided to start all over again in the neighboring Valle de la Ermita (Valley of the Hermitage), as the valley was known. An edict by Governor Martín Mayorga made the move official. It took a while for the new capital to catch on, as many Antigua residents refused to move despite Spanish decrees ordering the settlement of the new city. In 1800, the population of Guatemala City was only 25,000. The new city was laid out in a grid pattern,

much like every other town established by the Spanish, with the construction of major public buildings including the Catedral Metropolitana (cathedral), Cabildo (Town Hall), and Palacio de los Capitanes Generales. Of these, only the cathedral remains standing.

In addition to resistance from Antigueños (residents of Antigua), the city's growth would be stifled by competition from the large highland urban center of Quetzaltenango. Indeed, it even threatened at one time to secede from Guatemala and become the capital of a new territory known as "Los Altos." In the end, however, nature took care of its secessionist dreams by dealing the city a massive blow with a 1902 earthquake that left it in ruins. Though it would be reconstructed, many of the city's wealthy elite opted to move to Guatemala City. The new capital would also experience its own series of destructive earthquakes in December 1917, lasting into February of the following year. By this time, it seems, the population had come to terms with the fact that its city was built upon one of the world's most active fault lines. The fault line would again create widespread havoc with another earthquake in 1976. Ironically, the earthquake triggered widescale migration into the city, resulting in the establishment of many slums lining the city's numerous ravines, or *barrancos.*

The city grew tremendously throughout the 20th century, spreading from its original core (now known as the Centro Histórico) and spilling out into the surrounding barrancos and up into the mountains lining the western and eastern edges of the valley. Much of the country's industry is concentrated here, fueling economic migration from other parts of the country. The population of Guatemala City's metro area now reaches at least three million.

CLIMATE

Guatemala City enjoys a delightful climate almost year-round. Its location in a valley at an altitude of 1,493 meters (4,897 feet) above sea level ensures that it never gets excessively warm, as do some other, low-lying Central American capitals. This pleasant climate has earned it the nickname "Land of Eternal Spring." It should be noted, however, that the nickname was coined during a long-gone era before the city's exponential growth, which has given rise to urban microclimates such as the urban heat island. The latter is caused when the direct tropical sun heats large expanses of pavement, which in turn heat the surrounding air masses, causing a phenomenon not unlike a large convection oven. The truth is that it can get somewhat hot here during April and May, what locals generally call *verano,* or summer, with daytime highs in the mid- to upper 80s. Longtime residents frequently remark about the increasingly warm summers, which they say have become much warmer than what was once typical. This is also the driest time of year and the surrounding mountains can turn some rather parched shades of brown. Thermal inversions causing extreme haze are also quite typical this time of year, making Guatemala City look somewhat like a smaller version of Los Angeles. These occur frequently in valleys when a layer of warm air settles over a layer of cooler air lying close to the ground, holding this cooler air down and preventing pollutants from rising and scattering.

Between June and August, after the arrival of the rainy season, mornings are typically sunny and warm, giving way to increasing cloudiness and afternoon showers almost every day. September and October are increasingly rainy with entire stretches of cloudy or rainy days. In November the skies clear and become increasingly windy. Many people equate this time of year with kite flying, and indeed the giant kite festival in the nearby towns of Sumpango and Sacatepéquez take place on the first of the month. December through February can be chilly here and elsewhere in mountainous parts of Guatemala with the arrival from the north of frequent cold fronts coinciding with the northern hemisphere's winter season. Bring some warm clothes if you're traveling to Guatemala City or elsewhere in the highlands during this time of year, as concrete houses with tile floors are the most popular form of architecture and aren't typically heated or carpeted, making it feel even colder.

ORIENTATION

Guatemala City is divided into 21 *zonas,* or zones, purely for administrative purposes. Of these only a small number are really of any interest to visitors. These include the downtown areas encompassing Zonas 1 and 2 as well as newer sections of the city with high concentrations of restaurants and hotels in Zonas 4, 9, 10, and 11. The international airport is in Zona 13. Zonas 14, 15, and 16 are also attractive and are home to many of Guatemala's wealthy elite. You'll find several hotels, restaurants, and shopping malls in these areas. The wealthiest part of town can be found in the hillsides east of the city along the road climbing out of the valley, known as the highway to El Salvador. This area is commonly referred to as Carretera a El Salvador, and it has grown substantially in recent years. The downtown core (Zona 1) is also referred to as **El Centro Histórico** and occupies the northern part of the city. Zonas 13 and 14 are on its southern fringes, while Zona 11 lies west toward Antigua. Zona 10 lies in the eastern sector.

Pay special attention when looking for street addresses, as the same street and house number can exist in more than one zone. Addresses usually begin with an avenue, or *avenida,* followed by a number with a dash. A typical street address would be something like: 7a Avenida 8-34 Zona 10. In this case, the "8" corresponds to the intersecting street number, or *calle.* The number after the dash is the house number. So the above address would be house number 34 on the eighth block along 7th Avenue of Zona 10.

SAFETY

Guatemala City can be a rough place, though certain *zonas* are certainly safer than others. Most of the areas frequented by tourists are relatively safe, though the downtown area is considerably less safe than Zonas 10 and 14 and purse snatching and pickpocketing are serious problems. Exercise common sense and caution when in public areas. Riding public buses is not usually a good idea, though the newly unveiled transit system, the Transmetro, might prove safer. It is certainly more efficient. Pay careful attention when using ATMs. Some thieves have been so ingenious as to set up keypads at the entrance to ATM kiosks asking cardholders to enter their PIN numbers in order to gain access to the machine. You should never enter your PIN number anywhere other than on the ATM keypad itself.

Watch out for another common scam, particularly in the vicinity of the airport, whereby a "Good Samaritan" informs you of a flat tire on your car. If that is indeed the case, pull over in a well-lit, public place if you can but do not stop in the middle of the road to change the tire. He may try to carjack you. If you are able to make it to a public place such as a gas station, have someone in your party stay inside the car or keep an eye on it yourself while you have someone change the tire for you (it's common for gas station attendants to change tires in Guatemala). The im-portant thing is not to lose sight of the inside of your vehicle for a moment. Thieves can be extremely crafty at distracting you and getting into your car while you take care of the urgent business at hand. Locked doors may be a deterrent but are not going to stop the thieves if they've targeted you. For information on other precautions and common scams to watch out for while traveling in Guatemala, see the State Department's Consular Information Sheet online at http://travel.state.gov/travel/cis_pa_tw/cis/cis_1129.html.

Plans were to install INGUAT (Guatemala Tourist Commission) kiosks staffed with police officers in strategic points of the city frequented by tourists. These included four kiosks in Zona 10's Zona Viva commercial district, one along Avenida La Reforma in Zona 9, and another kiosk along the road into town from the international airport.

Sights

Sights will be listed by city zone, the official format for divvying up the city's land area. Most of the city's historic sites are found within the Centro Histórico. Some of the nicer museums are found near the airport in Zona 13 and in the Miraflores area west of the city center in Zona 11.

CENTRO HISTÓRICO

The original core of Guatemala City, dating to its foundation, is composed of 1a to 17 Calle and 1a to 12 Avenida, known today as the Centro Histórico. Most of the architecture is neoclassical, a sharp departure from the baroque architecture found in the previous capital of Antigua Guatemala. Few of the original buildings remain, having largely been destroyed by earthquakes in 1917 and 1976 or modified with the passing of time. Yet some excellent examples of the original architecture can still be found and there is an ongoing campaign to restore several historic buildings in the downtown core. This program, known as RenaCENTRO, is a collaboration between several entities, including the local municipality, INGUAT, the private sector, and Argentinean, Spanish, and French cooperation.

Guatemala City was once nicknamed "The Silver Teacup" for its urban Spanish Renaissance design and architecture, including elegant theaters, large colonial mansions, broad avenues, imposing churches, and charming side streets. Although its aesthetics are badly deteriorated, they are not beyond rescue and this is precisely RenaCentro's mission via a multifaceted, holistic approach to restoring the grandeur of Guatemala's colonial-era capital. The restoration inexorably hinges upon local economic reactivation. The area adjoining the central park along 8a Calle and the Portal del Comercio was being spruced up as a new pedestrian thoroughfare. Plans also call for the expansion of nearby Parque Centenario in addition to the widening of sidewalks and general cleanup of 6a Avenida between 8a and 9a Calles and along 9a Calle parallel to the central plaza. Things are starting to come around, as evidenced by the numerous new cafés opening on downtown streets. Given Guatemala's huge tourism potential, it seems only fitting that its capital would become a welcome stop along the visitor's path, though this has not been the case up until now.

Parque Central

In typical Spanish colonial fashion, the city was laid out around a central plaza with the Catholic church and government buildings surrounding it. It is also known as the Plaza de la Constitución. The central park encompasses a large area between 6a and 7a Avenidas and 6a and 8a Calles. Alongside it are the Palacio Nacional de la Cultura, Catedral Metropolitana, and Portal del Comercio. The park is usually abuzz with shoe shiners and folks enjoying a stroll through its grounds, now largely composed of concrete blocks with little greenery after being remodeled in the mid-1980s to include an underground parking lot. A large Guatemalan flag dominates the plaza near a small, sadly neglected monument to the 1996 peace accords; it consists of a glass case enclosing a flame which has long since burned out.

🔇 Palacio Nacional de la Cultura

Boston's Fenway Park has its Green Monster and so does Guatemala City. The former presidential palace, built between 1939 and 1943 during the time of maniacal dictator Jorge Ubico, is a large, green stone structure with elements of colonial and neoclassical architecture. With most of Guatemala's presidents preferring to live in other parts of the city, it has not housed a president during a term in office since the early 1990's.

The palace is one of Guatemala City's most interesting attractions, as it affords the visitor a glimpse into Guatemala's colonial and dictatorial legacy. After all, Guatemala City was once the capital of the entire Central American isthmus and nowhere else in the region were colonial institutions so embedded in the national fiber. Similarly, Guate-

mala's *caudillos* (military strongmen) needed a residence befitting their status as rulers of a quasifeudal kingdom, to which end the palace served them quite well. The 1996 peace accords were signed here and it was subsequently converted into a museum (tel. 2253-0748, 8 A.M.–3 P.M. daily, free). Today it is also used to host visiting dignitaries, most recently President George W. Bush during a visit in March 2007.

You can take a free guided tour of the palace (though it's always a good idea to tip) where you can admire the architecture including some Moorish courtyards and frescoed arches made of carved stone as well as artwork by several Guatemalan artists of the 1940s. As you climb the wood-and-brass main stairway, you can admire a mural by Alredo Gálvez Suárez depicting a romanticized take on Guatemalan history. Stained-glass windows by Julio Urruela Vásquez and Roberto González Goyri can be found in the second-floor banquet hall adorning Ubico's palace, depicting the virtues of good government in an ironic twist typical of the strongman immortalized in Nobel Prize winner Miguel Angel Asturias's *El Señor Presidente.* You might also be able to see the presidential balcony, which overlooks the plaza in classic dictatorial fashion.

A more modern-day attraction is the Patio de la Paz, where a stone sculpture of two hands commemorates the 1996 signing of the peace accords. A white rose held in the outstretched hands is changed at 11 A.M. daily by the palace guards or, on special occasions, by visiting dignitaries.

Catedral Metropolitana

The construction of Guatemala City's neoclassical cathedral (7a Avenida facing the plaza, 6 A.M.–noon and 2–7 P.M.) began in 1782 and was completed in 1815, though the bell towers would not be completed until 1867. It has survived two earthquakes, a testament to its sturdy construction, though it isn't exactly the prettiest of Guatemala's churches. The pillars on the church's facade are adorned with the

© NATHAN GOLDEN

Catedral Metropolitana

names of many of Guatemala's disappeared, etched into the stone as a testament to the desire for justice, whether in this lifetime or the next. Inside, many of the altars and paintings adorning the church were brought here forcefully when the capital, along with its institutions, was officially moved to its current site from Antigua. The standout is the image of the Virgen del Perpetuo Socorro, Guatemala's oldest, brought into the country by Pedro de Alvarado in 1524.

Parque Centenario

Adjoining the larger central plaza, to the west, is the smaller Parque Centenario, with the Biblioteca Nacional (National Library) and Archivo General de Centroamérica (National Archive) bordering it. It occupies the former site of the Palacio Centenario, built to commemorate 100 years of independence from Spain. It briefly housed the National Congress, whose building was burnt to the ground in 1927. Its most interesting feature is a small acoustic shell amphitheater.

Mercado Central

Behind the cathedral is the city's central market (8a Avenida and 6a Calle, 6 A.M.–6 P.M. Mon.–Sat., 9 A.M.–noon Sun.). The basement harbors produce, while the top two floors have a varied assortment of textiles, leather goods, and various handicrafts. It's a bit dark and bunkerlike, with the stalls packed to the ceiling with all kinds of goodies. It's a bit overwhelming. The current market replaced the one destroyed by the 1976 earthquake. Be wary of pickpockets here.

Museums

One block east of the market and one block south on 10a Avenida is the **Museo Nacional de Historia** (9a Calle 9-70 Zona 1, tel. 2253-6149, 9 A.M.–4:30 P.M. Mon.–Fri., $1.50) with historical documents, clothing, and paintings. Among the more interesting exhibits are some photographs by Eadweard Muybridge, who visited and photographed the country in 1875. The museum is housed in a very attractive colonial building.

An excellent newer addition to Guatemala City's list of museums is the **Museo del Ferrocarril** (in front of the intersection of 9a Avenida and 20 Calle, tel. 2232-9270, ferroguat@hotmail.com, 9 A.M.–5 P.M. Tues.–Fri., 10 A.M.–5 P.M. Sat./Sun., free), housed in a refurbished building that was once the city's train station. The state-run railways, known then as FEGUA, were privatized during the Arzú administration. Among the attractions are several steam engines, train cars, and exhibits of train paraphernalia, including some wonderful old photographs. Some fantastic classic cars are also on display here.

Churches

Several of the city's downtown churches have been restored in recent years and might be worth a stop to admire their noteworthy architecture. Construction on **Iglesia de San Francisco** (6a Avenida and 13 Calle Zona 1, 7 A.M.–noon and 2–7 P.M.) began in 1800 and wasn't completed until 1851. Outside, it looks charmingly worn down by the elements and is a light gray. Inside are 18 altars of impressive quality. Another beautiful church is that of **Iglesia Santo Domingo** (12 Avenida and 10a Calle), constructed between 1792 and 1808. In addition to its attractive architecture, it is known for its paintings, including one depicting the apparition of the Virgin Mary to Santo Domingo de Guzmán, after whom the capital of the Dominican Republic is named. (It is believed he received the rosary from her.) **El Cerrito del Carmen** (12 Avenida and 2a Calle Zona 1, 7 A.M.–noon and 2–6 P.M.) denominates both the name of this hermitage and the hill on which it rests, with wonderful views of the downtown area. It dates to 1620 and is known for its image of a virgin of the same name embossed in silver, a gift from Carmelite nuns in the 17th century. Oil paintings by Tomás de Merlo adorn the inside of **Iglesia San Miguel de Capuchinas** (10 Avenida 10-51 Zona 1, 6 A.M.–noon and 2–7 P.M.), with its transitional baroque-neoclassical architecture.

6a and 7a Avenidas

The heart of Guatemala City was traditionally the strip along 6a Avenida, or as locals refer to it, "La Sexta." Today, it's a busy commercial district, its sidewalks crammed with informal vendors and streets filled with noisy traffic. Some fine examples of architecture sit along this historic street, though you'd never know it because most of it is covered by a profusion of street signs and commercial advertising. The street is closed to all but pedestrian traffic on weekends. It's not the safest part of town for a stroll, so be extra careful if you do venture out this way, as it's rife with pickpockets and assorted other riffraff.

Paralleling 6a Avenida is 7a Avenida, with a variety of architectural highlights. Among these is the splendid **Palacio de Correos** (Central Post Office, 8:30 A.M.–5 P.M. Mon.–Fri., 8:30 A.M.–1 P.M. Sat.), at the corner of 7a Avenida and 12 Calle, featuring a large archway that reaches over to the building across the street. Also attractive is the nearby **Tipografía Nacional** (National Printing Press), at the corner of 7a Avenida and 18 Calle. It dates to 1894 and somewhat resembles a gingerbread house. Nearby is **Casa Mima** (8a Avenida 14-12 Zona 1, tel. 2253-4020, 9 A.M.–12:30 P.M. and 2–6 P.M. Mon.–Fri., 9 A.M.–5 P.M. Sat., $2.50), offering a fascinating peek into the lives of Guatemala's upper middle class. The splendidly restored 19th-century town house is furnished in art deco, Victorian and French neorococo styles. A quaint café on the back patio serves coffee and pastries. English-speaking guides are sometimes available to show you around.

Both 6a and 7a Avenidas continue their straight-on course southward through Zonas 4 and 9 before ending at a series of archways marking the northern extreme of the international airport's runway.

ZONA 2
Parque Minerva

As you head north along 6a Avenida and then Avenida Simeón Cañas, it's about 1.5 kilometers from the city center to Parque Minerva in the adjoing Zona 2 sector. The park here has some sporting facilities, including the **Estadio Nacional de Béisbol** (National Baseball Stadium), where there are games on weekends. Its informal atmosphere is a bit like that of old-time minor league parks in the U.S. Midwest. Baseball is nowhere near as popular in Guatemala as in other parts of Central America, namely Nicaragua, but if you're a fan of the game you might want to stop and check it out.

The park's main attraction, however, is also one of Guatemala's most unusual. The 2,000-square-meter **Mapa en Relieve** (Relief Map, 9 A.M.–5 P.M. daily, $2), is built to 1:10,000 scale and was created in 1905, well before the invention of Google Earth. It gives you a good idea of the country's mountain topography and the contrasting flatness of Petén and neighboring Belize, which, of course, is included as part of Guatemala in accord with the long-standing border dispute. The scale of the mountains is somewhat exaggerated, with the volcanoes and peaks looking steep and pointy. There are observation towers from which you can get a better vantage point. The rivers and lakes are sometimes filled with water from built-in taps, making for an even more authentic experience. It makes a good stop if you're in Guatemala City before heading out to the interior and want to get a feel for the country's unique geography.

ZONA 4

A revitalization program has given Zona 4 a distinct character in recent years with the establishment of a pedestrian thoroughfare known as 4 Grados Norte, lined with hip sidewalk cafés and restaurants during the day, doubling as bars at night. This warehouse district promises to grow in the next few years, as more and more places are being refurbished. The thoroughfare even has its own cultural center. The **Centro Cultural de España** (Vía 5 1-23 Zona 4, 4 Grados Norte, tel. 2385-9066/7, www.centroculturalespana.com.gt, 9:30 A.M.–1 P.M. and 2–7 P.M. Tues.–Thurs., 10 A.M.–7 P.M. Sat.) shows movies on Tuesday and Friday nights, hosts workshops and art exhibits, and has a small library. Zona 4's

other main attraction is a dilapidated bus terminal for second-class buses, though this was expected to fall into disuse with the municipal government's plans to move all bus traffic out of the city.

Centro Cívico

As you head south from the downtown sectors of Zonas 1 and 2, you'll come to a transitional area between the old city core and some of the newer parts of town. Some guidebooks refer to the latter as the "new city," which to the best of my knowledge has never been used by locals to describe their city layout. As the city spread south from the central area, urban planners and architects decided to build around a concept of a civic center to house some of the more important government buildings. Thus was born the Centro Cívico. Today it houses Guatemala's **Corte Suprema de Justicia** (Supreme Court), **Banco de Guatemala** (Bank of Guatemala), **Municipalidad de Guatemala** (City Hall), and the administrative offices of the **Guatemala Tourist Commission** (7a Avenida 1-17 Zona 4, 8 A.M.–4 P.M. Mon.–Fri.). There's the occasional exhibit in the lobby and you can get some tourist information, including maps, but you're probably better off picking these up at the information kiosks at the international airport.

Centro Cultural Miguel Angel Asturias

Inaugurated in 1968 and named after Guatemala's Nobel Prize–winning author, the capital's national theater is built on a hill once harboring the fort of San José de Buena Vista, destroyed by artillery fire during the October Revolution of 1944. It consists of a **Gran Sala** (Great Theater) with a seating capacity of 2,041, an outdoor amphitheater seating 2,500, the 320-seat **Teatro de Cámara** (Chamber Theater), and several smaller venues. It has some interesting architecture designed by architect Efrín Recinos, and its hilltop location overlooking the rest of the civic center gives it an air of grandeur. The center still hosts frequent events, including ballet and theater

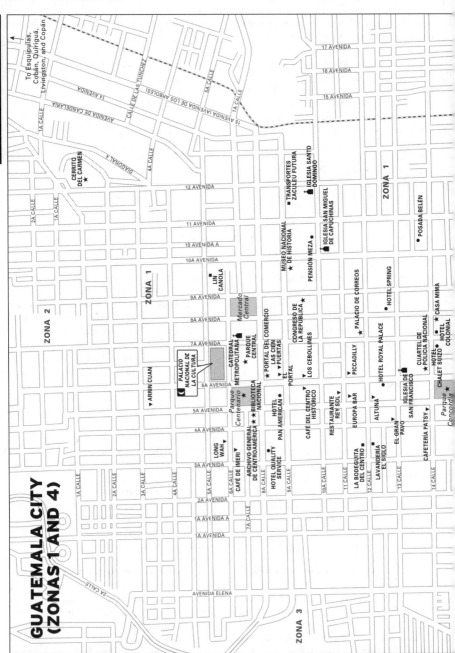

GUATEMALA CITY (ZONAS 1 AND 4)

GUATEMALA CITY

© AVALON TRAVEL PUBLISHING, INC.

productions. Check local listings for more information (or see the *Entertainment* section).

Iglesia Yurrita

This pretty rose-colored neo-Gothic chapel with ornate decor inside and out is one of Guatemala City's more offbeat tourist attractions. It was commissioned by don Felipe Yurrita Castañeda, a wealthy Spaniard, as a thank-you offering to Our Lady of Anguish for sparing his life and that of his family in the 1902 eruption of Santa María volcano, which blanketed areas in rock and ash near his San Marcos coffee farm. It was completed in 1941 just five months before his death. Situated at Ruta 6 8-52 and usually open to the public (8 A.M.–noon and 3–6 P.M. Tues.–Sun.), it's worth a look. It's an interesting mishmash of architectural styles in vogue at the time and capriciously admired by its creator. Note the interesting crooked cross at top.

ZONA 7
Parque Arqueológico Kaminaljuyú

This Mayan site occupied the valley where Guatemala City now stands. It was first settled sometime around 400 B.C. and grew to house an abundance of flat-topped pyramids (with the remains of nobility buried underneath) by A.D. 100. The first inhabitants of the site appear to have been some early cultures (Las Charcas, Miraflores, and Esperanza, dating from 1500 B.C. to A.D. 150), which developed a foundation for the later development of the Classic Mayan culture here. These early cultures are characterized by the development of agriculture, weaving, pottery making, and ritual burial of the dead in temple mounds and shrines. Central to the city's rapid population growth was the development of a series of irrigation canals drawing upon the ancient lake of Miraflores. Eventually the lake began to dry out, leading to widespread migration out of the city. Its Chol-speaking inhabitants are thought to have moved on to El Salvador and maybe even Copán, Honduras. The site's historical record fades out (momentarily) sometime between the 2nd and 3rd centuries A.D.

© AL ARGUETA

kite-flying over a Kaminaljuyú temple mound

With the rise of Central Mexico's Teotihuacán in the 5th century, the Guatemalan highlands received a large influx of invaders from the north. Here the invaders established their regional capital, constructing new temples and structures, and flourished with the control of trade networks around highly prized obsidian and jade. It is thought that, along with its powerful neighbor to the north, Kaminaljuyú exercised considerable influence over the Petén lowland sites, in particular Tikal. One of Tikal's rulers, Curl Nose, may actually have come from here in A.D. 387.

The site was first excavated in 1925 and yielded potsherds and clay figurines from the early cultures. Its larger extent and importance were discovered in 1935 when a local football team uncovered a buried structure after cutting away the edges of two inconspicuous mounds to lengthen their practice field. Today the site is really no more than a series of mounds. Though the site is in Zona 7 proper, the best place to see it is actually near the Museo Miraflores in adjacent Zona

11, where you can tour the excellent museum and see some temple mounds. (See the *Zona 11* section.)

ZONA 9

Part of the city's newer sector, Zona 9 adjoins Zona 4 and is crossed by 6a and 7a Avenidas. Along 7a Avenida, on 2a Calle, is an Eiffel Tower–like monument commemorating the rule of Guatemala's liberal reformer Justo Rufino Barrios (1871–1885), known as **Torre del Reformador.** Wonderfully illuminated at night with a large spinning spotlight at top, the steel tower serves as a nice backdrop for an annual December fireworks show. A bell at top is rung every year on June 30 in remembrance of the Liberal victory in the revolution of 1871. It was a project of the Ubico administration and was not a donation from France, as is commonly thought. The bell tower, however, was a gift from Belgium. Nearby, at the corner of 5a Calle and Avenida La Reforma is **Plaza Estado de Israel,** honoring the creation of the Jewish state with a giant Star of David sculpture.

Also along Avenida La Reforma, between 1a and 2a Calle, is the **Jardín Botánico y Museo de Historia Natural** (Botanical Gardens and Natural History Museum, 8 A.M.– 3 P.M. Mon.–Fri., 9 A.M.–noon Sat., $1.50), managed by the San Carlos University. It's really only recommendable for the botanical gardens, which offer a nice respite from the chaotic traffic just beyond its walls. The plant species are all labeled in Spanish and Latin. Give the natural history museum a skip unless you're really into bad taxidermy.

At 7a Avenida and 12 Calle is the **Plazuela España,** a circular miniplaza circumvented by traffic and featuring a pretty fountain built in honor of Spain's King Carlos III in 1789. It originally was in the city's central park, where it had a large equestrian statue that disappeared shortly after independence from Spain. Its current location was a move by the Ubico administration. Some very attractive tile benches are on the sidewalks opposite the fountain.

ZONA 10
Avenida La Reforma

Running between 1a Calle and 20 Calle, Avenida La Reforma is a classic example of the 19th-century trend, common throughout Latin America's major capitals, of emulating French architectural and urban design with wide, tree-lined boulevards adorned with statues. This broad thoroughfare separates Zonas 9 and 10 and features some of the city's better hotels, cafés, and restaurants along its path. The wide, grassy median contains some interesting sculptures and makes a great place for a stroll. La Reforma culminates at the spacious **Parque Obelisco,** featuring a large obelisk, a gigantic Guatemalan flag, palm trees, a fountain, and sitting areas.

◖ Zona Viva

Within Zona 10, east of Avenida La Reforma all the way to 6a Avenida and running north–south from 10a Calle to 16 Calle, the Zona

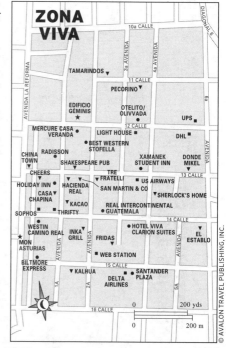

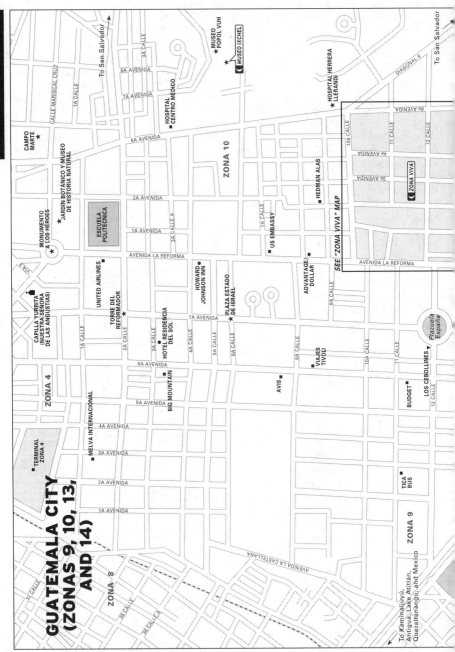

GUATEMALA CITY (ZONAS 9, 10, 13, AND 14)

SEE "ZONA VIVA" MAP

ZONA VIVA

To San Salvador

MUSEO POPOL VUH
MUSEO IXCHEL
HOSPITAL HERRERA LLERANDI
DIAGONAL 6
8A AVENIDA
10A CALLE
11 CALLE
12 CALLE
6a AVENIDA
4a AVENIDA
3a AVENIDA

8A AVENIDA
7A AVENIDA
3A CALLE
8A CALLE
1A CALLE
CALLE MARISCAL CRUZ
HOSPITAL CENTRO MÉDICO
6A AVENIDA

CAMPO MARTE
JARDÍN BOTÁNICO Y MUSEO DE HISTORIA NATURAL
MONUMENTO A LOS HÉROES
ESCUELA POLITÉCNICA
ZONA 10
2A AVENIDA
1A AVENIDA
3A CALLE A
AVENIDA LA REFORMA
HEDMAN ALAS
7A CALLE
US EMBASSY
9A CALLE
AVENIDA LA REFORMA

VÍA 9
CAPILLA YURRITA (NUESTRA SEÑORA DE LAS ANGUSTIAS)
TORRE DEL REFORMADOR
UNITED AIRLINES
HOWARD JOHNSON INN
PLAZA ESTADO DE ISRAEL
ADVANTAGE/DOLLAR
7A AVENIDA
5A CALLE
4A CALLE
5A CALLE
6A CALLE
8A CALLE

ZONA 4
1A CALLE
2A CALLE
HOTEL RESIDENCIA DEL SOL
6A AVENIDA
BIG MOUNTAIN
5A AVENIDA
AVIS
VIAJES TIVOLI
10A CALLE
11 CALLE
Plazuela España
LOS CEBOLLINES

TERMINAL ZONA 4
MELVA INTERNACIONAL
4A AVENIDA
3A AVENIDA
2A AVENIDA
1A AVENIDA
BUDGET
12 CALLE

3ª CALLE
ZONA 8
TICA BUS
ZONA 9

AVENIDA LA CASTELLANA

3ª CALLE A

To Kaminaljuyú, Antigua, Lake Atitlán, Quezaltenango, and Mexico

To San Salvador

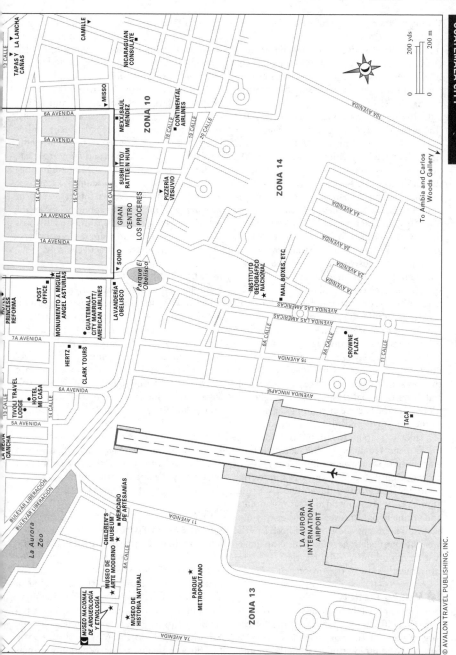

0   200 yds
0   200 m

To Ambia and Carlos
Woods Gallery

ZONA 10

ZONA 14

ZONA 13

CAMILLE ▼

TAPAS Y LA LANCHA
CANAS

13 CALLE

NICARAGUAN
CONSULATE

▼ MISSO

6A AVENIDA

5A AVENIDA

MEXX/SAUL
MENDEZ

18 CALLE

CONTINENTAL
AIRLINES

19 CALLE

20 CALLE

14 CALLE

15 CALLE

16 CALLE

SUSHI ITTO/
RATTLE N HUM

2A AVENIDA

1A AVENIDA

GRAN
CENTRO
LOS PRÓCERES

PIZZERIA
VESUVIO

4A AVENIDA

3A AVENIDA

2A AVENIDA

1A AVENIDA

▼ SOHO

Parque El
Obelisco

INSTITUTO
GEOGRÁFICO
NACIONAL

■ MAIL BOXES, ETC.

AVENIDA LAS AMÉRICAS

AVENIDA LAS AMÉRICAS

7A AVENIDA

HOTEL
PRINCESS
REFORMA

POST
OFFICE

MONUMENTO A MIGUEL
ÁNGEL ASTURIAS

GUATEMALA
CITY MARRIOTT/
AMERICAN AIRLINES

LAVANDERIA
OBELISCO

5 CALLE

7 CALLE

1S AVENIDA

3A CALLE

CROWNE
PLAZA

11 CALLE

HERTZ

CLARK TOURS

6A AVENIDA

AVENIDA HINCAPIE

13 CALLE

TIVOLI TRAVEL
LODGE

HOTEL
MI CASA

14 CALLE

5A AVENIDA

LA AURORA INTERNATIONAL
AIRPORT

TACA

LA MEDIA
CANCHA

BULEVAR LIBERACIÓN

BULEVAR LIBERACIÓN

La Aurora
Zoo

CHILDREN'S
MUSEUM

MERCADO
DE ARTESANÍAS

6A CALLE

11 AVENIDA

MUSEO DE
ARTE MODERNO

PARQUE
METROPOLITANO

MUSEO NACIONAL
DE ARQUEOLOGÍA
Y ETNOLOGÍA

MUSEO DE
HISTORIA NATURAL

7A AVENIDA

10A AVENIDA

Viva is Guatemala City's most pleasant commercial district, with a variety of hip cafés, trendy boutiques, lively bars and nightclubs, excellent restaurants, and expensive hotels. It's Guatemala City at its best and after long periods in the country's hinterlands, it can be downright refreshing.

Unlike in downtown Guatemala City, you'll find plenty of trees sheltering the streets from the harsh tropical sun in addition to wide, pedestrian-friendly sidewalks. Zona Viva's many high-rise buildings harbor banks, office buildings, the bulk of Guatemala City's international hotel chain properties, and condominiums. None of these buildings is more than 20 stories high, as the airport's proximity limits vertical expansion of the adjacent areas, giving the neighborhood a cosmopolitan feel without the claustrophobic concrete-jungle look found in larger international cities. Interspersed between office buildings are the area's many dining and entertainment options and tucked away into the side streets are some of Guatemala's nicest residences sheltered behind walls, barbed wire, and bougainvillea.

During the day, Zona Viva's streets are mostly the haunt of businessmen because of the area's prominence as the city's main financial district. By night, especially on weekends, it becomes the enclave of young folks heading to the area's bars and nightclubs or to dinner at a fancy restaurant. If you find yourself needing to spend a night or two in Guatemala City, you might make it a very enjoyable experience by checking into one of the area's attractive boutique or international chain hotels, eating at one of the recommended local restaurants, and taking in one or several of the nearby museums. The recent addition of a hostel to the area's accommodations means this is no longer just an option for wealthy travelers. It is also conveniently close to the airport.

◖ Museo Ixchel

The city's most fabulous museum (6a Calle Final Zona 10, tel. 2331-3739, www.museoixchel.org, 9 A.M.–5 P.M. Mon.–Fri., 9 A.M.–1 P.M. Sat., $3.50 adults, $2 students), on the grounds of the Francisco Marroquín University is dedicated to Mayan culture with an emphasis on weaving and traditional costumes. It's housed in a beautiful brick building built to resemble a Mayan *huipil,* or hand-woven, embroidered blouse. On display are Pre-Hispanic objects, photographs, hand-woven fabrics, ceremonial costumes, weaving tools, and folk paintings by Guatemalan artist Andrés Curruchich. You'll find interactive multimedia displays, a café, bookstore, and *huipiles* for sale in the excellent gift shop. Displays are in English and Spanish. This museum is a must-see for anyone with even a casual interest in Mayan weaving, as it manages to condense the country's rich weaving heritage spanning a fairly vast geographical range into a single place with excellent displays and an attractive setting.

Museo Popol Vuh

Next door and also on the university campus is the similarly high-caliber Museo Popol Vuh (tel. 2361-2301, www.popolvuh.ufm.edu.gt, 9 A.M.–5 P.M. Mon.–Fri., 9 A.M.–1 P.M. Sat., $3.50 adults, $2 students). Started in 1978 from a university donation by private collectors, it has been in its current location since 1997. The museum houses an impressive collection from Guatemala's archaeological record grouped in different rooms denoted by Preclassic, Classic, Postclassic, and Colonial times. The highlight is in the Postclassic room with a replica of the *Dresden Codex,* one of only three Mayan books to survive their postconquest burning by the Spanish (the other two are the Paris Codex and the Madrid Codex).

ZONA 11
◖ Museo Miraflores

The excellent Museo Miraflores (7a Calle 21-55 Zona 11, Paseo Miraflores, tel. 2470-3415/16/17/18, 9 A.M.–7 P.M. Tues.–Sun., $2 adults, $1 children/students) is dedicated to the history of the Mayan site of Kaminaljuyú. Just outside the museum's main entrance is a replica of an irrigation canal similar to those found throughout the Mayan city as early as 600 B.C. Inside, the large window panels provide fantastic views of the stark contrast between old and new, with the green temple mound of structure B-V-3 flanked by modern glass buildings in the background. Also at the entrance is a scale model of what the city probably looked like in its heyday, built into the museum floor under a glass case. In the main exhibit area, you'll find a comprehensive history of Kaminaljuyú in English and Spanish as well as a burial display, pottery, jade jewelry, stone sculpture, and obsidian blades. There are also old photographs of the site's excavation and maps showing the large area once occupied by the ancient city. You are free to explore the temple mounds outside (steps are built into them). A few more temple mounds can be found in the vicinity of the museum, having been completely closed in by one of the city's larger shopping complexes. Among the latter are the ever-growing Galerías Miraflores, Paseo Miraflores, and Las Majadas.

ZONA 13

This area was once the site of a large farm known as La Aurora, which today gives its name to the zoo and airport. The airport is undergoing a major renovation and expansion which, in addition to bringing the airport up to international standards, will bring about the creation of a very attractive city park on the grounds of what was once a horse-racing track. Details on the project were sketchy but it's expected to include sporting facilities and spacious grounds for strolling.

Zona 13 also houses a number of fairly good museums, all adjacent to each other in a large complex, and the city's zoo.

La Aurora Zoo

Guatemala City's La Aurora Zoo (Boulevard Juan Pablo II Zona 13, tel. 2475-0894, laurorazoo .centroamerica.com, 9 A.M.–5 P.M. Tues.–Sun., $2.50 adults, $1 children) is modern and well run. Its grounds are a popular weekend destination for city dwellers from all walks of life. About 900 animals representing 110 species are housed in re-creations of their natural habitats, including African savannah, Asia, and tropi-

cal forest. There are leopards, lions, giraffes, Asian pachyderms, Bengal tigers, and jaguars and other species found in Guatemala's tropical forests. A project is under way to remove all cages from the park so as to provide visitors with the opportunity to see the animals free of visual obstructions. Check out the English tea house dating to 1924.

Children's Museum

Right across the street is the Museo de los Niños (5a Calle 10-00 Zona 13, tel. 2475-5076, www .museodelosninos.com.gt, 8 A.M.–noon and 1–5 P.M. Tues.–Thurs., 8 A.M.–noon and 2–6 P.M. Fri., 10 A.M.–1 P.M. and 2:30–6 P.M. Sat./Sun., $5), housed in a pyramidal building, with educational exhibits and hands-on learning on themes such as civic values and teamwork. You'll also find a giant jigsaw puzzle of Guatemala, a hands-on music room, and trampolines. It's closed yearly from mid-December to mid-January and is a popular school field trip.

◖ Museo Nacional de Arqueología y Etnología

The city's Archaeology Museum (6a Calle y 7a Avenida Zona 13, tel. 2475-4399, 9 A.M.–4 P.M. Tues.–Fri., 9 A.M.–noon and 1:30–4 P.M. Sat./Sun., $4) houses an outstanding collection of original monuments from Guatemala's archaeological sites, including ceramics, carved rock sculptures and stelae from Kaminaljuyú, *barrigones* (Olmecoid stone figures with distended, bloated bellies) from the Pacific Coast sites, and stelae from the Petén sites. Among the latter are beautifully carved stelae and a spectacular hieroglyphic bench from Piedras Negras as well as stelae and hieroglyphic panels from Dos Pilas and Machaquilá. Another of the museum's highlights is a splendid jade mask made famous on the cover of the September 1987 issue of *National Geographic*. The ethnology section has displays on traditional costumes and housing. The displays are not quite as modern or well done as in some other of the city's top museums, but the sheer significance of the original pieces found here makes a visit more than worthwhile.

Museo Nacional de Arte Moderno Carlos Mérida

Across the street is the city's Museum of Modern Art (tel. 2472-0467, 9 A.M.–4 P.M. Tues.–Fri., 9 A.M.–noon and 1:30–4 P.M. Sat./Sun, $1.50), which focuses largely on the work of its namesake artist, including examples of his cubist art and large murals. He's Guatemala's most celebrated artist; his work also adorns the inside of several buildings in Guatemala City's Civic Center, including City Hall, with a giant mural known as *Canto a la Raza (Ode to the Race),* recently restored. Among the other interesting works found here is one titled *La Peste (Pestilence)* by Rodolfo Abularach, reminiscent of Picasso's *Guernica.*

Museo Nacional de Historia Natural Jorge Ibarra

For all of Guatemala's rich ecology, it still lacks a natural history museum to do it justice. The Natural History Museum (tel. 2472-0468, 9 A.M.–4 P.M. Tues.–Fri., 9 A.M.–noon and 2–4 P.M. Sat./Sun., $1.50), around the corner from the previous two, makes an attempt but falls a bit short. You'll find plenty of taxidermy as well as exhibits on several of the country's ecosystems. A standout is the photo exhibit on the Atitlán pied-billed grebe, extinct since 1987, and the attempt in the mid-20th century to save it.

ZONA 14

South of Zona 10's **Parque El Obelisco** is Zona 14 and the **Avenida Las Américas,** paralleling the airport runway and home to a growing concentration of expensive hotels and restaurants. It is somewhat similar to Avenida La Reforma and is flanked at its southern extreme by a deep ravine, the same one preventing the airport's runway from being lengthened. At this spot is **Plaza Berlín,** with wonderful views of Pacaya Volcano and a few snack and drink stands. Between the airport and Avenida Las Américas is Avenida Hincapié, where the hangars of some of the domestic carriers and helicopter flights are housed just off its juncture with 18 Calle.

a view of Zona 14 over Avenida Las Américas

© AL ARGUETA

Entertainment

NIGHTLIFE

Guatemala City has a fairly lively nightlife scene with bars, clubs, and music found mostly in the Zona Viva, Zona 4's hip 4 Grados Norte, and downtown. There are plenty of places to dance salsa and Latin beats in addition to rock and pop music. Electronica is also a big hit with Guatemalan partygoers. DJ Tiësto performed here in November 2004 and again in February 2007.

Bars

A good mix of bars in the downtown area caters to the city's bohemian population as well as to international travelers. In Zona 10, the Zona Viva sector centered around 16 Calle is the place to go if you want to hang out with the city's wealthy elite in the hippest establishments. Zona 4's 4 Grados Norte is also increasingly lively, with cafeés, bars, and restaurants along the pedestrian area usually packed on weekends.

Downtown, **El Portal** (Portal del Comercio, 9a Calle, between 6a and 7a Avenidas, 10 A.M.–10 P.M. Mon.–Sat.) is said to be the old stomping grounds of none other than Che Guevara, who lived in Guatemala City in the early 1950s. You'll find a long wooden bar and some wooden tables along with draft beers for about $2. The entrance is at the Portal del Comercio arcade entrance on the south side of the park along 6a Avenida. Nearby **Las Cien Puertas** (9a Calle between 6a and 7a Avenidas, Pasaje Aycinena, Zona 1, noon–2 A.M. Mon.–Sat.) is the city's quintessential bohemian hangout set in a beautifully beat-up colonial arcade. Enjoy tasty quesadillas and tacos when you get the munchies. **Europa Bar** (11 Calle 5-16, Edificio Testa, Local 201, tel. 2253-4929, 8 A.M.–midnight Mon.–Sat.) is a restaurant doubling as a bar that is popular with the expat crowd. CNN and sports are on the cable TV and the restaurant serves decent food, including the all-American staple breakfast of eggs, hash browns, bacon, and toast.

Zona Viva's motley assortment of upscale bars is constantly in flux. New places open and close all the time, and it's hard to keep up with all the changes, even if you live in Guatemala City. Among the old standby watering holes is **El Establo** (14 Calle 5-08 Zona 10, 8 P.M.–3 A.M. Wed.–Sat.), which has long been popular with locals and foreigners alike for its classy, publike atmosphere with a spacious wooden bar, tasty pub grub, and smart music mixes compiled by its German owners. A classic expat hangout, the **William Shakespeare Pub** (13 Calle and 1a Avenida, Torre Santa Clara II, Local 5, Zona 10, tel. 2331-2641, 11 A.M.–1 A.M. Mon.–Sat., 2 P.M.–1 A.M. Sun.) appropriately advertises, "No tragedy, no comedy, just good times." **Cheers** (13 Calle 0-40 Zona 10, tel. 2368-2089, 9 A.M.–1 A.M. Mon.–Sat., 1 P.M.–midnight Sun.) is the city's best sports bar with scrumptious buffalo wings, frosty beer on tap, dartboards, pool tables, foosball, big-screen TVs, and classic rock on the stereo. **Rattle and Hum** (4a Avenida and 16 Calle, Zona 10, 8 P.M.–3 A.M. Wed.–Sat.) is a lively and popular Australian-owned bar playing good music. Also in vogue and close by is **SOHO** (Avenida La Reforma 16-01, Plaza Obelisco, Segundo Nivel, Zona 10, tel. 2332-3242).

In the 4 Grados Norte part of town, **Vino Vino** (Vía 5, tel. 2385-9042, 12:30–3 P.M. and 6–11 P.M. Tues.–Thurs., 12:30–3 P.M. and 6–1 A.M. Fri./Sat.) is an American-owned wine bar with a pleasant Old World feel to it. Its chef prepares mouthwatering steak and chicken dishes. Across the street, **SUAE** is a funky warehouse-style bar with plastic sofas in vivid hues of green, a hip clientele, and electronic beats on the stereo. It's rather reminiscent of an Austin, Texas 6th Street bar.

Nightclubs

Like the bars, nightclubs are in constant flux, but here are some options that have been around for a while and don't look to be going anywhere. **Kalhua** (15 Calle and 1a Avenida, Zona 10, 8 P.M.–3 A.M. Mon.–Sat., $5 cover) is one of Guatemala City's most popular clubs with a wealthy clientele and hip atmosphere spread out on four floors. Near El Obelisco, **Sherlock's Home** (4a Avenida between 13 and 14 Calle Zona 10, 6 P.M.–3 A.M. Mon.–Sat.) is also popular with young adults and thirty-somethings. It's on the smaller side, but it's very stylish and contemporary and makes a good place to go if you're not up for anything too elaborate or on the hectic side. In 4 Grados Norte, a good underground venue for DJ-spun house and electronica is **La Ocupa** (Ruta 5 8-42 Zona 4, 8 P.M.–3 A.M. Fri. and Sat. only). There are also live bands on occasion.

Live Music

A popular place for live music in a wonderfully bohemian atmosphere is **La Bodeguita del Centro** (12 Calle 3-55 Zona 1, tel. 2230-2976, 8 P.M.–2 A.M. Tues.–Sat., $4 cover on weekends). Besides live folk, rock, and jazz music, there are poetry readings, forums, and movies some nights. Posters feature numerous artists the likes of the Bob Marley and Che Guevara, and there is tons of memorabilia relating to the Argentinean revolutionary. Food is also served, with tasty chicken sandwiches. In 4 Grados Norte, **TrovaJazz** (Vía 6 3-55 Zona 4, tel. 2334-1241) has live jazz in the evenings Thursday through Saturday. It also serves food and coffee beverages.

PERFORMING ARTS

The **Centro Cultural Miguel Angel Asturias** (24 Calle 3-81 Zona 4, tel. 2232-4042/3/4/5) hosts ballet and a number of cultural events throughout the year. Check listings in the *Prensa Libre* newspaper or *Recrearte*, a free monthly publication widely available in tourist shops and hotels.

Somewhat less cultured but extremely hilarious (if you understand Spanish) are some cheesy comedy productions featuring the antics of rural Guatemalans from the fictional town of Huité starring comedian Hugo Aldana as the character Teco. The productions change from time to time but are usually in the same venue, the **Teatro de la Cámara de la Industria** (Chamber of Industry Theater, Ruta 6, 0-21 Zona 4, tel. 2334-4848 or 2331-9191, showtimes 8:30 P.M. Fri. and Sat., 5 P.M. Sun., $8).

For other cultural events, check the entertainment section of the useful Spanish-language website at www.deguate.com/artman/publish/entretenimiento.shtml.

MOVIES

Guatemala City has a number of excellent movie theaters, with movies sometimes opening on the same day as their U.S. release. The newest addition to this listing is the **Circuito Alba** (tel. 2329-2550, circuitoalba.com.gt) IMAX movie theater with stadium seating at the new Pradera Concepción shopping mall along Km. 17.5 of *Carretera a El Salvador.* The same company also runs the movieplex at **Cines La Pradera** (18 Calle 25-85 Zona 10, tel. 2329-2575, www.circuitoalba.com.gt), housed in its namesake shopping mall. Another decent nearby option is **Cines Los Próceres** (Centro Comercial Los Próceres, 18 Calle 2-21 Zona 10, tel. 2332-8507). In the city's most popular shopping mall is **Cinépolis Miraflores** (Centro Comercial Miraflores, 21 Avenida 4-32 Zona 11, tel. 2470-8367, www.cinepolis.com.gt), widely regarded as the best movie theater in the city, also with stadium seating. Check the *Prensa Libre* newspaper or the theaters' websites for showtimes. Movies at all of the above generally cost between $4 and $5.

Shopping

Guatemala City has some excellent shopping malls carrying the most basic or most exclusive items one could want or need while on the road, in addition to fashionable boutiques and several venues for buying handicrafts and textiles.

RETAIL DISTRICTS
Zona Viva

In line with its fashionable cafés and expensive hotels, the Zona Viva also features a number of attractive stores for window-shopping or picking up an outfit should you need something nice to wear for a fancy dinner or night out on the town. Two of the most fashionable retail outlets are the European chain **Mexx** (16 Calle 5-86 Zona 10, Plaza Magnolia, tel. 2368-0757, www.mexx.com, 10 A.M.–8 P.M. daily) and the European-inspired menswear store **Saúl Méndez** (12 Calle 1-25 Zona 10, Edificio Géminis, tel. 2379-8722, 10 A.M.–8 P.M. daily). Saúl Méndez is also found in the same shopping center as the above-mentioned Mexx.

SHOPPING MALLS

As is to be expected, Guatemala City has a variety of modern shopping malls. Several house department stores, none of which (curiously) seem to result from Guatemalan investment. These include Simán (El Salvador), Carrion (Honduras) and Sears (United States). The newest and largest shopping mall is **Pradera Concepción** (Km. 17.5 Carretera a El Salvador, 10 A.M.–7 P.M. Mon.–Thurs. and 10 A.M.–9 P.M. Fri./Sat.), with a variety of familiar stores and restaurant chains including Sears and T.G.I. Friday's. Opened in 2003 and expanded in 2006, the large **Galerías Miraflores** (21 Avenida 4-32 Zona 11, 9 A.M.–9 P.M. daily) also harbors some of Guatemala's most exclusive stores, including a Simán department store, the international Zara boutique, a L'Occitane store, and an Apple Store. Across the way is the **Las Majadas** shopping center with a Sears, Fetiche perfume store, and a T.G.I. Friday's.

In Zona 10, east up the hill toward the Carretera a El Salvador, is **La Pradera** (20 Calle 25-85 Zona 10, tel. 2367-4136, 10 A.M.–8 P.M. Mon.–Sat. and 10 A.M.–7 P.M. Sun.), another upscale shopping mall. Though not as upscale as its Zona Viva location might suggest, **Gran Centro Los Próceres** (16 Calle 2-00 Zona 10, tel. 2332-8742) nonetheless has some good shops and eateries and is conveniently situated near the major Zona 10 hotels.

HANDICRAFTS

You can shop the jam-packed stalls in downtown Guatemala City's **Mercado Central** (8a Avenida and 6a Calle, 6 A.M.–6 P.M. Mon.–Sat., 9 A.M.–noon Sun.) for textiles, *típica* clothing, and leather goods. A safer and more enjoyable option can be found near the airport and Zona 13 museums at the open-air **Mercado de Artesanías** (Boulevard Juan Pablo II, 8 A.M.–6 P.M. Mon.–Sat., 8 A.M.–1 P.M. Sun.), with a fairly wide assortment of handicrafts and tourist souvenirs.

Recommended retailers include **Lin Canola** (5a Calle 9-60 Zona 1, tel. 2232-0858, www .lin-canola.com, 9 A.M.–6 P.M. Mon.–Fri.), where the assortment varies from home decorative items to jewelry and everything between. This store is especially recommended if you want to buy Guatemalan fabrics by the yard. Its Zona 10 location, **In Nola** (18 Calle 21-31 Zona 10 Boulevard Los Próceres, tel. 2367-2424, 8:30 A.M.–6:30 P.M. Mon.–Fri. and 8:30 A.M.–1:30 P.M. Sat.), is more modern and contains much the same in a better part of town.

Selling fashionable adaptations on traditional designs for the home, **Textura** (Diagonal 6, 13-63 Zona 10, tel. 2333-5496, 9 A.M.–5 P.M. Mon.–Sat.) is especially recommended for its beautiful and colorful hammocks.

ART GALLERIES

If you want to take in the work of local artists, head to Guatemala's oldest art gallery,

Galería El Túnel (Boulevard Los Próceres 15-60 Zona 10, 2nd Floor, tel. 2363-4744, galeriaeltunel@yahoo.com), featuring the work of more than 100 artists. Another good art gallery worth checking out is **el attico** (4a Avenida 15-45 Zona 14, tel. 2368-0853, elatticogal@msn.com). Next door to one of the finest restaurants in the city, **Carlos Woods Arte Antiguo y Contemporáneo** (10a Avenida 5-49 Zona 14, tel. 2366-6883/84, www.carloswoods arte.com, 10 A.M.–8 P.M. Mon.–Fri. and 10 A.M.–2 P.M. Sat.) features a variety of exhibitions from local artists in a well-lit minimalist setting. Check the website for current exhibitions.

BOOKS

For a great atmosphere for unwinding with a cup of coffee or tea and a large selection of books (though mostly in Spanish), try **Sophos** (Avenida Reforma 13-89 Zona 10, tel. 2334-6797, 9 A.M.–8 P.M. Mon.–Sat. and 10 A.M.–6 P.M. Sun.). Also with plenty of books in Spanish is **Artemis Edinter** (www .artemisedinter.com) with several locations

including Galerías Miraflores, La Pradera, Pradera Concepción, and the 4 Grados Norte pedestrian thoroughfare.

A number of bookstores cater to the expat community, stocking a variety of English-language books on their shelves. **Vista Hermosa Book Shop** (2a Calle 18-50, Vista Hermosa II, Zona 15, tel. 2369-1003, vhbookshop@ intelnet.net.gt, 9 A.M.–1 P.M. and 2–6 P.M. Mon.–Sat.) has books in English and Spanish and is in a quiet residential sector east of Zona 10. Another good option for books in English is **Géminis Bookstore** (3a Avenida 17-05 Zona 14, Edificio Casa Alta, tel. 2366-1031, geminisbookstore@hotmail.com, 9 A.M.–1 P.M. and 3–6 P.M. Mon.–Fri. and 9 A.M.–1 P.M. Sat.).

OUTDOOR GEAR

For anything you may have neglected to bring for your outdoor Guatemala adventures, head to **Big Mountain** (5a Avenida "B" 3-15 Zona 9, tel. 2332-1941, 9 A.M.–5 P.M. Mon.–Fri.), offering a good assortment of hiking, climbing, and camping gear, and name-brand outdoor clothing.

Recreation

PARKS

The idea of a greenbelt is relatively new to Guatemalan city planners. Most of the city's parks tend to be plazas centered around churches. An exception is the **Campo Marte,** a relatively well-executed park with facilities for playing soccer, baseball, and basketball as well as running around its spacious grounds. It was previously the city's military barracks and is east of Avenida La Reforma along 2a Calle. A better option might be the new **Parque Metropolitano,** scheduled for completion in late 2007 and tied closely to the project surrounding the airport's renovation and expansion in Zona 13. It should be the city's best park with plenty of space to get some fresh air and exercise.

HEALTH CLUBS

There are a number of good gymnasiums, mostly U.S. franchises, where you can pay a day rate of about $7 to work out if you don't have a membership. **World Gym** (www.worldgym .com) has three locations to choose from. Its Calzada Roosevelt location (Calzada Roosevelt 21-09 Zona 7, Centro Comercial Gran Vía Roosevelt, tel. 2475-2856) is conveniently across the street from Galerías Miraflores and the Grand Tikal Futura Hotel. It also has a Zona 10 location (Boulevard Los Próceres 25-74 Zona 10, Gran Vía Pradera, tel. 2423-6000), and a third location in the southwest suburbs of San Cristóbal (tel. 2424-4848). All have a full gym and swimming pool. You can also work out at **Gold's Gym** (Pradera Concepción Mall, Km. 17.5 Carretera a El Salvador, tel. 6634-1240, www.goldsgym.com).

GOLF

Fans of golf will find some excellent golf courses in and around the city housed in private country clubs but open to visitors. You can enjoy a round of golf surrounded by the country's spectacular mountain scenery as you play on narrow, sloping fairways lined with pine trees and a variety of other obstacles. Several of the sportfishing outfitters mentioned in the Pacific Coast chapter have combined fishing and golf packages. If you're interested in either or both of these, contact **The Great Sailfishing Company** (tel. 7832-1991, 5966-4528 Antigua, or 877/763-0851 U.S., www.greatsailfishing.com) or **Sailfish Bay Lodge** (tel. 2426-3909 direct or 800/638-7405 U.S. reservations, www.sailfishbay.com). It's also possible to arrange a round of golf through the concierges at some of the city's finer hotels, including the Marriott, Camino Real, and In-

terContinental. Entry to all of these clubs is by prior authorization only. You'll need to call ahead or email.

In 2006 and 2007, Guatemala City's San Isidro Golf Club hosted the **NGA/Hooter's Pro Golf Tour,** which has become an annual event between the last week of February and the first week of March. Guatemala is also a major stop along the annual *Tour de las Américas* in February.

San Isidro Golf Club

Still officially within the city limits in Zona 16, San Isidro Golf Club (tel. 2385-6524, www.clubsanisidro.com) is the city's most modern and is in a quiet residential section in its eastern extremes. The 18-hole, par-72 course measures 6,640 yards and offers some truly spectacular views of Guatemala City flanked by Agua, Acatenango, and Fuego Volcanoes. Greens fees are $75, clubs rent for $15, a cart rental costs $20, and caddies are $15. The splendid facilities here include a

Alta Vista Golf and Tennis Club offers Guatemala's most challenging course in addition to fantastic mountain views.

restaurant overlooking the greens featuring a beautiful dining room with vaulted wooden ceiling, a gym, squash court, and a swimming pool with lap lanes.

Hacienda Nueva Country Club

The 18-hole, 7,100-yard, par-72 golf course at Hacienda Nueva Country Club (Km. 25, Ruta Nacional 18, Carretera a Mataquescuintla, San José Pinula, tel. 6628-1000, www.haciendanueva.com, $75 Tues.–Fri., $90 weekends and holidays) is just outside the city near the Carretera a El Salvador and is set beautifully on the grounds of a 16th-century Jesuit monastery. There's a small chapel with original artwork where Mass is still held weekly. Facilities include nine tennis courts, two squash courts, tennis and golf pro shops, and a swimming pool that has won international design awards. The clubhouse has three dining areas, including a poolside snack bar, a casual dining room serving international dishes, and La Pérgola, an outdoor steakhouse overlooking the 18th hole. Fees include $15 for caddie service and $25 for cart rental. A limited number of golf clubs are available for rental at $15. There are also a driving range and putting green.

Alta Vista Golf and Tennis Club

The most challenging course can be found just down the road from Hacienda Nueva at Alta Vista Golf and Tennis Club (Km. 27, Ruta Nacional 18, Carretera a Mataquescuintla, San José Pinula, tel. 6641-5058, www.alta vistagolf.com, 7 A.M.–8 P.M. Tues.–Sun., $75), where the 18-hole, par-71, slope-122 course is divided into two nine-hole sections. Additional challenges include 74 sand traps and two water traps with a route defined by 1,800 trees of varying species adding a nice alpine touch to the incredible mountain views. The clubhouse is in a large and attractive three-story, English-style building with an elegant restaurant, a bar with pool table, an indoor swimming pool, three squash courts, and six tennis courts. Golf cart rentals cost $27, clubs are $12, and caddies $11.

Mayan Golf Course

South of the city in the neighboring district of Villa Nueva, Mayan Golf Course (Finca El Zarzal, Villa Nueva, tel. 6631-0045, www .mayangolf.com, $75) is Guatemala City's oldest, dating to 1918. The facilities here feel somewhat dated but have been well maintained. The 18-hole, par-72 golf course has exquisite views of Lake Amatitlán and Pacaya Volcano along its 7,092-yard length. Rental clubs and golf carts are available and there is a café with a terrace overlooking the course. Additional sporting facilities include a bowling alley, tennis courts, a soccer field, volleyball court, and swimming pool.

SPECTATOR SPORTS

Like other Latin Americans, Guatemalans are crazy about *fútbol*. The two most popular teams in the country's four-team national soccer league, denoted by the colors of their jerseys, are the *Rojos* (Municipales) and *Cremas* (Comunicaciones), who usually end up battling it out at the end of the season for the championship title. International games are also a big event, as Guatemala has never been to a World Cup. In recent years, it has gotten closer than it's ever been, and the postgame celebrations have spilled into the streets and lasted into the wee hours of the morning. Unfortunately, their high hopes have ended in bitter disappointment. Games can be seen at the **Estadio Mateo Flores** (10a Avenida, Zona 5), but be advised it can get quite rowdy. In 1996, things got so out of hand that a stampede ensued when stands collapsed, killing 100 people. The soccer stadium has been remodeled in the aftermath. If you've always wanted to see a Latin American soccer match, you might want to check it out.

You can see baseball games at Parque Minerva's ballpark. (See the *Sights* section.)

CITY TOURS

An excellent way to take in the downtown sites is on a narrated trolley tour offered by Antigua-based **Chiltepe Tours** (7a Calle Poniente #15, tel. 5907-0913 or 5709-2232, www.chiltepetours.com, $25 on arrival, $22 with prior booking). The three-hour tours (in English and Spanish) cover more than 30 sights in the historic downtown area and leave twice a day from the Zona 9 and 10 hotels Tuesday through Sunday. It's affiliated with Gray Line Tours. Traditional city tours can be arranged through any of the larger hotels or via **Clark Tours** (7a Avenida 14-76, Plaza Clark, Zona 9, tel. 2412-4700, www .clarktours.com). It has offices in the Westin Camino Real, Holiday Inn, and Marriott.

Accommodations

Guatemala City has a wide variety of accommodations for all budgets. The major U.S. hotel chains have properties in Zonas 10, 11, and 13—close to the airport. Downtown is home to most of the city's budget accommodations.

CENTRO HISTÓRICO
Under $10

There are some real cheapies in downtown Guatemala City, traditionally the city's budget accommodation headquarters, though there are also some nice budget options outside the downtown area now, so you have to stay in this slightly dodgy part of town only if you really want to. A longtime favorite with the backpacker crowd, **Pension Meza** (10a Calle 10-17 Zona 1, tel. 2232-3177) has shared-bath doubles for $7 and rooms with private bath for $12 d. It's somewhat dilapidated, though the graffiti-strewn walls have a certain charm and the beds are good enough. You'll find a courtyard, Ping-Pong table, and book exchange. **Hotel Fenix** (7a Avenida 15-81 Zona 1, tel. 2251-6625) is a good budget value with clean rooms. It's also quite secure. There are shared-bath doubles for $7 (upstairs and quieter) and rooms with private bathroom for $10 d. It has a bistro with excellent sandwiches and areas for hanging out.

$10-25

Hotel Ajau (8a Avenida 15-62 Zona 1, tel. 2232-0488) has 44 rooms, including shared-bath doubles for $12 and doubles with private bath for $19. **Hotel Spring** (8a Avenida 12-65 Zona 1, tel. 2230-2858, hotelspring@hotmail .com) is a good value with clean, pleasant rooms. It has doubles with shared bath for $18, older rooms with private bath for $23 d, and quieter, newly remodeled rooms with private bath for $33 d. A cheery three-level place, **Hotel Excel** (9a Avenida 15-12 Zona 1, tel. 2253-2709, $23 d) has rooms with private hot-water bath. The architecture at **Hotel Colonial** (7a Avenida 14-19 Zona 1, tel. 2232-6722, www.hotelcolonial.net, $19–30 d) is just as its name implies, with tile floors, wrought iron, and dark hardwood accents. Its spacious rooms come with shared or private bathroom.

$25-50

Across from the police headquarters is a perennial favorite in this budget category, **Chalet Suizo** (14 Calle 6-82 Zona 1, tel. 2251-3786, $27 d), with 47 spotlessly clean rooms, all with private bath, built around sunny courtyards. On a quiet side street, another fine choice is **◖ Posada Belén** (13 Calle "A" 10-30 Zona 1, tel. 2253-4530, www.posadabelen.com, $45 d), an 1873 home converted into a lovely museum inn. It has 10 rooms with tile floors tastefully decorated with Guatemalan bedspreads, paintings, and weavings. Its gracious hosts, René and Francesca, speak English and can help you plan your journeys into Guatemala's rugged interior. Amenities include telephone and Internet access. All rooms have private bath and rates include breakfast. Other delicious homemade meals are available upon request. **Hotel Quality Service** (8a Calle 3-18 Zona 1, tel. 2251-8005/6/7, www.qualityguate .com) has 22 recently renovated tile-floor rooms with private hot-water bath, cable TV, and desk. Rates include a Guatemalan breakfast of eggs, beans, bread, orange juice, and coffee or tea.

$50-100

Oozing with history is the landmark **Hotel Pan American** (9a Calle 5-63 Zona 1, tel. 2232-6807), which was once Guatemala City's go-to property, having been established by its namesake airline. It was due to become the latest addition to the Porta hotel chain and may include more services by the time of your visit. Rooms have tile floors and are nicely decorated with Guatemalan artwork and furnishings. The dining room, serving international and Guatemalan dishes, is well known for its antique charm and elegance, with waiters wearing traditional village attire. Another elegant downtown property is the **Hotel Royal Palace** (6a Avenida 12-66 Zona 1, tel. 2220-8980, www.hotelroyal palace.com, $55–65 d), where the spacious, comfortable rooms have attractive traditional paintings, reading lamps, cable TV, and wooden furniture. There are standard rooms and larger junior suites to choose from. Other amenities include a workout room and an executive floor. Rooms facing the street have balconies and the property is wheelchair-accessible.

ZONA 4
$50-100

Conquistador Hotel (Vía 5, 4-68 Zona 4, tel. 2331-2222) was formerly a Ramada property and has comfortable rooms for $90 d including breakfast. You'll find a lobby bar, the Café Jardín serving a breakfast and lunch buffet, and La Pérgola serving fine international dishes for dinner. Centered around a swimming pool in an art deco building with a newer motel-style wing is **Hotel Plaza** (Vía 7, 6-16 Zona 4, tel. 2332-7626, $65 d).

ZONA 9
Under $50

Hotel Mi Casa (5a Avenida "A" 13-51 Zona 9, tel. 5709-4466, www.hotelmicasa.com, $40–50 d), in a pleasant middle class neighborhood, has rooms with private bath and cable TV or

shared bath. All rooms include breakfast and transfer to or from the airport. The comfortable rooms have fans and reading lamps. In the same neighborhood, **Tivoli Travel Lodge** (5a Avenida "A" 13-42 Zona 9, tel. 5510-0032, www.tivolitravellodge.com, $40 d) has well-furnished rooms with private bath, cable TV, and reading lamps. The hotel can arrange shuttle transfers and guided tours of the city.

$50-100

In this price category is the **Howard Johnson Inn** (Avenida La Reforma 4-22 Zona 9, tel. 2360-7188 or 2361-6566, www.hojo.com, $70 d), with all the standard amenities you would expect from this international hotel chain, including air-conditioning, fan, nice wooden furniture, phone, and TV. Airport transfers are included and there's a small restaurant in the lobby. Your breakfast might be included in the room rate. Try to get a room facing the outside street. Just one block west of Avenida La Reforma is the excellent-value **Hotel Residencia del Sol** (3a Calle 6-42 Zona 9, tel. 2360-4823, www.residenciadelsol.com, $50 d). It has comfortable, carpeted rooms, some with city views and windows shaded by trees, with private bath and in-room Internet.

$100-200

Among Guatemala City's numerous international hotel chain options is the **Guatemala City Marriott** (7a Avenida 15-45 Zona 9, tel. 2339-7777, www.marriott.com, $120 d), with all the standard comforts usually found in its properties. The hotel swimming pool was being remodeled during my visit. American and Continental Airlines have offices in the lobby.

The Guatemala City location of a Guatemalan luxury hotel chain enjoying success throughout Central America, **◖ Hotel Princess Reforma** (13 Calle 7-65 Zona 9, tel. 2334-4545, www.hotelesprincess.com, $120 d) is a winner for its sophisticated old-time ambience. Amenities include a swimming pool, gym, restaurant, and English pub–style bar. Its 110 rooms have air-conditioning. It is curiously the only of its Central American counterparts that is not part of the Hilton chain.

ZONA 10
Under $50

Zona 10 was strictly high-budget options until the recent appearance of **Xamanek Student Inn** (13 Calle 3-57 Zona 10, tel. 2360-8345, www.mayaworld.net/xamanek, $14 p/p in dorms, $35 private doubles), a friendly sort of place with clean dormitories sharing spotless bathrooms with hot showers and two rooms with private bath. Services include laundry, airport pickup, Internet, bag storage, and free use of the kitchen. Room rates include pancakes and coffee. There are two gardens and a living room for chilling out. It makes a great place to stay if you're on a budget and don't want to stay downtown. Its Zona Viva location is excellent.

$50-100

Best Western Stofella (2a Avenida 12-28 Zona 10, tel. 2410-8600 or 2338-5600, www.stofella.com, $65–100 d), a solid choice for business travelers, has rooms with fan or air-conditioning with breakfast included in the nightly rate. You'll find a lobby lounge with some slot machines, a fitness room with whirlpool tub, a bar, and in-room Internet connection. **Santander Plaza** (15 Calle 3-52 Zona 10, tel. 2333-5857, www.santanderplaza.com, $100 d) has 26 comfortable rooms with stylish, well-appointed furnishings in executive rooms and junior and master suites. It has a lobby bar and restaurant. Guests enjoy access to the wonderful Hacienda Nueva Country Club (see *Golf* in the *Recreation* section). Offering many of the same services as its pricier sister hotels under the management of the Camino Real chain, **Biltmore Express** (15 Calle 0-31 Zona 10, tel. 2338-5000, www.caminoreal.com.gt) offers corporate rates for $65 d, including continental breakfast, and has comfortable rooms with broadband Internet. Guests can enjoy use of the nearby Westin Camino Real's swimming pool, whirlpool tub, and tennis and racquetball courts for an additional $10 a day.

$100-200

Guatemala City's hippest digs are at **◖ Otelito** (12 Calle 4-51 Zona 10, tel. 2339-1811, www.otelito.com, $120–160 d), with 12 rooms all named after local produce housed in a modern home turned upscale hotel. The decor is minimalist with a different color scheme in evidence during each of the year's four seasons. It offers chill-out music playing on the speakers throughout the property, wireless Internet throughout, a business center, and a book exchange. Movies are shown nightly. A hip, frosted-glass lounge and restaurant mean you don't even have to leave your hotel to enjoy some of Zona Viva's best food in a delightful atmosphere. (See the *Olivadda* entry in the *Food* section).

Rooms feature nice artwork, 300-thread-count Egyptian cotton sheets, down pillows, air-conditioning, flat-screen cable TV, hardwood floors, and in-room chill-out music. Some have a minifridge. Showers feature tempered glass in lieu of shower curtains. Check for Internet specials on room rates, which include a continental breakfast and transfer to or from the airport.

Another top choice is the fabulous, 239-room **◖ Real InterContinental Guatemala** (14 Calle 2-51 Zona 10, tel. 2379-4548 or 888/424-6835 toll-free U.S., www.intercontinental.com, $125–485 d) with a wonderful lobby featuring Guatemalan paintings and sculpture, a new sushi restaurant, a French café, and *boulangerie*/patisserie. The comfortable, stylish rooms feature in-room Internet access, down pillows, Egyptian cotton sheets, and flat-screen cable TV. Bathrooms have rain showerheads and the safety deposit boxes are large enough to accommodate a laptop. Guests have use of an in-room iPod. There are free airport shuttles and a pleasant swimming pool on a deck overlooking the city. President George W. Bush and his wife, Laura, spent the night here during their 24-hour visit to Guatemala in March 2007.

French chain Accor Hotels unveiled its Guatemala City property in March 2007. **Mercure Casa Veranda** (12 Calle 1-24 Zona 10, tel. 2361-0196, www.mercure.com, $100–150 d) features all the amenities you'd come to expect from a reputable international hotel chain. Among the unique features of the property's 99 spacious suites are hardwood floors, Persian rugs, wireless Internet and balconies with fantastic city views; some suites have full kitchens. Local contacts say the restaurant and bar are top-notch.

A number of other international hotel chains are in this price category. Among them is the ever-reliable **Holiday Inn** (1a Avenida 13-22 Zona 10, tel. 2332-2555 or 888/465-4329 toll-free U.S., www.holidayinn.com.gt, $120 d), the landmark 271-room **Westin Camino Real** (14 Calle and Avenida La Reforma Zona 10, tel. 2333-3000, www.caminoreal.com .gt, $120–160 d), and the business traveler–oriented **Viva Clarion Suites** (tel. 2421-3333, www.clarionguatemala.com, $105–125 d), which also has some good packages for couples traveling to Guatemala to adopt children.

The all-suite **Radisson** (1a Avenida 12-46 Zona 10, tel. 2332-9797 or 800/333-3333 toll-free U.S., www.radisson.com, $120 d) has a Family Floor with rooms specially equipped for couples adopting children, including cribs and carriages, bottle sterilizers, and nanny service (extra). There's also a floor exclusively for women with the business traveler in mind, featuring a beauty salon and free transportation to area shopping malls, among other perks. All rooms have minibar, in-room safe, large windows with great city views, and in-room Internet access. There are also a gym, sauna, business center, and sushi restaurant/bar open 11 A.M.–midnight daily.

ZONAS 11 AND 13 (AIRPORT)
Under $50

A number of inexpensive hotels all offering similar services are centered in a middle-class neighborhood near the airport. All offer free transport to and from the terminal as well as breakfast, though this varies from continental minimalist to a full-on Guatemalan feast. **Dos Lunas Guest House** (21 Calle 10-92 Zona 13, Aurora II, tel. 2334-5264, www.hoteldoslunas .com) has nine basic rooms, all with shared

bath, for $12 per person including a breakfast of eggs and toast. Reservations are necessary, as it's usually booked. **Hostal Los Lagos** (8a Avenida 15-85 Zona 13, tel. 2334-5311, www .loslagoshostal.com) has cheerful rooms with colorful paintings and several beds each. You can share a room and a bathroom for as little as $15 or share a room with private bathroom for $20. A double room with one bed and private bathroom costs $35. All rates include a complete breakfast of eggs, beans, cereal, toast, juice, and coffee or tea. You'll find Internet, cable TV, laundry, and baggage storage as well as two sitting rooms with bamboo furniture.

Hostal Los Volcanes (16 Calle 8-00, Colonia Aurora I, Zona 13, tel. 2360-3232, www .hostallosvolcanes.com) has seven rooms with private or shared bathroom. Rates start at $15 per person in a dormitory bed. There are private shared-bath singles for $20. A room with private bathroom, large bed and cable TV costs $25/$40 a single/double. The pleasant house in which the hostel is based has a pleasant garden patio with a colonial fountain, a balcony with volcano views, a living room with cable TV, VCR, games, a library, Internet, and free drinking water. It also provides rides to the bus terminals.

A notch above the rest of the lodgings in the airport neighborhood is the newly opened **Hotel Casablanca** (15 Calle "C" 7-35, Aurora I, Zona 13, tel. 2362-5655 or 2362-4460, www.casablancagt.com, $35–50 d), with pleasant, tastefully decorated rooms with big beds, reading lamps, framed photo art, and shared or private bathroom. It has wireless Internet throughout and a restaurant/bar that had not yet opened when I visited.

$100-200

The newly remodeled 183-room **C Crowne Plaza** (Avenida Las Américas 9-08 Zona 13, tel. 2422-5000 or 877/227-6963 toll-free U.S., www.crowneplaza.com/guatemalacity, $105–150 d) features rooms with the chain's Sleep Advantage, including deliciously comfortable beds, new duvets, and your choice of seven different pillows. The seventh floor is designated as a "Quiet Zone," with TVs that reach only a certain volume and a relaxation kit with aromatherapy products. The ninth floor is an all-suite executive floor. The staff assures me you can drink the tap water and everything, including the hotel food, is certified to the highest standards of hygiene. It has a business center with wireless Internet, a huge gym with excellent city views from the top floor, a sports bar with video poker and slot machines, and a heated pool with whirlpool tub. The Los Volcanes restaurant, on the ground floor, serves international and local dishes à la carte or buffet style. There's a piano player at night. **Video Lotería Monte Carlo** (video gambling, 1 P.M.–3 A.M. daily) is also based on the ground floor, featuring video poker and slot machines. Proceeds benefit the environmental foundation Monte Carlo Verde.

Formerly the city's Hyatt Regency, the ◖ **Grand Tikal Futura** (Calzada Roosevelt 22-43 Zona 11, tel. 2440-1234, www.grand tikalfutura.com.gt, $140–600 d) still maintains the same high-quality standards and has comfortable, well-furnished rooms varying from standard rooms to a stunning Presidential Suite. All have splendid views of the city and surrounding mountains. Restaurants include elegant La Molienda, serving international and Guatemalan dishes for breakfast, lunch, and dinner and the excellent Thai Grill, Bar, and Wok serving lunch and dinner in a fantastic tropically inspired casual atmosphere. There are a lobby bar, fitness center with health-food bar, and a covered swimming pool with poolside service and city views.

CARRETERA A EL SALVADOR (SUBURBS)
Over $100

Although a bit far from the action, the all-suite ◖ **Quinta Real Guatemala** (Km. 8.5 Carretera a El Salvador, tel. 2420-7720, www.quinta real.com.gt, $100–899 d) scores big points for its location on a bluff overlooking the city and its neocolonial architecture featuring Mexican artistic touches. Its 129 rooms are all comfortable and well furnished with some truly splendid

© AL ARGUETA

Mayan temple mounds and modern Grand Tikal Futura contrast in Zona 11.

features, including vaulted wooden ceilings and neocolonial archways in some rooms. The Suite Gran Clase rooms are a good value and substantially nicer than the Master Suites, which are only slightly less expensive. The Suite Presidencial is probably the nicest room in all of Guatemala. Check the website for special deals. Wireless Internet is offered throughout the property. There is a pleasant, though unheated, garden swimming pool.

Its Restaurante Las Ventanas is one of the city's most exclusive, with a variety of international dishes served in an elegant dining room overlooking the hotel's gardens. Its well-stocked Bar Quinta Real is open 5 P.M.–1 A.M. Monday–Saturday.

Food

Cosmopolitan Guatemala City features a variety of excellent eating establishments for every taste and budget, as well as some more familiar U.S. franchises. Its culinary prowess is confirmed by a spot for Jake's on *Travel and Leisure* magazine's list of Top 10 Restaurants in Latin America (2006). Two other establishments were finalists.

CAFÉS

A profusion of new cafés has appeared in the downtown area, providing further evidence of the resurgence of the city's downtown core. Among these is **Café del Centro Histórico** (6a Avenida 9-50 Zona 1, all meals daily), well situated on the second floor of a restored 1930s building. Old photographs and original tiles hark back to the golden age of Sexta Avenida. Inexpensive meals, including Guatemalan staples such as *tortillas con carne,* salads, pies, and excellent coffee are served. Also downtown is **Café de Imeri** (6a Calle 3-30 Zona 1, tel. 2232-9008), which enjoys a loyal following owed to its delightful old-fashioned atmosphere and efficiently elegant service. The cakes and baked goods are top-notch, and there are good breakfasts, tacos, pasta, and salads. It makes a great place for lunch with a set menu for $3.50.

4 Grados Norte also has some pleasant sidewalk cafés, including **Café Saúl** (Ruta 2, 4 Grados Norte, tel. 2379-8721, 11 A.M.–11 P.M. Tues.–Thurs., 11 A.M.–midnight Fri./Sat., 11 A.M.–8 P.M. Sun., $4–8), serving delicious sweet and salty crepes, ice cream, sandwiches, salads, smoothies, and coffee in an eclectic atmosphere with chill music. Beer and wine are also served. Across the street is the bistro-style **Del Paseo** (tel. 2385-9046, 11 A.M.–10 P.M. Mon.–Thurs., 11 A.M.–1 A.M. Fri./Sat., noon–8 P.M. Sun.), with cool music, a funky atmosphere, and some seating facing the street. It has a full bar and a Middle Eastern menu that includes gyros, *shwarma,* and falafel as well as cheesecake and baklava for dessert. There's live music on Thursdays.

Caffé dei Fiori (15 Avenida 15-66 Zona 10, tel. 2363-5888, www.caffedeifiori.com, $3–8) has been around since the 1970's in three different Zona 10 locations. Its current incarnation features a pleasant covered patio where breakfasts, pizzas, pastas, salads, and sandwiches are served. Desserts include delicious tiramisu and *empanadas de piña.* Great espresso drinks round out the meal.

LIGHT MEALS AND PASTRIES

Cafeteria Patsy (14 Calle 4-73 Zona 1, tel. 2232-6703, and Avenida La Reforma 8-01 Zona 10, tel. 2331-2435, 7:30 A.M.–8 P.M. daily) has burgers, subs, and salads in the $2–4 range served in a pleasant atmosphere. There are set lunch menus for around $4. For healthy vegetarian fare, check out **Restaurante Rey Sol** (11 Calle 5-51 Zona 1, 8 A.M.– 5 P.M. Mon.–Sat., $4–8) serving tasty spinach lasagnas, whole-wheat bread sandwiches, salads, and smoothies. It also sells soy milk, granola, and herbal teas. Popular with Guatemalans, **San Martin and Company** (13 Calle 1-62 Zona 10, 6 A.M.–8 P.M. Mon.–Sat.) is a bak-

POLLO CAMPERO AND THE CULT OF FRIED CHICKEN

If, like most people traveling home from Guatemala, you fly out on a commercial airline flight, don't be surprised by the distinct smell of fried chicken onboard your aircraft. One look at the overhead bins will quickly reveal that they are crammed tight with boxes of fried chicken. Meet Pollo Campero, which along with coffee and bananas may be one of Guatemala's main exports.

Guatemalans have always had an affinity for the stuff. It's actually quite good, though I've never taken it along as a carry-on. Many travelers take a box home for homesick relatives craving a taste of the land they left behind. Although Pollo Campero has opened up shop in recent years in several U.S. cities, expatriate Guatemalans still make a point of stopping at the store in La Aurora airport to pick up a box. To illustrate the utter hold it has on the Guatemalan masses, the closed-for-remodeling airport shop operated out of a street-side trailer during the airport's recent renovation at a time when all other businesses were simply closed.

You may be asked by U.S. Customs if you're carrying food and this question might specifically address your smuggling of Pollo Campero. Rest assured, Customs officials are happy to let the cooked chicken cross the American threshold after applying the requisite X-rays. Some Newark Airport Customs officers even claim to have the uncanny ability to distinguish chicken from a Guatemalan Pollo Campero versus a San Salvador outlet, though I've never taken them up on offers to verify their claims.

Pollo Campero is becoming more than just a Guatemalan phenomenon, however. An aggressive company expansion includes the opening of numerous new locations throughout North America, Europe, and even Asia in the coming years. In 2007, Campero opened outlets in Jakarta, Indonesia, and Shanghai, China, with ambitious goals to open 500 more restaurants in China by 2012. Campero already operates 220 restaurants in 10 countries, including 38 in the United States. It employs more than 7,000 people and is the largest fast-food chain in Latin America. With such aggressive expansion plans, Pollo Campero may be headed for a location near you, and I don't mean seat 25F.

---

ery and café with pleasant outdoor seating on a terrace or ceiling fan–cooled dining room inside. There are scrumptious croissant sandwiches for breakfast as well as a variety of sandwiches, salads, and soups for lunch and dinner in the $3–5 range.

MEDITERRANEAN

Tarboosh (Ruta 2, Cuatro Grados Norte, tel. 2385-9091, 5 P.M.–1 A.M. Tues.–Thurs., noon–1 A.M. Fri./Sat.) is an Arab restaurant serving hummus, falafel, *shwarma,* and kebabs ($6–20) in a fashionable atmosphere where you can sit on cushions at low tables overlooking the pedestrian thoroughfare below. At **Tapas y Cañas** (13 Calle 7-78 Zona 10, tel. 2367-2166 or 2366-7970, lunch and dinner daily) you can savor delicious Spanish tapas. Try the *pinchos españoles*

or the *albondigas de lomito.* A longtime local favorite, **Altuna** (5a Avenida 12-31 Zona 1, tel. 2251-7185 and 10a Calle 0-45 Zona 10, tel. 2332-6576, www.restaurantealtuna.com, noon–10 P.M. Tues.–Sat., noon–5 P.M. Sun., $7–22) is also one of the city's fanciest offerings with impeccable service and an elegant atmosphere. Specialties include fish and seafood dishes, including paella and lobster, but it also serves land-based fare, including *jamón serrano* and chorizo. **La Paella** (12 Avenida 17-64 Zona 10, tel. 2368-2368, lunch and dinner daily), specializes in Paella Valenciana.

STEAK HOUSES

You'll find a variety of excellent steak houses in Guatemala City, including **Hacienda Real** (13 Calle 1-10 Zona 10, tel. 2368-1168 or

2333-5408/9, lunch and dinner daily, $10–20), where the meals are served with tasty tortillas and savory side sauces. Try the peppered steak. Another good choice is the Argentinean-style steak house **La Media Cancha** (13 Calle 4-71 Zona 9, tel. 2331-6463, lunch and dinner daily, $7–15). It's popular on weekends. For absolutely astounding views of the city from its perch along Carretera a El Salvador, you can't top **C El Portal del Angel** (Km. 11.2 Carretera a El Salvador, tel. 2369-6007, noon–9 P.M. Mon.–Thurs., noon–10 P.M. Fri.–Sun., $8–35). The food is just as good as the views and the tasteful decor, with walls in vivid hues adorned with cool paintings of Catholic saints, make this place truly heavenly. It is also in Zona 11 at Paseo Miraflores, minus the city views.

MEXICAN

Always a popular downtown favorite, **El Gran Pavo de Don Neto** (13 Calle 4-41 Zona 1, tel. 2232-9912, 7 A.M.–11 P.M. daily) serves a wide variety of authentic Mexican dishes at reasonable prices. It has live mariachi music on weekends and another location at 6a Avenida 12-72 Zona 10 (tel. 2362-0608/9). Also with several locations is **Los Cebollines** (6a Avenida 9-75 Zona 1, tel. 2232-7750; 12 Calle 6-17, Plazuela España, Zona 9, tel. 2334-1485; and Condado Concepción, at Km. 15.5 Carretera a El Salvador, tel. 6634-5405; www.cebollines.com, 7 A.M.–11 P.M. Mon.–Thurs., 7 A.M.–midnight Fri./Sat., 7 A.M.–10 P.M. Sun.), serving tasty grilled meats, enchiladas, and tacos you can wash down with refreshing lemonades, smoothies, or cocktails. Try the delicious *tacos de pollo pibil*. Along with its branch in Antigua, **Fridas** (3a Avenida 14-60 Zona 10, tel. 2367-1611/14, www.vivafridas.com, lunch and dinner daily) serves Mexican dishes that include tasty fajitas and flautas at fairly reasonable prices ($5–10). The chicken in mango sauce is delectable and the bar makes excellent margaritas. Pick your poison from the long list of tequilas ($4–12). The most casual of all the Mexican food options is **Ta'Contento** (Ruta 2 and Vía 5, 4 Grados Norte, tel. 2362-8584, 11 A.M.–midnight Tues.–Sun.), where you can eat your Mexican food al fresco on a patio adjacent to the popular pedestrian thoroughfare on which it's situated.

FRENCH

There has always been considerable French influence on Guatemalan culture, which is also evident in the city's culinary offerings. Among the excellent options are **Saint-Honoré** (14 Calle 2-51 Zona 10, tel. 2379-4548, 11:30 A.M.–11 P.M. daily), inside the Inter-Continental hotel, a typical French bakery serving cakes and some of Guatemala's best coffee. Also in the hotel lobby is the excellent **C Café de la Paix** (6 A.M.–11 P.M. daily), the only franchise of the famous Parisian brasserie chain outside of France, serving heavier meals, including entrecôte and onion soup ($12–25). **C Jean Francois** (Diagonal 6, 13-63 Zona 10, tel. 2333-4785, noon–3 P.M. and 7–10:30 P.M. Mon.–Fri., noon–3 P.M. Sat., $8–25) is a longtime favorite with Guatemala's wealthy elite and is arguably one of the finest restaurants in Latin America. The atmosphere is elegant with tablecloths and flowers adorning the tables and antique colonial furniture in the lounge. Entrées include snook in a cream and lemon sauce with fine herbs and steak *bondelaise* with porcini mushrooms. Try the fantastic cold lemon soufflé with caramel sauce for dessert.

A more casual French dining option is **La Lancha** (13 Calle 7-98 Zona 10, tel. 2337-4029, lalanchavino@hotmail.com, lunch Mon.–Tues., lunch and dinner Wed.–Fri.) with a set lunch chalkboard menu in the $5–10 range and à la carte dinner options for $6–10. Choose from a mix of homemade semi-Guatemalan and French dishes and wash them down with all-natural fruit juices or a bottle of wine from the extensive wine list.

GUATEMALAN

For gourmet Guatemalan cuisine served in a classy atmosphere accented by a high-roofed thatch ceiling, head to **C Kacao** (2a Avenida between 13 and 14 Calle, Zona 10, tel. 2337-4188/89, lunch and dinner daily). You can try a variety of traditional Guatemalan dishes, including spicy beef and chicken dishes in *pepián* and *jocón* sauces as well as corn-based delicacies such as *chuchitos* and tamales. In the downtown area, another popular place for Guatemalan cuisine is **Arrin Cuan** (5a Avenida 3-27 Zona 1, tel. 2238-0242, or 16 Calle 4-32 Zona 10, tel. 2366-2660, www.arrincuan.com, lunch and dinner daily, $5–10), with many dishes from the Cobán region, including *kakik* stew, but also some tasty less adventurous recipes such as chicken in apple sauce. The atmosphere is charmingly simple. Another good place for hearty Guatemalan fare is **Casa Chapina** (1a Avenida 13-42 Zona 10, tel. 2337-0143), serving well-presented Guatemalan dishes such as *pollo en salsa de loroco* accompanied by fresh avocado and corn on the cob.

ASIAN

Sushi places seem to have sprung up all over town recently with the Holiday Inn and Radisson each having their own sushi restaurants in their respective lobbies. The best of the hotel lobby sushi places, however, is **Tanoshii** (14 Calle 2-51 Zona 10, tel. 2379-4548, noon–3 P.M. and 6:30–11 P.M. Mon.–Sat.), inside the InterContinental hotel, also serving Japanese dishes in a hip, ultramodern setting. Also in Zona 10 is **Sushi Itto** (4a Avenida 16-01 Zona 10, tel. 2474-5812, www.sushi-itto.com, lunch and dinner daily). In Zona 4's 4 Grados Norte district, **Kampai Sushi** (tel. 2385-1468, lunch and dinner Tues.–Sun.) also serves Japanese noodle dishes in a casual atmosphere. For excellent Thai food, head to the Grand Tikal Futura hotel's **Thai Grill** (Calzada Roosevelt 22-43 Zona 11, tel. 2440-1234, www.grand tikalfutura.com.gt) for pad thai noodles, fried rice, or chicken satay.

For Chinese food, downtown there's **Long Wah** (6a Calle 3-75 Zona 1, tel. 2232-6611, lunch and dinner daily) with reasonably priced staple dishes you can eat in or take out. It's the best of several Chinese places west of the central plaza. **China Town** (13 Calle and Avenida La Reforma Zona 10, tel. 2331-9574, lunch and dinner Mon.–Sat.) delivers to the Zona 10 hotels, or you can enjoy your meal in its pleasant atmosphere.

ITALIAN

◖ **Pecorino** (11 Calle 3-36 Zona 10, tel. 2360-3035, www.ristorantepecorino.com, noon–1 A.M. Mon.–Sat.) is an excellent choice for its authentic Italian food, including brick-oven pizza, seafood dishes, steak, pasta, salads, and *panini* served in an attractive Old World atmosphere. There's also a huge wine selection. In a more modern setting with attractive blue-and-white-checkered tablecloths, **Tre Fratelli** (2a Avenida 13-25 Zona 10, tel. 2366-2678, www.trefratelli .com, noon–1 A.M. daily) serves ample portions of very good food in a lively atmosphere with prices in the $5–10 range. It's part of a growing chain of restaurants with locations in the United States, Mexico, and Central America. Other Guatemala City locations can be found in Zona 11 and Carretera a El Salvador. For outstanding brick-oven pizza served in a casual atmosphere, it's hard to beat **Pizzeria Vesuvio** (18 Calle 3-36 Zona 10, tel. 2337-1697, lunch and dinner daily, $7–15).

Downtown, **Restaurante Piccadilly** (6a Avenida and 11 Calle Zona 1, tel. 2253-4522, 7 A.M.–10 P.M. daily, $5–10) has a great selection of Italian and Guatemalan dishes in a pleasant family atmosphere. It also has beer on tap and a second location in Zona 9 at the Plazuela España (tel. 2334-7442). In 4 Grados Norte, **L'Osteria** (Ruta 2 and Vía 5, tel. 2379-8719, lunch and dinner Tues.–Sat., noon–6 P.M. Sun., $6–9) has delicious pizza, pasta, calzone, and crepes among its wide assortment of dishes. There is live music on Thursdays.

FUSION CUISINE AND FINE DINING

Many Guatemalan chefs study overseas early in their careers, which is clearly evident in the international influence permeating the city's excellent fusion cuisine. In other cases, talented chefs from New York and other international cities have set up shop in Guatemala, completely raising the bar for everyone else. Such is the case of ◖ **Jake's** (17 Calle 10-40 Zona 10, tel. 2368-0351, noon–3 P.M. and 7–10:30 P.M.

© AL ARGUETA

Tamarindos is one of Guatemala City's finest restaurants.

Also serving as a culinary school, **Camille** (9a Avenida 15-27 Zona 10, tel. 2368-0048 or 2367-1525, noon–3 P.M. and 7–10 P.M. Tues.–Fri., 7–10 P.M. Sat., $10–15) serves creatively prepared fish, chicken, and seafood dishes. The steak in chipotle sauce served on a cheese *pupusa* (Salvadoran cheese-filled tortilla) is truly extraordinary. The atmosphere is pleasantly cozy with carbon sketches etched on the white plaster walls and also on ripped-out pages from spiral bound notebooks framed and hung.

On the list of runners-up for distinction by *Travel and Leisure*'s Latin American Top 10 list is (**Tamarindos** (11 Calle 2-19A Zona 10, tel. 2360-2815, reservaciones@tamarindos .com.gt, 12:30–3 P.M. and 7:30 P.M.–1 A.M. Mon.–Sat., $10–20), which makes some fine sushi and does an excellent job of combining Thai, Italian, and Guatemalan flavors into some irresistible dishes. There is pleasant indoor and outdoor garden patio seating and the hip ambience is set by postmodern decor and electronica music on the stereo. Try the vegetarian pad thai or the four-cheese gnocchi.

The latest arrival on the Guatemala City fusion cuisine scene is **Misso** (16 Calle 6-17 Zona 10, tel. 2368-1747, noon–3 P.M. and 7–11 P.M. Mon.–Sat., $13–25). In addition to well-prepared sushi, there are a variety of creative dishes on offer. The crowning achievement is the duck in cinnamon-raspberry-peach chutney sauce. You can dine in the hip lounge (which also includes one of the city's swankiest bars) or outside on the terrace overlooking the bustling Zona Viva.

Zona 14 also has some highly recommended restaurants. **Céfiro** (3a Avenida 15-43 Zona 14, Plaza La Rioja Local #2, tel. 2385-5212, 12:30–10:30 P.M. Mon.–Sat., $10–15), in a shopping center in a quiet upscale neighborhood, has some creative menu options, including a delicious pasta salad made with watermelon, fennel, feta cheese, red onions, and black olives; plantain soup; a lasagna with seasoned mushrooms and brie; salmon cooked in tequila; and the outstanding tenderloin and foie gras scallop in a Zacapa Centenario rum reduction.

Mon.–Sat., noon–4 P.M. Sun., $10–25), started by New York City artist-turned-chef Jake Denburg. *Travel and Leisure* magazine recently rated Jake's one of the Top 10 restaurants in Latin America. Several features combine to make a visit to Jake's something truly special, including its wonderful atmosphere in a converted house with tile floors and wooden ceilings, eclectic decor, including some interesting black-and-white photographs, tables covered in butcher paper (crayons supplied), and most of all, the food. Highlights include lobster tortellini and the signature dish, the Vaquero Chino (Chinese Cowboy), a tenderloin steak prepared in a base sauce of sweet soy, espresso, and anise. The wine list is also impressive and rounding out your meal with one of the delectable homemade cheesecakes is a must.

Housed in the Otelito hotel, **Olivadda** (12 Calle 4-51 Zona 10, tel. 2339-1811, lunch and dinner daily, $7–12) serves sushi and exquisite international dishes with Guatemalan flair in a wonderful garden courtyard. Try the *caldo de tortilla Moreno*.

In a much more exclusive shopping center amid spacious gardens set apart from the road is **⊄ Ambia** (10a Avenida 5-49 Zona 14, tel. 2366-6890/7, lunch and dinner Mon.–Sat., lunch Sun.), where the emphasis is on New Age cuisine consisting largely of Asian recipes, including Thai chicken and shrimp recipes, pad thai ($10–12), excellent soups, Italian pastas, and lobster Thermidor ($26). There are excellent desserts, including black-and-white chocolate mousse and pears in red wine. The wine list, incidentally, is extensive and includes a $278 bottle of Spanish Vega Sicilia Valbuena.

SEAFOOD

With a hip family atmosphere housed in a building resembling its namesake structure, **Light House** (12 Calle 3-46 Zona 10, tel. 2331-9866, noon–11 P.M. Mon.–Wed., noon–1 A.M. Thurs.–Sat., noon–6 P.M. Sun.) serves classic seafood dishes, including oysters Rockefeller, crab cakes, and lobster Thermidor. **Donde Mikel** (13 Calle 5-19 Zona 10, tel. 2323-1524, lunch and dinner Mon.–Sat.) serves some of the city's best seafood and grilled steak in a casual atmosphere. Its surf-and-turf plates are a popular favorite. Although officially Peruvian food, the menu at **Inka Grill** (2a Avenida 14-22 Zona 10, tel. 2363-3013, noon–10 P.M. Sun.–Wed., until 11 P.M. Thurs.–Sat.) is heavy on delicious seafood, including several types of grilled fish and a Chinese-Peruvian blend of flavors, as in the case of its tasty wonton soup.

Information and Services

TOURIST INFORMATION

The main office of the Guatemala Tourist Commission (INGUAT) is at 7a Avenida 1-17 Zona 4, and it is open 8 A.M.–4 P.M. Monday–Friday. Your best bet, however, is to stop by its kiosk in the airport arrivals area, which is open 6 A.M.–9 P.M. It also has smaller offices inside the Palacio Nacional de la Cultura (Parque Central, tel. 2253-0748), which keeps odd hours, and the historic Palacio de Correos (Main Post Office, 7a Avenida 11-67 Zona 1, tel. 2251-1898, 9 A.M.–5 P.M. Mon.–Fri.).

MAPS

The best maps of Guatemala are *Mapas de Guatemala* (www.mapasdeguatemala.com), a series of recently introduced, beautifully illustrated, full-color maps of Guatemala's main tourist regions that also include helpful information on local businesses. The free maps are available at INGUAT and at tourist gift shops and restaurants seemingly everywhere. If you need a good map before leaving for Guatemala, ITMB Publishing (530 W. Broadway, Vancouver, BC, Canada, 604/879-3621, www.itmb.com) publishes an excellent *International Travel Map of Guatemala* ($10.95), which is weatherproof and can be found at well-known bookstores in the United States.

COMMUNICATIONS

The main post office (8:30 A.M.–5 P.M. Mon.–Fri., 8:30 A.M.–1 P.M. Sat.) is downtown at 7a Avenida 11-67 Zona 1. There are also branches at the airport and the corner of Avenida La Reforma and 14 Calle Zona 9 with the same hours. It's called El Correo.

For more reliable service, many people prefer to use one of the international couriers, including FedEx (14 Avenida 7-12 Complejo Empre-Villa #20, Zona 14, tel. 2366-8536 or toll-free from Guatemala 1-801-00-333-39, www.fedex.com/gt_english), UPS (12 Calle 5-53 Zona 10, tel. 2360-6460, www.ups.com), and DHL (12 Calle 5-12 Zona 10, tel. 2332-7547, www.dhl.com). For an all-in-one shipping locale, try Mail Boxes (Avenida Las Américas 6-19 Zona 14, tel. 2337-4450, 8 A.M.–7 P.M. Mon.–Fri., 9 A.M.–1 P.M. Sat.).

Internet access is widely available throughout the city, but especially downtown, costing about $1–1.50 an hour. It's more expensive (like everything else) in Zona 10, though Web Station (2a Avenida 14-63 Zona 10, 10 A.M.–midnight Mon.–Sat., noon–midnight Sun.) is a cheaper option at $2.50 an hour.

MONEY

You can exchange dollars and cash travelers checks at virtually all of the city's banks, including the one in the arrivals hall of the international airport. ATMs linked to international networks can be found all over the city. Be especially careful when withdrawing money at ATMs in the downtown area. The safest place to hit up an ATM is probably one of the numerous Guatemala City shopping malls.

You can search for Visa ATM locations in Guatemala City online at http://visa.via.infonow .net/locator/global/jsp/SearchPage.jsp and MasterCard ATMs at www.mastercard.com/atm. A useful listing of **Banco Industrial** Visa ATM machines throughout Guatemala can be found at www.bi.com.gt/Cajeros-BI_body.htm.

The American Express Agent in Guatemala City is Clark Tours (7a Avenida 14-76, Plaza Clark, Zona 9, tel. 2412-4700, www.clark tours.com). It also has offices in the Westin Camino Real, Holiday Inn, and Marriott.

LAUNDRY

You can do laundry at some of the budget hotels, including the Xamanek Student Inn (13 Calle 3-57 Zona 10). Otherwise, downtown

---

GUATEMALA CITY EMBASSIES AND CONSULATES

Most embassies and consulates tend to be open only during weekday mornings.

- **Austria:** 6a Avenida 20-25, Edificio Plaza, Zona 10, tel. 2364-3460

- **Belize:** Avenida La Reforma 8-50, Edificio El Reformador, Suite 803, Zona 9, tel. 2334-5531

- **Canada:** 13 Calle 8-44, 6th Floor, Edificio Edyma Plaza, Zona 10, tel. 2333-6102

- **Colombia:** 5a Avenida 5-55, Edificio Europlaza, Torre I, Zona 14, tel. 2385-3432

- **Costa Rica:** 1a Avenida 15-52 Zona 10, tel. 2363-1345

- **Cuba:** 13 Calle 5-72 Zona 10, tel. 2333-7627

- **El Salvador:** 5a Avenida 8-15 Zona 9, tel. 2360-7660

- **France:** Edificio Marbella, 11th Floor, 16 Calle 4-53 Zona 10, tel. 2337-3639

- **Germany:** Edificio Plaza Marítima, 20 Calle 6-20 Zona 10, tel. 2364-6700

- **Honduras:** 19 Avenida "A" 20-19 Zona 10, tel. 2366-5640

- **Israel:** 13 Avenida 14-07 Zona 10, Colonia Oakland, tel. 2363-5665

- **Italy:** 5a Avenida 8-59 Zona 14, tel. 2337-4851

- **Mexico:** 15 Calle 3-20 Zona 10, tel. 2333-7254

- **Netherlands:** 16 Calle 0-55, 13th Floor, Torre Internacional, Zona 10, tel. 2367-4761

- **Nicaragua:** 10a Avenida 14-72 Zona 10, tel. 2368-0785

- **Panama:** 10a Avenida 18-53 Zona 14, tel. 2368-2805

- **Spain:** 6a Calle 6-48 Zona 9, tel. 2379-3530

- **Sweden:** 8a Avenida 15-07 Zona 10, tel. 2333-6536

- **Switzerland:** Torre Internacional, 16 Calle 0-65 Zona 10, tel. 2367-5520

- **United Kingdom:** Torre Internacional, 16 Calle 0-65, 11th Floor, Zona 10, tel. 2367-5520

- **United States:** Avenida La Reforma 7-01 Zona 10, tel. 2331-1541

there's Lavandería El Siglo (12 Calle 3-42 Zona 1, 8 A.M.–6 P.M. Mon.–Sat., $4 per load). In Zona 10 is Lavandería Obelisco (Avenida La Reforma 16-30), where self-service laundry costs about $3 per load to wash and dry.

MEDICAL SERVICES

Public clinics such as the Clínica Cruz Roja (Red Cross Clinic, 3a Calle 8-40 Zona 1, 8 A.M.– 5:30 P.M. Mon.–Fri., 8 A.M.–noon Sat.) offer free or low-cost consultations. There are also several private clinics with doctors who speak English, including the highly recommended 24-hour Hospital Centro Medico (6a Avenida 3-47 Zona 10, tel. 2332-3555) and the Hospital Herrera Llerandi (6a Avenida 8-71 Zona 10, tel. 2334-5959 or 2334-5955 emergencies).

EMERGENCY

Dial 120 from any phone for the police (6a Avenida and 14 Calle Zona 1). For emergency medical assistance, dial 125 for the Red Cross. For the fire department, dial 122 or 123.

IMMIGRATION

The offices of Migración (tel. 2361-8476, www.migracion.gob.gt) are on the second floor of the INGUAT building at 7a Avenida 1-17 Zona 4 and are open 8 A.M.–2:45 P.M. Monday–Friday.

TRAVEL AGENTS

For booking plane tickets and onward travel within Guatemala, a good choice is Viajes Tivoli (6a Avenida 8-41 Zona 9, tel. 2386-4200, or 12 Calle 4-55 Zona 1, Edificio Herrera, tel. 2298-1050, www.tivoli.com .gt), as is Clark Tours (7a Avenida 14-76, Plaza Clark, Zona 9, tel. 2412-4700, www .clarktours.com). Clark Tours also has offices in the Westin Camino Real, Holiday Inn, and Marriott.

Getting There and Around

GETTING THERE
Air

The once-wonky **La Aurora International Airport** (GUA) is undergoing a major expansion and renovation (see the sidebar *A New Airport for Guatemala City?*), with the passenger terminal having been completely emptied of all businesses to carry out the much-needed improvements. Its pre-modernization services included a bank, ATMs, various restaurants, excellent duty-free shopping, several souvenir stalls, and a post office. Look for these services and some newer selections to be available in the remodeled terminal, which will certainly outshine the previous port of entry.

Up-to-the-minute flight arrival and departure information can be found online at www .prensalibre.com.gt/app/vuelos/index.jsp and is the same information you'll find on the flight monitors at the airport.

Several U.S. and foreign carriers fly daily into Guatemala City, with new ones report-edly looking to start service pending the completion of the airport modernization project. (See the *Essentials* chapter for more detailed schedule and routing information.) Several of these airlines have city ticket offices, including **American Airlines** (Guatemala City Marriott, 7a Avenida 15-45 Zona 9, and Columbus Center, Avenida Las Américas 18-81, Nivel 2, Zona 14, tel. 2422-0000), **Continental Airlines** (18 Calle 5-56, Edificio Unicentro, Local 704, Zona 10, tel. 2385-9610 or 801/812-6684 toll-free), **Delta** (15 Calle 3-20 Zona 10, Centro Ejecutivo, Primer Nivel, Zona 10, tel. 2337-0642), **United Airlines** (Avenida La Reforma 1-50, Edificio Reformador, Zona 9, tel. 2336-9900), **US Airways** (13 Calle 3-40 Zona 10, Edificio Atlantis, Nivel 2, #27, tel. 2470-0880), **TACA** (Avenida Hincapié 12-22, Zona 13, tel. 2470-8222), and **Iberia** (Avenida La Reforma 8-60 Zona 9, tel. 2332-0911). American Airlines and Continental Airlines passengers can check in the day before at service centers in

A NEW AIRPORT FOR GUATEMALA CITY?

© GUATEMALAN CIVIL AVIATION

artist's rendering of remodeled La Aurora International Airport

Longtime travelers to Guatemala might be surprised to find a modern, gleaming new airport terminal when they next set foot in Guatemala City. Officials were busily executing a much-needed renovation and reconstruction of Guatemala City's La Aurora International Airport (GUA), and by the time you read this, the first phase of the $80 million project should be unveiled, including a completely revamped main terminal building with a covered access ramp fronted by a three-story, 500-car parking garage. Inside, it will house new check-in facilities on the expanded third floor and new immigration kiosks, customs operations, and baggage-claim carousels for arriving passengers. A brand-new terminal, known as the **North Finger,** will house 12 gates for arrivals and departures. The original international departures lounges running out from the main terminal building will have been demolished to make room for the four-gate **Central Finger,** parallel to the main terminal, with capacity for larger aircraft such as 747-400s and Airbus A340s. One carrier already flies A340s to Guatemala and had been having trouble maneuvering in the airport's cramped spaces. Runway improvements will allow for simultaneous takeoffs and landings with the separation of the main taxiway from La Aurora's runway 1-19. The final phase, which was to be completed in 2008, will be the construction of an additional five-gate complex known as the **South Finger,** bringing the total number of gates to 21, up from eight before the reconstruction program.

The improvements are partially the result of an ultimatum given to Guatemalan authorities by the International Civil Aviation Organization (ICAO); it required the needed improvements to be completed by 2007 to remove Guatemala from a Category 2 safety classification. Had Guatemala remained Category 2, travelers to the country may very well have started flying in to neighboring San Salvador, as U.S. carriers threatened to cease operations at La Aurora if the improvements were not made. The ICAO is managing the project and will also recertify the airport's safety classification after the renovations.

La Aurora's aging facilities had received substandard maintenance and minimal infrastructural improvements since first opening in 1968 as one of the finest airport terminals in Latin America. While the improvements will restore much of the airport's lost splendor, authorities realize the airport will eventually need to be moved out of Guatemala City altogether. A commercial district at its northern end and a deep ravine to the south hedge in La Aurora's sole runway and limit the airport's expansion. In addition to several mountains and volcanic peaks that make the approach into GUA difficult for pilots, Guatemala City's office buildings and condos flank the surrounding areas, leading to fears of a runway mishap of tragic proportions.

La Aurora Airport could not be any more conveniently situated, though its location very much within the confines of Guatemala City is both a blessing and a curse. Runway overruns, some fatal, have occurred. The most notable include the nonfatal 1993 TACA crash of a Boeing 767 and a Cubana DC-10 crash in 1999, which killed 26. Its safety in light of its location right in the heart of the city has always been

questioned but recent events have also cast doubt on the adequacy of its security measures, something that will have to be resolved before its recertification. In September 2006, thieves executing a well-planned heist made off with $8.6 million in cash that was awaiting transfer to a Miami-bound aircraft on the airport tarmac.

The new airport project has been talked about for decades but it may be scheduled for takeoff in the next few years. The Japan International Cooperation Agency (JICA) has donated feasibility studies for the new airport, including the determination of the best location based on several criteria, as well as blueprints for the terminal's architectural design. Authorities have announced Masagua, in the coastal department of Escuintla, as the ideal site for the new facility. The new site offers several advantages, including the absence of urban congestion, a runway at sea level to allow long-haul flights from Europe and Asia, more room to build facilities, and the opportunity to turn the airport into a magnet for economic development outside of the capital. The main disadvantages appear to be the project's hefty $565 million price tag and the greater distance from the capital. Authorities will need to incorporate public transportation and new access roads to the airport, which would be completed sometime in the next 15-20 years, when La Aurora is projected to definitively exceed its capacity even with the recent improvements. The Ministry of Communications announced the project in January 2006, calling it "feasible and necessary." It may take 10 years just to implement structures for the project's execution, including the purchase of needed lands, formalizing of design plans, and contracting the necessary construction work.

La Aurora International Airport

the Guatemala City Marriott (7a Avenida 15-45 Zona 9).

The only **domestic service** was to Flores, near the ruins of Tikal, though other routes may open thanks to an aggressive government project to revamp several smaller airports throughout the country. The only airline leaving from the main terminal for domestic flights is TACA, with several daily flights to Flores. There are 2–3 other carriers offering service from the other side of the runway at private hangars, for which you'll need to take a taxi.

A taxi from the airport costs $8–20 depending on what part of town you're going to. Frequent shuttle buses leave for Antigua, costing about $15–20. It's not a good idea to ride a public bus into the city, especially at night.

Bus

Guatemala City's unattractive Zona 4 bus terminal was being phased out thanks to a long-overdue plan to bring order to the chaos traditionally characterizing the state of public transportation, both within and into and out of the city. Accounting for 80 percent of the bedlam were buses arriving from and departing to the Western Highlands and the Pacific Coast. Details were sketchy, but it appears buses to and from both of these regions will now be based out of the **Central de Transferencias (CENTRA)** in Zona 12, on the southern outskirts of the city. From there, a series of modern, bright green interconnected buses known as *buses articulados* take passengers on a new system called the **Transmetro** into the city center. Plans call for other transfer centers for buses coming from the eastern part of the country to be built thereafter. The city's public transportation system, meanwhile, will be replaced entirely by the Transmetro, a sort of surface metro, which will cover the entire metropolitan area by 2015.

For now, the Transmetro's sole route starts at the CENTRA and heads downtown, making 12 stops along the way, including those at the Centro Cívico (Civic Center) and El Trébol, near the Zona 4 bus terminal. The latter's status as the transportation hub for many bus lines will probably remain in place pending the gradual transition to the new system based on transfer centers. Direct Transmetro buses (no stops) heading from downtown to CENTRA leave from **El Amate station** (4a Avenida and 18 Calle Zona 1, 5–9 A.M. and 4–9 P.M. Mon.–Fri.). Check locally for the latest on this interesting development and more detailed schedule information.

A number of the (mostly) **first class buses** still leave from their own depots spread throughout the city, and this will probably continue to be the case for some time. Here is the information on some of the more popular first class bus routes:

To Chiquimula: (3.5 hours, $4, 170 km) **Rutas Orientales** (19 Calle 8-18 Zona 1, tel. 2253-7282), departures every half hour 4:30 A.M.–6 P.M., or **Transportes Guerra** (19 Calle 8-39 Zona 1, tel. 2238-2917), every half hour 7 A.M.–6 P.M.

To Cobán: (4.5 hours, $5, 213 km) **Transportes Escobar Monja Blanca** (8a Avenida 15-16 Zona 1, tel. 2238-1409), has hourly buses 4 A.M.–5 P.M., stopping at El Rancho and the Quetzal Biotope.

To Esquipulas: (4.5 hours, $5, 222 km) **Rutas Orientales** (19 Calle 8-18 Zona 1, tel. 2253-7282), with departures every half hour 4:30 A.M.–6 P.M.

To Flores: (eight hours, $10–30 depending on service level, 500 km) Options include **Línea Dorada** (16 Calle 10-55 Zona 1, tel. 2232-5506, www.tikalmayanworld.com), with luxury buses departing at 10 A.M. and 9 P.M. ($30), or a more economical overnight bus leaving at 10 P.M. ($16). **Fuentes del Norte** (17 Calle 8-46 Zona 1, tel. 2251-3817) has about 20 daily departures ($10–20).

To Huehuetenango: (five hours, 266 km) **Los Halcones** (7a Avenida 15-27 Zona 1, tel. 2238-1929, $5), departs at 7 A.M., 2 P.M., and 5 P.M. **Transportes Velásquez** (20 Calle 1-37 Zona 1, tel. 2221-1084, $4) has nine buses daily. **Transportes Zaculeu Futura** (9a Calle 11-42 Zona 1, tel. 2232-2858, $5), has buses at 6 A.M. and 3 P.M.

To La Mesilla: (seven hours, $6, 345 km)

Transportes Velásquez (20 Calle 1-37 Zona 1, tel. 2221-1084, $5.50), every two hours 5:30 A.M.–1:30 P.M.

To Panajachel: (three hours, 148 km) **Transportes Rebuli** (21 Calle and 4a Avenida Zona 1, $2) has hourly buses 5:30 A.M.–3:30 P.M.

To Puerto Barrios: (five hours, 295 km) **Litegua** (15 Calle 10-40 Zona 1, tel. 2220-8840, www.litegua.com) has 16 buses daily 4:30 A.M.–7 P.M.

To Quetzaltenango: (four hours, $4.50, 205 km) **Transportes Álamo** (21 Calle 0-14 Zona 1, tel. 2251-4838) has six buses a day 8 A.M.–5:30 P.M. **Líneas América** (2a Avenida 18-47 Zona 1, tel. 2232-1432) has seven buses a day 5 A.M.–7:30 P.M. **Transportes Galgos** (7a Avenida 19-44 Zona 1, tel. 2253-4868) leaves seven times daily 5:30 A.M.–7 P.M. The newest option is a nonstop bus on an ultraluxurious coach aboard **Línea Dorada** (16 Calle 10-03 Zona 1, tel. 2220-7900 or 2232-9658, $6) at 8 A.M. and 3 P.M.

To Río Dulce: (six hours, $6–21, 280 km) **Línea Dorada** (16 Calle 10-55 Zona 1, tel. 2232-5506, www.tikalmayanworld.com) has luxury buses departing at 10 A.M. and 9 P.M. ($21), or a more economical bus leaving at 10 P.M. ($11). Both continue to Flores. **Litegua** (15 Calle 10-40 Zona 1, tel. 2220-8840, www.litegua.com) has buses at 6 A.M., 9 A.M., 11:30 A.M., and 1 P.M.

To Zacapa: (three hours, $3.50) **Rutas Orientales** (19 Calle 8-18 Zona 1, tel. 2253-7282) has 15 buses daily.

International Bus

To Copán, Honduras: (five hours, 238 km, $35) **Hedman Alas** (2a Avenida 8-73 Zona 10, tel. 2362-5072/3/4, www.hedmanalas.com) departs daily at 5 A.M.

To San Salvador, El Salvador: (five hours, 240 km) **Melva Internacional** (3a Avenida 1-38 Zona 9, tel. 2331-0874, $10) departs hourly 5 A.M.–4 P.M., with more expensive *especiales* ($12) leaving at 6:45 A.M., 9 A.M., and 3 P.M. **Tica Bus** (11 Calle 2-74 Zona 9, tel. 2331-4279, www.ticabus.com, $11) leaves at 1 P.M.

King Quality (18 Avenida 1-96 Zona 15, tel. 2369-0404, $22) has luxury buses departing at 6:30 A.M., 8 A.M., 2 P.M., and 3:30 P.M. **Pullmantur** (1a Avenida 13-22 Zona 10, Holiday Inn, tel. 2367-4746, www.pullmantur .com, $30–46) offers the most luxurious service on this route with double-decker buses and a choice of fare classes, departing at 7 A.M. and 3 P.M. daily with additional buses Fridays at noon and Sundays at 4 P.M.

To Tapachula, Mexico: (seven hours, 290 km) **Transportes Galgos** (7a Avenida 19-44 Zona 1, tel. 2253-4868, $22) has departures at 7:30 A.M. and 2 P.M. **Línea Dorada** (16 Calle 10-55 Zona 1, tel. 2232-5506, www.tikalmayan world.com, $22) departs at 8 A.M.

GETTING AROUND
Taxi
Getting around by taxi can be tricky, as there is really only one reliable taxicab company in the city and it requires you to call for a pickup if you wish to hire its services. **Taxis Amarillo Express** (tel. 2332-1515) is also one of the only companies to use meters. Otherwise, the airport taxis and those at the Zona Viva hotels are generally reliable. It's not usually a good idea to hail a cab from the street, as some of these are gypsy cabs and robberies do sometimes occur. If you find a reliable cab driver, you can always ask for a business card and hire his services for the rest of your stay or ask him to refer you to another reputable driver.

Car Rental
Several car rental agencies operate out of the airport and nearby Zona 10, including **Advantage** (Avenida La Reforma 8-33 Zona 10, tel. 2332-7525 or 2362-7202 or 800/777-5500 U.S. toll-free, www.advantagerentacar .com), **Avis** (6a Avenida 7-64 Zona 9, tel. 2331-0017 or 800/331-1212 U.S. toll-free, www.avis.com), **Dollar** (Avenida La Reforma 8-33 Zona 10, tel. 2331-7185 or 800/800-

4000 U.S. toll-free, www.dollar.com), **Budget** (6a Avenida 11-24 Zona 9, tel. 2332-7744 or 800/472-3325 U.S. toll-free, www.budget .com or www.budgetguatemala.com.gt), **Hertz** (7a Avenida 14-76 Zona 9, tel. 2470-3800 or 800/654-3001 U.S. toll-free, also with offices inside the Westin Camino Real, Intercontinental, and Marriott, www.hertz.com), and **Thrifty** (1a Avenida 13-74 Zona 10, tel. 2333-7444, 2379-8747, or 800/847-4389 U.S. toll-free, www.thrifty.com).

Public Buses
Guatemala City's chaotic public bus transportation is not recommended for international travelers, mainly for safety considerations, as armed robberies and purse snatchings are frequent. Buses are also particularly susceptible to the city's increasing gang-related violence and drivers are often harassed for money by gang members. A glimmer of hope is on the horizon, however, with the recent unveiling of the **Transmetro,** a completely revamped public transportation system, which will be in full operation by 2020. The first phase, including the first transfer center (in Zona 12) for buses coming in from other parts of Guatemala, is already up and running. Bus service via long, trainlike interconnected green units brings travelers from the transfer center to the downtown area. More transfer centers are in the works.

The system promises to provide Guatemalans (and foreign travelers) with a safe, comfortable, and fast option for getting around the city. Buses will stop at designated locations, drivers will no longer trundle the streets competing for passengers, a prepaid system will eliminate on-board cash, and buses and stations will be guarded by cameras and plainclothes police officers. It seems to be a good idea, in theory at least. Travelers riding on the new transportation system are encouraged to write in with their thoughts and observations.

Near Guatemala City

South of the city along Calzada Aguilar Batres, the city sprawl continues into the adjacent district of Villa Nueva, a suburban housing and industrial area that has been swallowed by the larger city. From here, the Carretera al Pacífico, or Pacific Highway (CA-9) leads south to Escuintla and the Pacific Coast.

LAKE AMATITLÁN

Amatitlán lies 30 kilometers south of Guatemala City on the road to the Pacific Coast. The lake is in the process of being rescued from what would have been certain ecological death caused by wastewater from nearby industry and uncontrolled urban growth. A new sewage treatment plant now filters the filthy waters of the Río Villalobos, which once flooded untreated sewage into the lake. Trees have been replanted and the lake is being pumped with oxygen and cleaned of plants in an effort to reverse its eutrophication. It's still not possible to swim in the lake's waters, though it may be some day.

Recreation

The public beach of **Las Ninfas** was being remodeled by tourism authorities to include boat docks (for sailboats and motorboats), new food stalls, walkways, and landscaping. The long-closed **Teleférico** (Aerial Tram, 9 A.M.– 5 P.M. Fri.–Sun., $2 adults, $0.85 children), was reopened in 2006, kicking off the rebirth of one of Guatemala City's oldest recreational enclaves. The funicular climbs 350 meters up a mountainside along a 1.5-kilometer route. There's a lookout point at the top of the mountain where you can get out, appreciate the view of the lake and Guatemala City, and grab a bite to eat at a small cafeteria serving tacos, hot dogs, chicken wings, and salads.

Another recreational option is **rock climbing** on the rock cliffs overlooking the lakeshore on 20 different routes ranging in difficulty from 5.8 to 5.13. **Vertical Expeditions** (tel. 5801-6871, ask for Manuel Vanegas, or 2232-0044, ask for Julioandre Piedra Santa, www.verticalexpeditions

.com.gt) does full-day climbing trips for $35 per person with a three-person minimum, including guide, gear, and transportation. It also offers a one-day rock climbing school for $50, covering all aspects of safety, equipment, and climbing techniques. Further options include climbing (5.8 to 5.13) and rappelling along a 70-meter (230-foot) waterfall in the eastern province of Jalapa, 100 kilometers from Guatemala City. You can also rappel down the actual waterfall, a practice commonly referred to as canyoning. Day trips cost $65 per person with a four-person minimum and include guide, transport, and gear. Antigua-based **Old Town Outfitters** (5a Avenida Sur #12C, tel. 5339-0440, www .bikeguatemala.com) also offers rock-climbing day trips to Amatitlán for $35 per person, including all gear, and can provide instruction.

If you'd rather just soak your weary bones in the warm waters of some pleasant hot springs, you can do that at **Baños Termales Santa Teresita** (tel. 6633-0225, www.santateresita .com.gt, 8 A.M.–6 P.M. daily). You can enjoy a private steam bath or a soak in a private tub filled with steaming hot water to your taste ($5). Several outdoor pools of varying temperatures are also available and there's a restaurant serving grilled meats and chicken, salads, sandwiches, and seafood. Rounding out the list of offerings is a spa, where you can enjoy a one-hour massage for about $13.

Parque Nacional Naciones Unidas

This 491-hectare park near the lakeshore is managed by private conservation group **Defensores de la Naturaleza** (tel. 6630-6421 or 6630-6153) and is open 8 A.M.–4 P.M. Monday–Friday and 8 A.M.–5 P.M. Saturday and Sunday. Admission is $3.50. Facilities include picnic areas with barbecue pits, hiking and mountain biking trails with lookout points over the lake, basketball courts, and soccer fields.

Getting There

You'll probably need to rent a car to get to Lake

Amatitlán, though you could also hire a cab to take you there from Guatemala City for about $25. If you're driving, take the Pacific Highway (CA-9) south out of the city. The main entrance to the Amatitlán lakeshore is at Km. 26. You'll see signs. The exit veers off from the right side of the highway. From the exit ramp, you'll come to a Shell gas station, where you turn left. Follow the road until it dead-ends just past the soccer fields on your left. Turn left at the dead end. You'll pass a bridge over the Río Michatoya on your right. The next left will take you to the Teleférico and farther up that same road is Parque Nacional Naciones Unidas. Turning right onto the bridge over the Río Michatoya followed by an immediate right will bring you to the Santa Teresita hot springs.

🏔 PACAYA VOLCANO NATIONAL PARK

Looming over Lake Amatitlán is this 2,552-meter-high active volcano spewing lava and ash for the amazement of tourists and locals alike.

Its current active phase began in 1965 and has barely ceased since. Activity varies from quiet gas, lava, and steam emissions to full-scale explosive eruptions hurtling rocks into the sky. It sometimes spews large ash clouds that prompt the closure of Guatemala City's La Aurora International Airport, as was the case when a 1998 eruption blanketed the airport runway in fine volcanic sand.

The volcano makes a convenient day trip from Guatemala City or Antigua. Logistically, it makes more sense from Guatemala City, but the tour operators offering the trip are almost entirely based in the old colonial city. It's possible to make the trip on your own, though going in a group with a local guide is highly recommended. (See the *La Antigua Guatemala* chapter for recommended guide companies.)

The volcano's national park status dates to 2001. A visitors center and ticket booth can be found at the trailhead in the village of San Francisco de Sales. Admission to the park is $3.50. There is safe parking for vehicles in

FIRE ON THE MOUNTAIN

Guatemala is one of few places in the world where you can get up close and personal with an active volcano in relative ease. From the town of San Francisco de Salas, the 3.7-kilometer trail up Pacaya Volcano (2-3 hours) climbs gradually through cornfields and secondary forest before arriving at a vast volcanic wasteland of old lava flows. After crossing a barren ridge, the trail then winds up the slopes of the volcanic crater itself. Hiking up the loose ash will give you the sensation of taking two steps forward and one step back. It's a good workout but worth the effort. At the summit, you're treated to a fine view of the main vent spewing lava, rocks, and ash. It may sometimes feel too close for comfort, as large chunks of lava rock often land nearby. You can also see Guatemala City, the Pacific Coast, and some of the neighboring volcanoes from here.

At the summit, avoid breathing in the clouds of sulfuric gases. Be especially careful where you step, as there are some hot zones and sometimes some slow-moving lava flows. The skilike descent down the same sandy ash can be tricky and you should exercise due caution to avoid a nasty face-plant into the jagged lava rocks alongside the trail.

If hiking during the day, bring plenty of sunscreen along with a hat, preferably with a chin strap that will prevent it from blowing away at the windy summit. Water and some snacks are always a good idea. Try not to carry excessive amounts of cash, but just what you'll need for the park admission, guide tip, and a drink and/or snack when you arrive back at the base of the trail. Rain gear (depending on the season) and some good, sturdy boots are also important. You'll especially appreciate the latter because you'll need ankle support and it's easy to get rocks and sand in your shoes, which can be extremely uncomfortable, during the final ascent up the sandy crater.

© AL ARGUETA

a view of smoking Pacaya Volcano from the south

San Francisco de Sales and the well-maintained trail has good signage, rest stops with trash receptacles, and outhouses. The trails are patrolled by park rangers and incidents of robbery, which once plagued this otherwise wonderful place, have become virtually unheard of in recent years.

To get here on your own steam, follow the CA-9 highway past Amatitlán to a signed turn-off at Km. 37.5 and heading east eight kilometers to the village of San Vicente Pacaya. The road continues from here another 10 kilometers to San Francisco de Sales and the trailhead. It's always possible to hire a guide at the visitors center.

Parque Natural Canopy Calderas

Three kilometers from San Francisco de Salas is the wonderful, privately owned Parque Natural Canopy Calderas (tel. 5538-5531, www.parque naturalcalderas.com, 8 A.M.–6 P.M. daily, $10 admission), where you can explore a volcanic caldera. Activities on and around the jungle-clad lagoon include cruising along a zip line through the forest canopy between six platforms ($10), four-wheeling ($13 per hour), horseback riding ($8), mountain biking, kayaking ($3.50), sailboarding ($7), rappelling, and guided hikes along nature trails or to the volcano. You can also safely camp here beside the lake for $7 in your own tent or you can rent one ($7).

LA ANTIGUA GUATEMALA

Its name means "the old Guatemala," and this is in fact what it is. The former capital of Guatemala was destroyed by an earthquake in 1773. Rather than rebuild, the country's aristocracy opted for a fresh start in the neighboring Valley of the Hermitage, the current site of Guatemala City. And so, by decree, the city and its inhabitants moved on. Still, some Antigueños stayed behind, choosing to live among the ruins, coffee farms, verdant hillsides, and sentinel volcanoes. The city's colonial architecture was maintained, as there were no plans to rebuild, and its ruined churches and convents remained just that. It is said the remaining residents of Antigua were so poor they had to subsist on avocadoes, earning them the nickname Panzas Verdes (Green Bellies).

Today, Antigua (as it is more commonly referred to) is a UNESCO World Heritage Site and is home to much of Guatemala's expatriate population along with scores of international students studying in its many Spanish schools. Its brightly colored houses and cobblestone streets harbor some of Guatemala's finest restaurants, shopping, and art galleries in a fantastic mountain setting that has inspired artists, writers, and wanderers for centuries. Antigua is a pleasant mixture of Mayan and Spanish colonial influences and is an excellent base from which to explore other parts of the country.

In addition to its colonial ruins, churches, and convents, Antigua offers a variety of recreational opportunities, including nearby coffee farms, where you can see the cultivation process of this singular bean, mountain biking through neighboring villages, and volcanoes

© AL ARGUETA

HIGHLIGHTS

◖ Parque Central: You can't miss the town's central plaza, easily Guatemala's loveliest and the heart and soul of Antigua (page 77).

◖ Arco de Santa Catalina: A beautiful colonial archway, which is also one of Antigua's most photographed landmarks, provides a suitable frame for views of Agua Volcano (page 80).

◖ Cerro de la Cruz: This large stone cross on a hill overlooking the valley and volcanoes makes a good afternoon stroll. Bring a camera (page 81).

◖ Iglesia y Convento de las Capuchinas: One of Antigua's best-preserved colonial monuments has many interesting features, including a tower and 18 nuns' cells built around a patio (page 81).

◖ Centro Cultural Casa Santo Domingo: The city's finest museum lies on the grounds of a fantastic restored monastery, which now functions as a five-star hotel (page 83).

◖ Casa Popenoe: This fully restored colonial mansion offers a rare glimpse into the life of a royal official in 17th-century Antigua in addition to wonderful city views from the second-story terrace (page 83).

◖ Volcano Climbs: Antigua's fantastic mountain scenery is dominated by the presence of Agua, Fuego, and Acatenango Volcanoes, affording excellent opportunities for mountaineering at a variety of difficulty levels. Active Pacaya Volcano, though not within sight of town, is not too much farther and is another popular day trip. It is also the easiest of these to climb (page 88).

◖ Centro Cultural La Azotea: This three-in-one coffee, music, and indigenous costume museum has excellent displays and offers an interesting glimpse into many aspects of modern-day Mayan culture (page 104).

LOOK FOR ◖ TO FIND RECOMMENDED SIGHTS, ACTIVITIES, DINING, AND LODGING.

LA ANTIGUA GUATEMALA

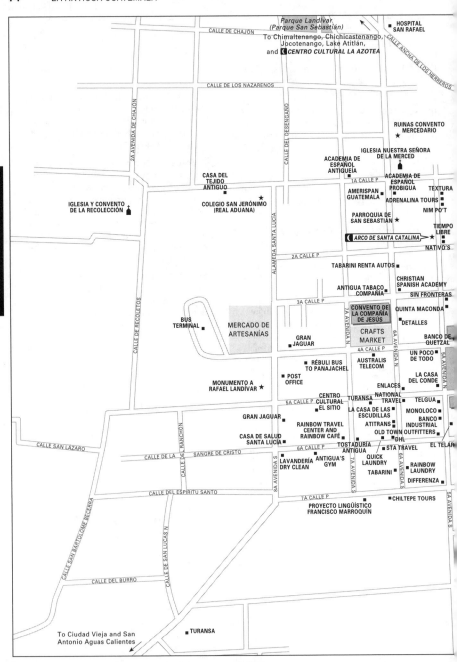

Parque Landívar
(Parque San Sebastián)
To Chimaltenango, Chichicastenango,
Jocotenango, Lake Atitlán,
and **◖ CENTRO CULTURAL LA AZOTEA**

CALLE DE CHAJÓN

HOSPITAL
SAN RAFAEL

CALLE ANCHA DE LOS HERREROS

CALLE DE LOS NAZARENOS

2A AVENIDA DE CHAJÓN

CALLE DEL DESENGAÑO

RUINAS CONVENTO
MERCEDARIO ★

IGLESIA NUESTRA SEÑORA
DE LA MERCED

CASA DEL
TEJIDO
ANTIGUO

ACADEMIA DE
ESPAÑOL
ANTIGUEÑA

1A CALLE P

ACADEMIA DE
ESPAÑOL
PROBIGUA   TEXTURA

IGLESIA Y CONVENTO
DE LA RECOLECCIÓN

COLEGIO SAN JERÓNIMO
(REAL ADUANA) ★

AMERISPAN
GUATEMALA

ADRENALINA TOURS

NIM PO'T

PARROQUIA DE
SAN SEBASTIÁN ★

TIEMPO
LIBRE

ALAMEDA SANTA LUCÍA

◖ ARCO DE SANTA CATALINA ★ →

NATIVO'S

2A CALLE P

TABARINI RENTA AUTOS ■

CHRISTIAN
SPANISH ACADEMY

ANTIGUA TABACO
COMPAÑIA ■

SIN FRONTERAS ■

3A CALLE P

CONVENTO DE
LA COMPAÑIA
DE JESÚS

QUINTA MACONDA ■

DETALLES ■

CALLE DE RECOLETOS

BUS
TERMINAL

MERCADO DE
ARTESANÍAS

7A AVENIDA N

CRAFTS
MARKET

BANCO DE
QUETZAL

GRAN
JAGUAR

4A CALLE P

AUSTRALIS
TELECOM

6A AVENIDA N

UN POCO
DE TODO

5A AVENIDA N

LA CASA
DEL CONDE

RÉBULI BUS
TO PANAJACHEL ■

MONUMENTO A
RAFAEL LANDÍVAR ★

POST
OFFICE ■

ENLACES ■

CENTRO
CULTURAL
EL SITIO

TURANSA ■

5A CALLE P

NATIONAL
TRAVEL ■

TELGUA ■

GRAN JAGUAR ■

RAINBOW TRAVEL
CENTER AND
RAINBOW CAFÉ ■

LA CASA DE LAS
ESCUDILLAS ■

ATITRANS ■

MONOLOCO ■

BANCO
INDUSTRIAL ■

OLD TOWN
OUTFITTERS ■

DHL ■

EL TELAR

CALLE SAN LÁZARO

CALLE DEL RANCHÓN

CASA DE SALUD
SANTA LUCÍA ■

TOSTADURÍA
ANTIGUA ■

STA TRAVEL ■

CALLE DE LA
SANGRE DE CRISTO

6A CALLE P

8A AVENIDA S

LAVANDERÍA
DRY CLEAN ■

ANTIGUA'S
GYM ■

QUICK
LAUNDRY ■

TABARINI ■

7A AVENIDA S

RAINBOW
LAUNDRY ■

DIFFERENZA ■

CALLE DEL ESPÍRITU SANTO

7A CALLE P

CHILTEPE TOURS ■

5A AVENIDA S

PROYECTO LINGÜÍSTICO
FRANCISCO MARROQUÍN

CALLE SAN BARTOLOMÉ BECERRA

CALLE DE SAN LUCAS N

CALLE DEL BURRO

To Ciudad Vieja y San
Antonio Aguas Calientes

TURANSA ■

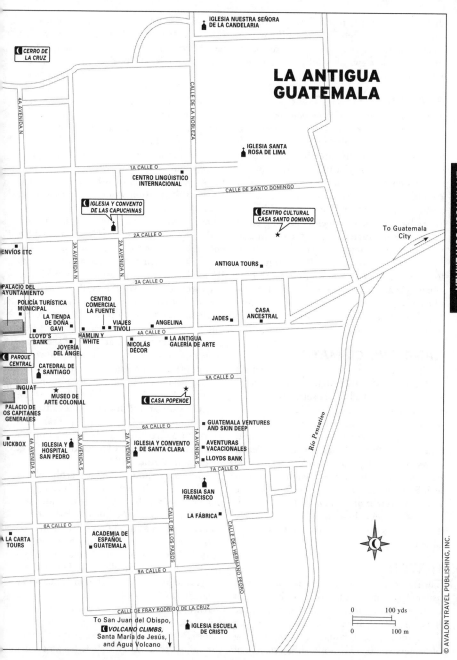

LA ANTIGUA GUATEMALA

IGLESIA NUESTRA SEÑORA
DE LA CANDELARIA

CERRO DE
LA CRUZ

CALLE DE LA NOBLEZA

4A AVENIDA N.

IGLESIA SANTA
ROSA DE LIMA

1A CALLE O

CENTRO LINGÜÍSTICO
INTERNACIONAL

CALLE DE SANTO DOMINGO

IGLESIA Y CONVENTO
DE LAS CAPUCHINAS

CENTRO CULTURAL
CASA SANTO DOMINGO

To Guatemala
City

2A CALLE O

3A AVENIDA N.

2A AVENIDA N.

ENVÍOS ETC

ANTIGUA TOURS

3A CALLE O

PALACIO DEL
AYUNTAMIENTO

POLICÍA TURÍSTICA
MUNICIPAL

CENTRO
COMERCIAL
LA FUENTE

LA TIENDA
DE DOÑA
GAVI

VIAJES
TIVOLI

ANGELINA

JADES

CASA
ANCESTRAL

LLOYD'S
BANK

HAMLIN Y
WHITE

4A CALLE O

NICOLÁS
DÉCOR

LA ANTIGUA
GALERÍA DE ARTE

JOYERÍA
DEL ÁNGEL

PARQUE
CENTRAL

CATEDRAL DE
SANTIAGO

5A CALLE O

INGUAT

MUSEO DE
ARTE COLONIAL

CASA POPENOE

PALACIO DE
OS CAPITANES
GENERALES

6A CALLE O

GUATEMALA VENTURES
AND SKIN DEEP

UICKBOX

IGLESIA Y
HOSPITAL
SAN PEDRO

3A AVENIDA S.

2A AVENIDA S.

IGLESIA Y CONVENTO
DE SANTA CLARA

1A AVENIDA S.

AVENTURAS
VACACIONALES

LLOYDS BANK

4A AVENIDA S.

7A CALLE O

IGLESIA SAN
FRANCISCO

Río Pensativo

LA FÁBRICA

8A CALLE O

A LA CARTA
TOURS

ACADEMIA DE
ESPAÑOL
GUATEMALA

CALLE DE LOS PASOS

CALLE DEL HERMANO PEDRO

9A CALLE O

CALLE DE FRAY RODRIGO DE LA CRUZ

To San Juan del Obispo,
VOLCANO CLIMBS,
Santa María de Jesús,
and Agua Volcano

IGLESIA ESCUELA
DE CRISTO

0   100 yds

0   100 m

that are just waiting to be climbed. Among the latter, Acatenango Volcano still enjoys a record relatively free of crime in addition to some fantastic views of nearby active Fuego Volcano from its twin-cone summit.

PLANNING YOUR TIME

A week in Antigua would give you ample time to explore the town, its ruins, museums, and churches, maybe climb a volcano, visit a coffee farm, and do some shopping. Depending on whether or not you plan to study Spanish, you could easily spend several weeks in Antigua. Some choose to study Spanish for a week just to brush up on their skills or get a very basic foundation before moving on to other parts of Guatemala. At the minimum, you should plan on spending two nights here. Some have even recommended Antigua as a long weekend getaway from cities such as Miami, Atlanta, Houston, and Dallas because of its proximity and ease of access. The Guatemala City international airport is about a 45-minute drive away.

LAND AND CLIMATE

Antigua lies 45 kilometers from Guatemala City via a good, paved highway. Its setting is spectacular, flanked on its southern extreme by towering 3,750-meter (12,325-foot) Agua Volcano. Colossal 4,235-meter (13,900-foot) Acatenango and active Fuego lie to the west. The surrounding hillsides provide wonderful views of the valley and the volcanoes and are excellent terrain for recreational pursuits such as hiking and mountain biking. The climate is similar to that of Guatemala City, as Antigua lies at about the same altitude, just over 1,500 meters. Days are warm and nights are pleasantly cool.

HISTORY

The former capital of Guatemala, now known as Ciudad Vieja, was the first of Guatemala's capitals to suffer merciless destruction at the hands of nature. It was built on the slopes of Agua Volcano; an earthquake on the evening of September 10, 1541, unleashed a torrent of mud and water that came tumbling down the volcano's slopes and destroyed the city. The new Muy Leal y Muy Noble Ciudad de Santiago de los Caballeros de Goathemala, as it would officially come to be known, was established on March 10, 1543, in the Panchoy Valley. The new capital would be no stranger to the ravages of nature, its first earthquake being endured by its inhabitants only 20 years after the city's founding.

An earthquake in 1717 spurred an unprecedented building boom, with the city reaching its peak in the mid-18th century. At that time, its population would number around 60,000. Antigua was the capital of the Audiencia de Guatemala, under the jurisdiction of the larger Viceroyalty of New Spain, which encompassed most of present-day Mexico and all of Central America as far south as Costa Rica. The Viceroyalty's capital was in Mexico City, which along with Lima, Peru, would be the only other New World cities exceeding Antigua's political, cultural, and economic importance. Antigua boasted Central America's first printing press and one of the hemisphere's first universities and was known as an important center of arts and education. Among its outstanding citizens were conquistador and historian Bernal Díaz del Castillo, Franciscan friar and Indian rights advocate Bartolomé de las Casas, bishop Francisco Marroquín, artist Tomás de Merlo, English priest/traveler Thomas Gage, and architect Juan Bautista Antonelli.

Antigua's prominence came crashing down in 1773. The city was rocked throughout most of the year by a series of earthquakes, which later came to be known as the Terremotos de Santa Marta. Two earthquakes occurred on July 29th. The final blows would be delivered on September 7 and December 13. The city was officially moved the following year to its present location in modern-day Guatemala City.

Antigua lay in ruins occupied mainly by squatters, its monuments pillaged for building materials for the new capital. It wasn't until the mid-19th century that it became once again populated and its buildings restored, in part with the money from the region's new-found coffee wealth. The city was declared a national monument in 1944 and came under the protection of the National Council for the Protection of Antigua Guatemala in 1969. It was declared a UNESCO World Heritage Site in 1979. The council has done a fairly decent job at protecting and restoring the city's cultural and architectural heritage, though building code violations are not at all unheard of. Still, many power lines have gone underground and truck traffic has been effectively banned from the city's streets, greatly reducing noise pollution.

ORIENTATION

Getting around Antigua is fairly straightforward. True to its colonial foundations, it was laid out in a grid pattern surrounding the central plaza with *calles* running east-west and *avenidas* running north-south. The plaza is bounded by 4a Calle and 5a Calle to the north and south, and 4a Avenida and 5a Avenida to the east and west. Street addresses are labeled according to their direction relative to the plaza: Norte (North), Oriente (East), Sur (South), and Poniente (West). Most streets are known by this method, though all have names dating to colonial times. Only a handful of streets are known solely in this manner.

Sights

Antigua is fascinating and easily manageable, as most everything you might want to see and do lies within a radius of a few miles.

◖ PARQUE CENTRAL

Antigua's central plaza is easily the most beautiful in the country and is the hub of activity for shoe shiners, strolling lovers, tour groups, ice cream vendors, and foreign visitors. Gracing the central part of the square is a lovely fountain dating to 1936, a re-creation of an earlier version from 1738 destroyed by earthquakes. It is bordered by the Catedral de Santiago, Palacio de los Capitanes Generales, Palacio del Ayuntamiento, and a commercial arcade known as the Portal del Comercio.

Catedral de Santiago

On its eastern side, the plaza is dominated by the beautiful Catedral de Santiago (9 A.M.–5 P.M.). It is wonderfully lit up at night. Its history, as is much of Antigua's, is one of constant destruction and reconstruction. The first cathedral built on this site dates to 1545, but its shoddy construction caused its roof to come crashing down during an earthquake in 1583. It was decided to build a new cathedral in 1670, a task that would require 11 years and the conscripted labor of indigenous Mayans. The scale of the new structure was astounding, with 18 chapels, a huge dome, five naves, and a large central chamber measuring 90 meters by 20 meters. It was graced by paintings and artwork of renowned European and colonial artists; its altar was inlaid with silver, ivory, and mother-of pearl. Although it withstood the earthquakes of 1689 and 1717, it finally succumbed to the earthquake of 1773.

The current church is not really a cathedral in the strict sense of the word, as it consists of two restored chambers known as the Parroquia de San José. You can visit the interesting interior entering from 5a Calle Oriente ($0.50), where you'll find splendid arches and towering columns. There is also a sculpted black Christ similar to the highly revered statue found in Esquipulas, both carved by Quirio Cataño. The remains of the rest of the colonial structure can also be seen here, a moss-covered mass of stones and rotting beams. The remains of some of the major players from colonial days are said to be buried beneath the church altar, including Don Pedro de Alvarado, his wife, Beatriz de la Cueva, Guatemala's first bishop, Francisco Marroquín, and conqueror/chronicler Bernal Díaz del Castillo. Steps behind the main altar lead to the former crypt turned chapel harboring the black Christ statue.

A WALKING TOUR OF ANTIGUA

This walking tour was developed by Martha Hettich, a native of Louisville, Kentucky, who has lived off and on in Guatemala for several years. Hettich moved back to Antigua in 2002 after a 12-year absence between 1978 and 1990 during the worst of the civil war violence. During her time away from Guatemala, she built a business dealing in ethnographic art and design from Asia and Latin America. She now escorts private tours for clients that have included *Condé Nast Traveler*, *Departures*, and *Continental* magazines, David Rockefeller, and Geoffrey Kent of Abercrombie and Kent, among others. She also serves as a consultant to museums and private collectors in the United States.

This tour is designed to incorporate many of the colonial ruins while not missing the things about the history of old Antigua that make the ruins so special.

Start early! I suggest between 8:30 and 9 A.M.

Start by stepping outside and giving thanks for waking up in this city of volcanoes, mountains, lush flora and fauna, unbelievable colonial heritage, and some of the most wonderful people in the world. Head to **Parque Central** to experience the heart and soul of Antigua. Buy a cup of steaming *café con leche* and some *pan dulce* (sweet bread) from one of the many coffee bars on or near the plaza. As you sit you can take in the **cathedral,** the **Captains General Palace,** the **Ayuntamiento (City Hall),** the **merchants' arcade,** and of course, Antigua's wonderful fountain of **Las Sirenas.**

After coffee, head north on 5a Avenida to the **Hotel Posada Don Rodrigo** at the corner of 3a Calle. Take a look around this wonderful old colonial home turned into a charming hotel. Get an idea of the courtyard style of living, in which all rooms lead to a central patio and not from room to room. Make sure you visit the kitchen garden, still complete with original *pila* (wash basin) and Moorish water garden originally used for growing herbs. Visit

the rooftop patio for a spectacular view of the volcanoes and rooftops of Antigua.

Continue north on 5a Avenida to the **Arch of Santa Catalina** (a major symbol of Antigua). It was built to provide a hidden passageway from one side of the street to the other so the cloistered nuns of the order would be hidden from the public's view. No matter how many earthquakes Antigua has suffered, the arch has suffered structural damage but has never fallen down.

Continue to the end of 5a Avenida to **La Merced.** Visit the ruins to see what many people call the most impressive fountain in Antigua. Climb to the second level for even more impressive views of Antigua. Afterward, visit the Church of La Merced, the only surviving piece of architecture built in the rococo style. This church plays an integral part in Antigua's Holy Week pageantry. The fountain outside the church was originally in the patio of the church of San Francisco El Grande. When you visit the ruins of San Francisco you will see where the fountain belongs.

After leaving the complex, turn right onto the street along the side of La Merced. This is 1a Calle. Walk east to 3a Avenida and turn right to see the ruins of the Carmelite convent and church, **Santa Teresa.** Go south on 3a Avenida to the corner of 3a Calle to see the ruins of **El Carmen,** home of the Carmelite order. Go back to 1a Calle and go to 2a Avenida, turning right to visit the ruins of **Las Cappuchinas,** which are at the corner of 2a Avenida and 2a Calle. This was home to the cloistered Capuchin nuns, an austere offshoot of the Franciscans. It is easy to spend 1-2 hours in these absolutely beautiful and extensive ruins. Return to 1a Calle and you will find yourself on a beautiful tree-lined boulevard in a quiet residential area.

Continue east on 1a Calle and it will intersect with 1a Avenida Norte. If you turn left you can walk about one block to the ruins of

Candelaria. Only the facade is left but it is quite impressive. Or you can turn right onto 1a Avenida Norte and go to 3a Calle. At this corner turn left and head east to the **Hotel Casa Santo Domingo.**

This hotel is built from and around the ruins of the old Dominican Monastery. At the hotel, visit the ruins and museums. Walk around the public spaces to take in the private art collection and to enjoy the wonderful gardens. Make plans to return for a candlelight dinner in the dining room. After leaving the hotel, turn left and then right onto Callejón de Concepción. Walk down to the museum entrance of **Jades, S.A.,** and visit the only museum dedicated to Holy Week in all of Antigua. The display of sawdust carpets, photos, and procession memorabilia will convince you of the need to return to see the spectacular events of Holy Week. While you are there visit the jade museum. Get a glimpse of ancient Mayan life and the importance of jade to the Mayans through the vignettes.

When you leave Jades, S.A., you will see the ruins of the **Convento La Concepción.** Turn left onto 4a Calle and walk past the ruins to the original entrance of the old convent. After standing in awe and taking as many photos as possible, return along 4a Calle heading west to the intersection of 1a Avenida. Turn left and walk south. There are many cafés and restaurants between Santo Domingo and the Church of San Francisco where you can stop and have lunch. Walk to the corner of 5a Calle and 1a Avenida and look for the large white house. This is **Casa Popenoe.** This restored colonial house is open only 2–4 P.M. Monday–Saturday. Make sure to visit the whole house – kitchen, bath, gardens, living rooms, dovecote, and rooftop.

Upon leaving Casa Popenoe continue south on 1a Avenida for two blocks until you reach the church of **San Francisco El Grande.** As you enter through the side gate you will see the entrance to the tomb of **Santo Hermano Pedro,** Central America's first saint. After visiting his tomb go into the church to see the spectacular works of art. This church also figures prominently in Holy Week activities. After leaving the church, go to visit the attached ruins of the old Franciscan monastery, where you have access to the museum dedicated to the life and works of Hermano Pedro and to the ruins of the multilevel monastery. These are my favorite ruins in all of Antigua. Take a book, pack a picnic, roam, and climb. These ruins are especially wonderful for children.

After leaving the grounds of San Francisco through the front gate, head south to the church of **Escuela de Cristo.** This church was originally built as the Church of San Francisco. When the Franciscans were granted a larger parcel of land it became the home of the foundation of the Oratorio de San Felipe Neri. After the earthquake of 1717 it was rebuilt using great, undecorated stone blocks to cover the massive damage done by the earthquake. After the baroque and rococo churches you have seen, this is like going back to medieval Europe. This is another important church during Holy Week.

Now take the side street and head east. You will walk into the park dedicated to Hermano Pedro. Face south and take in the facade of Iglesia El Belén. This is Antigua's only folk art church. Have you ever seen so many putti in one place? The inclusion of Hermano Pedro and his faithful burro in the nativity scene is especially delightful.

Since you have just spent 6–8 hours walking through Antigua, I think it's only fair to send you home to put your feet up and contemplate all you have taken in. Then realize there is so much more you haven't seen yet.

Contributed by Martha Hettich, who has been traveling in Guatemala for over 30 years. In addition to offering tours, she is an expert on local textiles.

© AL ARGUETA

view of the central plaza and Catedral de Santiago from Palacio del Ayuntamiento

Palacio del Ayuntamiento

Found on the north side of the plaza, this large structure functioned as the town hall, also known as the Casa del Cabildo. It has miraculously withstood the test of time, not having been damaged by earthquakes until the most recent one in 1976, despite its construction dating to 1740. Some fantastic views of the cathedral and Agua Volcano are framed by the building's beautiful arches from its second-floor balconies. Today the building houses the town municipal offices as well as the **Museo de Armas de Santiago** (9 A.M.–4 P.M. Tues.–Fri., 9 A.M.–noon and 2–4 P.M. Sat./Sun., $1.50 admission), set in the city's former town jail. It houses colonial artifacts, weapons, paintings, and furnishings. Perhaps a bigger draw than the museum itself is the quite interesting colonial fountain embossed with the emblem of Santiago (St. James), found in a quiet courtyard. Next door, the **Museo del Libro Antiguo** (Antique Book Museum, tel. 7832-5511, 9 A.M.–4 P.M. Tues.–Fri., 9 A.M.–noon and 2–4 P.M. Sat./Sun., $1.50 admission) fea-

tures exhibits on colonial printing and binding processes. There's a replica of the country's first printing press, brought to Guatemala in 1660 from Puebla, Mexico.

Palacio de los Capitanes Generales

On the south end of the plaza, the Palace of the Captains General dates to 1558 and was once the seat of government for the entire Central American territory from Chiapas to Costa Rica, of which Antigua was the capital, until 1773. Its imposing architecture is dominated by a row of 27 arches on both of its floors. It once housed colonial rulers, the royal mint, the judiciary, and tax offices, among other things. Today it houses the INGUAT tourist offices, the police department, and Sacatepéquez departmental government headquarters.

◖ ARCO DE SANTA CATALINA

Three blocks north of the park along 5a Avenida Norte (also known as Calle del Arco) is one of Antigua's most recognizable landmarks,

LA ANTIGUA GUATEMALA

© AL ARGUETA

Lovely Arco de Santa Catalina is one of Antigua's most easily recognizable landmarks.

the Santa Catalina archway. It is all that remains of a convent dating to 1613. As the convent grew, it expanded to include a structure across the street. The arch then was built to allow the nuns to cross to the other side while avoiding contact with the general populace in accordance with strict rules governing seclusion. Its current version with a clock tower is a reconstruction dating to the 19th century, as the original was destroyed in the 1773 earthquakes. The clock is a French model, which needed to be wound every three days. It stopped working after the 1976 earthquake but was repaired in 1991. Looking south through the archway, you'll find some nice framing for an unobstructed view of Agua Volcano. The archway is practically an Antigua icon and is beautifully painted in a rich orange hue with white accents that have become delightfully aged.

(CERRO DE LA CRUZ

In the hills north of the city stands this giant stone cross, from which there are sweeping views south over the city with Agua Volcano in the background. Robberies were once frequent here until the creation of the tourism police, which began escorting visitors to the site and pretty much put an end to these crimes. It's still a good idea to go along with a police escort and to visit during daylight hours. Escorts are available free from the tourism police near the central plaza. You'll want to bring along your camera and some water. It's about a 30-minute walk from the plaza. From the top of the hill, you can see the entire Antigua Valley and the cross makes for a nice foreground element.

CHURCHES AND MONASTERIES
(Iglesia y Convento de las Capuchinas

Las Capuchinas (2a Avenida Norte and 2a Calle Oriente, 9 A.M.–5 P.M. daily, $4) was abandoned after being destroyed in the earthquake of 1773. Restoration began in 1943 and is still being carried out today. The convent's foundation dates to 1726, making it the city's fourth, and is the work of renowned Antigua architect

SEMANA SANTA IN ANTIGUA

Semana Santa, or Holy Week, runs from Palm Sunday to Easter Sunday and is one of the best times to visit Antigua for the elaborate Catholic pageantry surrounding these holy days. Visitors come from around the world to see the colorful, solemn processions in which life-size images of Christ and other Catholic icons are paraded through the city's cobblestone streets. Before the processions pass through, Antigueños design and produce exquisite, though ephemeral, *alfombras*, or carpets made of colored sawdust and flowers. The parade floats, or *andas*, pass over the carpets, forever erasing their elaborate patterns under the feet of faithful *cucuruchos*, purple-clad bearers who carry the floats, which can weigh up to 3.5 tons and require 80 men to carry them. The bearers are accompanied by Roman soldiers and other robed figures who carry swaying, copal-laden incense burners. It can be quite a moving experience to see the swaying floats with images of a cross-bearing Christ bearing down on the men amid thick smoke.

A highlight of the week's festivities is a Good Friday event occurring at 3 A.M. in which Roman soldiers on horseback gallop through the streets proclaiming Christ's death sentence. Though several local churches participate in the festivities, the largest procession is the one leaving from La Merced on Good Friday with the 17th-century image of Jesús Nazareno (Jesus of Nazareth). Another well-known procession is that of the Escuela de Cristo, which features some striking images on its parade floats.

© AL ARGUETA

an incense burner used in a Holy Week procession

For specifics on Holy Week events, head to INGUAT's office on the central plaza, where you'll find free maps and event schedules. If you plan to take in the festivities, book far in advance, as word about Antigua's Holy Week events has been out for quite some time and accommodations fill up several months ahead with foreign visitors and vacationing Guatemalans.

Diego de Porres. There are beautiful fountains and courtyards flanked by sturdy stone pillars with stately arches and flowering bougainvillea. It is certainly the most elegant of Antigua's convents and well worth a look for those with even a casual interest in colonial Latin American architecture. The convent was the haunt of the Capuchin nuns from Madrid, a rather strict order limiting its numbers to 28 and requiring the nuns to sleep on wooden beds with straw pillows and sever all ties to the outside world.

The church consists of a single nave lacking side aisles. There are two choir areas, one adjacent to the altar on the ground floor and another on the second floor at the end of the nave.

After the 1773 earthquakes and the subsequent transfer of the Guatemalan capital to its new location, many of the convent's historical artifacts were likewise transferred to their new home in the San Miguel de Capuchinas convent in modern-day Guatemala City.

Iglesia y Convento de Santa Clara

The Santa Clara Convent (2a Avenida Sur #27, 9 A.M.–5 P.M. daily, $4) originally dates to 1702, with its current incarnation having been inaugurated in 1734 and destroyed in 1773. Its ruins are also pleasant for a stroll and in front of its main entrance is **Parque La Unión** with several wash basins, known as *pilas,* where women gather to do their laundry. The park's other outstanding feature is a large stone cross, a gift from the city of Santiago de Compostela, Spain. The church is beautifully floodlighted at night.

Iglesia de San Francisco

Southwest on 1a Avenida Sur, the church of San Francisco (8 A.M.–6 P.M. daily) is one of Antigua's oldest, dating to 1579. It once harbored a hospital, school, printing press, and monastery, among other things. Its main claim to fame nowadays is the tomb of Central America's first saint, **Hermano Pedro de San José de Betancourt,** a Franciscan monk who came to Antigua from the Canary Islands and founded the Hospital de Belén. He is credited with miraculous healings. The **Museo del Hermano Pedro** (8 A.M.–5 P.M., $0.50) is found on the south side of the church along with the ruins of the adjacent monastery. It houses church relics and some of Hermano Pedro's well-preserved personal belongings.

Iglesia y Convento de Nuestra Señora de la Merced

Known more commonly as La Merced, this is one of Antigua's most beautiful churches, painted in a bright yellow and adorned with white lily motifs on its columns. Inside are the ruins of its old monastery (5a Avenida Norte and 1a Calle Poniente, 9 A.M.–6:30 P.M., $0.50 admission) with the Fuente de Peces, said to be the largest in Latin America and interestingly in the shape of a water lily. The pools were once used for breeding fish. The upper level affords some wonderful city views and the fountain just outside the church is also worth a look.

Iglesia y Convento de la Recolección

On Avenida de la Recolección, this large church built between 1701 and 1715 was heavily damaged in 1717 in the same year it was inaugurated. The earthquake of 1773 finished the job and it has lain in ruins ever since.

MUSEUMS
Museo de Arte Colonial

On the former site of San Carlos University, the Colonial Art Museum (5a Calle Oriente #5, tel. 7832-0429, 9 A.M.–4 P.M. Tues.–Fri., 9 A.M.–noon and 2–4 P.M. Sat./Sun., $3.50 admission) harbors sculptures of saints, murals, furniture, and colonial paintings by Mexican artists. A beautiful Moorish courtyard dominates the surviving architecture.

◖ Centro Cultural Casa Santo Domingo

Antigua's finest museum is housed inside the Casa Santo Domingo hotel (3a Calle Oriente #28, tel. 7832-0140, 9 A.M.–6 P.M. Mon.–Sat., 11:15 A.M.–6 P.M. Sun., $5). The site was once the city's largest and wealthiest monastery, with a church completed in 1666, but it was damaged and eventually destroyed by the 18th-century earthquakes. Several museums are housed within the same complex, including the **colonial museum** harboring Catholic relics, among them an old Roman coin found during the excavations for the hotel's construction. Other highlights of this wonderful historic complex include a gorgeous monastery church, cleared of rubble and restored in the early 1990s. It is now frequently used for weddings. Below this area are two crypts. The first of these, the **Cripta del Calvario,** has a well-preserved Crucifixion mural. The other crypt harbors two graves with human bones.

There is also a small archaeological museum, but the highlight here is the **Museo Vigua de Arte Precolombino y Vidrio Moderno,** a fantastic, well-presented juxtaposition of colonial and pre-Columbian artifacts mixed with glass art. Rounding out the impressive list of attractions is the Casa de la Cera, an elaborate candle shop.

◖ Casa Popenoe

Authentically restored to re-create the living conditions of a 17th-century official, Casa

Popenoe (1a Avenida Sur #2, tel. 7832-3087, 2–4 P.M. Mon.–Sat., $1.50) was originally built in 1636 by Don Luis de las Infantas Mendoza. Like much of Antigua, it was left abandoned after the 1773 earthquakes until Dr. Wilson Popenoe and his wife, Dorothy, bought it in 1929. Dr. Popenoe, an agricultural scientist, worked with the United Fruit Company for much of his career and had a long history of adventures in plant collecting and botany in addition to his painstaking restoration of this fantastic cultural monument. He died in 1975, but two of his daughters still live in the house, including archaeologist Marion Popenoe Hatch. You'll see paintings of Bishop Francisco Marroquín and fierce conqueror Pedro de Alvarado. Also on display are the wonderfully restored servants' quarters and kitchen. A narrow staircase leads up to the roof terrace, from where there are gorgeous views of Antigua and the volcanoes off in the distance.

Arts and Entertainment

NIGHTLIFE

Antigua has a lively nightlife scene, particularly on weekends when wealthy Guatemala City youth flood the city streets in search of a good time.

Bars

A play on the Pink Floyd song, "The Wall," **El Muro** (3a Calle Oriente #19, tel. 7832-8849, 6 P.M.–1 A.M. Mon.–Sat.) is Antigua's newest gathering place, popular with the American expat crowd. It has cool chalk art on the walls and basic snacks for when the munchies set in, including pizza, grilled chicken, and hot dogs. You can also order food from Ni-Fu Ni-Fa next door. Another new addition to Antigua's bar scene is **El Mix** (4a Avenida Sur #4A, tel. 7832-8934, 7 A.M.–10 P.M. daily), serving tasty sandwiches and Israeli food in addition to a good selection of cocktails. It has a nice patio, free Internet access, games, and magazines to keep you entertained. Happy hour is 8–10 P.M. Also popular with the American expat crowd is **Café No Sé** (1a Avenida Sur #11C, tel. 5501-2680, 9 A.M.–1 A.M. daily), where you can enjoy drinks in a rustically charming setting, often with live music. There's also good pub grub, though the main attraction is the tequila/mescal bar. The second-hand bookstore next door is open until 4 P.M.

Just a few doors down, **Nokiate** (1a Avenida Sur #7, tel. 7821-2896, www.nokiate.com, 6:30 P.M.–1 A.M. Tues.–Fri., noon–3 P.M. and 6:30 P.M.–1 A.M. Sat., noon–9 P.M. Sun.) features a hip fusion of Japanese and Latin American styles in its very attractive, well-executed sake bar/lounge. Antigua's Irish pub is **Reilly's** (5a Avenida Norte #31, tel. 5672-7910, noon–1 A.M. daily), where there's also decent pub food, including fish 'n chips. You won't find Guinness on tap, however. You'll have to settle for a can ($8). Check out the weekly Sunday trivia quiz at 5 P.M., a veritable Antigua institution. **Monoloco** (5a Avenida Sur #6, 11 A.M.–1 A.M. daily) is also wildly popular and lively. It's set on two floors, and you can drink al fresco on the second-floor terrace. Reasonably priced burgers, nachos, and pizzas are served and there are sports on the downstairs TV.

The best place to grab a drink and watch the sunset with fantastic volcano views is the rooftop bar at **Café Sky** (corner of 6a Calle and 1a Avenida, tel. 7832-7300, 8 A.M.–11 P.M. daily). In addition to the rooftop terrace café bar, there's the downstairs Sky Lounge and Bamboo Bar, where you can enjoy drinks and a full menu of tasty food. **Onis** (7a Avenida Norte #2, tel. 7832-6812, 6 P.M.–1 A.M. Tues.–Sat.) is another two-story bar with nice views of the beautifully lit church of San Agustín from the second-floor terrace. It's popular with the student crowd and there are snacks and liquor shots available.

The ever-popular **Riki's Bar** (4a Avenida Norte #4, tel. 7832-1327, www.la-escudilla .com, 6 P.M.–1 A.M. daily) can be crowded and noisy at times. Locals tend to avoid it but it is a major stop with the backpacker crowd, particularly for its 7–9 P.M. happy hour. Housed in the same garden courtyard complex are the quieter **Paris Bistro,** toward the rear, and the hip **Cielos Lounge Bar** (6 P.M.–1 A.M. Tues.–Sat.), where you can enjoy Arab and Cuban beats as well as live music in a more comfortable setting. Finally, there's **La Sala** (6a Calle Poniente #9) which is spacious and nicely decorated with a good mix of locals and foreigners.

Dancing

Antigua's most popular and dependably fun disco is the two-story **La Casbah** (5a Avenida Norte #30, tel. 7832-2640, 9 P.M.–1 A.M. Mon.–Sat., free admission Mon.–Wed., $4 cover Thurs.–Sat.), where you can dance the night away in a classy atmosphere popular with the wealthy Guatemala City crowd. The admission price includes one drink. **La Sin Ventura** (5a Avenida Sur #8, tel. 7832-0581) is a popular disco bar with mostly Latin music and dancing on weekend nights.

Live Music

Restaurante Las Palmas (6a Avenida Norte #14, tel. 7832-9734, www.laspalmasantigua .com) has live jazz music on Wednesday nights,

as does **Mesón Panza Verde** (5a Avenida Sur #19, tel. 7832-2925, www.panzaverde.com) For more information, check out their listings in the *Food* section.

CINEMAS

Antigua has several cinemas where you can enjoy a movie along with dinner and drinks. You'll see weekly listings with schedules posted all over town. Features include Hollywood releases, art-house, and Latin American. Recommended cinemas include **Café 2000** (6a Avenida Norte #2, tel. 7832-2981), **Cinema Bistro** (5a Avenida Sur #14, four screenings a day), and **Maya Moon** (6a Avenida Norte #1A, three screens). **Proyecto Cultural El Sitio** (5a Calle Poniente #15, tel. 7832-3037, www .elsitiocultural.org) shows art-house movies at 6 P.M. Tuesdays for $2.

ART GALLERIES

Panza Verde (5a Avenida Sur #19, tel. 7832-2925, www.panzaverde.com) is a gallery housed inside its namesake restaurant/hotel; a new exhibit usually opens every second Wednesday of the month. **La Antigua Galería de Arte** (4a Calle Oriente #15, tel. 7832-2124, www .artintheamericas.com) exhibits the work of numerous local and international artists.

Shopping

Antigua is one of Guatemala's top places for shopping, with a wide assortment of excellent shops carrying quality items not found elsewhere in Guatemala. You'll be hard-pressed to find the same variety of home décor, textiles, clothing and jewelry anywhere else. Don't feel you have to confine your purchases to what you can fit in your checked airline baggage allotment, as there are a number of local companies that can help you ship your loot home.

HANDICRAFTS

Antigua's **Mercado de Artesanías** (4a Calle Poniente Final, 8 A.M.–7 P.M.) is an attractive,

safe place to shop for textiles, handicrafts, and souvenirs among several stalls. There is also an adjacent outdoor market selling fruits, vegetables, and wonderful fresh flowers. **Casa del Tejido Antiguo** (1a Calle Poniente #51, tel. 7832-3169, www.casadeltejido .com, 9 A.M.–5:30 P.M. Mon.–Sat., $1 admission) is entirely run by Mayan weavers selling and exhibiting authentic textiles and exclusive handicrafts. **Textura** (5a Avenida Norte #33, tel. 7832-5067, 10 A.M.–5:45 P.M. Mon.–Wed., 10 A.M.–6:45 P.M. Thurs.–Sat., 10 A.M.–5 P.M. Sun.) sells stylish home furnishings in updated versions of Mayan textiles, including gorgeous hammocks and table dressings. Selling similarly exquisite home furnishings is **El Telar** (5a Avenida Sur #7, tel. 7832-3179), with another location across the street from the Hotel Posada de Don Rodrigo at 5a Avenida Norte #18.

Nim Po't (5a Avenida Norte #29, tel. 7832-2681, 9 A.M.–9 P.M. daily) has a large selection of traditional Mayan dress items, including colorful *huipiles* (blouses), *cortes* (skirts), and *fajas* (belts). There is also a wide variety of artwork, masks, and other wooden carvings in the spacious warehouselike setting. Just down the street, **Nativo's** (5a Avenida Norte #25B, tel. 7832-6556, 10 A.M.–7 P.M. daily) also sells textiles and has some extremely rare, beautiful, and no-longer-produced textiles in the $600 range. Ask to see them. **Quinta Maconda** (5a Avenida Norte #11, tel. 7832-1480, www .quintamaconda.com, 9:30 A.M.–1 P.M. and 2–7 P.M. daily) sells its own brand of high-quality handcrafted leather travel gear and handwoven Guatemalan brocades in beautiful muted hues and earth tones. It also has a fine collection of Southeast Asian antiques and wooden furniture in its by-appointment-only showroom.

JEWELRY

Guatemala produces some of the world's finest jade, including rare black jade, found only in this part of the world. You can buy fabulous jade jewelry here tax-free. The best store for perusing wonderful jade creations in colorful hues, including emerald, yellow, and lilac, is **Jades, S.A.** (4a Calle Oriente #34, tel. 7832-0109, www.jademaya.com, 9 A.M.–7 P.M. daily), where you'll find a vast array of items varying from 18-karat gold/jade earrings to a unique $3,800 jade chess board. All of the jade found here is mined from a quarry in eastern Guatemala. The store doubles as a jade museum and you can also visit the factory behind the shop. Guided tours are available in German, Spanish, English, French, and Italian. For fashionable and exotic jewelry, handbags, and sunglasses, visit **Joyería del Ángel** (4a Calle Oriente #5A, tel. 7832-5334, 9 A.M.–6 P.M. daily).

BOOKS

Hamlin y White (4a Calle Oriente #12A, tel. 7832-7075, 9 A.M.–6:30 P.M. daily) has a good selection of books and international magazines. Under the same ownership is **Tiempo Libre** (5a Avenida Norte #25, tel. 7832-1816, 9 A.M.–7 P.M. daily), with a wider assortment of books in English and Spanish, including Moon Handbooks. On the west side of the plaza in the Portal del Comercio, **La Casa del Conde** (5a Avenida Norte #4, tel. 7832-3322, 9 A.M.–7 P.M. Mon.–Sat., 10 A.M.–7 P.M. Sun.) sells an assortment of travel guides in addition to material specifically relating to Guatemala, Central America, and the Mayan world, mostly in English. A few doors down in the same complex, **Un Poco De Todo** (tel. 7832-4676, 9 A.M.–1:30 P.M. and 3–6:30 P.M. daily) also sells books, though mostly in Spanish.

ART, ANTIQUES, AND FURNITURE

Differenza (5a Avenida Sur #24C, tel. 7832-1851, pierre@conexion.com.gt, 9 A.M.–6 P.M. Mon.–Sat.) features the work of French sculptor and designer Pierre Turlin. Among the unique finds are raku sculptures and bowls, blown-glass stemware and decanters, and wooden furniture. The store also carries extraordinary handcrafted jewelry from two other Antigua resident artists. **Nicolas Decor** (4a Calle Oriente #7, tel. 7832-5510, www .nicolas.com.gt) offers an eclectic mix of furniture and items for the home. **Angelina** (4a Calle Oriente #22, tel. 7832-1812, 10 A.M.–6 P.M. daily) sells primitive antique furniture, reproductions of colonial columns, and contemporary sculpted furniture. **La Casa de las Escudillas** (6a Avenida Sur # 4, tel. 7832-9257, 9 A.M.–8 P.M. daily) sells antique furniture and ceramics. The best place for antiques is **Casa Ancestral** (4a Calle Oriente #46, tel. 7832-9740, 9:30 A.M.–6 P.M. Fri.–Wed.).

COFFEE AND TOBACCO

For coffee, head to **Tostaduría Antigua** (6a Calle Poniente #26). You can buy Cuban and Honduran cigars, as well as enjoy them in a comfortable lounge, at **Antigua Tabaco Compañía** (3a Calle Poniente #12, tel. 7832-9420).

WELLNESS

One of Antigua's most interesting stores is **La Tienda de Doña Gavi** (3a Avenida Norte #2, tel. 7832-6514, noon–7 P.M. daily), where you can pick up a number of natural remedies, including Jacameb, a powerful concoction created from the jacaranda flower that does the trick on amoebas and assorted other parasitic problems.

Recreation

HEALTH CLUBS

Antigua's Gym (6a Calle Poniente #31, tel. 7832-7554, www.antiguasgym.ajaw.org) offers spinning, Tae Bo, cardiovascular equipment, free weights, and some weight-lifting machines. **La Fábrica** (Calle del Hermano Pedro #16, tel. 7832-0486) also has cardiovascular machines and weights in addition to aerobics and martial arts.

SPAS

Casa Madeleine (Calle del Espíritu Santo #69, tel. 7832-9348, www.casamadeleine .com) offers complete spa packages along with its swanky boutique accommodations. Services include massage, reflexology, aromatherapy, mud therapy, pedicures, manicures, and deep facial treatments. **Skin Deep** (1a Avenida Sur #15, tel. 7832-7182, 8 A.M.– 8 P.M. daily) is a well-run day spa and salon housed in the same building as Café Sky offering the usual assortment of spa services in a pleasing environment.

COOKING SCHOOL

If you acquire a taste for traditional Guatemalan cuisine and want to re-create the country's myriad flavors at home, you may want to check out **Antigua Cooking School** (5a Avenida Norte #25B, tel. 5944-8568 or 5990-3366, www.antiguacookingschool.com, $50 per class). The school is open Tuesday–Saturday and teaches five different menu items, including some desserts. Classes are in English and Spanish. Dishes include *tamalitos blancos, rellenitos de plátano, chiles rellenos, pepián,* and (the author's favorite) *chuchitos.*

MOUNTAIN BIKING

Antigua's mountain terrain and the variety of trails traversing it make mountain biking a popular recreational activity. **Old Town Outfitters** (5a Avenida Sur #12C, tel. 5339-0440, www.bikeguatemala.com, $35 half day) is a highly recommended outfitter offering rides for all skill levels. Half-day options include easy rides in the Almolonga Valley or in and around a coffee plantation to edge-of-your seat single-track rides careening down volcanic slopes or along narrow mountain ridges with fantastic views. Its equipment is top-notch and well cared for. **Guatemala Ventures** (1a Avenida Sur #15, end of 6a Calle Oriente, tel. 7832-3383, www.guatemala ventures.com) is another recommended outfitter for tackling the rugged terrain around Antigua by mountain bike. It also rents out mountain bikes for $8 a day. Both companies also offer a lot of other recreational options in addition to mountain biking, as you'll see by the frequency with which they are mentioned here.

HIKING

There is no shortage of rugged hiking trails for enjoying the spectacular mountain scenery and peaceful mountain villages found near Antigua. The same recommended mountain biking outfitters can point you to the best hiking trails. A guide is highly recommended, as robberies of solo hikers along remote mountain footpaths is sometimes an issue in rural Guatemala. The bulk of the hiking done around Antigua involves one of the volcanoes towering ominously over its streets.

Agua Volcano looms over Antigua to the south.

◀ Volcano Climbs

At 3,750 meters (12,325 feet) **Agua Volcano** is one of the most popular climbs because of its proximity to town, from which it invites hikers to attempt an ascent of its steep slopes to the near-perfect crater ringed with various radio antennas. The trailhead is in the nearby village of Santa María de Jesús, from where it's a five-hour ascent, though numerous tourist robberies have occurred through the years in the vicinity of this town. **Guatemala Ventures** drives farther up the road to a spot two hours from the summit and is the recommended way to go. A day trip costs $40 with this outfitter.

Just shy of 4,300 meters (14,000 feet), **Acatenango Volcano** is a safer and somewhat more interesting climb, as it has twin craters and often affords fantastic views of nearby Fuego Volcano, which entered a phase of increased activity in 1999. **Old Town Outfitters** offers a one-day ($49) or overnight ($69) trip to the volcano starting in the village of La Soledad, from where it's a 5–6-hour hike through cornfields and pine forests to the first cra-

ter. The overnight trip camps on the second peak, which stands at 13,900 feet. **Guatemala Ventures** also does the trip, driving to within two hours of the first summit and costing $59/$99 for the one-day and overnight trips.

By far the most popular volcano trip is to active **Pacaya Volcano,** near Lake Amatitlán and closer to Guatemala City. (See *Near Guatemala City* in the *Guatemala City* chapter for details on the climb.) There's no shortage of outfitters offering this trip, which generally leaves in the afternoon and costs $7–30 per person. Recommended companies include **Old Town Outfitters** ($30, including lunch), which leaves earlier than most other companies to avoid the crowds. **Adrenalina Tours** (5a Avenida Norte #31, tel. 7832-1108 or 5535-6831) leaves daily at 6 A.M. and 1 P.M. The trip costs $10–20 depending on whether or not you want a meal with your climb. The more expensive V.I.P. trip has a four-person minimum and also includes the $3 park admission fee. For your standard trip in the $5–7 vicinity, a good outfitter is **Gran Jaguar**

© AL ARGUETA

A photo tour is a great way to capture some memorable vacation pictures.

Tours (4a Calle Poniente #30, tel. 7832-2712), leaving at 6 A.M. and 1 P.M.

HORSEBACK RIDING
In the nearby village of San Juan del Obispo, toward Agua Volcano, **Ravenscroft Riding Stables** (2a Avenida Sur #3, San Juan del Obispo, tel. 7832-6229) offers three-, four-, or five-hour rides in the hills and valleys near Antigua for $15 per person per hour.

CITY TOURS
A La Carta Tours (8a Calle Oriente, inside Porta Hotel Antigua, tel. 7832-9636, www.alacartatours.com) offers creative thematic walking tours at 9 A.M. and 2:30 P.M. Monday–Saturday centered around subjects that include shopping, art, food, photography, and religious celebrations, among others. Prices range $14–39 per person. Practically an Antigua institution, **Antigua Tours** (3a Calle Oriente #22, tel. 7832-5821, www.antiguatours.net) are guided by Elizabeth Bell (author of *Antigua Guatemala: The City and Its Heritage*) Tuesday, Wednesday, Fri-

day, and Saturday at 9:30 A.M. Tours on Monday and Thursday at 2 P.M. are guided by Roberto Spillari. All tours meet at the fountain in Antigua's central park and cost $20. There is also a guided tour of nearby villages, including San Antonio Aguas Calientes, San Pedro Las Huertas, and San Juan del Obispo, going out at 2 P.M. Monday–Friday and lasting three hours. It costs $35 per person with a two-person minimum.

Antigua now also has narrated trolley tours offered by **Chiltepe Tours** (7a Calle Poniente #15, inside Centro Comercial el Búcaro, tel. 5907-0913 or 5709-2232). The tours go through parts of Antigua and outlying towns and last about two hours. Tickets are $25 per adult (children $15), but you can save $3 by booking in advance through the company's website. The tours run Tuesday–Sunday. **Martha Hettich** (1a Avenida Sur #4A, tel. 7832-2134 or 5792-2459, www.marthahettich.com) does recommended guided historical and shopping tours of Antigua and the highlands; by appointment only. She can also tell you stories garnered from years spent in Guatemala and is a wealth of historical information.

Accommodations

UNDER $10

Antigua has a number of excellent hostels offering comfortable accommodations at budget prices. **Hotel Mochilero's Place** (4a Calle Poniente #27, tel. 7832-7743, $14 d shared bath, $16 d private bath) is a friendly sort of establishment with 10 large, clean rooms. Among the amenities are free coffee and tea, laundry sinks, and luggage storage. The rooms facing south have decent views of Agua Volcano. Reservations are necessary, as it's very popular. **Hostal Día Verde** (1a Calle Poniente #14B, tel. 7832-3402) has seven clean rooms with shared bath ($7 p/p) or private bath ($8 p/p). Rates include breakfast and one free hour of Internet. Another popular choice is **Yellow House** (1a Calle Poniente #24, tel. 7832-6646), where the mattresses are somewhat soft but the attractive, private shared-bath rooms ($16 d) are well decorated and have cable TV. Dorm beds go for $8 p/p. The single rooms are very small. Rates include breakfast and half hour of Internet daily. Guests have free use of the kitchen.

A newcomer to Antigua's budget scene is the attractive **Black Cat Hostel** (6a Avenida Norte #1A, tel. 7832-1229, www.blackcat antigua.com), where there are shared-bath dorm beds ($7) and private doubles ($20). Amenities include wireless Internet, a substantial free breakfast, a movie lounge with more than 350 DVDs, a living room and hammock patio for hanging out, a restaurant serving breakfast and light meals (8 A.M.–11 P.M.), and a full bar. The hostel is partially British -owned and you can earn yourself a few free drinks by bringing an offering of Yorkie bars, Marmite, Branston Pickle, or HP sauce. **Jungle Party Hostel** (6a Avenida Norte #20, between 3a and 2a Calle Poniente, tel. 7832-0463) is a lively backpacker hangout with clean dorm rooms and shared baths for $6–8 p/p. There's a fun communal area that doubles as a bar and snack stand. The cheerfully painted, tiled floor **UmmaGumma Hostel** (7a Avenida Norte #34, tel. 7832-4413) has a wide range of accommodations, including dorms ($5 p/p) and private rooms with ($13 p/p) or without ($8 p/p) private bath. Guests enjoy use of two fully equipped kitchens, communal lounge areas with DirecTV, laundry service, wireless Internet, international phone calls, and luggage storage. The staff can also help with travel arrangements.

$10-25

A well-established budget hotel is the very pleasant and friendly **Posada Juma Ocag** (Calzada de Santa Lucía #13, tel. 7832-3109, $15 d) with seven tastefully decorated, well-furnished rooms featuring wrought-iron headboards, mirrors, and reading lamps, all with private bath. It has a rooftop patio and garden as well as some nice extras such as free drinking water. It's also conveniently situated near the bus terminal. The excellent value ◖ **Casa Cristina** (Callejón Camposeco #3A, between 6a and 7a Avenida, tel. 7832-0623, www.casa-cristina.com, $22–37 d) has beautifully decorated, colorful rooms with wrought-iron accents, Guatemalan bedspreads, tile floors, and private hot-water bathroom. Pricier "standard plus" rooms have cable TV, while deluxe rooms also have gorgeous volcano views and minifridge. Room rates include unlimited use of wireless Internet, purified drinking water, coffee, and tea.

Just north of the Arco de Santa Catalina, **Posada Asjemenou** (Calle del Arco #31, tel. 7832-2670, $23–31 d) has attractive rooms centered around a courtyard with or without private hot-water bathroom. The large rooms have nice antique tile floors and wooden furnishings and there's a restaurant on the premises where you can enjoy delicious pizzas and pastas in the $10–16 range. Room rates include breakfast. **Posada La Merced** (7a Avenida Norte #43, tel. 7832-3197, $20–25 d) is another good choice offering nicely decorated, furnished rooms with private or shared hot-water bathroom. It features a courtyard where you can help yourself to purified drinking water, baggage storage, and a communal kitchen. Candles add a nice touch in the evening. Just one block from the central plaza, **Hotel Casa Rústica** (6a Avenida Norte #8, tel. 7832-3709, www.casarusticagt.com, $26–36 d) has comfortable rooms with shared bathroom or private bathroom, with or without cable TV and garden view. Rates include breakfast, filtered drinking water, and use of the kitchen. It also offers laundry service, bag storage, and wireless Internet. There are nice gardens and hammocks for lounging.

$25-50

Hotel Posada del Sol (Calle de los Nazarenos #17, tel. 7832-6838, $35) is housed in a pretty yellow house and has six spacious, well-furnished rooms with orthopedic beds and private hot-water bathroom. There's laundry service and the friendly staff can help you plan onward travel throughout Guatemala. The excellent-value C **Hotel Posada San Pedro** (3a Avenida Sur #15, tel. 7832-3594, www.posada sanpedro.net, $35 d) is also stylish and comfortable, featuring 10 spotless rooms with firm beds, tile floors, wooden furnishings, attractive tile bathrooms, and cable TV. Guests also enjoy use of a living room and full kitchen. The staff here is friendly and the place is well-run with a laid back but efficient atmosphere. There's a second location at 7a Avenida Norte #29 (tel. 7832-0718) with the same rates but slightly smaller, less attractive rooms.

Friendly **Hotel Palacio Chico** (4a Avenida Sur #4, tel. 7832-0406, $50 d) is conveniently situated near the central plaza and has comfortable, attractive rooms painted with faux finishes and fitted with cable TV, nice furnishings, and electric hot-water private bathrooms. Rates include a continental breakfast. Also south of the park on the next street over, **Hotel La Sin Ventura** (5a Avenida Sur #8, tel. 7832-0581, www.lasinventura.com, $32 d) has 34 clean rooms spread out over three floors, all with private bathroom. There are excellent views of Agua Volcano from its rooftop terrace and it's conveniently (or not, depending on how you look at it) situated near several nightlife spots, one of which is in the hotel lobby.

Hotel San Jorge (4a Avenida Sur #13, tel. 7832-3132, www.hotelsanjorge.centroamerica .com, $53 d) has attractive rooms centered around a garden courtyard with a fountain and patio furniture. The well-furnished rooms are carpeted and have private hot-water bathroom, Guatemalan bedspreads and accents, chimney, cable TV, and reading lamps. Rates include a continental breakfast and guests enjoy free use of the nearby Porta Hotel Antigua's sprawling swimming pool. **Hotel Santa Clara** (2a Avenida Sur #20, tel. 7832-0342, $45 d) features 19 rooms, some with cable TV, and all with private bathroom, colorful decor and wooden furniture set around a courtyard. Newer rooms with less character, but slightly more cheerful, are at the rear.

$50-100

With many of the fine decorative touches and amenities of its pricier boutique counterparts **El Meson de María** (3a Calle Poniente #8, tel. 7832-6068 or 7832-0520, www.hotelmesonde maria.com, $75–135 d) is a good value. Its 20 brand-new, well-appointed rooms are attractively decorated with Guatemalan fabrics and beautifully carved wooden headboards. You'll feel the antique charm as soon as you enter the doorway of your room framed with antique wooden beams. Rooms on the second floor have skylights and some of the spacious tiled bathrooms have whirlpool tubs. There are gorgeous views of the town and volcanoes from the delightful third-floor terrace. Rates include breakfast at the nearby La Fonda de la Calle Real. Outside the city center on the way to Santa Ana is **Hotel Quinta de las Flores** (Calle del Hermano Pedro #6, tel. 7832-3721/25, www .quintadelasflores.com, $70–130 d), another excellent value. The lodge was built on the site of what were once public baths and you can still hear the soothing sounds of tinkling fountains throughout the property. The charming rooms, built around a peaceful garden, feature tile floors, chimneys, cable TV, Guatemalan bedspreads, and nice accents and furnishings along with a small porch with sitting area. Larger two-bedroom casitas comfortably sleep

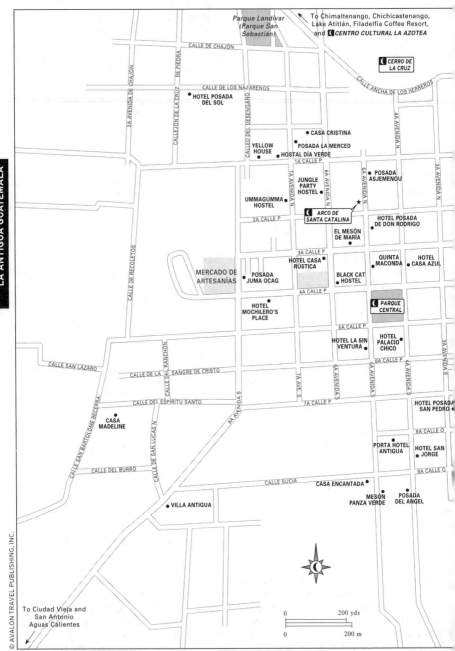

LA ANTIGUA GUATEMALA

Parque Landívar
(Parque San
Sebastián)

To Chimaltenango, Chichicastenango,
Lake Atitlán, Filadelfia Coffee Resort,
and ☾ *CENTRO CULTURAL LA AZOTEA*

☾ *CERRO DE
LA CRUZ*

CALLE DE CHAJÓN

CALLE DE LOS NAZARENOS

CALLE ANCHA DE LOS HERREROS

2A AVENIDA DE CHAJÓN

DE PIEDRA

CALLEJÓN DE LA CRUZ

CALLE DEL DESENGAÑO

4A AVENIDA N

3A AVENIDA N

• HOTEL POSADA
DEL SOL

• CASA CRISTINA

• POSADA LA MERCED

YELLOW
HOUSE •
• HOSTAL DÍA VERDE

1A CALLE P

7A AVENIDA N

6A AVENIDA N

5A AVENIDA N

• POSADA
ASJEMENOU

JUNGLE
PARTY
HOSTEL •

UMMAGUMMA
HOSTEL •

2A CALLE P

☾ ARCO DE
SANTA CATALINA

★

HOTEL POSADA
DE DON RODRIGO

• EL MESÓN
DE MARÍA

3A CALLE P

CALLE DE RECOLETOS

HOTEL CASA
RÚSTICA •

QUINTA
MACONDA •

HOTEL
• CASA AZUL

MERCADO DE
ARTESANÍAS

POSADA •
JUMA OCAG

BLACK CAT
• HOSTEL

4A CALLE P

HOTEL
MOCHILERO'S
PLACE •

☾ *PARQUE
CENTRAL*

5A CALLE P

HOTEL LA SIN
VENTURA •

HOTEL
PALACIO •
CHICO

3A AVENIDA S

6A CALLE P

4A AVENIDA S

CALLE SAN LÁZARO

CALLE DEL RANCHÓN

CALLE DE LA SANGRE DE CRISTO

7A AVE. S

6A AVENIDA S

5A AVENIDA S

CALLE DEL ESPÍRITU SANTO

7A CALLE P

HOTEL POSADA
SAN PEDRO •

8A AVENIDA S

8A CALLE O

CALLE SAN BARTOLOMÉ BECERRA

• CASA
MADELINE

CALLE DE SAN LUCAS N

PORTA HOTEL
ANTIGUA •

HOTEL SAN
• JORGE

CALLE DEL BURRO

9A CALLE O

CALLE SUCIA

CASA ENCANTADA •

• VILLA ANTIGUA

MESÓN •
PANZA VERDE

• POSADA
DEL ANGEL

To Ciudad Vieja and
San Antonio
Aguas Calientes

© AVALON TRAVEL PUBLISHING, INC.

0   200 yds

0   200 m

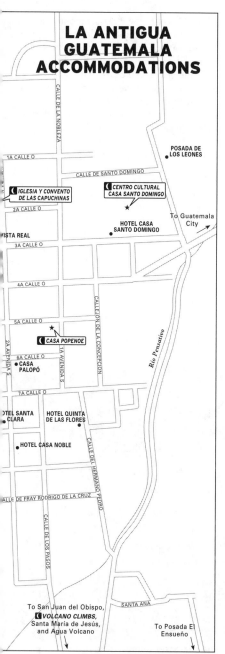

LA ANTIGUA GUATEMALA ACCOMMODATIONS

To Guatemala City

POSADA DE LOS LEONES

IGLESIA Y CONVENTO DE LAS CAPUCHINAS

CENTRO CULTURAL CASA SANTO DOMINGO

HOTEL CASA SANTO DOMINGO

VISTA REAL

CASA POPENOE

CASA PALOPÓ

HOTEL SANTA CLARA

HOTEL QUINTA DE LAS FLORES

HOTEL CASA NOBLE

Río Pensativo

CALLE DE LA NOBLEZA

1A CALLE O

CALLE DE SANTO DOMINGO

2A CALLE O

3A CALLE O

4A CALLE O

5A CALLE O

6A CALLE O

7A CALLE O

2A AVENIDA S

1A AVENIDA S

CALLEJÓN DE LA CONCEPCIÓN

CALLE DEL HERMANO PEDRO

CALLE DE FRAY RODRIGO DE LA CRUZ

CALLE DE LOS PASOS

SANTA ANA

To San Juan del Obispo, VOLCANO CLIMBS, Santa María de Jesús, and Agua Volcano

To Posada El Ensueño

five and have living room, dining room, and fully equipped kitchen. There's a large outdoor swimming pool just next to the hotel's restaurant, which serves Guatemalan dishes, including delicious *chuchitos* and *tostadas,* or salads, steak, and chicken. It's a good choice for vacationing families.

Hotel Casa Azul (4a Avenida Norte #5, tel. 7832-0961/62, www.casazul.guate.com, $83 d including breakfast) has comfortable rooms with cable TV and minibar, some with carpeting, decorated with an abundance of colorful hues and pretty tiles. There's a small pool with volcano views and a whirlpool tub. **Posada de Don Rodrigo** (5a Avenida Norte #17, tel. 7832-0291, $68 d) is one of Antigua's classic hotels, well situated near the Arco de Santa Catalina. Housed in a very old house, the inviting rooms have been updated with all the comforts of a modern hotel. The staff wears traditional costumes and marimba music can often be heard in the main courtyard. **Hotel Casa Noble** (2a Avenida Sur #29, tel. 7832-0864, www.hotel casanoble.com) has 11 beautifully decorated rooms, some with views of Agua Volcano, featuring electronic locks and cable TV starting at $80 d. There's a pleasant garden courtyard with tables and the management is extremely friendly. You'll feel right at home.

OVER $100
Resorts

The **Villa Antigua** (9a Calle Poniente, Carretera a Ciudad Vieja, tel. 7879-4444, www.villa antigua.com, $145–280 d) has 139 rooms and 45 suites, all of which are spacious and equipped with chimney, cable TV, and wonderful garden and volcano views. It has a swimming pool, restaurant, and all the usual amenities found at a large resort. It is the oldest of Antigua's resorts and ironically the one with the least colonial charm because of its more modern architecture. Part of the excellent Villas de Guatemala chain, **Villa Colonial** (Alameda del Calvario #28, tel. 7832-2039 hotel or 2334-1818 reservations, www.villasdeguatemala.com, $104–134 d) has 50 rooms housed in colonial buildings charmingly built to imitate a colonial Spanish town, complete with cobblestone streets, a town square garden, and fountain-style swimming pool. Rooms are tastefully decorated with Guatemalan fabrics and include cable TV in addition to the usual resort amenities. There are standard rooms and larger junior suites with a separate living room.

A Condé Nast Traveler Gold List property, **☾ Porta Hotel Antigua** (8a Calle Poniente #1, tel. 7832-2801, www.portahotels.com, $150–225) has 77 sumptuous rooms with chimney, colorful walls with faux finishes, Guatemalan decor and charming stained hardwood floors in its standard and deluxe rooms and suites. It features a restaurant serving excellent Guatemalan and international dishes overlooking the swimming pool set amid tropical gardens, as well as a fully stocked, quaint wooden bar. Candles provide atmosphere at night and a colonial fountain graces the entrance to the hotel. The service is excellent, as is the courteous and friendly staff. Another property that has put Antigua on the map of the world's finest accommodations is the exquisite **☾ Hotel Casa Santo Domingo** (3a Calle Oriente #28, tel. 7832-0140, www.casasantodomingo.com.gt, $200–550 d), built in the ruins of an old Dominican monastery. Its 125 rooms have all the comforts you could wish for and effortlessly merge colonial charm with modern comfort. Some rooms have a chimney and there are some newer rooms with chic glass and wooden showers. Other amenities include a charming swimming pool andthe city's best museum and wonderful colonial ruins at your doorstep. The restaurant here is also highly recommended.

Boutique Hotels

Antigua has an astounding assortment of boutique properties offering comfort and privacy in an atmosphere of elegance and style. Spending a night in one of Antigua's boutique properties is the real deal and can feel like waking up in a museum chock-full of interesting knick-knacks and artwork. President Clinton chose **☾ Posada del Ángel** (4a Avenida Sur #24A, tel. 7832-5303 Antigua or 305/677-2382 U.S., www.posadadelangel.com, $165–240 d) for his 1999 visit to Antigua for a summit meeting with Central American leaders. If you'd like

Posada del Ángel's exterior offers a glimpse of the character found inside.

to follow in his footsteps, stay in the exquisite Rose Suite, the largest of the lodge's five, with a private balcony offering gorgeous volcano views and fine antiques. Each of the suites is different but all are truly charming and include wood-burning fireplace, cable TV, and fresh flowers. Rates include a delicious breakfast served in the dining room looking out to the hotel's small lap pool. A luxurious private inn, **Quinta Maconda** (5a Avenida Norte #11, tel. 5309-1423 Antigua or 866/621-4032 U.S., www.quintamaconda.com, $130–165 d) has four comfortable bedrooms, all with private bath, tastefully decorated with rare textiles, colonial antiques, and primitive art that are the collection of long-term Antigua resident and world traveler John Heaton. Rates include breakfast served in a pleasant garden patio or in a formal dining room oozing with character and charm. Lunch and dinner are available upon request. There is wireless Internet throughout the house and gracious hosts Catherine and John arrange fantastic custom-tailored travel to explore any and all aspects of Guatemala's unique offerings in comfort and style, drawing on years of experience and first-hand knowledge.

Mesón Panza Verde (5a Avenida Sur #19, tel. 7832-2925, www.panzaverde.com, $75–200) exudes a distinct European atmosphere with an eclectic array of decor that includes Persian rugs, wrought-iron works, chandeliers, fresh flowers, Guatemalan textiles and wooden furniture, and tile or hardwood floors. There are nine suites, including the splendid Grand Suite, and three double rooms. There are wonderful private patios in some of the rooms and one of Antigua's finest restaurants is in the lobby. The 10 cozy, white-walled, wood beam–ceilinged rooms at **Casa Encantada** (9a Calle Poniente #1, tel. 7832-9715 Antigua or 866/837-8900 U.S., www.casaencantada-antigua.com, $75–225 d) are a more modern take on European decor with Guatemalan flair. Stylish accents include framed Guatemalan *huipiles,* oriental rugs, wrought-iron beds, feather and down comforters, and fine Italian linens. There is a rooftop bar perfect for enjoying the sunset over the colonial city streets. All rates include a scrumptious full breakfast, also served on the rooftop patio.

Antigua's newest boutique hotel, **Vista Real** (3a Calle Oriente #16A, tel. 7832-9715/16, www.vistareal.com, $150–225 d including breakfast) offers colonial style with distinction, excellent service, and attention to detail. Each of the five luxurious suites features four-poster beds, artwork, chimney, telephone, a private patio, and large bathroom decorated with Spanish tiles. The hotel's restaurant, Romarin, serves fine French cuisine amid restored colonial ruins. For the ultimate in private luxury, **Casa Palopó** (6a Calle Oriente #1, tel. 7762-2270, www.casapalopo.com) is a three-room villa inconspicuously housed in a white-walled structure on the south side of Parque La Unión. All of the suites are comfortable and tastefully decorated, but the master suite, Santa Clara, takes the cake. It has a walk-in shower, stained hardwood floors, oversized artwork, and a king-size bed. You can stay at Casa Palopó for as little as $175 a night, depending on the season, or rent the whole villa for $550 to $755. A friendly team offering impeccable service staffs the property. Wonderful extras include Aveda bath products. A lounge with TV and DVD player, library, heated lap pool, bar, dining room terrace, and lovely courtyard round out the list of amenities.

One of Antigua's most elegant properties, **◖ Posada de los Leones** (Las Gravileas #1, tel. 7832-7371, www.lionsinnantigua.com, $165–250 d) is set amid, coffee trees, and tropical gardens. Its six spacious, absolutely gorgeous rooms feature high ceilings, hardwood floors, and a delightful array of classy European and Guatemalan decorative touches. On the house's second floor is Antigua's loveliest terrace overlooking tropical gardens, the surrounding coffee plantation, and the volcanoes off in the distance. You can enjoy drinks on the terrace in addition to a lap pool, a comfortable living room, and library. There is wireless Internet throughout the house. If you're looking to combine your stay with an excellent spa experience, **Casa Madeleine** (Calle del Espíritu Santo #69, tel. 7832-9348, www.casamadeleine.com,

$95–205 d) is the place for you. Its six comfortable rooms feature wrought-iron beds and lamps and are decorated in different hues with Guatemalan bedspreads and artwork. Complete spa packages are available and services include massages, reflexology, aromatherapy, mud therapy, pedicures, manicures, and deep facial treatments. Room rates include a full breakfast you are welcome to enjoy in the comfort of your own room at no extra charge.

OUTSIDE OF TOWN

On a working 40-acre avocado farm, **Earthlodge** (tel. 5664-0713 or 5613-6934, www.earthlodgeguatemala.com, dorms $4 p/p, $13 d in tree house or cabin) is a sure bet for wonderful volcano views and the chance to get away from it all at a reasonable distance from town in the surrounding hillsides. Accommodations include a shared-bath, eight-bed dormitory, three A-frame cabins, and a tree house. The private cabins and tree house are wonderfully secluded in a grove of Spanish oaks and have fabulous views of the valley and surrounding mountains. Each has a large double bed. Bathrooms are shared.

Delicious vegetarian dinners are served family-style for $5, though carnivores need not despair as meat options are also available, including a fun weekend barbecue. Breakfast items include eggs, bacon, sausage, pancakes, and fresh fruit. Heaping sandwiches and salads are served for lunch. You can relax in a hammock and take in the valley views, hike nearby trails, or sweat out any remaining First World stress in the stone-and-mortar sauna. There are also books, movies, music, and games on hand should you need further entertainment. Spanish classes are also available and the owners accept volunteers to help out with chores in exchange for reduced rates on food and bed. The lodge is run by a friendly Canadian-American couple who will pick you up in town in their green VW bug with prior notice for a nominal gas charge, as they come into Antigua almost daily. Alternatively, you can hitch a chicken bus to the village of El Hato for about $0.50 or flag a pickup truck heading this way.

In nearby Santa Ana, **Posada El Ensueño** (Calle del Agua, Callejón La Ermita Final, Santa Ana, tel. 7832-7958, www.posadael ensueno.com, $95–115 d) is a splendid bed-and-breakfast in a quiet setting. Run by American expatriate Carmen Herrerias, the lodge has three tastefully decorated rooms with garden showers, one of which is a suite. It's a great place to relax away from the action in Antigua. Breakfast and home-cooked meals are served poolside, and Carmen loves to cook for her guests. There's also a small heated lap pool and bikes to get around. It's about a 25-minute walk to Antigua's central park.

Just minutes from Antigua in neighboring San Felipe de Jesús, **(Filadelfia Coffee Resort and Spa** (150 meters north of the San Felipe de Jesús church, tel. 7728-0800, hotel@rdaltoncoffee.com, $211–449 d including breakfast) is a working coffee farm where you can stay in a splendid neocolonial building harboring luxurious accommodations. The 20 spacious rooms have tile floors, king- or queen-size beds, classy Guatemalan furnishings, cable TV with DVD player, large two-sink bathrooms, glass showers with antique tiles, and nice patios with furniture. There are four standard rooms, 14 deluxe doubles, and two master suites with island kitchen and a living room with leather sofa and large desk. Coffee machinery and wooden carvings adorn the public areas, while the main building harbors a cozy lobby adorned with Persian rugs. Activities include twice-daily coffee tours lasting two hours each at 9 A.M. and 2 P.M. ($15), mule riding ($20), and a four-hour hike to a lookout point ($50, including sack lunch). An elegant restaurant in the main lodge serves international dishes with flair.

Closer to the farm's main entrance is **Cafetenango** (tel. 5219-9291, 7:30 A.M.–7 P.M. Mon.–Sat. and 7:30 A.M.–6:30 P.M. Sun.), offering a more casual dining atmosphere in a country setting with lovely volcano views. It serves eggs, fruit, and yogurt for breakfast ($4), grilled meats and sandwiches for lunch and dinner ($6–12). Traditional Guatemalan dishes ($10) include *pollo en jocón* and *pepián de pollo*.

Food

Antigua's status as one of Guatemala's main tourist destinations is evident in the variety and number of excellent restaurants for every taste and budget. The mix here is rather eclectic and restaurants can often be classified into more than one category. While the presence of a McDonald's in town hardly constitutes anything worth writing home about, Antigua's golden arches are the focus of some local lore completely in line with the magic seemingly everywhere in Guatemala. According to some folks, the Ronald McDonald sitting on the bench outside Antigua's McDonald's has at least on one occasion crossed its legs and come to life, scaring unsuspecting passersby out of their wits.

CAFÉS AND LIGHT MEALS

L'Espresso (6a Avenida Norte #4, tel. 7832-0539, 7 A.M.–8 P.M. daily) has decent crepes, salads, sandwiches, smoothies, and cold or hot espresso drinks. One of Antigua's best-known cafés, **Doña Luisa Xicotencatl** (4a Calle Oriente #12, tel. 7832-2578, 7 A.M.–9:30 P.M. daily) serves delicious breakfasts, snacks, pastries, and light meals in a delightful garden courtyard. There are fresh-baked breads and cakes available all day from the bakery at the front of the building. Next door, **La Fuente** (4a Calle Oriente #14, tel. 7832-4520, 7 A.M.–7 P.M. daily) is a good place for breakfast and vegetarian fare as well as for a cup of coffee accompanied by an ever-so-sinfully delicious chocolate brownie topped with coffee ice cream and chocolate syrup.

On the west side of the central park, **Café Condesa** (Portal del Comercio #4, tel. 7832-0038, 7 A.M.–8 P.M. Sun.–Thurs., until 9 P.M. Fri./Sat.) is a great place to get some pep in your step with an early breakfast and coffee or to refuel later in the day. There are excellent cakes, pastries, sandwiches, and salads served in a pleasing garden atmosphere or you can enjoy the all-day breakfasts. A Sunday brunch is served 10 A.M.–2 P.M. and includes scrambled eggs, home-fried potatoes, silver-dollar pancakes, quiche, homemade bread, and muffins, just to name a few items. If you're on the go, grab a cup of the excellent coffee at the **Condesa Express** next door.

For fresh bagels, bagel sandwiches, and great coffee, stop at **The Bagel Barn** (5a Calle Poniente #2, 6 A.M.–10 P.M. daily). There is wireless Internet if you're traveling with a laptop and movies are shown in the afternoons and evenings. Another Antigua standby is the **Rainbow Café and Bookshop** (7a Avenida Sur #8, tel. 7832-1919, all meals daily), serving delicious menu options including eggs Florentine, Israeli falafel, and the chocolate bomb for dessert. Try the outstanding Greek chicken fillet stuffed with spinach, bacon, raisins, feta cheese, and covered with a creamy oregano and lime sauce ($8). Live music, poetry readings, and other cultural events are held on-site. On the pricier side, **Caffé Opera** (6a Avenida Norte #17, tel. 7832-0727, www.cafe-opera.com, closed Wed., $6–15) is a popular place serving some delicious coffee frappé beverages in an eclectic atmosphere stuffed with opera-themed posters and artwork. The *panini* are recommended. Under the same ownership as the Café No Sé (which is more of a bar), **Y Tu Piña También** (corner of 6a Calle Oriente and 1a Avenida Sur) is a juice bar also serving snacks, pastries, and light meals. The mango chutney chicken is good if you're on the hungrier side. Finally, a trip to Antigua wouldn't be complete without a stop for some *dulces típicos* (typical Guatemalan sweets) from **Doña María Gordillo** (4a Calle Oriente #11).

STEAK HOUSES

Ni-Fu Ni-Fa (3a Calle Oriente #21, tel. 7832-6579, lunch and dinner daily) is a genuine Argentinean steak house serving tasty grilled meats on a pleasant raised wooden deck surrounded by lush gardens. **Restaurant Las Antorchas** (3a Avenida Sur #1, tel. 7832-0806, www.lasantorchas.com, lunch and dinner daily) offers a more elegant setting and a menu that includes grilled onions, cheese fondue, tortellini, salmon in orange sauce, and well-presented grilled steak and chicken dishes.

MEXICAN

Just like its Guatemala City counterpart, **Fridas** (5a Avenida Norte #29, tel. 7832-0504, www.vivafridas.com, lunch and dinner daily, $4–10) serves scrumptious Mexican classics such as fajitas, flautas, tacos, burritos, enchiladas, and nachos in addition to the best margaritas and *mojitos* in town, all in a lively atmosphere.

INTERNATIONAL

La Escudilla (4a Avenida Norte #4, tel. 7832-1327, www.la-escudilla.com, 8 A.M.–midnight daily) is a restored colonial home with several dining options all under one roof centered around a pleasant garden courtyard. La Escudilla Restaurant has a varied menu for breakfast, lunch, and dinner, including tasty omelets, *tortillas de pollo* (flour tortillas with chicken), salads, steaks, pastas, and apple strudel for dessert. Housed in the same building is **Helas** (6 P.M.–1 A.M. Tues.–Fri., 1 P.M.–1 A.M. Sat./Sun.), a tavern serving authentic Greek dishes in the $6–8 range. You can dine in a small but pleasant room decorated with fishing nets and Aegean themes.

The new owners of **Café Sky** (corner of 6a Calle Oriente and 1a Avenida Sur, tel. 7832-7300, 8 A.M.–11 P.M. daily, $4–8) are revamping the menu with a new chef onboard and a variety of tasty menu items, including sandwiches, lasagnas, and quesadillas. As always, there are wonderful volcano views from the restaurant's rooftop terrace location. **Perú Café** (4a Avenida Norte #7, tel. 7832-9121, www.perucafe.com, $6–10) serves appetizing Peruvian dishes in a colonial atmosphere. Try the tasty *causas,* which are essentially burgers with layers of mashed potatoes substituted for bread. For a lively atmosphere and great food, ◖ **Restaurante Las Palmas** (6a Avenida Norte #14, tel. 7832-9734, www.laspalmas antigua.com, 9 A.M.–10 P.M. daily, $7–12) makes

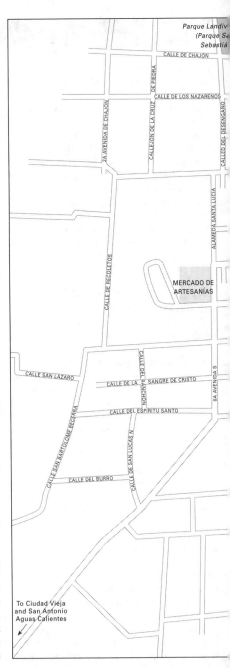

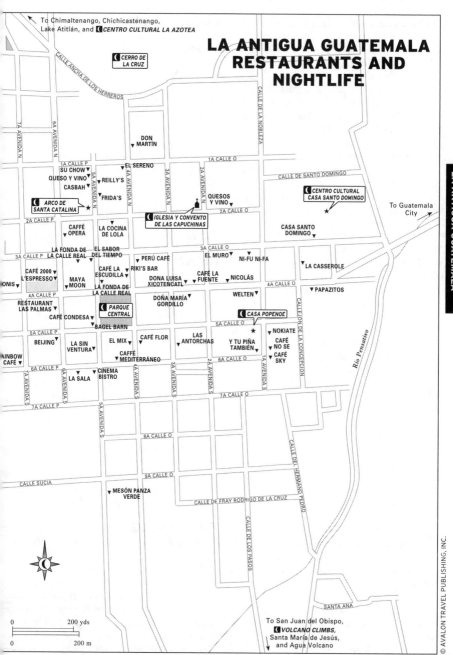

a fine choice. Among the varied menu items are fish in cilantro sauce, spinach lasagna, shrimp in Alfredo pasta, and filet mignon. There are whirring ceiling fans, a fully stocked bar, and vibrant tropical Latin decor.

For French food, **La Casserole** (Callejón de la Concepción #7, tel. 7832-0219, noon–3 P.M. and 7–10 P.M. Tues.–Sat., noon–4 P.M. Sun.) is hard to beat. In an appealing garden patio with a dozen or so tables, there are tasty soups, well-prepared pastas, and fish and chicken or meat dishes to satiate your hunger. For dessert, there are excellent crepes, tiramisu, sorbet, and mousse. For Spanish food, head to **La Cocina de Lola** (2a Calle Poniente #3, tel. 7832-6616, noon–3 P.M. and 6–10 P.M. Tues.–Fri., noon–10 P.M. Sat., noon–9 P.M. Sun., $5–10), where there are several rooms around a garden patio. You can feast on classic Spanish dishes the likes of paella, seafood, and grilled steaks. Just down the street from the Arco de Santa Catalina, **El Sabor del Tiempo** (Calle del Arco and 3a Calle, tel. 7832-0516, lunch and dinner daily, $5–11) offers a casual dining atmosphere and creatively prepared dishes, including rabbit steak, pastas, *panini,* and tasty Greek burgers.

ITALIAN

Antigua has a number of Italian restaurants popular with travelers and locals alike. **Queso y Vino** (5a Avenida Norte #32A, tel. 7832-7785, noon–3 P.M. and 6–10 P.M. Wed.–Mon., $5–10) has delicious pizza, pastas, and cheeses in addition to Chilean and Spanish wines. **Caffé Mediterraneo** (6a Calle Poniente #6A, tel. 7832-7180, noon–3 P.M. and 6–10 P.M. Mon. and Wed.–Sat., noon–4:30 P.M. and 6:30–9 P.M. Sun., $7–12) is small but serves excellent Italian food, including homemade pastas and delightful antipasti in addition to a good assortment of wines. For gourmet pizza, try **Papazitos** (4a Calle Oriente #39, tel. 7832-5209, 11:30 A.M.–11 P.M. daily). It also serves nachos, *panini,* calzones, pastas, vegetarian dishes, wine, and beer. It offers free delivery with a minimum $7 purchase; 10- to 18-inch pizzas go for $9–16.

GUATEMALAN

Another one of Antigua's legendary restaurants is **La Fonda de la Calle Real** (3a Calle Poniente #7, tel. 7832-0507, noon–10 P.M. daily; 5a Avenida Norte #5, tel. 7832-2629, noon–10 P.M. daily; 5a Avenida Norte #12, tel. 7832-3749, 8 A.M.–10 P.M. daily, $5–12), with three branches, the nicest of which is the one on 3a Calle Poniente. There is a varied menu of Guatemalan favorites, including *chiles rellenos* as well as tasty grilled meats. If you can't decide, do as Clinton did and order the filling sampler menu. **Don Martín** (4a Avenida Norte #27, tel. 7832-1063) features creative Guatemalan dishes, including *pepián* (a spicy meat or chicken stew), and has an international touch with pasta dishes.

ASIAN

Café Flor (4a Avenida Sur #1, tel. 7832-5274, 11 A.M.–11 P.M. daily, $5–10) does a reasonably good job with Thai food, though it won't taste familiar to fans of Asian cuisine. Other dishes include Thai curries, rice dishes, and Indian tandoori recipes. The portions are adequate, but not huge either. With a self-proclaimed Far Eastern "cool Zen" atmosphere, 【 **Nokiate** (1a Avenida Sur #7, tel. 7821-2896, www.nokiate.com, 6:30 P.M.–1 A.M. Tues.–Fri., noon–3 P.M. and 6:30 P.M.–1 A.M. Sat., noon–9 P.M. Sun., $5–10) pulls it off beautifully. The hip lounge, sake bar, and wonderful Asian garden patio make a suitably glamorous backdrop for enjoying the best sushi in town. For your standard Chinese food, head to **Su Chow** (5a Avenida Norte #36, tel. 7832-1344, noon–10 P.M. daily, $5–10). It also delivers.

FINE DINING

With a long tradition of excellence, **Welten** (4a Calle Oriente #21, tel. 7832-0630, www .weltenrestaurant.com, noon–10 P.M. Sun.–Thurs., until 11 P.M. Fri./Sat., closed Tues., $13–22) is one of Antigua's well-established dining options serving an impressive menu of gourmet Guatemalan, French, and Italian specialties in an elegant atmosphere. Menu highlights include creamy peppered steak (filet au poivre), seafood fettuccine, and fish fillet in a traditional salsa. There are delicious homemade ice creams for dessert. **(Mesón Panza Verde** (5a Avenida Sur #19, tel. 7832-2925, www.panzaverde.com, lunch and dinner Tues.–Sat., brunch and lunch Sun., $10–20) is easily one of Guatemala's finest restaurants thanks to the culinary prowess of its Swiss-born, French-trained chef, Cristophe Pache, and its sophisticated European ambience. The mostly French cuisine is heavy on meat and fish dishes. The wine list is impressive, as are the desserts. A Sunday brunch is served 10 A.M.–1 P.M. You can enjoy your meal in the main dining room surrounded by fine art under a vaulted ceiling or al fresco in La Cueva, a covered patio beneath baroque arches beside a fountain. *Chacun à son goût.*

On par with the exclusive digs in this landmark Antigua hotel, the restaurant at **Casa Santo Domingo** (3a Calle Oriente #28, tel. 7832-0140, www.casasantodomingo.com.gt, $15–25) serves delicious Guatemalan and international fare in the restored ruins of an old monastery. It makes a great spot for a romantic candlelit dinner. Another excellent hotel restaurant can be found at **Hotel Posada de Don Rodrigo** (5a Avenida Norte #17, tel. 7832-0291, all meals daily), which is popular with Guatemalans who come here for its wonderful ambience overlooking the hotel gardens and delicious Guatemalan and international cuisine. The tortillas are made fresh on the premises and you can watch the dough being patted and placed on the *comal,* where they are cooked over a fire. There is sometimes live marimba music to complete the authentic Guatemalan feel.

Nicolas (4a Calle Oriente #20, tel. 7832-0471, www.nicolas.com.gt, 12:30–3 P.M. Fri.–Sun., 7–10 P.M. daily except Wed.) is a relative newcomer to Antigua's fine-dining scene, but it has already made a name for itself with its Norwegian chef. The atmosphere is modern and the menu includes an interesting array of Asian fusion dishes, seafood, and meats. A longtime favorite is **(El Sereno** (4a Avenida Norte #16, tel. 7832-0501, www.elsereno.com.gt, lunch and dinner daily). The restaurant dates to 1980, but the wonderfully old colonial building in which it's housed dates to the 16th century and once housed the Spanish priests who built La Merced church. You can dine on gourmet international dishes in the elegant main dining room, in a romantic cavelike candlelit room, or al fresco either in a delightful covered garden patio or on the rooftop terrace.

Information and Services

TOURIST INFORMATION

The INGUAT office (Palacio de los Capitanes Generales, tel. 7832-0763, 8 A.M.–12:30 P.M. and 2:30–5 P.M. Mon.–Fri., 9 A.M.–12:30 P.M. and 2:30–5 P.M. Sat./Sun) is on the southeast corner of the plaza. Its friendly, helpful staff can help steer you in the right direction as well as provide free maps, bus schedules, and other useful information. A useful website with lots of information on hotels, restaurants, shops, and services is www.aroundantigua.com. Another useful publication is the monthly *Revue* magazine, available free at many hotels, restaurants, and shops.

COMMUNICATIONS

Antigua's main post office is near the bus terminal on the corner of 4a Calle Poniente and Calzada de Santa Lucía and is open 9 A.M.–5 P.M. There are also various international couriers with offices here, including UPS (6a Calle Poniente #34, tel. 7832-0073) and DHL (6a Avenida Sur #12, tel. 7832-1696). A number of companies can also help you ship home any purchases you're unable to fit in your check-in baggage allotment. These include Quickbox (6a Calle Poniente #7, tel. 7832-3825) and Envíos Etc. (2a Calle Poniente #3), which is also the local representative for FedEx.

Conexion (4a Calle Oriente #14, Centro Comercial La Fuente, tel. 7832-3768, 8:30 A.M.–7:30 P.M. daily) offers fast Internet on new machines with flat screens for $1.50 an hour. It also does printing, photocopying, and CD-burning in addition to phone and fax services. Enlaces (6a Avenida Norte #1, tel. 7832-5555, 8 A.M.–7:30 P.M. Mon.–Sat., 8 A.M.–1 P.M. Sun.) is another good setup offering many of the same services. Funky Monkey (5a Avenida Sur #6) is housed in the same complex as the Monoloco bar and has a decent Internet connection for about $1 an hour. Strictly for phone calls, your best bet is Australis Telecom (4a Calle Poniente #15, tel. 2381-0698, 8 A.M.–8 P.M. daily), where you can pretty much call anywhere on the planet for $0.09–0.10 a minute from a nice soundproof cabin.

MONEY

Banco Industrial (5a Avenida Sur #4), just south of the plaza, has a Visa/Plus ATM. On the north side of the plaza is Banco del Quetzal with a MasterCard/Cirrus ATM. Just off the square at the corner of 4a Calle Oriente and 4a Avenida Norte, Lloyd's TSB changes U.S. dollars and can cash travelers checks.

LAUNDRY

Detalles (6a Avenida Norte #3B, tel. 7832-5973, 7:30 A.M.–6:30 P.M. Mon.–Sat., 8 A.M.–4 P.M. Sun.) does dry cleaning and has coin-operated laundry machines. Lavandería Dry Clean (6a Calle Poniente #49, 7 A.M.–7 P.M. Mon.–Sat., 9 A.M.–6 P.M. Sun.) charges about $4 a load. Quick Laundry (6a Calle Poniente #14, tel. 7832-2937, 8 A.M.–5 P.M. Mon.–Sat.) charges about $0.85 per pound.

CHOOSING A LANGUAGE SCHOOL

Antigua has close to 100 language schools, and the task of choosing the right one can seem downright daunting. It really boils down to the quality of individual instructors, though some schools are definitely better than others. Look around and ask plenty of questions. If you decide midway through a weeklong course that you're just not jiving with the instructor, don't hesitate to pull out and ask for a new one. That being said, the following websites can help you out in your search: **www.guatemala365.com** and **www.123teachme.com**. Both have surveys and rankings of individual schools in Guatemala.

Among the recommended Antigua schools are **Academia de Español Antigueña** (1a Calle Poniente #10, tel. 7832-7241, www.spanish academyantiguena.com), a small, well-run school with space for 10 students at a time. **Escuela de Español San José El Viejo** (5a Avenida Sur #34, tel. 7832-3028, www.san joseelviejo.com) has its own very attractive campus where you can stay in comfortable accommodations with facilities that include a tennis court and swimming pool amid lovely gardens and coffee trees. A longtime student favorite is **Christian Spanish Academy**

(6a Avenida Norte #15, tel. 7832-3922, www .learncsa.com), a very well-run school set in a pleasant colonial courtyard. Antigua's oldest language school is **Proyecto Lingüístico Francisco Marroquín** (7a Calle Poniente #31, tel. 7832-2886, www.plfm-antigua.org), run by a nonprofit foundation working toward the study and preservation of Mayan languages. It comes highly recommended. **Academia de Español Probigua** (6a Avenida Norte #41B, tel. 7832-2998, www.probigua.conexion.com) is run by a nonprofit group working to establish and maintain libraries in rural villages. Another good choice with comfortable accommodations across the street from the school is **Centro Lingüístico Internacional** (1a Calle Oriente #11, tel. 7832-0391, www.spanishcontact.com).

The recommended schools range in price $140-225 per week, including 20-35 hours of instruction and a stay with local family. While the schools provide everything you will need to learn the language, it might be a challenge to have a total language immersion experience because of the overwhelming presence of foreigners in Antigua. If this is an issue for you, consider taking Spanish classes in Cobán or Petén.

MEDICAL SERVICES

Casa de Salud Santa Lucía (Calzada de Santa Lucía Sur #7, tel. 7832-3122) is a private medical hospital with 24-hour emergency services. Hospital Nacional Pedro de Betancourth is a public hospital two kilometers from town with emergency service. For serious issues, your best bet is to go to Guatemala City.

EMERGENCY

For the Bomberos Municipales (Municipal Fire Department), dial 7831-0049. The office of the Policía de Turismo (Tourist Police) can be found just off the central square at Palacio del Ayuntamiento on 4a Avenida Norte. They escort visitors to nearby Cerro de la Cruz and can help translate if you need to report an incident to the Policía Nacional Civil (National Civil Police, Palacio de los Capitanes Generales, tel. 7832-0251).

TRAVEL AGENCIES

Travel agencies are ubiquitous in Antigua. Among the recommended companies for shuttle buses is Atitrans (6a Avenida Sur #8, tel. 7832-3371 or 7832-0644, www.atitrans .com). For plane tickets and general travel needs, recommended travel agents include National Travel (6a Avenida Sur #1A, tel. 7832-8383 or 5715-1675 after hours), Viajes Tivoli (4a Calle Oriente #10, Edificio El Jaulón, tel. 7832-1370), and Rainbow Travel Center (7a Avenida Sur #8, tel. 7832-4202, www.rain bowtravelcenter.com). Specializing in student and youth travel is STA Travel (6a Calle Poniente #21, tel. 7892-3985).

Sin Fronteras (5a Avenida Norte #15A, tel. 7832-1017, www.sinfront.com) is another good all-around agency with package deals to Tikal in addition to local tours. It rents cars through Tabarini Rent A Car. Another good agency for packages to Tikal or other parts of Guatemala is Adrenalina Tours (5a Avenida Norte #31, tel. 7832-1108, www.adrenalinatours.com). It also has daily shuttle service to Quetzaltenango at 8 A.M. and 2:30 P.M. for $25 per person.

VOLUNTEER WORK

Proyecto Mosaico Guatemala (3a Avenida Norte #3, Casa de Mito, tel. 7932-0955, www .promosaico.org) places volunteers with organizations working to make Guatemala a better place. It also provides resources to more than 60 ongoing projects. Amerispan Guatemala (6a Avenida Norte #40A, tel. 7832-0164, www .amerispan.com) can also get you connected to volunteer opportunities throughout the country for a $60 fee.

LANGUAGE SCHOOLS

A major draw for visitors to Antigua are the city's excellent language schools, though the abundance of foreigners in and around town can sometimes hinder the total immersion experience. (See the sidebar *Choosing a Language School* for recommended schools and tips on finding a school that's right for you.)

Getting There and Around

BUS

The main **bus terminal** is found next to the market, three blocks west of the central plaza. It is separated from the heart of town by a broad, tree-lined street. There are connections to the highlands available by taking one of many frequent buses up to Chimaltenango (every 15 minutes, half-hour travel time) along the Pan-American Highway and a requisite stop for buses trundling along to the highlands from Guatemala City. You can also catch one of the slightly less frequent buses to San Lucas Sacatepéquez, which is closer to Guatemala City. There may be more seats available on the buses plying the same highway en route toward Chimaltenango. Buses for Guatemala City leave every 15 minutes or so 4 A.M.–7:30 P.M., taking about an hour and costing about $1.25. There is also a direct bus to Panajachel at 7 A.M. leaving from 4a Calle Poniente #34 (two hours, $5).

Otherwise, buses leave every 15 minutes for San Miguel Dueñas ("Dueñas," 30 minutes, $0.30) stopping along the way in Ciudad Vieja. There are also buses every 30 minutes for San Antonio Aguas Calientes and Santa María de Jesús.

SHUTTLE BUS

Many travelers opt for the comfort, convenience, safety, and hassle-free experience aboard one of the numerous shuttle buses. Destinations include frequent runs to the Guatemala City airport, at least one bus daily to Monterrico and Cobán, several daily to Panajachel and Quetzaltenango, and less frequently to Río Dulce. Recommended shuttle companies include **Atitrans** (6a Avenida Sur #8, tel. 7832-3371 or 7832-0644, www.atitrans.com) and **Adrenalina Tours** (5a Avenida Norte #31, tel. 7832-1108, www.adrenalinatours.com). **Moon-**

Ray Tours (tel. 7832-0198) has buses to San Salvador, El Salvador, on Monday, Wednesday, Friday, and Sunday at 9 A.M., costing $30 one-way and returning on alternate days.

TAXI

Taxis can be found on the east side of the park next to the cathedral by the bus terminal. The former is probably a safer place to board one. A ride to Guatemala City should cost around $30. You'll also see *tuk-tuks* (motorized rickshaws) throughout the city, costing considerably less and recommended for short distances.

CAR RENTAL

Tabarini (6a Avenida Sur #22, tel. 7832-8107) rents cars from its own office and also handles bookings via **Sin Fronteras** (5a Avenida Norte #15A, tel. 7832-1017).

Near Antigua Guatemala

JOCOTENANGO

Jocotenango lies just 3.5 kilometers northwest of Antigua. A pretty, pink stucco church adorns the main square. In colonial times, the town served as the official entry point into neighboring Antigua.

◖ Centro Cultural La Azotea

The town's main attraction is La Azotea Cultural Center (Calle del Cementerio, Final, 8:30 A.M.–4 P.M. Mon.–Fri., 8:30 A.M.–2 P.M. Sat., $4 adults, $0.85 children), which functions as a three-in-one coffee, costume, and music museum. The music museum, **Casa K'ojom** (www.kojom.org) features a wonderful assortment of traditional Mayan musical instruments, including *marimbas,* drums, a diatomic harp, and flutes in addition to masks and paintings collected by its dedicated administrator, Samuel Franco. There is also an audiovisual room where you can watch a video on traditional music as it would be played in Mayan villages. Traditional costumes and crafts of the Antigua Valley are

exhibited in a separate room dedicated to Sacatepéquez department.

The adjoining **Museo del Café** covers the history and evolution of coffee cultivation and is available as a self-guided or guided tour. You can see coffee beans in varying stages of production from recently harvested to fully roasted. The well-illustrated displays include information on wet and dry mills, some old roasters, and machinery. You can then tour an actual plantation on-site. There is also a shop where you can buy CDs, DVDs, handicrafts, and of course, coffee.

Also found here is the **Establo La Ronda,** where you can ride around the grounds on horseback for an hour in the mornings ($3). Call ahead.

You can get to Jocotenango by taking any Chimaltenango-bound bus leaving from Antigua's bus terminal.

SAN JUAN DEL OBISPO

Although this town itself is unremarkable, it bears mentioning for the impressive **Palacio**

del Obispo, the original home of Bishop Francisco Marroquín, which was restored in 1939. Though it's now used as a place for spiritual retreats, the nuns living there are happy to show you around if you ring the bell at a reasonable hour. The entrance is on the street behind the attached church. Marroquín arrived with Alvarado and temporarily assumed government leadership in the wake of the death of Alvarado's wife, Beatriz de la Cueva, who assumed power after his death. He also assumed a great deal of responsibility for the construction of the new capital at Antigua. The palace interior is quite lovely and still contains original furniture in addition to a 16th-century portrait of Marroquín and religious artwork imported from Europe. There is also an ornate baroque chapel. There are some nice views of Antigua

THE GIANT KITE FESTIVAL

If you're visiting the Antigua or Guatemala City area around November 1, you should certainly plan a trip to either of the highland Mayan towns of Santiago Sacatepéquez or Sumpango, home to the annual Giant Kite Festival. In addition to the lively atmosphere of a typical Mayan fiesta, you'll be treated to an awe-inspiring display of larger-than-life kites, typically 20–50 feet wide. The kites are painstakingly crafted from tissue paper and bamboo reeds incorporating colorful and elaborate designs. Preparations typically begin six weeks in advance, in mid-September, with teams working more hours as the deadline for completion draws closer. Judges are on hand at the festival to name the best entries in a variety of categories.

Kites under 20 feet in diameter are flown over the town cemetery later in the day and are believed to be a vehicle for speaking with the souls of departed loved ones. The flying kites are representative of the floating spirits of the dead. Larger kites are only for show and typically carry a message or theme, sometimes overtly political in nature. The weather is typically windy during this time of year, with the surrounding hillsides still tinged with verdant hues thanks to the recently ended rainy season. The colorful cemetery structures and the typical native dress of the Mayan people cap off a Technicolor dream of a day.

The festival in Sumpango, the larger of the two towns, takes place in a broad field adjacent to the cemetery. Santiago Sacatepéquez has a somewhat more cramped setting, its cemetery being perched on the edge of a plateau and extending down a gently sloping hillside.

© AL ARGUETA

one of the smaller kites at the Giant Kite Festival

Many Antigua travel agencies have special trips to both towns on these days, or you can go by bus. Santiago Sacatepéquez lies a few kilometers off the Pan-American Highway. You can take a direct bus from Antigua or get off from any Guatemala City-bound bus at the junction and continue from there. For Sumpango, your best bet is to get to Chimaltenango, also on the Pan-American Highway, and connect from there.

and the valley from here, just south of town. Buses leave hourly from the Antigua bus terminal, taking about 20 minutes to get here.

CIUDAD VIEJA

Ciudad Vieja served as Guatemala's colonial capital before its destruction by mudflows from Agua Volcano in 1541, after which the capital was moved to present-day Antigua, six kilometers north. Its former glory is long gone, its only outstanding landmark being the colonial church on the plaza. Beatriz de la Cueva, Don Pedro de Alvarado's second wife, perished in the ruins of a nearby chapel while seeking refuge from the storm, which brought mud and water clambering down the slopes of the volcano.

Just beyond Ciudad Vieja, on the road to San Miguel Dueñas, **Estación Experimental Valhalla** (Km 52.5 Carretera a San Miguel Dueñas, tel. 7831-5799, www.exvalhalla.net, 8 A.M.–5 P.M. daily) is an experimental macadamia nut–farming operation. You can tour the organic plantation, sample macadamia chocolates and macadamia oil skin-care products, or eat delicious macadamia nut pancakes served with blueberry jam and macadamia butter 8:30 A.M.–3:30 P.M. The owner is a visionary who sees macadamia trees as a sustainable agricultural and ecological alternative to coffee harvesting and may be on hand to show you around.

SAN ANTONIO AGUAS CALIENTES

This town is well known for its wonderful weavings incorporating geometric/floral patterns and for handicrafts, including *petates* (reed mats), wooden masks, reed dolls, and kites. At the time of its founding in the 16th century, San Antonio and other adjoining communities were lakeshore villages on Lago Quinizilapa, which has long since been drained. The town's prominence as a handicrafts production center has made it relatively prosperous and it enjoys one of the highest literacy rates in the Guatemalan highlands. There are frequent buses to San Antonio, just six kilometers from Antigua. **Antigua Tours** (3a Calle Oriente #22, tel. 7832-5821, www.antiguatours.net) includes a stop in San Antonio Aguas Calientes as part of its "Antigua Villages" tour. (See *City Tours* under *Recreation* in this chapter for details.)

SANTIAGO SACATEPÉQUEZ AND SUMPANGO

These towns, found between 20 and 25 kilometers north of Antigua, are noteworthy for their November 1 Giant Kite Festival. See the *Giant Kite Festival* sidebar for more information.

THE WESTERN HIGHLANDS

The Western Highlands are probably the region most travelers familiar with Guatemala think about when daydreaming about a trip to this country. The region is home to quaint and colorful mountain villages, highland lakes, pine forests, and the majority of Guatemala's indigenous peoples. Although other parts of Central America offer attractions similar to those found elsewhere in Guatemala, nowhere else in the region are age-old traditions, exquisite Mayan culture, and a history both proud and painful so remarkably evident and incredibly alive. From the Indian markets in Chichicastenango and the Mayan practices of the *costumbristas* (shamans practicing traditional Mayan rituals) in the hills just outside of town to the all-day November 1 horse races of Todos Santos, the region is steeped in rich culture.

In the Western Highlands, you'll find the ruined cities of the highland Mayan tribes encountered by Pedro de Alvarado and the Spanish when they arrived in 1524. The sites are still places of pilgrimage for the modern-day descendants of the various linguistic groups populating this part of the country. Traversing the pine tree–peppered mountain scenery, you'll also come across the region's spectacular volcanic chain, which runs like a spine heading west from Antigua all the way to the Mexican border. The water-filled caldera of an extinct volcano forms the basis for one of the country's most outrageously beautiful natural attractions, the singular Lake Atitlán. In addition to water-based recreational activities, unlike any other lake in Central America, it offers the opportunity to observe and interact with the

fascinating highland Mayan people inhabiting the dozen or so villages along its lakeshores. Farther west is Guatemala's second-largest city, Quetzaltenango, which has become a popular place for Spanish-language study as well as a hub of NGO activity in the aftermath of the civil war. It boasts some outstanding nearby natural attractions of its own and the cosmopolitan feel of a European city.

Throughout the highlands, you'll encounter the aftereffects of Guatemala's bloody civil war, which affected this region more than any other. But, like a brilliant springtime flower emerging through fertile soil from winter's icy chill, the highlands and its people are fast changing and rising from the ashes of the armed conflict. There's a new feeling in the air. Where once there was fear and apprehension (and rightfully so) on the part of its Mayan inhabitants, there is now curiosity and a desire to build a new future while holding on to the culture that is their inheritance. You are a big part of this, as your presence in these parts is a catalyst to substantial progress along the lines of sustainable development with tourism at the forefront. There are many community-based tourism projects in this area and your visit helps provide needed income but also positive interaction with the outside world.

It is so refreshing, years later, to be able to travel to areas that were once bombed out and cleared of vegetation but are now green and vibrant once again. This painful legacy intertwined with optimism is most evident in the Ixil Triangle, which stands poised to become a mecca for cultural and ecotourism, overseen by and to the benefit of, its Ixil inhabitants. Despite having suffered some of the most horrendous atrocities during the civil war, still they smile, a testament to their fortitude. Farther west toward the Mexican border, the department of Huehuetenango boasts fascinating Mayan villages of its own in addition to some seldom-visited natural attractions along the Sierra de los Cuchumatanes mountain chain. It's only a matter of time before visitors to Guatemala put this vast wilderness on the map.

HIGHLIGHTS

◖ **Iximché:** Conveniently situated close to the Pan-American Highway about an hour outside of Guatemala City, the ruins of the former capital of the Kaqchikel kingdom is worth a look to see what the Spanish encountered when they first arrived in Guatemala. It is the most easily accessible of all the highland Mayan centers brought under Spanish dominion at the time of the conquest (page 112).

◖ **Reserva Natural Atitlán:** Lake Atitlán is one of Guatemala's greatest natural wonders, and this private nature reserve offers a unique glimpse into its ecosystems. There are trails, waterfalls, plenty of animals, a butterfly farm, and a private lake beach in addition to comfortable accommodations (page 118).

◖ **Chichicastenango's Market:** Don't miss the chance to barter for goods and take in the chaotic atmosphere of this colorful Sunday and Thursday market at the center of a K'iche' town (page 141).

◖ **Acul:** One of the so-called "model villages" established by the military, Acul has come into its own in the aftermath of the armed conflict. It makes an excellent hike from Nebaj, though the pastoral scenery and Swiss-like ambience found in some of the local accommodations will probably have you planning on staying the night (page 154).

◖ **Laguna Chicabal:** Near Quetzaltenango, this enchanting, bowl-shaped crater lake makes

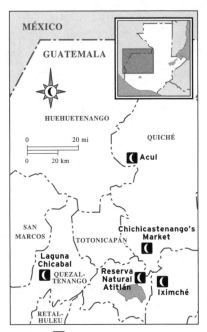

LOOK FOR ◖ TO FIND RECOMMENDED SIGHTS, ACTIVITIES, DINING, AND LODGING.

a worthy day hike. Mayan rituals still take place here, and the site is equally fascinating for the spectacular natural surroundings (page 184).

PLANNING YOUR TIME

The Western Highlands are home to many of Guatemala's main attractions and there is plenty here worth seeing. Although distances on a map may be short, the rugged mountain terrain means getting to places that look close on a map will often take longer than expected because of twisting mountain roads, some of which are not even paved. You could easily spend several weeks here or longer, as attested to by the sizeable expat population living on the shores of Lake Atitlán. But, since most folks tend to be on a tighter schedule you'll

probably end up choosing among the many wonderful attractions.

The region is traversed in several parts by the Pan-American Highway, meaning that if you're on a limited schedule, you should stick to areas near this paved main road. Along this road, coming up from Guatemala City or Antigua, you may want to spend an hour or so at the ruins of Iximché, the former Kaqchikel capital, which also served as the first capital of Guatemala when the Spanish set up shop here after the conquest. If you have only a few days, you should certainly not miss a visit to

Lake Atitlán, staying either in the large tourist and services hub of Panajachel or taking a boat across the lake to the village of your choice. Each has its own characteristics and tends to attract a certain crowd.

After the lake, you can continue along the Pan-American Highway to Quetzaltenango, Guatemala's second-largest city, where you can take in area villages or natural attractions, including the fantastic crater lake atop Chicabal Volcano. It's also a great place to sign up for a week (or more) of Spanish lessons if you have the time. If you can work it in to your sched-ule, plan on visiting the market (Sundays and Thursdays) in the K'iche' town of Chichicas-tenango, which is easily accessible from Quet-zaltenango and Panajachel. If you have more time, head north from Chichicastenango into the hills of Quiché department to the Ixil Tri-angle. You certainly won't be disappointed.

If you have still more time, consider head-ing west to Huehuetenango from the branch road in the town of Sacapulas (Quiché depart-ment) or east to Cobán and the Verapaces via a spectacularly scenic, and equally rugged, dirt road.

Chimaltenango Department and Vicinity

CHIMALTENANGO

The departmental capital of Chimaltenango is a major transit point between Guatemala City/Antigua and the highlands. You may find yourself changing buses here if you're head-ing up from Antigua going east to Guatemala City or west to the highlands, including Chi-chicastenango, Lake Atitlán, Quetzaltenango, and Huehuetenango. (See *Getting There* in the appropriate sections for details.) There's little else to keep you in this busy commercial town and transportation hub.

TECPÁN TO LOS ENCUENTROS

A much more pleasant alternative to the noise and pollution of Chimaltenango is a stretch of the Pan-American Highway (CA-1) heading through the Western Highlands from the town of Tecpán, about an hour from Guatemala City, all the way west to the Los Encuentros junction, from where a turnoff leads to a ver-tiginous drop down the sides of an extinct vol-canic caldera to out-of-this-world Lake Atitlán. Another road leads north from Los Encuentros to the department of El Quiché, with its color-ful markets and highland villages. Along the road from Tecpán to Los Encuentros, you'll find some interesting Mayan ruins and good eats, should you need to stop for sustenance or simply want a break from the drive to enjoy the wonderful sylvan settings.

Tecpán

The town of Tecpán proper is about half a ki-lometer from the main highway via a signed turnoff, though few people actually go into the town unless they're en route to the ruins of Iximché. You'll find plenty of roadside restaurants along this stretch of the highway, many with nearly identical menus. Some of these, such as **Katok** (Km. 87.5, tel. 7840-3384, www.ahumadoskatok.com) and **Kape Paulino's** (Km. 87.5, tel. 7840-3806, www.kapepaulinos.com) are perennial favorites with Guatemalans and are usually very busy, serving a variety of grilled steaks, chicken, Guatemalan dishes, and cured meats in a log cabin atmosphere.

If you're not a big fan of crowds, just across the road is the usually emptier and somewhat more charming atmosphere of **⬛ Hacienda Tecpán** (tel. 7840-3780, haciendatecpan@yahoo.es). The large, hacienda-style building is set among sprawling landscaped grounds tra-versed by small streams and grazed by sheep and goats. The pleasant dining room overlooking the grounds features tablecloths and somewhat more upscale country decor than its neighbors, with the emphasis on Guatemalan dishes.

THE WESTERN HIGHLANDS

© AL ARGUETA

highland scenery along the Pan-American Highway

At a turnoff from the main highway at Km. 90.5 heading to the village of Santa Apolonia, **El Pedregal** (tel. 7840-3055) has pleasant grounds in a country setting away from the noise of the busy Pan-American Highway. It also makes a great place for kids, with ducks, cows, and other farm animals for them to enjoy. Delicious home-cooked meals including sandwiches, fresh bread, and cakes are served in a lovely covered patio fronting the gardens. Farther along the road at Km. 102, **Restaurant Chichoy** (also at Km. 78 in the village of Chirijuyú) is another good choice, serving breakfast, lunch, and dinner. It was originally started by a cooperative of widows from the civil war.

◖ Iximché

Faced with the increasingly belligerent expansionist aims of their K'iche' rivals, the Kaqchikel moved their capital from present-day Chichicastenango to the more easily defended site of Iximché, surrounded on three sides by ravines, sometime around A.D. 1470. Like many other Postclassic Mayan sites, it bore strong in-

fluence from present-day Mexico, an influence evident in its Nahua name, Cuauhtemallan, a derivative of which eventually gave the country its modern-day name meaning "land of many trees." Societal organization here was based on lineages, with evidence of bitter rivalry between different lineages including ritual cannibalism and human sacrifice. The new capital had been established for only about 50 years before the arrival of the Spanish, who would enlist the Kaqchikels as allies in their quest to conquer the K'iche' and other Mayan peoples of the Western Highlands.

After the highlands were fully conquered, the Spanish established the first capital of Guatemala here on July 25, 1524. Alvarado, however, began demanding excessive tribute and the Kaqchikels soon revolted, eventually fleeing the town after Alvarado finally burned it to the ground. From the surrounding countryside (demonstrating a remarkable symmetry to the country's more recent history), the Kaqchikels launched a guerrilla war against the Spanish that lasted until 1530.

© AL ARGUETA

the ruins of Iximché

Iximché is the most easily accessible of Guatemala's highland Mayan ceremonial sites and makes an interesting stop for those with an interest in Mayan culture and history because of the differences it exhibits from the lowland Mayan sites of Petén, which date to much earlier times. Like many of its more remote highland counterparts (Mixco Viejo, K'umarcaaj, and Zaculeu), it was built on an isolated bluff surrounded and protected by ravines. Its smaller structures also exhibit much more Mexican influence, attesting to the population of the Guatemalan highlands by Toltec groups coming from the area near present-day Veracruz.

In March 2007, Iximché made a convenient stopover for President George W. Bush, the first lady, Laura Bush, and their Guatemalan hosts Oscar and Wendy Berger on their way back to Guatemala City from a visit to a nearby vegetable farming cooperative. They received a red carpet welcome of sorts, entering the ruins' main plaza on a specially made *alfombra* similar to the ones created for Anti-

gua's Holy Week processions. They were also treated to a marimba band, an exhibition of the Mayan ball game, and a traditional dance performed by local children. In an impromptu display rarely seen in international protocol, Presidents Bush and Berger even attempted to play some ball of their own before members of the Secret Service rushed them on to the next order of business.

Of the ruined temple pyramids, only a few features stand out. The small altar at the base of Temple II, on Plaza A, has faint traces of murals. Other features include two ball courts and Plaza B, which housed royals. The museum has some interpretive displays predominantly on Pedro de Alvarado and the Kaqchikel uprisings. There's also a 1:200 scale model of Iximché based on an 1882 map created by Alfred Maudslay. The ruins are open 8 A.M.–5 P.M. daily. Admission is $3.50. To get here, turn off the main highway to Tecpán. From the town center there are buses, minibuses, and taxis heading out to the ruins, less than 10 minutes away.

Los Encuentros

The road diverting to El Quiché department is found at this junction and, about one kilometer farther down, is the turnoff for the road to Lake Atitlán. The Pan-American Highway (also known as the Interamericana) continues west to Quetzaltenango and Huehuetenango through lovely alpine scenery.

Accommodations

West of Los Encuentros at Km. 145 of the Pan-American Highway, **(Corazón del Bosque** (tel. 7723-4140 or 5299-6915, www .corazondelbosque.com, $0.65 admission) is a community tourism initiative consisting of rustic wooden cabins, a *temascal* (Mayan sauna), plant nursery, and nature trails. There's also a restaurant/bar serving typical Guatemalan fare and highland Mayan alcoholic concoctions such as *kusha*. The quaint wooden cabins ($27 d) are well furnished and have nice views in addition to private wooden patios. True to its name, meaning "Heart of the Forest," it enjoys a sublime setting amid pine forests. The site is just 15 minutes from Los Encuentros, 45 minutes from Panajachel, and 1.5 hours from Quetzaltenango.

Panajachel and Lake Atitlán

From Los Encuentros, the road descends through beautiful agricultural fields tended by Mayan Indians, many of whom still wear traditional dress. After passing the departmental capital of Sololá, the road becomes steeper, descending to the Lake Atitlán shoreline with gorgeous views of the large, crescent moon–shaped lake bounded by three volcanoes on its southern shore. You'll also pass a waterfall or two along the way. For centuries the beauty of Lake Atitlán has captivated travelers, including Aldous Huxley, who called it "The most beautiful lake in the world," a statement often quoted by travel guides and tourist brochures promoting the country and its fantastic scenery. Although it's been quoted countless times, it really bears repeating, as words cannot begin to describe the magic felt when seeing the lake for the first time, its waters shimmering in the afternoon light. Picture Italy's Lake Como, only with volcanoes and quaint Mayan villages.

Lake Atitlán's origins can be traced back 85,000 years to a volcanic eruption that created the collapsed caldera the lake now fills, also spreading ash over a 1,000-mile radius. The lake was created when drainage to the Pacific Ocean was blocked after the emergence of the more recent Tolimán and Atitlán Volcanoes. It covers 125 square kilometers, being 30 kilometers long and 10 kilometers wide. Its maximum depth is more than 320 meters, though the 1976 earthquake that rocked much of Guatemala may have opened a drainage point somewhere, as the water level has been gradually declining ever since. A third volcano, San Pedro, which is just under 3,000 meters high, is somewhat lower than the other two but still offers a challenging climb on a path straight up its slopes.

The lake's main tourist town has always been Panajachel, once a requisite stop along the "Gringo Trail," as it was known in the 1960s, the path of American and European backpackers making their way down to South America. There are incredible views across the lake from "Pana," as it's often referred to by locals, though in recent years several of the outlying villages have started receiving their own fair share of visitors. Many foreigners like the more peaceful atmosphere of the other villages surrounding the lake. As one expatriate living in San Pedro put it, "Twenty minutes in Panajachel is enough for me." Still, Pana is worth at least a night's stay for the excellent shopping and decent restaurants.

ORIENTATION

Pana's main street is Calle Principal. Most buses coming in to town stop at the intersection of Calle Principal and Calle Santander, which leads directly to the lakeshore. Santander is lined with a plethora of banks, shops, restaurants, hotels, and other tourist services. You'll find that many of these don't use street addresses. The town hall, church, market, and a few other restaurants and hotels are found a half kilometer northeast along Calle Principal from the Calle Santander junction. East of Calle Santander and running parallel is Calle Rancho Grande, which also has some accommodations. Running roughly between the two along the lakeshore is Calle del Lago.

SIGHTS
Museo Lacustre Atitlán

Atitlán's Lake Museum (inside Hotel Posada de Don Rodrigo, Calle Santander, 8 A.M.–6 P.M. Sun.–Fri., 8 A.M.–7 P.M. Sat., $5 admission for nonguests) has well-displayed exhibits on the geological history of Lake Atitlán and its creation, along with subaquatic Mayan archaeology, including ceremonial urns and incense burners, mostly from Late Preclassic and Classic times.

Museo Raúl Vásquez

This funky museum (at the northeast end of

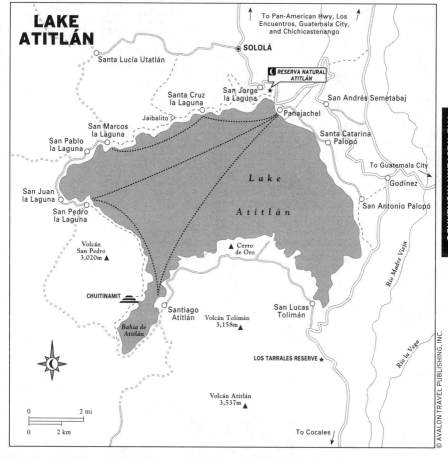

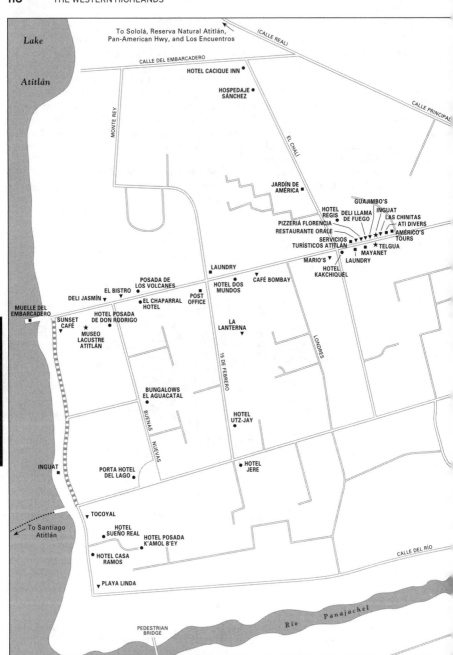

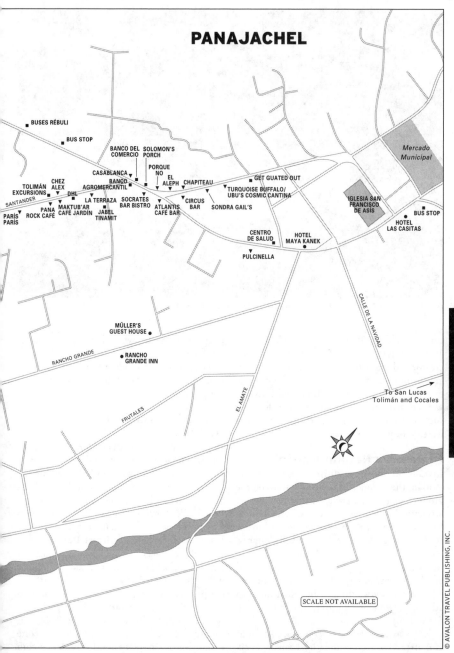

PANAJACHEL

BUSES RÉBULI

BUS STOP

BANCO DEL   SOLOMON'S
COMERCIO   PORCH

PORQUE
NO   EL
CASABLANCA   ALEPH   CHAPITEAU
BANCO   GET GUATED OUT
CHEZ   AGROMERCANTIL   TURQUOISE BUFFALO/
TOLIMÁN   ALEX   UBU'S COSMIC CANTINA
EXCURSIONS   DHL   LA TERRAZA
SANTANDER   SOCRATES   CIRCUS
PANA   MAKTUB'AR   BAR BISTRO BAR   SONDRA GAIL'S
PARÍS   ROCK CAFÉ CAFÉ JARDÍN JABEL   ATLANTIS
PARÍS   TINAMIT   CAFÉ BAR

Mercado
Municipal

IGLESIA SAN
FRANCISCO
DE ASÍS   BUS STOP

HOTEL
LAS CASITAS

CENTRO   HOTEL
DE SALUD   MAYA KANEK

PULCINELLA

CALLE DE LA NAVIDAD

MÜLLER'S
GUEST HOUSE

RANCHO GRANDE   RANCHO
GRANDE INN

To San Lucas
Tolimán and Cocales

FRUTALES

EL AMATE

SCALE NOT AVAILABLE

Atitlán, Tolimán, and San Pedro Volcanoes loom over Lake Atitlán.

© AL ARGUETA

town at 5a Calle Peatonal, east of Calle Real, 10 A.M.–6 P.M. daily, $1.50) is named after its creator and multifunctions as his home/studio and sculpture museum. Among the eclectic mix are statues of Jesus Christ and Shiva as well as characters from Guatemalan folklore such as El Sombrerón. There are whimsical watercolor paintings inside.

◖ Reserva Natural Atitlán

Just outside of town 200 meters past Hotel Atitlán, this wonderful nature preserve on the grounds of a former coffee farm offers myriad attractions including a visitors center, a zip line between trees in the forest canopy, a butterfly farm, a lakeside beach, and well-designed nature trails with hanging bridges leading to waterfalls, where you can spot monkeys and coatis (pizotes) along the way. The park (tel. 7762-2565, www.atitlan.com/resnat.htm, $5 adults, $2 students/children) is open 8 A.M.–5 P.M. daily.

Recently added to the reserve are spacious and attractive accommodations for up to six people with decks overlooking the surrounding forests. Rates are $55 s/d during the week and $65 s/d on weekends. You are also welcome to camp here for $14. Tent rentals cost $4.50 per person.

ENTERTAINMENT
Nightlife

Pana is a popular weekend playground for folks from Guatemala City and things are usually hopping on Friday and Saturday nights. There's a smattering of bars and dance places along Calle de los Arboles, which breaks off from Calle Principal just past its junction with Calle Santander. It's hard to beat the lively bohemian atmosphere at **Circus Bar** (Avenida Los Arboles, tel. 7762-2056, www.panajachel .com/circusbar, noon–midnight daily), popular with locals and foreigners alike. There are circus posters adorning the walls, a wide selection of drinks, and tasty food. Its pizzas are highly recommended. There's live music 8–11 P.M. nightly. Across the street and under the same ownership is **Chapiteau,** a lively dance club

© AL ARGUETA

visitors center at the Reserva Natural Atitlán

open until 1 A.M. **El Aleph** and **Porque No** are also along this corridor and worth checking out for live music. A more laid-back setup with a big-screen TV showing sports can be found at **Ubu's Cosmic Cantina,** farther up Calle de los Arboles.

As you head back toward Calle Santander, on Calle Principal is **Socrates,** a dance club frequented by a younger crowd for its Latin pop and merengue beats. On Calle Santander, **Pana Rock Café** (tel. 7762-2194, www.pana rockcafe.com, 8 A.M.–1 A.M. daily) serves Tex-Mex food, including delicious burritos, has live music daily, and a lively happy hour. There's also wireless Internet. **Maktub'ar Café Jardín** (Calle Santander, tel. 7762-2151, 10 A.M.–1 A.M. Tues.–Fri., 8 A.M.– 1 A.M. Sat./Sun.) is set in a pleasant open-air courtyard with bamboo trees. There's live music starting at 8:30 P.M. Wednesday–Sunday and a lively happy hour 7–9 P.M. nightly. It also serves delicious fruit smoothies and sandwiches. On the lakeshore at the end of Calle Santander is **Sunset Café** (tel. 7762-0003, 11 A.M.–midnight daily), with live music every night. It makes a great place to enjoy a cocktail while watching a gorgeous Lake Atitlán sunset. Decent tacos, nachos, quesadillas, burritos, and fajitas are served.

Cinemas

With a balcony overlooking Calle Principal, **Solomon's Porch** (tel. 7723-0751, noon–10 P.M. Tues.–Sat., 3–10 P.M. Sun.) shows digitally projected movies on its giant screen with surround sound. It also has an extensive DVD collection of movie titles available for rent. Complementing the audiovisual facilities is a full coffee bar. The **Carrot Chic** and **Turquoise Buffalo** cinemas, on Calle de los Arboles, also show movies.

SHOPPING

Pana is one of Guatemala's best places to shop for handicrafts with several stores along Calle Santander. Stalls also line the street jam-packed with goods from wall to wall. Street sellers expect you to bargain. Start at about half the asking price and work your way up from there. There are some nice, though somewhat pricier, shops in the small Centro Comercial Siquín on Calle Santander across the street from El Bistro.

RECREATION
The lake and mountainous surroundings afford a variety of recreational opportunities. Panajachel has a fairly clean public beach suitable for **swimming.** It was scheduled for remodeling by tourism authorities. A somewhat sophisticated water-treatment plant has been installed in Panajachel, as elsewhere around the lake. Some of the beaches in neighboring towns make much better places for swimming, however. Keep in mind the waters of this highland mountain lake tend to be a bit chilly. They also tend to get a bit rough in the afternoon because of the presence of a wind phenomenon known as the **Xocomil.** If you stop to look closely, you'll see it blowing across the lake, turning the glassy-smooth surface choppy in a matter of minutes. There are kayaks available for rent here.

Cycling
Hotel Utz-Jay (2-50 Calle 15 de Febrero, tel. 7762-0217, www.hotelutzjay.com) rents mountain bikes and also organizes mountain-biking trips on trails around the lake. Antigua-based **Old Town Outfitters** (5a Avenida Sur #12, Antigua, tel. 5399-0440, www.bike guatemala.com) runs a highly stimulating two-day Pedal and Paddle tour, dropping you 2,000 vertical feet along 20–25 miles of single track followed by sea kayaking across the lake for about four miles. You can add a third day of rock climbing and rappelling or climb San Pedro Volcano. The two-day trip costs $175 or $250 for three days.

Hiking
Tolimán Excursions (Calle Santander 1-77, tel. 7762-2455 or 7762-0334) offers guided hikes up San Pedro Volcano across the lake, leaving early in the morning (6 A.M.) and re-

turning late afternoon around 6 P.M. The trip costs $39 per person including food, transport, guide, and park entrance fee. The possibilities for hikes to surrounding towns and villages are virtually limitless, though you should never hike alone and always inquire about the security situation with the local tourist office before heading out.

Scuba Diving
Although based in the nearby town of Santa Cruz, **ATI Divers** has an office in Panajachel on Calle Santander in Plaza los Patios (tel. 7762-2621, ati_divers@yahoo.com). You can do a fun dive for $25 or take the PADI open water course for $205. A high-altitude diving certification course is $75. You'll have to spend at least one night at lake altitude before your first dive to avoid decompression sickness. The high-altitude lake offers a unique diving experience, including the chance to see underwater volcanic rock formations and a fault line where you can see and feel hot volcanic mud.

Paragliding
If you're the type who likes to fly by the seat of your pants, contact Canadian **Roger Lapointe** (tel. 5595-7732, paragliding@panajachel.com) for exhilarating tandem paragliding from the lake's steep mountainsides, costing $60.

Fishing
The waters of Lake Atitlán have been stocked with largemouth bass since 1958 thanks to the efforts of tourism promoters at now-absconded Pan American Airways. These same largemouth bass were also largely responsible for the extinction of the rare Atitlán pied-billed grebe, which disappeared in the late 1980s as their young increasingly fell prey to the large fish. In any case, you can try your hand at catching one of these elusive creatures. Most of the fish caught are in the five-pound range, though there are supposedly 20-pound fish here. The lake's 1,550-meter (5,100-foot) maximum depth further complicates matters, as the bigger fish tend to hang out at greater depths except during the annual spring spawn. Your

best chance of landing "the big one" is between March and May, before and after the spawn. If you're interested in learning more about Lake Atitlán largemouth bass fishing, email bass@panajachel.com.

ACCOMMODATIONS
Under $10

Mario's Rooms (Calle Santander, tel. 7762-2370, $9–11 d) is a long-running favorite with basic, clean rooms with shared bath. Rooms with private bathroom (really just a built-in cubicle) are just slightly more. **Hospedaje Sánchez** (Calle El Chalí, one block from Calle Santander, tel. 7762-2244, $5 p/p) is basic but clean and quiet. Try for an upstairs room with lake breezes from the back window. There's a nice view from the rooftop. Another well-run family-owned budget choice is **Villa Lupita** (Callejón Don Tino, tel. 7762-1201, $5 p/p), right in the town center. Its 18 rooms have good beds, rugs, reading lamps, clean shared hot-water bathrooms, and nice views from the property's terrace. Free coffee and drinking water are available. **Hospedaje El Amanecer** (Calle Ramos, tel. 7762-0636, $8–16 d) is a new hotel with two shared-bath rooms and four pricier rooms with private hot-water bathroom and TV. All the rooms are spotless.

$10-25

Near the lakeshore on Calle Ramos, **Hotel Casa Ramos** (tel. 7762-0413, $20 d) has 18 sparkling clean rooms with warm Guatemalan wool blankets set in a small, plant-filled courtyard. Along the same street, **❰ Hotel Sueño Real** (tel. 7762-0608, $24–33 d) is an excellent value featuring comfortable rooms beautifully decorated with Guatemalan accents, private hot-water bathroom, fan, and TV. There's a lovely second-floor terrace and Internet access on the first floor. The nicest room is on the second floor, just off the patio. The place and its guests are lovingly and well cared for by Pedro and Catarina Ramos, a charming Mayan couple. Well-situated on a quiet side street near the lake and Calle Santander, **Hotel Utz-Jay** (2-50 Calle 15 de Febrero, tel. 7762-0217, www.hotelutzjay.com, $25 d) has comfortable rooms housed in garden cottages decorated with traditional Guatemalan fabrics and equipped with fan and private hot-water bathroom. There are good breakfasts (not included) and the friendly, knowledgeable owners speak English, French, and Spanish. You can also enjoy a traditional Mayan sauna, or *chuj,* here. Internet access is available and you can rent mountain bikes for getting around or go mountain biking along the lake on an organized trip. **Hotel Jere** (Calle Rancho Grande, tel. 7762-2781, $12–15 d) has nine cheerfully decorated rooms with woven blankets and private hot-water bathroom, with or without TV. You can book shuttle buses from here. If you want to be closer to the action along Calle Santander, there's **El Chaparral Hotel** (Final Calle Santander, one block from the lake, tel. 7762-0540, $24 d), in a new multistory neocolonial structure. The comfortable rooms with private bathroom are well furnished with basic wooden furniture and cable TV.

$25-50

If you don't mind being a little far from the lakeshore, a good choice in the main town is **Hotel Las Casitas** (Calle Prinicpal, near the market, tel. 7762-1224, www.hotellascasitas .net, $36 d including breakfast and taxes) with attractive rooms featuring traditional furnishings and vaulted wooden ceilings along with private hot-water bathroom. **Posada de los Volcanes** (Calle Santander 5-51, tel. 7762-0244 or 7762-1096, www.posadadelos volcanes.com, $35–43 d) is an excellent value hotel in a neocolonial three-story building with spotless rooms, including tile floors, cable TV, patio furniture for relaxing on the balcony in front of your room, and private hot-water bathroom. Rooms on the top two floors are more expensive. The owners, Julio and Jeannette, are friendly and knowledgeable. They can arrange pickup from Guatemala City upon your arrival and bring you to Panajachel for $25 per person. The same service costs $12 from Antigua. **Hotel Playa Linda** (Calle del Lago, tel. 7762-0096) is just off the public beach and has spacious though somewhat spartanly decorated rooms for $40 d or $55 with lake views. **Müller's Guest House** (Calle Rancho Grande, tel. 7762-2442) has three comfortable rooms with hot-water private bathroom and attractive wooden floors and ceilings set around a pleasant garden. Rates include breakfast. **Hotel Posada K'amol B'ey** (Calle Ramos, tel. 7762-0219, hotelkamolbey@yahoo.com) is a large property with two different sections and prices ranging from $30–40 a double. The clean rooms have TV and private bathroom. There's a spacious apartment sleeping five people with living room, kitchen, dining room, cable TV, and private bathroom fronting attractive gardens for $78.

$50-100

⟨ **Rancho Grande Inn** (Calle Rancho Grande, tel. 7762-2255, www.ranchogrande-inn.com, $55–77 d) dates to the 1940s and has 12 attractive rooms, suites, and cabins housed in faux-thatched-roof villas fronting a well-manicured lawn and tropical gardens. There's a nice kidney-shaped swimming pool with a partial wooden deck. Rates include a deliciously filling breakfast featuring pancakes, eggs, beans, and good, strong coffee to put some pep in your morning step. **Hotel Cacique Inn** (Calle El Chalí 3-82, tel. 7762-2053, $60 d) fills up with vacationing Guatemalans during holidays and weekends. It has 34 rooms built around a garden swimming pool with Guatemalan blankets, weavings, and a fireplace. **Hotel Regis** (Calle Santander 3-47, tel. 7762-1152, $62 d) is set away from the street and has 25 comfortable rooms housed in a neocolonial building. The main attraction here is a hot spring set in the garden out back. **Hotel Dos Mundos** (Calle Santander, tel. 7762-2078, www.hotel dosmundos.com, $60 d) has comfortable rooms with tile floors and Guatemalan bedspreads set away from the street near a garden swimming pool. There's a recommended Italian restaurant on the premises as well as a street-side café/bar on Calle Santander. Also on Calle Santander, in a modern multistory building, **Hotel Kakchiquel** (tel. 7762-0634,

www.hotelkakchiquel.com, $50 d and up) has spacious modern rooms with a separate living room area, a heated pool and whirlpool tub, and Internet access.

$100-200

Outside of town on a lovely and quiet lakeside plot, **⟨** **Hotel Atitlán** (tel. 7762-1441, www .hotelatitlan.com, $120–190 d) does a wonderful job of combining old-school charm with modern amenities in its well-furnished, tastefully decorated rooms featuring tile floors, antiques, and colorful textiles. All rooms have balconies with gorgeous lake views. There are extensive tropical gardens, an attractive swimming pool, and boat docks. The hotel's restaurant is a favorite with well-to-do Guatemalans. **⟨** **Hotel Posada de Don Rodrigo** (at the lakeside end of Calle Santander, tel. 7762-2326, www.posadadedonrodrigo.com, $100–110 d) has rooms in two separate areas, one of which is more modern and is worth the extra splurge for the splendid lake views. The rooms are comfortable and well furnished. The restaurant/bar serves excellent Guatemalan and international dishes in a pleasant dining room with views to the lake and the swimming pool below.

The resort-style **Porta Hotel del Lago** (www .portahotels.com, $220 d all-inclusive) is an all-inclusive affair housed in a modern five-story building overlooking the public beach. The recently renovated rooms have all the usual amenities and the remodeled pool area has a pleasant deck for lounging and enjoying your favorite cocktail. Outside of town just past the Hotel Atitlán, **San Buenaventura de Atitlán** (tel. 7762-2559, hotelsanbuenaventura.net, $105–262) has quaint rooms housed in buildings with domed ceilings and adobe and brick walls with an upstairs kitchen or slightly less attractive one- or two-story concrete structures, also with kitchen. You can rent out the whole structure for 4–6 people or a single/double room. There's plenty to keep you busy, including a beautiful private beach with kayaks available for rent, a pool and hot tub, and bike rentals. It's a good choice for families. Farther along the same road, **La Riviera de Atitlán** ($122–342 d) is a resort-style hotel in a large high-rise building reminiscent of Acapulco. The 16-story building had stood abandoned for decades under a previous owner, but it has now been finished. There are 82 comfortable rooms with all the usual amenities among standard rooms and suites. The lobby has a nice terrace bar with a happy hour 7–8 P.M.

FOOD
Cafés and Cheap Eats

In a pleasant garden patio decorated with Asian-style spherical paper lamps, **([Deli Jasmín** (Calle Santander, close to the lakeshore, tel. 7762-2585, 7 A.M.–6 P.M. Wed.–Mon.) serves delicious all-day breakfasts, including bagels and English muffins in addition to healthy fares such as tofu and vegetarian dishes. It sells teas, jams, whole wheat bread, and cookies for you to take away. Farther up Calle Santander and under the same management is **Deli Llama de Fuego** (tel. 7762-2586, 7 A.M.–10 P.M. Thurs.–Tues.), with much the same menu and surroundings. Another good place for breakfast is **El Patio** (tel. 7762-2041, 8 A.M.–9:30 P.M. daily), set in a sunny patio right next to Calle Santander closer to the lakeshore end of the street.

París París (Calle Santander across from San Rafael Shopping Center, tel. 7762-0963, lunch and dinner daily) is a garden café with a pleasant atmosphere where you can enjoy steak, chicken, seafood, and foot-long French baguettes for around $7. There's also a bar with a happy hour 5–7 P.M. **El Bistro** (Calle Santander, closer to the lakeshore, tel. 7762-0508, 7 A.M.–10 P.M. daily, $6–10) is a pleasant, shady, café/bar serving steak, pasta dishes, and sandwiches in the $5–10 range. Try the fettuccine with spicy tomato sauce. A perennial favorite, **Café Bombay** (Calle Santander, 100 meters from the lake, tel. 7762-0611, 11 A.M.–9 P.M. Wed.–Mon., $2–7) is an inexpensive vegetarian restaurant serving a varied menu that includes tasty falafel, pita sandwiches, lasagna, burritos, curries, pad thai, and miso soup. For tasty,

reasonably priced Mexican dishes and steak there's **Restaurante Orale** (Calle Santander, tel. 7762-0017, lunch and dinner daily), popular for its friendly service and lively streetside atmosphere.

Though already mentioned as a recommended bar, **([Maktub'ar Café Jardín** (Calle Santander, tel. 7762-2151, 10 A.M.– 1 A.M. Tues.–Fri., 8 A.M.– 1 A.M. Sat./Sun.) bears special mention under this category for its atmosphere, excellent fruit smoothies, and delicious breakfasts. There are a number of eateries on Calle del Lago with similar seafood/meat menus and outrageous decor verging on the likes of a taxidermy museum, none of which I can bring myself to recommend. An exception is the well-staffed **Restaurante El Tocoyal** (8:30 A.M.–5 P.M. Sun.–Fri., 8:30 A.M.–8 P.M. Sat., $3–13), which also has some vegetarian fare.

American

Sondra Gail's (Calle de los Arboles, tel. 7762-2063, noon–10 P.M. Wed.–Mon.) is owned by an East Texas native who grew up on a farm. There are fresh salads and a varied Tex-Mex menu that includes nachos, tacos, burritos, corn bread, barbecued chicken, and tilapia stuffed with white wine sauce or fried.

International

([Circus Bar (Avenida Los Arboles, tel. 7762-2056, www.panajachel.com/circusbar, noon–midnight daily) has the best pizza in town as well as excellent pasta and seafood. There's a relaxed vibe and colorful decor that conveys the feeling of being under the big top. A reasonable alternative for pizza, particularly for carryout or delivery, is **Pizzeria Florencia** (Calle Santander, across from Telgua, tel. 7762-1055), where you'll also find Argentinean empanadas and cheeseburgers.

For authentic Italian food, head to **Restaurante La Lanterna** (inside Hotel Dos Mundos, Calle Santander, tel. 7762-2078), where there's excellent homemade pasta and a nice assortment of Italian wines. The large dining room has one of Panajachel's most pleasant atmospheres and the service is impeccable. For scrumptious Pan-Asian cuisine, check out **Las Chinitas** (Calle Santander, tel. 7762-2612, 8 A.M.–10 P.M. daily) where you can savor Malaysian curries and Thai dishes, among other dishes, at moderate prices. It's a busy spot for dinner. Also on Calle Santander, closer to Calle Principal, is **La Terraza** (Edificio Rincón Sai, tel. 7762-0041, lunch and dinner daily), with a second-floor balcony overlooking the street below and serving steaks, lake fish, and European fare including Spanish tapas.

Halfway down Calle Santander, **Guajimbo's** (tel. 7762-0063, 7 A.M.–10 P.M. Fri.–Wed.) serves South American–style *parrilladas* (barbecued meats) including steaks, chicken, and sausage. There are also vegetarian dishes and good breakfasts. On Calle Principal, close to the intersection with Calle de los Arboles, **Atlantis Café Bar** serves a good mix of international dishes, including decent burgers, pasta, pizza, and sandwiches along with a wide range of cocktails from its elegant wooden bar. The decor is eclectic and there are also some good desserts.

Fine Dining

Duck, escargot, lamb chops, and Wiener schnitzel are on the menu at **Chez Alex** (halfway down Calle Santander, tel. 7762-0172, noon–3 P.M. and 6–10 P.M. daily) in a tasteful atmosphere with prices in the $10–12 range. Repeatedly on the list of Central America's best restaurants, **(| Casablanca** (at the intersection of Calle Principal and Calle Santander, tel. 7762-1015, noon–11 P.M. daily, $8–22) serves delicious pastas, chicken, meat, and seafood dishes accompanied by Chilean wines in a sophisticated atmosphere. The dining room at the **(| Hotel Atitlán** (tel. 7762-1441, www.hotelatitlan.com, 6:30 A.M.–10 P.M. daily $7–20) makes a fine place for a splurge, surrounded by pleasant gardens overlooking the lake and fabulous views. Patrons enjoy free use of the swimming pool and there are Guatemalan and international dishes on the menu. There is a Sunday breakfast buffet for around $10.

INFORMATION & SERVICES

Tourist Offices

The INGUAT information office (Calle Santander, tel. 7762-1392, 9 A.M.–5 P.M. daily) has basic hotel information, transportation schedules, and friendly staff who can answer your questions.

Communications

The main post office is on the corner of Calle Santander and Calle 15 de Febrero. DHL is in Edificio Rincón Sai at the northern end of Calle Santander. For larger parcels, head to Get Guated Out (Calle de los Arboles, Comercial El Pueblito, tel. 7762-0595), an English-speaking company handling international air freight.

Telgua (7 A.M.–midnight) is halfway down Calle Santander near the junction with Calle 15 de Febrero. There is no shortage of Internet cafés along Calle Santander for making international phone calls. Typical rates are $0.30 per minute to North America and $0.50 per minute to Europe.

There are Internet setups all over town. Among the best are MayaNet (halfway down Calle Santander, tel. 7762-2092) and Café Pulcinella (Calle Principal 0-72). Both are open 9 A.M.–9 P.M. and charge about $1.50 per hour.

Money

About halfway down Calle Santander, Banco Industrial has a Visa ATM and can cash U.S. dollars and travelers checks. There's a Master-Card/Cirrus ATM outside Banco Agromercantil on the corner of Calle Principal and Calle Santander. Banco del Comercio is on the ground floor of the same building as Solomon's Porch, on Calle Principal. It has an ATM that accepts both Visa and MasterCard.

Laundry

Lavandería Viajero (Calle Santander, Edificio Rincón Sai, 8 A.M.–7 P.M.) charges about $0.50 a pound. Lavandería Automático (Calle de los Arboles 0-15, 7:30 A.M.–6:30 P.M. Mon.–Sat.) charges $4 for a full load.

Medical Services

Panamedic Centro Clínico Familiar (Calle Principal 0-72, tel. 7762-2174) has round-the-clock emergency medical attention. Doctors Francisco and Zulma Ordoñez both speak English. For an ambulance, dial 7762-4121.

Emergency

In case of an emergency, contact Policía de Turismo (Tourist Police, Calle Principal, in the town hall, tel. 7762-1120).

Travel Agencies

There are a number of travel agencies along Calle Santander that can book airline tickets, shuttles, and onward transport to other parts of Guatemala. Among the recommended agencies are Atitrans (Edificio Rincón Sai, tel. 7762-0146 or 7762-0152, www.atitrans.com), Unión Travel (corner of Calle Santander and Calle El Chali, tel. 7762-2426, www.igoguate.com), Servicios Turísticos Atitlán (Calle Santander, tel. 7762-2075), and Tolimán Excursions (Calle Santander 1-77, tel. 7762-2455 or 7762-0334).

Language Schools

There are a few language schools in Panajachel, including **Jardín de América** (Calle 14 de Febrero, 3a Avenida Peatonal 4-44, tel. 7762-2637, www.jardindeamerica.com) and **Jabel Tinamit** (Calle Santander, tel. 7762-0238, www.jabeltinamit.com). Rates are about $150 per week for four hours of one-on-one instruction Monday–Friday, including homestay with a local family at either school.

GETTING THERE AND AROUND
Bus

Buses stop at the junction of Calle Santander and Calle Principal both leaving and arriving Panajachel. Direct buses leave for Antigua ($5, 2.5 hours) at 10:45 A.M. daily except Sunday. You can also take a Guatemala City–bound bus ($2.50, 3.5 hours) and change at Chimaltenango. There are 10 daily buses to Guatemala City between 5 A.M. and 2:30 P.M. Six buses leave daily to Quetzaltenango ($2, 2.5 hours) and there are eight daily buses to Chichicastenango ($1.50, 1.5 hours).

Shuttle Bus

The convenience and, most of all, safety of shuttle buses cannot be overstated. In the course of researching and writing this book, it seems not a week went by without newspapers reporting some sort of incident aboard Guatemala's second-class buses, including armed robberies turning into shoot-outs between passengers and would-be thieves or tragic accidents on twisting mountain roads. That said, there are frequent shuttle buses to Antigua, Chichicastenango (on market days), Quetzaltenango, and Guatemala City. Recommended shuttle agencies include **Atitrans** (Edificio Rincón Sai, tel. 7762-0146 or 7762-0152, www.atitrans.com) and **Servicios Turísticos Atitlán** (Calle Santander near Calle 15 de Febrero, tel. 7762-2075).

Boat

There are two different boat docks for getting around to the surrounding villages. The first of these is at the end of Calle del Embarcadero and is for boats to Santa Cruz (15 minutes), Jaibalito (25 minutes), Tzununá (30 minutes), and San Marcos (40 minutes). Some boats continue to San Pedro, across the lake (just under an hour, with stops), but there are also direct boats from Pana taking about 20 minutes. All of the above routes are serviced by small, fast *lanchas*. The second boat dock is at the end of Calle Rancho Grande and is for ferry (one hour) and *lancha* service (25 minutes) to Santiago Atitlán. Expect to pay anywhere between $1.50 and $3 for the ride. Locals pay less than visitors. Ask around for the time of the last boat back to Pana from the outlying villages. Some may be as early as 4:30 P.M. **Lake tours** ($10, full day) from Pana visiting San Pedro and Santiago also leave from the second pier and can be booked at any travel agency.

Bike Rentals

Hotel Utz-Jay (2-50 Calle 15 de Febrero, tel. 7762-0217, www.hotelutzjay.com) rents mountain bikes.

Lake Atitlán Villages

Lake Atitlán is surrounded by a number of smaller villages, each with its own distinct feel. Across the lake, only San Pedro La Laguna rivals Panajachel in popularity. The other villages remain fairly quiet, though tourism has become a significant presence in almost all of them. Heading east of Panajachel along the lakeshore, the first village of note is Santa Catarina Palopó.

SANTA CATARINA PALOPÓ

Five kilometers east of Panajachel is the quaint lakeside village of Santa Catarina Palopó, a collection of adobe houses with tin and thatched roofs built into the surrounding hillsides. The streets near the church and the road leading to the lakeside are excellent places to pick up some of the colorful textiles and handicrafts produced here. Many of the villagers still sport the traditional attire.

As elsewhere on Lake Atitlán, many well-to-do Guatemalans (and increasingly, foreigners) have bought property and built houses on the slopes just outside of town.

Accommodations and Food

Santa Catarina is the site of a few moderate to high-end hotels offering some of the lake's best accommodations. Just off the street leading to the lakeshore, the 36-room **Villa Santa Catarina** (tel. 7762-1291 or 7762-2827, www .villasdeguatemala.com, $68–104 d) has attractive rooms and junior suites with gorgeous lake views, tile floors, TV, hot-water private bathroom, telephone, some with ceiling fan. There are lovely antique furnishings throughout the property, a swimming pool and the excellent **Restaurante Las Playas** (7 A.M.–10 P.M. daily), serving Guatemalan and international dishes in an attractive dining room overlooking the swimming pool. Meal prices are in the $5–10 range. Along the road leading out of town toward neighboring San Antonio Palopó, **Tzam Poc Resort** (tel. 7762-2680, www.atitlan .com/tzampoc.htm, $85–170 d) has accommodations varying from standard and deluxe rooms

in Mediterranean-style, thatched-roof villas to an entire, fully furnished villa for $400–1,000 per night. The beautiful rooms are nicely decorated. The resort's centerpiece is an exquisite infinity-edge swimming pool overlooking the lake below. There are tropical gardens throughout. Other amenities include a tropical lounge, sauna, and solarium. Credit cards are accepted but incur a 7 percent service charge.

The most splendid of the lake's accommodations is ◖ **Casa Palopó** (Km. 6.8 Carretera a San Antonio Palopó, tel. 7762-2270, www .casapalopo.com, $125–276 d), with rooms housed in a beautiful colonial-style villa featuring floor-to-ceiling windows with magnificent lake views. The rooms and common areas are loaded with antiques, brightly painted walls, exquisite furnishings, and wonderful extras such as Italian cotton sheets and Aveda bathroom products. There's also a charming swimming pool with peaceful angel carvings looking on from an adjacent wall. Farther up the hill is the even more alluring **Villa Palopó,** decorated with a tasteful mix of African tribal relics and Indonesian hardwood furnishings. There are hardwood floors and ceilings and fantastic lake views from each of the two suites ($199.50–235 d). You can rent the whole villa for $683–998, depending on the season. The villa has its own lap pool, also overlooking the lake, and butler service.

Casa Palopó's restaurant is a bit on the expensive side ($15–25 for a typical meal), but the food is certainly some of the best you'll find on the shores of Lake Atitlán, with spectacular lake views from an airy terrace. If you're not staying there, it makes a great place to stop for a drink and watch the sunset or enjoy a romantic candlelit dinner.

SANTA CRUZ LA LAGUNA

West of Panajachel and accessible only by boat is the quiet village of Santa Cruz La Laguna, more commonly referred to simply as "Santa Cruz." There are a number of good accommodations here with a range of prices for every budget. It's understandably huge with the backpacker crowd.

Recreation

Housed inside the Iguana Perdida lodge, **ATI Divers** (ati_divers@yahoo.com) is a PADI-certified **scuba diving** operation offering Altitude Specialty certifications for $75, fun dives for $25, or PADI open water certifications for $205. Due to altitudinal pressure changes and the lake's location at just over 1,500 meters above sea level, you'll have to spend at least one night at lake altitude before your first dive to avoid decompression sickness. The lake offers a unique diving experience, including the chance to see underwater volcanic rock formations and a fault line where you can see and feel hot volcanic mud.

Other activities include **hikes** up the hill to the village proper (20 minutes) to see the town church in addition to hiking along a trail skirting the lakeshore to the neighboring village of Jaibalito (45 minutes) or San Marcos (three hours). Check on the safety situation with local lodges if you plan on doing the latter, as there have been incidents of robbery in the past. Check with the Iguana Perdida for the location of a **cliff jumping** spot along the shoreline near town if that suits your fancy.

Accommodations and Food

El Arca de Noé (tel. 5515-3712, www.atitlan .com/arca.htm, $12–35 d) is run by friendly Wolfgang and Anna Kallab, an Austian and German couple who arrived early on the scene in the 1980's. The delightful lodge has 10 rooms, half of them with private bathroom. Three of the rooms are lovely stone-and-wood cottages. All of the rooms are rustic but nicely decorated with Guatemalan fabrics. Delicious breakfasts and lunches are served à la carte. Anna loves to cook and treats her guests to a delicious six-course dinner consisting of Guatemalan and European specialties for around $10, served family-style. The lodge is solar-powered.

Just next door is one of Guatemala's quint-essential backpacker hideaways, **La Iguana Perdida** (tel. 5706-4117 or 7762-2621, www

.laiguanaperdida.com, from $4 p/p in dorms to $50 d), which has recently added some very attractive private rooms for those of us who have gotten just a bit older. There are three dormitories with a total of 22 beds and rooms with or without private bathroom. Electricity was finally installed after years of making do without it and I am happy to report there are now hot showers and Internet access available. Still, the electricity can be spotty and kerosene lamps are on hand to provide agreeable ambient lighting after dark. Breakfast and lunch are served 8 A.M.–3 P.M. and consist of delicious sandwiches, salads, crepes, and other yummy dishes prepared by a staff of indigenous women. Dinner is a family-style affair and is a three-course spread, including soup and homemade bread, a main course, and dessert. Vegetarian options are always available. The dinner atmosphere is lively and it makes a great place to meet fellow travelers. The crowd is decidedly young. In addition to scuba diving (see *Recreation*), there are Spanish lessons available for $150 per week with dorm accommodations (upgrades available), a tandem kayak and snorkeling equipment for rent, waterskiing, and tons of board games. On Saturdays, there's a fun dress-up dinner party where you can eat chicken or veggie burgers and jam to a guitar and drums. If you get bored here, you should probably check your pulse.

Farther along the lakeshore heading back east toward Panajachel is **La Casa Rosa** (tel. 5416-1251 or 5803-2531, www.la-casa-rosa .com, $22–35), with modern, clean, and comfortable rooms with shared or private hot-water bath in addition to two suites housed in bungalows. An apartment with kitchen is available for rent for $120/week or $350/month. There are homemade jams and bread in addition to Guatemalan, international, and vegetarian dishes served in the main floor dining room. Spanish classes are also available for $150 per week.

You might stumble upon a few private villas as you make your way farther east a few hundred meters to the fantastic, American-owned ◖ **Villa Sumaya** (tel. 5510-0229, www.villa sumaya.com, $45–85 d). There are 14 beautiful rooms, all named after jungle animals. Some are housed in a thatched-roof complex; others are farther up the hill in separate cabins. All of the spacious rooms have private hot-water bathroom, warm Guatemalan wool blankets, and patios with furniture and lovely hammocks. The rooms up the hill have mosquito netting and larger bathrooms with tubs, one of which is impressively built into the side of the mountain with lava rock adorning the semioutdoor shower. There's an impressive, hardwood-floor and thatched-roof yoga center, which is often booked months in advance by groups from the United States. Other amenities include a massage parlor, library, and two hot tubs. The restaurant here is correspondingly excellent, consisting of vegetarian selections as well as fish, meat, and chicken dishes prepared by two talented chefs. Delicious baked goods are also produced daily. Breakfast and lunch are à la carte. Dinner is a set menu served family-style. The outdoor café is housed in a pretty wooden patio overlooking the lake.

From the main dock in Santa Cruz, heading west to Jaibalito, it's 400 meters to the private dock of **Islaverde Hotel** (tel. 5760-2648 or 5964-7419, www.islaverdeatitlan.com, $30–40 d), with eight comfortable wooden A-frame cabins with wonderful lake views and shared or private bath. There are pretty gardens with plumeria flowers, a beautiful wooden deck lounge with books and games to keep you entertained in addition to a sauna, hot tub, and meditation/massage platform. All of the food served at the lodge is fresh and well prepared. The property is the culmination of 12 years of travel by a young Spanish and British couple, who have put many of the ideas found along the road into this splendid place they see less like a hotel and more like a garden of delights.

Getting There

Santa Cruz is reached exclusively by boat. Boats leave from the dock at the end of Calle del Embarcadero in Panajachel. For the intrepid, there's a foot path from the departmental capital of Sololá.

JAIBALITO

West along the shoreline from Santa Cruz is the village of Jaibalito, which is even smaller than Santa Cruz and is also accessible only by boat or foot trail. A number of lodges have sprouted here in recent years, taking advantage of the remote location to offer a comfortable stay in a quiet environment.

Accommodations and Food

Wildly popular, **La Casa del Mundo** (tel. 5218-5332 or 5204-5558, www.lacasadelmundo.com, $27–60 d) is a charming inn built into the side of a rocky cliff. There are rooms with shared or private bathroom, all housed in wonderful stone cottages with outrageous lake views and decorated with tasteful Guatemalan accents. There's excellent swimming in a rocky cove where the water is an exquisite shade of emerald. There are kayaks for rent ($4–7) and mountain biking can be arranged via Antigua-based Old Town Outfitters with at least two days' notice. The trail to Santa Cruz or San Marcos passes right outside the lodge's back door. Meals are served at set times in a small dining room on the ground floor of the main house. Dinner is served family-style and costs $10. The service here is excellent and the Guatemalan-American owners are very friendly. In the village proper and away from the lake, **Vulcano Lodge** (tel. 5410-2237, www.vulcanolodge.com, $28–58 d) is a Norwegian-owned lodge with five rooms, all with private bath and smartly decorated. The largest is a family-size villa, which sleeps five and has a living room, kitchen, and a nice big terrace with lake views. The restaurant serves tasty meals for breakfast and lunch, with dinner ($12 for four courses) served family-style. Many of the fresh ingredients, including bananas, avocadoes, and limes, come right from the on-site garden plot.

West along the shore, the next village is Tzununá, home to the agreeable **Lomas de Tzununá** (tel. 5201-8272 or 7820-4060, www.lomasdetzununa.com, $70 d including breakfast and tax), high atop a steep hill. You can call the lodge for a pickup from the hotel's pier or make the 100-meter trek up the slope. Run by a Belgian-Uruguayan couple who discovered Guatemala while working with the United Nations, the lodge features 10 lovely stone-and-wood bungalows with tile floors and lake views greatly enhanced by their sheer height above the water. Amenities include Internet, a lap pool, library, board games, and a crafts shop. Meals are served al fresco on a wooden patio with superb lake views. Just the views of the volcanoes reflected in the placid swimming pool high above the lake are worth the price of admission.

SAN MARCOS LA LAGUNA

San Marcos is a unique lake town in that it harbors a strangely esoteric vibe, aided by its prominence as Guatemala's New Age center. It's about a three-hour walk from Santa Cruz and two hours from San Pedro. Most visitors arrive at a boat dock beside Posada Schumann, though boats stop first at the main dock a few hundred meters east. A road runs beside the lodge into town, which together with a parallel street 100 meters west, form the main pedestrian arteries into town.

Sights and Recreation

Among the spiritually inclined attractions is **Las Pirámides** (tel. 5205-7302 and tel. 5205-7151, www.laspiramidesdelka.com), offering a variety of New Age alternative psychology courses, including a one-month "moon course" beginning with the full moon and culminating in a full week of fasting and silence. With completion of the moon course there's further study, including a three-month sun course, featuring elements of Kabbalah, tarot reading, and lucid dreaming. Nonstudents can join in on hatha yoga sessions at 7 A.M., classes on various spiritual topics at 10 A.M., and meditation techniques at 5 P.M. A session costs $4. To get here, follow the path up the hill past Posada Schumann and then turn left along the signed pathway. It's about 200 meters on your left.

Back toward Posada Schumann is **San Marcos Holistic Centre** (www.sanmholistic centre.com, 10 A.M.–5 P.M. Mon.–Sat.), offering a wide assortment of massages and ho-

listic therapies. There are training courses in Reiki, shiatsu, massage, reflexology, and Bach flower remedies. English, Spanish, German, and French are spoken. A typical treatment costs somewhere around $15.

You can **hike** from San Marcos east to Jaibalito, but check on the safety situation with local sources, as hiker robberies in this neck of the woods have been frequent in the past. It's not recommended. Going west to Santa Clara La Laguna might be a safer bet. If you do go, leave the valuables behind. The waters here are excellent for **swimming**, as the lake is nice and clean in this area. The best swimming hole is a rocky beach on the western end of town near the Moonfish café.

Accommodations

♦ Posada Schumann (tel. 5202-2216, www .posadaschumann.com, $15–50 d) is the first place you'll come across if, like most people, you arrive into town at its dock. Most of the comfortable, well-furnished, and tastefully decorated rooms are housed in quaint stone-and-mortar cottages. An excellent value, room number 12 is a deluxe second-floor wooden bungalow ($25–36 d, depending on season) with its own deck. Numbers 8 and 10 have awesome volcano and lake views. The restaurant overlooking the well-tended gardens serves sandwiches, smoothies, and Guatemalan fare for breakfast and lunch, though the service can be slow. West along the lakeshore past Las Pirámides, **Aaculaax** (tel. 5577-5072, www.aaculax.com, $7–50 d) is a work of art constructed out of recycled building materials, including glass, carved pumice stones, and colorful papier-mâché. Each of the six rooms is unique, though all have private bathrooms with composting toilets and lovely terraces. The rooms are literally built around the rocks of the surrounding hillsides, which are prominently displayed in the architecture of some of the rooms. The glasswork in evidence throughout the property is simply delicious, as is the Middle Eastern food served in the hotel's restaurant/bar. There's also fresh bread baked daily in the lodge's own bakery. A gorgeous second-floor terrace caps off the hotel's atmosphere quite nicely.

The footpath continues farther west to **Hotel Jinava** (tel. 5299-3311 or 5406-5986, www.hoteljinava.com, $20–37 d), right on the lake with its own beach on the edge of town. The five rooms are housed in Spanish-style whitewashed, tiled-roof villas with private terraces and have private or shared bathroom and attractive decor with tile floors and colorful textiles. The restaurant serves decent meals, including Thai, Indian, Mexican, Greek, Italian, and Guatemalan dishes. There's also a full bar. Up the path into the main part of town is **Hotel Restaurante El Quetzal** (tel. 5350-0610, $7 d) with clean shared-bath rooms, good-value food, hot water, and a nice patio for lounging. Closer to the center of town at the top of the path leading up the hill from the dock at Posada Schumann is **Hotel y Restaurante Paco Real** (tel. 5918-7215, elpacoreal@hotmail.com, $16–24 d), with simple but comfortable shared-bath rooms in wooden thatched-roof cabanas with Guatemalan furnishings and woven reed floor mats in a peaceful garden setting. There's a small restaurant on the premises serving simple Mexican dishes. A few feet west of Paco Real, **Hotel La Paz** (tel. 5702-9168, $7 p/p) has two doubles and dorms housed in stone, bamboo, and mud structures with thatched roof amid spacious gardens. There's a *chuj,* or traditional Mayan sauna, and a vegetarian restaurant with a pleasant library above it.

Food

Enjoying a wonderful lakeside location west of Posada Schumann is French-owned **Tul y Sol** (tel. 5293-7997 or 5854-5365, all meals daily) offering decent sandwiches, grilled fish, and pasta. **Moonfish** is a pleasant lakeside café next to Aaculaax recommended for tasty hummus and falafel. (**Il Giardino** (tel. 7804-0186, up the path toward town from Posada Schumann, lunch and dinner daily), serves delicious burritos, pizza, and spaghetti dishes in a tranquil garden setting. It also has Internet access. Next to Las Pirámides, **Il Forno** is another recommended Italian restaurant. Heading into the

town center from the lakeshore and crossing the main road through town, you'll find its newest eatery, **Blind Lemon's** (tel. 5540-0399, 9 A.M.–10 P.M. Mon.–Sat.), inspired by blues musician Lemon Jefferson and housed in a pleasant colonial-style courtyard recommended for breakfast, light meals, and tasty sandwiches.

SAN JUAN LA LAGUNA

Serene San Juan La Laguna is a relative latecomer to the tourism scene and makes a good stop if you'd like to see a fairly sizable lakeside village that remains largely untouched by international tourism. It's accessible by boat or via a road that branches off from the Pan-American Highway, subsequently twisting and turning down the surrounding mountainside. If you'd like to stay here, **Uxlabil Ecohotel** (tel. 5990-6016 or 2366-9555, www.uxlabil.com, $48–72 d) has comfortable, tastefully rustic rooms housed in a large building overlooking the lake. There's a large dock for swimming among plentiful grass reeds dotting the lakeshore here as well as a sauna, whirlpool tub, kayaks for rent, and horseback riding available on request.

SAN PEDRO LA LAGUNA

On the lake's southwest corner and accessible by frequent boats or road, San Pedro is second in popularity only to Panajachel and has a hip international atmosphere. The town is a bit on the scruffy side and seems to have sprouted from the lakeshore almost overnight. If you're not already feeling decidedly immersed in the Third World, you soon will as you walk along some of the side trails leading into the heart of the village from the main road through town.

The town flanks the northern slopes of San Pedro Volcano, a popular climb for which the town is ideally suited as a base. It has increasingly become home to a number of language schools, some of dubious quality, collectively offering some of Guatemala's least expensive tuition rates. While it was originally a backpacker Shangri-La, there have been recent additions to the hotel infrastructure, making for suitable accommodations to house the non-backpacker crowd.

The bulk of the tourist hotels and services are between two docks, on the southeast and northwest sides of town, and in the areas adjacent to them. The first one serves boats to/from Panajachel and the rest of the lake towns; the other is for boats to Santiago Atitlán. They are about one kilometer apart. The area between them is known as El Otro Lado (The Other Side). Street numbers and names are not generally in use here. From the Santiago dock, turn right to get to El Otro Lado and continue to the Panajachel boat

dock. From the latter dock, turn left to get to the other side of town.

San Pedro Volcano

The volcano became a national park in 2006, so it is hoped that, as was the case with Pacaya Volcano, its newly protected status will result in greater police presence and an end to the robberies that frequently happen near the summit. For now, check with locals before heading up the volcano. Under no circumstances should

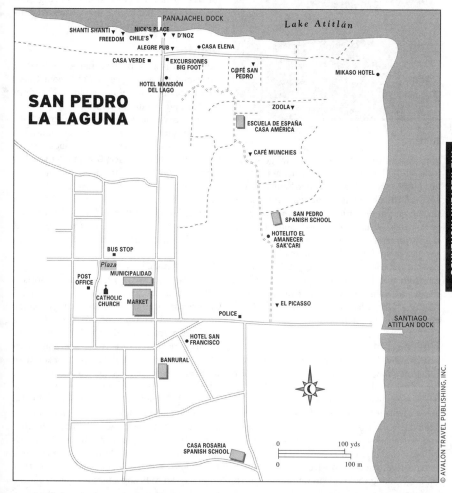

THE WESTERN HIGHLANDS

© AVALON TRAVEL PUBLISHING, INC.

© AL ARGUETA

San Pedro Volcano seen from Santiago Atitlán

you attempt this hike alone. Always go with a local guide. There is a visitors center at the trailhead, which is just off the road to Santiago. The hike is fairly strenuous, as the trail runs straight up the mountain with very little in the way of switchbacks. It takes about 4–5 hours to reach the summit, which is still very much covered in thick cloud forest. There's a small gap in the trees at the top from which there are views of Santiago and the lake. Start your hike early in the day to avoid the midday heat and the clouds that typically gather at the summit of the lake's volcanoes in the afternoon.

Recreation

Other activities include horseback riding and hikes up a mountain known locally as "Indian Nose," as its shape resembles the profile of a Mayan nose like those depicted on stelae. Horses are available in the vicinity of Nick's Place. You should have no trouble finding someone to offer you horseback-riding trips. Walking to other villages from here makes sense from a logistical perspective, though too-frequent reports of robberies along the trails prevent me from rec-

ommending this as a viable activity. If you do decide to go on any of the hikes, bring only that which you wouldn't mind losing.

Guide Companies

Excursiones Big Foot (tel. 7721-8202), on the main drag as you come up the hill from the Panajachel dock and turn left, is San Pedro's most reliable outfitter and has been in operation since 1995. It offers trips to San Pedro Volcano with knowledgeable guides and security for $14, including park admission. Big Foot can also guide you to Indian Nose with a four-person minimum for $5 p/p.

Nightlife

San Pedro is a lively town harboring several bars where the party goes on until about 1 A.M. East from the dock about a block, **Freedom** is a bar and restaurant housed in a thatched-roof terrace overlooking the lake. It serves light meals and it's particularly lively at night. Try the margaritas. To the left of the dock and directly above Nick's Place, **D'Noz** is a lively bar with good food, including baguettes and croissants, where movies are shown nightly. In the center of town between the two docks, check out the **Buddha Bar,** housed in a three-level building with a cool Asian atmosphere and pool tables and dartboards on the first floor.

Accommodations

A popular favorite with travelers of all sorts is **Casa Elena** (tel. 5310-9243, $5–11 d), found by turning left at the first corner as you come up the street from the main boat dock. Housed in a large peach-and-white building, it has clean rooms with shared or private bathroom. Two larger rooms on the top floor facing the lake have nice patios with hammocks, tables, and chairs. The hippest place in town is the friendly, Israeli-owned **Zoola** (tel. 5534-3111, agmon2003@yahoo.com, $3 in dorms to $10 d), found along a trail east of the dock where boats come in from Panajachel. It has eight rooms, half of them with private bathroom, and dorm beds. There are a movie lounge, book exchange, purified water from its own well, and a massage room, but the crowning achievement is the beautiful thatched-roof hammock lounge with comfortable pillows on wooden floors. Around the corner is **Jarachik** (jarachik@hotmail.com, $4–7 d), a smart budget choice with clean and pleasant rooms with shared bath. There's also an apartment available for $10 d. A very popular budget hotel is **Hotel San Francisco** (tel. 7721-8016, $4–8 d) with clean rooms, some with private bath and most with lake view balconies. All have kitchens. **Hotelito El Amanecer Sak'cari** (tel. 5964-3838 or 7721-8096, www.hotelsakcari .com, $16 d) feels a bit like a motel, though the rooms on the second floor have nice lake views with hammocks out front. All have private bathroom. It's near the San Pedro Spanish School.

Hotel Mansión del Lago (tel. 7811-8172, $10 d) has clean, spartan rooms with private bathrooms, some with lake views. It's just up the street from the Panajachel boat dock. The nicest place in town is the brand-new ◖ **Mikaso Hotel** (tel. 5973-3129, www.mikaso hotel.com, $8 p/p in dorm or $25–45 d) with 11 rooms and a dormitory housed in an attractive Spanish neocolonial-style building fronting the lakeshore. Rooms have tile bathrooms, ceiling fans, tile floors, and tasteful decor. The rooftop restaurant here is also quite smart, serving Mediterranean Spanish food, including delicious *bocadillos* (sandwiches), and open 7 A.M.–10 P.M. Movies are shown three times a week on Wednesday, Friday, and Sunday nights. Just outside of town near the Panajachel boat dock, **Casa San Pedro** (tel. 5963-6910 or 7736-8101, www.hotelcasasanpedrosa .com, $40 d) is a comfortable lodge housed in a large stone villa with Spanish tile roof. Rooms are well furnished and have lake views. The hotel has its own boat dock with kayaks and bikes for rent. There are a sauna, whirlpool tub, video library, and pool table.

Food

On your right as you arrive from the Panajachel dock is **Chile's** (tel. 5594-6194, 7 A.M.–1 A.M. daily, $4–7), a restaurant and bar serving good pastas, sandwiches, desserts, and French-pressed coffee on a nice patio overlooking the lake. There's live music on Saturday nights and salsa lessons Tuesday and Friday nights. As you head up the street into town, the **Alegre Pub and Restaurant** (tel. 7721-8100, 5 P.M.–1 A.M. Mon., 9 A.M.–1 A.M. Tues.–Sat., 9 A.M.–11 P.M. Sun.) serves authentic pub grub, including Indian curry, Cajun fare, chili, baked potatoes, and fish 'n chips. There's a nice rooftop garden. To the left of the boat docks, the first place you'll come across is **Nick's Place,** (7721-8065, 7 A.M.–midnight daily, $4-8) serving excellent-value Guatemalan and international dishes inside or outside on the terrace. Also in this area, **Shanti Shanti** (8a Calle 3-93 Zona 2, tel. 5561-8423, 7 A.M.–11 P.M. daily) has fantastic lake views, chill music, Israeli food, sandwiches, smoothies, and delicious breads and cakes.

There are a number of good eateries in the part of town inland between the two docks known as El Otro Lado. Among them is **Zoola** (all meals daily), housed in its namesake lodge and serving freshly prepared food, including vegetarian fare, though chicken salads and meat lasagnas are also on the menu. You can dine under a pleasant open-air, thatched-roof structure. Nearby is ◖ **The Buddha** (tel. 5967-6810, noon–1 A.M. daily), housed in a three-level building with a pool table and darts on the first floor, a dining area and chill-out lounge on the second floor, and a rooftop terrace bar. The restaurant serves authentic Asian and Guatemalan fusion cuisine with a variety of rice, noodle, and curry dishes, sushi, soups, wraps, and tasty desserts at reasonable prices. There's a hookah water pipe smoking lounge. Also in this neck of the woods is **Jarachik** (jarachik@ hotmail.com, all meals daily), a smart Dutch-owned place where you can dine on curry, kebabs, burritos, and delicious stuffed chicken in a garden patio just off the street. Across the way is **Café Munchie's,** (5875-2461) adorned with cosmically inspired murals and serving Indian and Thai curries in addition to Middle Eastern fare, including moussaka.

For delicious breakfasts, head to **Luna Azul** (9 A.M.–3 P.M. daily) on a quiet lakeside plot east of the main dock where you can feast on homemade biscuits, three-egg omelets, and

THE WESTERN HIGHLANDS

hash browns for under $5. San Pedro's newest restaurant, **El Picasso** (to the right of the Santiago Atitlán dock, tel. 5847-4850, www.el picasso.com, all meals daily, $2–5) is owned by a German-Nicaraguan partnership and opened to rave reviews in October 2006. There's a pleasant open-air dining room with a vaulted wooden ceiling that's artfully decorated. Breakfast, including crepes, omelets, and pancakes is served all day until 9 P.M. For lunch and dinner there are Spanish omelets, lemon-marinated chicken, and pastas with a good selection of Chilean wines to accompany them.

Information and Services

There's a Banrural in the heart of town, reached by heading straight up the street from the Panajachel dock for about a kilometer. You'll pass the town market on your right, two blocks before the bank, which will be on your left. From the Santiago dock, head up the street and turn left at the market. For Internet and phone calls, D'Noz is just off the Panajachel dock, or you can head up the street one block to Casa Verde, your all-in-one stop for Internet, laundry, international calls, and travel agency. On the main drag, turning left at Casa Verde as you come up from the Panajachel dock, you'll find C@fé San Pedro (tel. 7720-4056, 7:30 A.M.–9 P.M.), serving breakfast and snacks in addition to offering Internet access. All of the above charge about $1.50 for an hour online.

Language Schools

Recommended language schools include the following: **Casa Rosario** (up the street from Santiago dock, then left, tel. 7613-6401, www .casarosario.com) and **Corazón Maya** (first left up the street from Santiago dock, tel. 7721-8160, corazonmaya.com). Also along this street is **Sol de Oro Spanish School** (tel. 7614-9618). In the El Otro Lado sector between the two docks are **Escuela de Español Casa America** (tel. 7767-7718, casaamerica@ hotmail.com), **Mayab' Spanish School** (tel. 7815-7722, www.mayabspanishschool.com), and **San Pedro Spanish School** (tel. 7721-8176, www.sanpedrospanishschool.org).

Getting There

There are hourly boats to Santiago (45 minutes, $1.50) from the dock at the northwest part of town 6 A.M.–2 P.M. *Lanchas* leave throughout the day for the lakeshore villages of San Marcos, Jaibalito, Santa Cruz, and Panajachel. The last one usually leaves around 4 P.M. All leave from the dock on the southeast side of town. There are buses to Quetzaltenango ($3, 2.5 hours) leaving from in front of the church in the main part of town at 4:45, 6, and 7 A.M. There may be others leaving later. There are also four daily buses to Guatemala City from here and frequent pickups to the villages as far as the road goes to San Marcos and in the other direction to Santiago.

SANTIAGO ATITLÁN

Santiago Atitlán is a more traditional sort of place and has a very different feel from San Pedro. It's spectacularly set in an inlet with gorgeous views of San Pedro Volcano just across this small body of water. Atitlán and Tolimán Volcanoes rise behind it. It is the main enclave of Guatemala's Tz'utujil-speaking Mayans, whose wonderful painting and handicrafts can be seen along the main street coming up from the boat dock, which is lined with art galleries and craft shops. On display is a very distinct form of painting depicting various elements of indigenous life such as agricultural harvests and festivals.

Santiago suffered greatly during the civil war, as the area was a hotbed of activity for ORPA guerrillas, who established themselves in this strategic area between the highlands and the Pacific Coast. The Guatemalan military established a base here and began systematically searching for guerrilla sympathizers, killing hundreds. As the civil war waned, the military's presence became increasingly unnecessary, as was the case throughout much of Guatemala, and villagers became increasingly resentful of its presence. The massacre of 12 unarmed villagers (including three children) in 1990 unleashed a flood of local and international pressure to close the military garrison. A petition presented to the Guatemalan government asking for the base's closure was soon granted.

More recently, Santiago made world headlines in October 2005 after a number of devastating mudslides in the wake of Hurricane Stan left close to 1,000 victims. The neighboring village of Panabaj was completely wiped out by the mudslides, and the scars can still be seen on the mountainside. Many international organizations are still working in the area and Santiago has become a popular center for volunteer activities in the tragedy's aftermath.

Another Santiago curiosity is the presence of a highland Mayan deity known as Maximón, housed in the home of a different member of the local *cofradía,* or Catholic brotherhood, every year. The effigy is a wooden figure clad in colorful silk scarves and a Stetson hat, smoking a big cigar and receiving offerings of moonshine, cigarettes, and rum. Local village children will offer you their services to go see the idol, which you can photograph for a fee. It is not surprisingly a sore point between the Catholic syncretists and the increasingly prominent Evangelical Christian churches, which have won over many of Santiago's residents.

You will probably be approached by innocent-looking children as soon as you arrive from the boat dock offering any of a number of services, including a guided trip to see Maximón or assistance in finding accommodations. You have the right to politely refuse, but you might be surprised at the colorful language they can resort to (in English) if they're unhappy with you for not hiring their services or if you fail to provide an adequate tip. Internationally recognized finger gestures are also not out of the realm of possibility.

Sights

Santiago's colorful **market** really gets going on Fridays and Sundays, when the town's streets are filled with vendors and Mayan women dressed in the town's spectacular purple costume. The men wear interesting striped shorts, though it seems in fewer numbers every year. Standing prominently in the central plaza, the **Iglesia Parroquial Santiago Apóstol** was built between 1572 and 1581. Inside lining the walls are wooden saints dressed in clothes made by local women and renewed yearly. At the far end of the church are three sacred colonial altarpieces refurbished with more Mayan-inspired motifs by two local brothers between 1976 and 1981. The altarpieces represent the three volcanoes in the vicinity of Santiago, which are believed to protect the village. Local creation myths distinguish them as the first dry land to emerge from the early seas. The wooden pulpit has interesting carvings, including corn and animal figures. The town's newest attraction is the **Museo Cojoyla** (9 A.M.–4 P.M. Mon.–Fri, 9 A.M.–1 P.M. Sat., free), a block up the street

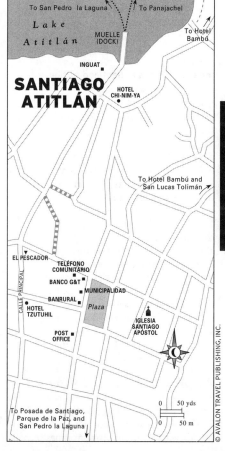

THE WESTERN HIGHLANDS

© AL ARGUETA

the church steps at Santiago Atitlán

from the main dock, on the left, with displays on Santiago's artful legacy of traditional backstrap weaving.

Recreation

Atitlán and Tolimán Volcanoes are tempting climbs from town but unfortunately have been the scene of robberies, a problem that unfortunately seems endemic in the Lake Atitlán area. Check with the local lodges on the security situation and for reliable guides who might be able to take you there, should you wish to venture on the path less traveled.

Jim and Nancy Matison (tel. 7811-5516 or 5742-8975, wildwest@amigo.net.gt) offer recommended horseback riding and wilderness hikes throughout the area, though they no longer offer trips to San Pedro Volcano because of the state of the trail in the aftermath of Hurricane Stan.

Accommodations and Food

Santiago's nicest accommodations are at the charming ◖ **Posada de Santiago** (tel. 7721-7366, www.posadadesantiago.com, $12 p/p to $95 d) with a variety of room types in comfortable stone cabins featuring tasteful Guatemalan decor. It has adjusted well to the recent influx of missionaries and volunteer groups, offering rooms for 4–5 people at budget prices. The lodge is run by Dave and Susie Glanville, a gracious American couple. Ironically, the hotel originally opened just weeks before the installation of the now-absconded local military garrison. It was closed for 10 years and did not reopen until June of 1991. If you're interested in the hotel's interesting history be sure to ask for Dave's "Smart Aleck Interview," which should answer most of your questions. The restaurant here is one of the lake's finest. Breakfast, lunch, and dinner are served at set times throughout the day. Dinner costs $8–21 and includes Cajun, Asian, and continental cuisine. All of the sauces, breads, pastries, and ice cream served here are homemade and the Glanvilles grow, process, and roast their own coffee. Activities include fishing or kayaking on the lake, Thai or deep tissue massages, lounging by the pool in a hammock overlooking the lake, and swimming. There is wireless Internet in the lodge.

Just outside of town, another nice place to stay is **Hotel and Restaurant Bambú** (tel. 7721-7333, www.ecobambu.com, $55–65 d) with two bungalows, eight rooms, and a villa housed in pretty thatched-roof stone cottages with fantastic lake and volcano views fronting beautifully landscaped grounds. The rooms are cheerful and bright with beautiful Guatemalan furnishings. There are a very nice swimming pool, a private dock, and kayaks available for rent at $5 an hour. The restaurant serves tasty international and Spanish cuisine. Be sure to take a taxi or *tuk-tuk* if you decide to go into town at night, as robberies have been reported on the isolated paths from the hotel into town after dark.

Right in the heart of town is **Turicentro Tiosh Abaj** (Cantón Tzanjuyú, tel. 7721-7165, www.turicentrotioshabaj.com, $55 d) built on sprawling grounds leading down to the dock with spacious, modern rooms housed in a large building. There's a large restaurant serving a variety of international dishes. Try to negotiate for a lower rate, as the hotel seems to be empty most of the time. A decent budget choice is

© AL ARGUETA

Santiago's market

Hotel Chi-Nim-Ya (turn left at the first intersection after coming up from the dock, tel. 7721-7131, $10–13 d) with 22 simple and clean concrete-floored rooms built around a central courtyard with shared or private bathroom. Another budget choice is **Hotel Tzutuhil** (four blocks up the hill from the dock, then left, tel. 7721-7174, $8–11 d) with basic, clean rooms housed in a five-story building.

For lake fish, snacks, sandwiches, and light fare, a good choice is **Restaurante El Pescador** (two blocks up the street from the dock, tel. 7721-7147, 7 A.M.–9 P.M. Mon.–Sat., 7 A.M.–4 P.M. Sun.).

Money
There's a Banrural right on the plaza where you can exchange dollars and travelers checks.

Getting There
Ferry service ($2.50) departs Santiago for Panajachel at 6, 7, and 11:45 A.M., 12:30, 1:30, 2, and 4:30 P.M. The ferry crossing takes about an hour and there is also faster *lancha* service. There are also frequent boats to San Pedro from here. There are seven daily buses leaving from the central plaza for Cocales and Guatemala City between 3 A.M. and 3 P.M. in addition to pickups for San Lucas Tolimán. Frequent pickups to San Pedro leave from Hotel Chi-Nim-Ya.

SAN LUCAS TOLIMÁN AND VICINITY
San Lucas is probably the least attractive of the lakeside villages, though the adjacent area is as gorgeous as the rest of the lake. It makes a good place to get away from it all. If you're looking for comfortable accommodations to host your escape, you might want to check out **Hotel Tolimán** (6a Avenida 1-26, tel. 7722-0033, www.atitlanhotel.com, $46–82 d) on a sprawling lakeside ranch run by a wonderful Guatemalan couple. The 22 comfortable rooms, including some splendid suites, all have private bathroom and a 17th-century hacienda ambience enhanced by numerous decorative touches that include delightful furniture and antiques. Rates include a delicious

WAKE UP AND SMELL THE COFFEE, AND THEN PICK SOME BEANS

Guatemala is known around the world for its excellent coffee. A recent trend in Guatemala's growing list of recreational alternatives is the opportunity to stay on a working coffee farm in comfortable accommodations. It provides a rare glimpse into the inner workings of one of the country's principal economic activities and an industry that largely shaped Guatemala into the nation it is today. Guatemala's coffee farms are largely centered in the Western Highlands, though coffee is also grown on the Pacific slopes, the Verapaces and the Eastern Highlands.

If you've always wanted to see the origins of the potent potable that provides the pep in your step, you'll want to check out one or more of the coffee farms covered throughout this book, including **Los Tarrales** and **El Retiro** (both near Lake Atitlán), **Finca El Patrocinio** and **Takalik Maya Lodge** (near Retalhuleu), **Finca Filadelfia** and **Casa K'ojom** (near Antigua), and **Finca El Cisne** (near Copán, Honduras).

Usual activities include touring the coffee plantation as well as observing the process from harvest to roasting. Some properties are on large private reserves and combine bird-watching, hiking, and other outdoor activities with the visit to the coffee farm.

For a fascinating read on the myriad ways in which coffee cultivation has affected Guatemala's history and societal relations, including events in the civil war as they took place on a plantation caught in the crossfire, check out Daniel Wilkinson's excellent book, *Silence on the Mountain*.

Guatemalan breakfast of eggs, beans, coffee, and fried plantains.

Just a few kilometers along Ruta Nacional 11, leading from San Lucas to the coastal town of Cocales, this is a gem of a place to stay. **(Los Tarrales** (Km. 164.2 RN-11, tel. 2478-4867 or 5208-0940, www.tarrales .com, from $6 camping to $30 per person in lodge) is a private reserve on the southern slopes of Atitlán Volcano named after the abundant bamboo trees that grow here. Altitudes range 700–3,000 meters (2,300–9,800 feet), providing for a wonderfully diverse array of ecosystems. Several locals are employed by the reserve, working on its coffee farm or in the ecotourism business and the lodge runs a school for local children. Activities include hiking and bird-watching with naturalist guides, climbing Atitlán Volcano, mountain biking, canoeing, horseback riding, and visits to the working coffee farm. Accommodations include camping, shared-bath rooms, beautiful rooms with private bathroom, or wonderful tree house cabins. Excellent, home-cooked meals are served ($6–8) for breakfast, lunch, and dinner including fresh salads, vegetarian and meat dishes, and bread from the on-site bakery. Buses heading to Cocales pass right by the entrance to the reserve, which is 15 minutes from San Lucas and about 45 minutes from Santiago.

Nearby, in the adjacent municipality of Pochuta, Chimaltenango, **El Retiro Finca and Lodge** (Finca El Retiro, Pochuta, tel. 2365-4468, www.elretirofinca.com, $35 d) is another wonderful place to stay with four comfortable rooms and a larger wooden cabin, all with private hot-water bathroom. The lodge is on the grounds of a working organic coffee and banana plantation and the surrounding cloud forests harbor trails leading to waterfalls and pristine mountain streams for you to explore. Horseback riding and mountain biking are also available. Meals are served in a charming wooden dining room and there's also a bar and swimming pool.

To get here, follow RN-11 south toward Cocales, turning left at the junction for the road heading east to Pochuta. It's about a 45-minute drive from San Lucas Tolimán.

Chichicastenango

At Chichi, tourism became voyeurism. There was always so much going on – the crowded, noisy market, the rituals on the steps of Santo Tomás, a ceremonial dance outside El Calvario chapel, the explosion of firecrackers in the morning, a procession – that it was easy to think it all a show put on for the tourists' benefit. But in Chichi it was not a show. The "spectacle" was part of daily life for the Indians, ritual that must be performed in spite of, not because of, the tourists. Wherever tourists went in Chichi they were treading on and through someone else's devotional rites. Two different worlds whirled past each other, momentarily inhabiting the same space but unable to comprehend each other. Bizarre scenes resulted from this encounter: a Quiché man walked on his knees over rough cobblestones, crying out his agony, while a tourist trailed behind him, filming the man's act of penance on a camcorder; a tourist group climbed the crowded steps of Santo Tomás, hoping to get a photo of the plaza from atop the church's platform, and in the confusion a heavy-set tourist kicked over an incense burner, apologized loudly in English to the woman kneeling there, then fumbled in her purse and waved a ten-quetzal note at the Indian woman; a cofrade, a member of a brotherhood devoted to the worship of a particular saint, was standing outside El Calvario, wearing the traditional outfit indicative of a special occasion and holding an ebony and silver staff, the symbol of his office, when a tourist approached and asked him how much he'd take for the staff: the tourist's money belt was already open when the cofrade without a word turned and disappeared into the sanctuary.

Stephen Connely Benz,
Guatemalan Journey

While you may or may not witness such blatant disregard for the local culture, Chichicastenango (Chichi, for short) will surely provide you with an opportunity to take in a unique highland market experience. There are certainly other, more authentic markets in highland Guatemala, at least one of which is larger, but Chichi's popular Sunday and Thursday market is unique in that it includes allowances for the very strong foreign presence here. It is the only highland market where you'll see large tour buses packed with camera-toting tourists negotiating the hairpin, dizzying mountain switchbacks along the road from Antigua and Guatemala City. The road to Chichi diverts from the Pan-American Highway at the Los Encuentros junction, along Km. 127.5.

The market, and Chichi's status as a bona fide tourist attraction, got their start in the 1930s when enterprising Alfred S. Clark opened the Mayan Inn and started busing folks in from the capital for a look at an authentic highland Mayan village. Chichicastenango, originally known as Chaviar, was an important Kaqchikel trading town long before the arrival of the Spanish. The Kaqchikel went to war with their K'iche' rivals based in K'umarcaaj (near present-day Santa Cruz del Quiché, 20 miles north) in the 15th century, moving their capital to the more easily defended site of Iximché. Spanish conquistador Pedro de Alvarado would play the K'iche'-Kaqchikel rivalry to his advantage, using the latter as allies in his final push against the K'iche', who comprised the only real opposition to Spanish conquest. Chichicastenango got its name, meaning "place of the nettles," from Alvarado's Nahuatl-speaking Mexican allies after the town's reestablishment here after the defeat of the K'iche' capital in 1524.

Today, Chichi is still very much a K'iche' town with strong adherence to the old ways. Its traditional fiesta, the **Fiesta de Santo Tomás,** takes place December 14–21. There are plenty of loud fireworks, traditional dances, moonshine, and the fascinating *palo volador* ritual

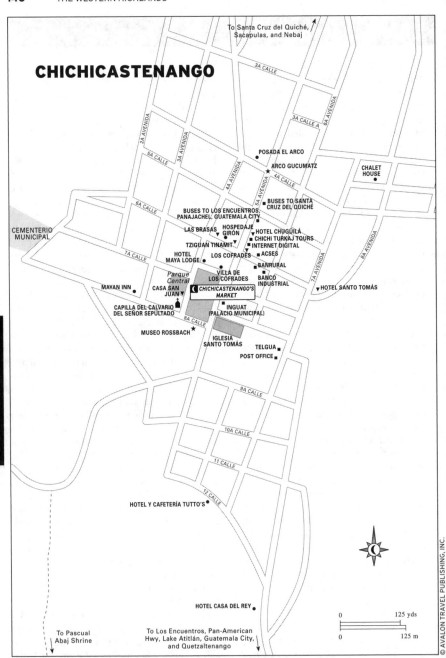

CHICHICASTENANGO

To Santa Cruz del Quiché,
Sacapulas, and Nebaj

3A CALLE

3A CALLE A

2A AVENIDA

3A AVENIDA

4A AVENIDA

5A AVENIDA

6A AVENIDA

8A AVENIDA

6A CALLE

8A CALLE

POSADA EL ARCO

ARCO GUCUMATZ

CHALET
HOUSE

BUSES TO SANTA
CRUZ DEL QUICHÉ

BUSES TO LOS ENCUENTROS,
PANAJACHEL, GUATEMALA CITY

LAS BRASAS

HOSPEDAJE
GIRÓN

HOTEL CHUGÜILÁ
CHICHI TURKAJ TOURS
INTERNET DIGITAL

CEMENTERIO
MUNICIPAL

7A CALLE

TZIGUAN TINAMIT

ACSES

HOTEL
MAYA LODGE

LOS COFRADES

BANRURAL

VILLA DE
LOS COFRADES

BANCO
INDUSTRIAL

Parque
Central

CHICHICASTENANGO'S
MARKET

HOTEL SANTO TOMÁS

MAYAN INN

CASA SAN
JUAN

CAPILLA DEL CALVARIO
DEL SEÑOR SEPULTADO

8A CALLE

INGUAT
(PALACIO MUNICIPAL)

MUSEO ROSSBACH

IGLESIA
SANTO TOMÁS

TELGUA

POST OFFICE

9A CALLE

10A CALLE

11 CALLE

12 CALLE

8A AVENIDA

7A AVENIDA

HOTEL Y CAFETERÍA TUTTO'S

HOTEL CASA DEL REY

To Pascual
Abaj Shrine

To Los Encuentros, Pan-American
Hwy, Lake Atitlán, Guatemala City,
and Quetzaltenango

0   125 yds
0   125 m

in which men spin from ropes attached to a 20-meter pole.

SIGHTS
Chichicastenango's Market

If you're a big fan of outdoor markets, you'll certainly enjoy this one. In addition to the crowds of vendors and potential buyers you'll find a dizzying array of good-quality weavings, pottery, fabrics, gourds, and masks, to name just a few. On the stairs of the adjacent church of Santo Tomás, you'll see Mayans waving incense burners, filling the air with the pungent smell of *corozo* palm and adding an additional aura of mystique to this chaotic market that is a feast for the senses. There are certainly more authentic indigenous highland markets, but what makes Chichi unique is its accommodation of visitors' needs and desires for traditional handicrafts into a twice-weekly event that would otherwise continue undeterred for the benefit of the locals it has always catered to.

Most of the better handicrafts are found in the central part of the plaza, but be prepared to rummage through piles of lesser-quality stuff, which is readily in abundance. In addition to the main part of the plaza, there are stalls peddling tourist-oriented trinkets along the streets to the north of it. The streets to the south and the *centro comercial* on the plaza's north side are home to the everyday items villagers come to market for, including fruits and vegetables, clothing, spices, household items, and baked goods. As in all of Guatemala's markets, haggling is in order. The best time to get a good deal on anything that might have caught your fancy is after 3 P.M., when the market starts to wind down. You can often score substantial price reductions simply by walking away and feigning disinterest. It's all a very complex game.

Iglesia Santo Tomás

The town's oft-photographed church dates to 1540 and is the site of syncretic Catholic-Mayan rituals both inside and out. On the steps, you'll find *chuchkajaues*—indigenous people at prayer, swinging incense-laden censers (usually just metal cans punctured with holes) and reciting incantations. Take care to enter the church through the side door to the right, as the main entrance is reserved for religious officials and *chuchkajaues*. Inside you'll find an astounding number of lit candles lining the church floor along with pine boughs and offerings of liquor bottles wrapped in corn husks, flowers, and maize kernels in remembrance of departed relatives, some of whom are buried beneath the church floor. Photography is strictly prohibited inside the church.

Found beside the church is a monastery, where the *Popol Vuh* Mayan book was found among church archives by Spanish priest Francisco Ximénez in the early 18th century.

On the west side of the plaza is **Capilla del Calvario,** another whitewashed church somewhat like a miniature version of Santo Tomás and with much the same feel. There is a glass-encased Christ statue inside, which is paraded through town during Holy Week processions.

Museo Rossbach

This small museum (5a Avenida 4-47 Zona 1, 8 A.M.–noon and 2–4 P.M. Tues., Wed., Fri., Sat., 8 A.M.–4 P.M. Thurs., 8 A.M.–2 P.M. Sun., $0.75) harbors a collection of jade objects, including necklaces and figurines in addition to historical objects such as ceremonial masks, obsidian spearheads, and incense burners. It's named after Hugo Rossbach, a German who served as the town's Catholic priest for many years until his death in 1944.

Pascual Abaj

On a hill just outside of town is this Mayan shrine dedicated to the earth god Huyup Tak'ah (Mountain Plain) where worshippers gather frequently to perform ceremonies. The idol is a blackened Pre-Columbian sculpture standing about a meter tall and lined with stones, candles, and sacrificial offerings of booze. It has been around for centuries. Ceremonies performed by a Mayan shaman usually involve much incense, liquor-drinking, chanting, and offerings of candles, flowers, and maybe even a sacrificial chicken. If you

THE *POPOL VUH*

Believed to have been written by an unknown Mayan scribe in the 1560s, the *Popol Vuh (Council Book)*, was found in the church archives in Chichicastenango early in the 18th century by parish priest Francisco Ximénez. Amazingly, it survived the burning and destruction most Mayan writings fell prey to at the hands of the Spanish and lives on as an important document recording K'iche' histories and legends. Ximénez painstakingly transcribed the document into Latin and then translated it into Spanish. It is now the only surviving copy of the Mayan text and resides in Chicago's Newberry Library.

The *Popol Vuh* contains the K'iche' peoples' creation myths as well as their history before the arrival of the Spanish. Although there are some striking similarities with Christian writings, including the Old Testament, scholars believe these are coincidences rather than evidence of overt Christian influence – this despite the fact that the text was written about 40 years after the conquest. It mentions Christianity only at its beginning and its end, framing the narration (as opposed to the events themselves) of the *Popol Vuh* as taking place within the context of the Christian era, for better or worse.

The book describes the moment of creation as having been spurred instantly by the words of the gods themselves describing the moments preceding creation with, "Whatever might be is simply not there: only murmurs, ripples, in the dark, in the night." It also describes how the gods attempt to create humans to give meaning to creation and have beings that can speak, praise, and keep the passing of time, first forming them out of earth and mud, which soon dissolves. The second version of humankind, the text relates, was created out of wood, but these beings were dull and could not speak in words.

The gods decide to annihilate them by sending a flood and other devastations, including the revolt of the beings' own possessions, which turn and destroy their owners. The book explains that the remains of this previous version of mankind are the monkeys and humanlike creatures we see today. The gods finally create mankind using corn, which is not surprising given its importance as a Mayan subsistence crop to this day.

Other similarities shared with the Bible's Book of Genesis include the explanation of astronomical features, including the Big Dipper, the assertion that woman was created after man, and the conclusion that man at one point had come too close to being like the divine, resulting in a confusion of languages to disperse humankind into different linguistic groups. The *Popol Vuh* is not without its own tales of heroics, the most prominent being the myth of the Hero Twins, who journey into the underworld (known as Xibalba), ruled by seven lords, and endure great hardships.

In addition to the interesting metaphysical speculation provided throughout the text, another fascinating feature of the *Popol Vuh* is that it may have served as a book of divination, with some hidden meaning if read in a certain way that allowed the reader to predict future events – hence its being referred to as the "Council Book." In a more literal sense, it also tells quite matter-of-factly of the impending difficulties that will arrive with the coming of "enemies, hidden behind mountains and hills," a possible allusion to the civil war and its atrocities. Despite the hardships, the book concludes that, "Our people will never be scattered. Our destiny will triumph over the ill-fated days which are coming at a time unknown. We will always be secure in the land we have occupied."

happen to stumble upon one of these ceremonies during your visit, be sure to keep your distance and refrain from taking photographs. You can always ask for permission, but don't be surprised if the answer is a firm "no." To get to the shrine, walk down 5a Avenida from the main plaza turning right onto 9a Calle. At the bottom of the hill found along this street, head left onto a path through the signposted *morerías* (mask workshops) found there. The path continues uphill from there to the hilltop site. It's best to go in a group and earlier in the day, as robberies of tourists along this route are not infrequent.

ACCOMMODATIONS
Under $25
Hospedaje Girón (6a Calle 4-52 Zona 1, tel. 7756-1156) has basic, passable rooms for $7 d with shared bath or $13 d with private bath. The rooms downstairs can feel a bit damp. Friendly **Hotel y Cafetería Tutto's** (12 Calle 6-29 Zona 1, tel. 7756-1540, $18 d) has spotless rooms with private bathroom and cable TV in addition to a downstairs café with beautiful mountain views. The excellent-value (**Posada El Arco** (4a Calle 4-36 Zona 1, tel. 7756-1255, $25 d) has friendly English-speaking owners and seven spacious rooms with attractive decor, fireplace, and private hot-water bathroom; some have balcony views. There are splendid mountain views from the garden. **Chalet House** (3a Calle "C" 7-44, tel. 7756-1360, $20 d) is on a quiet street and has pleasant rooms with private bathroom, warm wool blankets, and eye-catching textiles.

$25-50
The **Maya Lodge** (6a Calle 'A' 4-08, tel. 7756-1167, $26 d) is rather "plain Jane," though it's right on the plaza. **Hotel Chugüila** (5a Avenida 5-24 Zona 1, tel. 7756-1134) has 15 rooms, all except one with chimney, and it is expanding. Rooms are set around a courtyard and have TV and nice patios.

$50-100
At the entrance to town on the left-hand side is **Hotel Casa del Rey** (Km. 144, entrance to Chichicastenango, www.hotelcasadelrey.com, tel. 7756-1053, $45–60 d) in simple motel style with a restaurant/bar and swimming pool. You'll see large tour buses parked here, as it's a favorite for folks on overnight package tours, giving the property some semblance of atmosphere. In the heart of town, (**Hotel Santo Tomás** (7a Avenida 5-32 Zona 1, tel. 7756-1051, $100 d) is a lovely colonial-style hotel with rooms centered around a graceful courtyard fountain complete with squawking macaws. There are a pool, hot tub, gift shop, a lively bar, and restaurant. A longtime favorite with travelers to Chichicastenango is the (**Mayan Inn** (8a Calle "A" 1-91 Zona 1, tel. 7756-1176, www.mayaninn.com.gt, $100 d), established by Alfred S. Clark, founder of Clark Tours, in 1932. The 30 rooms are beautifully decorated with antique furnishings and have fireplaces. Most of the bathrooms have tubs. Each room has its own attendant dressed in traditional village costume, as there are no locks on the doors from the outside. Rest assured, you can lock yourself in at night. There's a good restaurant here. The market is literally at your doorstep.

FOOD
Tziguan Tinamit (5a Avenida 5-67 Zona 1, tel. 7756-1144, 7 A.M.–10 P.M. daily) serves a variety of light meals and has particularly tasty baked goods. **Los Cofrades** (corner of 6a Calle and 5a Avenida, tel. 7756-1647, 9 A.M.–10 P.M. Wed.–Sun.) has pleasant outdoor seating on a balcony overlooking the busy street below. There are delicious, large set-menu lunches and dinners for $5–7. **Restaurante Las Brasas** (6a Calle 4-52, Comercial Girón, tel. 7756-2226, 7 A.M.–10 P.M. daily, $4–9) is a good-value steak house also serving decent breakfasts. Beside El Calvario church, (**Casa San Juan** (4a Avenida, on the main plaza) serves creatively prepared sandwiches and Guatemalan food in a stylish environment that includes wrought-iron chairs and artwork. **La Villa de los Cofrades** (6a Calle "A" and main plaza, tel. 7756-1643)

is a café/restaurant serving good breakfasts, grilled meats, coffee, and even crepes. The town's most stylish eateries are at the restaurants housed inside the **Mayan Inn** and **Hotel Santo Tomás,** where a three-course meal runs somewhere in the vicinity of $10–15. The waiters at both places wear elaborate traditional costumes, though the food at Hotel Santo Tomás outshines that of its closest competitor, albeit slightly.

INFORMATION AND SERVICES
Communications
For post, you'll find Correos on 7a Avenida between 8a and 9a Calles. ACSES (6a Calle 4-52 Zona 1) has Internet for $1.75 an hour, as does Internet Digital (5a Avenida 5-60 Zona 1).

Money
Conveniently, Chichi's banks stay open on Sundays. Among the options are Banco Industrial (6a Calle 6-05 Zona 1, 10 A.M.–2 P.M. Mon., 10 A.M.–5 P.M. Wed. and Fri., 9 A.M.–5 P.M. Thurs. and Sun., 10 A.M.–3 P.M. Sat.) with a VISA/Plus ATM. Banrural (6a Calle east of 5a Avenida, 9 A.M.–5 P.M. Sun.–Fri., 9 A.M.–1 P.M. Sat.) has a MasterCard/Cirrus ATM.

GETTING THERE
Bus
Chichi lacks a bus terminal, though bus arrivals and departures are centered around 5a Avenida and 5a Calle. There are buses to Guatemala City leaving every 30 minutes between 4 A.M. and 5 P.M. (three hours, $2), eight daily buses to Panajachel (1.5 hours, $1.50) between 5 A.M. and 2 P.M., and seven daily buses to Quetzaltenango (three hours, $1.75). Alternatively, you can take any of the above to the Los Encuentros junction and change there for connecting service. If you're heading north, there are frequent buses to the departmental capital of Santa Cruz del Quiché leaving every 30 minutes.

Shuttle Bus
Adrenalina Tours (www.adrenalinatours .com), with offices in Quetzaltenango and Antigua, offers shuttle service from Chichi to Panajachel, Antigua, Quetzaltenango, and Guatemala City on market days. **Chichi Turkaj Tours** (5a Avenida 5-24, tel. 7756-1579) offers departures to the above cities plus Huehuetenango, the Mexican border, and others, though it's best to inquire as to specific schedules and routes, as these tend to be somewhat elastic.

Santa Cruz del Quiché and Vicinity

The capital of the Quiché department holds little of interest for foreign visitors when compared to Chichicastenango, just 18 kilometers away, though facilities and services are adequate if you should find yourself needing to spend the night. There is quite a bit of history surrounding this town, including the old K'iche' capital of K'umarcaaj, also known as Utatlán thanks to Pedro de Alvarado's Mexican allies. It was here that Alvarado and his men were invited to sign a formal surrender by the defeated K'iche's after the showdown near Quetzaltenango. The surrender turned into wholesale slaughter when Alvarado suspected

a trap and enticed the K'iche' rulers outside the safety of their city walls and then charged them with treason and burned them at the stake.

More recently, Quiché, as it's better known, housed an army garrison and the surrounding countryside was the site of intense battles between guerrilla and army forces during the civil war. The villages to the north suffered greatly during the conflict, particularly those in an area known as the Ixil Triangle. Today, the city serves mostly as a transit point for travelers heading north to these exquisite villages and their fantastic surroundings, which have become increasingly attractive in the advent of peace.

SIGHTS

The military barracks that once occupied the northeast corner of the plaza was closed by President Berger in 2004. The plaza is dominated by, as usual, the church, said to have been constructed by Dominican friars using stones from K'umarcaaj's Templo Tohil. The local market is held on Thursdays and Sundays, just as in neighboring Chichicastenango. Other than that, there's little in the way of sights in the town proper.

K'umarcaaj (Gumarcaj)

The former capital of the K'iche' empire enjoys a splendidly sylvan setting surrounded by deep ravines, though little has been carried out in the way of restoration since it was destroyed by the Spanish conquerors in 1524. Only a few structures are still recognizable and the site consists mostly of unexcavated grassy mounds. The K'iche' established themselves here sometime around A.D. 1250 after a migration from the Gulf of Mexico lowlands (previously Toltec territory) to the Yucataán Peninsula and up the Río Usumacinta. They were able to dominate and subdue the less-complex highland societies they encountered along the way, eventually establishing a sizable kingdom that stretched as far east as the lands occupied by the Rabinal of modern-day Alta Verapaz, west to present-day Momostenango, north to the Sierra de Chuacús, and south to Chichicastenango. The population of the immediate urban area is thought to have numbered 20,000. The formal founding of K'umarcaaj, signaling the consolidation of K'iche' power, dates from about A.D. 1400. It fell briefly under the dominion of the Mexica (Aztec) of Central Mexico, with whom they maintained a peaceful coexistence, until the arrival of the Spanish two decades later.

Of the city's 80 structures, few are recognizable, these being limited to the area around the central plaza. The partially restored **Templo Tohil** is the site's tallest structure and featured a sacrificial stone altar that was once the site of ritual human sacrifice. It is dedicated to a deity of thunder and lightning. Modern-day worshippers still perform rituals here, as it remains an important site for the Mayans. Much of the temple's exterior stonework has been vandalized and removed for use in local construction. The circular foundations of **Templo K'ucumatz** can also be seen and are all that remains of a previous building about four meters in diameter with a doorway in the shape of a snake head. A ball court lies to the east of here. Beneath the ruins on the site's southern escarpment is a long, 100-meter tunnel. It's debated whether it was built by the K'iche' to hide the women and children pending the Spanish arrival or as a representation of the mythical caves of Tula mentioned in the *Popol Vuh*. The site is revered by modern-day Mayans and is also a place for frequent rituals, including candle and flower petal offerings and chicken sacrifices. Bring a flashlight if you go into the cave, as there are a number of side tunnels, at least one of which ends in a dark, deep chasm. Watch your step.

The ruins are open 8 A.M.–5 P.M. daily and admission costs about $2. There's a small museum at the entrance displaying some Pre-Hispanic art. The easiest way to get here is to take a cab from the center of town, which should cost about $9 round-trip including an hour's wait time. You can also walk for about 45 minutes from the center of town, heading south from the plaza along 2a Avenida and turning right onto 10a Calle, from where it's a straight shot to the ruins.

ACCOMMODATIONS

Quiché's basic smattering of accommodations includes **Hotel Rey K'iche'** (tel. 7775-0827, 8a Calle 0-39 Zona 5, $10–13 d), two blocks north of the bus terminal, where the 22 spotless rooms mostly have private hot-water bathroom and cable TV. There's also a decent cafeteria. Friendly **Hotel Maya Quiché** (3a Avenida 4-19 Zona 1, tel. 7755-1464, $10–13 d) is conveniently situated a block west of the plaza and has large rooms with or without private bathroom. With several rooms in a multistory building around a parking lot/courtyard, the 42-room **Hotel Monte Bello** (4a Avenida 9-16 Zona 1, tel. 7755-3948, $25–35 d) is probably the nicest place in town. **Hotel San Pascual** (7a Calle 0-43 Zona 1, tel. 7757-1107, $7–13 d), between the bus terminal and central plaza, has clean rooms with or without private bathroom with the added bonus of pleasant plant-filled courtyards.

FOOD

El Torito Steakhouse (3a Avenida 4-35 Zona 1), one block west of the plaza, has decent-value set lunches for about $4 and a somewhat interesting cowboy ambience complete with stuffed animal heads. There's good filet mignon for about $6 and grilled chicken with rice, potatoes, and vegetables. **La Pizza de Ciro,** on the west side of the plaza, serves edible pizzas but certainly nothing to write home about. If all else fails there's always Guatemala's ever-popular answer to KFC, **Pollo Campero** (2a Avenida 7-35 Zona 1), serving tasty fried chicken, sandwiches, and some decent breakfasts in a sit-down environment with wait staff.

SERVICES

Banrural, on the plaza's northwest corner, changes dollars and travelers checks and has a MasterCard ATM. Another bank may have taken over the Visa ATM machine of recently absconded Bancafé, also on this side of the plaza.

GETTING THERE

The city bus depot is four blocks south and then two blocks east of the central plaza. Several of the buses heading to Chichicastenango from Guatemala City continue this way. There are buses every 30 minutes between 3 A.M. and 5 P.M. heading back toward Guatemala City, stopping at Chichicastenango and the Los Encuentros junction along the way. If you're heading north, there are eight daily buses to Nebaj (2.5 hours, $2) between 8:30 A.M. and 5 P.M. All of these stop in Sacapulas (one hour, $1) along the way, meaning there is also hourly service to this city during the same period.

A new road linking Santa Cruz del Quiché directly to Huehuetenango, to the west, might be a reality by the time you read this. It reportedly traverses some fantastic scenery.

EAST OF SANTA CRUZ DEL QUICHÉ

The road east from El Quiché runs along the Sierra de Chuacús through some villages set in verdant agricultural fields and is newly paved, ultimately winding up in Guatemala City some 160 kilometers away. The first of these villages, 10 kilometers away, is **Chiché,** which shares similar characteristics with Chichicastenango and has a Wednesday market. Farther along are the towns of **Chinique** and **Zacualpa.** Known as Pamaca in Postclassic times, Zacualpa has Thursday and Sunday markets and features the restored **Iglesia del Espíritu Santo,** with an elegant facade featuring twin bell towers punctuated by a third atop a curved central rise.

Next along this road is **Joyabaj,** which was practically leveled to the ground in the 1976 earthquake. It was rebuilt and is the main regional market center. It is one of three places in Guatemala where you can witness the *palo volador* ritual in which two "dancers" twist around a pole while tied with ropes, eventually descending to the ground. The event takes place during the annual fiesta, usually the second week in August.

Pachalum

A highlight of this back-door route to Guatemala City is Pachalum, a prosperous town only 21 years old; it has become a development model for the rest of Guatemala, having received international acclaim for its widespread citizen participation in local government, decentralization of local political power structures, and financial transparency. It should be noted that much of this development has taken place with assistance from USAID, which chose Pachalum as a project site because of its young age and the chance to start off with a clean slate. Access to potable water, electricity, health care, and education are widely available and there are municipal offices dedicated to Women's Vocational Training and Children and Youth. The town even has its own website, found at www.pachalum.com. It is just

72 kilometers from Guatemala City and, while not necessarily a tourism destination in the traditional sense, it is certainly worth a look if you go this way, at least for the chance to see what a developed Guatemala might someday resemble.

Should you need to stay here, **Hotel Nancy** (northwest of the plaza) or **Hotel Posada del Sol** (150 meters from city hall on Avenida Los Geranios and Calle Las Ilusiones, Zona 4) are good, inexpensive hotels.

Mixco Viejo

The paved road from Pachalum to Guatemala City also provides convenient access to the site of Mixco Viejo, about 12 kilometers south of Pachalum and 59 kilometers northwest of Guatemala City. Situated on a promontory overlooking the Río Pixcayá and surrounded by spectacular ravines on all sides, Mixco Viejo is the former Poqomam capital and ceremonial center, consisting of several low-rise pyramids and two ball courts. There is only one way in or out of the city, this being a narrow causeway.

Although it came under Kaqchikel influence shortly before falling to the Spanish in 1525, it shows heavy Toltec and Aztec influences, including a pair of sculptures of open-mouthed serpents with small human skulls adorning the ball court. The latter is a replica, with the original having been removed to Guatemala City.

The site, consisting of about 120 structures, was restored in the 1950s and '60s by a French expedition. It is thought to have harbored a population of about 10,000 at the time of Spanish contact. According to Spanish accounts of the city's siege, the battle was fought in the plains near the city after Poqomam warriors from Chinautla attacked the Spanish from behind. The few survivors then pointed the way to a secret entrance to the city, which the Spanish entered practically unopposed to destroy and kill in typical merciless fashion.

Mixco Viejo is open 7 A.M.–4:30 P.M. daily. Admission to the site is $3.50. To get here, hop on any of the buses headed to Pachalum from Guatemala City (four daily); they stop at the

THE HAUNTED HILL OF PACHALUM

Between Pachalum and the ruins of Mixco Viejo, the Río Motagua traverses forested hillsides and fields. One of these hills, **Cerro Potosí**, is thought by locals to be haunted. Townsfolk ascribe a number of mysteries to this seemingly innocuous hill, including the presence of animals seen but never heard, an airplane crash for which wreckage was never found, and the seeming disappearance of people who walk into the mountain's forests.

One of the most popular tales is that of a woman who decided to take a shortcut across the mountain while walking to her village, never to be heard from again. Family members and neighbors sent a search party but found nothing. Townsfolk also tell of a plane crash many years ago, clearly taking place on the mountain. When they went looking for the wreckage, there were no signs of the plane or its passengers. Although the hill is not very densely forested and is covered mostly in scrub forest, locals often hear the sounds of turkeys, dogs, and roosters coming from the mountain. Some local hunters have even been lured into its expanses looking for animals they hear but can never find.

The secret to the origins of the strange happenings on this mysterious mountain may lie buried with its former landowner, Don Serbando Rosales, a wealthy man from Pachalum who is said to have ever worn only white and to have ridden only white horses. He was seen every Friday evening, villagers say, carrying a black chicken up the side of the mountain. Townsfolk also say black birds made of smoke flew over his house 40 days after he was buried and that during Rosales's burial, astonished funeral-goers realized he was no longer in his coffin.

Similar legends abound throughout Guatemala, a country with a long tradition of supernatural mystery, magic, and folklore.

entrance to the ruins. It's also accessible from the town of San Juan Sacatepéquez, a satellite town of the capital, via pickups. It's about a 10-minute walk up the hill from the roadside drop-off point to the ruins.

NORTH OF SANTA CRUZ DEL QUICHÉ
Sacapulas

This town, on the banks of the Río Negro, sits at the crossroads of newly paved roads heading west to Huehuetenango, east to Uspantán and Cobán (partially paved), and north to Nebaj. If you need to spend the night here, a decent choice is **Tujaal** (tel. 5529-8609, $10 s/d), on the right side just before crossing the bridge over the river for the road to Nebaj. Rooms were still under construction during my visit, but some of them looked to have nice views to the river and surrounding mountains. There's a restaurant on the ground floor serving basic Guatemalan fare. A second option is **Hospedaje y Restaurante Río Negro** (tel. 5410-8168, $3 p/p) with basic rooms and shared, cold-water bath. It's on the southern bank of the river next to the Cruz Roja (Red Cross).

If you should need to exchange cash dollars, Banrural is on the north side of the plaza uphill from the bridge.

From here, there are seven daily buses to Nebaj (1.5 hours), two buses to Huehuetenango at 4:30 and 5:30 A.M. (1.5 hours), and seven daily buses to Uspantán, in addition to pickups throughout the day. Buses leave from the north side of the bridge over the river.

SACAPULAS TO COBÁN
Uspantán

A very scenic road leads east toward Alta Verapaz. If you're traveling by bus, you'll probably need to overnight in Uspantán, a small town nestled in the Cuchumatanes Mountains, which is actually a very pleasant place with clean streets and friendly folk. Hoping you may wind up staying here by choice, the local government has installed a **Municipal Tourism Office** (Municipal Palace, 1st Floor, tel. 7951-8125, www .uspantan.com) to help you make the most of your visit. Recreational opportunities include

hikes through the backcountry to the wonderful waterfall of **Los Regadillos,** hikes to **Peña Flor** and the neighboring site of **Tzunun Kaab'** along streams to another waterfall, witnessing a Mayan ceremony on the **Xoqoneb'** hillside just outside of town, and hiking or biking to the agricultural village of **Cholá,** where you can bathe in a refreshing spring-fed pool. Perhaps the most alluring option is a visit to **Laj Chimel,** the birthplace of Nobel Peace Prize winner Rigoberta Menchú and the gateway to Guatemala's fourth-largest cloud forest, where you can try your luck at spotting the elusive quetzal.

There are some good options for accommodations, all except one in the range of $10–15 d, including **Casa Blanca** (2a Avenida and 6a Calle Zona 3, tel. 7951-8049), where the rooms have cable TV and hot water. There's also ample parking if you've brought a car. **Hotel Montana** (5a Avenida 4-60 Zona 3, tel. 7951-8025) has clean rooms with hot-water private bath and cable TV housed in a pleasant peach-colored building. Offering minibus service to Cobán at 5 A.M., **Hotel La Villa** (tel. 7951-8046) has rooms with private or shared bathroom centered around a patio/parking lot. Centrally located **Hotel Posada de Doña Leonor** (6a Calle 4-09 Zona 1, tel. 7951-8045) has well-furnished rooms around a garden courtyard with shared or private bath and cable TV. Entirely with shared-bath rooms, a good budget option is **Hotel Uspanteka** (4a Calle 5-18 Zona 1, tel. 7951-8078, $6 d).

For food, there's **Café Don David** (5a Calle 3-27 Zona 1, tel. 7951-8169) serving light meals, dinners, and snacks that include sandwiches and Guatemalan food. **Comedor San Miguel** (4a Avenida 3-29 Zona 1, tel. 5592-1833) serving basic Guatemalan fare is another decent option. Across from the soccer stadium, **TV Café El Golazo** (tel. 7951-8027) is a good place for breakfasts, cakes, and sandwiches.

Banrural (7a Avenida Zona 4), two blocks from the central plaza, changes cash dollars.

Buses to Cobán (four hours, $3.50) leave early at 3 A.M. and 5 A.M. Heading west to Sacapulas are six daily buses continuing to El Quiché starting at 3 A.M. until about 4 P.M.

THE LIFE AND TIMES OF RIGOBERTA MENCHÚ

Rigoberta Menchú captured world attention in 1992 (the 500-year-anniversary of Columbus's landing in America) when she was awarded the Nobel Peace Prize for her work in bringing awareness to the plight of Guatemala's indigenous Mayan population. Her book *I, Rigoberta Menchú*, tells the story of her experiences growing up in a Mayan family in Guatemala's Western Highlands and of how several family members, including her father, mother, and brother, were murdered during the civil war at the hands of the military. Menchú herself had been persecuted by the military and eventually fled to exile in Mexico.

Much of her story was contested in author David Stoll's book *Rigoberta Menchú and the Story of All Poor Guatemalans*, published in 1999. After painstaking research and agonizing over whether or not to publish his findings, Stoll questions the veracity of several items appearing in Menchú's account. Among these are land conflicts with a neighboring ladino family portrayed by Menchú as the product of class struggle which, according to Stoll, were more like a family feud between Rigoberta's father and his in-laws. The book also casts doubt on Menchú's claims that she personally witnessed the death of her brother, burned alive at the hands of the military in the village of Chajul, claiming she probably was not in fact there. Eyewitness testimony, meanwhile, contends the victims were machine-gunned to death. Underlying the issues of supposed embellishments and distortions was Stoll's contention that Menchú's autobiography served purposes aimed at gaining the support of the Mayan peasantry for the guerrilla movement. Stoll concedes that Menchú's story is valuable in that it is a compelling version of events that can be generally applied to the plight of Gua-

temala's Mayan population during the civil war. Somehow, Menchú managed to escape the controversy with her reputation largely unblemished. In any case, Menchú's book is a fascinating read, in the very least for the insights it provides into highland Mayan culture and the atrocities committed during the civil war.

More recently, Menchú's Rigoberta Menchú Tum Foundation presented former accusations of torture, murder, and genocide in a Spanish court against several prominent Guatemalan military officials for their role in the atrocities during the civil war. The case centers around the firebombing of the Spanish embassy, which killed Menchú's father, a prominent activist, after he and several other protesters occupied the foreign government outpost. In 2006, the Spanish court issued arrest warrants for the accused, including Efraín Ríos Montt and Oscar Humberto Mejía Víctores, after a fruitless visit to Guatemala by a Spanish judge to record eyewitness testimony. The accused presented injunctions preventing their court summons and have also presented various appeals to prevent the arrest warrants from being carried out. As is always the case in Guatemala whenever prominent figures are involved, they had some help from technicalities that prevented the courts from issuing warrants for their arrest because of a supposed mixup in the paperwork coming from Spain, which mysteriously left out specific orders of apprehension for Ríos Montt and Mejía Víctores.

Menchú has also announced plans to form an indigenous political party to go along with her presidential aspirations, though she ran as a candidate for the Encuentro Por Guatemala party in the 2007 presidential election.

The Ixil Triangle

North of Sacapulas via a newly paved road is the Ixil Triangle, a name given to the area comprising the villages of Santa María Nebaj, San Juan Cotzal, and San Gaspar Chajul. The scenery here is spectacular, as are the weavings made by its Ixil-speaking inhabitants. Set in the foothills of the lush Cuchumatanes, the area was the scene of heavy fighting during the country's civil war. Its inhabitants suffered greatly during the violence, undoubtedly more than any other region in Guatemala. Peace has returned, but the region remains remote, drawing visitors with its colorful traditional Mayan culture, some of the country's best hiking, and breathtaking scenery.

HISTORY

The area populated by the Ixil-speaking peoples shows signs of having been inhabited since the latter part of the Classic period, between the 6th and 9th centuries A.D., including various stelae, pyramids, and monuments unearthed in this region. The Ixil didn't come under Spanish authority until 1530, having managed to successfully repel earlier invasions from their fortresses in Nebaj and Chajul with help from their neighbors and allies in Uspantán. When the Spanish did finally conquer the region, they burnt Nebaj to the ground and enslaved its people. After Spanish priests felt confident they had secured the souls of the newly conquered peoples, the region fell into a period of neglect until Dominican friars arrived on the scene in the 19th century seeking to convert the remaining outlying mountain villages. Guatemala's burgeoning coffee trade and its insatiable need for cheap labor had become fully established by this time, and the region's inhabitants were soon conscripted to work on the coastal plantations using debt peonage, among other tactics.

By the mid-20th century several wealthy families had firmly established themselves in the lower elevations of the Ixil region, owning huge cattle, coffee, cacao, and sugar plantations. Among the local landowning families, the Brol and Arenas families were notoriously cruel masters and the subject of eventual retribution during the civil war. The Brols owned thousands of acres as far as Uspantán, employing as many as 4,000 resident and seasonal workers at their Finca San Francisco in the northern lowlands near Cotzal. Many of its workers were held captive to debt peonage.

The Ejército Guerrillero de los Pobres, or EGP, moved into the region in 1972, crossing the border from Mexico and finding in the Ixil a populace willing to cooperate with them in the hopes of being finally liberated from the tyranny of the landowning elite. The swift acceptance of the EGP in the hearts and minds of the Ixil was further aided by weak government and military presence throughout the region. Eventually, the Guatemalan military moved into the region and began indiscriminately executing and "disappearing" suspected guerrilla sympathizers.

Although the EGP quickly displayed the ability to enlist thousands of peasants to its cause, the ideological momentum was not matched with a logistical capacity to arm or supply its followers. Villagers were soon caught in the middle of a scorched-earth campaign, with entire villages being massacred and destroyed, the guerrillas being largely unable to protect their followers.

An amnesty was declared under the subsequent government of Efraín Ríos Montt in 1982, bringing in thousands of refugees who had fled to the hinterlands trying to escape from the military. Between 1982 and 1984, 42,000 peasants turned themselves in. Other policies included the establishment of local Civil Defense Patrols, known as PACs, aimed at curtailing the influence of the guerrillas among the local population, and the rounding up of displaced citizens into so-called "model villages" closely guarded by the military.

By the time democratic rule finally returned to Guatemala in 1986, the guerrillas had been

splendid scenery along the road from Nebaj to Acul

pushed back to the northern reaches of the El Quiché department. There were occasional skirmishes until the signing of the 1996 peace accords. Almost all the smaller villages and hamlets of the Ixil Triangle and neighboring Ixcán were destroyed during the 1970s and '80s, with 25,000 Ixil murdered or displaced during the atrocities.

NEBAJ

Nebaj is the largest of the three villages and has grown substantially through the last few years since the end of the civil war. I still have pleasant memories of my first visit to this enchanting town, at the ripe old age of 18, riding on the roof rack of a crowded chicken bus on twisting mountain (dirt) roads. The location of this hamlet, nestled in a valley among the Cuchumatanes mountain chain, is superb, and you'll surely remember the first time you see its quaint houses and whitewashed church coming into view from the mountains above. As elsewhere, the town is centered around the plaza with the church and government offices built around it. A peek inside Nebaj's church reveals a multitude of small crosses as a memorial to civil war victims.

During the worst of the violence Nebaj was pretty much off-limits, with military checkpoints in Santa Cruz del Quiché, Sacapulas, and along the road north keeping close tabs on the activities of sojourners to these parts. Today it's become increasingly popular with foreign volunteers working with one of many NGOs helping out with postwar reconstruction and community development projects throughout the area. Despite its violent history, the region is remarkably safe, with reports of tourist robberies in these parts being virtually unheard of.

The women of Nebaj wear one of the most colorful and beautiful of Guatemala's indigenous costumes; they're imbued with animal and bird motifs and worn with an elaborate headdress adorned with purple, yellow, and green pom-poms. You can pick up colorful weavings with these motifs from several stalls along the plaza and at some of the local restaurants.

Hikes

The opportunities for hikes around Nebaj are virtually limitless. Two of the nicest hikes are to the villages of **Acul** and **Cocop.** One of the easiest hikes is along green pastures and meadows to some nearby waterfalls known as **Las Cataratas,** about 20 meters (60 feet) high. There are also several sites that are sacred to the Mayans where you might witness ceremonies, though their locations are not well known and it's best to go with a guide. There are several multiday hikes offered by a number of outfitters that afford you the opportunity to really get off the beaten path. These include a fantastic three-day hike over the Cuchumatanes mountain range to the village of **Todos Santos,** hikes across highland plateaus dotted with meadows and lagoons, and two- or three-day treks to the remote villages of **Xeo** and **Cotzal.**

Another nearby attraction of sorts is an old military landing strip still pockmarked with bomb holes that was a settlement for displaced war victims. Found four kilometers west of town, it's also known by its Ixil name **Ak'Txumb'al,** meaning "New Mentality," certainly as a way of adding insult to injury by its military creators.

Guide Companies

Because of the remoteness of most of the locales mentioned here, as well as the chance to contribute directly to the well-being of local inhabitants, guides are strongly recommended. Among the local outfitters is **Guías Ixiles** (3a Calle Zona 1, tel. 5311-9100, www .nebaj.com/ixilguides.htm), housed inside El Descanso, which offers hikes to all of the above-mentioned locales. A share of the proceeds goes to finance community projects. Next door, **Pablo's Tours** (tel. 5416-8674) offers hikes to nearby waterfalls, a river cave near a magnificently pristine blue river, horseback riding ($5 per hour), and multiday hiking from Nebaj to Todos Santos. Quetzaltenango-based **Quetzaltrekkers** (Diagonal 12 8-37 Zona 1, inside Casa Argentinas, Quetzaltenango, tel. 7765-5895, www.quetzaltrekkers.com) is another recommended outfitter for the Nebaj–Todos Santos trek, with proceeds being donated to fund projects benefiting Quetzaltenango's street children. The six-day trip ($150) leaves from Quetzaltenango, though it might be possible to meet up with a group if you already happen to be in Nebaj. Trips leave every other Wednesday.

If you prefer to hike without a guide, pick up a copy of the very useful *Trekking en la Región Ixil* guide ($2) from Guías Ixiles.

Shopping

Nebaj's busy **market** is one block east of the church and sells basic items mostly of interest to local residents. It's substantially busier on Thursdays and Sundays, when merchants come from out of town peddling cheap First World goods. For weaving and handicrafts, there are several stalls near the church. Another good spot is the **Centro Cultural Ixil y Mercado de Artesanías** (3a Avenida Zona 1, right off the park), where you can shop for handicrafts in a pretty neocolonial courtyard.

Accommodations

Most of Nebaj's accommodations are rather basic, though there is now at least one decent option for more discriminating travelers. **Hotel Ilebal Tenam** (Calzada 15 de Septiembre, Salida a Chajul, Cantón Simocool, tel. 7755-8039, $7–13 d) has rooms with shared or private hot-water bathrooms and basic furnishings centered around a courtyard. Rooms with private bath have cable TV. The garden sitting areas with thatched-roof shelters for shade are a nice touch. Nebaj's attractive new hostel is **(MediaLuna MedioSol** (tel. 5749-7450, $4 p/p in dorms or $7 p/p in private room), half a block from El Descanso on 3a Calle, with several amenities, including wireless Internet, a comfortable DVD lounge, a dartboard, Ping-Pong table, and a Mayan sauna in addition to clean rooms. Guests have use of the kitchen and you get the fourth night free if you spend three nights.

Hotel Shalom (corner of Calzada 15 de Septiembre and 4a Calle, tel. 7755-8028, $16

d) has spacious and attractive well-furnished rooms with private hot-water bathroom, cable TV, and wood-paneled walls. **Anexo Hotel Ixil** (tel. 7756-0036, corner of 2a Avenida and 9a Calle, $16 d) is basic but clean with rooms centered around a courtyard. All have private hot-water bathroom. The budget-friendly version of this property is **Hotel Ixil** (four blocks south of the plaza on 5a Avenida, tel. 7756-0036, $4 p/p) with simple shared-bath rooms. **Hotel Turansa** (corner of 5a Calle and 6a Avenida, tel. 7755-8487, $18 d) has a secured parking lot around which are centered 16 clean rooms with private hot-water bathroom and cable TV. The nicest place in town is (**Hotel Villa Nebaj** (Avenida 15 de Septiembre, just north of the plaza, tel. 7756-0005 or 7755-8115, $26 d), where the comfortable rooms have big wooden beds with Nebaj quilts, private hot-water bathroom, cable TV, and tile floors. There's also plenty of parking.

Food

For wonderful views overlooking the central plaza and tasty Guatemalan dishes, head to **Café Restaurante Maya Ixil** (tel. 7755-8168). It's also a good place for breakfast. Nebaj's main gathering spot is (**El Descanso** (3a Calle Zona 1, tel. 5311-9100, 6:30 A.M.–10 P.M. daily) where there are good Guatemalan dishes, sandwiches, nachos, and pastries. There's upstairs seating as well as a bar/lounge on the lower level. Movies are shown here nightly. (**Restaurante Maya-Inca** (5a Calle 1-90 Zona 1, 7 A.M.–9 P.M. daily) serves tasty, filling food at great prices (mostly in the $4 range). Dishes include Guatemalan favorites, Peruvian cuisine such as tasty *papas rellenas* (baked potatoes stuffed with beef, raisins and hard-boiled eggs), and hearty breakfasts. For decent pizza, there's **Pizza del César** (2a Avenida, tel. 7755-8095). Just off the square is the town's newest eatery, **Papi's** (tel. 5906-5780), serving healthy American-style food the likes of soy burgers. The bread is freshly baked on the premises. For steaks, fajitas, and tasty sandwiches, **Restaurante El Rancho** (Cantón Xalacul, Barrio Tipepala, tel. 7755-8019, all meals daily) is a good bet and is popular with the NGO crowd. On the road out of town heading out to Sacapulas, **Asados El Pasabién** (tel. 5701-2222, noon–11 P.M. daily) serves scrumptious grilled meats and chicken in a simple environment.

Information and Services

Nebaj's de facto tourist information office is El Descanso. It also serves as an all-in-one travel clearinghouse and services center providing Internet access ($1.50 per hour). Guías Ixiles is also based here.

The post office is at 5a Avenida 4-37, one block north of the central plaza.

For money, Banrural, on the north side of the plaza, has a MasterCard/Cirrus ATM. The Visa ATM managed by Bancafé (which went the way of the dodo bird) is (or was) at 2a Avenida #46, east and then north of the plaza, and has probably been taken over by another bank.

Language Courses

Established by the same folks who began El Descanso, **Nebaj Language School** (www.nebaj.com/nls.htm) offers 20 hours of one-on-one teaching per week for $130, including homestay with a local family (including two meals a day), two guided treks, and discounted Internet and food at El Descanso.

Volunteer Opportunities

Volunteer opportunities are available through **Community Enterprise Solutions (CES),** a nonprofit organization working with local businesses in Nebaj and started by two former Peace Corps volunteers. CES seeks to get local business enterprises up and running for the benefit of local inhabitants and acts as a consulting service to those already on their feet. These businesses are featured on the very useful website found at www.nebaj.com, which it manages. Volunteer opportunities are listed on the website at www.nebaj.com/volunteer.htm and include teaching, marketing/business planning, and translating with commitment times ranging from one week to three months or longer.

Getting There

Bus schedules in Nebaj, as in most small rural towns, are somewhat elastic. The bus depot is two blocks southeast of the plaza. There are seven daily buses to Santa Cruz del Quiché, with the last bus leaving sometime around noon. All of these stop in Sacapulas along the way. Buses to Chajul leave at 10 A.M. and 3 P.M. (one hour). Cotzal-bound buses (one hour) leave at 12:30 and 3:30 P.M. Again, verify these times locally. The roads between Nebaj and its sister towns, Chajul and Cotzal, were being paved.

◖ ACUL

Originally established as one of the "model villages" under the authoritarian hand of Efraín Ríos Montt, Acul is starting to come into its own. It features friendly folk and a spectacular Swiss-like mountain setting enhanced by the presence of quaint dairy farms. There are fairly frequent buses and pickups heading out this way from Nebaj, though it seems most gringos prefer to walk out this way through the lovely countryside.

Accommodations

If you'd like to stay in town, there's **Posada Doña Magdalena** (tel. 5782-0891), with beds in the dorm for $4 p/p or in the private double room for $7 p/p. All of the simple rooms share a bathroom. The hostel is run by a friendly Nebajense woman who lived in Las Vegas and speaks English, Spanish, and Ixil. Meals here are served family-style. There are textiles for sale as well as a Mayan sauna, or *temascal,* out back.

Among the local dairy farms is **Finca San Antonio** (tel. 5305-6240 or 2439-3352), started in 1938 by Italian immigrant José Azzari, who died in 1999. The finca is a pleasant working farm run by Azzari's sons and grandsons and producing some delicious cheeses made using centuries-old methods brought over from the old country. They're happy to

show you around and you're welcome to stay in the charming wooden cabanas featuring tile floors, simple but pleasing decorative touches, and shared ($11 p/p) or private hot-water bathroom ($13 p/p). One of the rooms upstairs has a deck with gorgeous views of the surrounding farmland. Activities include nature hikes in the surrounding countryside and there were plans to buy mountain bikes, maybe by the time of your visit.

Just next door along the road into town is ◖ **Hacienda Mil Amores** (tel. 5704-4817), also owned by members of the Azzari family. The four lovely, spacious tile-roofed cottages are a step above its neighbor's and are built of stone or wood. Each of the rooms is different and has elaborate tree-trunk or terracotta floors and private bathroom, some with chimney. Room rates are $47 d. The property has several connections with well-known tour operators and has no trouble filling its rooms, so book well in advance if you wish to stay here. This is also a working farm where you can buy cheeses. Kids will love the opportunity to see farm animals and even milk cows if they're so inclined. Other activities include hikes to neighboring villages and horseback riding. Meals are served family-style in the main farmhouse, which is beautifully decorated with orchids grown on-site and has wonderful views of the surrounding pasturelands from a pleasant wooden deck.

SAN JUAN COTZAL

Cotzal is the southernmost of the three towns comprising the Ixil Triangle and was actually its largest town until the road to Nebaj was built in the 1940s. It's a rather small town, though its setting is (as everywhere else in these parts) gorgeous, surrounded by the imposing Cuchumatanes mountain chain. There's little to see in the town itself, though the weavings here are some of Guatemala's finest. Check out its **Iglesia San Juan,** containing 500 small symbolic crosses commemorating kidnapped, tortured, murdered, and disappeared victims of the civil war. There is virtually nothing here in the way of accom-

© AL ARGUETA

Acul

modations save an extremely basic and un-marked posada two blocks from the church. You may find enterprising weavers offering you a place to stay or you could ask one of the local aid workers in these parts. Things may have changed by the time of your visit, as this region is growing up fast. There are likewise a few basic *comedores,* the best of which is **La Maguey,** behind the church.

Chimel and Santa Abelina Waterfalls

Some pretty waterfalls out this way make a good day hike, 10 and 12 kilometers from town, though there are not as of yet any out-fitters to take you here. You can take pick-ups or minibuses to the villages of Chichel and Santa Abelina, from where it's a much shorter walk to the falls. The first water-fall, near Chichel, is Chimel, which cas-cades down a rocky cliff into a small river. There are some tables and benches in the surrounding grassy hillside beneath the falls

and it makes a pleasant place for a picnic. You can drive part of the way on a rugged dirt road, but you'll find yourself hiking the last half mile or so to the falls through beau-tiful pastureland.

The second waterfall is reached by going a further two kilometers along the main road out of Cotzal to the village of Santa Abelina. The town is built on a hillside and if you go to the base of this hillside via the main road, you'll find a small *tienda* on the outskirts of town. You walk straight uphill from here on a very steep trail, turning left onto a smaller footpath, which eventually traverses cornfields for about 20 minutes to the falls. The water tumbles over a rock that is pitched just over the edge of the cliff and produces quite a bit of spray. There's a small tile-roofed changing room by the pool at the base of the falls and a friendly caretaker who will collect a $1 ad-mission price. You can ask any of the locals how to get here and they can point you in the general direction.

GUATEMALA: FAST-FORWARD

For decades, intrepid travelers have come to Guatemala to experience this mythical pocket paradise: a compact, diverse nation in the middle of the Americas with 33 volcanoes, Lake Atitlán – "the most beautiful lake in the world," steamy jungles, ancient Mayan temples, and colorful indigenous villages.

The volcanoes are still here; the lake is still here; much of the steamy jungles are still here, with their enigmatic ancient Mayan temples. However, the villages of Guatemala's highlands are experiencing a major transition thanks to remittance money sent back from Guatemalans working in the United States.

Whitewashed adobe houses with terra-cotta-tiled roofs are being exchanged for concrete block walls and corrugated tin roofs. Electricity, indoor plumbing, rebar, satellite dishes, asphalt, and concrete are just some of the newcomers to these villages.

In one of my favorite, rather remote, highland villages, Chajul, young women in traditional regalia blithely sip colas and chat on cell phones in Ixil Mayan. Boys play soccer in the street wearing Beckham jerseys, Yankees baseball caps, calling to each other in Ixil, Spanish, and English. In Sololá, speakers broadcast evan-gelical radio shows that compete with hip-hop and rap coming from the local fruit market. It appears that more people own pickup trucks, cell phones, and televisions than toilets.

Why the dramatic change? Guatemala welcomes $3.5 billion annually from the Guatemalan workforce living in the United States. Thanks to these greenbacks, traditional, often indigenous communities are on fast-forward, hurtling into a brave new modern world. All this has happened in the past few years and perhaps because of the distance between what was and what has become, the results can be overwhelming: sometimes wonderful, sometimes painful, often humorous, and always interesting for the traveler, especially to those who are students of human nature.

Enrique V. Iglesias (former longtime president of the Inter-American Development Bank) lauds the direct and democratic attributes of remittances. However, witnessing remittances in action, I do not find it always pretty what they are doing to village life in Guatemala. It sounds so good on paper: Courageous Guatemalans enter the United States, work hard, send money home, and help to sustain their country: direct, democratic, family to family.

CHAJUL

About 15 kilometers northeast of Nebaj, Chajul is a picturesque collection of quaint adobe houses with tiled roofs. Of the three Ixil Triangle towns, it certainly has the most traditional feel, though a new paved road to Nebaj has many traditionalists fearing the end is near for one of the country's most pleasantly isolated villages. In any case, it still offers spectacular weavings you'll undoubtedly see everywhere. Though there is no scheduled market day, sellers will most certainly find you to offer their wares in brilliant hues of red and blue embroidered with animals and plants.

The town's **Iglesia de San Gaspar Los Reyes** has been restored with new front doors carved by local artists and is a major pilgrimage site on the second Friday of Lent for its *Cristo de Golgotha.*

Chajul's plaza was also the site of a grisly public execution of EGP guerrillas carried out by the Guatemalan military in retaliation for the 1979 murder of landowner Enrique Brol, an event which is narrated in Nobel Peace Prize winner Rigoberta Menchu's autobiography. While the basic facts of the army's extra-judicial murders has not come into question, Menchú's testimony certainly has. An investigation by author David Stoll has since revealed Menchú may not have been there at all and is also at odds with her claims that the prisoners were burnt alive, claiming instead that they were mowed down with machine guns. The research and evidence supporting his claims and questioning much of Menchú's autobiography

However, early-stage capitalism produces the most voracious consumers and with limited leadership, law enforcement, zoning, education, or planning, these new dollars create new consumers who are left to learn as they go.

Yet, as travelers in the early 21st century, count your anthropological blessings – you get to be voyeurs on a whirling dervish of change and culture clash. While it is not always beautiful or charming, if you are from the developed "First" World, it is strangely fascinating and perhaps even important to see.

I have interviewed Guatemalans living in the United States who say (some with great relish, some with dejected nostalgia) that they no longer recognize their villages. They tell me that the families they left (to better support by working in the United States) have used their hard-earned cash to transform the highlands into something new. But few know just what that is.

The signs of progress are everywhere: A proud grandma's adobe house is now a three-story concrete house faced in shiny tile and paned with reflective glass. Old-time swimming holes have become water parks. Pagan shrines and ritual have diminished as evangelicals re-weave the religious fabric and build Christian churches in these communities. A pickup truck is much easier to carry products with than a forehead tumpline but one notices expanded waistlines. Televisions provide a window to the war in Iraq, China's environmental issues, American pop culture, giraffes in Kenya.... Women do not spend hours hand-spinning wool blankets anymore; the ones arriving from China are much cheaper and just about as warm.

One of the great Guatemala travelers explains it to me this way: "The Guatemala I met 20 years ago was a slow, enchanting melody. Guatemala today is the same melody; it is now just being played on fast-forward."

After living in and writing about Central America for almost 10 years, I still encourage travelers to go to the Guatemala highland villages: Look, explore, listen, absorb – no longer for their simple charms, but as a fascinating window into the fast changing lives and vernacular of Central America.

Contributed by Catherine Docter
Writer and consultant
Contributing editor, Departures Magazine
www.mesoamericanconsulting.com
Antigua, Guatemala

are presented in his book, *Rigoberta Menchú and the Story of All Poor Guatemalans.*

Practicalities

There's not much in the way of accommodations here. In a pinch, head to the somewhat dodgy **Hospedaje Cristina.** Again, you will likely be approached by locals offering food and shelter in their homes, which is probably a better bet. You can also eat at **Café La Cabaña,** two blocks east of the church. There's a Banrural on the plaza for changing cash dollars.

THE IXCÁN

North of Chajul, foot trails lead to the summit of 2,700-meter (9,000-foot) **Cerro Bisís** and some hamlets scattered throughout a roadless wilderness that has been proposed for special protection. Beyond this lies the Ixcán, a jungle wilderness extending northwest to Huehuetenango and the Mexican border settled by landless peasants during the 1960s with the help of Maryknoll missionaries. It was hotly contested during the civil war with virtually every village being razed to the ground in a scorched-earth campaign by the Guatemalan military. Today it remains largely untamed and many settlers have moved back from exile in Mexico. An interesting read on this subject is *Paradise in Ashes,* by Beatriz Manz.

The region holds excellent possibilities for ecotourism and remains one of Guatemala's great wilderness areas. It's quite literally the end of the road. If you're the explorer type, you may want to head out this way and if you do, feel free to write in with your experiences.

THE WESTERN HIGHLANDS

Huehuetenango and Vicinity

Affectionately called "Huehue" (WAY-way) by locals, this somewhat busy coffee-trading town sits in a valley overlooking the glaciated peaks of the Sierra de los Cuchumatanes. Because of its location in the mountain chain's rain shadow, the town and surrounding areas are somewhat drier than the Quiché highlands to the east, which lie on the mountain chain's windward side. The departmental capital is busy with travelers heading to or from the western border with Mexico as well as with coffee farmers and traders heading to or from nearby farms. Since first coming here at the age of three, I watched the town grow up into a somewhat disorganized agglomeration of trade and commerce, though there has been a remarkable improvement in the level of its services. It makes a great jumping-off point for deeper explorations of the very diverse department of Huehuetenango and even includes a worthwhile site of its own, this being the ruins of Zaculeu just outside of town.

Access to Huehue is mainly via the Pan-American Highway, with the turnoff into town at Km. 264, from where it's another three kilometers to its center via a boulevard. A recently paved road now also leads east to Sacapulas, passing the town of Aguacatán (and wonderful mountain views) along the way.

SIGHTS

As always, the town is centered on the **parque central,** which is actually one of Guatemala's prettiest. At its center is a colonial fountain along with well-tended gardens and even a **relief map** of the department of Huehuetenango. On the plaza's southern end, facing 5a Avenida, is its neoclassical church, the **Catedral Templo de la Inmaculada Concepción.** It dates to 1874. The town's **Municipalidad** (City Hall) is on the west side of the plaza and is curiously topped with an oyster-shaped band shell. On the park's eastern side, in early 20th-century architecture and notable for its clock tower, is the building housing **Gobernación Departamental,** the regional seat of government.

the ruins of Zaculeu

© AL ARGUETA

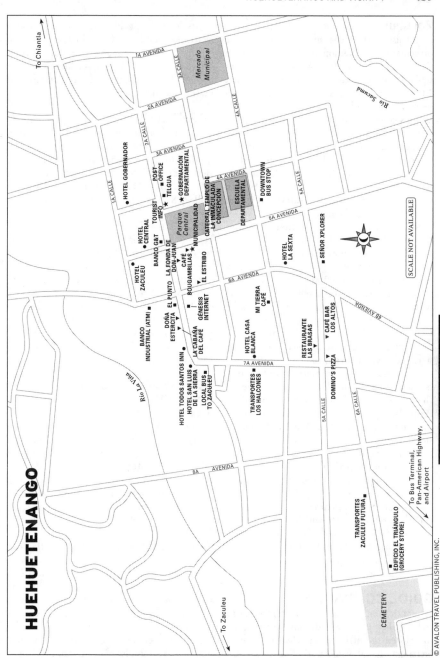

HUEHUETENANGO

THE WESTERN HIGHLANDS

SCALE NOT AVAILABLE

© AVALON TRAVEL PUBLISHING, INC.

To Chiantla

1A AVENIDA

3A CALLE

Mercado Municipal

2A AVENIDA

2A CALLE

Río Sacuná

1A CALLE

3A AVENIDA

4A CALLE

● HOTEL GOBERNADOR

POST OFFICE
★ TELGUA
● GOBERNACIÓN DEPARTAMENTAL

TOURIST INFO

4A AVENIDA

DOWNTOWN BUS STOP ■

● ESCUELA DEPARTAMENTAL

5A CALLE

5A AVENIDA

● HOTEL CENTRAL

Parque Central

BANCO G&T ■
CAFÉ ● MUNICIPALIDAD
LA FONDA DE DON JUAN

CATEDRAL, TEMPLO DE LA INMACULADA CONCEPCIÓN

● HOTEL LA SEXTA

■ SEÑOR XPLORER

● HOTEL ZACULEU

EL PUNTO ■
EL ESTRIBO ■
● BOUGAMBILIAS

6A AVENIDA

DOÑA ESTERCITA ■
■ LA CABAÑA DEL CAFÉ
● GÉNESIS INTERNET

MI TIERRA CAFÉ

CAFÉ BAR LOS ALTOS ▼

8A AVENIDA

BANCO INDUSTRIAL (ATM) ■

Río La Viña

● HOTEL CASA BLANCA

RESTAURANTE LAS BRASAS ▼

HOTEL TODOS SANTOS INN ■
HOTEL SAN LUIS DE LA SIERRA ■
LOCAL BUS TO ZACULEU ■

7A AVENIDA

5A CALLE

6A CALLE

DOMINO'S PIZZA ▼

TRANSPORTES LOS HALCONES ■

8A AVENIDA

To Bus Terminal, Pan-American Highway, and Airport

TRANSPORTES ZACULEU FUTURA ■

EDIFICIO EL TRIANGULO (GROCERY STORE) ■

CEMETERY

To Zaculeu

Zaculeu

Zaculeu (8 A.M.–6 P.M. daily, $3.50) was the principal Mam ceremonial site. Dating to the Early Classic period (A.D. 400–700), it shows signs of having been occupied for more than 1,000 years until it was conquered by Gonzalo de Alvarado, brother of Guatemala's other infamous conquistador, in October 1525. It was starvation that eventually did the local population in, as Alvarado and his troops simply staked out the fortified city (surrounded by ravines) for two months, cutting off rescue attempts from neighboring Mam villages with the help of the Spanish cavalry and 2,000 Mexica and K'iche' allies.

More than any of the other highland Mayan sites such as K'umarcaaj and Iximché, Zaculeu somehow manages to evoke the feel of the city as it might have looked in its heyday, thanks to a 1950s restoration project covering the restored temples in graying white plaster. At the same time, the temples lack the bright coloring they most certainly would have had and similarly lack any of their decorative details. The highest of its temple pyramids, **Structure I,** rises to about 12 meters. Another somewhat impressive structure is **Structure 13,** on the southeast corner of the main plaza. The site also has an interesting I-shaped ball court. There's an on-site museum with some interesting displays on the siege of the city as well as burial pieces found beneath Structure I.

Snacks and refreshments are available from a couple of simple eateries across from the main entrance to the park.

To get here, you can hire a cab from the central plaza for about $6, which includes about an hour at the ruins. Otherwise, there are frequent, cheap local buses heading out this way from 2a Calle and 7a Avenida near Hotel San Luis de la Sierra.

GUIDE COMPANIES

Quetzaltenango-based **Adrenalina Tours** (tel. 7761-4509, www.adrenalinatours.com) has closed the office it once had in Huehuetenango, though you can still hire the services of its knowledgeable local driver, Mario Martínez, and his 4WD vehicle to take you to any of Huehuetenango's remote natural attractions. You can contact him by phone at 5762-1903 and 7764-6897 or by email at mario_huehuetenango@yahoo.com.

NIGHTLIFE

When Huehuetecos want to party, they tend to head to Xela. Still, there are a few good places in town for enjoying an evening cocktail, including **El Estribo** (6a Avenida between 3a and 4a Calle Zona 1) and **Café Bar Los Altos** (5a Calle 6-85 Zona 1).

SHOPPING

You can pick up good-quality handicrafts at **Artesanías Ixquil** (6a Avenida, Cerrito del Maíz, Zona 4, tel. 5543-5661, ixquilhuehue@hotmail.com), which has a wide assortment of products representing the department's excellent weavings and singular traditional costumes. From the plaza, walk north up 6a Avenida to the top of a hill and then right on 1a Calle, where it's number 1-115. It's about a 15-minute walk.

ACCOMMODATIONS
Under $10

Hotel Gobernador (4a Avenida 1-45 Zona 1, tel. 7764-1197, $7–12 d) is a solid family-run budget choice with good-size rooms, some with private bath. Some rooms are better ventilated than others. **Hotel Central** (5a Avenida 1-33 Zona 1, tel. 7764-1202, $6 d) is a reasonable budget option with large, if aging, rooms, all with shared bath.

$10-25

Friendly **Todos Santos Inn** (2a Calle 7-64 Zona 1, tel. 7764-1241, $10–16 d) has 16 rooms with shared or private bath cheerfully painted in hues of red and orange with passable mattresses and reading lamps, some with cable TV. There's an upstairs sitting area as well as a third-floor patio. Downstairs rooms are not as well ventilated and tend to feel moldy, a common issue throughout the highlands. Indifferent **Hotel La Sexta** (6a Avenida 4-29 Zona 1, tel. 7764-6612, $17 d) has stiff beds and smallish rooms with cable TV and medieval-looking hot-water heaters. On the south side of the bus terminal, **Hotel Guatemex** (tel. 7769-0398, $10–20 d) is your best bet for late bus arrivals into town, with rooms in a variety of price categories, all with cable TV and good beds.

$25-50

Half a block north of the plaza, **Hotel Zaculeu** (5a Avenida 1-14 Zona 1, tel. 7764-1086, $37 d) was undergoing renovations at the time of my visit. The planned changes include a new lobby, Internet lounge, and bar. There are attractive ground-floor rooms with tile floors beside a garden courtyard. The top-floor rooms in a newer section have been upgraded with carpeting, accent lighting on the walls, and other pleasant decorative touches. All rooms have cable TV, great beds, and private hot-water bathroom. There's a dining room serving breakfast and dinner. Conveniently situated across from the Los Halcones bus depot, ◀ **Hotel Casa Blanca** (7a Avenida 3-41 Zona 1, tel. 7769-0777, $37 d) has personal sentimental value, as it was once my grandfather's home and office. All mushiness aside, there's plenty here to recommend it, including attractive rooms in the original house (with plenty of character) or beside the back patio (more modern and spacious). All 15 rooms have hot-water private bathroom, phone, and cable TV. There are two restaurants, each fronting one of the house's two patios.

Just up the street, **Hotel San Luis de la Sierra** (2a Calle 7-00 Zona 1, tel. 7764-9217, hsanluis@intelnet.net.gt, $28 d) is lovingly cared for by María Rosa Calderón, a former grade-school teacher who once lived in Guatemala City and taught Spanish to a future Moon Handbooks author. The spotless rooms have fan, attractive furnishings, hot-water private bathroom, cable TV, and reading lamps. There's a dining room serving breakfast and dinner. ◀ **Hotel Premier** (2a Calle 5-37 Zona 8, tel. 7764-9200 or 7769-0927, $33 d), on the way out to Zaculeu, has 36 rooms set around a pretty, opaque plastic–covered courtyard graced by a fountain. The rooms have the comfiest beds in town, tile floors, cable TV, wireless Internet, and hot-water private bathroom; some have views of the Cuchumatanes. The attractive lobby has a restaurant/bar serving international dishes.

There are a number of hotels along the entrance into town near the bus terminal, including the **Hotel California** (3a Avenida 4-25 Zona 5, Colonia Alvarado, tel. 7769-0500, $33 d), with clean, modern rooms with cable TV and private hot-water bathroom. There's also a dining room and lobby lounge. Don't let its name scare you; unlike the famous hotel in the Eagles tune, you can check out anytime you like and you can certainly leave. Also along the entrance into town is **Hotel San Francisco** (Km. 260, Cantón San José, tel. 7764-9987/88, $30 d), which is not as fancy as the armed guards posted at its doors would have you believe. It has 51 spotless rooms with somewhat bland decor and private hot-water bathroom and cable TV. There are an Internet center, a pool table, and a small gym as well as a restaurant next to the parking lot. The main lobby is housed under a pleasant opaque-ceiling courtyard, allowing for ample ambient light. The hotel's gardens are also the home of an unfortunate caged spider monkey.

FOOD

Conveniently situated across from the main plaza's cathedral, **Café Bougambilias** (tel. 7764-0105, 6:45 A.M.–9:30 P.M.) is a great place for a quick snack or cheap eat with set dishes that include steak or chicken, salad, and a drink for $3.50 or tortillas, burgers, and sandwiches for $1.50. The cooking is done on the ground floor, which you can see as you come in, with tables on the top two floors overlooking the park. Just off the square, **La Fonda de Don Juan** (2a Calle 5-35 Zona 1, tel. 7764-1173, 6 A.M.–10 P.M.) serves an excellent and varied menu including Italian, Mexican, and Guatemalan dishes the likes of pizza, pasta, and burgers in a lively atmosphere that

THE WESTERN HIGHLANDS

includes checkered tablecloths. **⟨ Mi Tierra Café** (4a Calle 6-46 Zona 1, tel. 7764-1473, 7 A.M.–9 P.M. Mon.–Sat., 2–9 P.M. Sun.) is a friendly little restaurant that is ever-popular with locals, serving tasty nachos, pizza, and fajitas in addition to delicious breakfasts, including delectable croissant sandwiches. Try the "muffin ranchero," essentially a salsa-bathed egg sandwich with fried tortillas instead of bread. The strong coffee is locally grown and extraordinary. For steaks, seafood, and even some Chinese fare, check out **Restaurante Las Brasas** (5a Calle 6-104, on the corner of 5a Calle and 7a Avenida, tel. 7764-6200, 10 A.M.–11 P.M. daily, $4–15). There's even duck on the menu. **Domino's Pizza** is across the street.

Just down the street is one of the best places in town, **⟨ Hotel Casa Blanca** (7a Avenida 3-41 Zona 1, tel. 7769-0777, 6 A.M.–10 P.M.), where you can dine al fresco in the backyard garden or inside facing the house's original courtyard. On the menu are steaks, grilled chicken, good soups, and salads as well as sandwiches. It makes a great place for breakfast. **Especialidades Doña Estercita** (2a Calle west of 6a Avenida, tel. 7764-2212, 8 A.M.–10 P.M. Mon.–Sat.) is the place to go for sweet or salty crepes, croissants, pies, empanadas, and sandwiches. Just a few doors down, **La Cabaña del Café** (2a Calle 6-50 Zona 1, tel. 7764-8903, 8 A.M.–9 P.M. daily) has probably the best coffee in town, including great espresso drinks, in addition to a range of light fare including sandwiches, breakfasts, and cakes, housed in a homey log cabin.

INFORMATION AND SERVICES
Tourist Information

Huehue's Centro de Información Turística (tel. 7694-9354, 8 A.M.–noon and 1:30–5 P.M.) is on 2a Calle housed inside the Gobernación Departamental building fronting the plaza. The staff speaks English and has a variety of maps and printed information that can help you get around town and explore the surrounding attractions throughout the department.

Communications

The central post office is at 2a Calle 3-54 Zona 1 just east of the plaza. Telgua has pay phones and international calling right next door.

With fast connections and abundant computers, Señor Xplorer (5a Calle 5-97 Zona 1, Centro Comercial La Plazuela Local 4, tel. 7768-1185/86) offers Internet service for about $1 an hour. Interhuehue (3a Calle 6-65 Zona 1) also charges about $1 an hour. Another large operation with about 20 computers is Techno Café Internet (2a Calle Zona 1, across from La Fonda de Don Juan, tel. 7762-6353, 9 A.M.– 9 P.M. Mon.–Sat.). On 2a Calle next door to Especialidades Doña Estercita is El Punto (tel. 7764-7826), charging about $0.65 an hour. Across the street, Génesis Internet (tel. 7764-7021) charges the same.

Money

The ATM at G&T Banco Continental on the north side of the plaza fronting 2a Calle works with both Visa and MasterCard. Banco Industrial (6a Avenida 1-26 Zona 1) has a Visa/Plus ATM. Both banks can change cash dollars and travelers checks.

Language Schools

Huehue makes a good place to learn Spanish and become immersed in the language, as the gringo presence here is not as prevalent as in other parts of Guatemala. Its sole language school is **Academia de Español Xinabajul** (4a Avenida 14-14 Zona 5, Los Encinos, tel. 7764-6631, academiaxinabajul@hotmail.com), which charges $150 per week for 20 hours of instruction and stay with a local host family. It gets good marks from former students. For private lessons, contact Faby Castro at tel. 7762-7730 or 5348-1676.

GETTING THERE

The bus terminal is about two kilometers southwest of the city center, halfway along the boulevard leading out to the Pan-American Highway. There are frequent buses to many outlying towns and villages, most notably:

• **Aguacatán:** (one hour, $1), 10 daily buses between 6 A.M. and 4 P.M.

- **Barillas:** (seven hours, $4), 10 daily buses 2 A.M.–10 P.M.

- **La Mesilla (Mexican border):** (two hours, $2), 20 daily buses 6 A.M.–6 P.M.

- **Nenton:** (three hours, $2), six daily buses between 3:30 A.M. and 1 P.M.

- **Sacapulas, Quiché:** (1.5 hours, $2), at 11:30 A.M. and 12:45 P.M.

- **Soloma:** (three hours, $2.50), 16 daily buses between 2 A.M. and 10 P.M.

- **Todos Santos Cuchumatán:** (two hours, $2), leaving at 4:30 A.M., 5 A.M., 12:45 P.M., 1:30 P.M., 2:45 P.M., and 3:45 P.M. There may be others.

Frequent second-class bus departures also include **Guatemala City** (20 daily buses until 4 P.M., five hours, $5) and **Quetzaltenango** (16 daily buses until 2:30 P.M., two hours, $1.75).

Pullman bus service to Guatemala City is available via **Transportes Los Halcones** (7a Avenida 3-62 Zona 1, tel. 7764-2251, $5) at 4:30 A.M., 7 A.M., and 2 P.M. **Transportes Zaculeu Futura** (3a Avenida 5-25 Zona 1, tel. 7764-1535) has departures at 6 A.M. and 3 P.M. **Transportes Velásquez,** operating from the main terminal, is another option, with buses every half hour or so between 8:30 A.M. and 3:30 P.M.

NEAR HUEHUETENANGO

The following towns are close to the department capital and might make for interesting day trips if you lack the time to go deep into the heart of this remote corner of Guatemala.

Chiantla

Chiantla lies five kilometers north of Huehuetenango along a paved road that continues into the Cuchumtanes mountain chain. It was once a silver mining center and is known for its **Iglesia Nuestra Señora de Candelaria,** harboring the Virgen de Chiantla, adorned in the town's silver. There are some interesting murals in the church's nave depicting an *encomendero* watching over Mayan workers in the silver mine. The church is a pilgrimage site through-

out the year, but especially on February 2 during the annual town festival. Chiantla's town center features two adjacent plazas, with one of them graced by a municipal building with a clock tower very much like the one in Huehuetenango. There are buses from Chiantla to Huehuetenango (and vice versa) about every 20 minutes. Heading out from Huehue, the buses stop at 1a Calle and 1a Avenida on the way out of town, which is much closer to the city center than the bus terminal.

Aguacatán

Heading east from Chiantla on the paved road toward Sacapulas, you'll pass this small agricultural town at the base of the Cuchumatanes. The village is the product of a merger of two distinct groups of people, the Chalchitek and Awakatek, into a single community by Dominican friars during colonial times. Today, they still speak separate languages. Gold and silver were mined here during colonial days, though nowadays its economic activities are centered around the production of abundant crops, most notably garlic. The weekly market is held on Sunday, with traders arriving and setting up shop on Saturday afternoon. The town's other claim to fame is the *nacimiento* (source) of the Río San Juan, which bubbles up from the underbelly of a rocky hillside about 20 minutes' walk outside of town.

For accommodations and food, your best bet is two blocks north of the plaza at **Hotel y Restaurante San Juan** (tel. 7766-0110, $7–15 d), with clean rooms with or without private bathroom.

El Mirador

The road winds its way out of Chiantla up the vertiginous face of the Cuchumatanes, with the superimposed quilt pattern of corn- and wheat fields upon the countryside transitioning to one of grasses and hearty maguey plants at about 2,700 meters (9,000 feet). At the top of the rise is a lookout point known as El Mirador or La Cumbre (The Summit), from where there are views of Huehuetenango and Guatemala's impressive volcanic chain to the south.

Huehuetenango Frontier

From the lookout, the road continues along the 3,300 meter (11,000-foot) Paquix plateau, characterized by smooth, rounded hills with scant vegetation that conjure images of the Peruvian Andes or Alaska. Windblown grasses, black granite rocks, sturdy maguey plants, and herds of sheep pepper the surrounding countryside with the occasional adobe house occupied by ruddy Mayans more closely resembling their South American Inca relatives. The recent introduction of llamas to these areas adds further similarity.

About one kilometer north from the lookout, a dirt-road turnoff heads east to the village of Chancol and the **Unicornio Azul** equestrian center. Back along the main (paved) road another nine kilometers or so is the **Paquix Junction,** with its westbound turnoff heading to the village of **Todos Santos Cuchumatán.** Its northbound turnoff leads to the villages of **San Juan Ixcoy, Soloma, Santa Eulalia, San Mateo Ixtatán** and, eventually, **Barillas.**

UNICORNIO AZUL

Not so much a hotel as a professionally run equestrian center, **◖ Unicornio Azul** (tel. 5205-9328, www.unicornioazul.com, $33 d) enjoys a spectacular location on the grassy plateau atop the rugged Cuchumatanes from where you can embark on horseback rides as short as one hour to as long as several days throughout the sprawling countryside. About 25 kilometers northeast of Huehuetenango, the operation consists of 11 well-cared-for horses, stables, and wonderful accommodations meticulously managed by its French-Guatemalan owners. Prices for rides range from $80 for one day to $970 for nine days, though they vary depending on the number of riders in a group. The accommodations here are rustically beautiful, consisting of five rooms housed in two separate tiled-roof houses. All of the rooms are distinctly decorated and furnished with unique touches such as gorgeous lamps fashioned from Honduran Lenca pottery. At night, gas lamps provide wonderful ambience, though there is electricity for showers and cooking. Room rates include breakfast and one hour of horseback riding. Lunch and dinner are served family-style and cost $7 each. If you're not keen on riding, there are also mountain bikes for exploring the rugged roads and trails all around.

TODOS SANTOS CUCHUMATÁN

Todos Santos sits on the dry western slopes of the Cuchumatanes. Remote and largely retaining its traditions, it is a fine place to take in Mayan culture, do some hiking, and shop for unique weavings. It is one of only a few places in the highlands where you'll still see men wearing traditional attire, consisting of bright red pants with thin white stripes paired with a zany striped shirt featuring oversize, elabo-

the church at Todos Santos

© AL ARGUETA

ALL SAINTS' DAY IN TODOS SANTOS

If you're in Todos Santos November 1 (All Saints' Day) and love a good party, you may not want to miss the three-day annual town festival, at the center of which is a series of horse races. There's plenty of drinking, dancing, and marimba music during this time. The race begins with costumed riders galloping from one end of the 600-yard course, drinking *aguardiente* upon their arrival at the course's other extreme before heading back once again. The back-and-forth pattern is a survival of the fittest with riders struggling to hang on as the race (and drunken stupor) reach a crescendo. Traditionally, the riders hit the horses with live chickens, though in recent years they have begun switching to whips. The races sometimes continue well into the afternoon.

By the end of the day, most people are lying passed out in the streets or in bars (if they're lucky) in a drunken spectacle rivaled in few places in Guatemala. There are always a few drunken brawls and some folks who wind up in the town jail. The next day is Day of the Dead, and the festivities transition to the local cemetery, where locals visit departed relatives, marking their gravestones with candles and flowers. There's also more music and dance as part of the final day of celebration.

rately embroidered collars. The costume also includes a straw hat with a wide, blue, grommeted ribbon. The women wear equally stunning purple *huipiles* and embroider many items with the town's signature designs. Contributing to the remarkable preservation of local customs and dress is the intense local pride of Todos Santos's Mam-speaking residents, who stand a full head taller than most other Mayan indigenous peoples.

The village first gained notoriety after social scientist and world traveler Maud Oakes spent two years here starting in 1945 and wrote two books about her experiences, *The Two Crosses of Todos Santos* and *Beyond the Windy Place*. The local Mam hold four local mountain peaks sacred and some of her neighbors reputedly believed the foreign-born female shaman to be the guardian of one of these.

The main market day here is Saturday. Don't be surprised to find inebriated men (mostly) stumbling through the streets or passed out on the sidewalk, an unfortunately common sight throughout the highlands. As in the Ixil Triangle, the population here suffered greatly during the civil war. The army marched on the town in 1982 in the days following a brief occupation by EGP guerrillas, carrying out the torture, disappearance, and murder of suspected guerrilla sympathizers.

Many villagers fled to the hillsides to wait out the troubles or went north to Mexico.

Todos Santos certainly remains very poor. Many of its residents have traditionally made ends meet by traveling to the Pacific lowlands to work in the annual harvests. Many Todosanteros now have family in the United States, a fact that becomes readily apparent as you walk the town's streets and see new construction funded with dollars sent from abroad by expatriate relatives. Despite its remoteness, it's not uncommon to see groups of villagers in their distinctive attire at Guatemala City's international airport waiting on the arrival of a returning family member. Huehuetenango supposedly sends more of its inhabitants abroad than any other of Guatemala's departments.

As always, you should be careful not to photograph Mayan people (especially children) without permission, nor should you show undue interest. It can be tough at times, because Mayan children (and Mayan people in general) can provide some wonderful opportunities for portraiture. In 2000, a Japanese tourist and the Guatemalan tour bus driver who tried to protect him were lynched in Todos Santos by an angry mob after the tourist tried to photograph a child. The incident was certainly an isolated one and was attributed to a rumor about satanists who were supposedly in the area snatching local children at the time. If anything, it serves as a grim reminder that the old photographer's rule contending that it's easier to apologize (for taking a candid photo) than to ask permission doesn't really apply in Guatemala.

Sights

Museo Balam (tel. 5787-3598, 7 A.M.–9 P.M., $0.65) is to the left 150 meters off the main street one block from the park. Run by a friendly local family, it features marimbas, costumes for traditional village dances, and old leather sandals, bags, plows, and saddles, affording a glimpse into the town's history and traditions.

Todos Santos is one of very few places in Guatemala that still largely adheres to the 260-day Mayan calendar known as the Tzolkin. There are frequent rituals, including animal sacrifices, performed at a small Mayan site just above town known either as **Cumanchúm** or **Tojcunenchén.** The ruins look out onto the 3,650-meter (12,000-foot) **Chemal** peak (also known as "La Torre" for the radio mast atop it), which is the highest nonvolcanic peak in Central America. To reach the summit, hike or take a bus east to the neighboring village of La Ventosa, from where a trail leads past adobe houses through sylvan settings to the top, a journey of about 1.5 hours. Your reward on a clear day is a breathtaking view of Guatemala's volcanic chain from Tacaná on the Mexican border all the way east to Agua and Acatenango, near Antigua.

Todos Santos is well known for its annual November 1 horse races capping off weeklong festivities that include plenty of drinking, dancing, and general merriment. (See the sidebar *All Saints' Day in Todos Santos.*)

Hiking

There are numerous opportunities for hikes. If you want a guide or printed information to make the most of your walk, head to either of the town's two language schools. One of the most popular walks is to the site of **Las Letras,** the town's equivalent of the "Holly-wood" sign overlooking California's famous neighborhood. The Todos Santos version is a series of white painted rocks above town, with an arrangement that might be illegible depending on when they were last reassembled. It's about a two-hour hike round-trip. From there, you can continue another five hours to the villages of **Tuicoy** and **Tzichim. La Puerta del Cielo** is another amazing lookout point accessible via a detour from Tuicoy. A five-hour trek from Todos Santos is the village of **San Juan Atitán,** up the ridge looming over the village and down into a valley, crossing streams and verdant forests along the way.

Accommodations

Most of the town's accommodations can be found in a cluster up the hill about a block from the plaza. Only a few have phones to contact for reservations. **Hotel Casa Familiar** (tel. 7783-0656, $4 p/p) is a favorite with backpackers for its simple wooden rooms with shared hot-water bathroom run by a local family. The family also serves food. The best place in town (and that's not saying much) is **Hotelito Todos Santos** ($12–13 d) with basic tiled-floor rooms with shared or private hot-water bathroom. There's a basic café in the lobby. Next door is the bare-bones **Hotel Mam** ($3.50 p/p). Turning right up the hill at the end of this same street, you'll find **Hospedaje El Viajero** (tel. 7783-0705 or 5754-9760, $4 p/p), featuring rooms with bare concrete-block walls, hard beds, and little else, though there's a small terrace fronting some of them. All rooms share baths.

Food

There are a few decent places for food along the main street heading out from the plaza toward the main road and Huehuetenango. Among these is **Restaurante Cuchumatlán,** serving pizzas ($8 for a large pie), curry dishes, and fruit smoothies. It also has a book exchange. **Rebecca's,** just east of the park, is American-owned and serves sandwiches, stir-fry, and pastas. It's also a bookstore. For simpler fare, **Comedor Martita,** across the street from Hotel

Mam, and **Casa Familiar,** are both acceptable choices. Both of these places are inexpensive—expect to pay about $2–4.

Information and Services
For your banking needs, Banrural is on the trapezoidal plaza at the center of town. The post office and policep are also here. Along the main street leading out of town is Café Internet (tel. 5781-1059), charging $1.50 per hour for a somewhat slow Internet connection.

Language Schools
Todos Santos's two language schools charge about $120 per week for 4–5 hours of instruction per day plus homestay with a local family. Living conditions are very basic and most host families speak Mam, with a select few opportunities for homestay with Spanish-speaking families. Both schools also offer instruction in the local Mayan dialect. The two schools are **Academia Hispano Maya** (opposite Hotelito Todos Santos, www.hispanomaya.org) and **Nuevo Amanecer** (150 meters west of the plaza, escuela_linguistica@yahoo.com).

Getting There
There are seven daily buses to Huehuetenango (2.5 hours), the last one leaving at 3 P.M. They leave from the plaza.

SAN JUAN IXCOY TO BARILLAS
From the Paquix Junction, the spectacularly scenic road heads north to several mountain towns in the heart of the Cuchumatanes. Along the road are some exquisite pastures, which have been grazed since colonial times. Large, gray boulders are also strewn about and the frigid mountain scenery is at once beautiful and inhospitable. At the edge of the plateau, the road begins its steep descent shortly after passing a local limestone outcropping in the shape of two pointy teeth known as the **Piedras de Captzín.** The stones are sacred to the local Q'anjob'al.

San Juan Ixcoy is the first village you'll come across as you begin the descent from the plateau. Its women wear long, white *huipiles* with embroidery at the collar. In the vicinity of town are the **Los Jolotes** waterfalls, which got their name from a corruption of the Spanish word *tecolotes,* meaning "owls," which are said to be abundant in the surrounding forests. The waterfalls are part of the Río San Juan, a tributary of the Río Ixcán, which eventually flows into the mighty Río Usumacinta.

San Pedro Soloma
Another seven kilometers down the road is San Pedro Soloma, a fairly prosperous and surprisingly sizable town given its remote location deep in the mountains. It looks rather attractive from the surrounding mountainside as you descend into the green valley it occupies. The Mayans here also speak Q'anjob'al. Many of them have family members living in the United States, adding to the town's prosperity.

Soloma is a good place to break up the journey if you're headed north to Barillas. Among the options for accommodations is **Hotel Caucaso** (3a Calle 3A-37, tel. 7780-6179, $7 d), one block northeast of the plaza, with barebones rooms. The nicest place in town is **Hotel Don Chico** (4a Avenida 3-65 Zona 1, tel. 7780-6087, $20 d), where the comfortable rooms have hot water and cable TV. There's also underground parking and an Internet access center next door on the edge of a large parking lot bordering the hotel. Also found facing this lot is **Restaurante El Eden** (all meals daily), which serves good Guatemalan fare as well as pastas, sandwiches, and decent breakfasts. Another decent choice is **Restaurante Alma Latina,** on the plaza.

The pavement ends in Soloma, the rest of the way being a fairly well-maintained dirt road.

San Mateo Ixtatán
Continuing north, you'll pass the small village of **Santa Eulalia** before eventually arriving in the Chuj-speaking village of San Mateo Ixtatán, perched on the side of a mountain at 2,560 meters (8,400 feet). While the residents of neighboring villages travel to the coast for seasonal labor, those in San Mateo tend to work

their own lands tending sheep and growing coffee, cardamom, and grains. Like most other towns in Huehuetenango, however, a large percentage of its men travel to the United States in search of work. Another source of local prosperity are the community-owned salt mines. The town is well known for the production of its exotic black salt and its very name is a derivation of the Nahuatl word Ixtatlán, meaning "abundance of salt."

The town's pretty **church** somewhat resembles a giant birthday cake and is supposedly painted every year in different bright colors. I remember catching my first glimpse of its Technicolor facade in a *National Geographic* magazine from the late 1980s, but on my recent visit it was painted a rather unremarkable cream and white. The traditional *huipil* worn by San Mateo's women is one of Guatemala's finest, with concentric woven star patterns in reds, purples, and blues that verge on the psychedelic. Some of the men still wear the *capixay,* a thick, black-wool, open-sided pullover. The town's annual fiesta runs September 17–21. Market days are Thursdays and Sundays.

Just below the village are the unrestored ruins of **Wajxaklajunh,** which look out to a valley and surrounding mountain ridges. There are a few temples, some stelae, and a ball court.

Hotels here are very basic. If you should find yourself needing to spend the night here, head to **Hotel Ixtateco** (tel. 7756-6586), which at the very least has hot water.

A good source of information on San Mateo is the website of the Ixtatán Foundation (www.ixtatan.org), a development organization that has helped the town build its very first high school and has a variety of other projects in the works. It also runs an Internet cafá, Wajxaklajunh.com, charging about $1 per hour.

Barillas

The road out of San Mateo Ixtatán heads east and descends 28 kilometers to the ladino frontier town of Barillas, which lies at about the same altitude as Guatemala City. The town itself is fairly unremarkable, though it's interesting in that it borders the Ixcán wilderness to the north and west. There is one daily bus and several pickups heading east to Playa Grande via a rough road. The government has announced plans to construct a transversal highway stretching east–west from Izabal department through Alta Verapaz and Quiché all the way to Huehuetenango's Mexican border. If all goes to plan, it would be complete sometime around 2010.

Another 18 kilometers north from Barillas is the aquamarine **Laguna Maxbal,** surrounded by forests and a worthy, if little-explored, adventure option.

WEST TO MEXICO
La Mesilla

Heading northwest from Huehuetenango, the Pan-American Highway leads to La Mesilla border and, beyond that, Mexico. Border formalities here are pretty straightforward, though the Mexican border crossing lies four kilometers away on the other side at Ciudad Cuauhtémoc, for which you'll need to take a collective taxi ($0.50) if you're not in your own car. There are basic services here, including banks, a post office, police station, and ubiquitous money changers. If you get stuck here, head to **Hotel Mily's** (500 meters uphill from the border, $15 d), with fan-cooled rooms, cable TV, and private hot-water bathroom. Another alternative is **Hotel y Restaurante Maricruz** (about 200 meters from the border, tel. 7685-0532, $10 d), also with private bathrooms.

Nentón to Gracias a Dios

A few kilometers east of La Mesilla along the Pan-American Highway, a turnoff branches north down a newly paved road to the town of Nentón and continues to a new border crossing at Gracias a Dios. Along the way, you could stop to admire **El Cimarrón,** a cavernous, 300-meter-deep limestone sinkhole harboring a forest at its base that has only recently been descended and explored. From the main road about three kilometers from the village of **La Trinidad,** 35 kilometers north of Nentón, a network of trails leads through surrounding farmland and cattle pastures to the sinkhole. It's about a 30-minute walk from the road.

From La Trinidad, a dirt road leads east to the village of **Yalambojoch,** where you can grab a pickup to San Mateo Ixtatán. It also serves as the transit point for visits to the wonderful **Laguna Yolnabaj,** also known as Laguna Brava, five kilometers north of here. There are many returned refugees from Mexico living in these parts and you should be aware that the activities of foreign mining companies here and in other parts of northern Huehuetenango have locals a bit on edge. Exercise due caution. Bet-

ter yet, go with a guide. Quetzaltenango-based **Chilli Tours** (tel. 7761-2800) runs trips to El Cimarron and other attractions in the vicinity of Nentón, including Laguna Yolnabaj and the pristine **Río Azul,** which is a dazzlingly exotic hue of blue, as its name implies.

Border formalities at Gracias a Dios are also fairly straightforward and the friendly immigration agents might grant you a day pass to cross into Mexico to see the spectacular, nearby **Lagunas de Montebello,** a national park with pristine emerald lagoons surrounded by luxuriant forests.

Quetzaltenango (Xela) and Vicinity

Head southeast from Huehuetenango on the Pan-American Highway, some 80 kilometers toward Guatemala City, to the highland city of Quetzaltenango. The country's second-largest city is the main population center of the country's K'iche' Mayans and an increasingly popular destination with language school students and NGO workers. Its original K'iche' name is Xelajú, still widely in use today, though in its abbreviated form, Xela. Set in a sprawling valley dominated by the near-perfect cone of 3,770-meter (12,375-foot) Santa María Volcano and the adjacent (active) Santiaguito, the city has a population of about 300,000. It sits at a rather high altitude of 2,400 meters (8,000 feet) and can be correspondingly chilly.

Xela is very cosmopolitan and has all the feel of a European highland city. It is considerably safe for a city of its size and has a lively cultural scene peppered by the presence of an ever-increasing number of foreign visitors. There are also good hotels and restaurants, along with interesting day trips to neighboring highland Mayan villages that still adhere strictly to the old ways. Nearby natural attractions include a wonderful crater lake, climbs to the surrounding volcanoes, and soaking in warm hot springs. If you really start to long for the warmer climates, the sweltering Pacific

coastal lowlands are just about an hour away and beaches lie not much farther.

History

Quetzaltenango was originally a Mam-speaking Mayan town before coming under the influence of the K'iche'-speaking Mayans of K'umarcaaj

Pasaje Enríquez

© AL ARGUETA

THE WESTERN HIGHLANDS

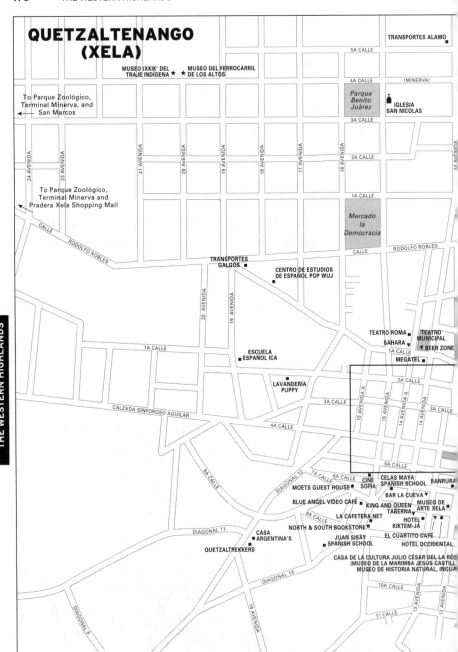

QUETZALTENANGO (XELA)

TRANSPORTES ALAMO ■

5A CALLE

MUSEO IXKIK' DEL
TRAJE INDÍGENA ★   ★ MUSEO DEL FERROCARRIL
DE LOS ALTOS

4A CALLE   (MINERVA)

*Parque
Benito
Juárez*

⬥ IGLESIA
SAN NICOLAS

To Parque Zoológico,
Terminal Minerva, and
San Marcos

3A CALLE

24 AVENIDA
23 AVENIDA
21 AVENIDA
20 AVENIDA
19 AVENIDA
18 AVENIDA
17 AVENIDA
16 AVENIDA

2A CALLE

To Parque Zoológico,
Terminal Minerva and
Pradera Xela Shopping Mall

1A CALLE

*Mercado
la
Democracia*

CALLE
RODOLFO ROBLES

CALLE   RODOLFO ROBLES

TRANSPORTES
GALGOS ■

CENTRO DE ESTUDIOS
DE ESPAÑOL POP WUJ

20 AVENIDA
19 AVENIDA

TEATRO ROMA ■   TEATRO
MUNICIPAL
SAHARA ▾   ▾ BEER ZONE

1A CALLE

1A CALLE
■ ESCUELA
ESPAÑOL ICA

MEGATEL ■

2A CALLE

LAVANDERÍA
PUPPY

15 AVENIDA A
15 AVENIDA A
14 AVENIDA A
14 AVENIDA

3A CALLE   3A CALLE

CALZADA SINFOROSO AGUILAR

4A CALLE

8A CALLE

5A CALLE

DIAGONAL 12

7A CALLE   6A CALLE   CINE   CELAS MAYA
SOFIA   SPANISH SCHOOL   BANRURAL

MOETS GUEST HOUSE ●
BAR LA CUEVA ▾
BLUE ANGEL VIDEO CAFÉ ■   KING AND QUEEN   MUSEO DE
TABERNA▾   ARTE XELA★

LA CAFETERA.NET   HOTEL ●
8A CALLE   ■ KIKTEM-JÁ   ▾ ▾

NORTH & SOUTH BOOKSTORE ■

CASA
● ARGENTINA'S   JUAN SISAY   EL CUARTITO CAFÉ
■ SPANISH SCHOOL   HOTEL OCCIDENTAL

QUETZALTREKKERS

DIAGONAL 11

CASA DE LA CULTURA JULIO CÉSAR DEL LA ROS
(MUSEO DE LA MARIMBA JESUS CASTILL
MUSEO DE HISTORIA NATURAL, INGUA

DIAGONAL 13

10A CALLE

13 AVENIDA
12 AVENIDA

DIAGONAL 8

19 AVENIDA

11 CALLE

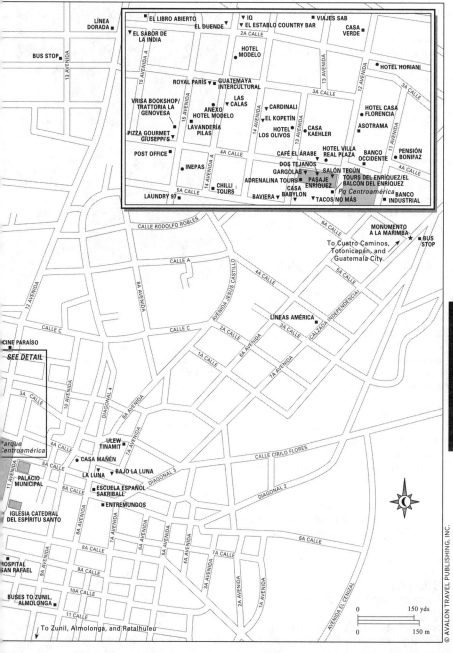

during their 14th-century expansionist wars. K'iche' leader Tecún Umán was defeated by Spanish conquistador Pedro de Alvarado in 1524 at a site known as Llano del Pinal, southwest of town at the base of Santa María Volcano. The town became quite prosperous during the 19th-century coffee boom. Its newfound prosperity, coupled with the abatement of Spanish power in the aftermath of independence, contributed to strong separatist sentiments shared with highland areas to the west. Guatemala City would bring the renegade region back into the fold in the latter part of the century, though Quetzaltenango remains a strong focal point for regional identity.

Like other Guatemalan population centers, it is no stranger to earthquakes, having been rocked by an earthquake and a volcanic eruption courtesy of Santa María Volcano in 1902. It was subsequently rebuilt, largely in neoclassical style. Its strategic location at a crossroads for trade and transport between the highlands and agriculturally rich Pacific slope have continued to ensure the city's prosperity despite any setbacks along the way. A regional railway once connected Xela to the Pacific slope, but natural disasters and political manipulation from Guatemala City made the railway, known as the Ferrocarril de los Altos, extremely short-lived.

Parque Centroamérica

© AL ARGUETA

Orientation

Quetzaltenango lies a few kilometers south of the Cuatro Caminos Junction, found along the Pan-American Highway. Its Zona 1 downtown core houses most of its important monuments, as well as the bulk of its tourist services, and is laid out in the standard grid pattern. Avenidas run roughly north–south and calles run east–west. Zona 2 covers an area to the northeast, while Zona 3 sprawls to the north and northwest. You'll find the city's bus station at this end of town.

SIGHTS
Parque Centroamérica

Like the rest of Guatemala's important urban centers, Xela is built around a central park. The city's sprawling Parque Centroamérica

is lined with government offices, museums, and a shopping arcade, among other buildings, and is itself splendidly shaded by trees and adorned by neoclassical monuments and flower beds. It gives the city a decidedly European feel, enhanced by the presence of several Greek columns, and is a fine place for people-watching or enjoying the warm afternoon sun amid the surrounding buzz of activity. An artisans' market is held here the first Sunday of every month.

At the western end of the park, between 12 and 13 Avenidas, is **Pasaje Enríquez,** a pedestrian thoroughfare and commercial arcade originally built to house fine shops but now home to several good bars and restaurants. One of these is on the second floor, from which there are wonderful views of the plaza below. Downhill toward the southern end of the plaza but still on its western borders is the **Museo de Arte Xela** (7a Calle 12-12 Zona 1, inside the Taller de Artes Plásticas, 8 A.M.–noon and 2–6 P.M. Mon.–Fri., 9 A.M.–1 P.M. Sat., $1), where the focus is on modern art exhibited by mostly young local talent. It's on the second floor of a building dating to 1909. The **Museo del Ferrocarril de los Altos,** dedicated to the early 20th-century railroad that briefly connected Xela to the coastal town of Retalhuleu, once occupied the first floor of this building. It was being moved to the site of the original train station, in Zona 3.

On the park's southern end is the Casa de la Cultura, housing the **Museo de Historia Natural** (Natural History Museum, 8 A.M.–noon and 2–6 P.M. Mon.–Fri., 9 A.M.–1 P.M. Sat., $1). The museum is an odd collection of taxidermy and rooms dedicated to the Liberal Revolution of 1871 which, together with the **Museo de la Marimba Jesús Castillo** (also housed here), were collectively christened "Museum of the Kitchen Sink" by this guide's previous author for its antique dealer's garage sale feel. I have to concur, and unless you have a rainy afternoon with nothing else to do, you're probably better off skipping this one.

On the eastern end of the park is the original facade of **Iglesia Catedral del Espíritu Santo,** which dates to 1535 and was constructed by Bishop Francisco Marroquín. The facade is all that remains of the original church, as a new church was erected behind it in 1899 and was very heavily damaged in the earthquake of 1902. The current cathedral building is the latest reconstruction. The neighboring **Municipalidad** (City Hall) was likewise reconstructed after the 1902 earthquake in grand neoclassical style.

Outside the City Center (Zona 3)

The legacy of maniacal dictator Manuel Estrada Cabrera's quest to emulate all things European, the neoclassical **Templo Minerva** is a monument to the Greek goddess of wisdom. It stands at the corner of Calle Minerva and Calle Rodolfo Robles. The temple looks over the city's bus terminal and busy market. Farther along, in Parque Minerva proper, is the **Parque Zoológico Minerva** (9 A.M.–5 P.M. Tues.–Sun., free), where there's an unimpressive collection of animals housed in cages. Buses to this part

of town leave from Pasaje Enríquez at 13 Avenida and 4a Calle Zona 1.

Formerly the Zona Militar 1715, the old building that once served as the train terminal for the defunct Ferrocarril de los Altos was slated to be the new home of the museum dedicated to its memory. It should be pretty spectacular, if a similar museum in Guatemala City is any indicator. It's now known as the Centro de Desarrollo Intercultural y Deportivo de Quetzaltenango, and there are plans for several other museums to open here in the coming years. Already housed in this complex is the **Museo Ixkik' del Traje Indígena** (4a Calle and 19 Avenida Zona 3, tel. 7761-6472, 9 A.M.–noon and 2–6 P.M. Mon.–Fri., $1), housing a collection of indigenous costumes.

ENTERTAINMENT
Bars

Beer drinkers will want to try Cabro, an excellent local brew sold widely in Xela. Among the liveliest and most popular places in town is **Casa Verde** (12 Avenida 1-40 Zona 1, tel. 7763-0271, 4 P.M.–midnight Tues.–Sun.), where the attractions alternate between live music, poetry readings, theater, and open-mike nights. There's also Thursday-night salsa dancing, pool, and board games to keep you stimulated at this restaurant-bar. Undergoing an expansion to include a second-floor bar-lounge and next-door restaurant, **Salón Tecún** (Pasaje Enríquez, on the west side of Parque Centroamérica, tel. 7761-2832) is a popular gathering spot with a great location and funky decor. There's also outdoor seating fronting the attractive Pasaje Enríquez pedestrian thoroughfare. Menu items include pizzas, pastas, vegetarian, and Thai dishes.

King and Queen Taberna (7a Calle 13-27 Zona 1, tel. 5493-1112, 7 P.M.–1 A.M. Mon.–Sat.), two blocks west of Parque Centroamérica, is a popular hangout with the language school and volunteer crowd. **Gargolas** (4a Calle 12-49 Zona 1, Pasaje Enriquez, 5 P.M.–1 A.M. daily) has a hip atmosphere and plays good music. You can drink at the bar or step into the stylish lounge areas to enjoy your evening under baroque, cathedral-like columns. **Iq** (14 Avenida "A" 1-37 Zona 1, tel. 5471-9222, 3 P.M.–1 A.M.) is a small bar where there are beers on tap and light fast-food–style pub fare for you to snack on. Also with beer on tap is **Beer Zone** (1a Calle 14-64 Zona 1, tel. 5336-1882, 7 P.M.–1 A.M.) with an eclectic music mix and beer also available by the meter. The bar inside **Pensión Bonifaz** (4a Calle 10-50 Zona 1, tel. 7765-1111) is the place to go for high-brow socializing.

Dancing
Sahara (14 Avenida "A" A-80 Zona 1, tel. 5554-0785, 8:30 P.M.–1 A.M. Thurs.–Sat.) is the town's salsa hot spot, tucked behind Del Teatro restaurant, which serves mainly pasta dishes. **Bar La Cueva** (13 Avenida 6-20 Zona 1, Pasaje Colonial, tel. 7741-8586, 9 A.M.–1 A.M. Tues.–Sat., 9 A.M.–5 P.M. Mon.) has a fun cave-like atmosphere with nice lounge areas and a dance floor. It's popular on weekends and it also serves light meals. If you enjoy dancing to Quebradito and Tejano music, check out **El Establo Country Bar** (14 Avenida "A" 1-49 Zona 1, tel. 5304-8481, 7:30 P.M.–1 A.M.) with cool country-western decor that includes saddle seats, popular with the city's *finquero* (farm and ranch-owning) crowd. For a more modern atmosphere reminiscent of a college dance club, head to **El Duende** (14 Avenida "A" 1-42 Zona 1, tel. 7765-1264, 7 P.M.–1 A.M. Wed.–Sat.), where you'll also find snacks and an antihangover soup. Let me know if it does the trick.

Performing Arts
There are sometimes cultural performances at the elegant **Teatro Municipal** (1a Calle between 14 Avenida and 14 Avenida "A"), which dates from 1908.

Cinemas
Blue Angel Video Café (7a Calle 15-79 Zona 1, 1–11 P.M. Mon.–Sat., 3–10 P.M. Sun.) shows movies at 8 P.M. nightly and serves vegetarian fare and smoothies. **Cinema Paraíso** (1a Calle 12-20 Zona 1, tel. 5408-1963, $1.50) is another café screening nightly movies. The newest video cinema in town is **Cine Sofia** (6a Calle 15-12 Zona 1, $1.50) showing international nonmainstream movies at 6 P.M. Monday–Friday, sometimes on a large screen if there's enough demand. **Teatro Roma** (14 Avenida "A" across from Teatro Municipal) sometimes screens movies. For the latest releases, head to **Cines Pradera Xela** (Avenida Las Américas y 7a Calle Zona 3, www.circuitoalba.com.gt, $3) inside its namesake shopping mall.

SHOPPING
Compared to Panajachel and Antigua, Xela is not a big shopping destination. A standout in this regard is **Asotrama** (12 Avenida 3-39 Zona 1, tel. 7765-8564), a women's cooperative of Mam, Cakchiquel, Ixil, Tzutuhil, and Quiché weavers that produces and sells high-quality products that are prewashed, preshrunk, and completely colorfast. There are scarves, purses, table runners, and some truly exquisite pillowcases for sale. For all your First World shopping needs, **Pradera Xela Shopping Mall** (10 A.M.–9 P.M. Mon.–Sat., 11 A.M.–8 P.M. Sun.) is on Avenida Las Américas between 7a and 8a Calles Zona 3, outside the city center.

Books
North and South Bookstore (8a Calle and 15 Avenida 13-77 Zona 1, tel. 7761-0589, 9:30 A.M.–6 P.M. Mon.–Fri., 9:30 A.M.–5 P.M. Sat.) sells a good selection of books in English with subjects including Guatemalan politics and history, travel guides, birding manuals, maps, Spanish textbooks, and dictionaries. **Vrisa Bookshop** (15 Avenida 3-64 Zona 1, tel. 7761-3237, 9 A.M.–7 P.M. Mon.–Sat.) sells mostly used books with some new titles, mostly in English. **El Libro Abierto** (15 Avenida "A" 1-56 Zona 1, tel. 7761-5195, 9:30 A.M.–5:30 P.M. Mon.–Fri., 11 A.M.–5 P.M. Sat.) has a wide selection of books in English and Spanish.

RECREATION
Volcano Climbs
Accessible from Xela are a variety of volcano hikes, including **Tajumulco Volcano,** which is Central America's highest and is in the neighboring department of San Marcos. Closer to

CLIMBING SANTA MARÍA VOLCANO

Santa María Volcano with smoking Santiaguito beside it

Santa María is one of the most popular volcano climbs from Xela, with spectacular views from its 3,772-meter summit. The trailhead is at the end of a paved road in the village of Llanos del Pinal. To get there, take one of the hourly pickups leaving from Xela's Cementerio General (General Cemetery) at 20 Avenida and 4a Calle 7 A.M.–5 P.M. Heading out of Llanos del Pinal, the road soon turns into a trail up the steep volcanic slopes, with painted arrows leading the way along this initial section of the footpath. About two hours from the starting point, you reach a flat grassy area known as "La Mesa," where the trail diverts to the right and then switchbacks up the mountainside through pine forests. This part of the climb is somewhat steeper, with the summit about three hours from this point. A few hundred meters from the summit, you'll see the end of the tree line and the summit itself, providing a much-needed mental boost for the end of your climb.

The best time to arrive at the summit is at sunrise, affording opportunities to take in the magnificent views before clouds start to roll in. From there, you can look southwest into the smoking crater of 2,500-meter Santiaguito Volcano, which has been belching out smoke and ash since its birth in 1902. To the east you'll see the cones of San Pedro, Tolimán, Atitlán, Acatenango, Agua, and Fuego. If you look west, you'll see the two highest volcanoes in Central America, Tajumulco and Tacaná, on the Mexican border.

Santa María's last major eruption took place on October 24 and 25, 1902, when it coughed up 10 cubic kilometers of ash into the stratosphere, covering much of the Pacific Coast and destroying a large section of the volcano's south face. Ash from the eruption is reported to have reached as far north as California.

The safety situation on the volcanoes in Xela's vicinity is markedly better than on those around Lake Atitlán, though robberies are by no means unheard of. It's best to go with a guide. **Quetzaltrekkers** (www.quetzaltrekkers .com) runs a fantastic once-a-month overnight trip up the slopes of Santa María in the light of the full moon, arriving on the summit just in time for sunrise. If peering into the summit of smoking Santiaguito has you itching for more volcanic adventures, you'll be happy to know it also runs trips to the challenging, ashy slopes of this smaller active volcano.

Xela is **Santa María Volcano,** affording excellent views all the way to Lake Atitlán as well as over its active, much smaller neighbor **Santiaguito Volcano.** Several local companies offer trips to all of these. (See *Guide Companies*). It is very easy to get lost on these peaks so a guide is strongly recommended. Hikers have gotten lost on the slopes of Volcán Santa María.

Rock Climbing

The **Cerro Quemado,** near Xela, offers good rock climbing on its 45-meter (150-foot) rock faces known locally as "La Muela." Routes include traditional climbs as well as sport climbing and are rated 5.07 to 5.13. **Vertical Expeditions** (tel. 5801-6871 or 5412-6717, www.verticalexpeditions.com.gt) offers one and two days of climbing with a minimum of four people for $75 and $80, including transport from Guatemala City or Antigua, guide, gear, meals, and overnight camping on the latter option. Antigua-based **Old Town Outfitters** (5a Avenida Sur #12C, Antigua, tel. 5339-0440, www.bikeguatemala.com) does a two-day trip for $150, leaving from Antigua and staying overnight in a Xela hotel. Locally based **Quetzaltrekkers** (Diagonal 12 8-37 Zona 1, inside Casa Argentinas, tel. 7765-5895, www.quetzaltrekkers.com) does a day trip for $20 p/p (minimum of four) including gear, transport, food, water, and guides.

Guide Companies

Highly recommended for volcano climbs as well as excellent tours to area attractions is **Adrenalina Tours** (13 Avenida and 4a Calle Zona 1, Pasaje Enríquez, tel. 7761-4509 or 7767-2474, www.adrenalinatours.com). Trips leave with a minimum of four people and include Santa María Volcano ($20 p/p), Chicabal Lagoon ($20), the Santiaguito Volcano lookout ($20), Tajumulco Volcano ($43), and a fantastic three-day hike to Lake Atitlán ($67). Adrenalina Tours can also book plane tickets and Tikal tours. The company operates shuttle bus service to Antigua, Guatemala City, Panajachel, the Mexican border, and Chichicastenango.

On the first floor as you go up to El Balcón del Enríquez restaurant, **Tours del Enríquez** (Pasaje Enríquez, tel. 7765-2296) does trips to Santa María Volcano with a minimum of two people for $25 p/p in addition to half-day visits to area hot springs and Mayan villages. It also offers transfer services in private vehicles.

With excellent guides and proceeds that go directly to fund projects that benefit Xela's street children, **Quetzaltrekkers** (Diagonal 12 8-37 Zona 1, inside Casa Argentinas, tel. 7765-5895, www.quetzaltrekkers.com) is highly recommended for its two-day volcano trips to Santiaguito and Tajumulco ($50), three-day treks to Lake Atitlán ($79), and a wonderful six-day highland trek between the villages of Nebaj and Todos Santos ($150). It also does a unique full-moon climb to Santa María Volcano to watch the sunrise ($17). Most trips leave on Saturdays and every other Wednesday depending on demand, but you can always get your own group together.

Chilli Tours (14 Avenida "A" 4-85 Zona 1, tel. 7761-2800, www.chillitoursguate.com) runs one- and two-day trips to the volcanoes as well as trips to off-the-beaten-path areas in neighboring Huehuetenango department and coastal Retalhuleu's coffee farms and beaches.

ACCOMMODATIONS
Under $10

Hotel Quetzalteco (12 Avenida, one block north of Parque Centroamérica, tel. 7765-8461, $9–13 d) is a decent-value hotel in an old colonial home where the 20 basic rooms have desks and reading lamps along with shared or private bathroom. The rooms upstairs are slightly nicer and there's a squawking parrot on the premises to keep you company.

Hotel Horiani (12 Avenida 2-23 Zona 1, tel. 7763-0815, $8 d) is another good value with better beds than others in its price range and clean rooms with shared bath. The woman who runs the place also does a good job of screening would-be troublemakers. It's a good choice for solo women travelers. **Moets Guest House** (7a Calle 15-24 Zona 1, tel. 5585-4213, $4 p/p) has just five rooms, all with shared bath, that are slightly nicer than others in this price range. There's a pleasant courtyard sitting area and a café-bar in the front lobby. **Casa Argentina's** (Diagonal 12 8-37 Zona 1, tel. 7761-2470, $3 in dorms, $4 p/p shared-bath room to $10 d with private bath) is a solid budget choice with 27 clean rooms. Some have cable TV and there are always tea, coffee, and purified water available. Guests have use of the kitchen. It's run by the very friendly and hospitable Leonor Morales and her charming mother. Quetzaltrekkers is housed here.

$10-25

Casa Kaehler (13 Avenida 3-33 Zona 1, tel. 7761-2091, $13–17 d) has pleasantly simple rooms, all but one with shared bathroom, furnished with reading lamps. It's run by a friendly Guatemalan woman and you can use the kitchen for $0.65. She'll also do your laundry for you (hang dried) for $2.75. Another good choice is **Hotel Kiktem-Ja** (13 Avenida 7-18 Zona 1, tel. 7761-4304, $21 d), housed in an old colonial building with wooden floors and a plant-filled courtyard. Some rooms have chimney and desks; all have reading lamps, hot-water bathroom and cable TV. **Hotel Occidental** (7a Calle 12-23 Zona 1, tel. 7765-4069, $16 d) has 10 spartanly decorated rooms with cable TV and private hot-water bathroom conveniently situated near Parque Centroamérica.

$25-50

Los Olivos (13 Avenida 3-32 Zona 1, tel. 7761-0215 or 7765-3469, $27 d) is a good choice if you're traveling with a rental car, thanks to a large covered parking lot. All rooms have private hot-water bathroom and cable TV housed around a covered opaque-ceiling courtyard. Basic meals are also available and the owners are quite friendly. **Hotel Modelo** (14 Avenida "A" 2-31 Zona 1, tel. 7761-2529, $40 d) is a well-situated, excellent-value hotel in an old colonial home run by a friendly Guatemalan family. The nicest rooms are in a section fronting the street and opening to a pleasant garden courtyard. All have private bathroom, tiled floors, cable TV, charm-

ing antique furniture, and warm wool blankets. The restaurant here serves excellent breakfasts. Down the street is the equally pleasant and somewhat quieter **Anexo Hotel Modelo** (tel. 7765-1271, $30 d). The rooms facing the street here are brighter and tend to feel airier, as they get sun and breezes all afternoon, which is more comfortable for those of us with rainy-season mold allergies. **Hotel Villa Real Plaza** (4a Calle 12-22 Zona 1, tel. 7761-4045, $43 d) is housed in a 19th-century building that once served as a prison. Some of the rooms tend to feel a little bit dark, but that's a common thing in Xela's older constructions. All have private bath, cable TV, and closets. Some have a chimney. The lobby has a nice restaurant set in a courtyard under an opaque roof. There are rooms in a newer section with somewhat bland decor that tend to get loud thanks to the presence of the hotel's conference center in this part of the lodge. **Hotel Casa Florencia** (12 Avenida 3-61 Zona 1, tel. 7761-2326, $32 d) has nice rooms with private bath, cable TV, wood paneling, tungsten reading lights, and nice extras such as shampoo and soap. The friendly innkeeper, Celeste, keeps it spotless.

$50-100

A gorgeous flower garden and rock waterfall set the mood as you enter Xela's most wonderfully atmospheric hotel, **Casa Mañen B&B** (9a Avenida 4-11 Zona 1, tel. 7765-0786, www.comeseeit.com, $50–100 d), with nine tastefully decorated rooms featuring exquisite furnishings, wool blankets and throw rugs, terra-cotta floors, cable TV, and private bathroom. There's a rooftop terrace bar with wonderful city views. The delicious breakfast is served in a pleasant dining room looking out to the peaceful garden courtyard.

The haunt of Guatemala's oligarchy on visits to Xela, **Pensión Bonifaz** (4a Calle 10-50 Zona 1, tel. 7765-1111, $65–100 d) is a beautiful hotel, though it tends to feel stuffy thanks to the pretentious front desk staff. It has spacious, well-decorated rooms with private bathrooms, desks, and cable TV. There are a restaurant, small gift shop, and a heated swimming pool in a pretty garden courtyard under an opaque ceiling letting in just enough sunlight. There's wireless Internet on the first floor and the rooms just above it (numbers 123-130) get a signal. More modern rooms are housed in a newer section, but those in the original building harbor all the charm.

Outside of Town

If you have your own car and find it more convenient to stay outside of town near the Cuatro Caminos Junction, your best bet is **Hotel del Campo** (Km. 224 Carretera a Cantel, tel. 7763-1665, $38 d), with cozy rooms equipped with hot-water private bathroom and cable TV. There's a business center with Internet, a pleasant dining room lined with overhanging ferns, and a heated, covered swimming pool.

FOOD
Cafés and Light Meals

Café El Árabe (4a Calle 12-22 Zona 1, tel. 7761-7889, noon–midnight daily, $4–10) serves delicious Middle Eastern fare, including fresh hummus and tasty falafel. It's conveniently situated just off the plaza and can also be a lively place at night. **Café Baviera** (5a Calle 13-14, tel. 7761-5018, 7 A.M.–8:30 P.M. daily, $3–5) has a decidedly German atmosphere chock-full of antiques where you can enjoy scrumptious pastries, sandwiches, crepes, and shakes in addition to some of the best coffee in town. **Café La Luna** (8a Avenida 4-11 Zona 1, tel. 7761-2242, 9:30 A.M.–9 P.M. Mon.–Fri., 4–9 P.M. Sat./Sun.) is wonderfully decorated with an eclectic mix of antiques, including old signs, gas lamps, cash registers, and even pre-Columbian artifacts. Menu options include great coffee, snacks, and desserts and there are daily specials of various Guatemalan dishes, including delicious enchiladas on Sundays. Try the scrumptious chocolate cake.

Around the corner and under the same ownership is **Bajo La Luna** (tel. 7761-2242, 8 P.M.–midnight Tues.–Fri.), a cozy wine cellar with a charming Old World feel where there's a good mix of bottled wines ranging in price $9–50. There are also various cheeses on offer. With wonderful views of Parque Centroamérica from its second-floor terrace, **El Balcón del Enríquez** (12 Avenida 4-40 Zona 1, tel. 7765-2296, all meals daily) is a good place to start the day or wind it up with a cup of coffee or cocktail while people-watching over the plaza below. There are good sandwiches, breakfasts, and pastries. For a quaint coffee-bar atmosphere, check out **El Cuartito Café** (13 Avenida 7-09 Zona 1, 10 A.M.–11 P.M. Wed.–Sun.), serving organically grown fair trade coffee, tea, and chocolate beverages in addition to tempting cookies and baked goods. There are books and board games to keep you entertained as well as live music some nights.

International

Your mouth will water as soon as you set foot inside **Casa Babylon** (corner 5a Calle and 13 Avenida, tel. 7761-2320, 11:30 A.M.–11 P.M. daily), with its ground-floor kitchen where you can watch your food being prepared. On offer are a variety of cocktails, a good Italian and French wine list, and nonalcoholic beverages, including fresh-fruit smoothies. Menu items include falafel, salads, tacos, quesadillas, pita pizzas, pastas, and vegetarian dishes. There are two more floors, including a nice third-floor lounge; you should call ahead and reserve, as it tends to get busy during dinner hours. **Restaurante Las Calas** (14 Avenida "A" 3-21 Zona 1, tel. 7765-1270, 7 A.M.–11 P.M. Mon.–Sat.) is tastefully decorated with a variety of art on rotating and permanent displays. Menu items include salads, Guatemalan food, steak, chicken, and seafood dishes. **Restaurante El Kopetín** (14 Avenida 3-51 Zona 1, tel. 7761-8381, 11 A.M.–10 P.M. daily) is a fairly stylish spot popular with locals serving a varied menu that includes tasty Cuban sandwiches.

Indian

Very much in vogue, **Sabor de la India** (2a Calle between 16 Avenida and 15 Avenida "A," tel. 7765-0101, 11 A.M.–9 P.M. Tues.–Sat., 5–9 P.M. Sun., $2–7) serves delicious vegetarian and nonvegetarian Indian dishes in generous portions.

Mexican and Tex-Mex

Xela now boasts an excellent Tex-Mex restaurant with the recent addition of 【 **Dos Tejanos** (4a Calle 12-33, Pasaje Enríquez, 7 A.M.–11 P.M. daily), where you can dig into authentic Texas barbecue ribs, chicken, and brisket. Serving Mexican food in the same commercial arcade is **Tacos No Más** (5a Calle 12-46 Zona 1, Pasaje Enriquez).

Italian

For authentic Italian food in a wonderful Old World family atmosphere, head to 【 **Restaurante Cardinali** (14 Avenida 3-25 Zona 1, tel. 7761-0922, 11:30 A.M.–10 P.M. daily). There's a large wine selection and various entrées in the $9 range. **Giuseppe's Gourmet Pizza** (15 Avenida 3-68 Zona 1, Edificio Santa Rita Segundo Nivel, tel. 7761-2521 or 7761-9439, 11 A.M.–9:30 P.M.) has fairly decent hand-tossed pizza and pastas. **Trattoria La Genovesa** (15 Avenida 3-64 Zona 1, tel. 5915-3231, dinner Tues.–Sun., $4–7), next to the Vrisa bookshop, has a front-side bakery selling pizzas, cakes, and tomato sauces. The Italian chef, Alfredo, cooks up some authentic recipes served al fresco in a pleasant garden courtyard.

Fine Dining

The dining room at the upscale **Pensión Bonifaz** (4a Calle 10-50 Zona 1, tel. 7765-1111, all meals daily) is a good place for a splurge with a variety of Guatemalan and international dishes served in a classy atmosphere frequented by the city's elite. 【 **Royal Paris** (14 Avenida "A" 3-06 Zona 1, tel. 7761-1942, noon–11 P.M. Tues.–Sun., 6–11 P.M. Mon., $5–15) is a very popular, highly authentic French restaurant with dishes that include crepes, baked camembert, and onion soup as well as meat and chicken that you can enjoy accompanied by excellent wines. There's live music on Friday and Saturday nights and French or Italian movies are shown on Tuesdays at 8 P.M.

INFORMATION AND SERVICES
Tourist Information

The INGUAT tourism information center (tel. 7761-4931, 9 A.M.–5 P.M. Mon.–Fri.) is on the southern end of Parque Centroamerica next to Casa de la Cultura, though you might have better luck getting information from local travel agencies such as Adrenalina Tours just a few steps away in Pasaje Enríquez.

Useful websites with some helpful information include www.xelapages.com, www.xelapages.net, www.xelawho.com, and Spanish-language www.xelaenlinea.com.

Communications

The main post office is at 4a Calle 15-07 Zona 1. Couriers include DHL (corner of 12 Avenida and 1a Calle Zona 1, tel. 7763-1209). Some travelers have complained of incorrect import duties for packages shipped to Guatemala via DHL.

There are dozens of places where you can access the Internet in Xela, with most places charging somewhere around $1.25 per hour. La Cafetera.net (corner of 15 Avenida and 8a Calle Zona 1, tel. 7761-0588, 8 A.M.–8 P.M. daily) is an Internet café next door to the North and South Bookstore serving snacks, coffee, sandwiches, and breakfasts. Online access costs about $0.85 an hour. Chilli Tours (14 Avenida "A" 4-85 Zona 1, tel. 7761-2800, 9 A.M.–8 P.M. Mon.–Sat.) also serves light fare and provides Internet access. Celas Maya (6a Calle 14-55 Zona 1, tel. 7761-4342, 8 A.M.–7:30 P.M. Mon.–Fri., 9 A.M.–7:30 P.M. Sat.) is a Spanish school with an Internet café charging about $0.85 an hour for online access. Infinito Internet (7a Calle 15-16 Zona 1) provides phone service to the United States for about $0.25 a minute, $0.40 per minute to Europe. Megatel (1a Calle 14-35 Zona 1, 8 A.M.–8 P.M. Mon.–Sat., 8 A.M.–6 P.M. Sun.) has slightly higher rates.

Money

There are several banks, some with ATMs, on Parque Centroamérica, including Banco de Occidente, on the north end of the park, where you can change cash dollars and travelers checks. Banco Industrial, on the east side of the plaza, has a Visa ATM, while Banrural, on its west side, has both a Visa and Master-Card ATM.

Laundry
It costs about $2.25 to wash and dry a load at Lavandería Pilas (15 Avenida 3-51 Zona 1, tel. 7765-4039, 8 A.M.–1 P.M. and 2–6 P.M. Mon.–Sat.). It's also at 7a Avenida 5-48 Zona 1 (tel. 7765-3220). Near the post office, at the corner of 5a Calle and 15 Avenida, Laundry 97 (tel. 7761-7923, 8 A.M.–8 P.M.) charges about $0.65 per kilo to wash and dry. Lavandería El Puente (7a Calle 13-29 Zona 1, 8 A.M.–6 P.M. Mon.–Sat.) charges $2 for a four-kilogram load, washed and dried. Lavandería Puppy (2a Calle 16-61 Zona 1, 7:30 A.M.–5:30 P.M. Mon.–Sat., 9:30 A.M.–3 P.M. Sun.) charges similar rates for laundry washed, dried, and folded.

Medical Services
Private hospitals include Hospital Privado Quetzaltenango (Calle Rodolfo Robles 25-31 Zona 3, tel. 7761-4381/82), Hospital La Democracia (13 Avenida 6-51 Zona 3, tel. 7763-6760/62), and Hospital San Rafael (9a Calle 10-41 Zona 1, tel. 7761-4414 or 7761-2956), with 24-hour emergency service.

Emergency
For the firefighters *(bomberos),* dial 122 or 7761-2002. For the Red Cross (Cruz Roja), dial 125 or 7761-2746. The Policía Nacional Civil (National Civil Police) can be reached at 120, 110, or 7765-4991/2. The number for the Municipal Police (Policía Municipal) is 7761-5805.

Travel Agencies
Viajes SAB (1a Calle 12-35 Zona 1, tel. 7761-6402) is a good all-around agency for plane tickets, tours to Tikal, and the like. Adrenalina Tours (13 Avenida and 4a Calle Zona 1, Pasaje Enríquez, tel. 7761-4509 or 7767-2474, www.adrenalinatours.com) is also

recommended for these and other services. Guatemaya Intercultural (14 Avenida "A" 3-06 Zona 1, tel. 7765-0040) is a good place for youth and student airfares as well as general travel arrangements.

Language Schools
Xela has become increasingly popular as a place to learn Spanish, even rivaling Antigua, and the days when Xela hosted few foreigners are long gone. Still, it's a much larger city than any other in Guatemala, save the capital, and affords an opportunity for the foreign population to more easily blend into their surroundings, providing an adequate Spanish-language immersion experience. Schools in Xela were charging between $135 and $180 per week for 25 hours of instruction and room and board with a local host family. Xela also tends to attract a rather humane crowd and so there are plenty of operations that allow you to combine your language instruction with some time working with charitable organizations. The following schools are recommended for their consistently good marks on student evaluations. If you're a college student, you may be able to get college credit with several of these language schools. Ultimately, you'll have to check the schools out to see which one works best for you. This is just one of the many things to consider when visiting potential schools. Rates go up between June and August, when college students come down in droves. Useful websites for checking out schools include www.123teachme.com and www.guatemala365.com.

Proyecto Lingüistico Quetzalteco de Español (5a Calle 2-40 Zona 1, tel. 7763-1061, www.hermandad.com) is an extremely popular school often booked months in advance. Students have the opportunity to volunteer with the school's Luis Cardoza y Aragon Popular Culture Center, next door, providing art, music, and computer skill instruction to underprivileged local children. There are also opportunities to work in reforestation projects and meet with human rights workers, former guerrilla combatants and union leaders. **Celas Maya** (tel. 7761-4342, www.celasmaya.edu

.gt) is another fairly popular school and is set around a pleasant garden courtyard. There's an adjacent Internet café.

Run by a cooperative of experienced teachers who are very active in social projects, **Centro de Estudios de Español Pop Wuj** (1a Calle 17-72 Zona 1, tel. 7761-8286, www.pop-wuj .org) is another highly recommended school. **Escuela de Español Sakribal** (6a Calle 7-42 Zona 1, tel. 7763-0717, www.sakribal.com), a school founded and run by women, has a project benefiting civil war widows and orphans. **Inepas** (15 Avenida 4-59 Zona 1, tel. 7765-1308, www.inepas.org) combines quality language instruction with a widely recognized service-learning program.

In business for more than 30 years, **Escuela de Español ICA** (19 Avenida 1-47 Zona 1, tel. 7763-1871, www.guatemalaspanish.com) runs social welfare projects that include a medical clinic, adult literacy education, and reforestation. **Juan Sisay Spanish School** (15 Avenida 8-38 Zona 1, tel. 7765-1318 or 7761-1586, www.juansisay.com) is named after a self-taught indigenous *primitivista* painter who was massacred in his home village on the shores of Lake Atitlán in 1989. It's run by a teachers' collective involved in numerous social projects. **Ulew Tinimit** (7a Avenida 3-18 Zona 1, tel. 7761-6242, www.spanishguatemala.org) is a good setup, allowing plenty of one-on-one instruction time with your individual teacher.

Volunteer Opportunities

There are several volunteer opportunities available in and around Xela, as there's plenty of work to be done in Guatemala's impoverished Western Highlands. Any of the town's language schools can help you get plugged in to volunteer projects. A particularly helpful organization for volunteer opportunities is EntreMundos (El Espacio, 6a Calle 7-31 Zona 1, tel. 5606-9070 or 7761-2179, www.entremundos .org), which publishes a widely available free publication (*EntreMundos*) and has several resources on its website, including a database with contact information and descriptions for more than 150 NGOs in Xela and vicinity.

GETTING THERE AND AROUND
Air

Xela's airport terminal is being upgraded as part of a Guatemalan governmental plan to revamp several domestic airports and should be completed by the end of 2007. The airport will be international with probable flights to parts of Mexico and daily flights to Guatemala City. Flights to GUA should cost in the vicinity of $65-70 one way and take about 22 minutes.

Bus

Xela is a transportation hub for many buses heading to and from highland destinations. Upon arriving in town, you can avoid ending up at the Minerva bus terminal, which is well outside the city center, by getting off at a stop at 7a Avenida and 7a Calle. You'll see a giant monument to the marimba with a Mayan woman atop it at a traffic circle on Avenida de la Independencia. Most buses stop here and you can grab a taxi or minibus to the city center. If you do end up at the terminal, you can grab a taxi or bus into town from an area three blocks south of the market stalls. Look for the bus labeled "Parque." As elsewhere, Pullman, or first-class buses, leave from their own stations throughout town. Second-class bus routes include the following:

To Antigua: Take any bus heading to Chimaltenango (including first-class buses to Guatemala City) and change buses there.

- **To Chichicastenango:** 10 daily buses, 2.5 hours, $1.50.

- **To Coatepeque:** Buses every 30 minutes, just under two hours, $1.25.

- **To Guatemala City:** Frequent buses from 3 A.M.–4:30 P.M., $5.

- **To Huehuetenango:** Buses every 30 minutes 5 A.M.–5:30 P.M., 1.5 hours, $1.

- **To La Mesilla (Mexican border):** Six daily buses, 3.5 hours, $2.

- **To Momostenango:** Every 30 minutes 6 A.M.–5 P.M., 1.25 hours, $0.60.

- **To Panajachel:** Buses at 5 A.M., 6 A.M., 8 A.M., 10 A.M., noon, and 3 P.M., 2.5 hours, $2.

- **To Retalhuleu:** Every 30 minutes 4:30 A.M.–6 P.M., one hour, $1. The bus will most likely read "Reu."

- **To San Pedro La Laguna (Lake Atitlán):** Six daily buses, 2.25 hours, $2.

- **To Totonicapán:** Buses every 30 minutes 6 A.M.–5 P.M., one hour, $0.50.

- **To Tecún Umán (Mexican border):** Buses leave hourly 5 A.M.–2 P.M., 3.5 hours, $2.50.

- **To Zunil:** Every 30 minutes 7 A.M.–7 P.M., 30 minutes, $0.35.

First-class bus lines with service to Guatemala City include the following: **Líneas Américas** (7a Avenida 3-33 Zona 2, tel. 7761-2063), with six daily buses; **Transportes Alamo** (14 Avenida 5-15 Zona 3, tel. 7761-7117), six daily buses; **Transportes Galgos** (21 Calle 0-14 Zona 1, tel. 7761-2248), seven daily; and the ultraluxe, nonstop service of **Línea Dorada** (12 Avenida and 5a Calle Zona 3, tel. 7767-5198 or 7761-4509), with departures at 4 A.M. and 2:30 P.M.

Shuttle Buses

There are also a number of companies running shuttle buses to destinations that include Guatemala City, Antigua, Panajachel, the Mexican border, Chichicastenango, and Huehuetenango. **Adrenalina Tours** (13 Avenida and 4a Calle Zona 1, Pasaje Enríquez, tel. 7761-4509 or 7767-2474, www.adrenalina tours.com) is recommended for dependable shuttle-bus service.

Car Rental

Adrenalina Tours (13 Avenida and 4a Calle Zona 1, Pasaje Enríquez, tel. 7761-4509 or 7767-2474, www.adrenalinatours.com) rents vehicles, as do **Tabarini** (9a Calle 9-21 Zona 1, tel. 7763-0418, www.tabarini.com) and

Tours El Enríquez (Pasaje Enríquez, tel. 7765-2296).

Bike Rentals

For bike rentals, head to **Vrisa Bookshop** (15 Avenida 3-64 Zona 1, tel. 7761-3237, 9 A.M.–7 P.M. Mon.–Sat., $6/14/27 for daily/weekly/monthly rentals.

NEAR QUETZALTENANGO

The towns and villages surrounding Quetzaltenango make for some interesting day trips. Found nearby are the Santa María and Santiaguito Volcanoes (see *Volcano Climbs* under *Recreation*), hot springs, Indian markets, colorful churches, and an exquisite crater lake.

Almolonga

Just five kilometers southeast of Xela is the pleasant town of Almolonga, which has become quite prosperous by commercializing its excellent and abundant vegetables grown in a fertile valley. It has a lively market on Tuesdays, Thursdays, and Saturdays, where you can see its rich produce selection, including the largest carrots you've ever laid eyes on and baseball-size radishes. The cultivated plots here, as in neighboring Zunil, are irrigated by canals from which farmers scoop out water with large shovel-like contraptions.

The town's yellow and blue church, **Iglesia de San Pedro,** dates to 1608 and is now more of a tourist attraction with 90 percent of the local populace claiming conversion to Evangelical Christianity. Evangelicals point to the town's prosperity and uncommonly rich produce as evidence of the town's unique blessing. Its annual **Festival de San Pedro y San Pablo** takes place from June 27 to 29. Buses leave Xela's Minerva bus station every 15 minutes for Almolonga.

Just below the village, the road passes several hot springs known as **Los Baños** and popular with locals, though I can't bring myself to recommend them, as they are rather dilapidated and dirty, and there are better places to soak farther along the highway.

Zunil

A few kilometers farther along the same road is the spectacularly set town of Zunil. You'll see the white **Iglesia de Santa Catarina** gleaming from a distance as it towers above the tiled- and tin-roofed houses around it. Lovely mountains flank its surroundings. Zunil is one of a handful of towns in Guatemala where there is still strong adherence to the worship of the **Maximón** idol, as in Santiago Atitlán. The idol's location is rotated yearly, but it's easy to find out its whereabouts from any local resident, assuming the local children don't first intercept you and offer their guiding services for a small tip. It's known locally as San Simón and, unlike elsewhere, visitors here can actually pour liquor offerings down the effigy's throat. You'll probably be charged around $1 to see it, more if you want to take photographs.

Zunil's annual fiesta takes place on November 25.

Las Cumbres

About half a kilometer south of town is **(Las Cumbres** (tel. 5399-0029, www.ecosaunaslas cumbres.com, 7 A.M.–7 P.M. daily), a superb establishment harboring steam baths, beautiful accommodations housed in quaint red-tiled-roof cottages with mountain views, and a restaurant (all meals daily) serving mostly Guatemalan dishes but also sandwiches and wine. Thermal pools were in the planning stages and may be up and running by the time you read this. Its 11 rooms range $33–47 d and have nice wooden furnishings with warm wool blankets, private bathrooms, cable TV, CD player, and plenty of rustic charm. Some have their own in-room hot tubs. If you don't want to stay but just want a steam bath, you can have a private sauna for $3.50. Room rates include sauna access. There are also a squash court, pool table, and a small gym.

Fuentes Georginas

A popular day trip from Xela with locals as well as visitors, the Fuentes Georginas hot springs (tel. 5704-2959, 8 A.M.–6:30 P.M. Mon.–Sat., 7 A.M.–5 P.M. Sun., $2.75) were hit hard by Hurricanes Mitch and Stan in the past few years. The first of these wiped out a Hellenic statue that once gazed upon the pools and the second hurricane filled its main pool with mud and debris. It's all up and running, however, and in addition to the wonderfully warm thermal pools you can enjoy a fairly decent restaurant serving cocktails overlooking the emerald-green waters surrounded by tropical ferns and flowers. There are also sheltered picnic areas with barbecue pits for which you'll need to bring your own fuel. Trails lead to the Zunil and Santo Tomás Volcanoes with guides available at the restaurant for about $10. The hikes require about 3–5 hours one-way. There are accommodations available but they are not recommendable. The management assures me there are plans to invest some money into upgrading the accommodations once they've fully recovered financially from the last hurricane.

To get here, you can first take a bus to Zunil leaving frequently from Xela's Minerva bus terminal and then take a pickup the rest of the way (eight kilometers) to the hot springs. You can also walk from Zunil in about two hours. Head out from the plaza going uphill to the Cantel road (about 60 meters), turning right, and then going downhill to where you'll see a sign for the hot springs indicating their distance eight kilometers away. The easy way to get here is to book a trip through any of the local guide companies, including Adrenalina Tours, which runs transfers to the site at 8 A.M. and 2 P.M. for $10.

Cantel

Along an alternate route heading from Xela to Zunil via Las Rosas junction and bypassing Almolonga, Cantel lies 10 kilometers east of Xela and about three kilometers east of Zunil. It became an industrial suburb and one of the principal economic engines behind Xela's late 19th-century prosperity with the establishment of the **Fábrica de Hilados y Tejidos de Cantel,** which was somewhat like a modern-day sweatshop providing European technology and production methods to an already established weaving tradition. It began operations in 1883 and once employed 500 workers from Xela's total population of 30,000 inhabitants. The textile factory is still in operation and continues to put out a vast array of good-quality fabrics.

Today the town is better known as the site of the **Copavic Glass Factory** (Carretera al Pacífico, Km. 217.5, Cantón Pasac II, tel. 7763-8038, www.copavic.com), found along the road to Zunil and producing outstanding hand-blown glass made exclusively from recycled materials and exported around the world. The factory is open for tours 10:30 A.M.– 1:30 P.M. Monday–Friday and 10:30 A.M.–12:30 P.M. on Saturday. The sales floor is open 9 A.M.–6 P.M. Monday–Friday and 9 A.M.–1 P.M. Saturday.

Salcajá

Coming into Quetzaltenango from the Pan-American Highway, you'll pass this somewhat ugly town which nonetheless has a few noteworthy features. Among them is Central America's first Christian church, the **Iglesia de San Jacinto,** found two blocks west on 3a Calle from the main road (3a Avenida). It dates to 1524 and has a pretty facade with some interesting carvings. The interior boasts an ornate altar and some colonial-era paintings. Salcajá's other claim to fame is a pair of fermented beverages, including a uniquely fruity concoction made from pears, apples, peaches, and *nances* (white cherries), known as *caldo de frutas.* Its other adult beverage is *rompopo,* essentially a Mesoamerican eggnog made from egg whites, rum, sugar, crushed almonds, and assorted spices, including vanilla and cinnamon. It tastes much better than it looks. You can pick up small bottles of either of these drinks from local stores, including **Rompopo Salcajá** (4a Calle 2-02), a block east of the main road.

West to San Martín Sacatepequez

Head west from Xela 15 kilometers through the valley to the prosperous farming village of San Juan Ostuncalco, with a lively Sunday market. From the adjacent town of Concepción Chiquirichapa, the road climbs into the surrounding mountainside before once again descending into a fertile agricultural valley occupied by the village of San Martín Sacatepequez, also known as San Martín Chile Verde. Much of the land's fertility is owed to its proximity to Santa María Volcano, which provides ash-rich soil. It's a mixed blessing, however, as demonstrated by a 1902 eruption that buried the village in several feet of ash and volcanic rocks. San Martín, a Mam-speaking village, is a standout for its beautiful village costume consisting of a long white tunic with red stripes and elaborate embroidery around the cuffs, worn by village men. The look is completed with a bright red sash worn around the waist. The women wear bright red *huipiles* with blue *cortes.*

◖ Laguna Chicabal

From San Martín, it's a two-hour hike to the magical Chicabal Lagoon, ringed by lush cloud forest in a spectacular volcanic crater at an altitude of 2,700 meters (8,900 feet). It can be reached by taking the signed path on the right side of the road from where the bus drops you off heading into town. From there you'll go uphill through fields, cresting and descending a hill. You'll soon see the rangers' station, where you pay a $2 park entrance fee. If you've driven out this way, parking costs an additional $1.30. There's a rustic visitors center here where you can get food. There are also some very rustic bungalows with a (cold-water) shared bathroom. Bring your own sleeping bag if you're thinking of staying here. You can camp on the shore of the lagoon for $1.30, though most folks end up camping at the visitors center.

From the visitors center it's about 30–45 minutes, uphill, to a wonderful lookout point where you might catch a glimpse of the fantastic crater lake ringed by verdant cloud forest. Most of the time, however, the clouds have the view completely socked in. From the lookout, a trail of stairs descends to the lakeshore and the gorgeous lagoon, which is caressed by wisps of cloud just barely glancing the waters' surface. You'll soon realize why it's considered sacred by modern-day Mayans and a central element of their creation myths. An annual event includes 40 continuous days of prayers for rain and healing, ending on May 3. During the last few days culminating on this date, the lagoon is essentially off-limits to outsiders so as to allow the ceremonies to proceed undisturbed. Bathing in the lagoon's waters is strictly off-limits at all times and, as always, you should be careful to respect the native culture by not photographing any ceremonies that might be in progress throughout the year. You'll find the locals extremely friendly and willing to answer your questions if you put forth the effort to inquire amicably. As always, a smile goes a long way.

San Andrés Xecul

A road branches off to the west from a crossroads between Salcajá and the Pan American Highway junction at Cuatro Caminos leading to San Andrés Xecul, home to a stunning Technicolor dream of a church festooned with vines, saints, and assorted other characters. It's easily one of Guatemala's most photographed churches, and certainly one of its most bizarre. It's certainly worth a look.

Totonicapán

From the Cuatro Caminos Junction, the road heads northeast for 30 kilometers through pine-studded forests to the departmental capital of Totonicapán, also known as San Miguel Totonicapán. It's a fairly laid-back town with few foreign visitors. Sights include the ubiquitous town church, on a plaza superjacent to a second one below it harboring a statue of indigenous leader Atanasio Tzul, who led a peasant rebellion in 1820 spurred by government demands for taxation. Also on the upper plaza is a far less common **municipal theater,** built in 1924 in neoclassical style. It has been recently restored and painted in bright orange. The town's other main attraction is the **Casa de la Cultura Totonicapense** (8a Avenida 2-17 Zona 1, tel. 7766-1575), which was closed for remodeling. It should continue to house displays, including audiovisual presentations of local indigenous culture, history, and crafts, upon reopening.

San Andrés Xecul

© AL ARGUETA

The visitors center also offers tours to local artisans' workshops and the opportunity to try some Mayan dishes in local homes.

Totonicapán is especially lively during its annual **Festival Tradicional de Danza,** usually late in October. It is also kicking during its annual fiesta dedicated to the archangel Michael from September 24–30. The day marking the apparition of said heavenly figure, May 8, is also celebrated with dancing and fireworks.

If you need to stay in Totonicapán, a good budget choice is just next door to the Casa de la Cultura Totonicapense. **Hospedaje San Miguel** (8a Avenida 7-49 Zona 1, tel. 7766-1452, www.hoteltotonicapan.com, $8–16 d) has rooms on the third floor with shared bath or on the second floor with private bathroom, TV, and slightly more cheerful surroundings. The 23 rooms are clean and have some furniture, including desks. Try to get a room facing the street. On the pricier side is the nicest place in town, **Hotel Totonicapán** (8a Avenida 8-15 Zona 4, tel. 7766-4458, $28 d), with well-furnished rooms painted in cheery yellow pastel tones housing handcrafted wooden furniture, cable TV, city views, and private hot-water bathroom. Its pleasant lobby restaurant serves Guatemalan and international dishes. Closer to the town center, a decent place to grab a bite to eat is **La Hacienda** (8a Avenida 3-25 Zona 1), a steak house also serving some lighter Guatemalan dishes.

San Francisco El Alto

Just north of the Cuatro Caminos Junction, San Francisco El Alto is the site of the country's largest market, an extremely authentic affair that takes place on Fridays. It is not at all a tourist market like the one in Chichicastenango and you'd be hard-pressed to find touristy handicrafts and *típica* here. But, if you're in the mood to see an authentic Indian market, this is certainly the place. An added bonus is the wonderful view of Xela from here, thanks to a splendid hilltop location overlooking the larger city. The best views are from the top of the town's church. The caretaker should let you up there.

Momostenango

Another few kilometers along a beautifully pine-forested mountain road brings you to the town of Momostenango, famous for its delightfully warm wool blankets, which you can shop for at the twice-weekly markets on Wednesday and Sunday. Adherence to the Mayan calendar and traditional Mayan ceremonies are still very much in evidence here.

Among the attractions here is an interesting geological formation known as **Los Riscos,** essentially like large outdoor stalagmites, and made of eroded clay and crystalized stone. They're worth a look, though you might find the litter in the vicinity of the rock formations a bit unnerving, as is often the case in rural Guatemala. They're about 500 meters outside of town. Anyone can point the direction, and there are signs to guide you once you're on the way.

Momostenango's annual fiesta, the **Octava de Santiago,** takes place July 28–August 2. There are also dances held a few times a year, most notably on Christmas and New Year's Eve, when townsfolk performing the displays dress up in devil costumes and drink copious amounts of liquor.

Momostenango is accessible via frequent second-class bus from Xela's Minerva bus depot as well as from the Cuatro Caminos Junction and San Francisco El Alto. If you find yourself needing to spend the night here, your best bet among the ramshackle list of accommodations is **Hotel Estiver** (1a Calle 4-15 Zona 4, tel. 7736-5036, $5–7 d), which actually looks nicer from the outside. There are 12 spartan rooms with shared or private bathroom with hot water, some with balconies. A backup plan is the centrally located **Hospedaje Posada de Doña Pelagia** (2a Avenida "A" Zona 1, tel. 7736-5175, $2 per person), where you get a roof over your head and a room lit by a solitary lightbulb hanging on a wire. Bathrooms are shared. The rooms are centered around a courtyard and if you've brought a deck of cards you'll have to play elsewhere, as a sign clearly denotes that card-playing is strictly *verboten*. For food, there are a number of very basic *comedores* near the plaza.

THE PACIFIC COAST

Long-overlooked by travelers to Guatemala because of the absence of wide sandy beaches, the country's Pacific Coast is increasingly finding its way onto many travelers' itineraries. Cruise ships now regularly dock at Puerto San José, taking day-trippers inland to Antigua and some area attractions. While many of the Pacific Coast beaches are not particularly good for swimming because of riptides, they are noteworthy because of their dark sand, the product of nearby volcanoes, which can be seen in the distance on a clear day.

The Pacific slope is a very distinct geographic region characterized by a rather dramatic decrease in elevation from the mountainous highlands to the north. The daily high temperatures here hover at around 85°F year-round, but they are cooled by a fairly constant breeze the closer you get to the ocean. The region is home to vast sugarcane, coffee, and cotton plantations, which have dominated the local economy for centuries. Adding to its economic prominence is the presence of some important ports, including Puerto San José and Puerto Quetzal. The Canal de Chiquimulilla runs from the coastal town of Sipacate east all the way to Las Lisas near the Salvadoran border, forming a large barrier island along much of the coast. You'll have to cross this canal to get to many of Guatemala's beach towns. Tourism is just now becoming an important player in the regional economy.

The Pacific Coast has several attractions to recommend it, including the world-class theme parks of Xocomil and Xetulul, the archaeological sites of Takalik Abaj, El Baúl and

© AL ARGUETA

HIGHLIGHTS

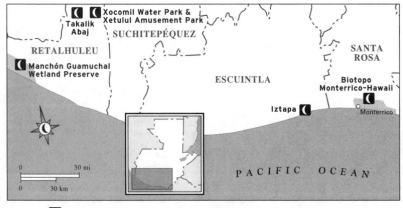 **Xocomil Water Park and Xetulul Amusement Park:** This amazing recreational center and its unique accommodations have quickly become Guatemala's top tourism draw and are certainly worth a stop if traveling to Guatemala with children or if you just need to indulge your inner child (page 192).

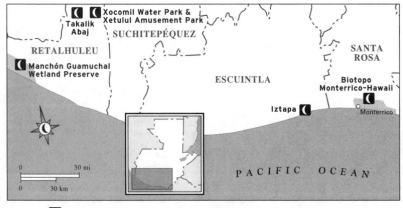 **Takalik Abaj:** This unique site spread over a series of terraces and coffee farms reveals interesting elements of Olmec influence in early Mayan culture. Adding to its allure is a wonderful lodge found on its ninth terrace (page 194).

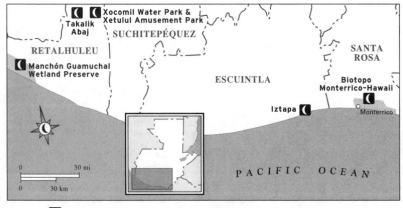 **Manchón Guamuchal Wetland Preserve:** These important protected wetlands are an excellent spot for birdwatching, which you can do along the canals lining the dense mangrove forests. The clean,

gently sloping dark-sand beaches here are also among Guatemala's best-kept secrets (page 197).

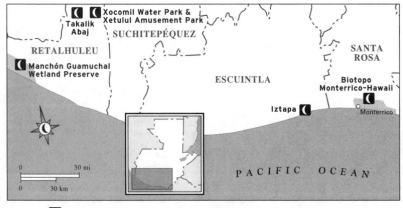 **Iztapa:** Guatemala is undoubtedly the sailfishing capital of the world, with several world records for single-day catch and release in the waters just off the coast of Iztapa. Several new outfitters and lodgings have sprung up to accommodate the wishes of this very distinct class of adventure travelers (page 203).

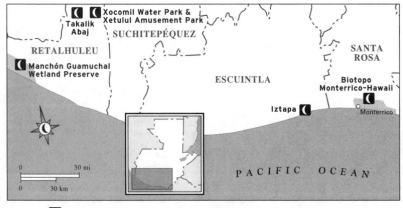 **Biotopo Monterrico-Hawaii:** Here is one of Guatemala's most popular, accessible beaches with a wide range of nearby accommodations. In season, you'll have the rare chance to spot a nesting sea turtle or interact with baby sea turtles at the local turtle hatchery before their initial voyage out to sea (page 209).

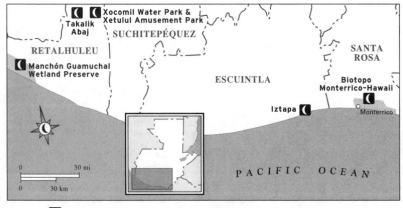

LOOK FOR TO FIND RECOMMENDED SIGHTS, ACTIVITIES, DINING, AND LODGING.

THE PACIFIC COAST

La Democracia, the Monterrico sea turtle preserve with its black-sand beaches, an emerging surf scene in Sipacate, and some of the best sailfishing in the world centered around Iztapa. All of these are becoming more easily accessible with plans for a trans-Pacific highway, at least two regional airports and, eventually, the construction of a new international airport to serve Guatemala City.

In addition to the dark-sand beaches and volcanoes, the Pacific Coast offers the chance to enjoy a holiday in warm tropical weather, relaxing in a hammock strung between graceful coconut palms. This can be a welcome respite from an extended stay in the more temperate (and sometimes chilly) Guatemalan highlands.

Border towns, beginning with El Carmen and then moving south and east from the Mexican border, are not covered in depth, as they are generally unattractive and increasingly unsafe. There is no reason to linger in these parts.

PLANNING YOUR TIME

Two nights would be optimal to explore and enjoy the twin parks of Xetulul and Xocomil. A few hours is enough time to explore the ruins of Takalik Abaj, but the excellent accommodations at Takalik Mayan Lodge might keep you busy for another two days. From here or nearby Retalhuleu, you can explore the Manchón Guamuchal wetlands for some bird-watching or just unwind at its beautiful beaches. Retalhuleu also makes an excellent base for exploring some of the surrounding countryside by bike, thanks to the presence of an excellent outfitter based here.

If you are in search of sand and sun, you might find yourself spending several nights at Monterrico. If your interest lies in surfing, you'll certainly want to spend a few days in Sipacate or Iztapa. For sailfishing, Iztapa is the place to go and you'll probably spend at least three days here. The 25-kilometer road between Iztapa and Monterrico is shaping up to be the closest thing to a Guatemalan Riviera and will certainly undergo some drastic changes in the next few years. For now, it's still a sleepy seaside area largely dedicated to the production of loofah. East toward El Salvador is another small seaside town, Las Lisas, with a couple of noteworthy accommodations, but unless you're heading out in this direction it's a bit out of the way.

WESTERN BORDER CROSSINGS

The northernmost and quieter of the two border crossings is found at **El Carmen,** where a bridge across the Río Suchiate connects it with Talismán, Mexico.

The more active (and preferable) border crossing is at **Ciudad Tecún Umán,** 39 kilometers south. A bridge links this city to its Mexican counterpart at Ciudad Hidalgo. There are frequent buses from here to points along the Pacific Coast Highway (CA-2) including Coatepeque, Retalhuleu, Mazatenango, and Escuintla. Buses also depart from here to Guatemala City and Quetzaltenango. You can connect to either of the latter two via Retalhuleu, a better place to linger if a bus is not immediately available.

Both borders are open 24 hours, but you should try to be out of border areas by dark. As elsewhere in Central America, border areas here are rife with crime thanks to immigrants trying to make their way northward and those who prey on them. There are some basic hotels and restaurants here.

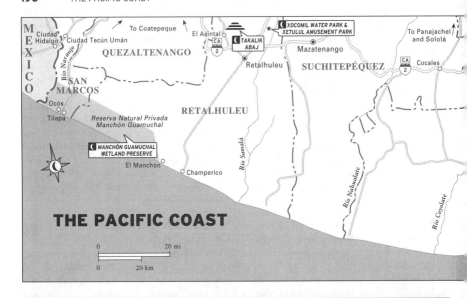

THE PACIFIC COAST

```
0        20 mi
0     20 km
```

Retalhuleu and Vicinity

East from the Mexican border, the first town of any real interest to visitors is a rather pleasant place with a newfound importance as the gateway to some increasingly popular attractions. The most prominent of these are also Retalhuleu's newest: the twin amusement parks of **Xocomil and Xetulul,** just a few minutes outside of town. Adding to its prominence as the southern coastal region's new recreational hub is the proximity of the ruins of **Takalik Abaj** and some decent stretches of beach within a relatively short distance.

Commonly referred to as "Reu" by locals, the town has always been the playground of local coffee and sugarcane farmers, a fact that will be readily apparent by the prevalence of roadside hotels with sparkling swimming pools and pleasant outdoor restaurants. The weather here is warm year-round, but you can always find shelter from the scorching sun under the abundant palm trees, as you will see from the palm-lined boulevard leading to the town center from the main highway.

Reu is becoming increasingly attractive as a hub for exploring this seldom-visited area of Guatemala. Even if amusement parks aren't your thing, there is plenty to keep you busy here and very comfortable accommodations from which to base your explorations. At least one outfitter has begun to unravel the beauties of this pleasant sun-kissed stretch of the Pacific lowlands.

SIGHTS

Downtown Retalhuleu's main attraction, aside from the central square, is the **Museo de Arqueología y Etnología** (6a Avenida 5-68 Zona 1, 8 A.M.–5:30 P.M. Tues.–Sat., 9 A.M.–noon Sun., $1.50 admission,) featuring archaeological relics on the ground floor and a collection of historical photographs from various stages of the city's past on the second floor.

GUIDE COMPANIES

Retalhuleu is home to one of Guatemala's better outfitters. **Reuxtreme** (4a Calle 4-23 Zona 1, tel. 5202-8180 or 5205-1132, www.reuxtreme.com) offers a variety of activities for the active

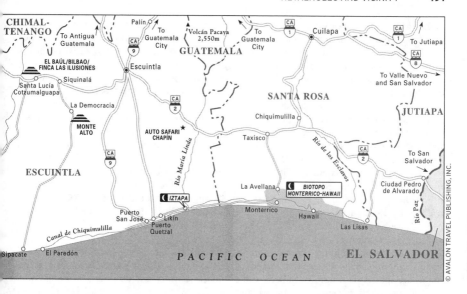

© AVALON TRAVEL PUBLISHING, INC.

traveler, including mountain biking to Champerico along the old railroad tracks passing over some very old bridges, kayaking in Manchón Guamuchal Wetland Preserve, treks to Quetzaltenango's Chicabal Volcano and Lagoon, coffee tours to local farms, and nighttime trips to Takalik Abaj. The outfit is run by Alejandro and María Mercedes Ravanales, a friendly Guatemalan brother-and-sister team who also manage the Hostal Casa Santa María.

SHOPPING

Retalhuleu's impressive outdoor shopping mall, **Centro Comercial La Trinidad,** is near the bus depot at 1a Calle and 5a Avenida "A" Zona 5, and has a modern grocery store, cell phone stores, banks, ATMs, and even a Radio Shack for all your technological needs while on the road. A large condominium complex is also planned here, attesting to the town's prosperity and its status as an enclave of the agricultural elite.

ACCOMMODATIONS

There are several motel-style places lining the main highway just outside of town where Guatemalan families like to stop and visit while

en route from chillier locales in the highlands. These places tend to get a bit noisy on weekends, but during the week they tend to be quite silent. **Hotel La Colonia** (at Km. 178, Carretera al Pacífico, tel. 7772-2048 or 2426-3894) is an old standby with spotless, comfortable, air-conditioned rooms. There is a swimming pool with a pleasant restaurant and bar. Rooms in duplex bungalows go for $50 d on weekends and $32 d during the week. You can use the pool for the day at a cost of $1.25. At the intersection where roads split off toward Champerico and Quetzaltenango is **Hotel Siboney** (tel. 7772-2174 or 7772-2176, $40 d) with pleasant rooms centered around two swimming pools. All have air-conditioning, firm mattresses, cable TV, phone, hot water, and a desk. Rooms are in older and newer sections, so ask to see a room first. It costs $2 to swim here. Also outside of town are the excellent Hostales del IRTRA. (See *Xocomil Water Park and Xetulul Amusement Park* under *North and West of Retalhuleu* for more information.)

In the heart of town, the most atmospheric of Retalhuleu's accommodations can be found at the family-run **(Hostal Casa Santa María** (4a Calle 4-23 Zona 1, tel. 5202-8180 or

THE PACIFIC COAST

5205-1132, www.hostalcasasantamaria.com), where eight tastefully decorated rooms in a colonial home come with private hot-water bath, cable TV, wireless Internet, air-conditioning, and/or ceiling fan. Room rates are $25 for a double with fan or $35 d with fan and air-conditioning. There is a nice breakfast room and a café/bar with Internet and book exchange. The young Guatemalan brother-and-sister team who own it also run Reuxtreme, Retalhuleu's finest outfitter, which operates weekend shuttles to Guatemala City and Antigua, among other things.

Another fine place to lay your head is the friendly **(Posada de Don José** (5a Calle 3-67 Zona 1, tel. 7771-0180 or 7771-0841, donjose@terra.com.gt, $42–55 d), in an attractive two-story building centered around a small swimming pool and courtyard. Standard rooms are spotless and have good beds, cable TV, air-conditioning, ceiling fan, phone, and private hot-water bath. The larger suites have a sitting area and some nice furniture. The hotel's restaurant, managed by Don Josée's wife, serves some of the town's tastiest food. The Mexican consulate is also based here. Nearby, at the corner of 5a Avenida and 5a Calle, is the smaller **Anexo Posada de Don José** (tel. 7771-4182), run by the same owners, with pleasant rooms for $25 d, breakfast included.

The well-furnished rooms in **Hotel Astor** (tel. 7771-0475, $37 d), are set in a colonial building and centered around a pretty garden courtyard and swimming pool. All rooms have air-conditioning, ceiling fan, and cable TV in addition to private hot-water bath. There is a restaurant in the lobby and a small sports bar. For budget accommodations, try **Hotel Modelo** (3a Avenida "A" 5-14 Zona 1, tel. 7771-0256), where rooms with ceiling fan and cable TV go for $15 d.

FOOD

A variety of decent restaurants are downtown. An excellent choice is the restaurant at **(Posada de Don José** (5a Calle 3-67 Zona 1, tel. 7771-0180 or 7771-0841), serving international cuisine with Guatemalan flair.

Cafetería La Luna (5a Avenida 4-97 Zona 1, all meals daily), just off the plaza's west corner, is a local favorite serving inexpensive Guatemalan fare. For a drink and pub fare, stop by **Lo de Chaz** (5a Calle 4-83 Zona 1). Reu's newest café is the **Café Rústico** (4a Calle 4-23 Zona 1 inside Hostal Casa Santa María, tel. 5202-8180), serving good coffee and snacks along with Internet access.

Among the culinary options you'll find in Centro Comercial La Trinidad is **Caffé Saúl** (tel. 7771-7918, 10 A.M.–9 P.M.Mon.–Thurs., 10 A.M.–10 P.M. Fri.–Sun.). There's also a **Domino's Pizza** and a **Tacos 3XQ10.** A large air-conditioned supermarket, **La Torre,** rounds out the list of options.

SERVICES

Banco Industrial has Visa ATMs at its locations on the central plaza (6a Calle 5-17 Zona 1) and at Centro Comercial La Trinidad (1a Calle and 5a Avenida "A" Zona 5). Banco Agromercantil, also on 5a Avenida facing the plaza, has a MasterCard ATM. Both banks change U.S. dollars and travelers checks.

For Internet access, check out Internet at 5a Calle and 6a Avenida, where an hour online costs $1.50. Hostal Casa Santa María (4a Calle 4-23 Zona 1, tel. 5202-8180 or 5205-1132) also has an Internet café.

GETTING THERE

Most buses plying the Pacific Coast Highway (Carretera al Pacífico) stop in Retalhuleu's main bus depot at 7a Avenida and 10a Calle. There are regular buses to Guatemala City, Quetzaltenango, the Mexican border, Champerico, and El Tulate.

NORTH AND WEST OF RETALHULEU
(Xocomil Water Park and Xetulul Amusement Park

The first of these, **Parque Acuático Xocomil** (Km. 180.5 on the road to Quetzaltenango, tel. 7772-5780, www.irtra.org.gt, 9 A.M.–5 P.M. Thurs.–Sun. Jan. 8–Oct. 31, Wed.–Sun. Nov. 1–Dec. 15, daily Dec. 15–Jan. 7, $10 adult,

© AL ARGUETA

tubing at Parque Acuático Xocomil

$7 children) is a wonderful water park on par with the world's best and a must-see if you are traveling with children. Among the attractions are 14 water slides, a wave pool, and a lazy river meandering through the complex of re-created Mayan ruins and monuments. The main restaurant showcases a Mayan pyramid painted in ochre, green, and yellow, as it would have looked in the Classic period. Additional food stands are scattered throughout the park.

The second phase of an eventual four-park plan is **Parque de Diversiones Xetulul** (tel. 7722-9450, www.irtra.org.gt, 10 A.M.–6 P.M. Thurs.–Sun. Jan. 8–Oct. 31, Wed.–Sun. Nov. 1–Dec. 15, daily Dec. 15–Jan. 7, $27 adult, $13 children), where a variety of amusement park rides are spread out among seven plazas, each with its own restaurant and gift shop showcasing a variety of replicated world monuments. Among the highlights are Paris's Moulin Rouge, Rome's Trevi Fountain, and Guatemala's own Gran Jaguar Temple from Tikal. The park is also home to Central America's largest roller coaster.

A new convention center and 18-hole golf course were in the planning stages.

Hostales del IRTRA

Just across the road from the two theme parks are the lodgings created specifically to house visitors. The Hostales del IRTRA (tel. 2423-9100, www.irtra.org.gt) encompass a virtual leisure city with various lodges, restaurants, bars, swimming pools, and a minigolf course. There are four separate lodging concepts ranging in price from $40 a night in the simplest accommodations without air-conditioning to $300 a night for a suite. The newest of the four *hostales,* 【 **Palajunoj,** was inspired by the cultures inhabiting the world's tropical rainforests and is the popular favorite with guests. The five buildings in this complex each have a different theme: African, Polynesian, Thai, Indonesian, and Mayan. All rooms have air-conditioning, cable TV, private bathroom, and wonderful wooden furnishings. The buildings housing the rooms at Palajunoj are worth a look for their unique architecture. The *hostales* outside

© AL ARGUETA

well-designed architecture of Hostal Palajunoj

this complex feature Spanish Colonial, Greek, and rustic cabana architecture.

There are three restaurants, the nicest of which is **Restaurante Kapa Hapa,** inspired by the cultures of Asia and the Pacific. A beautifully luminescent Polynesian sailboat graces the entrance as you make your way up the stairs to the second-floor dining room. Try the chicken satay and wash it down with a Mai Tai. Main dishes cost $7–12. Outdoor seating overlooking the Moana swimming pools is also available and is a great place for breakfast, which includes a delicious menu of croissant sandwiches or lighter fare such as yogurt and pancakes.

Any bus traveling along the Quetzaltenango–Retalhuleu road can drop you off here.

Finca El Patrocinio

Farther north along the road heading to Quetzaltenango, in the area known as Las Palmas, lies Finca El Patrocinio (tel. 7771-4393 or 5203-5701, www.patrocinioplantation.com), an agro-ecological tourism destination. So-called "agro tourism" is an increasingly popular

form of recreation in Guatemala encompassing natural areas adjacent to farms. The main attraction at El Patrocinio is bird-watching in and around its 25-hectare forest reserve. Other areas are dedicated to the cultivation of coffee, cacao, macadamia nuts, and exotic flowers, among others, which visitors are free to check out. There are three rooms in a farmhouse each renting for $60 d with shared bath. The farm is on the slopes of Santiaguito Volcano and has fantastic views of its smoldering cone. You can call the owner, Mario Aguilar, for a pickup ($12) from the Cuatro Caminos crossroads just outside of Retalhuleu, from where it's another 14 kilometers down a good paved road to the farm. Otherwise, birding packages can be arranged by booking in advance directly through El Patrocinio or through **Cayaya Birding** (tel. 5308-5160, www.cayaya-birding.com).

◖ Takalik Abaj

The site of Takalik Abaj (7 A.M.–5 P.M. daily, $3.50), meaning "standing stones," is particularly interesting because it reveals elements of Olmec influence in early Mayan culture. It made headlines as recently as 2002 with the discovery of an intact royal burial tomb thought to be that of the site's last Mayan ruler, a discovery featured in the May 2004 issue of *National Geographic.*

Formerly known as Abaj Takalik because of an error in translation, the site is spread out over 6.5 square kilometers along nine terraces. Its ceremonial center, at the city's core, is open to visitors but the remains of the city's outskirts are now on lands occupied by five coffee farms. One of these, on the ninth terrace, is home to an ecolodge.

In its heyday, between 800 B.C. and A.D. 200, Takalik Abaj was an important commercial and political center at the heart of a far-ranging trade network in which cacao and salt were exchanged for obsidian, quetzal feathers, pyrite, and jade.

More than 275 structures have been unearthed here. Now being restored in an area once belonging to a private coffee and banana plantation is Structure 5, the tallest

A GUATEMALAN TAKE ON DISNEY WORLD

The twin theme parks of Xocomil and Xetulul sprouted seemingly out of nowhere just a few years ago on the outskirts of Retalhuleu along the road to Quetzaltenango. The first of these, Xocomil, opened its doors in 1997, with Xetulul being added in 2002. Both parks are operated by IRTRA, the Institute for the Recreation of Guatemalan Private Industry Workers, a private entity created by the Guatemalan Congress. It operates three other parks near Guatemala City.

Xocomil and Xetulul opened to much fanfare and are beloved by Guatemalans and foreigners alike for the quality of the parks' attractions, their cleanliness, and the friendliness of the staff. By any standard, the parks are impressive, and they are special because they showcase the excellent quality and amazing potential of the Guatemalan service sector. The theme parks and the accommodations built to house their guests truly have nothing to envy similar attractions in developed nations. If you are traveling in this part of Guatemala with children, a stop at Xocomil and/or Xetulul is almost obligatory.

Xocomil and Xetulul receive more than one million visitors annually, making them Guatemala's top tourist draw. There are plans to build two more parks in the lands adjacent to them. Retalhuleu itself has already begun a transformation inspired by the parks' creation. Though it has always been a regional recreational center, the arrival of more visitors to the area has vastly improved the quality of local hotels, though prices have likewise increased. In addition to its popularity with Guatemalans, visitors from Southern Mexico, El Salvador, and Honduras also flock to the parks in droves. There are plans to build an airport, allowing those visitors to arrive by plane on package tours.

All this might sound suspect, like crass consumerism or the makings of mass tourism, brought home by the fact that the top tourism draw in a country of incredible natural beauty is a man-made theme park. But you should keep in mind that it's a far cry from Las Vegas and it really goes to show that Guatemala, and her people, are entirely capable of competing with better-known tourism destinations and creating something that is professional, high quality, and yet entirely Guatemalan.

structure at 16 meters high. It occupies Terrace 3. East of here is Structure 7, thought to have been an astronomical observatory. Structure 4 contains some very clear engraving in Mayan style. There are many sculptures scattered throughout the site. Among them are smaller versions of the giant Olmecoid heads seen elsewhere, as well as the pot-bellied *barrigones* that are also typical of Olmec influence. Also noteworthy is Structure 12, the largest structure with a base measuring 56 by 42 meters and dating to A.D. 300. Standing before it are seven carved monuments, including Altar 8, and Stela 5, which shows two kings presiding over bound captives. Olmecoid heads and zoomorphs compose the other finely carved monuments at this structure. Structure 11 is similar, also with seven monuments before it.

Takalik Abaj was sacked sometime around A.D. 300 and its Mayan-style monuments were ritualistically defaced. Some were rebuilt after A.D. 600. The site is still an important ceremonial site and many highland Mayans perform ceremonies there.

To get to Takalik Abaj, drive or take a bus heading out from Retalhuleu to the town of El Asintal, 12 kilometers northwest of Reu and 5 kilometers north of the Carretera al Pacífico (Pacific Coast Highway, CA-2). The turnoff is at Km. 190.5. Buses leave from 5a Avenida "A" southwest of the town plaza about every half hour during daylight hours. From El Asintal, pickups cover the remaining four kilometers to the site. You can also take a taxi from Reu's main plaza for about $30 round-trip, including waiting time.

THE PACIFIC COAST

© AL ARGUETA

Altar 9 at Takalik Abaj

Takalik Maya Lodge

Just two kilometers up the road, on the site's ninth terrace, is the exquisite (**Takalik Maya Lodge** (tel. 2333-7056 or 2337-0037, www .takalik.com), where you have your choice between two different concepts, both on lands occupied by the working Montes Eliseos coffee farm. The **Kacike Maya** concept is built in a heavily forested area near the lodge's restaurant. There are two beautiful and comfortable rooms, each with unique interior paint and decor. Both have a winding staircase leading to a second-floor balcony, where you can lounge away soothed by the sounds of the surrounding jungle. The rooms are truly a work of art and the walls are painted with motifs inspired by the natural beauty all around. Indigenous bedspreads, gas lamps, and tile floors complete the ambience. You can stay at the Kacike Maya for $80 d, but there are packages including one night's stay, three meals, and a tour to Takalik Abaj by tractor for $87 per person based on double occupancy.

At the **Paseo del Café,** just up the road, you

can stay in the heart of a 19th-century coffee farm in comfortable wooden buildings with charming red tin roofs centered around a small plaza. The seven rooms here have electricity and share a bathroom. They are also just steps from a refreshing swimming pool surrounded by lush jungle and coffee bushes. Rooms here cost $32 d and include breakfast. A package including one night's stay, three meals, a coffee tour, and a visit to Takalik Abaj by tractor-pulled cart costs $57 per person in a double room.

The restaurant, on the Kacike side of the lodge, serves a somewhat limited menu, though the food is quite good, with entrées in the $6–9 range that include kebabs and salads. The homemade lemonade is particularly thirst-quenching after a visit to the ruins.

Numerous nature trails wind their way through the farm and there is a small but refreshing waterfall just a 10-minute hike away. In addition to Takalik Abaj tours, the lodge can also arrange bird-watching and visits to the Manchón Guamuchal Wetland Preserve and Chicabal Lagoon.

From Takalik Abaj archaeological site's roadside entrance, it's a further two kilometers up the main road to Takalik Maya Lodge, about 30 minutes' walking.

Coatepeque

This rather unattractive town lies farther west toward the Mexican border and, as such, is the haunt of the usual rag-tag group of felons inhabiting shady border towns. It also doubles as a busy commercial center for the surrounding coffee farms. If you need to stay here, your best bet is the **Hotel Villa Real** (6a Calle 6-57 Zona 1, tel. 7775-1939, $20d), housed in a building dating to the early 1900s, featuring very clean rooms with ceiling fan, cable TV, and comfortable beds. There is also an *anexo* down the street with newer, single-bed rooms. The owner claims 80 percent of the local population is armed in this Guatemalan "red zone" and may be closing his doors in the next few years.

◖ Manchón Guamuchal Wetland Preserve

This wild, 13,500-hectare private wetland reserve harbors the last remaining undisturbed mangrove swamps in the country. The Manchón Guamuchal is included in the Ramsar Convention on Wetlands, encompassing a list of globally important sites, particularly those that provide habitat for aquatic birds. The convention was adopted in 1971 and signed by more than 100 countries. Guatemala ratified the convention in June 1990, and in 1998 the Manchón Guamuchal was added to the list of sites with international importance.

According to a recent study by a Brazilian biologist, the wetlands are an important stop along the path of migratory birds coming from Canada and the United States. Among the varied bird life are 14 duck species, 12 of which are migratory, sparrow hawks, buzzards, falcons, and 20 species of egrets. Birds arrive sometime in October to November, leaving in March after wintering in the lagoons. In addition to birds, there are crocodiles, iguanas, and an abundance of fish.

The reserve is just now being made accessible to tourism, though access to the park is fairly straightforward. The only facilities are in the towns of Tilapa and neighboring Tilapita. You'll find several simple *comedores* lining a pleasantly clean stretch of black-sand beach in Tilapa. For tours of the mangrove swamps, negotiate with one of the local boatmen found at the dock. You can catch a boat through the mangrove lagoons over to Tilapita for $0.50 or hire your own for about $3. There you'll find the wonderful **El Pacífico** beach hotel ($20 d) with screened-in rooms with fan, some with private bath.

To get to Tilapa, take one of the hourly buses leaving from Coatepeque. It's about a 1.5-hour drive from Retalhuleu, if you're driving. Take the Pacific Coast Highway (CA-2) west past Coatepeque and head south at the turnoff just past the town of Las Palmas.

The reserve is accessible on its eastern flank from Champerico along a dirt road heading west 25 kilometers to the village of El Manchón. There is one daily bus leaving for Retalhuleu at 5 A.M. and making the return journey to El Manchón at 3 P.M.

Outfitter **Reuxtreme** (tel. 5202-8180 or 5205-1132, www.reuxtreme.com) runs trips to the reserve for kayaking along the tranquil mangrove swamps and lagoons on this side of the park, where there is also a wide sandy beach.

SOUTH OF RETALHULEU
Champerico

Built as a shipping port during the late-19th-century coffee boom, this old port features a uniquely dilapidated wooden pier. The beaches here are not all that enticing, though there are some better ones nearby. Lining the beach in the area adjacent to the pier are a variety of cheap eateries serving mostly seafood. The old pier is worth a look and you can still walk on it for an out-of-this-century experience. Sportfishing outfitters and tourism authorities are trying to restore some of this town's old glory and infrastructure as a place from which to run deep-sea fishing trips. A new marina, built partially with Dutch capital, was being planned. In the meantime, it remains a quiet seaside town.

A fun day trip from Retalhuleu is a 55-kilometer mountain-bike ride along old railroad tracks and wooden bridges. **Reuxtreme** (tel. 5202-8180 or 5205-1132, www.reuxtreme .com, info@reuxtreme.com) runs the trips, costing $30 per person and including all gear. It also does surfing lessons here.

For accommodations and food, your best bet is **Hotel Posada del Mar** (tel. 7773-7101, along the highway into town at Km. 222, $25 d), where the comfortable rooms have air-conditioning and cable TV. There is a restaurant serving mostly seafood dishes along with a swimming pool. Alternatively, there's the **Hotel Montelimar** (2a Calle and Avenida Coatepeque, tel. 7773-7231, $13 d), where the wooden bar outshines the small, dark rooms.

Playa El Tulate

A much better bet for hitting the beach near Retalhuleu is El Tulate, about an hour from town. The beach isn't as clean as the one at Tilapa, but there's at least one serviceable hotel here. The

rooms at **Playa Paraíso** (tel. 5988-4084, $40 d) have big, cushy beds, ceiling fan, thatch roof, and a porch with bamboo furniture. There are two swimming pools and a restaurant.

To get to the beaches, you'll have to cross the **Canal de Chiquimulilla.** The cheapest crossing, if you're coming to Playa Paraío, is found by turning left when the main road dead-ends at the canal and continuing for 100 meters. It should cost about $0.25 to make the crossing. Local ferry boat operators will try to charge you $2 to cross closer to the end of the main road.

EAST TO ESCUINTLA

East along the Pacific Coast Highway to the department of Escuintla and its capital of the same name is Mazatenango, a coffee and sugarcane hub with little of interest for the international traveler. If you need to stop for a bite to eat your best bet is Plaza Americas, a new shopping center conveniently situated just off the Pacific Coast Highway outside the town center. Choose from Pollo Campero, Sarita, and Burger King There's even a movie theater.

Escuintla Department

SANTA LUCÍA COTZUMALGUAPA

In and of itself, the rather nondescript town of Santa Lucía Cotzumalguapa has little to recommend it. There are, however, some nearby archaeological attractions evidencing the influence of the Olmec culture and its expansion into coastal Guatemala from lowland Mexico. They might be worth a stop if you are passing this way as you travel along the coast. The sites, in the cane fields just outside of town, can be a bit difficult to reach and you'll probably find yourself hiring a cab if you're coming from town on your own.

What you'll see here are the remains of the Late Classic Pipil culture, which flourished here between A.D. 500 and 700. In 1880 more than 30 of the large stones found at the site were re-

moved, with nine of them being shipped off to Germany. Four sets of stones can still be found on-site. Unless you are a die-hard fan of pre-Columbian culture, I don't suggest traipsing through the cane fields to see them, as some of the highlights can be easily and conveniently viewed from museums on two different farms occupying the original site. In general, it's not a good idea to wander in and around the fields of tall sugarcane stalks, as they are prime territory for thieves and other assorted riff-raff.

Museo El Baúl

Although parts of this site lie among the sugarcane fields of Finca El Baúl, the highlights can be seen at Museo El Baúl (tel. 5312-1073, 7 A.M.–5 P.M. daily, $1.50), an open-air, roofed-in exhibit housing Pipil stone sculptures, including a jaguar, several skulls, and a smiling head. The museum is being preserved as an eco-archaeological attraction by private landowners and there are plans to remodel an old building to house visitors, build interpretive trails through the surrounding jungle, and establish a steam engine museum. The remains of old steam engines, one of which dates to 1914, can be found strewn about the grounds.

To get here, take the road heading north of town from El Calvario church. An intersection just past this landmark takes you about three kilometers to a fork in the road just past a bridge. The fork is marked by a sign, which reads "Los Tarros," where you make a left and follow the road another three kilometers to the headquarters of Finca El Baúl. An armed guard will greet you at the gate, where you'll have to identify yourself. Tell him you're visiting the museum. The museum is on the right another half kilometer or so past some old buildings. Buses carrying farm workers make their way out here from town at variable frequencies.

Museo Cultura Cotzumalguapa

On the site of Finca Las Ilusiones, the Museo Cultura Cotzumalguapa (7 A.M.–noon and 2 P.M.–4 P.M. Mon.–Fri., 7 A.M.–noon Sat., $1.50) has a variety of obsidian arrow points, ceramic pots and figurines, and several monuments on display. Among these are several Olmecoid statues and a glass fiber copy of Monument 21—the original still stands among the sugarcane fields of Finca Bilbao. The stone depicts a scene involving a ball-game player, a shaman, and a noble holding a heart. There are also photographs of stelae moved to Berlin's Dahlem Museum in 1880. The museum has some interpretive material and the caretaker is usually on hand to show you around.

The museum is one kilometer east of town along the Pacific Coast Highway. The signed entrance is on the left just before an Esso station. The turnoff leads another half kilometer to the museum along a dirt road.

Accommodations and Food

Along the highway on the western edge of town

at Km. 90.4 of the Pacific Coast Highway is **Hotel Santiaguito** (tel. 7882-5435/6/7, $26–50 d). The large, comfortable rooms have cable TV, phone, air-conditioning, and private bathroom set on spacious grounds with a swimming pool. Nonguests can use the pool for $3 and there is a good restaurant where fish, seafood, or meat dishes range $6–9. About 200 meters east along the highway is **Hotel El Camino** (tel. 7882-5316, $23–40 d), featuring bright rooms with tile floors, large bathrooms, balconies, cable TV; some have air-conditioning. Fan-cooled rooms on the first floor are less attractive but cheaper. There's also a decent restaurant here. Head east and then down a short signposted lane to **Hotel Internacional** (tel. 7882-5504, $20 d) with 14 large rooms and cold-water showers, fan, and cable TV. Try for an upstairs room.

Getting There

Most buses trundling along the Pacific Coast Highway no longer go into town thanks to a bypass constructed a few years back. If heading out here you might find yourself changing buses in Escuintla or Mazatenango. Santa Lucía is also accessible from Lake Atitlán via Cocales.

LA DEMOCRACIA

East from Santa Lucía Cotzumalguapa, a turn-off near the town of Siquinalá heads south to this small town. There's little to see and do other than admire the peculiar Olmecoid heads adorning the town's small central plaza. There is a certain Far Eastern mystique to these large grinning heads with swollen eyelids, some of which are attached to smaller, rotund bodies and known as *barrigones* because of their swollen bellies. They bear a striking resemblance to Olmec sculptures found in the Mexican lowlands of Villa Hermosa, near the Gulf Of Mexico. The stones date to the middle Pre-classic period sometime around 500 B.C. and come from the nearby site of Monte Alto, on the outskirts of town.

Also on the central plaza, a small museum, the **Museo Regional de Arqueología** (8 A.M.–noon and 2 P.M.–5 P.M. Tues.–Sun.,

$1.50) harbors some more stone heads, carvings, pottery, grinding stones, and an exquisite jade mask.

SIPACATE

If you continue south toward the coast from La Democracia you'll find Guatemala's surfing capital, Sipacate. Nowhere near as popular as in Costa Rica or even neighboring El Salvador, surfing nonetheless has some aficionados in this neck of the woods and there are some perfectly surf-worthy waves on the Guatemalan shores. International travelers are just now starting to get a clue, but for the meantime the lucky few can still surf these waves undisturbed by throngs of fellow wave enthusiasts, despite international travel magazines' best attempts to make these sites more widely known.

The drive south to Sipacate is almost as good as the beaches, with palmettos lining the road on either side of the well-paved, fast highway. Once in town, it should cost you about $1.40

YOU *CAN* SURF IN GUATEMALA

While neighboring countries such as Costa Rica, Nicaragua, and even El Salvador have acquired relative status as Central American surf spots, Guatemala has remained relatively obscure in this regard. Although the country's Pacific shores have perfectly surf-worthy breaks, the coast has always taken a back seat to the scenic and cultural wonders of the highlands, among other areas. A relative lack of tourism infrastructure in this region has also contributed to keeping the Pacific Coast on the periphery of Guatemala's emerging status as a destination for outdoor-loving, adventurous travelers.

The newfound popularity of beach destinations such as Monterrico and Iztapa has resulted in the corresponding development of coastal areas near these beach towns. As more and more people visit, locals and foreigners alike are discovering that you can, in fact, surf in Guatemala. The Guatemalan surfing community can be found mostly in small villages along the coast and numbers only about 100 people, according to local estimates. Surfing Guatemala's breaks means you won't have to share a wave with 20 other people, as is the case with other, more popular regions along the Central American coast. The best surfing beaches in Guatemala can be found at Iztapa and Sipacate, both of which have more-than-adequate accommodations.

United States travel magazines have put the word out concerning El Paredón Surf Camp, a bare-bones surfing paradise on one of Guatemala's best breaks. Still, you wouldn't know it cruising around the sandy streets of this quiet village where chickens roam freely and you can still show up on almost any given day with nary another surfer in sight.

The biggest waves can be found during swells occurring between mid-March and late October with wave faces sometimes as large as 18 feet. During other times of year, waves average 3–6 feet, with the occasional 10-foot swell.

If you want to check out the surfing scene in Guatemala, a useful website is www.surfin guatemala.com, established by Pedro Pablo Vergara, a local surfer who costarted Maya Extreme Surf School and offers trips to Guatemala's surf spots. The site lists about 20 breaks along the Pacific Coast with area maps to help you find them, along with information on accommodations varying from budget surf camps to stays in private villas. The school can also arrange transportation for you and your surfboards to various surf spots from Guatemala City.

Along with Maripaz Fernandez, Vergara started **Maya Extreme Surf School** (www .mayaextreme.com) in 2001 and **Maya Extreme Surf Shop** (Centro Comercial Pradera Concepción Local 308, tel. 6637-9593) in 2005. The shop sells the company's own brand of "G-land surfboards" and is based in one of Guatemala City's nicest shopping malls. A one-day "learn to surf" package costs $125, including transfers, food, equipment, and instruction.

to cross the Canal de Chiquimulilla over to the beaches. Sipacate's recommended accommodation, **Rancho Carrillo** (tel. 5517-1069 or 5413-9395, www.marmaya.com) is on a clean stretch of private beach. There are a restaurant, pool, and bungalows with air-conditioning, private bath, minifridge, and cable TV. The bungalows house up to four people and cost $60 regardless of occupancy. A family-size unit for up to eight people costs $108. Smaller, more basic rooms without air-conditioning but with outdoor hammock on a deck fronting the beach cost $40 d. There are deals available if you're here Sunday–Thursday.

El Paredón Surf Camp

East from Sipacate about five kilometers is the village of El Paredón Buena Vista, home to Guatemala's surfing mecca. Featured in *National Geographic Adventure* and *Outside,* El Paredón Surf Camp (tel. 7812-3387 or 5744-9342, www.surf-guatemala.com) is a barebones surfing hideaway where you can stay in a bed or hammock with meals for $12 a day. The meals are provided by a local family and are heavy on seafood. Surfboards are available for rent at $15 a day. You can put them to good use on the sea, which dishes out 1.5–2-meter (5–6-foot) rollers opposite the lovely beach at your doorstep.

The owners insist you book in advance. Transport from Antigua or Guatemala City takes two hours and costs $45. It is highly recommended, as getting here by public bus involves changing buses four times.

El Paredón is inside **Sipacate-Naranjo National Park,** home to large extensions of mangrove forests. Little has been done to make the park an authentic ecotourism attraction. The emphasis at El Paredón is decidedly on the surfing aspects, though the owners can arrange kayaking in the neighboring lagoons.

ESCUINTLA

The departmental capital of Escuintla is a sweltering, busy place and mainly a pit stop along the road to the coast from Guatemala City, or if you're heading east–west along the Pacific Coast Highway. A four-lane *autopista* starts just outside of Guatemala City and leads from Palín to Escuintla, with fantastic views of Agua, Fuego, and Acatenango Volcanoes along the way. Another four-lane highway continues south from Escuintla to Puerto San José, Puerto Quetzal, and Iztapa. A bypass means you don't need to even pass through town unless it's absolutely necessary.

Your best bet for a decent cheap hotel is along 4a Avenida. Otherwise, try **Hotel La Villa** (3a Avenida 3-21 Zona 1, tel. 7888-0395, $20 d), containing adequate rooms with fan or air-conditioning, cable TV, and private bathroom. There are also a swimming pool and restaurant. Nicer accommodations with swimming pools popular on weekends with Guatemalan families can be found along Avenida Centro América in Zona 3. The best of these is **Hotel Sarita** (Avenida Centro América 15-32 Zona 3, tel. 7888-1959, $50 d), offering some of the usual amenities such as ceiling fan, cable TV, air-conditioning, and private hot-water bathroom centered around the swimming pools. The restaurant here is a favorite with Guatemalan families and has opened other locations throughout the country. Its menu is similar to that of U.S.-based *Denny's* and includes burgers, sandwiches, and grilled meats. There is another one in Escuintla on the *autopista* heading back toward Guatemala City, just past the northbound toll booths.

As for banks, Banco Industrial has a Visa ATM in its branch office at 4a Avenida 6-14 Zona 1. The main bus depot is on the southern end of town, at the end of 4a Avenida, from where there are half-hourly buses to Guatemala City, Puerto San José, and east toward El Salvador as well as hourly departures for Antigua. Buses coming into Escuintla sometimes leave you at the north end of town along 2a Avenida, meaning a long walk through the sweltering town center. Splurge for a cab ride if you need to get to the bus terminal.

Near Escuintla

East on the road to Taxisco is one of the most unusual attractions in Guatemala and indeed all of Central America, the **Auto Safari Chapin** (Km. 87.5 Carretera a Taxisco, tel. 5517-1705, www.autosafarichapin.org, 9:30 A.M.–5 P.M. Tues.–Sun., $7 adults, $6 children), where you can drive through grounds harboring a variety of animals, including zebras, hippos, rhinos, giraffes, and a lion. There are also local species such as macaws and monkeys, which you can see in a small zoo, and an aviary. There is a rest area partway through the drive where you can get up close and personal with the park's giraffes. A swimming pool and restaurant round out the list of amenities.

PUERTO SAN JOSÉ

Puerto San José is where Guatemala City dwellers escape to for a quick dip in the sea. Try to avoid coming here during Holy Week, as droves of Guatemalan families descend upon the town and its beaches like shoppers at a Filene's Basement day-after-Christmas sale, leaving a trail of trash in their wake. Otherwise, the town makes an acceptable place to enjoy some time by the sea, though nearby Iztapa and Monterrico are certainly better alternatives.

Once Guatemala's main shipping port, it has been displaced by the newer **Puerto Quetzal** just a few kilometers away along the same stretch of coast. Cruise ships dock at Puerto Quetzal, which has its own cruise ship terminal. Most visitors either stay at the terminal, where they can eat and shop, or are quickly whisked away on package tours to a local resort; others go sailfishing or visit Antigua for the day.

Ostrich Farm

If you're spending some time in Puerto San José or just passing through, you may want to stop by the local ostrich farm for a look. **Avestruces Maya** (tel. 5608-0835 or 5608-8075, www.avestrucesmaya.com, 10 A.M.–6 P.M. daily, $3.50 adults, $2.65 children 10 and over, children under 10 free) occupies 27 acres, mostly devoted to raising ostriches, but also includes a small petting zoo, plant nursery, and riverlike swimming pool where you can relax in an inner tube.

A restaurant (open weekends) specializes in ostrich meat and a small shop sells ostrich-leather wallets, boots, purses, and assorted eggshell trinkets. The surprisingly supple leather can be very expensive.

The park is at Km. 100 along the old road from Guatemala City to Puerto San José. You can camp here for $3.25.

Also at the farm, you'll find **light aircraft rides.** Contact Christopher at 5651-6908 for details.

Aqua Magic

Another recreational option well suited to escaping the characteristic heat of Guatemala's Pacific plains is Aqua Magic (tel. 7881-1648, 10 A.M.–5 P.M. Wed.–Fri., 9 A.M.–6 P.M. Sat. and Sun., $8.75 adults, $6 children), where you'll find a small water park with numerous water slides, a wave pool, and beach access. There are also several restaurants and snack bars spread throughout. Though nowhere near as big or elaborate as Xocomil, in Retalhuleu, it is certainly adequate. You'll find the park by turning left after you cross the bridge across the Canal de Chiquimulilla leading to the beachfront part of town.

Accommodations

Most of the town's acceptable accommodations are oddly not found beachside. An exception is **Posada Quetzal** (along the main drag in Barrio Miramar, tel. 7881-1892 or 7881-2493), where you'll find a pleasant beachside restaurant on a covered wooden deck, a swimming pool, and simple but clean bungalows with ceiling fan and cable TV. The beach fronting the property is somewhat dirty, as it's right in town.

Some nicer options can be found in the heart of town. **Turicentro Martita** (tel. 7888-4848) has a very good restaurant with indoor or outdoor (poolside) seating and a varied menu of sandwiches, soups, grilled meats, and seafood. Its spotless rooms have comfortable beds, private bath, and air-conditioning, among other amenities. Rates vary, ranging from $65 s/d midweek to $80 per night s/d on weekends.

Guests enjoy half-off admission to Aqua Magic water park.

Heading west outside of town along Km. 113 on the road to the beachside development of Chulamar, you'll find **Hotel Costa Verde** (tel. 2367-0571 or 7881-1161, www.hotel costaverdeguatemala.com, $65–85 depending on day of week), a very nice property offering rooms with all the standard amenities as well as fully equipped suites. There are a restaurant and a swimming pool.

Food

Turning right after the Chiquimulilla Canal bridge (coming from the mainland) into the beachfront part of town, you'll find **Rancho Costa Grande,** a popular place with a varied menu that is predictably heavy on seafood. All of the other recommended places to eat are in the hotel properties. The best restaurant in town is hands-down that of **Turicentro Martita** (tel. 7888-4848).

Getting There

Buses to Puerto San José leave Guatemala City's bus terminal every half hour or so. It's also possible to arrange a private transfer with almost any travel agency in Antigua.

Chulamar

West of Puerto San José, Chulamar is home to many of the weekend vacation homes of wealthy folks from Guatemala City. Here you'll find one of the Pacific Coast's most luxurious lodging options, built to satisfy the demands of the Guatemalan elite. The **Villas del Pacífico** (tel. 2277-7777, www.villasdelpacifico.com), formerly a Radisson property, is a huge all-inclusive resort complex on a clean private beach with all the feel of an Acapulco beachside megaresort. Although it's popular on weekends, you may just have the place all to yourself if you visit during the middle of the week. There are two swimming pools and a variety of dining options. Double rooms start at $160 per room per night, all-inclusive, Sunday–Thursday or $200 on weekends. There are also deluxe suites and bungalows for $300 and $400 a night, re-spectively. You can get a day pass to enjoy the swimming pool and the hotel grounds for $50 per person, a popular option with cruise-ship passengers. Many of the sailfishing outfits also accommodate their clients here. Transport to the hotel is available from Guatemala City and Antigua with prior arrangement. Its sister hotel is the Villa Antigua.

PUERTO QUETZAL

The main attraction here is the **Puerto Quetzal Cruise Ship Terminal,** where an increasing number of boats calling on Guatemala's Pacific Coast make landfall. Within the larger terminal area is the **Marina Pez Vela,** harboring boats for sailfishing adventures. Cruise-ship passengers will find several amenities, including Internet access, telephone communications, and stands selling a variety of local handicrafts. An excellent restaurant, **7 Caldos del Mar (Seven Soups of the Sea),** is run by the amiable Dimitris Moliviatis. You'll find more than seven soups on the menu, including *tapado, sancocho,* and *kakik,* as well as a variety of meat and seafood dishes and a fully stocked bar. Order a Cuba Libre (rum and coke) with Guatemala's famous Zacapa Centenario rum.

◖ IZTAPA

Farther west along the coastline are the lovely beaches of Iztapa, which are remarkably clean, wide, and sandy. Although the town itself is a dilapidated old port town, it is becoming increasingly popular as the jumping-off point for some of the world's best sailfishing. Iztapa is Guatemala's original port, used by the Spanish conqueror Pedro de Alvarado to build boats and set sail for his onward journey to Perú. Anglers will find world-class accommodations to complement the world-class fishing just off the coast. Surfers will find plenty of waves to ride here, as there is a fairly decent break.

Sailfishing Outfitters

Among the recommended outfitters is **Sailfish Bay Lodge** (tel. 2426-3909 direct or 800/638-7405 U.S. reservations, www.sailfishbay.com),

© AL ARGUETA
Sailfish Bay Lodge

the right direction when planning a sailfishing trip to Guatemala. Guests stay at Villas del Pacífico Resort or a private villa within the same compound.

Following my visit to Guatemala, **Pacific Fins Resort & Marina** (tel. 888/700-3467 U.S., www.pacificfins.com) opened its doors as the rebooted version of the former Fins 'N Feathers sailfishing operation. The lodge works exclusively with Captain Hook Charters and accomplished angler Captain Ron Hamlin, who in November 2006 set a new world record for single-season billfish releases with 2,809 fish caught and released in 180 fishing days over a one-year period. Among the large boats in the company's fleet are a 2007 40-foot Cabo Flybridge *(The Captain Hook),* a 2007 35-foot Cabo Express *(Hooked Up),* and a 43-foot Willis *(The Circle Hook).* Guests stay at the company's excellent lodge fronting the Canal de Chiquimulilla. (See the following *Accommodations and Food* section).

Accommodations and Food

In town, adequate accommodations can be found at **Sol y Playa Tropical** (1a Calle 5-41, tel. 7881-4365, $22 d), which has rooms with private bath and ceiling fan or air-conditioning built around a nicely landscaped swimming pool. Across the Canal de Chiquimulilla and right on the beach, Iztapa's nicest accommodations are at the **Sailfish Bay Lodge** (tel. 2426-3909 direct or 800/638-7405 U.S. reservations, www .sailfishbay.com, $125 d), run by American expatriate Robert Fallon. Accommodations here are usually sold as part of a sailfishing package, but you are more than welcome to stay on your own. The Guatemalan Pacific Coast's best-kept secret is a modern, well-designed lodge featuring a thatched-roof seaside bar and swimming pool with whirlpool bath, comfortable ocean-view rooms with all the usual amenities, and an excellent restaurant fronting the canal. You can enjoy fantastic views of three volcanoes rising above the surrounding mangroves as you dine. There are surfboards for guests' use. Transportation to the lodge from Guatemala City or Antigua is also available.

owned and operated by American expatriate Robert Fallon. Packages include food and accommodations at a beautiful eight-room lodge right on the beach across the canal in Iztapa. Robert has lived in Guatemala for several years and is very knowledgeable about its culture and history. He has lived in and fished Costa Rica but believes the country pales in comparison to his new home. Another option is the upstart **Buena Vista Sportfishing Lodge** (Calle Baja Mar, Aldea Buena Vista, tel. 7832-1991/05, www.buenavistasportfishing.com), also owned by an American expatriate. The lodge was still in the making at the time of my visit. Its developer sees huge potential along the Guatemalan coast after having drifted here from Costa Rica.

Based in Antigua, and a joint Guatemalan-American venture, is **The Great Sailfishing Company** (tel. 7832-1991, 5966-4528 Antigua, or 877/763-0851 U.S., www.greatsail fishing.com). You can fish using conventional methods as well as fly-fishing and the company's informative website can point you in

THE SAILFISH CAPITAL OF THE WORLD

A unique swirling of ocean currents between Mexico and El Salvador creates an eddy unusually rich in pelagic fish (such as herring and mackerel) right on Guatemala's doorstep, where billfish, including sailfish and marlin, gather to feed along with large concentrations of dorado, yellow-fin tuna, and wahoo. The result is some of the world's best sailfishing waters.

Enthusiasts of Guatemala's emerging sailfishing scene are quick to point out that it is the true "Sailfish Capital of the World" and have the numbers to back up their claims. The world records for conventional and fly-fishing single-day catches have been set here, at 75 and 23. In March 2006, a single vessel carrying five anglers caught and released a whopping 124 sailfish. While the records are indeed impressive, anglers plying the Guatemalan Pacific Coast need not worry about any "feast or famine" phenomenon, as catch-and-release numbers are quite consistent. In terms of billfish releases per angler, a statistic compiled by The Southwest Fisheries Science Center in California, Guatemala ranks at the top. Its Catch Per Unit of Effort (CPUE) for Pacific sailfish in 2005 was 5.83 compared to Costa Rica's 2.57 and Panama's 2.25. On average, you can expect to catch 15-20 fish per boat per day, but catches of 25 fish aren't uncommon.

Guatemala's strength is certainly in its numbers. Unlike most of its competitors, it's not known as a beach destination with impressive resort accommodations. All that is starting to change, however, and there are now some very comfortable accommodations where you can stay right on the beach and relax after a long day at sea. Some of the outfitters accommodate anglers in their own lodges; otherwise there are private luxury villas on the beach or the large Villas del Pacífico resort. Many outfits combine fishing packages with a round of golf on one of Guatemala City's excellent golf courses. All of the outfitters listed here practice catch-and-release and use circle hooks, as mandated by Guatemalan law.

Fishing is active year-round, but most anglers come between November and May seeking a respite from colder climates. Prices for fishing packages vary by the size of the boat used and can be fairly expensive in Guatemala, as boats generally travel 40-80 kilometers (25-50 miles) offshore to a deep, 600-meter (2,000-foot) basin where sailfish tend to congregate around its rim, translating into higher fuel costs. Boats heading out this way are usually in the 28-foot range, but there are also a few 42- and 43-foot boats. Expect to pay about $2,100 per person for two people on a two-day/three-night fishing package on a 28-foot boat. Most packages include food and drink, accommodations, boat and captain, gear- and transfers to and from the Guatemala City airport. Anglers often spend their last night in Antigua or Guatemala City.

A newer alternative and a beacon to the tourism potential of this region is the still-under-construction **Buena Vista Sportfishing Lodge** (Calle Baja Mar, Aldea Buena Vista, tel. 7880-4203/05, jody@buenavistasportfishing.com, www.buenavistasportfishing.com), which promises to pamper anglers in luxurious accommodations after a day spent fishing. Plans call for a 36-boat marina and six villas housing two luxury rooms and two suites apiece. The complex fronts the lagoon from the mainland.

Pending the new lodge's completion, the owner's house, Casa Amarilla, is available for rent at $1,000 per night. Part of the same complex, across the street, is the **Sailfish Club** ($75 d), where there are 10 rooms with private bath and air-conditioning centered around a swimming pool. There's also a restaurant and bar. The lodge and sailfishing operation work out of this location until the completion of the new facilities.

Iztapa's best restaurant is popular with anglers and locals alike. **El Capitán** (tel. 7881-4403, 7 A.M.–9 P.M. daily) serves large portions of tasty seafood and meat dishes under a thatched-roof *palapa* facing the lagoon. It also has a lively bar.

Next door, the former Fins 'N Feathers Lodge, once the hub of Iztapa's sailfishing activity until its closure in 2005, reopened under new ownership in November 2006 as **(Pacific Fins Resort & Marina** (tel. 888/700-3467 U.S., www.pacificfins.com, $125-500 d). The attractive lodge was expanded to include 2 new guest rooms with double beds, complementing four existing two-bedroom/two-bath villas with kitchenette and living room. Room upgrades include satellite flat-screen televisions, wireless internet, and brand-new furniture. All rooms have air conditioning. The bar and restaurant, facing the lodge's swimming pool, were also upgraded and offer a varied menu that includes sandwiches, pasta, grilled, sautéed, or breaded fish, chicken Florentine, and Argentinean-style *parrilladas*. The restaurant serves a lighter menu until 4 A.M., and you can round out your evening with a Cuban cigar and your favorite after-dinner drink. Stays at the resort are usually part of a multiday fishing package. If you're not in Guatemala to fish and just want to stay here, your best chance for scoring a room is during the off-season (May–Oct.).

Getting There

The same buses that leave Guatemala City's bus terminal for Puerto San José more often than not continue to Iztapa. Most anglers arrive on all-inclusive packages booked directly through their operation of choice, covering transportation logistics.

ALONG THE IZTAPA-MONTERRICO ROAD

Heading east from Iztapa, a smooth paved road travels along the coastline for about 25 kilometers to Monterrico. A ferry in Iztapa's *Colonia 20 de Octubre* transports you to the beachside at Puerto Viejo, from where the road begins, and costs $2.65 per vehicle. You'll see loofah farms lining the side of the road and the occasional turnoff toward the beach, where numerous small hotels have begun to spring up on

oceanfront Cayman Suites, along the road from Iztapa to Monterrico

what is probably the finest stretch of sand on Guatemala's Pacific shores. There are rumors of a luxurious 18-hole golf course planned somewhere along this route in the not-too-distant future.

Accommodations and Food

The first of these lodgings, at Km. 8.5, is **Pantanal Resort** (tel. 5918-4366 or 5511-3679, www.pantanalresort.com, $38 d) with five bungalows spread out around a small pool by a nice stretch of beach. Farther along the road is the brand-new ❰ **Cayman Suites** (Km. 10.5, tel. 5529-6518/19 lodge or 2362-1708/9 reservations, www.caymansuites.com .gt, $85–155 d), set on a spectacular beach flanked by a kidney-shaped swimming pool and open-air *palapa*-roofed restaurant and bar. Its 22 rooms feature all the usual amenities, some with gorgeous sea views, and include deluxe rooms, junior suites, and spacious, fully furnished suites. All rooms have wireless Internet, DirecTV and fine hardwood accents. The restaurant serves excellent fusion cuisine and seafood. ATVs are available for rent.

Closer to Monterrico, at Km. 14.5, is **Portete Beach Bungalows** (tel. 2366-2924 or 2337-3787, portete@intelnet.net.gt), with two simple beachfront bungalows and a main house equipped with fan, refrigerator, private bath, and some decor. Each of the two bunga-

lows can be rented for a weekend at a cost of $60 d. The main house is available for $133. There is a small restaurant/bar. You might be able to get a deal for midweek stays and have the place all to yourself, though you might have to bring your own food.

A good place to stop for a snack or pick up any needed groceries is **Las Garzas** (Km. 17.5, tel. 2425-8500, 7:30 A.M.–9 P.M. daily). The owners of this friendly roadside minimart can help you get your bearings. They also serve snacks, including pizza and sandwiches, which you can enjoy in a pleasant outdoor patio with chairs.

The last place you'll come to along this road is **Utz Tzaba** (Km. 21.8, tel. 5318-9452, info@ utz-tzaba.com, www.utz-tzaba.com), which has 10 rooms in a large main building as well as four bungalows. All rooms have tile floors, private hot-water bathroom, wireless Internet, air-conditioning, and ceiling fan. There are plans to install cable TV. The bungalows include two bedrooms and a living room and come fully furnished with minifridge, gas range, kitchen sink, and dining room table. There is a bar by the infinity-edge swimming pool with whirlpool bath and the hotel's restaurant serves excellent meals, including sandwiches, pasta, and seafood in the $6–10 range. The lodge is closed yearly on Christmas Eve and Christmas Day. Call ahead, as it's also closed for fumigation about every two months.

Monterrico

Monterrico, once a sleepy fishing village with one hotel run by an ex-Peace Corps volunteer is fast becoming popular with foreigners looking to get some time by the beach on their trip to Guatemala. The village has grown considerably in the last few years, as has the quality of its accommodations. It is a popular weekend destination with folks from Guatemala City and students from Antigua's Spanish schools. The same architects who gave Xocomil and Xetulul Parks their outstanding visual appeal have been hired by INGUAT and local tourism authori-

ties to provide Monterrico with an urban face-lift, including a new tree-lined entrance to the main beach, pedestrian walkways, and a boat marina. The work was completed in 2007.

Although it's easy to see Monterrico as a beach destination, it should be noted that it was a protected sea turtle nesting site long before it became the haunt of beach-seeking vacationers. Visitors can contribute to the conservation efforts of the local sea turtle conservation site via their paid admission to tour its grounds. In addition to the beaches,

Monterrico offers the opportunity to interact with nature in some unique ways, whether it's touring the mangrove canals, holding a baby sea turtle in your hand before its maiden voyage out to sea, or watching a mother turtle come ashore to lay eggs in total darkness. Try to engage in at least one of these ecologically responsible activities while keeping in mind the ecological significance of this site. The sea turtles here have a fighting chance, though they are being wiped out elsewhere by the indiscriminate harvesting of their eggs.

As for the beaches themselves, there are, in all honesty, better and cleaner stretches elsewhere along Guatemala's Pacific seaboard. The waves break very close to the sand here, meaning you don't have a particularly wide stretch of beach, unlike at Iztapa or Tilapa farther west. The undertow here, as along much of the Pacific Coast, is severe and drownings are not uncommon. Exercise due caution.

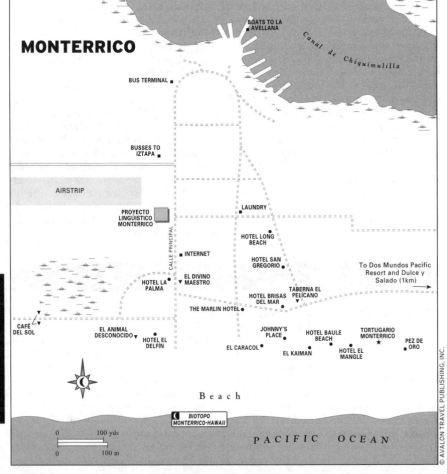

MONTERRICO-HAWAII AND ITS SEA TURTLES

If you're traveling to the Monterrico-Hawaii area between June and December, you might have the opportunity to witness a sea turtle coming ashore to lay its eggs or watch baby sea turtles making their maiden voyage out to sea.

Turtle nesting peaks during August and September, when you might be able to catch a large leatherback (baule) or the smaller olive ridley (parlama) coming ashore to lay eggs. Unfortunately, locals are also on the lookout for egg-laying sea turtles to snatch up the eggs and sell them, but under an agreement with the CECON monitoring station at Monterrico and ARCAS in Hawaii, they donate part of their stash toward conservation efforts. Your best bet for seeing a nesting turtle is to go with one of the CECON-trained guides or volunteer with ARCAS.

Volunteers are welcome at both stations. Among the duties are the collection of turtle eggs after the mothers have come ashore and moving them to a protected nesting site, where they are reburied and allowed to hatch. Typical incubation periods for olive ridley eggs is 50 days, 72 for leatherbacks. After a few days in a holding pen, the young turtles are released, either at sunrise or sunset, and make their way across the sand and into the ocean.

As the young turtles scamper across the sand, they are being imprinted with the unique details of the beach and its sand, where they will return and nest when they are adults. All this assumes they make it to adulthood, a big assumption when taking into account that only one turtle in 100 makes it to adulthood. Sea turtles are threatened not just by the collection of their eggs but also by fishing activities, where they often end up in nets, and sea pollution. Plastic bags, for example, are often mistaken for jellyfish by hungry sea turtles.

The CECON station at Monterrico releases about 5,000 sea turtle hatchlings per year. If you're there on a Saturday night between September and February, don't miss the sunset sea turtle race sponsored by the CECON turtle hatchery. For just a $2 donation, you can pick a winner from a batch of recently hatched baby sea turtles. Set it at the starting line and wait for the "go" signal before watching it make its dash across the sand and into the sea. If your turtle is the first to make it across a string near the waterline, you'll win free dinner for two at one of the local hotels. Whether or not your turtle wins, you can't beat the feeling of holding one of these remarkable creatures in your hand and pondering its fate against the elements and overwhelming odds.

SIGHTS
◖ Biotopo Monterrico-Hawaii

This protected biotope encompasses the beaches and mangrove swamps of Monterrico and those of adjacent Parque Hawaii, which are the prime nesting sites for sea turtles on Guatemala's Pacific seaboard, including the giant leatherback and smaller olive ridley turtles. Locals are involved in a conservation project with the local turtle hatchery whereby they are allowed to keep half of the eggs they collect from nests and turn in the other half to the hatchery. In the heart of town and run by the San Carlos University Center for Conservation Studies (CECON), the **Tortugario Monterrico** (on the sandy street just behind Johnny's Place, 8 A.M.–noon and 2 P.M.–5 P.M. daily, $1) encompasses a turtle hatchery right on the beach, where collected eggs are reburied and allowed to hatch under protected conditions. There's also a visitors center. In addition to baby sea turtles, the hatchery has enclosures housing green iguanas, crocodiles, and freshwater turtles bred on-site for release into the wild. The staff at CECON is always on the lookout for Spanish-speaking volunteers. (For more on this park, see the sidebar *Monterrico-Hawaii and Its Sea Turtles*.)

Parque Hawaii

Eight kilometers east along the sandy shoreline is Parque Hawaii, a more remote turtle nesting and iguana/crocodile breeding site on a pretty beach marked by the presence of sand dunes. The Wildlife Rescue and Conservation Association (ARCAS, www.arcasguatemala.com), has a sea turtle, crocodile, and mangrove conservation project here. Volunteers are welcome for a minimum one-week commitment ($50 per week for accommodations only) and assist in various projects, including caring for the animals, construction projects, mangrove reforestation, environmental education, and turtle egg collection/hatchery management. Turtle nesting season runs June–November with the peak of the action in August and September.

You can get to the park from Monterrico via public bus ($0.50), pickup ($5), or via a 20-minute boat ride through the canals ($20). Buses leave at 6 A.M., 11 A.M., 1:30 P.M., and 3:30 P.M.

NIGHTLIFE

For a Central American beach town, the nightlife scene in Monterrico is pretty tame. This is certainly not your average "spring break" destination. Most places close at 10 P.M., with only a few exceptions. The liveliest place in town is **El Animal Desconocido** (8 P.M.– 1 A.M. Thurs.–Sat.), where you can chill out to an eclectic mix of dance and rock music in a colorful atmosphere. The best place for a sunset drink is by the beach at **El Caracol,** where the strawberry daiquiri is a rare treat. It closes at 10 P.M. Another good option for a drink is **Taberna El Pelícano,** behind Johnny's Place, but it also closes early. The poolside bar at **The Marlin Hotel** is another popular watering hole. It sometimes closes late.

RECREATION

You won't find a whole lot to do around here other than the beaches. Whether from a lack of entrepreneurial initiative or what have you, the recreational options aside from sunbathing, swimming, and walking along the beach are pretty limited. You can always tour the mangrove-lined canals and perhaps do some bird-watching, but there are curiously no outfitters offering such trips in these parts, unlike elsewhere along the Pacific Coast. For **boat tours,** ask at the CECON station for recommended boatmen and tour guides (trained by CECON) who can take you around to see birds and, with some luck, iguanas and anteaters. Some of the beachfront hotels rent boogie boards.

ACCOMMODATIONS
Under $10

Monterrico's original backpacker spot, **Hotel Baule Beach** no longer holds much appeal because of the availability of much better options. Beds in unattractive rooms consist of a concrete slab with thin cushioning. Numerous thefts have also been reported. Stay here only if in dire need. West from here, the next place over is **El Kaiman** (tel. 5617-9880), where for $7 per person you get a bed, a cold-water shower, and not much else. The hotel pool looked somewhat funky. A few doors down is **El Caracol** (tel. 5918-3632 or 5693-0430), a small three-room hotel that feels somewhat like a bed-and-breakfast inn. Two rooms have private bath and fan ($20 d); the third room is a six-bed dorm ($5 per person). There is soothing decor and candlelight by evening and a hammock/couch area for lounging. The rooms are spotless. Another option in this price range is **Hotel El Delfín** (tel. 5702-6701), just west of Calle Principal, where rooms with shared bath go for $6 per person or $8 per person with private bath. All the rooms have mosquito netting and fan, keeping out critters from an open *palapa*-style roof. The beds here consist of a mattress on a concrete slab. The place is kind of shabby but it has a nice enough restaurant and small swimming pool. There are hammocks on the beach.

A good value in this price range can be found at **Hotel Long Beach** (tel. 5863-4419), down the street from Taberna El Pelícano, with spotless rooms with firm beds built next to a pool for $10 per person. There are hammocks for lounging outside your door.

$10-25

An old standby, **Johnny's Place** (tel. 5812-0409), is set right on the beach. The rooms are built so as to share a swimming pool with the unit next door and have cold-water showers, foamy beds, and some spartan furnishings under a thatched roof. Rooms with fan cost $25 d on weekends. Larger rooms with air-conditioning, kitchen, and cable TV go for $40 on weekends. Rates are considerably less during the week. There's a restaurant/bar on the beach and a sand volleyball court. Heading farther west along the beach toward Calle Principal, on a quiet side street you'll find **The Marlin Hotel** (tel. 5851-1687), a fairly new place seemingly popular with a younger crowd. There are a bar and a small pool with tables in the courtyard. The rooms have ceiling fan, private cold-water shower, cable TV, and thin mattresses. There are hammocks outside your door. Rates are $12 per person and it is open only on weekends outside of holidays.

On Calle Principal near the beach is **La Palma** (tel. 5817-3911 or 2363-4905, $13 d), with seven rooms with ceiling fan set around a pretty garden with a pleasing fountain. There are a small swimming pool, a hammock lounging area, and a restaurant serving very good French food. Directly behind Johnny's Place on the sandy street parallel to the shoreline is **Hotel Brisas del Mar** (tel. 5517-1142), offering simple rooms with air-conditioning ($33 d) or fan ($13 d). There's a restaurant serving basic, cheap fare upstairs.

East from the heart of town and right on the beach is **Hotel El Mangle** (tel. 5514-6517), where very basic rooms with cold-water private bath, fan, mosquito-netted beds, and unscreened thatched roof cost $22 d on weekdays and $27 d on weekends. There are newer rooms with air-conditioning for $37 and $43. There are a small pool and restaurant/bar by the beach.

$25-50

West of Calle Principal along the beach you'll find pleasant **C Café del Sol** (tel. 5810-0821, www.cafe-del-sol.com), where rooms in the original building with cold-water showers in private bath, fan, and mosquito netting cost $27 d. There's a newer section behind the hotel across the street where slightly nicer rooms

painted in cheerful yellows featuring some decor cost $33 d. The rooms also have a small patio fronting the street. The restaurant here is quite good.

East again from Calle Principal, around the corner and down the street from Taberna El Pelícano, is **Hotel San Gregorio** (tel. 2238-4690 or 5415-4361), with somewhat generic new rooms centered around a swimming pool for $40 d, all with air-conditioning, some with fan. Along the beach heading east from Johnny's Place, you'll find **C Hotel Pez de Oro** (tel. 2368-3684 reservations or 7920-9785 hotel, www.pezdeoro.com), an excellent choice with tastefully decorated rooms built around a swimming pool with wooden deck. The 11 attractive bungalows, all with private bath, feature terra-cotta floors, nice decorative accents, and firm beds. Rates are $40 d weekdays and $52 d on weekends. Equally well decorated and furnished raised-platform bungalows with nice decks (or patio) and hammock in a separate area with its own swimming pool cost the same. The restaurant here is excellent.

Farther east along the beach about a kilometer on a much quieter and cleaner stretch of beach outside of town is **Dulce y Salado** (tel. 5817-9046), with eight simple and spotless rooms housed in thatched-roof cabins centered around a swimming pool. All rooms have private bath, fan, and mosquito netting with a hammock for lounging out front. Rates for weekday stays are $28 d. On weekends, you can buy a package for $30 per person per day including room, breakfast, and lunch (but not drinks or gratuity). Weekend packages are sold on a minimum double-occupancy basis, but call ahead and speak to the friendly Italian owners if you're traveling solo.

$50-100

If you're looking for stylish beachside digs look no farther than Monterrico's newest hotel, also Italian-owned, next door to Dulce y Salado. Under the same ownership as Panajachel's Hotel Dos Mundos, **C Dos Mundos Pacific Resort** (tel. 7762-2078, h2mundos@ intelnet.net.gt, www.hoteldosmundos.com,

$80–140 d) was nearing completion. This fabulous property features 14 luxurious beachfront villas with terra-cotta floors, hot-water shower, and air-conditioning housed in ecochic thatched-roof structures with private patio. The bathrooms feature artsy ceramic sinks and oversize "rain" showerheads. The fine restaurant serves excellent Italian cuisine overlooking an infinity-edge swimming pool and the sea.

FOOD

Most of Monterrico's hotels, particularly those that are on the beach, serve food. The following are the best of the hotel restaurants, along with a few nonhotel eateries serving decent food. **⟨ Café del Sol** (all meals daily), in its namesake hotel, serves excellent seafood dishes ($4–8) under an airy *palapa* or on a pleasant beachside patio. The restaurant at **Hotel La Palma** serves excellent French cuisine cooked by its French owner/chef for breakfast, lunch, and dinner. For Italian fare, you can't beat the atmosphere at **Pez de Oro** ($5–7), but the food at **⟨ Dulce y Salado** ($4–7) is just slightly better. Its Italian owners prepare tasty pasta at affordable prices. On the fancier side, the restaurant at the new **Dos Mundos Pacific Resort** next door, overlooking the sea and an infinity-edge swimming pool, is probably also quite good thanks to its Italian chef, though the restaurant was yet to be finished. Write in and let me know if it's worth the splurge.

Hotels aside, there are also a few decent stand-alone eateries in town. On Calle Principal across the street from La Palma is **El Divino Maestro,** which does inexpensive seafood. Behind Johnny's Place on the sandy street parallel to the shore is **Taberna El Pelícano** (noon–2 P.M. and 6:30–9:30 P.M. Mon.–Fri., 6:30–10 P.M. Sat., noon–3 P.M. and 7–9:30 P.M. Sun.), where there are good pasta dishes and seafood for $4–8 and a fully stocked bar.

SERVICES

There are no banks or ATMs in town. Monterrico's post office is on Calle Principal. You'll also find a nameless Internet communications center on this street.

Language Schools

If you want to learn Spanish at the beach, head to **Proyecto Lingüístico Monterrico** (Calle Principal, tel. 5619-8200, www.playade monterrico.com/proyling.htm), where 20 hours of one-on-one instruction per week cost $75. Accommodations with a local family are available for $50 per week for room and board.

GETTING THERE

There are two ways to get to Monterrico. The first of these is via the 25-kilometer road from Puerto Viejo (Iztapa). The other option is via the town of Taxisco, from which you continue south for 17 kilometers to La Avellana. At La Avellana you make a ferry crossing ($7 per vehicle), traveling for about 20 minutes through the mangrove swamps. Most people seem to prefer the route via Iztapa, as the road is smooth and fast and there are some new, enticing accommodations options along this route. Buses leave from Guatemala City's Zone 4 bus terminal every 30 minutes for Taxisco on their way to Chiquimulilla between 5 A.M. and 6 P.M. Connecting buses make the trip down to La Avellana. **Transportes Cubanita** leaves the Zone 4 bus terminal directly for La Avellana at 10:30 A.M., 12:30 P.M., and 2:30 P.M. There are five buses a day from Puerto Viejo (Iztapa) to Monterrico leaving at 8 A.M., 10 A.M., noon, 1:30 P.M., and 4 P.M. As always, there's the occasional pickup truck heading this way.

Increasingly popular are daily shuttle buses from Antigua costing about $25 on weekdays and $15 on weekends. Among the options is **Aventuras Vacacionales** (tel. 7832-6056, www .sailing-diving-guatemala.com/guatemala-tours/ shuttles.php) and **Turansa** (tel. 7832-2928, info@ turansa.com, www.turansa.com).

East to El Salvador

From Taxisco, the road continues east parallel to the coastline, passing near the town of Chiquimulilla before heading into higher elevations, from which there are fantastic panoramas of the ocean below.

CHIQUIMULILLA

Chiquimulilla is an adequate place to stop should you need to regroup after crossing the border from El Salvador or if you need a place to stay on the way there. If you need to hit an ATM, your best bet is the 5B ATM at Banrural (1a Calle and 1a Avenida Zona 3). There's also a Banco Industrial Visa ATM at 1a Avenida and 3a Calle Zona 2. Should you need to stay, try the **Hotel San Carlos** (Barrio Santiago, tel. 7885-0187, $13 d).

Outside of town at Km. 99 of the Pacific Coast Highway (CA-2) is **Erhco Park** (tel. 7885-0139), a fairly decent ecological park and working farm occupying almost 70 acres.

There are nature trails, horseback riding, waterfalls, and farm animals. There's a small restaurant and you can camp or spend the night here in simple bungalows.

LAS LISAS

As you head east from Chiquimulilla close to the Salvadoran border, a turnoff from the Pacific Coast Highway (CA-2) at Km. 144 heads south to the small village of Las Lisas, which has some nice beaches on the other side of the Canal de Chiquimulilla. The town itself is unremarkable and tourism infrastructure virtually nonexistent, though there are at least two hotels in the area that merit mention.

Isleta de Gaia

Near Las Lisas is one of Guatemala's most exotic hideaways. Isleta de Gaia (tel. 7885-0044, www.isleta-de-gaia.com, $67–144), on a sandy spit between the Chiquimulilla Canal and the

© AL ARGUETA

a rainy day in Las Lisas

Pacific Ocean known as Barra del Jiote, is a great place to get away from it all. There are 12 attractive bamboo bungalows of varying sizes facing the clean, sandy beach or the lagoon; all are built around a nice swimming pool. The restaurant is open for breakfast, lunch, and dinner, and serves excellent international fare in the $5–12 range. The service is second to none. Your gracious host, Francois, will stop at nothing to make your stay enjoyable and keep things running smoothly, including emptying the rapidly filling swimming pool in the middle of a torrential tropical downpour to save its filter system.

The only drawback is accessibility. To get there you must hire a boat from the main dock in Las Lisas at a cost of $13 each way, as the lodge does not provide a pickup service from Las Lisas. You can sometimes hitch a ride back if someone is running in to town for supplies. It's about a 20-minute ride to the lodge from Las Lisas.

Caleta Azul
Divers will want to check out Caleta Azul (Barra del Jiote, tel. 5715-2849 or 5715-4101, www.caletaazul.net, $145 d all-inclusive), fronting a nice stretch of wide, sandy beach.

In the waters just off the coast are the remains of two sunken vessels, one dating to the 1950s, which scuba divers can explore with the help of the lodge's diving outfit. The lodge itself features 10 rooms in comfortable thatched-roof cabanas with private bathroom, fan, a patio, and hammocks. There's also a two-bedroom furnished apartment with air-conditioning. Meals are included in the room rate and feature tasty Caribbean dishes, including seafood stews, served in an airy *palapa* structure with lovely sea views. There are also a bar and swimming pool. Other recreational options include visits to the surrounding mangrove swamps and deep-sea fishing. If you call ahead, the lodge can help you out with transportation from the boat dock at Las Lisas.

CIUDAD PEDRO DE ALVARADO
The border crossing to El Salvador is found at Ciudad Pedro de Alvarado, which is fairly quiet. Most traffic uses the crossing farther north at Valle Nuevo/Las Chinamas. There are frequent buses from here to Escuintla and onward to Guatemala City. There are basic accommodations and eateries on both sides of the border.

EL ORIENTE AND IZABAL

These two very different geographical regions comprise the part of Guatemala east of Guatemala City all the way to the Honduran border and the Caribbean Sea. Izabal is a sweltering jungle coastland with rainforests and beaches sharing some similarities with Belize to its north. The region known as *El Oriente,* meanwhile, is a mix of temperate mountains and semiarid plains. As you head east from Guatemala City on the *Carretera al Atlántico* (CA-9), the road descends into this region of dusty plains and cactus-studded hills. Farther along, in the department of Izabal, the terrain becomes lush and green before ending at Puerto Barrios, on the Caribbean Sea, just about 300 kilometers from the capital.

The Izabal region features a unique kind of Caribbean experience not at all like Cancún or the West Indies but nonetheless beautiful. Tourism promoters have labeled this, "A different Caribbean." Cruise ships regularly dock at Puerto Santo Tomás de Castilla, just across the bay from Puerto Barrios. Its new cruise-ship terminal is fast becoming a motor for the tourism development of this long-overlooked Caribbean coastal region. Cruise-ship day-trippers can explore a rainforest and pristine jungle river with waterfalls and pools in the lush green mountains looming over the port. From Puerto Barrios, it's just a quick hop to remote beaches on the peninsula of Punta de Manabique, the intriguing Caribbean town of Lívingston, or the exotic jungle canyon of the Río Dulce.

The little-explored beaches and wetlands of Punta de Manabique are protected as a wildlife refuge and offer some unique opportunities for

© AL ARGUETA

HIGHLIGHTS

LOOK FOR ◖ TO FIND RECOMMENDED SIGHTS, ACTIVITIES, DINING, AND LODGING.

◖ **The Ruins of Copán:** This wonderful Mayan city just across the border in Honduras is home to some of the finest carved stelae in the Mayan world and to an outstanding museum housing several original monuments (page 228).

◖ **The Ruins of Quiriguá:** Also harboring beautifully carved stelae set amid luxuriant banana plantations and jungle, this small Mayan site is one of only three UNESCO World Heritage Sites in Guatemala (page 239).

◖ **Cerro San Gil and Río Las Escobas:** This fantastic rainforest preserve harboring a protected watershed with waterfalls and pristine pools is just minutes away from the cruise-ship terminal at Puerto Santo Tomás de Castilla (page 245).

◖ **Punta de Manabique Wildlife Refuge:** A remote peninsula abounding in wildlife and pristine nature, it also offers deserted beaches and the opportunity to explore adjoining wetland canals for excellent bird-watching (page 246).

◖ **The Zapotillo Cayes:** Sail or motor-boat to the picture-postcard beaches of this remote island chain on the southern fringes of the Belize Barrier Reef for scuba diving, swimming, or just plain relaxation (page 255).

◖ **Bocas del Polochic Wildlife Refuge:** Another excellent spot for bird-watching, this seldom-visited park has excellent visitor facilities from where you can explore jungle trails, wetland canals, caves, and sinkholes (page 265).

ecotourism, wildlife-viewing, and beachcombing. Lívingston is a standout for its unique Garífuna culture brought to coastal Guatemala from the Caribbean island of St. Vincent by way of Roatán, Honduras. This Black Carib influence provides a fascinating contrast to Guatemala's largely Mayan heritage with rhythmic dancing and musical customs that complete the Caribbean experience. The Río Dulce canyon connects Lívingston (and the Caribbean Sea) to Lake Izabal, Guatemala's largest lake. Along the Río Dulce, you'll find lush jungle canyons, hot springs, and side streams offering unique options for jungle accommodations. In the town of Río Dulce, at the mouth of Lake Izabal, you'll find a variety of tourist services and boat marinas, as it's become a popular shelter for boats sailing the Western Caribbean. The homes of wealthy Guatemalans also dot the river's banks. Lake Izabal harbors some intriguing natural attractions of its own, including a vast, little-explored wetland preserve of astounding biological diversity and a funky Spanish castle built to repel the attacks of 17th-century pirates.

Back on Highway CA-9 closer to Guatemala City, a branch road heads southeast to El Oriente, partially occupied by Guatemala's Eastern Highlands. The road continues east to Honduras, where you can visit the incredible ruins of Copán, just 12 kilometers across the border. Along with the nearby Mayan site of Quiriguá (Guatemala), Copán showcases some of the Mayan world's finest stelae, carved monuments depicting historical events in the life of Mayan dynasties. Copán's museum is among the finest attractions in the Mayan world, along with its restored temple pyramids, palaces, hieroglyphic stairway, and ball court. The surrounding mountainous countryside is also becoming increasingly popular with travelers exploring coffee farms, a jungle bird park, and hot springs. Also near the border, on the Guatemalan side, is the town of Esquipulas, a popular pilgrimage site with Central American tourists for its Black Christ, believed to have miraculous healing powers.

Radically different from the department of Izabal, Guatemala's other eastern departments comprising the region of El Oriente are semi-arid and populated by ladino cowboys, attracting few international travelers. A standout in this area is the odd crater lake atop the Ipala Volcano, near the town of Chiquimula.

THE LAY OF THE LAND

The eastern department of El Progreso is dominated by the presence of the Motagua River Valley, a region of cactus-studded plains lying between the rain-soaked Sierra de las Minas to the north and the Sierra del Espíritu Santo, along the Honduran border to the east. The Carretera al Atlántico passes through much of this terrain. South of here, the low-lying departments of Jalapa and Jutiapa have some green hills and a volcano or two, though they are not of the dramatic, conical kind found in the Western Highlands. The Ipala Volcano and crater lake is this region's best-known geographical feature. East of here, the areas along the Honduran border near Copán and Esquipulas have some pretty mountain scenery where coffee is grown.

The department of Izabal is one of Guatemala's most attractive for those who enjoy coastal environments. There are still large expanses of tropical rainforests, which receive ample rainfall when warm, moist air from the Caribbean Sea rises on mountain slopes. The Montañas del Mico stand as silent sentinels dominating a biological corridor between the Bahía de Amatique and the lazy Río Dulce to the north, which empties into the Caribbean. Guatemala's Caribbean coastline lacks the aquamarine beaches of Cancún and Belize, but the peninsula of Punta de Manabique stands out for its wild and scenic white-sand coastline. Farther out to sea is the tail end of the Belize Barrier Reef and some easily accessible cayes. Inland, Lake Izabal is a huge body of water with some nice beaches of its own and some impressive wetlands.

CLIMATE

The overall climate in these parts is warm, even in the Eastern Highlands, which lack the dramatic altitude of their western counterparts. The Motagua Valley is arid, whereas the Izabal region is warm and humid year-round. During the warmest months of April and May, the temperature and humidity can seem unbearable, though coastal regions get a lightly refreshing sea breeze that helps alleviate some of the tropical swelter. Temperatures can hover round 100°F during this time of year. At other times, it hovers somewhere between 85°F and 95°F. Izabal is particularly rainy and is sometimes battered by storms or the occasional hurricane.

PLANNING YOUR TIME

Copán can be done in a day or two, while Quiriguá requires only a couple of hours at most. It makes a good stop on the way to Puerto Barrios. If you really want to see Ipala Volcano and crater lake, you can probably do it as a day trip from Chiquimula or Esquipulas. I would recommend most foreign visitors give the latter town a miss, unless you really want to see the Black Christ statue housed in the town's basilica. There is plenty to see and do on the Caribbean Coast. Puerto Barrios is not

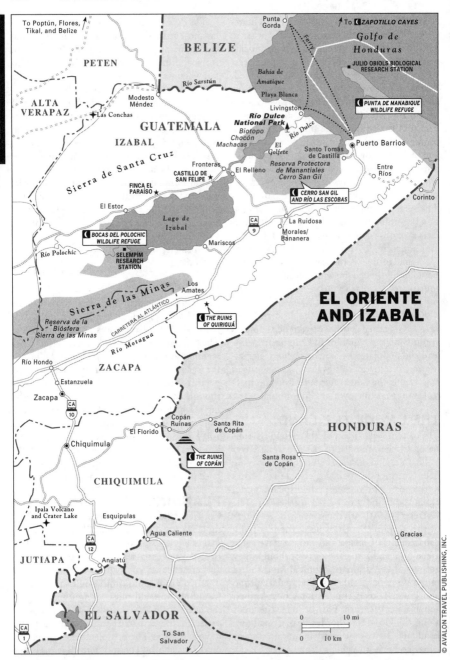

To Poptún, Flores, Tikal, and Belize

BELIZE

PETEN

ALTA VERAPAZ

Las Conchas

Modesto Méndez

Río Sarstún

GUATEMALA

IZABAL

Sierra de Santa Cruz

Fronteras

CASTILLO DE SAN FELIPE ★

FINCA EL PARAÍSO ★

El Estor

El Relleno

Lago de Izabal

CA 9

BOCAS DEL POLOCHIC WILDLIFE REFUGE

SELEMPÍM RESEARCH STATION

Río Polochic

Mariscos

La Ruidosa

Morales/ Bananera

Los Amates

Sierra de las Minas

CARRETERA AL ATLÁNTICO

THE RUINS OF QUIRIGUÁ

Reserva de la Biósfera Sierra de las Minas

Río Motagua

EL ORIENTE AND IZABAL

Río Hondo

ZACAPA

Estanzuela

Zacapa

CA 10

Chiquimula

Copán Ruinas

El Florido

Santa Rita de Copán

HONDURAS

THE RUINS OF COPÁN

Santa Rosa de Copán

CHIQUIMULA

Ipala Volcano and Crater Lake

Esquipulas

CA 12

Agua Caliente

Gracias

JUTIAPA

Angiatú

CA 1

EL SALVADOR

To San Salvador

Punta Gorda

To ZAPOTILLO CAYES

Golfo de Honduras

JULIO OBIOLS BIOLOGICAL RESEARCH STATION

Bahía de Amatique

Playa Blanca

Livingston

Río Dulce National Park

Biotopo Chocón Machacas

El Golfete

Río Dulce

Santo Tomás de Castilla

Reserva Protectora de Manantiales Cerro San Gil

CERRO SAN GIL AND RÍO LAS ESCOBAS

Puerto Barrios

Entre Ríos

Corinto

Ferry

PUNTA DE MANABIQUE WILDLIFE REFUGE

0   10 mi

0   10 km

© AVALON TRAVEL PUBLISHING, INC.

the most pleasant town, but there's no need to stay here as there are now better alternatives for exploring the Cerro San Gil Reserve and Río Las Escobas across Bahía de Amatique in Santo Tomás de Castilla. It's worth at least a half day for exploring, though you could easily spend the night in a comfortable lodge or take a few days to cross the rugged Montañas del Mico to Río Dulce for the ultimate jungle adventure. Puerto Barrios merits an hour or two at best as a transit point to Lívingston or Río Dulce.

A few days in Lívingston will allow you time to explore nearby waterfalls, beaches, and rainforests. For a real treat, sail the Caribbean to the outlying Belize cayes for a week or explore the remote peninsula of Punta de Manabique. The latter requires at least one night's stay because of its remote location. From Lívingston, you can also explore the Río Dulce canyon in a few hours while traveling to Río Dulce town, but it's also possible to stop over midway and spend a night or two at some comfortable lodgings on the Río Tatín tributary. Río Dulce will probably captivate you with its tropical charm and location at the mouth of Lake Izabal. It makes a great place to chill out for a few days before heading north to Petén or before or after some exploring on the lake.

Río Hondo to Esquipulas

The town of Río Hondo is an oasis of fun, featuring excellent restaurants, refreshing swimming pools, and even a water park. Many travelers heading between Guatemala and Puerto Barrios like to break up their journey here. Heading south from the Río Hondo Junction, the road passes through the hot lowland towns of Zacapa and Chiquimula before climbing into the mountains and into a bowl-shaped valley dominated by Esquipulas. There's really not much here for international travelers, so the towns along this corridor won't be covered in depth, aside from a few hotel and restaurant listings should you need to stop while passing through en route to other attractions. A worthy side trip is the Ipala Volcano and crater lake.

RÍO HONDO JUNCTION

The hotels and restaurants lining highway CA-9 (the road to the Atlantic Coast) at Río Hondo are popular places to stop and eat for travelers heading to or from faraway Puerto Barrios or Esquipulas. The dry, warm climate lends itself marvelously to swimming and other water-centered activities.

Accommodations and Food

All of the options listed here are found at Km. 126 and offer comfortable air-conditioned rooms with private bathroom and cable TV. All have swimming pool. Among the options is old standby **Hotel Longarone** (tel. 7934-7126, $45 d). Its large swimming pool has diving boards and a water slide. Some of the rooms can be dark. The restaurant/bar serves international food ($6–12) with excellent service and cleanliness. In addition to a large, attractive palm-lined swimming pool, **Hotel El Atlantico** (tel. 7934-7160, $45 d) boasts lovely gardens, a gym, and children's play areas. The indoor and outdoor restaurant/bars serve international cuisine. **Hotel Santa Cruz** (tel. 7934-7075, $50 d) has beautifully landscaped, flower-filled gardens around its swimming pool, spotless rooms, and an excellent restaurant serving (you guessed it) international dishes.

Valle Dorado Water Park

Another 23 kilometers east from Río Hondo along highway CA-9 is Valle Dorado Water Park (Km. 149, tel. 7943-6666, www.hotelvalledorado.com, 6 A.M.–6 P.M. Tues.–Sun., $7 adults, $5 children), well worth the wait if you can curb your appetite, as there are a variety of food options inside the park and tons of fun stuff for the kids (or the kid in you). The large theme park has a variety of pools and water slides as well as a very comfortable hotel with room rates starting at $70 d.

ESTANZUELA

Continuing southeast about six kilometers from Río Hondo along Highway CA-10 (the junction is at Km. 135), the first town you'll come across is Estanzuela. The terrain here is decidedly dry, resembling parts of Arizona, making for an excellent environment for the preservation of fossils. Sure enough, you can see some dinosaur bones, including the skeleton of a 50,000-year-old mastodon and that of a prehistoric whale at **Museo de Paleontología Bryan Patterson** (tel. 7941-4981, 9 A.M.– 5 P.M. daily, free admission). To get here, go through the town and follow the blue signs to the *museo*.

ZACAPA

The next stop along Highway CA-10 is the departmental capital of Zacapa. Its redeeming quality is the award-winning **Ron Zacapa Centenario,** sold in a festive woven-straw bottle holder. You don't have to go all the way to Zacapa to pick up a bottle, as it's available from its own duty-free shop at Guatemala City's international airport. You can pick up a bottle before your flight home.

CHIQUIMULA

Chiquimula is a hot, dry town and also a departmental capital. Like Zacapa, there is very little here for the international traveler. It does, however, serve as a transit point for southwest travel to the Ipala Lagoon or east to Copán, Honduras.

Accommodations and Food

Should you need to stay here, your best bet is **Hotel Hernandez** (3a Calle 7-41 Zona 1, tel. 7942-0708), with various types of rooms ranging from $6–20 d. The most expensive rooms overlook the swimming pool and have air-conditioning. A backup plan is **Hotel Posada Perla de Oriente** (2a Calle and 12 Avenida, tel. 7942-0014, $25–45 d), with tropical gardens, a swimming pool, and large, clean rooms with fan, hot-water bathroom, and cable TV. There are also rooms with air-conditioning. The restaurant serves decent food.

Other options for food include **Pollo Campero,** on the corner of 7a Avenida and 4a Calle, serving the fried chicken so beloved by Guatemalans in an air-conditioned environment. A fancier option is **Restaurante Chiquimulja** (3a Calle 6-51 Zona 1), part of its namesake hotel, serving pasta dishes, grilled meats, and other international fare ($5–8) in an attractive two-story palm-roofed building. It overlooks the central plaza. Guatemala's best-known supermarket chain, **Paiz** (recently acquired by Wal-Mart), is next door on the corner of 7a Avenida and 3a Calle.

Services

Among the services you'll find here are a bank, Banco G&T Continental (half a block south of the plaza at 7a Avenida 4-75 Zona 1. The post office is on 10a Avenida between 1a and 2a Calle. For phone calls, Telgua is on 3a Calle east of the central plaza. Internet is available at Email Center (6a Avenida 4-51, 9 A.M.–9 P.M. daily).

Getting There

The town bus terminal is midway between the plaza and the highway on 1a Calle between 10a and 11a Avenidas. There are hourly buses to Guatemala City (3.5 hours) and Puerto Barrios (four hours), half-hourly minibuses to Esquipulas (one hour), hourly buses and minibuses to Ipala (one hour) and the Salvadoran border at Anguiatú (one hour). Buses to the El Florido border (1.5 hours, for Copán, Honduras) leave from a separate terminal one block north every 45 minutes until 4:30 P.M.

NEAR CHIQUIMULA
Ipala Volcano and Crater Lake

It's a pleasant drive southwest of Chiquimula to the wonderful crater lake of the 1,650-meter-high Ipala Volcano. The summit is most easily accessible from the village of Agua Blanca (you'll see blue INGUAT signs leading the way), from which a paved road continues to an area near the top. Once at the crater lake, you'll see a visitors center, where the park rangers collect a modest park fee of $1.50.

A series of nature trails wind their way around the lagoon. You'll pass a lookout with an excellent view of the 3.5-kilometer-wide lake as well as the entrance to the **Cueva de la Leona** (Cave of the Lioness). The volcanic crater and its lake were designated as national parks in 1998. Water for four local villages continued to be extracted until very recently, meaning that the lake has lost much of its original water volume. The lake is filled entirely with rainwater.

There are hourly buses and pickups from the village of Ipala, on the north side of the volcano, to Agua Blanca. Minibuses run between Chiquimula and Ipala every half hour. You can camp at the lake or stay in a basic *hospedaje* in Ipala.

Esquipulas

The town of Esquipulas is popular with travelers from other parts of Central America who come here on a pilgrimage to see the miraculous Black Christ. Although the large white basilica is somewhat impressive, there is really little else of interest for the non-Central American traveler. If you really wish to see the Black Christ, by all means do so, but your time in Guatemala is probably best spent elsewhere. Nearby, there are a few natural attractions, but little that's been developed for tourism as in the Verapaces or Izabal regions. Esquipulas's other main claim to fame is the 1987 signing of an accord between area leaders outlining the establishment of peace processes to end the civil wars in El Salvador and Guatemala.

SIGHTS
Basilica
You'll see the large white church as soon as you enter the proximity of Esquipulas, as it dominates the view of town as you approach it from the road. Once you're in town, the basilica can be reached by crossing a large, pleasant palm-lined park leading to a flight of steps. A side entrance leads to the **Black Christ** (6 A.M.–7 P.M. daily), where you can shuffle into the line and follow pilgrims to a glass case behind the church altar for a brief glimpse. The height of veneration occurs during an annual festival on January 15, with week-

ends and religious holidays also popular. You may have the place all to yourself during the week, contrasting sharply with the melee seen on weekends. Inside the church is the usual atmosphere of hushed reverence and incense found throughout Guatemala's churches. For a real treat, check out the vending stalls near the church where you'll find a motley assortment of religious kitsch.

Cueva de las Minas
This cave complex lies about 300 meters south of the turnoff into town along the road heading to Honduras. It's a further 500 meters from the entrance gate to the complex (6:30 A.M.–4 P.M. daily). There are a fifty-meter-deep cave and the Río El Milagro, which folks say holds miraculous healing powers. Bring your own flashlight.

RECREATION
Chatun
After a visit to the Black Christ, many pilgrims feel the need to unwind for the rest of their stay. Among the recreational options for devotees and their families is Chatun (tel. 7943-0498, 9 A.M.–6 P.M. Wed.–Sun., $8 adults, $4 children), a very pleasant nature park three kilometers outside of town in the direction of Honduras. Among the many attractions are a nine-station canopy tour, a petting zoo, duck pond, inviting swimming pools, camping area,

climbing wall, horseback riding, and nature trails. You'll probably work up an appetite with all there is to do, for which there are a restaurant and several snack bars. If you're traveling with kids, this would most certainly be an obligatory stop.

ACCOMMODATIONS

Avoid staying in Esquipulas's low-budget accommodations, as they are the hideout of large groups of men from elsewhere in Central America, including gang members, who hang out in these parts seeking to make their way north. Esquipulas is somewhat close to the Honduran border and so has become a transit point for illegal immigration.

$10-25

The first option in this category is the **Hotel y Restaurante Aposento Alto** (3a Avenida 10-66 Zona 1, tel. 7943-1115, $20 d), where the rooms have hot water, cable TV, fan, and fluorescent lighting. The restaurant downstairs serves inexpensive Guatemalan and international dishes for breakfast, lunch, and dinner. Among several options facing the park from the southwest is **Hotel Posada Santiago** (tel. 7943-2023, 2a Avenida 11-58 Zona 1, $20 d), with comfortable rooms with hot-water bath, cable TV, and fan. One double room has a view of the basilica and there is a good restaurant serving Guatemalan and international fare in the lobby. At the upper end of this price category is **Hotel Villa Zonia** (10a Calle 1-84 Zona 1, tel. 7943-1143, $25 d), very close to the bus terminal and surrounded by budget accommodations. The smallish rooms have private bath with cable TV and hot water, but there are better values elsewhere. The single room prices, in particular, are a rip-off.

$25-50

An excellent value in this price category is ❰ **Hotel Portal de la Fe** (tel. 7943-4124, info@portaldelafehotel.com, www.portaldelafehotel.com, $34 d), with 29 attractive, spotless rooms with comfortable beds with wrought-iron headboard, ceiling fan, and

private hot-water bath. Rooms are distributed on three floors around a pretty courtyard fountain lit from above by an opaque roof opening. Nightly rates include free half-hour use of Internet. It's on the main street heading into town (11a Calle) on the right. Another good value is **IV Centenario** (tel. 7943-1751, info@ivcentenariohotel.com, www.ivcentenariohotel.com, $34 d), also along 11a Calle toward the park, in a colorful building painted in shades of yellow and blue with rooms built around the swimming pool. All have cable TV and hot-water private bathroom.

Facing the park from its southwest side is popular **Hotel Payaquí** (tel. 7943-1143, $50 d), where there are two restaurants, one by the swimming pool, the other with a big-screen TV. They serve Guatemalan and international dishes including sandwiches and steaks. Meals are in the $5–8 range. Rooms are comfortable and spacious and include a fully stocked minifridge, fan, and private bath. Next door is the also-popular **Hotel El Peregrino** (tel. 7943-1054, $30 d), featuring cheerful rooms with fan, cable TV, and private bath. In-room furniture includes a plastic table and chairs. Directly behind, on 1a Avenida, is **Hotel Vistana al Señor** (tel. 5958-8426, $40 d), in a modern colonial-style building with comfortable beds and an upstairs sitting area with chairs and umbrellas.

$50-100

The attractive ❰ **Porta Hotel Legendario** (9a Calle y 3a Avenida Zona 1, tel. 7943-1022, www.portahotels.com, $75 d) has 42 rooms, including standard and deluxe rooms as well as suites, in a large building centered around the swimming pool. All are comfortable and spacious. There are a restaurant and bar. Online rates are substantially higher. Try to book by calling directly if you can. The other option in this category is **Hotel El Gran Chortí** (tel. 7943-1148, Km. 222 on the road into town, $85 d), where the rooms have all the usual comforts you'd expect to find in this price category. There are a nice restaurant and swimming pool.

FOOD

The restaurant at the **Porta Hotel Legendario** (9a Calle y 3a Avenida Zona 1, tel. 7943-1022, 7 A.M.–9 P.M.) serves international fare including decent breakfasts, steaks, pasta, and salads. Some of the best light fare in town can be found at ◖ **Eco Moda Spa and Eco-Café** (Calle Real 3-48, tel. 7943-2764, ecomoda@esquipulas .com.gt, www.esquipulas.com.gt/ecomoda, 8 A.M.–9 P.M. Mon.–Sat.), set in a wonderful 250-year-old home. You can enjoy delicious sandwiches, salads, coffee, and pastries in a delightful garden courtyard. Before your meal, you can enjoy a relaxing massage in a quaint adobe parlor or opt for a sauna or hot-water whirlpool bath. The owners also arrange visits to their working coffee farm, **Finca Las Nubes** ($17 per person for accommodations), about an hour away via a rugged dirt road into the mountains, where you can sleep in a rustic but comfortable cabin and enjoy rappelling, walks to the nearby Río Frío and mountain biking, or do nothing at all.

Other culinary options closer to the center of town include **La Rotonda** (11 Calle, opposite Rutas Orientales, tel. 7943-2038, 7 A.M.–10 P.M. daily), where the pleasant circular dining area is arranged under a large awning. The menu includes pizza ($10 for a large pie), pasta, and burgers. Breakfasts ($2–4) are also quite good. **La Hacienda** (corner of 2a Avenida and 10a Calle, 8 A.M.–10 P.M.) is your best bet for grilled steaks, chicken, and seafood with prices in the $10–20 range. The perennial favorite with Guatemalans is **Pollo Campero,** just off 2a Avenida southwest of the park, where you can get your fried-chicken fix.

SERVICES
Communications

The post office is a bit far from the town center (about 10 blocks north) at 6a Avenida 2-15. Telgua is on the corner of 5a Avenida and 9a Calle with plenty of card-operated telephones. For Internet, try Global.com on 3a Avenida across from Banco Internacional.

Money

Banco Industrial (3a Avenida and 9a Calle) has a Visa ATM and can change dollars and cash travelers checks. Banco G&T Continental, across the street, will change money and cash travelers checks. Banco Internacional (3a Avenida 8-87 Zona 1) has a Visa ATM and is the local American Express agent.

GETTING THERE

The most comfortable bus service is via **Rutas Orientales** (11 Calle and 1a Avenida), with service to Guatemala City every half hour. Minibuses for the Honduran border post at Agua Caliente ($2) leave from across the street every half hour 6 A.M.–5 P.M. Taxis also leave from here. Minibuses to the Salvadoran border at Anguiatú ($2) and Chiquimula ($1.50) leave from an area farther east along 11 Calle, near the market, with similar frequency. If traveling to Copán via the El Florido border post, you'll have to take a minibus to Chiquimula and then connect onward.

Copán Archaeological Site (Honduras)

The Mayan site of Copán, just 13 kilometers across the border in Honduras, features some of the Mayan world's greatest artistic treasures, including numerous stelae and a hieroglyphic stairway that is the longest known Mayan inscription. Whereas Tikal has been likened to the Manhattan of Mayan cities for its grand scale and a population once thought to have numbered 100,000, Copán is likened to Paris for the exquisite quality of its artwork, unmatched in the Mayan world. It is thought to have harbored 25,000 inhabitants in its heyday.

Archaeologists are still busy excavating and restoring this site in addition to deciphering the jumbled mess of a hieroglyphic stairway (found tumbled and out of order). In recent years, they have undertaken the ambitious enterprise of digging tunnels beneath existing

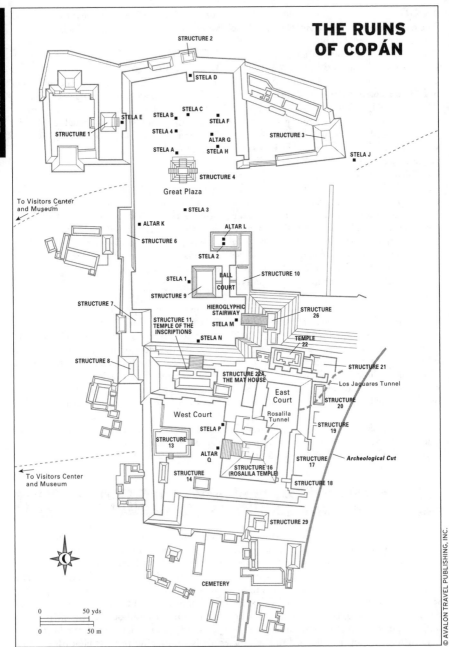

THE RUINS
OF COPÁN

STRUCTURE 2
STELA D
STELA C
STELA B
STELA F
STRUCTURE 3
STRUCTURE 1
STELA E
STELA 4
ALTAR G
STELA A
STELA H
STELA J
STRUCTURE 4
Great Plaza
To Visitors Center
and Museum
STELA 3
ALTAR K
ALTAR L
STRUCTURE 6
STELA 2
STELA 1
BALL
COURT
STRUCTURE 10
STRUCTURE 9
STRUCTURE 7
HIEROGLYPHIC
STAIRWAY
STRUCTURE
26
STRUCTURE 11,
TEMPLE OF THE
INSCRIPTIONS
STELA M
TEMPLE
22
STELA N
STRUCTURE 8
STRUCTURE 21
STRUCTURE 22A,
THE MAT HOUSE
Los Jaguares Tunnel
East
Court
STRUCTURE
20
West Court
Rosalila
Tunnel
STRUCTURE
19
STELA P
STRUCTURE
13
ALTAR
Q
STRUCTURE
17
Archeological Cut
STRUCTURE
14
STRUCTURE 16
(ROSALILA TEMPLE)
STRUCTURE 18
To Visitors Center
and Museum
STRUCTURE 29
CEMETERY
0   50 yds
0   50 m

© AVALON TRAVEL PUBLISHING, INC.

structures to uncover previous constructions. Among the magnificent finds are the well-preserved Rosalila (Rose-lilac) Temple and the tombs of several of Copán's rulers. You can see a wonderful reconstruction of the temple in all its Technicolor glory at Copán's excellent Sculpture Museum, in addition to several of the original finely carved stelae and monuments found in situ.

In addition to the ruins, the nearby town of **Copán Ruinas** has become increasingly popular as a destination unto itself for its excellent restaurants and accommodations. From here, you can explore the ruins and the surrounding countryside with ease.

CROSSING THE BORDER

The bare-bones border crossing at **El Florido** (open 6 A.M.–6 P.M.) includes some basic services but little else. There are some snack and soda stands and a Banrural which changes dollars and travelers checks. Ubiquitous money changers are also on-hand to help you change your quetzales for Honduran lempiras. Note that many tourist places in Copán take quetzales.

Crossing the border is fairly straightforward. If you're driving a rental car, you'll need to present a written letter from your rental-car agency allowing you to take the vehicle into Honduras. Otherwise, you'll have to leave it at the border. As at other border crossings, you may be asked to fork over a dollar or two in the form of an "unofficial" exit tax. Most Western nationalities, including U.S. citizens, need only a passport to get into Honduras; no visas are required. You can either get a three-day permit to enter and visit Copán and vicinity only or request a 30-day or 90-day entry permit by filling out an official request form. It all depends on your nationality what length of stay you're allowed. In either case officials will probably try to extract a dollar or two from you, both on the Guatemalan and Honduran sides. If on a three-day permit, you can still use your original entry stamp into Guatemala upon your return to continue traveling for the rest of your stay in the country.

Once in Honduras, there are onward buses

from the border to Copán Ruinas every 30 minutes or so ($2). Heading back, the last bus from El Florido to Chiquimula leaves at 4:30 P.M., but you are exhorted to cross the border much earlier in the day. To call Honduras, the country code is 504. Phone numbers are seven digits long. As in Guatemala, there are no area codes or city codes.

HISTORY
Early Copán

Although the fertile Copán Valley is thought to have been inhabited as early as 1,400 B.C., archaeological evidence points to its not having been occupied by the Mayans until around A.D. 100. Recorded history at the site does not begin until A.D. 426 with the establishment of Copán's royal dynasty. The site's early history was unearthed as recently as 1989, when excavations under the hieroglyphic stairway revealed a chamber subsequently nicknamed the **Founder's Room**. The chamber is thought to have been built by Copán's second ruler, **Mat Head** (after the odd-looking headdress with which he is depicted on stelae) in honor of his father, Copán's first ruler, in power A.D. 426–435. Subsequent kings appear to have revered this king, **Yax K'uk'Mo'**, and thought him to be semidivine. Archaeological evidence has found that he was indeed a great shaman. The tomb of Yax K'uk'Mo' was discovered in 1993 under the East Court of the Acropolis and the findings have yet to be fully revealed.

Little is known about the next several leaders in the dynastic line established by Yax K'uk'Mo', which ruled Copán throughout the entirety of its Classic Mayan history. It appears this dynasty was consolidating its rule at this time and establishing trade routes within the Mayan world and farther afield to powerful cities such as Teotihuacán. We know some of the names of Copán's leaders before A.D. 628: Cu Ix, the fourth king; Waterlily Jaguar, the seventh; Moon Jaguar, the 10th; and Butz' Chan, the 11th.

The Height of Power

The height of Copán's power came with the ascension to the throne of **Moon Jaguar** on May

26, 553. Moon Jaguar is credited with the construction of the **Rosalila Temple,** found buried beneath Structure 16 in 1993. Ruling A.D. 628–695 was one of Copán's greatest kings, **Smoke Imix,** the city's 12th ruler, who consolidated Copán into a regional commercial and military power. A stelae at the nearby site of Quiriguá bears his name and image, attesting to his probable takeover of the site. A prolific monument builder, Smoke Imix left behind the most inscribed monuments and temples out of all of Copán's rulers. His successor, **18 Rabbit** (A.D. 695–738), was also a prolific builder and pursued further military conquest. He came to a very unfortunate end, however, being captured and beheaded in a war with Quiriguá by its ruler, Cauac Sky.

Decline

Next in line was **Smoke Monkey** (A.D. 738–749), the 14th ruler of Copán, who built only one temple and erected no self-promoting stelae. The crushing blow suffered against Quiriguá may have resulted in the king's sharing power with a council composed of the city's nobility. Smoke Monkey's successor, **Smoke Shell** (A.D. 749–763), commissioned the creation of Copán's magnificent **Hieroglyphic Stairway,** containing 2,500 glyphs narrating the city's glorious past in an attempt to recapture the brilliance of the dynasty's heyday. By this time, however, it was evident that the city was in decline, a fact attested to by the subpar construction of the monument, which was later found collapsed, its narrative left scattered and out of order like a messy game of Jenga.

Yax Pac (A.D. 763–820) was Copán's 16th ruler, who continued along the same lines of beautifying the city. He left behind a fantastic monument known as **Altar Q,** depicting the city's 16 kings carved around a four-sided square monument with Copán's first king, Yax K'uk'Mo', passing the baton of leadership on to Yax Pac, thus legitimizing his rule.

Copán's 17th and final leader was **U Cit Tok',** assuming the throne in A.D. 822. His only legacy is the unfinished Altar L, of rather lackluster quality. Some believe this to be evidence of a sudden abandonment of Copán rather than a gradual collapse. As elsewhere in the Mayan world, Copán's collapse is thought to have been at least partially the result of exhausting the local ecosystem's carrying capacity, with a population thought to have reached 25,000 at its zenith. Agricultural areas were forced from the central part of the valley by urban expansion and the surrounding, less fertile hillsides eventually came under heavy cultivation. Soil erosion, droughts, deforestation, and rainy season flooding became the inevitable result. Though the city's core was abandoned, the valley was still somewhat heavily populated after this time. Archaeological evidence suggests another drop in population around 1200, after which the settlement patterns reverted to the small villages found by the Spanish in 1524. The ruins were left to be reclaimed by the jungle.

Rediscovery

The first known European to lay eyes on the ruined city was Diego García de Palacios, a representative of Spanish King Felipe II living in Guatemala and traveling through the Copán Valley. He described the ruins in a letter written to the king on March 8, 1576, and related that there were only five families living in the valley at the time, knowing nothing of the ruins' history or the people who built them. A Spanish colonel by the name of Juan Galindo would be the first to map the ruins almost 300 years later. Inspired by Galindo's report, John L. Stephens and Frederick Catherwood included a stop in Copán in 1839 during their famous journey to Mayan lands chronicled in *Incidents of Travel in Central America, Chiapas and Yucatán,* published two years later. Inspired by this book, British archaeologist Alfred P. Maudsley would make his way down to Copán in 1881. He returned four years later to fully map, excavate, photograph, and reconstruct the site off and on until 1902. Other scholars, among them Sylvanus Morley and J. Eric Thompson, would follow on his heels.

Present Day

In 1975, Harvard's Peabody Museum continued the investigations it had previously supported through Maudsley. Among its goals was the excavation of temples lying beneath existing structures, a product of the customary manner in which the Mayans built atop existing temples and pyramids. They embarked on a project to tunnel through Copán's numerous layers of construction and so have a glimpse into the city's history. Among the fascinating discoveries was the 1989 unearthing of the Rosalila Temple by Honduran archaeologist Ricardo Agurcia. An even earlier temple, Margarita, lies beneath it. Rosalila was found with its vivid ochre paint still visible. You can visit the excavation tunnel nowadays and/or see a replica of Rosalila in the Sculpture Museum.

Tunneling farther into the East Court, archaeologists came across a glyph panel paying homage to Copán's original ruler, Yax K'uk'Mo'. His tomb was found in 1993, buried far below the East Court by a team led by Robert Sharer of the University of Pennsylvania. This area remains closed to the public. Teams from Harvard, Tulane, and the University of Pennsylvania continue to work in different areas of the site.

EXPLORING THE PARK

The ruins of Copán lie about 1.5 kilometers from the town of Copán Ruinas, a 20-minute walk along a footpath running parallel to the highway. The **Visitors Center** houses the ticket office, where you pay a $15 admission fee for entry to the park (open 8 A.M. to 4 P.M. daily), including entry to the neighboring site of Las Sepulturas. Another $15 gets you admission to two underground tunnels where, among other attractions, you can see the Rosalila Temple in its original context. The tunnels are recommended for serious Mayan archaeology buffs, but not so much for the casual visitor. You can also buy your $7 ticket for admission to Copán's excellent Sculpture Museum. As far as Mayan sites go, Copán is certainly one of the most expensive (admission to Tikal is $7, for example), but the exquisite art on exhibit here is unmatched elsewhere in the Mayan world.

It's well worth it. There's a small exhibit placing Copán's importance in the context of the larger Mayan world at the Visitors Center.

Also at the Visitors Center are registered **guides** for hire, costing about $20 for a two-hour tour. There are English-speaking guides, though their skill levels vary, so be sure to assess their mastery of the English language before sealing the deal. Across the parking lot in front of the Visitors Center is a small **eatery** serving drinks and basic meals. There's also a small gift shop.

It's a few hundred meters' walk from the Visitors Center to the ticket checkpoint where you enter the ruins. A short **nature trail** winding its way through the surrounding forest diverts from the main path just before this checkpoint. A few semi-domesticated scarlet macaws sometimes hang out in this area. Try to visit the site right at opening time, as the crowds tend to get larger as the day goes on, especially on weekends. You'll also have better-angled light for photography.

one of Copán's magnificently carved stelae

© AL ARGUETA

A giant head sits amidst the rubble of Copán's ruins.

◖ THE RUINS OF COPÁN

Enthusiasts of Mayan archaeology will find some of the best hieroglyphic carvings in the whole of the Mayan world along with well-restored structures, including palaces, temple pyramids, and a ball court. The hieroglyphic stairway alone is worth the price of admission, not to mention the chance to see the buried section of temple pyramids from tunnels (Rosalila and Los Jaguares) originally used by archaeologists excavating the ruins.

Great Plaza

The first place you'll come to as you walk along the forest path from the main entrance to the park is the Great Plaza. You'll see a variety of stelae in a spacious grassy area, which was once paved. Traces of red paint (created by mixing mercury sulfate and tree resins) can still be seen on **Stela C,** which dates to A.D. 730. Most of the stelae date to the rule of Smoke Imix (A.D. 628–695) and 18 Rabbit (A.D. 695–738). The latter ruler is depicted on Stelae A, B, C, D, F, H, and 4. The plaza's standout is **Stela A**

(A.D. 731). Among its 52 glyphs are the emblem glyphs of Palenque, Tikal, Calakmul, and Copán, establishing Copán's position as one of the great cities of the Mayan world. As with many other important monuments, the original now resides in the Sculpture Museum. Another beautifully carved monument is **Stela H,** depicting what looks to be a woman wearing a skirt with a leopard skin underneath, wrists weighed down with jewelry, and an intricate headdress. It may have been 18 Rabbit's wife.

Copán's **ball court** is south of the Great Plaza after you cross what is known as the Central Plaza (Plaza Central). Completed in A.D. 738, it was the third ball court to have been erected at the site. There are three elaborate macaw heads on each side. It is one of the most often-photographed buildings in Copán.

Hieroglyphic Stairway

Farther south from the Great Plaza is the Hieroglyphic Stairway, which rises up the southeast corner of the plaza up the side of the neighboring Acropolis. The impressive structure, now covered with a roof for protection from the elements, contains 2,500 glyphs on its 72 steps and is the longest known hieroglyphic inscription found anywhere in the Mayan world. Commissioned in A.D. 753 by Smoke Shell, its substandard construction was evident in that it collapsed and was found by archaeologists as a jumbled mess, which they reassembled in 1940. Only about 15 steps, primarily on the bottom section, are thought to be in the correct order. Archaeologists are working on getting the correct order and deciphering the long message encoded on the steps. Its construction came at a time when Copán's rulers were attempting to once again instill confidence in their city's power and glorious history after the gruesome death of 18 Rabbit at the hands of neighboring Quiriguá.

At the base of the Hieroglyphic Stairway is **Stela M** (A.D. 756), with a figure presumed to be Smoke Shell dressed in a feathered cloak along with glyphs telling of a solar eclipse in that year. An altar in front depicts a feathered serpent with a human head emanating from its jaws.

© AL ARGUETA

the Great Plaza seen from the Acropolis

A tomb thought to belong to a royal scribe and possibly one of the sons of Smoke Imix was discovered underneath the Hieroglyphic Stairway in 1989. It was laden with painted pottery and well-carved jade objects. Digging ever deeper below the stairway, in 1993 archaeologists uncovered an earlier temple called **Papagayo,** erected by Mat Head. Farther below was a chamber dedicated to Yax K'uk'Mo', the city's original king. Archaeologists called it the **Founder's Room** and believe it was used as a place of reverence for the shaman king believed by subsequent kings to have been semidivine.

The Acropolis

Copán's dominating architectural feature is the massive Acropolis, which rises about 30 meters above the ground south of the Great Plaza. It is here that some of the more interesting archaeological finds have been unearthed in recent years by digging tunnels under existing structures to reveal what was originally beneath them.

South of the Hieroglyphic Stairway is a flight of steps running along the **Temple of the Inscriptions.** Walls atop the stairway are carved with various glyphs. Toward the top of the hieroglyphic stairway is a temple curiously adorned with engravings resembling woven mats and appropriately named the **Mat House,** also known as Structure 22A. It was built in A.D. 746 by Smoke Monkey shortly after the death of his predecessor, 18 Rabbit, and provides further evidence of the new power-sharing arrangement with the city's nobility after the shocking defeat at the hands of Quiriguá. It was thought to have operated as a council house, the mats being a symbol for authority and community. South of here is the **East Court,** the city's original plaza, underneath which were found the tombs of Yax K'uk'Mo' and his wife. It is also known as the "Patio de los Jaguares." Also buried in the East Court, below **Structure 18,** was Yax Pac, though it was unfortunately discovered and looted long before the arrival of archaeologists.

Between the East Court and nearby West

Court lies **Structure 16,** which was dedicated to the themes of death, war, and veneration of past rulers. The well-preserved **Rosalila Temple** was found buried underneath here in 1989.

In the **West Court** at the base of Structure 16 is a replica of the magnificently carved square monument known as **Altar Q,** depicting Yax Pac receiving the baton of rulership from Yax K'uk'Mo' himself. The altar is adorned with four kings on each side, giving us a complete line of succession for Copán's ruling dynasty of 16 kings from Yax K'uk'Mo' to Yax Pac, who commissioned its carving in A.D. 776. It was once thought to have portrayed a gathering of astronomers, but recent advances in glyph decipherment have shed light on its true meaning. The original can be seen in the Sculpture Museum. Behind the altar is a sacrificial vault, which contained the remains of 15 jaguars and several macaws sacrificed in honor of Yax Pac and his royal lineage.

Túnel Rosalila and Túnel de los Jaguares

Opened in 1999 to much fanfare, the original excavation tunnels used by archaeologists to discover the hidden gems of Copán are available for visitors to explore. The first of these, Túnel Rosalila, brings you to the Rosalila Temple found buried under Structure 16, still with some of its original brilliant hues. Only about 25 meters of the tunnel are open to visitors. Sheltered behind Plexiglas windows to protect it from the elements and human touch, you'll find small patches of the temple peeking out from underneath the outer layers of newer structures. Considered by some to be the best-preserved stucco structure in the Mayan world, the carvings are surprisingly crisp. To fully appreciate the scale, magnificence, and brilliant hue of this temple, you'll have to go to the Sculpture Museum, where it dominates the edifice and is beautifully lit from above by opaque sunlight.

The second tunnel, Túnel de los Jaguares, brings you to the Tumba Galindo beneath Structure 17 in the southern part of the East

Plaza. About 95 meters of this tunnel, fully comprising 700 meters, are open to visitors. It is somewhat less dramatic than the Rosalila Tunnel, comprising burial tombs and niches for offerings, though there is also a nice macaw mask to be seen. The tomb's discovery dates to 1834.

At $15, admission to the tunnels is a bit on the pricey side and is recommended for serious enthusiasts of archaeology but not so much for the casual visitor.

Las Sepulturas

This smaller residential complex is connected to the main group by a *sacbe,* or elevated causeway, running through the forest. This path is closed to visitors and so you must exit the archaeological site and head up the main road for two kilometers toward San Pedro Sula. You'll see a sign on the right (bring your admission ticket, as you'll need it to get in).

Las Sepulturas was ignored by archaeologists earlier in Copán's history but recent work here has revealed some information about the daily lives of the city's ancient inhabitants. Meaning "the tombs," the complex was named by local farmers who uncovered the remains of long-departed Mayan nobles who had been buried here.

This area is not of much interest to the casual visitor, though you might like walking along the quiet forest trails. Little remains of the original structures. An exception is the Hieroglyphic Wall found on Structure 83, comprising a group of 16 glyphs telling about events in the rule of Yax Pac and dating to A.D. 786. This site contains the remains of the **Palacio de los Bacabs** (Palace of the Officials), which is thought to have once housed 250 nobles. Only 18 of about 40 residential compounds have been excavated. In Las Sepulturas's Plaza A, archaeologists uncovered the tomb of a shaman from about A.D. 450, which can be seen in the town's Museo Regional de Arqueología. Traces of human settlement have been found here dating to 1,000 B.C., long before the Copán dynasty's rise to power.

Los Sapos

An outlying part of Copán even farther away is Los Sapos, in the hills opposite the main site. A rock outcrop carved in the form of a frog gives it its name, though the years have worn it down considerably. An even more badly degraded carving is thought to depict a woman with her legs spread and possibly giving birth. The site is believed to have been a birthing center. The hillside setting overlooking the valley is more dramatic than the carvings, which are set on the grounds of the fabulous **Hacienda San Lucas.** The property harbors a fantastic upscale farmhouse lodge and the owner has built a network of trails through the farm leading to the site. Admission is $2. If you're worn out from the walk, stop in for a drink or lunch at the friendly hacienda or, better yet, spend the night.

THE SCULPTURE MUSEUM

Copán's on-site museum (8 A.M.–3:45 P.M. daily, $7) is surely the best museum of its kind in the Mayan world. Other sites would do well to follow its lead for the sheer variety of original monuments well presented in a spacious and airy environment. Dominating the large, two-story building is a full-scale replica of the outrageously Technicolor Rosalila Temple, decorated in hues of red, green, and yellow, and offering the visitor a rare opportunity to admire the full grandeur of what the ancient Mayan temples may have looked like during the fullness of the civilization's splendor.

Entrance to the museum is via the mouth of a serpent. Winding through a dark cavelike tunnel, you are greeted at once as you emerge from the darkness by the arresting view of the Rosalila Temple lit from above by a giant opaque skylight. On the first floor are various sculptures of skulls, bats, and assorted images of death and violence. Also found here is the splendidly carved **Altar Q,** showing Yax Pac receiving the ceremonial ruler's baton from the highly revered first king of the Copán dynasty Yax K'uk'Mo'. The second floor contains original building facades, stelae, and other carved monuments. A reconstruction of Structure 22A, with its curious woven mat facade, should be open by the time you read this.

Copán Ruinas Town (Honduras)

Set amid the lush hills of the Río Copán Valley, this pleasant town of cobblestone streets serves as the perfect gateway for exploring the nearby archaeological site and some natural attractions, which include hot springs, a bird park, and coffee farms. The range of accommodations and places to eat here is excellent.

The Copán Valley is also the site of tobacco plantations, some of which supply the well-known Flor de Copán factory in Santa Rosa de Copán, east of here. The hillsides surrounding the Copán Valley grow good-quality coffee and cardamom. If you're visiting the ruins of Copán, try to spend at least one night in Copán Ruinas.

SIGHTS

As elsewhere in Central America, the town is built around its *parque central,* recently remodeled in questionable architectural style, but with a pretty colonial church. On the north end of the town's plaza is the **Museo Casa K'inich** (8 A.M.–noon and 1–5 P.M. Mon.–Sat., free admission), which is an interactive children's museum on Mayan subjects such as music and the Mayan number system. Few museums in the Mayan world live up to Copán's on-site museum, though the **Museo Regional de Arqueología** (651-4437, 8 A.M.–noon and 1–4 P.M. daily, $2), on the southwest corner of the plaza, is worth a look. There are exhibits of carved jade, painted pottery, and figurines. The

EL ORIENTE AND IZABAL

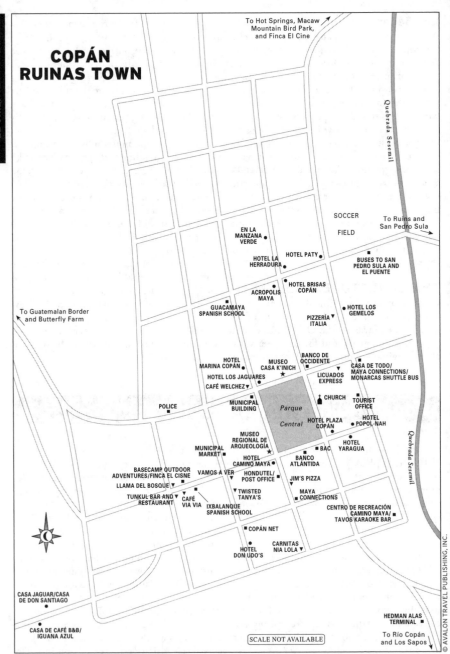

COPÁN RUINAS TOWN

To Hot Springs, Macaw Mountain Bird Park, and Finca El Cine

Quebrada Sesemil

SOCCER FIELD

To Ruins and San Pedro Sula

To Guatemalan Border and Butterfly Farm

EN LA MANZANA VERDE

HOTEL PATY

HOTEL LA HERRADURA

BUSES TO SAN PEDRO SULA AND EL PUENTE

HOTEL BRISAS COPÁN

ACROPOLIS MAYA

GUACAMAYA SPANISH SCHOOL

PIZZERÍA ITALIA

HOTEL LOS GEMELOS

HOTEL MARINA COPÁN

MUSEO CASA K'INICH

BANCO DE OCCIDENTE

CASA DE TODO/ MAYA CONNECTIONS/ MONARCAS SHUTTLE BUS

HOTEL LOS JAGUARES

LICUADOS EXPRESS

CAFÉ WELCHEZ

POLICE

MUNICIPAL BUILDING

Parque Central

CHURCH

TOURIST OFFICE

HOTEL POPOL-NAH

HOTEL PLAZA COPÁN

MUSEO REGIONAL DE ARQUEOLOGÍA

MUNICIPAL MARKET

HOTEL CAMINO MAYA

BANCO ATLÁNTIDA

BAC

HOTEL YARAGUA

BASECAMP OUTDOOR ADVENTURES/FINCA EL CISNE

VAMOS A VER

HONDUTEL/ POST OFFICE

JIM'S PIZZA

LLAMA DEL BOSQUE

TUNKUL BAR AND RESTAURANT

CAFÉ VIA VIA

TWISTED TANYA'S

MAYA CONNECTIONS

IXBALANQUE SPANISH SCHOOL

CENTRO DE RECREACIÓN CAMINO MAYA/ TAVOS KARAOKE BAR

COPÁN NET

CARNITAS NIA LOLA

HOTEL DON UDO'S

CASA JAGUAR/CASA DE DON SANTIAGO

CASA DE CAFÉ B&B/ IGUANA AZUL

Quebrada Sesemil

HEDMAN ALAS TERMINAL

To Río Copán and Los Sapos

SCALE NOT AVAILABLE

© AVALON TRAVEL PUBLISHING, INC.

museum's highlight is the Tumba del Brujo, the tomb of a Mayan shaman said to have died around A.D. 700 and found buried under the Plaza de los Jaguares.

ENTERTAINMENT

Two of the most popular watering holes include **Twisted Tanya's,** with its happy hour 4–6 P.M., and **Carnitas Nia Lola,** where you can find happiness 6:30–8 P.M. A popular after-dark option is **Café Via Via,** where you'll find plenty of fellow travelers. Next door, **Tunkul Bar** has a happy hour 7–8 P.M. and beer on tap. **Café Bar Xibalba,** inside the Hotel Camino Maya, is a quiet place with a cozy atmosphere where you can sample local coffees or enjoy your favorite cocktail.

The **Centro de Recreación Camino Maya** (6 A.M.–10 P.M. Sun.–Thurs., 6 A.M.–2 A.M. Fri. and Sat.), includes a swimming pool ($2), restaurant, and disco (cover charge) in addition to **Tavos Karaoke Bar.** It's two blocks south and one block east from the plaza on a pleasant riverside location beside the Quebrada Sesemil.

For weekend movies, head to **Hacienda El Jaral,** a few kilometers outside of town on the road to San Pedro Sula. You'll see signs around town with current shows and schedules.

GUIDE COMPANIES

Locally owned **Yaragua Tours** (inside Hotel Yaragua, tel. 651-4147, www.yaragua.com), under the same ownership of its namesake hotel, offers a variety of active tours, including caving, visits to hot springs, horseback riding, river tubing, waterfall hikes, and coffee farm visits at prices ranging $15–45 per person with a two-person minimum. A newer option is **Basecamp Outdoor Adventures** (651-4695, www.base camphonduras.com), which is under the same management as the Via Via across the street and offers a variety of alternative recreational options, including 2–6-hour hikes in and around the hills surrounding Copán Ruinas, motorcycle riding, and three- or five-hour horseback rides. It also runs daily shuttle buses to Antigua ($12) and Río Dulce ($20) with a 40-minute stop in Quiriguá along the way to the latter.

ACCOMMODATIONS
Under $10

Copán Ruinas's hippest budget accommodations are at **《 En la Manzana Verde** (651-4652, www.enlamanzanaverde.com, $4 dorm bed), a clean hostel two blocks north from the park where you'll find 18 beds in dorms named after personalities the likes of Fred Flintstone, 18 Rabbit, and Al Bundy, each with its own footlocker. There are two shared hot-water bathrooms. Guests have use of the kitchen (with fridge) as well as a TV lounge and hammocks. There are daily shuttles to Antigua and Guatemala City ($12) and you can book tours to Finca El Cisne with its nearby hot springs and mountain trails for horseback riding. The hostel is run by the same Belgian owners as the Café Via Via. Another fine choice in this category is **Hotel Los Gemelos** (one block east and half a block north of the park, 651-4077, $9 s/d), a popular backpacker spot centered around a pretty courtyard with orchids and run by a wonderful woman who keeps it spotless. She prefers her guests to be back at the hotel by 11 P.M. All rooms have shared bath. There are daily noon shuttle van departures to Antigua. You'll have to walk a few blocks southwest of the plaza to find the **《 Iguana Azul** (651-4620, www.iguanaazulcopan.com, $4 dorm bed, $11 d), but it will be well worth it. There are excellent-value dorm beds and private rooms sharing a hot-water bathroom. The same Honduran-American owners run the beautiful La Casa de Café next door.

$10-25

Among the options in this category is **《 Hotel Via Via** (651-4652, www.viaviacafe.com, $14 d), two blocks southwest of the park. Housed in the café of the same name, the hotel has spotless rooms with private hot-water bath and fan. There's a thatched-roof lounge on the second floor where movies are shown amid tropical foliage. On the southeast corner of the plaza, **Hotel Yaragua** (641-4147, info@yaragua .com, www.yaragua.com, $25 d) has rooms with private bathroom, tile floors, and cable

TV. Look out for some beds with concrete slabs beneath them. There's a restaurant/bar in the lobby and Internet access. On the edge of town on the street leading off to the ruins is **Hotel Patty** (651-4021, $22 d), in a modern building centered around the hotel's parking lot. Rooms have firm beds, tile floors, cable TV, and ceiling fan. Down the street as you head west is **Hotel Brisas de Copán** (651-4566, $18–32 d) with 22 large rooms, orthopedic beds, fan, hot-water bathroom, and cable TV. The cheaper rooms have smaller twin-size beds.

North of town near En la Manzana Verde, **Hotel La Herradura** (651-4771, www.herradura hotel.com, $15 d) has rooms with clean tile floors, private bath, mosquito netting, ceiling fan, and cable TV.

$25-50

The enchanting 【 **La Casa de Café** (651-4620, www.casadecafecopan.com, $45 d, breakfast included) is Copan Ruinas's premiere bed-and-breakfast inn, set in a quiet neighborhood a few blocks southwest of the plaza. The rooms are well furnished and tastefully decorated. You can enjoy fantastic views of the Copán Valley and Guatemala, farther west, from your patio hammock in a wonderful garden setting. The friendly Honduran-American owners also rent out fully furnished private villas across the street, including the **Casa Jaguar** (www.casajaguarcopan.com, $70 per night) and **Casa de Don Santiago** (www.casade donsantiagocopan.com, $90 per night).

A block north of the plaza across from the Hotel Brisas de Copán and run by the same family is the **Acropolis Maya** (651-4634, acropolis@copanhonduras.org, $45 d), with well-decorated rooms featuring nice, firm beds, tile floors, ceiling fan, reading lamp, air-conditioning, cable TV, and private hot-water bath. There's a small courtyard on the ground floor, along with a small living room in the lobby. Across the street from Hotel Yaragua, **Hotel Popol-Nah** (651-4095, www.hotel popolnah.com) is a comfortable and modern 12-room hotel that has rooms with fan and cable TV for $25 d or upstairs rooms with balcony views and air-conditioning for $45 d. All rooms have good mattresses and private hot-water bathroom. **Hotel Los Jaguares** (651-4451), on the plaza's northwest corner, has rooms that make a stab at decor with air-conditioning, private bath, firm beds, and cable TV.

$50-100

Hotel Camino Maya (651-4518, info@camino mayahotel.com, www.caminomayahotel .com, $55 d) has comfortable rooms with all the usual amenities, including air-conditioning and telephone. There's also a small lobby with wicker furniture. In a large building on the southeast corner of the plaza is the similarly priced **Plaza Copán** (651-4508, www.hotel plazacopan.com, $55 d), where well-furnished rooms have tile floors, air-conditioning, mini-fridge, TV, and private hot-water bathroom. There are a restaurant and small swimming pool. The town's fanciest accommodations are found at 【 **Hotel Marina Copan** (651-4070/71, 877/893-9131 toll-free U.S., www .hotelmarinacopan.com, $85–250 d, including breakfast), built in the old family home of Doña Marina Welchez about 60 years ago. All rooms have cable TV, ceiling fan, air-conditioning, and telephone. There are standard rooms and suites. Amenities include a sauna, gym, swimming pool, bar, and the excellent Glifo's restaurant. 【 **Hotel Don Udo's** (651-4533, www.donudos.com, $50–85 d) scores major points for atmosphere with comfortable tiled-floor rooms tastefully decorated with Guatemalan furnishings and accents centered around a delightful garden courtyard. There are rooms with or without air-conditioning and TV; all have fan and private hot-water bath. Some bathrooms have a tub. There's a lobby lounge where you can watch DVDs. Alternatively, you can relax in a sauna or the whirlpool tub. The restaurant here is highly recommended.

Outside of Town

On the outskirts of Copán Ruinas are a variety of excellent lodging options. On a pleasant hilltop setting overlooking town is **Posada Real de Copán** (651-4480/81/82, www.posadareal decopan.com, info@posadarealdecopan.com, $85 d), with 80 rooms equipped with purified tap water, air-conditioning, and cable TV, and with a swimming pool, two bars, and a restaurant. You may hear about [**Hacienda San Lucas** (651-4106, info@haciendasanlucas .com, www.haciendasanlucas.com, $85 d) even before your arrival in town, as it has a well-earned reputation for excellent service. The fantastic accommodations are set on a renovated 100-year-old hacienda, the brainchild of Honduran Flavia Cueva. The lodge's eight rooms, spread about the beautifully landscaped grounds, manage to be comfortable and yet stylishly rustic at the same time. At night, candles provide additional atmosphere. Enjoy a drink and watch the sunset over the Copán Valley before settling down to a delicious five-course dinner ($20) served in a gorgeous garden patio. Another wonderful old farm-turned-chic-hotel can be found along the road to San Pedro Sula near the village of Santa Rita at **Hacienda El Jaral** (552-4457 or 552-5067, $50 d), where you can stay in cozy wooden cabins near a lagoon. The rooms have ceiling fan, TV, private hot-water bathroom, and hammocks on a small porch. Choose from activities including hiking, mountain biking, horseback riding, or tubing on the Río Copán. Its owners also run a small shopping center, water park, and movie theater just down the road.

FOOD
Snacks, Light Meals, and Coffee
[**La Casa de Todo** (651-4185, www.casa detodo.com, 7 A.M.–9 P.M. daily) serves delicious snacks all day, including delicious *baleadas,* flour tortillas filled with beans and cheese, or scrumptious homemade yogurt with granola and fruit ($3.50). The breakfasts here are excellent ($2–4) with good, potent coffee and you can enjoy your meal in a sunny garden courtyard. Another great place for a snack is **Licuados Express** (651-4152, www.licuados express.com, 6:30 A.M.–5 P.M.Mon.–Sat.,

6:30 A.M.–noon Sun.), just up the street toward the plaza, blending healthy shakes and smoothies *(licuados)* plus sandwiches, bagels, waffles, yogurt, and excellent hot or cold espresso beverages ($1.50). Try the filling waffle breakfast ($3). Right on the plaza next to the Hotel Marina Copán, **Café Welchez** (7 A.M.–9 P.M. daily) is Copán's best coffee shop, with espresso drinks and delicious cakes, pastries, and assorted other baked goods. One block southwest of the plaza, **Vamos a Ver** (651-4627, 7 A.M.–10 P.M. daily) is a cozy covered-patio café that is a good bet for soups, homemade breads, a variety of international cheeses, salads and vegetarian dishes, smoothies, and strong coffee. There are very good sandwiches ($2–4) and it's a popular happy-hour venue 5–7 P.M.

Pizza
Across the street from Hotel Los Gemelos **Pizzería Italia** (651-4172, 10 A.M.–9:30 P.M. Tues.–Sun.) serves decent pizzas with a variety of toppings averaging around $6 for a medium pie. It also serves beer and wine in an agreeable cobblestone courtyard lit by quaint paper lamps. **Jim's Pizza** (651-4381, 11 A.M.–9 P.M. daily), a block south of the plaza, makes tasty pizzas ($6–10) and yummy rotisserie chicken with mashed potatoes and corn on the cob for $5.

Honduran Fare and Steak
[**Carnitas Nia Lola** (651-4196, 7 A.M.–10 P.M. daily), two blocks south of the Museo Regional de Arqueología, is a hugely popular gathering spot for its scrumptious quesadillas, nachos, large *baleadas,* and savory *carnitas* served in a funky restaurant/bar. Stop in for happy hour 6:30–8 P.M. and stay to satiate your beer munchies. Popular with locals is **Restaurant Llama del Bosque** (651-4431, 6 A.M.–10 P.M.), across from the Via Via, where the varied menu includes steak and seafood entrées for around $6. Go here for traditional breakfasts of eggs and beans or fondue cooked in a clay pot with beans and sausage ($4). It also sells Honduran cigars.

International

There are a variety of good choices for international fare. **⟨ Twisted Tanya's** (651-4182, www.twistedtanyas.com, 3 P.M.–10 P.M. Mon.–Sat.) manages to be classy and yet casual at the same time in a pleasant, second-story balcony setting overlooking the street. For $15, you get a soup or salad starter, main course, and dessert. Typical dishes include such creations as curry shrimp, Chinese dumplings with wasabi, fish fillet with sautéed vegetables, and seafood pasta with crab. The desserts are equally creative and appetizing. It's a block west and then half a block south of the plaza. Stop in for happy hour 4–6 P.M.

Serving *baleadas muy grandes* is **Tunkul Bar and Restaurant** (651-4152, 7 A.M.–midnight daily), where the atmosphere includes a stone floor and saddles suspended from the roof. There's a nice covered patio where you can enjoy a varied menu that includes half-pound burgers, fajitas, quesadillas, and *chilaquiles,* all for around $4. Things really get fired up at 6 P.M. when the open-air grill cranks out quarter chickens, *pinchos,* and barbecue chicken wings. Next door, **Café Via Via** (651-4652, 7 A.M.–midnight daily) is a popular watering hole with travelers and that doubles as a hip and trendy café. You can substitute vegetarian options for many of its dishes, including veggie burgers ($4). It also makes a good stab at Thai curry ($5). There are tables overlooking the street where you can enjoy the wonderful organically grown coffee.

Fine Dining

One of the finest restaurants in town can be found inside the Hotel Marina de Copán. **⟨ Glifo's** (6:30 A.M.–9:30 P.M. daily, $8–14) serves a variety of international dishes with a distinctly Mayan slant in a pleasing blue and yellow dining room. For a local treat, try the Pollo al Loroco, cooked in a savory sauce of pungent edible flowers. The house specialty is Glifo's Traditional Chicken, cooked in a sauce of roasted, ground sesame and squash seeds flavorfully seasoned with Mayan herbs. International dishes include curry chicken, steak in mushroom wine sauce, and tarragon fish. **Don Udo's** (651-4533, www.donudos .com, entrées $6–10) has a stylish restaurant to accompany the hotel's tasteful atmosphere. Among the excellent dishes are steak and seafood dishes, homemade pastas, and Mayan cuisine. Outside of town, the delightful restaurant at **⟨ Hacienda San Lucas** (tel. 651-4106) is the perfect place to catch the sunset from a perch overlooking the Copán Valley before digging into a scrumptious five-course dinner ($20). Much of the produce used in preparing the meals comes right from the farm. Typical dishes include cream of corn soup, tamales, chicken in adobo sauce, and flan for dessert. Reservations are required for dinner, though you can drop in for breakfast or lunch anytime.

INFORMATION AND SERVICES

Copan Ruinas's tourist office (651-4394, 8 A.M.–7 P.M. daily) is just east of the plaza on the same street as La Casa de Todo.

Communications

The post office (8 A.M.–noon and 1–5 P.M. Mon.–Fri., 8 A.M.–noon Sat.) is half a block west of the plaza.

For Internet, the most popular spot is Maya Connections (651-4077, 8 A.M.–8 P.M., $1.75 for one hour) at La Casa de Todo a block east of the park and near Jim's Pizza a block south of the park. Another option is Copan Net (one block south and one block west of the park, tel. 651-4460, 9 A.M.–9 P.M.), where a lightning-fast connection costs $1.50 an hour.

For phone calls, Hondutel (7 A.M.–9 P.M. Mon.–Fri., 7 A.M.–noon and 2–5 P.M. weekends) can be found just south of the square but you can also make phone calls from the Internet places.

Money

On the south side of the park, Banco Atlántida and BAC both have Visa ATMs and cash travelers checks, dollars, and quetzales. Banco de Occidente, on the park's northeast corner, changes dollars and quetzales as well as cashing travelers checks and issuing cash advances on Visa cards.

Laundry

For laundry, head to Casa de Todo, where a load costs about $1.

Language Schools

Spanish instruction is slightly more expensive than in Guatemala here, with two schools to choose from. **Ixbalanque Spanish School** (651-4432, www.copanruinas.com/ixbalenque .htm) offers five days of one-on-one instruction for $125 or $185 including homestay with a local family. The other option is **Guacamaya Spanish Academy** (651-4360, www.guacamaya .com), where a week's worth of instruction costs $130 alone or $200 including room and board with a local family.

GETTING THERE

Minibuses to the El Florido border leave town from the corner next to the market about every half hour for the 20-minute, 12-kilometer trip. There are hourly onward buses from there to Chiquimula, taking about an hour. A much more comfortable and increasingly popular option is to book a shuttle bus. **Monarcas Travel** (www.mayabus.com), in the Casa de Todo shop, runs two daily buses to Guatemala City and Antigua for $20 one-way. **Hedman-Alas** (651-4037, www.hedmanalas.com) operates a direct first-class bus to Guatemala City ($35, four hours) and Antigua ($41, five hours) from its terminal on the road south of town heading toward the river. There are also onward buses to Tegucigalpa and San Pedro Sula.

If driving a rental car to Copán from Guatemala, be aware that you'll need written permission from your car-rental agency.

NEAR COPÁN RUINAS
Enchanted Wings Butterfly House

On the road from Guatemala, just before the turnoff into town, Enchanted Wings Butterfly House (651-4133, www.hondurasecotours

.com, 8 A.M.–4:30 P.M., $5 adults, $2 children under 12) is run by former Peace Corps volunteer Robert Gallardo and his wife. There are between 30 and 35 species of butterflies being bred here in a screened-in facility by a river. Included in the admission price are a tour (you'll get a laminated placard with various pictures of butterflies to help you follow along) and a visit to an orchid nursery on the other side of the river. Robert should be putting out a guide to Honduran orchids in 2007. There are snacks and drinks available for purchase. It's best visited in the morning, when butterfly hatchings are frequent.

Macaw Mountain Bird Park

A few kilometers outside of town in the surrounding hillsides, Macaw Mountain Bird Park (651-4255, www.macawmountain.com, 9 A.M.– 5 P.M., $10 adults, $5 children) has a collection of birds, including macaws, parrots, and toucans, housed mostly in cages found along a trail and wooden walkways winding through the park's splendidly sylvan riverside setting. In one area, you can interact freely with domesticated birds outside of their cages. There's a restaurant at the main entrance serving mostly meat and seafood dishes ($5–8) as well as a café along the trail. There's also a gift shop.

Hot Springs

About 22 kilometers from town along this same road are a series of pleasant hot springs ($1.50), where you can soak in man-made pools or take a trail to the water's source. There is a nice mix of cool river water combining with the boiling hot water from the springs to make the water perfect for a soak. You can catch a pickup here from town, but a better way to get here is to combine a visit to the springs with a trip out to Finca El Cisne, preferably overnight, when you can use the springs after they have closed to other visitors.

Finca El Cisne

Farther along this same road and a 45-minute drive from Copán Ruinas is a century-old, 1,000-hectare coffee farm where you can ride horseback, tour the coffee and cardamom plantations, and bathe in warm jungle hot springs. Cowboy Carlos Castejón, whose family owns the farm, leads most trips and speaks good English. He can show you around the farm and show you everything you ever wanted to know about coffee cultivation. The farm also produces breadfruit, beans, avocados, corn, plantains, and oranges, among other crops.

Day trips (leaving at 8 A.M. and returning at 6 P.M., $50) include horseback riding, visits to the cardamom and coffee fields, lunch, and a visit to the nearby hot springs. You can also stay overnight in a cozy solar-powered cabin with all of the above plus meals for $75. The booking and information office is across the street from the Via Via in a shared office with Basecamp Outdoor Adventures.

Quiriguá to Puerto Barrios

QUIRIGUÁ

Set amid banana plantations, the Mayan site of Quiriguá is smaller but somewhat similar to Copán, particularly in regard to its inhabitants' skill and propensity in the carving of stelae. It's just 50 kilometers from Copán as the macaw flies, back on the Guatemalan side, though getting here from Copán is a bit more complicated than it looks on a map because the roads are structured so as to make you loop west, north, and then finally east on the highway leading to the Caribbean Coast (CA-9). Coming from Guatemala City, it's just a few kilometers down a dirt road turnoff from the main highway (CA-9), making it a worthy side trip along the road to Puerto Barrios or Río Dulce. Restoration of the site was conducted by the University of Pennsylvania in the 1930s and in 1981 Quiriguá was declared a UNESCO World Heritage Site. The only other sites of this kind in Guatemala are Tikal and Antigua. It boasts the tallest known Mayan stela.

History

Quiriguá's history largely mirrors that of Copán, of which it was a vassal state for much of its history. In A.D. 653, for example, Copán's very own king Smoke Jaguar erected Altar L in Quiriguá's Great Plaza in his own honor after installing the city's new ruler. Quiriguá's stelae were carved with help from Copán's artisans using beds of brown sandstone brought from the nearby Río Motagua. The sandstone was

soft when first cut, allowing the artisans to create the excellent-quality carvings, which hardened through time and can still be seen today.

Quiriguá's subservient status changed dramatically under the leadership of its king Cauac Sky with the capture and subsequent beheading of Copán's ruler 18 Rabbit in A.D. 737, an event which would mark the beginning of Copán's gradual downward slide. Cauac Sky quickly embarked on his own plan to expand the greatness of Quiriguá, carving most of the stelae in evidence there today. He can be seen on Stelae A, C, D, E, F, H, and J. Cauac Sky was succeeded by his son, Sky Xul (784–800), who lost his throne to Jade Sky, Quiriguá's last great king, who embarked on his own grandscale reconstruction of the city's Acropolis. Quiriguá managed to remain independent of Copán for the remainder of its history until its own silent and mysterious demise in the middle of the 9th century.

Like Copán, Quiriguá captured the attention and fascination of John L. Stephens, who compared it to "the rock-built city of Edom, unvisited, unsought and utterly unknown." Stephens even attempted to buy the site in 1840 and cart it off to New York City via the Río Motagua and out to sea. Assuming that Stephens was negotiating on behalf of the U.S. government, the landowner quoted an exorbitant price and the deal was never made. The noted archaeologist Alfred Maudsley followed up with his own visit and excavations between

1881 and 1894, making some fine illustrations of the site's stelae and zoomorphic rock figures. In the early 1900s, the site and surrounding lands became the property of the United Fruit Company, which preserved the ruins and the area in its vicinity. The rest of the land was converted to banana plantations, miles and miles of them.

◖ The Ruins of Quiriguá

What is left of Quiriguá is limited to its ceremonial center. As you enter the park from the main entrance, you'll see the **Acropolis** straight ahead and the various stelae and zoomorphs (stone sculptures depicting animals and hybrid human-animal forms) in the **Great Plaza** to your left. The stelae are housed under thatched-roof structures to protect them from further deterioration from the elements. It can be somewhat difficult to view the carvings and even more difficult to get a good photograph. The most impressive is **Stela E,** standing almost 11 meters high, making it the tallest known Mayan stela. Noteworthy features in the carvings include their bearded subjects with elaborate headdresses, the staffs of authority clutched in their hands, and glyphs running up and down the monuments' sides. The various zoomorphs can also be seen here, depicting turtles, jaguars, frogs, and serpents. Near the Acropolis, **Altar P** depicts a figure seated in a strange, Buddhalike pose. The Acropolis itself is rather unimpressive, failing to rise in height above the treetops of the surrounding jungle, though it is somewhat spread out. There's a small ball court on its western side.

Practicalities

The park is open 7:30 A.M.–5 P.M. daily. Admission is $4. There's a small museum housing displays on the site's significance in relation to Mayan history and geopolitics along with a model showing the extent of the site's boundaries and unexcavated sections.

The site lies four kilometers from the main road with frequent transport heading up and down thanks to the activities of the nearby banana plantations. At the entrance to the site are a ticket office, the museum, and a few simple soda stands as well as some folks selling coconuts. The turnoff to the park from the main road (Highway CA-9) is between Km. 204 and Km. 205, about 70 kilometers northeast of the Río Hondo Junction. The village of Quiriguá lies two kilometers back along the road toward Guatemala City and has some basic accommodations, though a better option is the town of Los Amates, at Km. 200 of Highway CA-9, if you should need to spend the night in these parts. Any bus heading along Highway CA-9 can drop you off at the junction to the road leading to the park.

MORALES (BANANERA) AND ENTRE RÍOS

Just north of this roadside town is the **La Ruidosa Junction,** where those heading to Río Dulce will have to change buses. Morales was formerly known as Bananera when it was the United Fruit Company town. Farther down, at about Km. 280, is the Entre Ríos Junction, from where the road heads east to Honduras.

JARDÍN BOTÁNICO Y RESTAURANTE ECOLÓGICO EL HIBISCUS

Near Puerto Barrios, at Km. 284 of Highway CA-9, is the Jardín Botánico y Restaurante Ecológico El Hibiscus (tel. 7294-0397 or 5514-9525, www.hibiscusprojectizabal.com, 6 A.M.–5:30 P.M. Mon.–Sat.), a pleasant restaurant tastefully furnished with tropical wicker furniture and Mayan textiles that serves excellent breakfasts ($3–4), seafood, steaks, sandwiches, salads, and Guatemalan dishes. A tasty *caldo de gallina criolla* (chicken soup) is served on Saturdays. You can enjoy your meal in a pleasant wooden dining room or outside on one of two patios. Visitors can also enjoy a stroll through the botanical gardens housing a wide variety of flowers and tropical plants. It makes a pleasant stop on the way to Puerto Barrios or a good place to eat outside of town if you're staying there. The restaurant also serves as an information center for the Cerro San Gil and Punta de Manabique protected areas.

Puerto Barrios and Vicinity

This hot, humid port city holds little of interest for travelers except as a jumping-off point to surrounding attractions such as Punta de Manabique, Lívingston, and resorts across the Bahía de Amatique. It was once Guatemala's main Caribbean shipping port but has been replaced by Puerto Santo Tomás de Castilla across the bay. It has had a slight resurgence in recent years thanks to the opening of a new shipping container port competing for business with a similar facility in Omoa, Honduras.

Construction of the port that now bears his name was initiated by reformist President Justo Rufino Barrios in the 1880s and was linked to Guatemala City via a railroad completed in 1908. Puerto Barrios was important during the long-past glory days of the United Fruit Company. The company financed much of the railroad's completion and linked its banana plantations to Puerto Barrios, which served as the company-controlled shipping center for produce bound for New Orleans and New York. United Fruit was sold to Del Monte in the 1970s and Puerto Barrios sank into a tropical slumber.

NIGHTLIFE

Just across the street from the Hotel del Norte and right next to the water, **Container** (7a Calle, 10 A.M.–10 P.M. daily) is curiously housed in two steel shipping containers. Simple fare including burgers and tacos are served, but it's mainly a place to enjoy a few beers. Next door, **Jeffrey's Place** is a simple snack and beer stand. The bars at the **Hotel del Norte,** across the street, or **Safari** (northern end of 5a Avenida, tel. 7948-0563, 10 A.M.–9 P.M.) make good places for a drink while enjoying the bay views. If you really want to get a feel for Puerto Barrios's sleazy, after-dark honky-tonk bars, head to the area around 8a Avenida between 6a and 7a Calle west of the post office, where you'll find a collection of a dozen or so bars and other "establishments."

GUIDE COMPANIES

Until recently, there were no organized tours of Puerto Barrios, as it's not really a major stop on the tourism circuit. With the installation of a new cruise-ship terminal across the bay fronting the port town, however, there is now at least one option for organized tours. Antigua-based **Chiltepe Tours** (7a Calle Poniente #15, Centro Comercial El Búcaro, Antigua, tel. 5907-0913, www.chiltepetours.com) is a Gray Line affiliate offering Unimog (military-style open-sided truck) tours of Puerto Barrios for $34 per adult or $29 per child. You can save $4 off each ticket by booking through the website. The price includes two beverages of your choice, including frosty beer to beat the heat. It also does jeep transfers from the cruise-ship dock to Río Las Escobas.

ACCOMMODATIONS

Many of the ultralow-budget accommodations in this town are used for prostitution, which is rampant in this sweltering coastal town, so backpackers beware. For Caribbean atmosphere and antique charm, you can't beat the 100-year-old (**Hotel del Norte** (7a Calle and 1a Avenida, tel. 7948-2116, $20–33 d). Its quaint, crooked wooden floors evoke another time and have a certain dilapidated charm. Rooms in the original building cost $20 d, have cold water, fan, and fluorescent lighting. Newer rooms in a separate building cost $33 d and have hot water, ceiling fan, warmer tungsten lighting, air-conditioning, and hot water. The restaurant, housed in a pleasant open-air thatched-roof building overlooking the hotel pool and sea, serves seafood, grilled meats, pasta, and other international dishes for $5–10. Just 1.5 blocks from the municipal docks, **Hotel Europa 2** (3a Avenida and 12 Calle, tel. 7948-1292, $13 d) is friendly and family run with clean rooms with bathroom around a parking lot/courtyard. Next door is the friendly and family-run **Hotel Miami** (tel. 7948-0537, $12–20 d), containing clean rooms with or without air-conditioning.

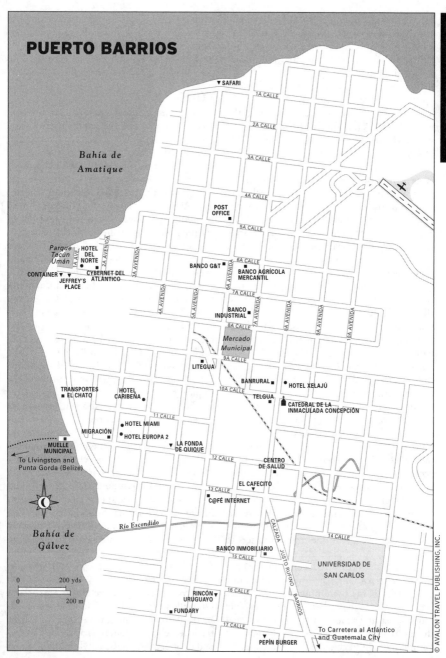

PUERTO BARRIOS

EL ORIENTE AND IZABAL

Bahía de
Amatique

▼ SAFARI

1A CALLE
2A CALLE
3A CALLE
4A CALLE

POST
OFFICE

5A CALLE

Parque
Tecún
Umán

HOTEL
DEL
NORTE

CYBERNET DEL
ATLÁNTICO

CONTAINER ▼
JEFFREY'S
PLACE

1A AVE.
2A AVENIDA
3A AVENIDA

BANCO G&T ■

6A CALLE

BANCO AGRÍCOLA
MERCANTIL

7A CALLE

4A AVENIDA
5A AVENIDA

BANCO
INDUSTRIAL

6A AVENIDA
7A AVENIDA

8A CALLE

8A AVENIDA
9A AVENIDA
10A AVENIDA

*Mercado
Municipal*

9A CALLE

LITEGUA ▼

BANRURAL ■   ● HOTEL XELAJÚ

10A CALLE

TELGUA ■

✝ CATEDRAL DE LA
INMACULADA CONCEPCIÓN

TRANSPORTES
■ EL CHATO

HOTEL
CARIBEÑA ●

11 CALLE

MIGRACIÓN ■   ● HOTEL MIAMI
● HOTEL EUROPA 2

▼ LA FONDA
DE QUIQUE

12 CALLE

CENTRO
DE SALUD

■ ■
MUELLE
MUNICIPAL

To Lívingston and
Punta Gorda (Belize)

EL CAFECITO ▼

13 CALLE

C@FÉ INTERNET ■

Río Escondido

Bahía de
Gálvez

BANCO INMOBILIARIO ■

15 CALLE

14 CALLE

UNIVERSIDAD DE
SAN CARLOS

CALZADA JUSTO RUFINO BARRIOS

0   200 yds
0   200 m

RINCÓN
URUGUAYO ▼

16 CALLE

■ FUNDARY

17 CALLE

To Carretera al Atlántico
and Guatemala City

▼ PEPÍN BURGER

Another budget option is **Hotel La Caribeña** (4a Avenida between 10 and 11 Calles, tel. 7948-0384, $11–20 d), with bare-bones but clean rooms with bathroom and fan and/or air-conditioning.

On the outskirts of town are some pricier options that are conveniently near the main highway should you not want to stay in the heart of town. **C Hotel Marbrissa** (25 Calle y 20 Avenida, Colonia Virginia, tel. 7948-0940, www.marbrissa.com, $85–140 d) has comfortable rooms centered around the hotel's large swimming pool with all the amenities you would expect in this price range, including air-conditioning and minifridge. There are also larger suites with a kitchenette and living and dining room. The open-air *palapa*-style restaurant here is one of the nicest in town for its tranquil atmosphere overlooking the swimming pool.

On the main road into town at the junction leading to Puerto Santo Tomás de Castilla, **Hotel Puerto Libre** (tel. 7948-3064/65, www.hotelpuertolibre.com, $28–40 d) has rooms with air-conditioning, private hot-water bath, and TV. There's a lively swimming pool and the hotel restaurant serves mainly seafood dishes but also does delicious *parrilladas*. Entrees are priced $5–12.

Outside of town just past the airstrip on tropical grounds bordering the sea is the outstanding **C Amatique Bay Resort and Marina** (tel. 7948-1800, www.amatiquebay .net, $120–250 per room), where comfortable accommodations are housed in neocolonial villas. There are standard rooms and larger suites with full kitchen; the largest of these have additional sofa beds and a living room. All have air-conditioning and the usual amenities. There's a white-sand beach on the tranquil waters of the Bahía de Amatique and a swimming pool complete with a Spanish galleon. Three restaurants keep vacationers happy, including one that's right by the swimming pool and serves lighter fare and sandwiches. The other two are more formal and serve a variety of international dishes. All in all, this complex is a self-contained leisure city built in colonial style somewhat re-sembling a seaside version of Antigua, complete with a whitewashed church. It is a popular day trip with cruise-ship passengers docking at nearby Puerto Santo Tomás de Castilla. The hotel is affiliated with Interval International.

FOOD

Local dishes include *tapado,* a seafood stew made from prawns, fish, and shellfish, seasoned with plantains, yucca, and coriander, and cooked in coconut milk. *Tortillas de harina* are flour tortillas stuffed with cheese, or anything else for that matter.

As for restaurants, **C Safari** (northern end of 5a Avenida, tel. 7948-0563, 10 A.M.–9 P.M.) is popular with locals for its large portions of excellent seafood dishes ($7–10) served in style on an open air, thatched-roofed platform over the sea. It also dos excellent chicken and meat dishes ($4–6). Another good seafood option is the restaurant at **Hotel La Caribeña** (4a Avenida between 10 and 11 Calles, tel. 7948-0384), known for its *caldo de mariscos* and **tapado.** For lighter fare, try the rice and beans. For burgers, *tortillas de harina* and delicious fajitas, head to **Pepín Burger** (17 Calle between 8a and 9a Avenida, closed Tues.) in a second-floor terrace where you can catch the tropical breezes.

The only real coffee shop in town is **El Cafecito** (13 Calle between 6a and 7a Avenidas, 7:30 A.M.–11 P.M. Mon.–Sat.), where you can enjoy espresso beverages and pair them with tasty pastries and bagels. Another stylish option for seafood and international dishes is **La Fonda de Quique** (corner 12 Calle and 5a Avenida) in a pleasant air-conditioned dining room with formal tablecloths. The best steak house in town is the **Rincón Uruguayo** (7a Avenida and 16 Calle, closed Mon.) serving excellent *parrilladas* (grilled meats South American–style), *papas asadas,* and *cebollines* (grilled spring onions).

If you're staying at the **Hotel Marbrissa** (25 Calle y 20 Avenida, Colonia Virginia, tel. 7948-0940, www.marbrissa.com) or nearby, try its excellent restaurant/bar set on the second floor of a large *palapa*-style building above the hotel lobby and overlooking the swimming pool. Parrots roam the premises while you dine on excellent seafood, grilled steaks, pasta, and other international dishes. There are a pool table and a large flat-screen TV.

SERVICES
Communications

The post office is on the corner of 8a Avenida and 6a Calle. Telgua is at 8a Avenida and 10a Calle.

Internet costs about $1.50 an hour at most places. Options for Internet use include Café Internet (13 Calle and 6a Avenida, 9 A.M.– 9 P.M. daily), Cybernet del Atlántico (7a Calle, east of Hotel del Norte), and Red Virtu@l (17 Calle and Calzada Justo Rufino Barrios, 8 A.M.–9:30 P.M. daily).

Money

Banco Industrial (7a Avenida Norte #73) has a Visa ATM and changes U.S. cash dollars and travelers checks. Banrural (8a Avenida and 9a Calle) has a MasterCard ATM and also changes dollars and travelers checks.

Immigration

The offices of *migración* are on the corner of 12 Calle and 3a Avenida, a block from the municipal docks. This is where you get your entry or exit stamp when arriving from or heading to Belize. There is a $10 departure tax. The offices are open 7 A.M.–8 P.M.

GETTING THERE
Air

Puerto Barrios's long, paved runway has been inaugurated several times and even supported frequent flights to Guatemala City at one time. That service is suspended for the moment, but things may change soon with the government's plans to build a network of domestic airports. The field is equipped to receive jet aircraft, including Boeing 737s.

Bus

Most of the transport in and out of Puerto Barrios is via the excellent **Transportes Litegua**

(6a Avenida and 9a Calle, tel. 7948-1172, www .litegua.com), which operates comfortable, modern buses departing every half hour to and from Guatemala City. Some buses stop in Morales en route, where you get off for Río Dulce.

It's also possible to travel overland to Honduras by bus. Minibuses depart from the marketplace every half hour between 6:30 A.M. and 4:30 P.M. heading to the town of **Entre Ríos,** where there's an immigration post, and then continue to the border (one hour). Once in Honduras, take an awaiting pickup or minibus for the town of **Corinto,** four kilometers away. From Corinto there are buses every 90 minutes to Puerto Cortés (2.5 hours), stopping in Omoa along the way. There are frequent departures from Puerto Cortés to San Pedro Sula and onward in Honduras.

Boat

Boats leave from the municipal dock at the end of 12 Calle. There is **ferry** service to Lívingston ($1.50, 1.5 hours) Mon.–Sat. at 10 A.M. and 5 P.M. Try to get there at least 30 minutes prior to departure time to secure your seat. *Lanchas* taking 30 minutes to make the journey depart when they have a dozen people or so and cost about $5 one-way. Most of the traffic heading to Lívingston is in the morning hours.

There are also departures to Punta Gorda, Belize ($20 one-way) via **Transportes El Chato** (1a Avenida between 10a and 11a Calles, tel. 7948-5525 or 7948-8787, www.transportes elchato.com) leaving Puerto Barrios at 10 A.M. daily and taking about an hour. You'll need to stop by the immigration office to get your passport stamped prior to getting on the boat.

PUERTO SANTO TOMÁS DE CASTILLA

Cruise ships dock in Santo Tomás de Castilla, just across the bay from Puerto Barrios, where those wishing to go ashore will find some of the country's best bird-watching, lush tropical rainforests, and refreshing jungle rivers. In August 2006, Carnival Cruise Lines announced the construction of a $40 million **cruise ship**

THE GUATEMALA-BELIZE BORDER DISPUTE

During your travels, you might be surprised to find the neighboring country of Belize included as part of Guatemala on many maps produced in-country. It would seem that Belize is just another Guatemalan *departamento* despite its status as an independent nation since 1981. Guatemala did not in fact recognize its neighbor's independence until 10 years later in a highly criticized and unconstitutional move by then-president Jorge Serrano Elías. Guatemala's constitution clearly states that any decision regarding the independence or territorial integrity of Belize must be submitted to a public referendum. And so the debate continues over the "Belize question." It seems to be one of those issues that just won't go away, with succeeding governments always promising a final solution to this centuries-old problem.

Several governments have used the issue as a diversionary tactic during times of civil unrest, particularly during the military regimes of the 1970s. Matters came to a head in 1977 when Great Britain sent 6,000 troops to the border in anticipation of an invasion by Guatemalan troops during the presidency of military strongman Romeo Lucas García. Today, there are occasional reports of incidents along the northern Petén region's eastern border with Belize when Guatemalan peasants are forcefully evicted from the "no-man's land" along the border in clashes with Belizean security forces. The border is often referred to as a *zona de adyacencia,* or "imaginary border" area. Guatemalan newspapers love to publicize these incidents of supposed injustice against unarmed peasants, calling for a final solution to the long-standing problem.

The dispute dates to colonial times, when Spain officially claimed all of the Central American coast but was unable in practice to enforce its claim. English privateers and traders established a beachhead along the southern coast of Belize and extracted valuable timber products, including mahogany. The English presence was officially recognized by Spain in 1763, granting the British the right to extract forest products but refusing them the right of permanent settlement. The first permanent settlements came soon after Central American independence from Spain, the British clearly taking advantage of the power vacuum created in the aftermath of Spanish rule. The weakness of Guatemala's early governments was evident in an 1859 treaty, which officially recognized the British presence and "lent" the Belize territory to them for further resource extraction in exchange for a payment of £50,000 and the construction of a road from Belize to Guatemala City. Great Britain never held up its end of the bargain on either point and so the treaty was rendered null and void. British occupation of the lands continued, however, and the land eventually became known as the colony of British Honduras, which was granted its independence from England in 1981.

In recent years, Guatemala has limited its claims to the southern half of Belize, from the Río Sibún to the Río Sarstún, arguing that historical documents support its claims and include this territory as part of the region of "Las Verapaces." Some Guatemalan analysts believe there might be a case here, though the reasons for Guatemala's insistence in this matter remain a mystery. The current government has expressed its interest in getting its case settled once and for all by international arbitration, which would mean bringing it to the International Court in The Hague if all other avenues fail. Belize has tried to get the matter resolved in the Organization of American States (OAS), so far unsuccessfully, and has repeatedly stated that it will not cede "a single inch of its territory."

It's doubtful Guatemala will ever be able to recover its full claim, though the possibility for comanagement of the Sapodilla Cayes Marine Park (also claimed by Honduras) as a trinational park might be the most realistic outcome of any internationally mediated settlement on this matter. It would give Guatemala the one thing its geography and tourist offerings lack: white-sand Caribbean beaches with clear, turquoise waters.

terminal. The facility is expected to bring in about 200 cruise ships and about 200,000 visitors per year. Local tourism authorities in nearby Lívingston and Río Dulce are improving the quality of their services to cater to these new arrivals, and it seems the once-sleepy Guatemalan Caribbean Coast may soon be abuzz with travelers. The terminal should be completed in 2008.

The history of Santo Tomás de Castilla actually dates to 1604, when it was founded as the coast's original colonial port. It was abandoned within a few years but later became the site of an ill-fated Belgian colony in 1843 after Guatemala's independence from Spain.

A paved road from Puerto Barrios leads to the main shipping center. From there, a dirt road continues along the coast to some of the area's natural attractions.

Cerro San Gil and Río Las Escobas

This idyllic park, centered around the Cerro San Gil mountain, comprises more than

Río Las Escobas

7,700 hectares (19,000 acres) of lush rainforest. Bathed in rainfall throughout most of the year (averaging 255 inches) as warm, humid air rises over the mountains from the sea to elevations in excess of 1,100 meters (3,900 feet), the preserve harbors an astounding level of biodiversity. Among the wildlife protected here are 56 species of mammals, including tapir and jaguars, 50 species of reptiles and amphibians, and more than 350 species of birds, including toucans, black and white hawk eagles, and keel-billed motmots. More than 90 neotropical migrants winter in the area and include the blue-winged warbler and wood thrush.

The park also protects the important watershed of the Río Las Escobas, which supplies water to Puerto Barrios. Part of the watershed is open to visitors ($8, including guided tour), who can bathe in Las Escobas's cool, clear waters and hike a series of nature trails winding through the park. The park is administered by private conservation group **FUNDAECO** (tel. 7948-4404, www.FUNDAECO.org .gt), which in partnership with The Nature Conservancy has been able to buy large tracts of this rainforest ecosystem for preservation. Facilities for visitors include an excellent system of **trails** winding through the river and waterfalls and which include wooden bridges with stops along the way for swimming in stunning turquoise pools. More adventurous types can explore areas deeper into the reserve beginning at a trailhead just up the mountain and going from there to the Río Las Escobas through a dense stretch of forest (one hour) or to Cumbre Las Torres (four hours there and back), or encompassing multiple days of strenuous jungle hiking to the village of Carboneras and down the mountain to Río Dulce. Contact FUNDAECO if you wish to explore these options, as you will need prior authorization. A guided trek of either of the first two options costs $20 per person. Rates for the longer trip are negotiable.

The park is an increasingly popular day trip with cruise-ship passengers, many of whom reportedly state this to be their favorite stop after the crass commercialism of places such as

Cancún and beaches that all pretty much look the same. The park lies just off the road, hugging the coastline from Puerto Santo Tomás de Castilla to the beach of Punta de Palma.

Antigua-based **Chiltepe Tours** (7a Calle Poniente #15, Centro Comercial El Búcaro, Antigua, tel. 5907-0913, www.chiltepetours .com) is a Gray Line affiliate offering jeep tours from the cruise-ship terminal to Río Las Escobas in fully restored American M151A2 jeeps with quarter-ton trailers hitched on to the back. The trips leave the cruise-ship terminal hourly at the bottom of the hour starting at 8:30 A.M., taking about 30 minutes. You can stay as long as you like at Las Escobas, with the last jeep heading back to the cruise-ship terminal at 4 P.M. Other return trips from Las Escobas leave hourly at the top of the hour. The tour costs $39 (adults) or $34 (children), but you can save $4 off each ticket by booking on the website.

Green Bay Hotel
Farther along this same road is the 50-room Green Bay Hotel (tel. 7948-2361, www .greenbay.com.gt, $60 d room-only or $130 d all-inclusive), which was built way ahead of its time in the early 1990s but now seems perfectly situated to cater to cruise-ship day trippers. The comfortable thatched-roof duplex bungalows are built into the side of a beautifully forested hillside near the water's edge and have all the comforts, including air-conditioning, TV, private hot-water bathroom, and bay windows looking out to the jungle. Although the exteriors are thatched-roof, it's really only for show, as the room interiors pretty much look like any standard modern hotel room. There is an airy, thatched-roof restaurant and bar overlooking the swimming pool and Bahía de Amatique. In addition to seafood, the restaurant serves international dishes including pasta, sandwiches, and grilled steaks. It's a bit overpriced at about $8 for pasta.

Out front is a dock from where you can book a tour of the bay or a motorboat transfer to Punta de Palma, Punta de Manabique,

Lívingston, or Río Dulce. Call 7948-1067 and ask for Bobi or inquire at the hotel's boat dock. Otherwise, you can catch some rays on the lagoon-front beach or explore the waters in a kayak. Two small mangrove islets, known as the Cayos del Diablo, lie just off the coast. Mountain bikes are also available for rent and there's a sandy beach volleyball court. As at most of Guatemala's Caribbean beaches, the water here is not clear like that along the Yucatán Peninsula, but more emerald in color. It's what the tourism promoters have called, "A different Caribbean."

Punta de Palma Beach
The road continues north from here to the beaches of Punta de Palma, a popular weekend getaway for folks from Puerto Barrios and where a sliver of sand meets the Caribbean Sea. There are some refreshment stands but little else here. Although locals might try to talk it up, you'll probably be very disappointed. If you really want to hit the beach, there are some better options near Lívingston and across the bay at Punta de Manabique.

◖ PUNTA DE MANABIQUE WILDLIFE REFUGE
Some day the white-sand Caribbean beaches along this remote peninsula on the northeast extreme of Bahía de Amatique may be home to resort hotels, but for now they remain largely uninhabited and lovely. The seas on the outer extreme of the peninsula can be particularly rough, as the land mass takes a bashing from the Atlantic Ocean while sheltering the waters of Bahía de Amatique, keeping them comparatively calm. In addition to the white sandy beaches where four species of sea turtles lay their eggs, there are mangrove swamps inhabited by manatees and more than 300 bird species, including the endangered yellow-headed parrot (*Amazona oratrix*). Savannahs and flooded swamp forests harbor jaguars, tapir, and howler monkeys. Also protected are coral reef outcrops, the only ones of their kind in Guatemala, at the tip of the peninsula. All in all, it's one of

Guatemala's most wonderful and least-visited wild places.

The reserve is managed by conservation organization Fundary, which is working with some of the approximately 2,000 people inhabiting this area in an effort to involve them in the conservation of the wonderful marine ecosystem they live in. Locals live mostly from fishing, particularly *manjua*, a type of small sardine. The waters off the coast of Honduras, Belize, and Guatemala have been somewhat overfished and so economic alternatives, including ecotourism, are being sought to provide a livelihood for the local population.

As fishing continues to be an important part of the local economy, new ways to make existing fishing operations more efficient have come into play. Together with USAID, Fundary has recently been able to bring solar power to the area, allowing locals access to heretofore uneasily obtained luxuries, such as ice, in a sweltering coastland. The availability of ice and refrigeration, in turn, makes it easier to cater to visitors and keep food for their consumption. The community of San Francisco del Mar, about halfway down the peninsula, now has its own solar-powered freezer and fish-processing plant. The women are making some extra cash producing and selling ice cream. It's all a bit reminiscent of Paul Theroux's *The Mosquito Coast*.

Recreation

It's a great time to explore this area, as it's clear tourism is still in its infancy. That all might change soon, however, with the new cruise-ship terminal just a few miles away in Puerto Santo Tomás de Castilla. For now, your best bet is to contact Fundary (tel. 7948-0435, Puerto Barrios or 2232-3230, Guatemala City, www .guate.net/fundarymanabique), which is working with local communities to promote ecotourism. Among the activities are visits to the mangrove-lined canals of **Bahía La Graciosa, Laguna Santa Isabel,** and adjacent **Canal Inglés** for bird-watching and manatee-spotting. The canal is named after British

loggers who dug the 10-kilometer trench connecting Laguna Santa Isabel to the Río Piteros. Along this canal is the small community of **Santa Isabel,** with a solar-powered visitors center, where you can fish with the locals or sit in on a demonstration of the local charcoal-making process. You can also kayak in the mangrove swamps and canals near the small community of **Estero Lagarto,** farther north and closer to the Punta de Manabique outcrop. Farther east, the Río Motagua marks the border with Honduras. Near the mouth of this river is the small settlement of **El Quetzalito,** where you can also do some bird-watching or crocodile-spotting. It's reached by road one hour from Puerto Barrios and then by traveling for half an hour downstream on the Motagua.

Accommodations and Food

Fundary runs a small basic lodge, **El Saraguate,** in the community of Punta de Manabique, just before you round the tip of the peninsula. Accommodations are in dorm-style bedrooms and cost $8 per person. It also offers package deals costing $75/95/120 (double, per person) for 1/2/3 nights' accommodations, food, and transport from Puerto Barrios. Food is heavily centered on seafood and is prepared by local families. Nearby is a fantastic trail with wooden bridges giving you a glimpse of the peninsula's largely flooded forest environment. A large dock goes out over the emerald-green waters fronting the lodge from where you can snorkel in the clear shallow waters. There's not much sand here and the locale feels very lagoonlike.

It's also possible to stay at the **Julio Obiols Biological Research Station,** run by Fundary, on the north end of the cape at Cabo Tres Puntas, where there's also a lighthouse. It has recently installed solar-powered electricity at the station and now hosts research teams with greater frequency. Accommodations ($100 for two nights per person, double occupancy, including transport from Puerto Barrios and meals) are in basic but clean rooms with 2–4 beds and mosquito netting.

The ambience here is somewhat more typical of a Caribbean seaside setting, with a nice stretch of white, sandy beach against which the waves come crashing from the Atlantic Ocean. The months of March–May offer somewhat calmer seas.

The community of Estero Lagarto has a very basic, three-bedroom lodge for accommodating guests. Santa Isabel is putting together a community-run lodging of its own and may be in operation by the time you visit.

Getting There

There is no regularly scheduled service to Punta de Manabique, though you might get lucky and hitch a ride out with a group going out on any given day. A better option is to book a package trip with Fundary with food, lodging, and transport included. Your money helps support conservation efforts. If you want to explore the area on your own, you can hire a boat to take you there from the municipal dock in Puerto Barrios. It's about an hour's ride. **Transportes El Chato** (1a Avenida between 10a and 11a Calles, tel. 7948-5525 or 7948-8787, www .transporteselchato.com) charges $180 for the trip. It's also possible to make the trip from Lívingston and it might be slightly cheaper.

Lívingston

A bit of an anomaly in Mayan and ladino Guatemala, Lívingston is an interesting Caribbean enclave of Garífuna culture and completes Guatemala's list of offerings with the authentic feel of a West Indian coastal town. This characteristic is made even more poignant by the fact that it's accessible only by boat. The town's setting is as exotic as its culture, splendidly situated at the mouth of the Río Dulce on the shores of the Bahía de Amatique. It makes a great base for upstream explorations of the Río Dulce canyon as well as nearby beaches, waterfalls, and pools, or the outlying Zapotillo cayes. The sounds of *punta* rock and reggae drifting out from the town's numerous restaurants and bars complete the Caribbean atmosphere. You can find some useful information on the town at www .livingston.com.gt.

SIGHTS

Museo Multicultural de Lívingston

The recently inaugurated Museo Multicultural de Lívingston (tel. 7947-0944, 9 A.M.–5 P.M. daily, $0.70 admission) is just to the left of the municipal docks and features displays on the local Garífuna, Kekchí, and Cagey cultures in addition to the local flora and fauna. There are some interesting old fishing nets as well as some old and new photographs on display. It's worth a quick stop and the friendly staff can answer your questions.

Los Siete Altares

A clean side stream forms this series of seven waterfalls and pretty emerald-green pools known as Los Siete Altares (Seven Altars, $1.50 admission) lying five kilometers northwest of town. (Picture a smaller version of Dunn's River Falls in Ocho Ríos, Jamaica.) Robberies have been reported here in the past, so it's safest to go as part of a group. Any of the recommended guide companies can get you there, though Exotic Travel runs an adventurous option on mountain bikes. The river falls can be reached by walking along the shore northwest of Playa Quehueche for a few kilometers and then wading across a side stream before turning left onto a path leading to the first of the falls. The seventh waterfall and pool is the nicest. You'll have to clamber up the slippery rocks to get there, but it's worth it.

Beaches

Lívingston has some acceptable beaches nearby, though the ones adjacent to town are

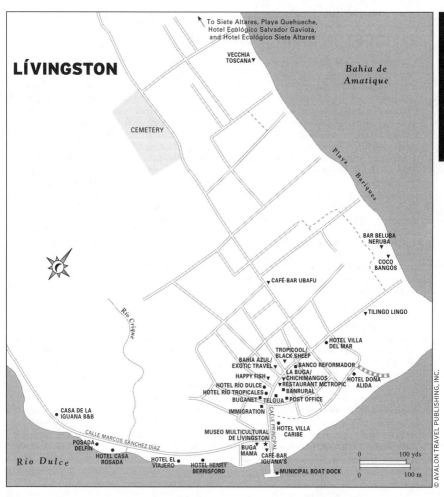

To Siete Altares, Playa Quehueche,
Hotel Ecológico Salvador Gaviota,
and Hotel Ecológico Siete Altares

LÍVINGSTON

VECCHIA TOSCANA ▼

Bahía de Amatique

CEMETERY

Playa Bariques

BAR BELUBA NERUBA ▼

COCO BANGOS

CAFÉ-BAR UBAFU ▼

TILINGO LINGO ▼

Río Crique

HOTEL VILLA DEL MAR ▼

TROPICOOL/ BLACK SHEEP ▼

BAHÍA AZUL/ EXOTIC TRAVEL ▼

BANCO REFORMADOR ●

LA BUGA/ CHICHIMANGOS ▼

HAPPY FISH ▼

RESTAURANT MCTROPIC ▼

HOTEL DOÑA ALIDA

HOTEL RÍO DULCE ●

HOTEL RÍO TROPICALES ●

BANRURAL ■

BUGANET ■ TELGUA ■ POST OFFICE ■

IMMIGRATION ■

CASA DE LA IGUANA B&B ●

CALLE PRINCIPAL

HOTEL VILLA CARIBE

MUSEO MULTICULTURAL DE LÍVINGSTON

CALLE MARCOS SÁNCHEZ DÍAZ

POSADA DELFÍN ●

BUGA MAMA ▼

Río Dulce

HOTEL CASA ROSADA ●

HOTEL EL VIAJERO ●

HOTEL HENRY BERRISFORD ●

CAFÉ-BAR IGUANA'S ▼

MUNICIPAL BOAT DOCK ■

0   100 yds

0   100 m

© AVALON TRAVEL PUBLISHING, INC.

generally not the cleanest and have had some security issues in the past. Locals insist the group perpetrating past robberies has been caught, with at least one of them having met an unfortunate end. The nicest beach close to town is that of **Playa Quehueche,** about two kilometers west along Bahía de Amatique. There are a couple of comfortable hotels here, allowing you the opportunity to stay right on the beach. Both have nice wooden docks for swimming in the placid Caribbean

waters. The beaches here are of white sand, unlike those on the Pacific Coast. It's not the talcum-powder white typically found on Caribbean shores elsewhere and the water is not turquoise as in the Belize cayes, mostly because silt from the surrounding jungle rivers flowing into the bay conspires to keep the waters a greenish-brown color. But they're still perfectly nice for swimming. A boat ride here costs about $3.

Another 12 kilometers or so northwest is

LÍVINGSTON'S GARÍFUNA CULTURE

Lívingston is one of Guatemala's most cultur-ally diverse regions, with Garífuna, Hindu, Q'eqchi', and ladino cultures peacefully coex-isting here. Of these, the Garífuna and Hindu influences are particularly interesting because they are not found elsewhere in Guatemala, giving this region a unique flavor. Guatema-lans are often surprised to see Afro-Caribbean people when they visit the Atlantic Coast, as they are not readily in evidence elsewhere in the country, looking upon them with a certain sense of wonder simultaneously fueled by a form of racism familiar to the country's Mayan people. A number of far-fetched myths have been affixed to Garífunas, including the belief that seeing an Afro-Caribbean person on the street (outside of Lívingston) means you will soon come in contact with a long-lost acquain-tance. Also common is the general suspicion of widespread practice of voodoo and cannibal-ism by Garífuna peoples.

Guatemala's Garífuna population numbers about 4,000 and traces its history to the Ca-ribbean island of St. Vincent. Ethnically, they are a mix of Amerindian and African peoples and their language comes from the Brazilian Arawakan language family. These Arawak-speaking peoples migrated from northern Brazil long before the arrival of Europeans in the New World and lived peacefully on the island until they were subdued by Carib speak-ers from the South American mainland. The African element of their bloodline came about after intermingling with the survivors from the wreck of a Spanish ship carrying Nigerian slaves just off the coast of St. Vincent. These people eventually became known to the British as Black Caribs – in their own language, Gari-nagu. Garífuna is the Spanish translation of this word. In the 1760s, the British tried to take St. Vincent but were driven off by the Caribs with help from the French. The Caribs would continue to oppose the British on and off for several years until finally being defeated in 1796, when they surrendered. The Garífuna were subsequently captured and imprisoned

by the British before being shipped off to the island of Roatán, off the coast of Honduras. One of the ships transporting the prisoners was captured by Spanish forces and sent to the Honduran mainland. Only 2,000 Garífuna made it to Roatán, as many died during their imprisonment on St. Vincent or along the sub-sequent journey.

Pleas for help from the Garífuna stranded on the tiny island of Roatán were answered by the Spanish forces who arrived some time later to take survivors to Trujillo (Honduras), where they were conscripted to serve in the armed forces or work in agricultural fields. The Garífuna continued to move along the coast, eventually settling other parts of Hon-duras as well as Nicaragua. Some were taken to southern Belize to work in logging opera-tions, from where they spread to Guatemala, establishing Lívingston in 1806. Today, the largest population of Garífuna can be found along the coast of Honduras (100,000), but there are also sizable populations in New York (50,000), New Orleans, and Los An-geles. Like other ethnic groups in Central America, they have been emigrating to the United States in increasing numbers since the 1970s.

Modern Garífuna speak Spanish, English, and the Garífuna language, which melds French, Arawak, Yuroba, Swahili, and Banti. Central to their culture are music and dance, namely *punta*, a form of musical expression with obvious West African influences incor-porating ritual chanting, mesmerizing drum-beats, and rhythmic dancing. A traditional Garífuna band consists of three large drums, a turtle shell, a large conch shell, and maracas. You will probably hear live *punta* music at least once during your visit to Lívingston. Also com-mon is *punta* rock, a more modern version of popular Garífuna music. Another fascinating traditional dance is the *yancunu* New Year's dance, similar to those of indigenous South American rainforest peoples with distinctly West African musical origins.

Playa Blanca

NIGHTLIFE

If you're the kind of person who likes to spike the punch at the party, you might want to try a *coco loco*, a rather fun concoction consisting of a coconut with the top chopped off and enhanced with a generous helping of rum. The simple bars along Calle Principal as you come up the street from the municipal docks, including **La Buga** and **Chichimangos,** across from the Bahía Azul restaurant, can usually satiate your thirst should the fancy take you.

Lívingston has a fairly vibrant nightlife scene befitting of its tropical location by the sea. Down by the beach on the northern end of town (Playa Bariques) is **Bar Beluba Neruba** with a small dance floor and tables right on the sand. Another lively spot in this neighborhood is **Coco Bongo's,** playing Jamaican reggae and Garífuna *punta* rock. They can both be reached by heading west along the beach at the end of Calle Principal.

Along a side street also heading west from Calle Principal, **Café-bar Ubafu** is usually hopping, with live music on weekends. On Calle Principal, **Tropicool** is a disco that opens at 8 P.M. on weekends.

The **Black Sheep,** next to the Bahía Azul restaurant, shows movies nightly at 8. A good place to hang out in a more relaxed environment can be found at **Café-Bar Iguana's** in an open-air patio overlooking the river next to the town's museum just to the left of the main dock.

GUIDE COMPANIES

Highly recommended for its knowledgeable guides and the variety of interesting tours, **Exotic Travel** (Calle Principal, inside Restaurante Bahía Azul, tel. 7497-0133 or 7497-0151, www.bluecaribbeanbay.com) has daily transport to Río Dulce ($11) as well as a daily Jungle Trip. The latter encompasses a walk through town past Garífuna neighborhoods before heading up to a lookout spot with wonderful views of the town and sea. You then take a canoe ride down the Río Quehueche to Playa Quehueche before hiking through the jungle to Siete Altares, where you have a few hours

the area's nicest beach, **Playa Blanca** (entrance $1.50), with a pretty stretch of white sand and palm trees along a tranquil stretch of the Caribbean Sea. The private beach is under the same ownership as the Villa Caribe and it wouldn't be surprising to see a hotel here within the next five years. For now, it remains pleasantly quiet, though it's becoming increasingly popular as a day trip from Lívingston. There are bathrooms and showers here.

Several outfitters including La Casa Rosada, Happy Fish, and Exotic Travel do trips to Playa Blanca for $13 per person with a six-person minimum and including a box lunch. The Exotic Travel tour stops at the waterfalls of **Siete Altares** and the **Río Cocolí** along the way. The river is a pleasant side stream suitable for swimming with a small sliver of beach along the bay. Trips leave around 9 A.M. and return in the afternoon around 5 P.M. If you're looking to hook up with a group, try Exotic Travel first, as it seems to be the popular favorite and might have a group already going out.

to relax and eat lunch at an on-site restaurant. The last leg of the journey is a five-kilometer hike back to town along the beach. The trip leaves daily at 9:30 A.M., returning at around 4:30 P.M., and costs $7. Entry fee to Siete Altares ($1.50) is additional. Another option is a twice-daily half-day mountain bike ride to Río Quehueche, continuing to Siete Altares and returning via the beach. This trip leaves at 8 A.M., returning at 12:30 P.M., or at 1 P.M., returning around 5 P.M. This trip costs $10, including gear, box lunch, and hydration fluid. A final option is a full-day horseback-riding trip to Finca Río Blanco, where there are some waterfalls. The trip costs $25, including horses, guide, entrance to the farm, and a box lunch. There's a 400-meter zip line at the finca, costing an extra $15, if you want to zip between the trees on a metal cable. Exotic Travel also does trips to Playa Blanca with a six-person minimum, stopping at Siete Altares and Río Cocolí along the way.

Hotel Casa Rosada (tel. 7947-0303, www.hotelcasarosada.com), **Happy Fish** (tel. 7947-0661 or 7947-0268, www.happyfishresort.com, $5–25), and **Hotel Río Dulce** (tel. 7947-0764) do trips to Siete Altares ($10) and Playa Blanca ($13) with a minimum of six people. Hotel Río Dulce's Playa Blanca trip also stops at Siete Altares and Río Cocolí along the way.

Hotel Posada El Delfín (tel. 7947-0056, www.turcios.com/eldelfin) offers a number of adventurous itineraries, including a full day of deep-sea fishing, an overnight scuba-diving trip to San Nicolás caye (in the Belize cayes), and a hike up a nearby mountain for an overnight stay in a jungle villa.

ACCOMMODATIONS

Despite its location right on the Caribbean Sea, Lívingston lacks beachside resort properties, though there are some midrange accommodations on a serviceable beach just north of town. Most of the accommodations are found in the heart of town.

Under $10

The most pleasant budget accommodations are found at the rustically charming **Casa de la Iguana B&B** (tel. 7947-0064, $5–8 per person), about one kilometer from the center of town along Calle Marcos Sánchez Díaz, where fan-cooled rooms housed in thatched-roof bungalows with somewhat stiff mattresses, private bath, and hot water go for $8 per person or $5 per person in a shared-bath dormitory. Breakfast ($2) is served 7–10 A.M. in a thatched-roof dining room overlooking a pleasant tropical garden and includes a choice of scrambled eggs, pancakes, or cereal. There's also a book exchange. If you're in a pinch, head to the no-frills **Hotel El Viajero** (tel. 5718-9544), closer to the center of town along the same street where rooms sharing a bathroom cost $2 per person or $6 d with private (cold-water) bathroom. Continuing toward town the next place you'll come across is **Hotel Henry Berrisford** (tel. 7947-0471/72), offering basic rooms spread out among several floors with ceiling fan, spongy foam mattresses, TV, and private cold-water shower for $10 per person or $7 minus the TV.

On Calle Principal, **Hotel Río Dulce** (tel. 7947-0764) has excellent-value rooms with shared bath for $5 or with private cold-water bath for $6. The shared-bath rooms are upstairs, are somewhat more cheerful, have balconies with street views, and get more ventilation than rooms with private bathroom, which are all on the first floor. All rooms have fan and spongy mattresses. A serviceable cheapie can be found farther north on Calle Principal at **Hotel Villa del Mar** (tel. 7947-0260), where rooms let for $4 with private cold-water bathroom or $3 with shared bath. All rooms have fan and somewhat hard beds but are fairly cheerful and bright.

$10-25

On Calle Principal, **Hotel Ríos Tropicales** (tel. 7947-0158) has basic shared-bath accommodations for $7 per person as well as nicer rooms with private bathroom for $25–27 d. There is hot water and an attractive courtyard with hammocks. The more expensive rooms have ceiling fan and some nice furniture. There's a small café serving breakfasts.

Along the waterfront is **Hotel Doña Alida** (tel. 7947-0027, $25 d), with 10 large, modern rooms with private bath on a quiet street overlooking a beach. Rooms 10 and 11 are worth requesting for the sea views. To get here, turn right on the street just behind the Villa Caribe and walk north 2.5 blocks.

Along Calle Marcos Sánchez Díaz, about 400 meters west of the boat docks, is **(Hotel Casa Rosada** (tel. 7947-0303, www.hotelcasa rosada.com, $20 s/d), a delightful place to stay with 10 rooms, all with shared bath, centered around a pretty pink wooden house on the shores of the Río Dulce. The rooms are housed in attractive wood-and-thatch cabins with nice furnishings and hand-painted accents. Amenities include ceiling fans and mosquito netting. Some rooms are brighter than others. There is a dock leading out to the river where you can get dropped off. The restaurant here is excellent.

Out of town northwest toward Siete Altares is Playa Quehueche, a sliver of a beach that holds a few comfortable lodgings. The first of these is **Hotel Ecológico Salvador Gaviota** (tel. 5514-3275 or 5514-7933, www.hotel salvadorgaviota.com), which has simple rooms in thatched-roof cabins, including shared-bath doubles ($20), rooms with private bath ($13 p/p), and bungalows sleeping up to five for $57. There is a simple seaside café serving local fare and there's a pier out front over the ocean where you can swim or lounge in a hammock. A boat ride into town costs about $3. Also in this neck of the woods and farther west is **Hotel Ecológico Siete Altares** (tel. 5514-3339 or 5205-7864, www.geocities .com/sietealtares, $15 p/p), where thatched-roof beachfront bungalows sleeping 2–6 people have ceiling fan and private bathroom. A restaurant serves a variety of menu items from hot dogs and barbecue chicken wings to grilled meat and seafood dishes, along with cocktails to enjoy by the beach.

$50-100

Right at the entrance to town near the main dock, the **Hotel Villa Caribe** (tel. 7947-0072, www.villasdeguatemala.com, $79–110 d) is a large white building with a commanding presence over the waterfront. Standard rooms have tile floors, fan, and private hot-water bath, while three attractively furnished suites housed in separate bungalows come with air-conditioning, TV, minibar, and lovely sea views. There's a large swimming pool and a restaurant that serves bland international fare. Splurge for the suite.

About 500 meters west of town along Calle Marcos Sánchez Díaz is the **(Posada El Delfín** (tel. 7947-0056, www.turcios.com/ eldelfin, $75–150 d), where the modern, comfortable rooms have air-conditioning, private bath, ceiling fan, phone, and wooden furniture. All upstairs rooms have carpeting. There are also larger suites, including the wonderful honeymoon suite on the end of the two-story dock with a balcony overlooking the river below. It comes equipped with fridge, TV, and a CD player. Guests can relax in a lounge on the second floor, in the small swimming pool, or in hammocks on the dock over the river. For overall comfort and relaxing riverside ambience amid refreshing breezes, this place can't be beat.

On the other bank of the Río Dulce and at its mouth, **Sierramar Eco-Lodge** (tel. 5590-0789 or 7832-3885, www.sierramar.com, $25 d) is a comfortable eight-room lodge with bungalows fronting a pretty beach on Bahía de Amatique.

FOOD

The specialty here and elsewhere in Izabal is a dish known as *tapado,* a seafood stew prepared using coconut milk and bananas.

On par with the wonderful accommodations at **(Hotel Casa Rosada** (tel. 7947-0303, www.hotelcasarosada.com, 6:30 A.M.–9 P.M. daily) is its excellent restaurant, where delicious meals are served on charming hand-painted tables in a thatched-roof covered patio overlooking the Río Dulce. Dinner is a three-course set menu, including fresh salad and coconut bread, main course, and dessert costing about $11. Typical entrées include lobster, shrimp, filet mignon, Thai curry, and fish. Lunch and breakfast are served à la carte and include sandwiches, fruit salads, and quesadillas. Try the banana pancakes for breakfast. Excellent coffee and espresso drinks are also served here.

A few doors down Calle Marcos Sánchez Díaz, heading west, **Malena's** (inside the Hotel Posada El Delfín, tel. 7947-0056, www .turcios.com/eldelfin, 6 A.M.–9:30 P.M. daily) is one of Lívingston's finest restaurants, serving a varied menu of international dishes at reasonable prices, including vegetarian nachos with Provençal sauce, chicken, burgers, and veggie burgers. Seafood entrées include *tapado,* ceviche, fish chowder, and sea bass. There are delicious homemade desserts, coffee, and espresso beverages to top off your meal. The restaurant is on the second floor of a two-story dock jutting over the Río Dulce with pleasant modern decor, sea breezes, and the unmistakable feel of the tropics.

Along this same street close to the municipal dock, **Restaurant Buga Mama** (tel. 7947-0891, 10 A.M.–10 P.M. Tues.–Sun., noon–10 P.M. Mon., $5–25) is a good place for reasonably priced fish, shrimp, and pasta dishes. The restaurant, housed in a bright-blue wooden building, is wonderfully staffed by tourism industry students from a local school run by grassroots development organization Ak' Tenamit. Try the spicy pasta.

Calle Principal has a number of eateries. One of the first places you'll see as you come up the hill from the main dock is **Café Dugú** (11 A.M.–10 P.M. Tues.–Sun.), adjacent to the Villa Caribe, serving coffee, smoothies, pizza, and baked goods. Up the street, **Happy Fish** (tel. 7947-0661 or 7947-0268, 7 A.M.–10 P.M.) serves reliable seafood and salads in a pleasant patio setting just off the street. It's a good bet for breakfast. Across the street is **Restaurante McTropic** (7 A.M.–10 P.M. daily), under the same ownership as the Hotel Ríos Tropicales, where the specialty is Cantonese food, including chop suey and fried rice. A few doors down and across the street is the popular **Restaurante Bahía Azul** (tel. 7947-0151, 7 A.M.–10 P.M. daily), where meals are also served on a patio overlooking the street. The creative menu includes curry, sweet and sour or soy sauce chicken. There is live music some nights. It's also a good bet for breakfast. Try the "Gangster" breakfast sandwich with ham, cheese, hot cakes, and honey—a bit like a McGriddle. Farther up the same street toward Bahía de Amatique, **Tilingo-Lingo** serves good pasta, curries, fish, and *tapado.*

If you crave authentic Italian cuisine, look no farther than **Vecchia Toscana** (tel. 7947-0883/84, 8 A.M.–1 A.M. daily), in Barrio París on the beach north of town toward Playa Quehueche. There are delicious pastas and wood-fired-oven pizzas with prices in the $4–9 range.

SERVICES

For money, Banrural is on Calle Principal, just past Villa Caribe, with an ATM. Farther up the street is Banco Reformador, also with an ATM.

The immigration office (6 A.M.–7 P.M. daily) is also on Calle Principal across the street from the Villa Caribe. You'll need to stop here first if heading out to or arriving from Belize. Telgua and the post office are right next to each other just up the street on the right side.

For Internet access, try La Buganet (8:30 A.M.–9 P.M. Mon.–Sat.) or Happy Fish (7 A.M.–10 P.M. daily), both on Calle Principal and costing about $2 an hour. La Casa Rosada does laundry for about $0.35 an item.

GETTING THERE

The only access to and from Lívingston is by water, either from the Caribbean Sea to Puerto Barrios, Belize, or Honduras or via the Río Dulce. There is daily ferry service to Puerto Barrios at 5 A.M. and 2 P.M. (1.5 hours, $1.50), along with motorboats leaving when they have a full load of people. There is also service to Punta Gorda, Belize, on Tuesdays and Fridays at 7 A.M. (one hour, $20). Any of the town's travel agencies can book tickets for you, but you must have the confirmed ticket the night before, along with your exit stamp from the immigration office. There's a $10 departure tax when leaving Guatemala by sea. From Punta Gorda to Lívingston, the boat leaves Tuesdays and Fridays at 12:30 P.M. **Exotic Travel** also runs shuttle transport directly to Placencia for $50 per person with a six-person minimum. If you're heading to Honduras and have at least four people, it can also take you to La Ceiba for $65 per person, including boat to Puerto Barrios and then a minibus for the rest of the way.

There are also boat transfers to Río Dulce (2.5 hours, $10), usually leaving at 9 A.M. and 1:30 P.M. available from any of the Lívingston travel agencies.

NEAR LÍVINGSTON
Río Sarstún

As you head northwest along the Caribbean coast past the beaches of Playa Blanca, the last stop along the Guatemalan Caribbean shores is the Río Sarstún, which forms the border between Belize and Guatemala. This beautiful jungle river has just recently become a viable option for exploration now that it is fully protected as a park administered by conservation group FUNDAECO (www.fundaeco.org

.gt). The park ($20 admission) protects 2,000 hectares of tropical rainforest, flooded forest, wetlands, and mangroves. You can kayak and explore wetland canals, see the recently discovered Cerro Sarstún cenote, swim in the emerald-green waters of a small lagoon, or hike along well-maintained nature trails, all of which are included in the price of admission.

Accommodations are in the recently built **Río Sarstún Biological Station,** a modern facility with clean dormitories and bunk beds where you can stay for $7. There are also bathrooms and showers here. You can buy meals from the local community for $3–5. To get here, contact FUNDAECO's Lívingston office at 7947-0152. You can also hire a boatman to bring you, which will cost about $200 for a day trip.

◖ The Zapotillo Cayes

For the ultimate Caribbean adventure, cruise out to the Zapotillo Cayes, part of the famous Belize Barrier Reef. As you head out to

SAILING TO THE BELIZE CAYES

One of the highlights of many visitors' travels in the Guatemalan Caribbean is the unique opportunity to sail down the Río Dulce canyon and out to the Belize cayes. Trips last about a week and there are stops en route to swim and enjoy the magical beauty of the jungle river and canyon before stopping in Lívingston for immigration formalities. From there, the trip rounds the cape at Punta de Manabique before continuing to the open seas, where the water morphs into luminescent shades of aquamarine. You can enjoy learning the ins and outs of sailing, lounging on the deck under the sun or stars, delicious meals of fresh-caught seafood, snorkeling, scuba diving ($35 per dive), and lounging on pretty white-sand beaches. Typical stays on the cayes are about three days, with the rest of the time spent sailing to and from these wonderful offshore islands.

The islands you'll sail to are part of Belize's Sapodilla Cayes Marine Park, also known as the Zapotillo Cayes, and consisting of Lime Caye, Hunting Caye, Nicholas Caye, Seal Caye, and French Caye. The islands form a hook shape and are the southern extreme of the world-famous Belize Barrier Reef, second in length and marine splendor only to Australia's Great Barrier Reef. Divers will be delighted to find a variety of beautiful coral gardens, double reefs, canyons, and steep drop-offs in these waters.

At least two companies operate the trip out of Río Dulce. **Aventuras Vacacionales** (tel. 7832-6056, www.sailing-diving-guatemala .com, $380 per person, double occupancy) has been sailing to the cayes since 1990. Its office is in Antigua. Sailing is on *Las Sirenas,* a 46-foot Polynesian catamaran captained by its owner, John Clark, and by Guatemalan captain Raúl Hernandez. This company also offers a shorter, four-day version of its sailing trips encompassing the Río Dulce canyon and Lake Izabal for $165 per person, double occupancy. Sailing adventures are also available on ***"That"*** (tel. 5529-0829), a 62-foot trimaran. Its office and meeting point in Río Dulce is at the Sundog Café.

sea from the mainland, the waters transfuse into gorgeous hues of emerald green. The talcum-powder beaches along the small cayes are the stuff of Caribbean postcards with inviting turquoise waters perfect for swimming. The cayes are protected as a nature preserve, meaning there are no hotels on these islands. Camping is allowed. The reef is particularly well preserved with excellent opportunities for scuba diving.

Several of the Lívingston travel agencies go out to the cayes with a minimum of four people. **Exotic Travel** (tel. 7497-0133 or 7497-0151, www.bluecaribbeanbay.com) runs a day trip to the cayes, taking two hours to get there from Lívingston by a fast boat and including a stop along the way for deep-sea fishing. A box lunch and snorkel gear are also included. The trip costs $40 per person with a five-person minimum, plus a $10 entry fee to the park. You'll have to check out with immigration and pay a $10 exit tax for your brief departure from Guatemala, something that has only recently begun to be enforced. Have your group together by 5 P.M. the night before, along with your immigration formalities.

Overnight stays are available by booking highly recommended **sailing adventures** starting in Río Dulce, taking you up the lush jungle river and out to the cayes for a memorable weeklong experience. (See sidebar *Sailing to the Belize Cayes* for details).

Río Dulce National Park

One of Guatemala's oldest parks, the waterway connecting the Caribbean Sea with Lake Izabal is protected as Río Dulce National Park, covering 7,200 hectares along the river's 30 kilometer (19-mile) course. Much of the riverbank is shrouded in dense tropical forest punctuated at its most dramatic point by a large jungle canyon with hundred-meter rock faces known as **La Cueva de la Vaca.** The canyon is a 15-minute boat ride upstream from Lívingston. Along this route you'll also come across a graffiti-covered rock escarpment known as **La Pintada** with the earliest painting in evidence dating to the 1950s.

RÍO TATÍN

This small tributary diverts north from the Río Dulce just upstream from the canyon. Along its course, you'll find some excellent accommodations built into the surrounding jungle and in complete harmony with their environment.

Finca Tatín

⬛ Finca Tatín (tel. 5902-0831 or 5776-5156, www.fincatatin.centroamerica.com) is a wonderfully secluded jungle camp and backpackers' haven about half a kilometer up the river where

you'll find a variety of accommodations, including shared-bath dormitory beds for $5 per person, shared-bath doubles for $12, and bungalows with charming stone showers in the

© AL ARGUETA

view of the Río Tatín from the dock at Rancho Corozal

© AL ARGUETA

the jungle-clad Río Dulce canyon

private bath for $20 d. Couples might want to splurge for the bungalow, as the shared-bath double rooms have very thin walls. All rooms have mosquito netting and fan. The lodge gets major props for ecological consciousness. Water for the showers comes from the river, while water for the bathroom sinks is collected rainwater. All the bungalows have their own septic tanks with all waste material being buried.

Excellent meals are served in the lodge's open-air restaurant housed under a thatched roof. Dinner is a family-style affair, allowing for opportunities to meet fellow travelers. Breakfast, lunch, and dinner cost $3.50, $4.50, and $6.50. The menu is a varied palette of creative vegetarian, Guatemalan, and international dishes.

Activities include bird-watching in the surrounding forests, hikes lasting from 30 minutes to four hours all the way to Lívingston, and kayaking in the Chocón Machacas Biotope or down the Río Dulce to Lívingston. A

two-person kayak rental costs $6 per day plus gas for the return *lancha* pickup. The lodge is run by a friendly Argentine. Italian, English, and French are spoken.

Rancho Corozal

A little farther down the Río Tatín is ⟨ **Rancho Corozal** (tel. 5309-1423 in Guatemala, 866/621-4032 toll-free U.S., www .quintamaconda.com), an absolutely astounding private villa that can be yours for $250 d per night including breakfast. The owners are quick to point out that it's not a hotel but rather a private hideaway. It can sleep up to 10 people in five double beds with stylish safari netting. The beautiful house, designed with soaring thatched roofs and attractive ceramic and stucco accents, is set right beside the river on its own 20-acre forest reserve. There are tastefully landscaped tropical gardens, a short nature trail, open-air living and dining rooms, and a hammock patio. The house is wonderfully watched over by its live-in caretaker, Sabino, who can show you

© AL ARGUETA

Rancho Corozal, a private hideaway on the Río Tatín

around and take you to area attractions aboard the house skiff ($125 per day). At night, the villa is lit by the warm glow of gas lamps and torches. Food can be arranged at the house or at one of a few local eateries. Try the freshwater crab cooked in coconut milk at neighboring Doña Lola's.

Ak' Tenamit

Heading back downstream toward the Río Tatín's confluence with the Río Dulce, you'll find Ak' Tenamit (tel. 7908-3392 or 7908-4358, www.aktenamit.org), a grassroots health and development organization helping to provide a better living for the local Q'eqchi' Maya who inhabit the area in several villages. Thanks to this organization's efforts, these extremely impoverished communities now have access to health care and education, among other basic necessities. There is a women's handicraft cooperative, a 24-hour clinic, primary and secondary schools (including curricula in tourism and social welfare), and an ecotourism center. At the visitors center you can buy locally made crafts

and enjoy light meals in a pleasant *palapa*-style café, which is open 7 A.M.–4:30 P.M. Volunteer doctors, dentists, and nurses who can commit for at least one month are always welcome.

RÍO LÁMPARA

Continuing upstream, on the south bank of the Río Dulce, is another tributary known as the Río Lámpara. You'll see a small island known as Cayo Quemado at the mouth of this small river. This area is seldom explored, though a new jungle camp has put this remote area on the map.

Accommodations

The exquisite little jungle lodge, **El Hotelito Perdido,** (tel. 5725-1576 or 5785-5022, www .hotelitoperdido.com; dorm beds $4, bungalows $13-20 d) lies on the quiet banks of the Río Lámpara hidden away (as its name implies) from civilization. If you're looking for an exotic, affordable escape to the outer limits of civilization, El Hotelito Perdido might just do the trick. The accommodations are built in typical thatch roof jungle style and include a dorm and shared or private bath bungalows with typical Guatemalan fabric accents. Solar panels provide electricity, while rainwater is collected for showers. Breakfast, lunch, and dinner ($1.50-5.50) are available at the hotel's restaurant and include a variety of dishes including vegetarian fare. There's a nearby waterfall for exploring in addition to gorgeous views of the Río Dulce canyon from the grounds, kayaks for rent, hammocks for lounging and a swimming dock. Other activities include full-moon kayaking trips to nearby hot springs, jungle hikes, and bird-watching.

To get here, hitch a ride on any of the boats heading in either direction between Río Dulce town and Lívingston. They should have no problem dropping you off here. The lodge also offers a pick-up service for $4 per person from the Lívingston municipal dock.

EL GOLFETE

Back along the Río Dulce, another kilometer or so upstream, is a spot where warm sulfurous waters bubble from the base of a cliff, providing a pleasant place to swim. Shortly thereafter, the river widens into a lake known as El Golfete. The lake is home to a dwindling population of manatees protected on its northern shore by the **Chocón Machacas Biotope** (7 A.M.–4 P.M. daily, $5). The large, slow-moving aquatic mammals (also known as sea cows) are extremely elusive creatures and fewer than 100 are thought to inhabit these waters. The walruslike animals are threatened throughout their range by long reproductive cycles (they reach sexual maturity late in life) and collisions with motorboats. The 186-square-kilometer (72-square-mile) park is run by CECON and there are aquatic routes through several jungle lagoons as well as a nature trail running through the park and its protected forests.

The river continues its course upstream past the expensive villas of Guatemala's oligarchy to the town of Río Dulce, at the confluence of the river and Lake Izabal. A long bridge connects both shores along Highway CA-13, which continues north to Petén.

Río Dulce Town

The town of Río Dulce is the community centered around a long bridge crossing over the river near its meeting point with Lake Izabal. You'll find most of the town's accommodations on the north side of the bridge, also known as Fronteras.

RECREATION

Although the river and jungle are all around you, exploring this area may not be so easy on your own. It's always possible to hire a *lanchero* to take you around. Bargain hard. A more viable alternative is to stay at one of the more ecologically oriented lodges, which usually offer a full range of options for exploring. The two best places to stay in this regard are **Hacienda Tijax** and **El Tortugal,** which both do an excellent job of providing engaging nature hikes as well as supplying equipment (kayaks, for example) to explore on your own. (See the *Accommodations* section for more information.)

Sailing to the Belize Cayes
Aventuras Vacacionales (tel. 7832-6056, www.sailing-diving-guatemala.com) offers sailing trips up the Río Dulce and out to the Belize cayes on *Las Sirenas,* a 46-foot Polynesian catamaran. Sailing adventures are also available on *"That"* (tel. 5529-0829), a 62-foot trimaran. (See the sidebar *Sailing to the Belize Cayes* for more details.)

ACCOMMODATIONS

Most of Río Dulce's accommodations can be found on the north side of the bridge, starting from there and spreading west a few kilometers along the riverbank. Directly underneath the bridge is **Bruno's Hotel and Marina** (tel. 7930-5175, www.mayaparadise.com), a popular establishment with the sailing set containing rooms in shared-bathroom dormitories for $5 per bed, rooms with shared bath for $20 d, or rooms with air-conditioning, hot-water private bath, and porch overlooking the gardens and river for $40 d. There's a small swimming pool next to the river, which makes a great place to hang out. A few doors down along the busy road leading out of town, the **Riverside Hotel** (tel. 7930-5668) makes an acceptable budget choice with shared-bath rooms on the first floor going for $5 d or upstairs with private bathroom for $10 d. All rooms are barebones but clean enough.

About one kilometer farther west along the river is **❰ Hacienda Tijax** (tel. 7930-5505/6/7, VHF channel 09, www.tijax.com), one of Guatemala's most enjoyable places to stay. The least expensive rooms are above the restaurant and cost $13 d with shared bath, though the quaint little A-frame cabins on the riverfront are what this place is all about. Cabins with shared bath go for $24 d, or $39 d with private bathroom. There are six private-bath cabins with air-conditioning available for an extra $10. Spacious bungalows cost $70 d. All rooms have comfortable beds with mosquito netting and fan. There is an excellent restaurant housed under a large *palapa* structure, an inviting swimming pool, and Internet access. Activities include a guided tour around the hacienda's working rubber plantation to a lookout tower with gorgeous views of the river and El Golfete, passing a hanging bridge over the forest along the way, two-hour horseback riding tours around the farm, kayaking, and sailing. Tours cost $10–25 per person. There's a boat marina here.

Farther west along the river, the next place over is the fancier, 35-room **(Catamaran Island Hotel** (tel. 7930-5494, www.catamaran island.com), set on a splendid private island. Rooms are housed in comfortable wooden cabins with ceiling fan, air-conditioning, and private bath. There are rooms on land for $85 d including breakfast or set over the water for $91 d, also including breakfast. There's a fancy restaurant serving seafood and international dishes, a tennis court, and a poolside bar with a happy hour 4–7 P.M. There are sports on its DirecTV-equipped units. There's also a marina here.

A fine choice for budget travelers is **Casa Perico** (tel. 7930-5666 or 7909-0721, VHF channel 68), another few kilometers farther west. Situated beside the Río Bravo, a small tributary of the Río Dulce, the lodge offers rooms in a dormitory above the restaurant/ bar for $5 per person or wooden cabins with private bath for $15 d. It's a bit out of the way, which is precisely what brings most guests here. The Swiss owners cook good meals (dinner is about $5–6) and will pick you up from Río Dulce for free and drop you off at the end of your stay.

Back near the bridge, on its south side, is **Hotel Backpackers** (tel. 7930-5480, www .hotelbackpackers.com). Another budget travel-

ers' hideout, it has rooms in shared-bath dorms for $3 per person, double rooms with shared bath for $8, or doubles with private bath for $16–20. It's run by Casa Guatemala, a nonprofit that manages a center on El Golfete for abandoned and malnourished children. There's a restaurant/bar here serving inexpensive international dishes, beers, sodas, and cocktails. Services include laundry, phone, fax, and email. You can inquire here about volunteer opportunities with Casa Guatemala. If arriving on the bus from Guatemala City, get off before crossing the bridge so as to avoid a long walk back from its other end. Also on this end of the bridge is **Hotel Ensenada Planeta Río** (tel. 2473-0317, www.planeta-rio.com, $61d). It has spacious modern rooms, air-conditioning, private bath, and some decor as well as a large restaurant that is open for three meals a day next to a substantial swimming pool. This is the kind of place that seems to be most popular with Guatemalans on holiday.

On the right side southwest about one kilometer from the bridge toward the Castillo de San Felipe is **(El Tortugal** (tel. 5306-6432 or 7742-8847, VHF channel 68, www .tortugal.com), where a splendid setting, beautiful accommodations, and attention to details make this one of the best places to stay in Río Dulce. You can stay in rustically comfortable, tastefully decorated thatched-roof cabins ($30 d), some with adjoining sun deck, others on raised platforms. Some of the cabins come with tables and chairs, a couch, and hammocks. There are also two dormitories with beds for $10 per person, one of which is directly over the water on a raised platform over a dock. All beds have reading lamps. The accommodations all share a bathroom, where the showers are hot and wit good pressure. The filtered tap water here is drinkable. There's an excellent restaurant serving vegetarian fare and Guatemalan takes on international dishes in a lovely soaring thatched-roof structure built on a platform over the water. Above the restaurant is a clubhouse where there's a big-screen TV with satellite connection, pool table, and computers with high-speed wireless Internet. Activities include catching some rays on the docks, kayaking (free for guests), sailing, and Rover tours to the jungle hot springs of nearby Finca El Paraíso.

FOOD

Bruno's Hotel and Marina (tel. 7930-5175, www.mayaparadise.com, 7 A.M.–10 P.M. daily) is especially popular with boaters for its varied menu of international dishes and snacks in the $5–10 range as well as its TV news and sports in an open-air dining room right by the water. There are pancakes, omelets, and hash browns for breakfast; burgers and ribs for lunch and dinner. Just up the street, (**Restaurante Río Bravo** (tel. 7930-5167, 7 A.M.–10 P.M. daily) serves a similar menu, including good seafood, pasta dishes, and pizzas ($11) on an open-air deck over the water. There's a full bar and it's a popular place for meeting fellow travelers. Along the same side street as Otitours and Atitrans, **Sundog Café** (tel. 5529-0829, $3–6) has delicious hot sandwiches, including an avocado melt, baguettes, and pastrami sandwiches. There's a 5:20 happy hour and it is the local booking agent for sailing trips aboard *"That,"* a 62-foot trimaran.

Whether or not you're staying at **Hacienda Tijax** (tel. 7930-5505/6/7, VHF channel 09, www.tijax.com), it makes a great place to eat for its rugged jungle ambience and delicious sandwiches, seafood, salads, pasta, and steak dishes in the $5–13 range served in an airy high-ceilinged *palapa* structure. It brews excellent coffee and has a full bar. Farther out this way, about two kilometers downstream from Río Dulce, is **Mario's Marina** (tel. 7930-5569/70, www.mariosmarina.com), which has a restaurant/bar that is popular with the sailing crowd and serving a variety of seafood and international dishes. Bar patrons can browse the book exchange or enjoy a game of darts.

West from the Río Dulce bridge toward the Castillo de San Felipe, the restaurant at (**El Tortugal** (tel. 5306-6432 or 7742-8847, VHF channel 68, www.tortugal.com, 7 A.M.–10 P.M.) is worth a stop for its deliciously prepared, creative menu options and superb

location right on the water away from the noise and traffic closer to town. Prepared using fresh ingredients, the menu includes a harmonious blending of authentic Guatemalan cuisine with American and European flourishes. Try the Cannoli de Rosa ($6), a flavorful Guatemalan crepe stuffed with grilled chicken, sweet onions, peppers, and a salsa cream sauce that will make you swoon. Other dinner options range $5–12 for items varying from a quarter-pound barbecue burger to seafood stew. It's also a great place for breakfast ($2.50–6) or lunch ($4–6). The bar here serves some excellent cocktails that you can enjoy along with the gorgeous jungle river scenery.

SERVICES
Communications

Restaurante Río Bravo and Bruno's, on the north end of the bridge, both have Internet access. Next door to Bruno's, Captain Nemo's Communications (tel. 7930-5174), offers phone, fax, and Internet services. Several local hotels, including Hacienda Tijax, Backpackers, and El Tortugal, are all wired.

Money

All of the banks are on the main road on the north side of the bridge. Banco Industrial has a visa ATM and Banrural has Visa and MasterCard ATMs.

Travel Agencies

You can book shuttle buses, sailing trips, and boat transfers from three very similar travel agencies on a small alleyway just north of Bruno's along the main road. These are Otitours (tel. 7930-7674), Atitrans (tel. 7832-0644 or 5218-5950), and Tijax Express/Gray Line Tours (tel. 7930-5196/97, www.grayline guatemala.com).

GETTING THERE
Bus

The north end of the bridge, also known as Fronteras, is a hub for transport heading out in several directions from here. Buses heading north to Petén all stop here before continuing to Poptún and Flores ($7, four hours). The same is true for the return trip south from Flores to Guatemala City ($6, six hours). Bus lines covering this route include Línea Dorada and Fuente del Norte. Both companies also have some more expensive luxury coaches plying this route. **Litegua** buses can take you to and from Puerto Barrios directly or by changing buses at La Ruidosa Junction near Morales. From there you can catch a westbound bus to Guatemala City or east to Puerto Barrios. All of these companies have offices in Río Dulce. There are

shuttle buses to Guatemala City ($30), Antigua ($37), and Copán Ruinas ($37) that can be booked through the local travel agencies. Buses to El Estor (1.75 hours) leave from here about every 90 minutes.

Boat

Boats to Lívingston leave from underneath the north side of the bridge via **ASOCOLMORAN** (tel. 5561-9657), the local water taxi association, at 9 A.M. and 1:30 P.M., taking about 90 minutes and costing $13 one-way or $21 round-trip.

Lake Izabal

Guatemala's largest lake is a mostly undiscovered region. Of particular note are the Bocas del Polochic Wildlife Preserve, centered around the Río Polochic's delta, and the 17th-century fortress of Castillo de San Felipe de Lara.

CASTILLO DE SAN FELIPE DE LARA

More commonly known as "El Castillo de San Felipe," (8 A.M.–5 P.M., $1.50), the fortress also gives its name to a small community on the northern shores of Lake Izabal. The castle was originally built by the Spanish in 1652 in an attempt to deter the activities of pirates, who would come up the Río Dulce to raid supplies. It would later serve as a prison but was finally abandoned and left to deteriorate. The present fortress was reconstructed in 1956. It's worth a look around for its thick walls enclosing a maze of small rooms as well as its old cannons. There are some nice lake views, a picnic area, and green grounds.

Accommodations and Food

One of the fancier options along the shores of the lake near the Castillo de San Felipe is **Mansión del Río** (tel. 7930-5020, www.mansiondelrio.com.gt, $109–133 d), a large, 95-room resort-style property popular with vacationing Guatemalans. Large and attractive rooms have air-conditioning, ceiling fan,

cable TV, minifridge, gorgeous bay views, and nice decorative touches, including marble counters in the private bathrooms. There are a large swimming pool, a restaurant, two bars, a fairly well-equipped gym, and well-cared-for gardens. Paddle boats and a playground will keep the kids busy. The Cocodrilo Creek restaurant serves international dishes and has both an indoor, air-conditioned section, or a breezy outdoor dining room under a thatched roof with beautiful bay views. The Bonito River Bar has a nice lounge for relaxing as well as foosball and Ping-Pong tables. A similar property, **Banana Palms Resort and Marina** (tel. 7930-5023 or 2331-2815, www.bananapalms.com.gt), can be found just down the road to the west. Here you'll find modern rooms housed in attractive units with two rooms on the ground floor and one deluxe suite on the top floor. Rates range from $92 d for a standard room to $129 d for a deluxe suite. Junior suites ($116 d) have ceiling fan, large bathroom, living room, small kitchen, and a deck with lake views. The deluxe suite has all of the above plus a whirlpool bath with lake views. All rooms have DirecTV and air-conditioning. The pleasant thatched-roof lobby leads out to a thatched-roof bar next to a swimming pool with foosball and pool tables and DirecTV. There are a nice dock and marina, game areas, a fitness center, and a large, airy restaurant housed under a high-roofed *palapa* structure. The restaurant/bar serves seafood, Guatemalan, and international dishes.

From the castle, a road heads northwest to its juncture with the road back to Río Dulce. Along this road you'll find **Hotel Chang-Gri-La** (tel. 7930-5467, hotelchangrila@yahoo.com, $39 d), with modern rooms and bungalows (sleep six, $152), including hot-water private bath, air-conditioning, and cable TV. There are a swimming pool and a restaurant serving simple international fare. A few paces away to the west, **La Cabaña del Viajero** (tel. 7930-5412) has charming tin-roofed cabins centered around a swimming pool. There are simple rooms with shared bath ($12) and much nicer rooms with private bath, air-conditioning, and TV for $22 d. All have mosquito netting and fan. There's a restaurant here.

Getting There

Castillo de San Felipe is three kilometers along the lakeshore from Río Dulce or four kilometers by road, which you can walk in about 45 minutes. Heading north out of town on the main road, turn left after the Banco Industrial. After a few kilometers, you'll pass the turnoff for El Estor on the right. Continue straight on the main road for another kilometer or so from here to the castle. Minivans ($0.50) leave every 30 minutes from the north end of the bridge, or you can hire a water taxi ($5).

EL ESTOR

El Estor is a pleasant, friendly lakeside town on the western shores that is becoming a gateway to some natural attractions in its vicinity. The town supposedly gets its name from a corruption of the English word "store," as it was referred to in the days of old when British pirates sailing up the Río Dulce and across the lake would come here to buy supplies.

The town is also home to a nickel mine, which functioned here in the 1970s but was later closed. Under the current government's push to exploit Guatemala's mineral wealth, the mine has been revived and there was debate on whether or not to allow minerals and

heavy equipment to be transported up the Río Dulce between Lake Izabal and the port of Santo Tomás de Castilla. It's all rather reminiscent of a similar push some years back to log the Río Dulce and float the wood downstream on large boats. The loggers failed in their attempt to gain approval for their plans, and at last check the Ministry of Agriculture and Natural Resources (MARN) had not decided what approach to take in this latest case based on the National Protected Areas Council's (CONAP) assessment of the activities as not in compliance with the park's management plan. It remains to be seen what effect the renewal of strip mining will have on the environment in the region surrounding El Estor. The mine was expected to resume production in 2008.

In any case, locals have spent some time working to make El Estor a viable ecotourism destination. A website showcases the nearby natural attractions, which include an impressive canyon, the **Bocas del Polochic Wildlife Refuge,** and the eastern end of the **Sierra de las Minas Biosphere Reserve.** The address is www.senderonatural.com/elestor. There is also a tourism information office (tel. 5415-1516 or 5818-0843) right on the main plaza.

Accommodations

El Estor has a variety of comfortable accommodations, all in the budget category. **Hotel Vista al Lago** (6a Avenida 1-13, tel. 7949-7205, vistalago@intelnett.com, $20 d) is an attractive, clean lodging overlooking the lake. Housed in an old wooden building dating to 1815 and originally owned by an English-Dutch business partnership, it is supposedly the original "store" that gives El Estor its name. All rooms have fan and private bath, but the best ones are those on the second floor fronting the lake. **Cabañas Chaabil** (west end of 3a Calle, tel. 7949-7272 or 5544-1066, $20 d) has four attractive wooden rooms with private bathroom, mosquito netting, and fan.

Under the same ownership as Hugo's Restaurant, **Hotel Ecológico Cabañas del Lago** (tel. 7949-7245, $30 d) is peacefully set aside on its own lakeside oasis one kilometer east of town in Barrio La Corroza. Its seven rooms housed in large, attractive bungalows have ceiling fan and private bath. There's a private beach and a dock for swimming and sunbathing. A small restaurant serves local food and cocktails, which you can enjoy in its pleasant lakeside setting. The owners can bring you here from Hugo's Restaurant in the center of town.

Right on the town's central park, **Posada de Don Juan** (5a Avenida 3-08, tel. 7949-7296) has simple, clean rooms housed in a cheerfully painted concrete building built around a parking lot courtyard. Rooms with private bath cost $9 d and rooms with shared bath cost $7 d. All rooms have fan. From the central park 1.5 blocks toward the lake is the motel-style **Hotel La Playa** (2a Calle 4-23, tel. 7949-7407), housed in a neocolonial concrete building (or a pink and green wooden annex) with simple, clean rooms with shared bath ($5) or private bath ($8) and fan.

Four blocks from the park on the road heading out to Lanquín and right on the lakeshore, **Posada Valle Verde** (tel. 5901-8907, www .posadalasmarias.com) has rooms housed in large, wooden A-frame cabins, including dorm beds ($4), shared-bath doubles ($10), and doubles with private bathroom ($20). The restaurant/bar serves Guatemalan and international dishes. Trips to the Bocas del Polochic Wildlife Refuge can be arranged through the hotel, which is under the same ownership as the Posada Las Marías in Lanquín.

Food

Chaabil (west end of 3a Calle, tel. 7949-7272 or 5544-1066, all meals daily, lunch and dinner $4–9) means "good" in Q'eqchi' and the food here lives up to its name with family recipes specializing in seafood served in a pleasant thatched-roof dining room with quaint handmade wooden furniture and right on the lake. On the plaza, **Café Portal** (5a Avenida 2-65, tel. 7818-0843, 6:30 A.M.–10 P.M. daily) and **Restaurante Hugo's** (tel. 7949-7245, all meals daily) serve a wide range of Guatemalan and international dishes, including vegetarian dishes and fast-food munchies such as burgers and sandwiches.

Information and Services

Banrural (3a Calle and 6a Avenida) can exchange cash dollars and cash travelers checks. In addition to the tourism information office on the central plaza, some folks at Hugo's Restaurant (Hugo Fajardo) and Hotel Vista al Lago (Oscar Paz) can answer your questions on local attractions and getting around.

Getting There

There are buses from Río Dulce to El Estor leaving every 90 minutes or so from the north end of the bridge. The buses leave hourly from El Estor for the return trip 6 A.M.–4 P.M. The dirt road continues west from here to Panzós, Tucurú, and Tactic, just south of Cobán, though it is not recommended because it's notorious for highway holdups. Check on the situation if you choose this route by inquiring at Hugo's Restaurant. If driving your own vehicle, you'll need a 4WD for this road.

A better option for getting to Las Verapaces is to take a truck leaving the town's central plaza at 9 A.M. daily for the village of Cahabón ($2, five hours). From there, you can take a pickup or bus to Lanquín, all the while being careful not to get stranded in Cahabón because it's not the safest place after dark. Coming back east to El Estor though here, the bus leaves at 4 A.M., so unless there's a later bus running at the time of your visit it would be ill-advised to take this route, as you'd have to spend the night in Cahabón. You'll also need 4WD on this road if you've got your own set of wheels.

A direct bus leaves for Guatemala City daily at 1 A.M., taking six hours and costing $7. The same bus leaves Guatemala City's bus terminal at 10 A.M.

There are no public boat routes between El Estor and any other of the lakeside settlements, but local *lancheros* would be happy to take you anywhere you like. Bargain hard.

NEAR EL ESTOR
Finca El Paraíso

On Lake Izabal's northern shore, between El Estor and Río Dulce, is the wonderful waterfall hot springs of Finca El Paraíso (tel. 7949-

7122), a working farm easily accessible from either town. Here a wide, 12-meter-high warm-water fall plunges into a clear pool cooled by flows from surrounding streams. If you think soaking in warm water in a tropical climate wouldn't be inviting, think again. Above the falls are some caves worth exploring, for which you'll need to bring a flashlight. Two kilometers west from the falls is a comfortable lodge and restaurant. The wooden bungalows have private bathroom and you can catch the cool lake breezes from a hammock on your very own patio. The restaurant is housed in a bamboo-and-thatch open-air structure with a menu that includes pasta and meat dishes.

The farm lies along the Río Dulce–El Estor bus route, about an hour from Río Dulce and 40 minutes from El Estor. Buses and pickups go by about every hour in both directions, with the last of these around 4:30 P.M. Hacienda Tijax and El Tortugal, in Río Dulce, can also bring you here on a tour.

El Boquerón

Roughly six kilometers east of El Estor, the dramatic limestone canyon of El Boquerón lies 500 meters off the road to Río Dulce. For about $3, locals can take you up the Río Sauce in a wooden canoe to explore the canyon and admire its 250-meter-high rock faces. There's a small beach in the canyon not too far from where the trip begins. They can leave you here and pick you up at an agreed upon time. The canyon extends for another five kilometers or so from here, should you want to do some more exploring.

◀ Bocas del Polochic Wildlife Refuge

This park encompasses the Río Polochic delta and includes wetlands, flooded forests, and savannas harboring a wide range of resident and migratory bird species as well as Lake Izabal's remaining manatee and crocodile populations. There are abundant populations of freshwater turtles and green iguanas. Larger mammals include tapir, howler monkeys, and three species of cats, including jaguars. The park is man-aged by **Defensores de la Naturaleza** (office in El Estor at 5a Avenida and 2a Calle, tel. 7949-7237 or 7949-7130, www.defensores .org.gt), which also manages the Sierra de las Minas Biosphere Reserve beginning just south of Bocas del Polochic and running west all the way to Baja Verapaz. (See the *Las Verapaces* chapter for more information). Together, both parks account for about 80 percent of Guatemala's biodiversity. Their management by a private conservation group translates into more-than-adequate facilities for tourism and scientific investigation. They afford great opportunities to explore some of Guatemala's most remote expanses with relative ease from a comfortable base.

If you want to explore either of these remote wilderness parks from here, call or stop by Defensores's office in El Estor, one block from the park. Defensores runs the highly recommended **Selempím Biological Station,** near its namesake community and river midway between both parks, where there are comfortable accommodations in screened-in private wooden cabins or dorms ($15 per person), shared bathrooms with showers, a hammock lounge, research facilities, and solar power. Meals can be arranged through the local community ($3–5) or you can bring your own food and use the station's cooking facilities ($2). Guides ($7 per group) can take you around by canoe or kayak through various canals for wildlife-viewing or land-based explorations along two nature trails. One of these offers a fantastic lookout point from where you can see the river's delta and fully appreciate the scale of the surrounding wilderness. Hidden in the pockmarked karst landscape of this rugged terrain are a number of sinkholes in addition to a cave near the biological station, where you can view some interesting stalactites and stalagmites.

To get here, your best option is to take one of the community-run boat transfer services ($8, 1.25 hours) leaving from El Estor at 11 A.M. on Mondays, Wednesdays, and Saturdays. The return trip leaves Selempím at 7 A.M. on the same days. Or you could hire a private boat transfer by inquiring in El Estor at Defensores's office. The typical rate is about $100 round-trip. The folks at Hugo's Restaurant or Hotel Vista del Lago might be able to hook you up with a local boatman for a little less. Admission to the park is $5.

MARISCOS

Things have gotten substantially quieter at the lake's main south-shore town, which once provided access to El Estor by way of a ferry boat but which has taken a backseat now that there's a road to El Estor from Río Dulce. The main attraction here is the fantastic ◖ **Denny's Beach** (tel. 5398-0908, www.dennysbeach .com), a lakeside resort four kilometers east of town, which has grown substantially from its humble beginnings as a restaurant and a few simple cabanas. A wide range of accommodations includes dorms ($7 per person), rustic cabanas ($16–20 d, with shared or private bathroom), beach-house rooms ($20–27 d, with shared/private bath and air-conditioning), beachfront cabanas ($40–67 d, with private bath, air-conditioning, and hot-water showers) or newly added luxurious villas with their own patios and lovely lakeside views ($80–100 d). The restaurant here has a varied menu in the $3–11 range for breakfast, lunch, and dinner, including excellent seafood, pastas, sandwiches, nachos, quesadillas, and creative shrimp burritos. There's a fully stocked beachside bar where you can hang out and meet other travelers. The available activities are as varied as the lodging options and include wakeboarding, horseback riding, beach volleyball, basketball, horseshoes, and Ping Pong. There are trips to the Sierra de las Minas, Finca Paraíso, Quiriguá, Río Obscuro, Río Dulce canyon, and Lívingston, or you can explore a nature trail meandering through the surrounding forests.

The easiest way to get here is by taking a daily water taxi leaving from Bruno's in Río Dulce between 4 and 4:30 P.M. (call ahead to confirm). By bus, travel along the Caribbean-bound highway (CA-9) and get off at the Las Trincheras Junction (Km. 221), from where you take a connecting minibus for the remaining 15 kilometers northwest to Mariscos. Once there, look for the **Ferretería de Doña Judith,** on the road leading out of town toward Playa Dorada. A hotel-owned water taxi can take you from there to the hotel. If you've driven your own car, you can also leave it here. The lodge can be reached on VHF channel 63. Many businesses in Mariscos use radios and can contact the lodge for you to arrange a pickup if you get lost along the way or if the water taxi isn't there.

LAS VERAPACES

Collectively known as "Las Verapaces," the departments of Alta and Baja Verapaz are mostly mountainous, remote, and clothed largely in verdant forests. Guatemala's national bird, the resplendent quetzal, and its national flower—a rare orchid known as the *monja blanca*—inhabit the cool cloud forests of this region. This is probably Guatemala's most overlooked area in terms of tourism potential, as it sees surprisingly few visitors. The recreational opportunities and natural attractions are boundless and include spectacular waterfalls, cool mountain forests, mysterious caves, Mayan ruins, turquoise lagoons, and white-water rivers. Perhaps because Guatemala has always had more fame as a cultural destination, its equally splendid natural attractions have been overlooked. This tendency seems to be changing.

Although it might seem the Verapaz Highlands are a continuation of the rugged Western Highlands, they are unique in a number of ways, including their settlement patterns, history, climate, geology, and population. You won't find much traditional attire being worn in these parts, particularly among the men. The women tend to wear traditional skirts with white blouses not nearly as colorful or intriguing as those worn elsewhere in the highlands. Still, Mayan culture is very much alive and well in the mountain towns and villages of the Verapaz Highlands. The stunning mountain scenery is on par with that found in the Western Highlands.

Perhaps most exciting for the visitor is the palpable sense of the Verapaces's being a well-kept secret just waiting to be told. It's easy to fall

© AL ARGUETA

HIGHLIGHTS

El Salto de Chilascó: This waterfall, among Central America's highest, can be reached with moderate effort from a nearby community on the fringes of the Sierra de las Minas Biosphere Reserve (page 276).

Biotopo Mario Dary Rivera: Also known as the Quetzal Biotope, this beautiful mountain park conveniently situated along the road to Cobán is the easiest way to explore the region's cloud forests and try your luck at glimpsing Guatemala's national bird, the resplendent quetzal (page 277).

Rafting the Río Cahabón: Adventurers won't soon forget a white-water rafting trip down the Class III-IV Río Cahabón, where you can battle rapids with names such as Rock and Roll, Sex Machine, and Corkscrew Falls between more peaceful stretches. You can also explore caves and thermal hot springs along the forested riverbanks (page 290).

Semuc Champey Natural Monument: The turquoise limestone pools and waterfalls of Semuc Champey are among Guatemala's most exquisite natural attractions. Don't miss a somewhat difficult trail up the side of a mountain for a fantastic view of the pools from above (page 292).

Cancuén: This Mayan site, still being excavated and restored, has yielded new insights into the last days of the Classic Mayans and lies in the remote jungles straddling the border between Alta Verapaz and Petén (page 294).

Candelaria Caves National Park: This large cave complex is among the most impressive in all of Latin America. Don't miss the chance to explore underground rivers by cave tubing or rafting into its depths (page 295).

Laguna Lachuá National Park: This exquisitely beautiful and remote lagoon lies in the northwest corner of Alta Verapaz surrounded by dense rainforest and is thought to have been the site of a prehistoric meteor impact. The surrounding forests and the azure jungle river known as Río Ikbolay are worth some exploration (page 299).

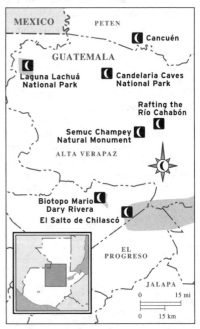

LOOK FOR **[** TO FIND RECOMMENDED SIGHTS, ACTIVITIES, DINING, AND LODGING.

in love with all that this wonderful area has to offer. New and increasingly comfortable accommodations with greater sophistication in services make this Guatemala's ecotourism frontier.

THE LAY OF THE LAND

Baja (Lower) Verapaz is the name given to the southernmost of the two departments. It is fringed by semiarid plains at its southern extremes before mountains, most notably the impressive **Sierra de las Minas,** rise and give way to lush cloud forests. The department is bisected by a number of flat valleys, the most important being the lush river valley that is home to its departmental capital of Salamá. A number of other interesting towns can be found along this corridor extending west toward the department of El Quiché. To the east, the Sierra de las Minas extends into Alta (Upper) Verapaz before descending into the neighboring flatlands of Izabal department. The two regions' unique ecosystems together comprise the bulk of all biodiversity found in Guatemala.

To the north, Baja Verapaz again meets the department of Alta Verapaz. Its departmental capital, Cobán, lies north of this boundary in a lush valley flanked by green hills and coffee farms at a comfortable altitude of 1,500 meters (5,000 feet). To the north, the mountains give way to smaller limestone hills and flatlands pockmarked by a variety of caves and sinkholes. The jungle flatlands extend west into the Ixcán region of Quiché and northward into Petén.

The entry point for most travelers making their way into this region is from the south via highway CA-14, which branches off from the semiarid plains west of Guatemala City at El Rancho Junction and climbs its way northward into the mountains of Baja Verapaz. An excellent paved highway also leads south from Petén into Alta Verapaz, from where you can see the rugged limestone peaks off in the distance. It is one of Guatemala's most wonderfully scenic stretches of highway.

CLIMATE

As elsewhere in Guatemala, the main determinant of climate is the altitude. As both Alta and Baja Verapaz are largely dominated by the presence of mountain chains, you can expect to find some chilly weather at high altitudes. The Sierra de las Minas reaches altitudes of 2,375 meters (7,800 feet), while Cobán displays similar temperatures to those in Guatemala City, which sits at the same altitude. It is considerably damper in these parts, as much of the year sees the *chipi chipi,* a misty drizzle that often dampens the atmosphere for entire days. The Baja Verapaz capital of Salamá is in a valley at about 1,065 meters (3,500 feet) and so is slightly warmer. Its climate is among the most agreeable in the country. Farther north, toward Chisec and the jungle flatlands extending northward, the temperature is substantially warmer and it can be extremely humid. All of these conditions are further influenced by the seasons (rainy and dry) dominating the entire country, though this area tends to see much more rainfall throughout the year with a shorter dry season (Dec.–Apr.) than elsewhere in Guatemala.

HISTORY

The history of the Verapaces is also quite different from elsewhere in Guatemala. The region was populated by the fierce Achi' Mayans, who were historically at war with the K'iche' of the Western Highlands before the Spanish conquest. The Spanish themselves were unable to conquer the Achi' and eventually gave up on this task, declaring the area a *tierra de guerra,* or "land of war." The church eventually succeeded where the conquerors had failed. Convinced by Fray Bartolomé de las Casas, the Spanish military forces agreed to leave the region for five years to give de las Casas and his men a chance to pacify and convert the Indians. De las Casas and three friars set out for the Verapaz Highlands in 1537, quickly befriending the Achi' chiefs and learning the local dialects. New converts were made and the Mayans living in scattered hamlets were convinced to move into Spanish-style settlements. After this five-year term, the Achi' were officially recognized as subjects of the Spanish crown, partially as a result of the passing of

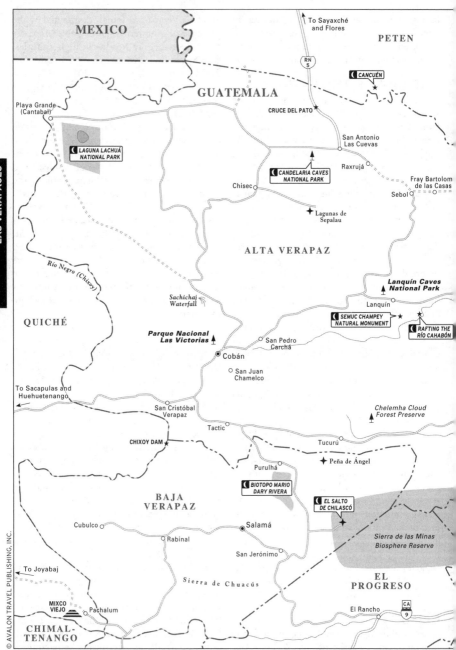

© AVALON TRAVEL PUBLISHING, INC.

LAS VERAPACES

To Poptún, Flores, Tikal, and Belize

Las Conchas

Cahabón

Río Cahabón

Sierra de Santa Cruz

IZABAL

El Estor

Lago de Izabal

Refugio de Vida Silvestre Bocas de Polochic

Río Polochic

Sierra de las Minas

CA 9

ZACAPA

Río Hondo

Río Motagua

CARRETERA AL ATLÁNTICO

Estanzuela

Zacapa

CA 10

0   5 mi

0   5 km

the New Laws in 1542 granting Indians basic rights and prohibiting their enslavement. The Spanish crown renamed the region Verapaz, or "true peace."

The region began to grow and develop with the arrival of coffee cultivation in Guatemala, aided by its proximity to the Caribbean port via the Río Polochic and across Lake Izabal. A railroad would eventually be built along this corridor. In the early 1900s, a flood of German immigrants snapped up large pieces of land and began cultivating coffee and cardamom, thus further altering the regional demographics. By 1915, half of all Guatemalan coffee was grown on land owned by these German immigrants, who sold a large percentage of the harvest to their fatherland. Cobán in particular was greatly altered by this demographic shift, as it took on the appearance of a German mountain town. The vestiges of this Old World influence can still be seen here and there. German economic and cultural dominion over the region was abruptly put to an end during World War II, when the United States prevailed upon Guatemala to deport the German farm owners, many of whom were unabashed in their support for the Nazis.

Today, the Achi' still inhabit Baja Verapaz in the area around Rabinal, with a largely Q'eqchi' and Poqomchi' population inhabiting the lands of Alta Verapaz. The region is still very much rural, much like the rest of Guatemala. Coffee and cardamom cultivation are still at the heart of the economy, with tourism beginning to make some significant inroads.

PLANNING YOUR TIME

You could easily spend your entire Guatemalan holiday in Las Verapaces and it would be entirely worth it. But, time being the finite entity that it is, you'll probably have to narrow your stay to your particular interests. If you're entering the region from the south along Highway CA-14, you might want to take a detour west to **Salamá** if your visit coincides with its annual fiesta during September. The nearby town of **San Jerónimo** is certainly worth a stop for its pleasant atmosphere and an excellent museum dedicated to the history of sugar production, of which it was the first center in Central America. North along Highway CA-14, the newly established **Cloud Forest Biological Corridor** is shaping up as a wonderful spot to explore a variety of natural attractions along the road to Cobán. Among these are some of the highest waterfalls in Central America at **El Salto de Chilascó,** on the border of the well-preserved cloud forests of the **Sierra de las Minas Biosphere Reserve.** Cobán still serves as the most convenient base for exploring all that the region has to offer and has some wonderful restaurants and hotels in addition to a pleasing mountain atmosphere. East of Cobán are the must-see turquoise pools and waterfalls of **Semuc Champey** and the nearby caves of Lanquín.

Lovers of cave exploration will want to spend some time in the area around Chisec, north of Cobán, where there are numerous cave formations, including the sinkhole of B'onb'il Pek and the spectacular **Candelaria Caves National Park** just a little farther north. Archaeology buffs will not be left wanting for attractions here, as the Mayan site of **Cancuén,** still being excavated and restored, lies north of here just across the border of Petén.

Last but certainly not least is the almost perfectly circular **Laguna Lachuá,** a magnificent azure lagoon in the flat jungles of northwestern Alta Verapaz.

Salamá and Vicinity

The road from the El Rancho Junction (CA-14) winds its way through the dry hill country, eventually making its way into the lush Baja Verapaz hillsides. Along Km. 132 is a turnoff known as "La Cumbre," from where the road branches west (CA-17) and begins its descent into the lush Río Salamá Valley. Fifteen kilometers down this road is the departmental capital of Salamá. There are some absorbing villages in these parts, and the town fiestas are among Guatemala's finest.

SALAMÁ

Salamá is mostly a ladino town, which really comes alive during its annual fiesta (Sept. 17–21). Other than that, there's really not much going on here. The old crumbling pedestrian bridge on the edge of town is worth a look, as is the ornate church of **San Mateo Apóstol,** on the east side of the plaza.

Guide Companies

For exploring the areas of Baja Verapaz, a good bet is **Eco-Verapaz** (8a Avenida 7-12 Zona 1, tel. 7940-0146). It offers mountain biking, caving, horseback riding, guided hikes, and cultural tours with prices somewhere around $40 per day for most itineraries.

Accommodations and Food

The best place to stay in town is the **Hotel Real Legendario** (8a Avenida 3-57, tel. 7940-0187 or 7940-0540, $15 d), with clean rooms, all with private bath, firm beds, and cable TV. There is a small café on the premises. Another good choice is **Hotel Argentina** (Diagonal 4, 2-57 Zona 2, Barrio San José, tel. 7940-1004, $15 d), featuring fan-cooled rooms with private hot-water bath and cable TV. An acceptable backup plan is **Hotel Tezulutlán** (Ruta 4 4-99 Zona 1, Barrio El Centro, tel. 7940-0141, $8–12 d), with 13 rooms set around a courtyard full of greenery, some with private bath. Just across the street is **Hotel San Ignacio** (4a Calle "A" 7-09 Zona 1, tel. 7940-0186, $5–9 d), with 18 bright, airy rooms with or without private hot-water bathroom. There's a pleasant *palapa* sitting area overlooking the street.

There are several places to eat near the plaza. For coffee, cakes, and snacks try **Café Deli-Donas** (15 Calle 6-61). **Cafetería Central** (corner of 15 Calle and 9a Avenida) is another good choice, particularly for lunch. A fancier option is **El Balcón de los Recuerdos** (8a Avenida 6-28, 8 A.M.–8:30 P.M. Mon.–Sat., $5–7), half a block west of the plaza on the way out of town, serving grilled meats and seafood in a fan-cooled dining room. Though its name evokes images of fast food, **Pollo to Go** (on the north side of the plaza) serves pretty decent burgers, chicken, and good breakfasts.

Information and Services

For banking, there's a Banrural on the south side of the plaza with a MasterCard ATM. The police station is one block west of the plaza. Telgua, just east of the plaza, has Internet access for $1.50 an hour. Lavandería 2000, next door to Hotel San Ignacio, does reasonably priced laundry.

Getting There

There are hourly buses leaving for Guatemala City from in front of Deli-Donas between 3 A.M. and 8 P.M. The 4 A.M. bus is a nicer, more expensive Pullman. Buses coming from Guatemala City continue west to Rabinal and Cubulco. Buses and minibuses for San Jerónimo leave from in front of the town hall every half hour 6 A.M.–5:30 P.M. There are also departures for the La Cumbre Junction with onward connections to Cobán departing from this same location about every half hour from early morning until 4 P.M.

SAN JERÓNIMO

About 10 kilometers from Salamá, back toward the La Cumbre Junction, is the wonderfully atmospheric town of San Jerónimo. This is about as clean and pleasant as highland Guatemalan towns get. The weather, at a comfortable altitude around 1,100 meters (3,600 feet), is just warm enough. San Jerónimo has an interesting history, as it was here that sugarcane cultivation first made inroads into the local economy with the establishment of Central America's first sugar mill by Dominican friars in 1601. The new crop came from Jamaica, along with new technology and 700 slaves from the island nation.

During the 17th century, the friars built a Roman-style aqueduct with **124 archways** to bring water to the sugar mill and town as production continued to increase. Wine and moonshine were also eventually produced in addition to sugar. The growth of these industries would be checked in 1829 with the expulsion from Guatemala of various religious orders under the liberal government of the time. You can still see the old remains of the archways scattered throughout town, giving San Jerónimo a unique feel.

Among the town's most interesting attractions is its beautiful 17th-century baroque **church,** set on the plaza. Inside, there's an altar brought from France and crafted with sheets of 18-karat gold. The plaza also harbors some ancient carved stones.

There are minibuses every half hour from Salamá to San Jerónimo between 6 A.M. and 7:30 P.M.

Museo del Trapiche

The town's most interesting attraction is the Museo del Trapiche (tel. 5514-6959, 8 A.M.–4 P.M. Mon.–Fri., 10 A.M.–4 P.M. Sat. and Sun., donation), set on the grounds of the old Hacienda San Geronimo, Central America's first sugar mill. It once housed 1,000 workers and boasted a production of 90 tons of processed sugar per year, a figure matched only by the great sugar mills of Mexico and Brazil. Among the relics you'll find here are a giant press and metallic waterwheel measuring seven meters in diameter and weighing a ton. There are displays on popular art and handicrafts, including old costumes, baskets, and woven items as well as archaeological relics, including pre-Columbian pottery.

With the expulsion of the Dominican friars, San Geronimo became state property and was later auctioned off. It was eventually abandoned in 1893 but has now regained some of its former splendor.

Accommodations and Food

Complementing the town's lovely provincial atmosphere are some nice hotels, should you wish to stay here. **Hotel Hacienda Real del Trapiche** (tel. 7940-2542, $20 d) is right at the entrance to town and has 10 pleasant rooms with good beds, private hot-water bath, and cable TV. There is a restaurant with excellent home-cooked meals. Another excellent option is the ❰ **Hotel Posada de los Frayles** (tel. 7723-5733, $28 d), with 10 comfortable rooms in a beautiful colonial-style building set among nicely landscaped gardens with tropical flowers and plants. Rooms have private hot-water bathroom, comfortable beds, and cable TV. There's a swimming pool and the restaurant serves decent meals for breakfast, lunch, and dinner.

SALAMÁ TO CUBULCO

West from Salamá are some interesting villages known for their weavings and annual fiestas. The first of these is **San Miguel Chicaj,** where the annual fiesta is held September 25–29.

To the west along a wonderfully scenic road, the next town over is **Rabinal,** founded in 1537 by Fray Bartolomé de las Casas. Rabinal is known for the quality of its pottery and its citrus products as well as for its observance of pre-Columbian traditions, dance, and folklore. The annual fiesta is held January 19–25 and it is by all means dramatic. The highlight is a dance performed on January 23 known as the **Rabinal Achi,'** which reenacts a battle between the Achi' and Quiché tribes.

The small **Museo Comunitario Rabinal Achi'** (4a Avenida and 2a Calle Zona 3, 8:30 A.M.–5 P.M. Mon.–Sat.) features exhibits on the history and culture of the Achi' Mayans living in this area. The most interesting exhibit pertains to the effects of the civil war, as the region was particularly hard-hit during the violence. Several mass graves dot the hillsides around Rabinal and about 4,400 victims have been exhumed and reburied in the past few years.

There are a few basic accommodations here. Try **Posada San Pablo** (3a Avenida 1-50 Zona 1, tel. 7940-0211, $7–12 d), where some of the clean rooms have private bath. The **Hospedaje Caballeros** (1a Calle 4-02) is another good alternative. Also on 1a Calle is the **Gran Hotel Rabinal Achi,** harboring large rooms with private bath and a small eatery.

As for services, there is a Banrural on 1a Calle and 3a Avenida, which can exchange your cash dollars. There are hourly buses to Salamá and five daily frequencies to Guatemala City via La Cumbre.

West from Rabinal the road continues up a high mountain pass along some uninhabited territory before plunging into yet another valley to the isolated Achi' Mayan and ladino town of **Cubulco.** The main attraction here is (you guessed it) the annual fiesta, with the peak of the action on July 25. This is one of the few places in Guatemala where you can witness the **palo volador,** a rather dodgy ritual in which dancers spin around a pole with a rope tied around their legs, eventually making it to the ground (most of the time, alive).

Along the Cloud Forest Biological Corridor

The Cloud Forest Biological Corridor (Corredor Biológico del Bosque Nuboso) is a relatively new creation that encompasses a forested area bisecting the Quetzal Biotope and Sierra de las Minas Biosphere Reserve. Its purpose is to provide an uninterrupted biological corridor for many species of animals living in these protected cloud forests. The area along the road to Cobán (CA-14) between Km. 144 and Km. 170 is part of this corridor, and it is clearly marked at its beginning and end. The corridor covers 28,640 hectares and includes nine communities and eight private reserves. A number of these private reserves are part of local hotels and restaurants that have begun catering to visitors interested in exploring all that

WHAT IS A CLOUD FOREST?

Cloud forests are essentially high-altitude rainforests, though the biological characteristics and corresponding classification are much more complicated than a matter of mere altitude. In Guatemala, cloud forests average an annual precipitation of between 2,000 and 6,000 millimeters and are found at altitudes between 1,000 and 2,500 meters. The forests essentially serve as a large sponge, retaining water that is later distributed to surrounding areas by means of evaporation or the formation of small streams. More than 60 small streams originate in Guatemala's Sierra de las Minas, for example.

A distinct characteristic of these forests is the presence of low-lying cloudbanks forming on the mountains, under which the forest is immersed for much of the time. Large amounts of water are deposited directly onto vegetation from the clouds and mist, with the leaves of trees at higher elevations often drip-ping water. Cloud forests serve as the habitat for many species of plants and animals, including epiphytes, which grow on other plants. You'll see tree branches thick with bromeliads, orchids, and tree ferns. As for wildlife, the forests support an abundance of rare and endangered species, including quetzal birds, howler monkeys, jaguars, and wild boars.

The Verapaz Highlands still contain many of these forests, including the largest protected cloud forest in Central America, the Sierra de las Minas Biosphere Reserve. The cloud forests that once covered much of the Western Highlands have been largely lost to subsistence agriculture by indigenous peasants who seek to make a living by clearing the forests and cultivating crops on steep hillsides. Outside of the Verapaces, there are still some patches of cloud forest left in the Sierra de los Cuchumatanes as well as on the slopes of Guatemala's volcanoes.

this exuberant highland forest ecosystem has to offer. The result is an emerging ecotourism development area, which may serve as a model for other areas in Guatemala with roads adjacent to protected areas.

The initiative is managed by an association based at Restaurante Montebello, at Km. 164 in the vicinity of Purulhá, which can provide additional resources and information. It can be contacted at tel. 7953-9234. Ask for Marlen de Moino.

Accommodations

The first stop along this ecotourism corridor is (**Hacienda Río Escondido** (Km. 144, tel. 5308-2440 or 5208-1407, ecorioescondido@ yahoo.com, $20 per person), where you'll find family-size bungalows on a private nature reserve bisected by the cool, clear waters of the Río San Isidro. There are several kilometers of nature trails, horseback riding, and inner tubing to keep you busy should you not want to just relax and unwind. The best of the cabins are set along the creek and there are plans for smaller cabins catering to independent travelers in the works. The restaurant here does barbecued meats and has some delicious smoothies you can enjoy in an open-air patio.

SIERRA DE LAS MINAS BIOSPHERE RESERVE

The Sierra de las Minas is a vast, 242,642-hectare mountain park harboring an astounding diversity of plant and animal life and encompassing a motley assortment of ecosystems, including cloud forests harboring several species of endemic conifers, as well as tropical moist forests and rainforests. The park extends 130 kilometers eastward (it's 30 kilometers wide) into the neighboring department of Izabal, where it meets with the lowland forests and grasslands of the Río Polochic delta. The biosphere reserve ranges in elevation from 400 to 2,400 meters and is composed mainly of cloud forests throughout its mountainous core in Baja Verapaz. Sixty-two permanent streams have their source in the upper slopes of the biosphere reserve, making it an important watershed supplying the Motagua and Polochic Rivers. It is home to healthy populations of quetzals and jaguars, among other exotic species. Together with the adjacent Bocas del Polochic Wildlife Refuge, the parks account for 80 percent of Guatemala's biodiversity.

The biosphere reserve is privately administered by **Defensores de la Naturaleza,** a well-known local conservation group with ties to The Nature Conservancy, among others. Although you may contact this organization for trips to the reserve, your best bet is to go via one of the local **community tourism cooperatives** in the villages near the park, which have trained guides who can take you on trips of a few hours or several days. Contacting this NGO proved virtually impossible despite repeated attempts and some help from the folks at INGUAT.

San Rafael Chilascó

San Rafael Chilascó is a small agricultural settlement that serves as the rallying point for visits to nearby waterfalls and into the biosphere reserve. The town's well-organized, friendly, and professional Chilascó Community Tourism Organization has stepped in to cater to visitors' recreational needs where NGOs have fallen short. It runs the local Tourist Information Office (tel. 5301-8928 or 5776-1683, elsaltodechilasco@yahoo.es, www.chilasco .net.ms, 7 A.M.–4 P.M. daily) at the entrance to town. The visitors center charges the $2 admission fee for entry to the falls, rents horses, can set you up with a guide, and provide you with comfortable accommodations with a local family or in its own basic lodge ($5 per person). Meals are available at local *comedores.*

San Rafael Chilascó is reached via a 12-kilometer dirt road branching east from the main highway heading northward toward Cobán (CA-14). The turnoff is at Km. 146. There are daily buses to Salamá leaving at 5:45 A.M., 8:30 A.M., 12:30 P.M., and 3 P.M., all of which pass by the Highway CA-14 turnoff ($0.50). You can flag down a northbound bus

to Cobán or southbound to Guatemala City from the turnoff.

◖ El Salto de Chilascó

Among the places local guides can take you is the spectacular El Salto de Chilascó, which they claim is the highest waterfall in Central America, at 130 meters. Other sources, however, place the falls at 70 meters and claim the highest waterfall in Guatemala is Tzuul Tak'a, recently discovered in a remote corner of the Sierra de las Minas, with a height of 115 meters. To the best of my knowledge, the highest waterfall in Central America is still Belize's Hidden Valley Falls, at more than 450 meters.

In any case, the Chilascó falls are certainly one of the region's highest and are well worth a visit. They can be reached via an excellent trail in about 1.25 hours. From the tourist information center in town (where you pay a $2 admission fee), it's two kilometers to a parking lot and the trailhead. It's another three kilometers from there to the falls. You'll first come to a smaller waterfall known as El Saltito before

El Salto de Chilascó

reaching the point where you descend to the larger waterfall via a separate trail. You'll be treated to wonderful vistas along the way and to an opportunity to see the gradual progression from agricultural fields dotted with potato, broccoli, and cabbage patches to dense cloud forest with wonderful bromeliads, orchids, and ferns. There are two lookout points from where there are fantastic views of the spectacular waterfall. A guide is recommended and costs about $4.

Lomo del Macho

If you wish to go farther into the reserve, guides can take you on single- or multiday hikes to such places as Lomo del Macho, eight kilometers down a trail crisscrossing the mountains on the fringes of the biosphere reserve. There are two smaller waterfalls along the way, one of which forms a pleasant swimming hole. The trail continues to the trail's namesake mountain ridge, where you have a breathtaking view of the forested slopes of the rugged mountain chain at the heart of this biosphere reserve. Horses are available for rent at about $4 for both of these hikes, but they can take you only part of the way, as the trail eventually gets quite steep and narrow.

Albores

A five-hour hike from San Rafael Chilascó deep into the heart of the reserve brings you to the farming community of Albores, on the southeastern side of the mountain range. Defensores has built comfortable **cabins** ($30 per person) to house visitors at its **biological research station** nearby. You can also stay in the community with a local family for $5 per person. There are about 70 families living in Albores, most of which have traditionally made a living from cultivating coffee, cardamom, and vegetables. Ecotourism is a relatively new source of income for these families and they welcome visitors with open arms. They can provide you with meals for about $5.

A park admission fee of $5 applies for exploring this part of the reserve. From Albores, there are two trails into the surrounding cloud forest. The first trail takes you to the magnificent **Peña del Angel,** an igneous rock formation at an altitude of 2,400 meters, from where you have an incredible view of the surrounding cloud forest and the Polochic and Motagua River Valleys. The rock gets its name from its appearance, like that of two extended angelic wings, thanks to the 1976 earthquake, which broke the rock in two. The second trail takes you to a lookout point built by Defensores to monitor forest fires, from which there are also fabulous views.

For visits to this part of the reserve, you should technically contact **Defensores de la Naturaleza** (tel. 7936-0566 or 7959-5341, sminas@defensores.org.gt or info@defensores .org.gt, www.defensores.org), though you may never hear back. A better option is to contact **Ecotourism and Adventure Specialists** (tel. 2337-0009 Guatemala, 415/762-3996 U.S., info@ecotourism-adventure.com, www .ecotourism-adventure.com). If you don't mind making arrangements until you are in Guatemala, try planning a visit with the **Chilascó Community Tourism Organization** (tel. 5301-8928 or 5776-1683, elsaltodechilasco@ yahoo.es, www.chilasco.net.ms).

◖ BIOTOPO MARIO DARY RIVERA

Also known as the Quetzal Biotope ($3.50, 7 A.M.–4 P.M. daily), this 1,044-hectare protected area is one of several biotopes administered by San Carlos University's Department of Conservation Studies (CECON) and is conveniently situated along Highway CA-14 at Km. 160.5, about an hour from Cobán. Though quetzal birds are easier to spot in Sierra de Las Minas, the elusive creatures are said to frequent the yard of some local eating establishments (Biotopín Restaurant and Ranchitos del Quetzal), where they like to feast on the fruits of the *aguacatillo* tree. The Quetzal Biotope's convenient roadside location means that if you're on your way to or from Cobán, you should at least stop in for a look. You might just get lucky and see one of Guatemala's most beloved national symbols,

MARIO DARY RIVERA

Considered by many to be the patriarch of Guatemala's environmental movement, Mario Dary Rivera was a biologist who served as rector of the University of San Carlos in 1981, the same year in which he was assassinated. Dary succeeded in getting the municipality of Salamá to donate part of the land for the creation of the Quetzal Biotope, which was subsequently named after him, and served as the new park's director from 1977 to 1981. Dary also founded the university's Center for Conservation Studies (CECON) in 1981, along with its system of protected areas known as biotopes, set aside for the protection and scientific study of endangered plants and animals.

Today there are at least half a dozen of these biotopes throughout Guatemala. Among the animals being protected and studied are the quetzal bird, sea turtles, jaguars, bats, deer, and Petén turkey.

Although the urban militant wing of the leftist Guatemalan Workers Party (PGT) has been attributed with Dary's assassination, some believe his conservation activities stirred the waters with local logging interests, who may have also played a part in his assassination. Unlike most political killings at the height of the violent civil war, Dary's stands out because he was generally perceived to be right of center in his political inclinations.

while *Los Musgos* (The Mosses) trail is twice as long. While you may or may not see a quetzal bird, you'll certainly see a dense growth of epiphytes, mosses, ferns, and orchids along the well-maintained trails. Both trails pass by some nice waterfalls where you can swim.

Trail maps are available for $0.75 at the visitors center, where there is also an exhibit. A small shop sells snacks and drinks and there are camping and barbecue areas. Check with the guards before camping, as it may or may not be allowed at the time of your visit.

Accommodations and Food

A number of comfortable lodgings are alongside the road in the vicinity of the biotope. The first place you'll find, coming from Cobán, is **Ranchitos del Quetzal** (tel. 2434-5919), where eight basic rooms in thatched-roof huts or concrete structures with electric hot-water heater cost $7 per person. The restaurant here serves basic, inexpensive meals ($1.50–4) and there is a trail to a waterfall and swimming hole 40 minutes away. Quetzals are sometimes seen here. Across the street from the biotope is **Restaurante Biotopín** (tel. 5202-0528 or 2473-9017, 7 A.M.–5 P.M. Fri.–Sun.), serving snacks, barbecued meats, burgers, hot dogs, and other picnic fare in an open-air dining room facing the woods. Farther along the highway at Km. 158.5 is **Hotel y Restaurante Ram Tzul** (tel. 5908-4066, ramtzul@intelnet.net.gt, www.m-y-c.com .ar/ramtzul, $40 d), with comfortable accommodations in wooden cabins, all with private bath. A large restaurant tastefully constructed using 3,500 bamboo shoots serves good food three meals a day. The lodge is on a private 150-hectare forest preserve. A 45-minute hike leads to a pretty waterfall. Another lodge on a private forest reserve is **Posada Montaña del Quetzal** (Km. 156.5 on the road to Cobán, tel. 6620-0709 or 2332-4969, reservaciones@ hposadaquetzal.com, www.hposadaquetzal .com, $36–46 d), where you have a choice of staying in standard rooms or family-size bungalows. There are firm beds and an on-demand hot-water heater. The rooms can

with its exotic green plumage, long tail feathers, and bright red breast. Your best chances are between February and September. Plan on being up early if you want to see them.

Exploring the Park

Only a small part of the reserve is open to visitors, though there is plenty to keep you busy. There are two trails beginning at the visitors center, winding their way through the exuberant vegetation. The shorter *Los Helechos* (The Ferns) trail is two kilometers long,

be moldy, which is common in these cold, humid parts. There are two swimming pools, a Ping-Pong table, and a trail leading to a waterfall 30 minutes away.

Getting There

Any bus heading along the Cobán–Guatemala Highway can let you off at the biotope, though be sure to let the driver know you're getting off here. The entrance is at Km. 160.5.

PURULHÁ AND VICINITY

As you continue along the road toward Cobán, the next sizable town is Purulhá. Though the town itself is unremarkable, there are several important stops on the biological corridor along the road in the vicinity of town and farther east from the town itself.

Reserva Natural Privada Montebello

This private nature reserve and restaurant (tel. 7953-9234 or 7953-9215) sits along Km. 164 of Highway CA-14. The specialties are a tasty chicken stew and traditional pastries. A small shop sells locally made handicrafts and there are nature trails for hiking amid several pleasant streams crisscrossing the property.

Accommodations

At Km. 166.5, **▌ Reserva Natural Privada Country Delight** (tel. 5514-0955, country delight@hotmail.com, 7 A.M.–7 P.M. daily) is a quaint family-run inn and café. The delicious homemade food includes sandwiches, breads, cookies, and cakes. There are also smoked meats for sale. Rooms in the main house with tiled floor, cable TV, large, firm beds, tasteful decor, and private hot-water bath go for $45 d. Bungalows range from $30 for a unit accommodating two people to $100 for a large, six-bed cabin. Camping in a covered area with cooking facilities, shower, bathroom, and a common area with Ping-Pong table, foosball table, and swimming pool is a great value at $7 per person. Bonfires and nighttime lightning bug shows between April and June are among the fun activities available.

© AL ARGUETA

LAS VERAPACES

comfortable cabin at Reserva Natural Privada Country Delight

The restaurant and lodge are on Country Delight's own private reserve, but there are also other reserves adjacent to the property: **Reserva Natural Privada Llano Largo** and **Reserva Privada Santa Rosa.** Combined, they are roughly the same size as the Quetzal Biotope. The lodge can arrange visits to both.

East from Purulhá

A number of beautiful natural attractions in the vicinity of Purulhá have begun making their way onto travelers' radar screens with the establishment of the biological corridor. A turnoff at Km. 166 heads east to Purulhá and then continues for 32 kilometers to **Peña del Ángel,** a dramatic limestone canyon surrounded by tropical moist forest and bisected by the **Río Panimá.** To get to Peña del Ángel, contact the local *comité de turismo* (tel. 5317-6344), which operates a restaurant and some simple cabanas at the site. You can also get there by foot via an 11-kilometer trail starting just off the road at Km. 164. (Note that this is not the same Peña del Ángel mentioned under *Sierra de las Minas Biosphere Reserve.*)

Another option is to arrange a visit via the **Reserva Natural Privada San Rafael** (tel. 5475-1236, ask for Beatriz Thomae), one hour away from Purulhá along a 27-kilometer stretch of road descending into lower elevations. It offers trips to local coffee and cardamom plantations in addition to inner tubing on the Río Panimá and hikes to Peña del Ángel along hanging bridges used by villagers to cross the river. Lodging and food are also available here.

Chicoy Cave

As you head toward Tactic at Km. 167.5 of Highway CA-14 you'll reach the Chicoy Cave ($2.50), with a depth of 70 meters and some large stalagmites. Locals still come to this place to perform Mayan rituals dedicated to the earth, seeking blessings upon their harvest.

CHELEMHÁ CLOUD FOREST PRESERVE

A turnoff at Highway CA-14's Km. 180 heads east for 22 kilometers to the town of Tucurú, from where it's another 26 kilometers via a rugged dirt road passable only in 4WD vehicle to the fantastic Chelemhá Cloud Forest Preserve. This privately managed protected area comprises 500 hectares of primary cloud forest and is part of the Sierra Yalijux mountain range, said to harbor Guatemala's highest density of quetzal populations. The reserve forms part of an important migratory corridor to and from the Sierra de las Minas.

On the outskirts of the reserve, the ◖ **Maya Cloud Forest Lodge** (tel. 7951-0365, www .chelemha.org, $50 per person) is a comfortable, well-equipped wooden cabin built right into the side of the mountain in an environmentally friendly manner. Each of its four rooms comes with private hot-water bath and two beds. There are a lounge, dining area, and an observation deck with outrageous views of the forest-clad mountains in the vicinity. Its Swiss-born manager serves delicious European and international dishes for breakfast ($7), lunch ($10), and dinner ($12). Activities include hikes through the reserve along trails with local Kekchí guides, visits to a local

village, wildlife-viewing and, of course, bird-watching. The owners virtually guarantee you will see a quetzal during your visit as well as raucous howler monkeys.

Volunteer opportunities in the reserve are available by contacting Unión Para Proteger el Bosque Nuboso (UPROBON), which manages the park, at 7951-0365 or via email at uprobon@ chelemha.org. It also offers opportunities for scientific study and research.

TACTIC

Back on Highway CA-14 northbound, the next town over is Tactic, 32 kilometers north of Cobán. The turnoff into town is at Km. 183. The town's best-known attraction is the so-called **Pozo Vivo** (Living Well), named as such because its muddy waters supposedly bubble up when there are people nearby. It has unfortunately become very polluted, as it's a popular destination for locals, who aren't always environmentally conscious. It also may be dry depending on the time of year. It's just off the highway directly opposite Gasolinera Tactic, at Km. 184, should you want to take a gander.

A far more interesting attraction is the **Chi-ixim church,** which overlooks the town from a high hill reached by a steep staircase. The main attraction for pilgrims here is a visit to the black saint of Chi-ixim, also known as **El Dios del Maíz** (Maize God), to give thanks for ascribed miracles.

On the town plaza, the **Cooperativa de Tejedores** sells its wares and demonstrates weaving techniques. The plaza's ornate colonial-era church is decorated on its facade with jaguars and mermaids.

Accommodations and Food

For a place to stay, you could do far worse than **Chi'ixim Eco Hotel** (Km. 182.5 on Highway CA-14, tel. 7953-9198, $20 d), where there are eight cozy bungalows complete with fireplace, dining room, and private hot-water bath. There's a good restaurant at the lodge serving sandwiches and local dishes. Delicious food is also served at the log cabin–style **Café La Granja,** at Km. 187. Among the menu options you'll find salads, sandwiches, and Guatemalan specialties.

Cobán and Vicinity

Pleasant Cobán sits amid evergreen forests and coffee-studded mountains, making an excellent gateway for exploring nearby natural attractions. It has good hotels and food, as well as a tranquil country atmosphere. A small national park lies square in the middle of town. Though it is no stranger to urban sprawl and noise, the tranquility of this small town quickly reveals itself to you as you walk down its quieter side streets away from the noisy central area.

Cobán can sometimes feel a bit dreary, as much of the year sees the presence of a rainy mist known as *chipi chipi,* though it's not nearly as prominent nowadays because of local climate change from deforestation. Still, there's something upbeat about this place and the abundance of nearby natural wonders gives it an entirely different feel from towns in the Western Highlands.

The town and its surroundings are an important gourmet coffee–growing center and also produce cardamom and allspice for export. The town is often referred to as the "Imperial City," owing to its charter by Emperor Charles V in 1538. More recently, in the 19th century Cobán saw an influx of German families, who came to dominate the local culture and economy owing to their fortunes made growing coffee for export. The United States pressured the Guatemalan government to remove the Germans from the country during World War II. There are still bits of German influence here and there, giving the city its distinctive air.

Cobán is home to a yearly folklore festival taking place in late July or early August known as **Rabin Ajau,** in which a Mayan beauty queen is selected from among various hopefuls. Another important event is the annual **orchid show** held here in December.

A number of excellent outfitters have regular departures for the Lanquín caves and Semuc Champey as well as the Quetzal Biotope and points farther afield. Cobán makes a great place to regroup and get information before heading out on deeper explorations of all that Las Verapaces have to offer.

An excellent resource for planning a trip can be found online at www.cobanav.net.

SIGHTS
Parque Central

Cobán's triangular central park is interesting in that it is on a hilltop from which the rest of the town drops off in all directions. The cathedral contains the remains of a large, cracked church bell. A block behind the cathedral is the town's market.

Templo El Calvario

For many, this whitewashed church dating to 1810 holds greater significance than the town's cathedral because of its prominence as a site for Kekchí religious rituals on altars lining the long staircase leading up to it. Among the themes represented at its different altars are the granting of wishes for love and health, among others. The inside of the temple is virtually covered with votive candles, while hundreds of corncobs hang from the roof. Outside, there are fantastic views of Cobán and the rolling green hillsides all around. To the southeast is Mount Xucaneb, the highest point in Alta Verapaz. To get there, head west from the main plaza up 1a Calle and then north two blocks on 7a Avenida. You'll see the long, winding staircase heading up to the temple.

Parque Nacional Las Victorias

Next door to the church is Parque Nacional Las Victorias (11 Avenida and 3a Calle Zona 1, 8 A.M.–4:30 P.M. daily, $0.75), an 84-hectare national park right in the middle of town where you can take a walk on nice paths through mostly evergreen forests, passing a lagoon along the way. Try not to visit alone, as there have been isolated incidents involving muggings at the hands of local gangs.

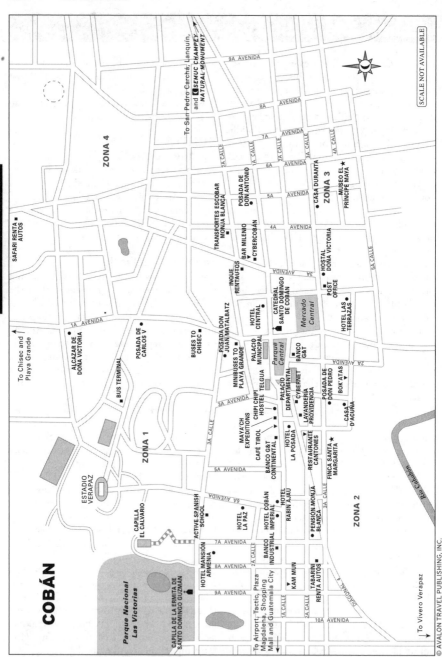

COBÁN

SCALE NOT AVAILABLE

Parque Nacional
Las Victorias

ZONA 4

ZONA 1

ZONA 2

ZONA 3

Río Cahabón

To San Pedro Carchá, Lanquín, and ◀ SEMUC CHAMPEY NATURAL MONUMENT

To Chisec and Playa Grande

To Airport, Tactic, Magdalena, Shopping Mall and Guatemala City

To Vivero Verapaz

SAFARI RENTA AUTOS
ALCAZAR DE DOÑA VICTORIA
POSADA DE CARLOS V
BUS TERMINAL
ESTADIO VERAPAZ
CAPILLA EL CALVARIO
CAPILLA DE LA ERMITA DE SANTO DOMINGO GUZMÁN
ACTIVE SPANISH SCHOOL
HOTEL MANSION ARMENIA
HOTEL LA PAZ
BANCO INDUSTRIAL IMPERIAL
HOTEL COBÁN
RABIN AJAU
KAM MUN
TABARINI RENTA AUTOS
PENSIÓN MONJA BLANCA
HOTEL LA POSADA
CAFÉ TIROL
BANCO G&T CONTINENTAL
MAYA'CH EXPEDITIONS
CHIPI CHIPI HOSTEL
RESTAURANTE CANTONES
FINCA SANTA MARGARITA
CASA D'ACUÑA
POSADA DE DON PEDRO
BOK ATAS
LAVANDERÍA PROVIDENCIA
CYBERNET
PALACIO DEPARTAMENTAL
BANCO G&T
Parque Central
TELGUA
PALACIO MUNICIPAL
POSADA DON JUAN MATALBATZ
BUSES TO CHISEC
MINIBUSES TO PLAYA GRANDE
HOTEL CENTRAL
CATEDRAL SANTO DOMINGO DE COBÁN
Mercado Central
HOTEL LAS TERRAZAS
POST OFFICE
HOSTAL DOÑA VICTORIA
INGUE RENTAUTOS
BAR MILENIO
CYBERCOBÁN
TRANSPORTES ESCOBAR MONJA BLANCA
POSADA DE DON ANTONIO
CASA DURANTA ★
MUSEO EL PRÍNCIPE MAYA ★

9A AVENIDA
8A AVENIDA
7A AVENIDA
6A AVENIDA
5A AVENIDA
4A AVENIDA
3A AVENIDA
2A AVENIDA
1A AVENIDA

2A CALLE
3A CALLE
5A CALLE
7A CALLE
8A CALLE
9A CALLE
10A AVENIDA
DIAGONAL 4

1A CALLE
2A CALLE
3A CALLE
4A CALLE
5A CALLE
6A CALLE
7A CALLE

© AVALON TRAVEL PUBLISHING, INC.

Museo El Príncipe Maya

This excellent private museum (6a Avenida 4-26 Zona 3, tel. 7952-2809, museoprincipemaya@ yahoo.es, 9 A.M.–6 P.M. Mon.–Sat., $2) harbors an impressive collection of artifacts, including carvings in mother-of-pearl and jade, polychromatic pottery, ceremonial objects, tools, and weapons. Among the highlights is a Classic-period hieroglyphic panel from Cancuén and an Olmec crystal figurine with decidedly Asian features. The museum gets its name from a figurine of a Mayan prince dressed in full regalia, including a quetzal-feather headdress.

Finca Santa Margarita

Cobán has some of Guatemala's best coffee, so it's only fitting that you might have the opportunity to go behind the scenes and see the process of how the morning elixir makes it from a bush to your Bodum. The Dieseldorff family's Finca Santa Margarita (3a Calle 4-12 Zona 2, tel. 7951-3067, 8 A.M.–12:30 P.M. and 1:30 P.M.–5 P.M. Mon.–Fri., 8 A.M.–noon Sat., $2.50) is a working coffee farm where excellent, 45-minute guided tours are available in English or Spanish, thanks to a knowledgeable Guatemalan guide who once lived in New York. You will get up-close and personal with the process governing the planting, picking, roasting, packaging, and exporting of these wonderful beans. At the end of the tour, you're treated to a cup (or two) of coffee fresh from the roaster and can buy a bag (or several) of the farm's excellent coffee. The more exclusive "special" selection is a steal at just $5 per pound.

Vivero Verapaz

Lovers of orchids will find nirvana at Vivero Verapaz (Carretera Antigua de Entrada a Cobán, tel. 7952-1133, 9 A.M.–noon and 2 P.M.–4 P.M. daily, $1.50). This wonderful nursery is just outside of town and has several hundred species of orchids on display. The best time of year to visit is between October and February, when many of the flowers are in bloom. The national orchid show is held here in December and is reportedly magnificent. A guide is on hand to show you around and will lend you a magnifying glass for viewing miniature orchids. Guatemala's national flower, the rare *monja blanca,* can be seen here in season. Otto Mittelstaedt, the original collector of the nursery's orchids, has died but the nursery lives on. Vivero Verapaz is about a 40-minute walk from the central plaza, two kilometers southwest. A taxi costs about $3.

NIGHTLIFE

A good place for a drink and some decent music is **Bok'atas** (4a Calle 3-34 Zona 2, tel. 5204-1353, www.bokatas.net, 4 P.M.–1 A.M. Mon.–Fri., noon–1 A.M. Fri. & Sat.), an open-air tapas bar. There is live music some weekends and it serves Mediterranean (Spanish) food. **Bar Milenio** (3a Avenida 1-11 Zona 4, no cover charge) caters mostly to an older crowd, serves food, and has pool tables and TV screens to watch sports. The fanciest place to go after dark is **Keops** (3a Calle 4-71 Zona 3, $5 cover charge, open Fri. & Sat. nights), where the music is a mix of mostly Latin tunes catering to a high-class clientele.

If you're in the mood for a movie, the complex at **Plaza Magdalena Shopping Mall** (1a Calle 15-20 Zona 2) west of the town center on the road out to Guatemala City screens new releases.

SHOPPING

Plaza Magdalena Shopping Mall (1a Calle 15-20 Zona 2) is where you can go to find First World goods you might need while on the road or indulge in a fast-food binge at McDonald's. Run by a handicrafts cooperative, **Aj K'uubanel** (Diagonal 4, 5-13 Zona 2, tel. 7951-4152) has a variety of textiles, maize and wax art, and silver jewelry for sale.

RECREATION

Cobán has a variety of nearby attractions that can be visited in one day as well as numerous outfitters that can get you there. Popular day trips include the **Semuc Champey** pools and the **Lanquín caves.** Although these can certainly be done in a day, they are worth a stay of at least one night, as there are comfortable accommodations and plenty to see and do. If you have the time, stay overnight in Lanquín.

Other day-trip options include the **Quetzal Biotope, Chicoy cave,** and **Chixim church,** all south of Cobán.

North of town, along Km. 24 on the road heading to Chisec, is the **Sachichaj waterfall,** another increasingly popular attraction. Most of the following tour operators can get you there.

Guide Companies

Housed inside the Hostal de Doña Victoria, **Aventuras Turísticas** (3a Calle 2-38 Zona 3, tel. 7951-4213/14, www.aventurasturisticas .com) does the usual day trips to the nearby sites and adventurous options in destinations farther afield, including rappelling in the Bombil Pek caves near Chisec, backdoor treks to Semuc Champey, and trips to Lagunas de Sepalau. This is *the* place to contact for caving, trekking, inner tubing, and kayaking, among other exciting options. It also does the usual daily tour of Semuc Champey ($35 per person), leaving at 7:30 A.M. and returning by nightfall.

A newcomer to Coban's adventure travel scene is **Maya'ch Expeditions** (1a Calle 3-25 Zona 1, across from Hotel La Posada, tel. 7951-4335), offering one- and two-day trips to Semuc Champey in comfortable vans with breakfast and lunch included. Overnight visitors stay at the outfitter's lodge, Casa El Zapote, 2.5 kilometers from Semuc Champey. You can also book transport-only to Semuc Champey or a package including round-trip transport and lodging at Casa El Zapote.

Casa D'Acuña (4a Calle 3-11 Zona 2, tel. 7951-0482 or 7951-0484, casadeacuna@ yahoo.com) also does trips to Semuc Champey and has some excellent guides. It has daily shuttles to Tikal and Antigua leaving at 6 A.M. and costing $28 one-way. Unlike on other shuttles, however, you can get off at intermediate points such as Chisec, Candelaria, Sayaxché, and Flores on the trip north, or at the Quetzal Biotope heading to Antigua.

Proyecto EcoQuetzal (2a Calle 14-36 Zona 1, tel. 7952-1047, bidaspeq@hotmail .com, www.ecoquetzal.org) is a local NGO working with indigenous people in two communities near well-preserved areas of cloud and rainforest in Chicacnab (southeastern Alta Verapaz) and Rokjá Pomtilá (near Laguna Lachuá) to offer economic alternatives to deforestation via sustainable tourism. Guides are rural Kekchí Mayans who know the forest intimately and have received thorough training as nature guides. Trekkers to these remote parts stay in the guides' homes, which have been fitted with beds, toilets, and boiled drinking water, among other basic comforts. It allows for a true cross-cultural experience as well as a means for providing locals with a viable alternative to the destruction of the fragile ecosystem they call home. Your chances of spotting a rare quetzal bird are also fairly good. A two-night trip to Chicacnab costs about $45 per person, including guide, food, and accommodations with additional nights available for about $15 apiece. A two-night stay at Rokjá Pomtilá also costs $45.

Discovery Nature (3a Calle 1-46 Zona 1, tel. 7951-0811), inside the Posada Don Juan Matalbatz, does trips to Semuc Champey and Laguna Lachuá.

ACCOMMODATIONS
Under $10

In the budget range is one of the best values you'll find anywhere in Guatemala. **Casa D'Acuña** (4a Calle 3-11 Zona 2, tel. 7951-0482 or 7951-0484, casadeacuna@yahoo .com) lies at the bottom of a steep hill south of the main plaza and has four comfortable dormitories with four beds apiece ($7 per person) as well as two private double rooms ($13 d). All rooms have shared bath. There is also an excellent restaurant built around the main courtyard of the colonial building in which the lodge is housed. On the next street over toward the park is **Posada de Don Pedro** (3a Calle 3-12 Zona 2, tel. 7951-0562), with acceptably comfortable beds and five rooms with shared bath at $5.50 per person along with two rooms with private bath for $8 per person. The main entrance doubles as a small corner store. Though not a budget accommodation per se, █ **Hostal de Doña Victoria** (3a Calle

2-38 Zona 3, tel. 7951-4213/14) has a shared-bath, bunk-bed dormitory where you can stay for $3.50 per person. North of the main plaza and conveniently situated near the bus terminals (though not in the best part of town) is **Posada Don Juan Matalbatz** (3a Calle 1-46 Zona 1, tel. 7951-0811). It has rooms around a pretty courtyard in a neocolonial building with somewhat saggy beds, cable TV, reading lamps, and ancient hot-water heaters. There are rooms with shared bath for $8 per person and some with private bath going for $26 d. There's also a café downstairs with a pool table. It doesn't get any cheaper or more basic than **Chipi Chipi Hostel** (1a Calle 3-25 Zona 1, tel. 5226-0235), just off the main plaza, where a bed in a shared-bath dormitory can be had for $3.50. It has an Internet lounge and hammock area.

A few blocks west of the plaza is **Pensión Monja Blanca** (2a Calle 6-30 Zona 2, tel. 7952-1712), run by a charming elderly couple who keep the place spotless. Centered round a lovely garden are comfortable tiled-floor rooms with shared bath ($7 per person) or private bath ($26 d). There are a balcony with a sitting area, a pay phone, and a pleasant tea room where you can have breakfast. Friendly **Hotel La Paz** (6a Avenida 2-19 Zona 1, tel. 7952-1358) is another good budget option with basic but clean, cheerful rooms with electric hot-water heater for $10 d. **Hotel Cobán Imperial** (6a Avenida 1-12 Zona 1, tel. 7952-1131) is an old standby popular with Guatemalan families and has rooms with TV and shared bath for $8 d or rooms with private bath with electric hot-water heater for $17 d.

$10-25

An excellent value in this price range is **Hostal de Doña Victoria** (3a Calle 2-38 Zona 3, tel. 7951-4213/14, $25 d), in a 400-year-old colonial home radiating with atmosphere. Its eight rooms centered round a pretty courtyard and café are tastefully decorated and have TV, desk, and private hot-water bathroom. Around the corner at 2a Avenida and 4a Calle, **Hotel Las Terrazas** (tel. 7951-2763, $20 d) is under the same management

but is a different concept altogether with 22 rooms in a modern building with private bath and electric hot-water heater. It's clean but not nearly as charming as the hostel. West of the plaza, the **Hotel Rabin Ajau** (1a Calle 5-37 Zona 1, tel. 7951-4296, $17 d) has rooms with private bath and ancient electric hot-water heaters, firm beds, and cable TV. The rooms are lit by a single fluorescent bulb and tend to feel dark. Just off the plaza and centrally situated, as its name would indicate, is **Hotel Central** (1a Calle 1-79 Zona 1, tel. 7952-1442, $23), with clean rooms built around a garden courtyard. All rooms have private hot-water bathroom and cable TV.

$25-50

Cobán has several excellent choices in this category. The newest option is the beautiful **Casa Duranta** (3a Calle 4-46 Zona 3, tel. 7951-4188, info@casaduranta.com, www.casaduranta.com, $47 d), with 10 tastefully decorated, well-appointed rooms—all with private bath—with Guatemalan indigenous blankets, tiled floors, and wrought-ironworks inside and outside the rooms. There are a TV lounge, a reading area, and wireless Internet throughout the colonial house centered around an appealing courtyard. An on-site café is open for three meals daily. West of the central plaza is **Hotel La Posada** (1a Calle 4-12 Zona 2, tel. 7952-1495, www.laposadacoban.com, $50 d), in a 400-year-old colonial mansion with tiled floors, Guatemalan accents, and attractively tiled private hot-water bathrooms. Try for a room away from the busy main street on the front end of the hotel. There is an excellent restaurant here. Under the same management as the Hostal de Doña Victoria, the **Alcazar de Doña Victoria** (1a Avenida 5-34 Zona 1, tel. 7952-1143, $35 d) is a much larger, 50-room operation. The spacious, tastefully decorated rooms centered around a courtyard have firm beds and cheerful private hot-water bathroom, though rooms on the first floor can be a bit damp. All have tile floors and cable TV. There are a café and bar as well as an events salon, which was recently moved to an area away from the main building, greatly enhancing the guest experience. Near the bus terminal is **Posada de Carlos V** (1 Avenida 3-44 Zona 1, tel. 7951-3501/2, www.hotel carlosvgt.com, $26 d), which has homey rooms housed in a large wooden house reminiscent of a rural Swiss chalet, all with firm beds, private hot-water bath, and cable TV. Downstairs there are a lounge with a big-screen TV and a restaurant serving three meals daily. A newer section of 10 additional rooms housed in a separate concrete building is equally comfortable though not as quaint.

Just a block from the Iglesia El Calvario, **Hotel Mansión Armenia** (7a Avenida 2-18 Zona 1, tel. 7951-4244, $30 d) is housed in a modern concrete-block building and is clean and neat throughout. Rooms have firm beds, private hot-water bathroom, cable TV, and in-room phone. Hot water is available 5 P.M.–8 A.M. Under the same ownership as Transportes Monja Blanca, the pleasant **Posada de Don Antonio** (5a Avenida 1-51 Zona 4, tel. 7951-4287, posadadedonantonio @yahoo.com, $35 d) has 21 rooms in a two-story colonial building centered around a beautiful garden with a pretty fountain. There are nice tiled floors and decorative tiled stairs throughout. Rooms have firm beds, cable TV, and hot-water private bath. There's also a restaurant open daily for breakfast and dinner. This hotel is a good value.

In a class all by itself on the road into Cobán from Guatemala City, Italian-owned **☙ Park Hotel** (tel. 7952-0807, www.parkhotelresort .com) is situated on its own 15-acre forest preserve and has many excellent amenities, including a gym, tennis courts, nature trails, and even a small zoo. Its 96 comfortable and well-decorated rooms are an excellent value starting at $28 d for a standard room with all the usual amenities, though they are right by the road and tend to be noisy. A better option is a junior suite ($47 d). Try to book one in the Firenze building, where odd-numbered rooms have a view of sprawling gardens and a fishpond under a quaint wooden bridge. Suites with a living room and chimney are also available ($50 d),

but these tend to feel smaller than the junior suite. Italian food is the specialty at one of its restaurants, while the other is a Uruguayan steak house. The gift shop sells orchids.

FOOD

On the road to Cobán from Guatemala City, **Hotel y Restaurante la Lupa di Roma** (Km. 200 on the road to Cobán, tel. 7951-4444, www.otupactours.com) serves authentic Italian cuisine in an attractive country setting. Arguably the best food in town, Casa D'Acuña's peaceful courtyard restaurant, **☙ El Bistro** (4a Calle 3-11 Zona 2, tel. 7951-0482 or 7951-0484, 6:30 A.M.–10 P.M. daily), serves a variety of excellent international dishes, including great pasta ($5–6), pizzas, meat dishes, homemade breads and pastries, salads, and sandwiches. Another excellent place to eat is the café inside **Hostal de Doña Victoria** (3a Calle 2-38 Zona 3, tel. 7951-4213/14), though the menu is not as intricate as that at El Bistro and leans more toward Guatemalan dishes. It's always a good bet for breakfast. A good option for fine dining can be found at **☙ Café and Restaurant La Posada** (1a Calle 4-12 Zona 2, tel. 7952-1495, www.laposadacoban.com), inside the Hotel La Posada. The café (1 P.M.–8:30 P.M. Wed.–Mon.) is at the far end of the building and looks out onto the plaza. The fancier restaurant (7 A.M.–9:30 P.M. Mon.–Sat., 7 A.M.–11 A.M. Sun.) is set in an attractive dining room with a fireplace and two terraces facing a garden. The food at both is excellent, though the service is notoriously slow. It's a good place to relax and unwind if you have a few hours to kill or aren't in a hurry. The menu includes Guatemalan and international dishes.

For paella and other Spanish/Mediterranean specialties, head to **Bok'atas** (4a Calle 3-34 Zona 2, tel. 5204-1353, www.bokatas.net, 4 P.M.–1 A.M. Mon.–Fri., noon–1 A.M. Fri. and Sat.). There's also a lively bar playing good tunes.

There are a variety of decent cafés in Cobán, among them the café at **Casa Duranta** (3a Calle 4-46 Zona 3, tel. 7951-4188, www.casa duranta.com, 7 A.M.–10 A.M. and 3 P.M.–8 P.M. daily), where the specialty is crepes (sweet and salty) as well as sandwiches and pastas. West of the plaza, **C Café El Tirol** (1a Calle 3-13 Zona 1, tel. 7951-4042, 7:30 A.M.–9 P.M.Mon.–Sat.) is a great place for breakfast or a light meal and coffee enjoyed in a pleasant terrace. The smoothies and sandwiches are particularly tasty. On the south side of the plaza, **Cafeto** (tel. 7951-2850, 9 A.M.–9 P.M. daily) is a pleasant wine and coffee shop serving an affordable daily set lunch menu, including soup, half a sandwich, and salad, as well as European dishes such as bratwurst with mustard and sauerkraut. **Xkape Kob'an** (Diagonal 4, 5-13 Zona 2, tel. 7951-4152) does a variety of coffee drinks but specializes in local dishes such as chicken stew, tamales, and *kaq-ik* in addition to pastries in a pleasant atmosphere with rustic wooden tables in a garden setting. There is artwork for sale and the café is managed by the Artisans' Association of Verapaz.

For Asian food, try the clean and tidy **Restaurante Kam Mun** (1a Calle 8-12 Zona 2), where heaping portions of Chinese dishes ($5–10) are served in a pleasant atmosphere. Another alternative is **Restaurante Cantonés** (behind Hotel La Posada at Diagonal 4, 4-24 Zona 2, tel. 7952-1592, 11:30 A.M.–10 P.M. daily), where a tasty large plate of fried rice can be had for $4.

There are several cheap eats lining the central plaza, the best (and safest) of which is **Empanadas Argentinas,** on the north end next to Telgua, where you can savor a tasty chicken empanada for just $0.85.

INFORMATION AND SERVICES
Tourist Information
Cobán doesn't have an INGUAT office but you can find out everything you might need to know from the friendly staff at Casa D'Acuña (4a Calle 3-11 Zona 2, tel. 7951-0482) and Hostal de Doña Victoria (3a Calle 2-38 Zona 3, tel. 7951-4213/14), which act as the de facto tourism information offices.

Communications
The post office is on the corner of 2a Avenida

and 3a Calle one block southeast of the main plaza. Telgua is right on the plaza, on the north side, with card phones outside.

You'll find several options for access to the Internet in Cobán, with the going rate at about $1.75 an hour. Among the options are Access Computación (1a Calle 3-13 Zona 1, tel. 7951-4040, 9 A.M.–7 P.M. Mon.–Fri., 8 A.M.–6 P.M. Sat.), Hostal de Doña Victoria (3a Calle 2-38 Zona 3, tel. 7951-4213/14), CyberCoban (3a Avenida, 1-11 Zona 4, tel. 7951-1777, 8:30 A.M.–7 P.M. daily), and Cybernet (on the south side of the plaza at Diagonal 4, 3-12 Zona 2, tel. 7951-4390). Navega.com. (8 A.M.–8 P.M.) is right next door to Café Tirol and has lightning-fast connection speeds. Mayan Internet (6a Avenida 2-28 Zona 1, tel. 5694-7696, 8:30 A.M.–8 P.M. Mon.–Sat., 2:30 P.M.–9 P.M. Sun.) is another option.

Money
Banco Industrial has a Visa ATM at 1a Calle and 7a Avenida, Zona 1. Banco G&T Continental has a branch at 1a Calle and 4a Avenida, across the street from Hotel La Posada, with a versatile 5B ATM. There's another branch at 1a Calle and 2a Avenida, Zona 3. You can change travelers checks and dollars at all of these.

Laundry
Lavandería La Providencia (8 A.M.–noon and 2 P.M.–5 P.M. Mon.–Sat.) is on the south side of the plaza. It costs about $3.50 to wash and dry a load. Otherwise, it's about $5 to wash and dry a load at Casa D'Acuña (4a Calle 3-11 Zona 2, tel. 7951-0482).

Language Schools
Though Spanish-language instruction isn't nearly as prolific in Cobán as elsewhere in Guatemala, the increasing number of visitors to these parts has translated into the opening of a number of schools in the past few years. Among the options are **Active Spanish School** (3a Calle 6-12 Zona 1, tel. 7952-1432, $110 per week including room and board with host family), known for its instructor who is an invaluable source on the local nightlife

scene and organizes day trips to outdoor attractions. Another option is **School of Arts and Language** (16 Avenida 2-50 Zona 1, tel. 7953-9062, alftujab@intelnett.com, $140 per week with local host family). Outside of town on a tranquil farm is **Eco Cabaña Spanish School** (Km. 6 Carretera a Chamil, San Juan Chamelco, tel. 7951-5898, ecocabana@yahoo .com), where four hours of daily instruction cost $90 per week. An additional $70 gets you a homestay with a local family or on-site.

GETTING THERE
Bus
The situation with public bus transport in Cobán is rather chaotic, as different buses heading for different places leave from various parts of town despite the presence of (in theory) a central bus terminal. You can find complete bus schedules for virtually any place you might want to go from Cobán at www .cobanav.net/bus.php. Check the Cobán map in this book for pickup locations for the various destinations. That being said, buses to Guatemala City via **Transportes Escobar Monja Blanca** (tel. 7951-3571) depart from a pleasant bus station at 2a Calle 3-77 Zona 4 every 30 minutes between 2 A.M. and 5 P.M. Departures from the so-called "Terminal Nueva" (New Terminal) near the soccer stadium are limited to Tactic (every 30 minutes), the Quetzal Biotope (every 30 minutes), El Estor (six buses daily), and Fray Bartolomé de las Casas via Pajal (five buses daily).

Microbuses to Lanquín leave from 3a Calle near the Posada de Don Juan Matalbatz. Buses for San Juan Chamelco (4a Calle and 4a Avenida Zona 3) and San Pedro Carchá (2a Calle and 4a Avenida Zona 4) leave every 20 minutes. Buses to San Juan Chamelco also reputedly leave from the Wasen Bridge, Diagonal 15, Zona 7, every half hour.

Shuttle Bus
Casa D'Acuña (4a Calle 3-11 Zona 2, tel. 7951-0482 or 7951-0484, casadeacuna@ yahoo.com) runs daily shuttles to Tikal and Antigua leaving at 6 A.M. and costing $28 one-

way. You can get off at intermediate points such as Chisec, Candelaria, Sayaxché, and Flores on the trip north, or at the Quetzal Biotope heading to Antigua.

Car Rental
Several car-rental companies (though none of international stature) have offices in Cobán: **Inque Renta Autos** (3a Avenida and 2a Calle Zona 4, tel. 7952-1994 or 7952-1431), **Tabarini Rent A Car** (8a Avenida 2-27 Zona 2, tel. 7952-1504, www.tabarini.com), and **Safari Renta Autos** (3a Avenida 8-47 Zona 11, tel. 7952-1175).

NEAR COBÁN
San Pedro Carchá
This small town lies six kilometers east of Cobán, though the urban sprawl around both towns means they are gradually merging into a single agglomeration. In the center of town, you'll find the small, recently renovated **Museo Regional** (9 A.M.–noon and 2 P.M.– 5 P.M. Mon.–Fri., $1) beside the church. There are stuffed birds and animals as well as Mayan artifacts and dolls in traditional costume. The town's other main attraction is the **Balneario Las Islas,** a 10-minute walk from the center of town, where a river runs down into a natural pool.

There are some decent places to stay on the outskirts of town that make a nice alternative to staying in Cobán proper, if you seek a more natural environment. Along Km. 216 of the road from Cobán to San Pedro Carchá is **Hotel Mansión Santo Domingo de Guzman** (tel. 7950-0777, www.mansionsantodomingo deguzman.com, $40 d), a wonderful colonial hacienda-style property set on forested grounds. The rooms and common areas are tastefully decorated with antiques. All rooms have private hot-water bath, comfortable beds, cable TV, and a desk. There is also a good restaurant with outdoor patio seating overlooking well-manicured lawns. Also out this way near the *arco* bridge at the entrance to town along Km. 217.5 is **Hotel Posada de Don Francisco** (tel. 7951-3356, $44 d), also featuring comfortable rooms in a similar setting, some with river views.

Access to the cloud forests of **Chicacnab** (see the *Proyecto EcoQuetzal* entry under *Guide Companies* in the *Cobán* section) is from San Pedro Carchá via bus to the village of Caquipec and then on to San Lucas. There are buses every 20 minutes from Cobán to Carchá.

San Juan Chamelco

Seven kilometers southeast of Cobán, San Juan Chamelco is a Q'eqchi' town whose women are known for their traditional costume, which includes the wearing of earrings made from a layered series of old coins. The church here sits on a small hill and provides wonderful views of surrounding areas. There are paintings inside depicting the arrival of the Spanish conquerors. Outside, it is interestingly decorated with Mayan adaptations of the Hapsburg double eagle, providing further evidence of the historic German influence in this region. The church's bell was a gift to local villager Juan Matalbatz from the Holy Roman Emperor Charles V. Mass here is held in Spanish and Q'eqchi'.

In nearby Aldea Chajaneb is the wonderful $\blacklozenge$ **Don Jeronimo's** (tel. 5301-3191, www .dearbrutus.com/donjeronimo), run by amiable expat Jerry Makransky, where you can get away from it all and enjoy a relaxing stay at a working blueberry farm. There are rooms in the main house with fabulous balcony views of the surrounding countryside as well as quaint bungalows with private bathroom. For $25 you get a room and three delicious vegetarian meals daily. There are guided hikes available to a mountain with commanding views of the highlands as well as inner tubing on a pretty stretch of the Río Sotzil. A series of paths winds its way through the property and around the river to two swimming holes.

Don Jeronimo's lies five kilometers outside of Chamelco down a signposted road 150 meters west of the plaza. You can walk or take a bus headed for the village of Chamil and ask the driver to let you off at the turnoff for Don Jeronimo's. From there it's a short walk

for 300 meters along a path. You'll see the farmhouse after you cross the bridge and walk into a clearing.

Half a kilometer from Don Jeronimo's are the **Grutas del Rey Marcos** (8 A.M.–5 P.M. daily, $3 including guide and hard-hat and boot rental), worth a look for some interesting stalagmites reached by wading across an underground river. Though the caves are a kilometer long, you'll see only a small part of the complex on the tour.

San Cristóbal Verapaz

Nineteen kilometers west of Cobán is the Poqomchi' Mayan town of San Cristóbal Verapaz, set beside Lake Chicoj. The Holy Week festivities here are similar to those in La Antigua, with processions and the making of colorful sawdust-and-flower petal carpets. The **Museo Kitanamit** (tel. 7950-4039, cecep@intelnet.net.gt, $1), run by the local Centro Comunitario Educativo Pokomchi (CECEP), features exhibits on the Poqomchi' way of life, including art, textiles, and tools used in everyday life. The organization also runs the **Aj Chi Cho Language Center** (www .ajchicho.50g.com), which teaches Spanish and Poqomchi'.

If you need a place to stay, try the Poqomchi'-owned **El Portón Real** hostel (tel. 7950-4604).

Sachichaj Waterfall

From Cobán, as you head north on the road to Chisecis, is the Sachichaj waterfall at Km. 24. This beautiful, 15-meter-high cataract spills from the mouth of a cave into a gorgeous cobalt lagoon. You can get here via a tour booked with Casa D'Acuña or Hostal de Doña Victoria. To get here on your own, drive to the point where the Río Sachichaj crosses the road at Km. 24 of the road to Chisec. Just past this point on the left-hand side is Tienda y Comedor Reina, where you can hire a guide, which is highly recommended as it's easy to get lost in the twisting maze of paths. It's a 40-minute walk from here to the falls.

Lanquín and Semuc Champey

LANQUÍN

From San Pedro Carchá, a paved road diverts northeast through coffee and cardamom plantations to El Pajal, where there is a turnoff for a dirt road that twists and turns for another 12 kilometers to the small town of Lanquín. Lanquín is home to some interesting caves and has some comfortable accommodations to use as a base for exploring the nearby countryside.

Lanquín Caves National Park

The Lanquín caves (8 A.M.–6 P.M. daily, $4) lie one kilometer northwest of town. They are several kilometers long, though only a small part is open to visitors. Although there are diesel generator–powered lights, these sometimes fail so bring a flashlight and good shoes for the slippery, guano-laden surfaces inside. The entire cave system has yet to be fully explored or mapped, so don't wander too far into the cav-

ern's core. There are some interesting stalactites to be found here.

Another highlight of a visit to these caves is the thousands of bats flying out from the cavern at dusk. The Río Lanquín also flows out of this cave and forms a turquoise ribbon meandering through the surrounding jungle. It's perfect for a refreshing swim.

🄲 Rafting the Río Cahabón

In addition to the caves, Lanquín serves as a departure point for white-water rafting trips down the Class III–IV Río Cahabón. **Maya Expeditions** (tel. 2363-4955, www.maya expeditions.com), pioneered white-water rafting in Guatemala starting in 1987 and was named one of the "Top 20 Eco-Outfitters in the World" by *Condé Nast Traveler* in the 1990s. It does both the upper and lower gorges as day trips ($115/155), but it also has various options for 3–6-day adventures ($210–678). The com-

Corkscrew Falls on the Río Cahabón

© AL ARGUETA

THE RAGING RAPIDS OF THE RÍO CAHABÓN

Guatemala's best white-water river is the Class III-IV Río Cahabón. In addition to the exhilarating rapids, the traverse downstream on its emerald waters is interspersed with more tranquil stretches that afford opportunities to view several species of birds and explore caves, waterfalls, and hot springs along its forested banks.

The Cahabón is the same river that flows into a cave under the limestone pools of Semuc Champey, reemerging several hundred meters downstream. Most river trips begin at a put-in point near Lanquín. There are some rather menacing rapids along this stretch of the Upper Cahabón, including Rock and Roll, Entonces, and Las Tres Hermanas, making for an adrenaline-filled ride. The Middle Gorge has some nice jungle scenery and continuous Class III rapids. There are a few more challenging rapids after passing the bridge at a place called Oxec before reaching an obligatory takeout point at Takinkó to portage the Class VI (not possible to run) Chulac Falls. A dam was once planned here, but dam builders seem to have gone cold on the idea after discovering a fault line running right beneath the proposed dam site. The two-day trip camps here.

The Lower Gorge is a boatload of fun with titillating rapids such as Saca Corchos (Corkscrew) and Saca Caca. There are stops along the way to explore caves and enjoy lunch at "El Pequeño Paraíso," a small side stream with delightful waterfalls and hot springs flowing into the Cahabón. The next rapid is appropriately named Lose Your Lunch, shortly after which the river widens and you are treated to a serene stretch of river with mountainous jungle-clad banks. The takeout is at Cahaboncito, where the intrepid can take a plunge into the river from a 30-foot bridge.

Rafting the Cahabón affords the opportunity to see some remote natural attractions and come in contact with the local people inhabiting the area. As is often the case in Guatemala, the beauty coexists with a sobering reality. In addition to still-forested areas you will see some steep, badly deforested slopes given over to corn cultivation, shedding light on the desperate plight of peasants willing to live and grow their crops anywhere they can.

plete six-day adventure begins in Guatemala City and includes stops at the Quetzal Biotope, Cobán, Lanquín, Semuc Champey, and the Candelaria caves in addition to rafting both the upper and lower gorges of the Cahabón. A newer option is **Guatemala Rafting** (tel. 7983-3056, www.guatemalarafting.com), offering one- and two-day trips on the river ($50/140). It is based at El Retiro lodge. Bring your own tent if you're going on the overnight trip with this outfitter, as it provides only a shelter. Both outfitters provide all the basics such as food, transport, and equipment.

Accommodations and Food

One of the hippest hotels in all of Central America lies 500 meters along the road from Lanquín toward the village of Cahabón. **(℃ El Retiro** (tel. 7983-0009) offers a variety of accommodations for all budgets in a splendid setting beside the Río Lanquín. The so-called "posh block" has tastefully decorated rooms with private bath and electric hot-water heater ($24 d). There are hammocks out front for taking in the wonderful vistas toward the river and surrounding hillsides. A bed in one of the four-person dormitories costs $4. Rooms with shared bath are also available, and range $10–13 d. You can camp here or sleep in a hammock for $2. The *palapa*-style bar plays great music and is lined with rope-swing bar seats. The restaurant serves excellent food, with dinner being a nightly communal experience. There are barbecues on Wednesday nights; Saturday night is Mexican. The lodge can arrange a variety of activities for you, including inner tubing on the river for $1.50 and horseback riding ($5–16).

In town, **Hotel Rabin Itzam** (tel. 7983-0076) has 14 clean rooms with somewhat hard beds and shared bath for $4 per person. On the other end of town as you come in to Lanquín from the El Pajal Junction is **Hotel El Recreo** (tel. 7983-0056), with rooms in a wooden main house or in an adjacent concrete structure. The main house has a lower-level section with shared-bath rooms for $20 d. The lighting is fluorescent. Nicer rooms with private bath are $31 d. This lodge is usually empty unless there's a tour group in town. There's a restaurant here too.

Other options for food include **Comedor Shalom,** near the Hotel Rabin Itzam, with set-menu lunches and dinners comprising mostly meat and rice dishes for around $2.

◖ SEMUC CHAMPEY NATURAL MONUMENT

These gorgeous limestone pools (6 A.M.–6 P.M. daily, $4) lie at the end of a rough dirt road nine kilometers from Lanquín. Although they were once a remote attraction way off the beaten path, they are now one of Las Verapaces's

the wonderful limestone pools of Semuc Champey

top tourist draws. Accordingly, infrastructure has improved to keep up with the rising numbers of visitors. Try not to visit on a weekend, as there are day-trippers in droves from Cobán and vicinity.

A giant, 300-meter-long limestone bridge forms the backbone for the descending series of pools and small waterfalls that make up Semuc Champey. The water that fills the pools is the product of runoff from the Río Cahabón, churning as it plunges into an underground chasm from where it reemerges downstream at the end of this massive limestone overpass.

Recreation

In addition to **swimming** in the perfectly placid pools, there is a series of **trails** and hanging wooden bridges taking you to the sites where the river makes its underground plunge and where it reemerges downstream. It is truly awe inspiring to see the force of nature as the raging river is crammed into an underground cavern. A more recent addition is a longer, 1.2-kilometer trail heading straight up the side of a mountain to a fantastic **lookout point,** where you can see the pools from above. It's worth the substantial effort required to climb on the steep mountainside, sometimes with the help of vines and tree roots.

Another recent addition is that of a visitors center, across from the park entry booth, where you can buy drinks and food. The latter is a set menu consisting mainly of local dishes and grilled meats costing between $2.70 and $5.50. Vehicle parking costs $1.30. Guides are available here to take you around. As always, tipping is a good idea.

Accommodations and Food

You can camp at Semuc Champey, where there is security round the clock, for $5. There are also two hotels just minutes away from the park entrance. Coming from Semuc Champey, the first place you'll come across (one kilometer) is **Posada Las Marías** (tel. 7861-2209, www.posadalasmarias.com), which enjoys a wonderful riverside location and offers accommodations in dorms with shared bath ($3.50 per person), five-bed cabanas ($26), or rooms with shared bath ($10 d). The restaurant serves three meals a day ($2–4) and the menu includes sandwiches, nachos, and barbecued steak. Activities include inner tubing on the Río Cahabón and visits to the nearby caves of K'anba ($5), where you can explore an underwater river. The other option near Semuc Champey lies another couple of hundred meters away at **Casa El Zapote** (tel. 7861-2639/40, mayachexpedition.com). There are private rooms ($7 p/p shared bath, $12 p/p with private bath and fan) along with six-bed and 12-bed dorm rooms ($2 p/p, shared bath). The dorm beds consist of a small mattress on a wooden floor and are above the restaurant/bar. Otherwise, the beds are firm and there is hot water. Breakfast here costs $3 and lunch or dinner cost $4; all are set-menu options.

Getting There

There are several tour companies in Cobán operating day and overnight trips to Lanquín and Semuc Champey. Shuttle-only options are available and are highly recommended as the best way to get here. From Antigua, **Old Town Outfitters** (tel. 5399-0440, info@adventure guatemala.com, www.bikeguatemala.com) runs a four-day trip to Lanquín, Semuc Champey, and the cave of Can Ba for $295 per person with a two-passenger minimum, including transport, meals, and accommodations. There are stops in Cobán and the Quetzal Biotope along the way.

If you're driving, you'll need a 4WD vehicle for the road from El Pajal to Lanquí. Bus schedules change frequently so check current schedules at El Retiro (Lanquín) or Casa D'Acuñ and Hostal de Doña Victoria (in Cobán). There are six microbuses and at least two shuttles a day to Cobán.

Northern Alta Verapaz

Northern Alta Verapaz is quickly gaining momentum as the site for a varied assortment of ecotourism options thanks to the presence of some well-organized community tourism initiatives and its location along the corridor connecting Alta Verapaz and Petén on a good paved road. Among the highlights in this neck of the woods are the Candelaria Caves National Park, Lagunas de Sepalau, Cuevas B'onb'il Pek, and Laguna Lachuá National Park. It will be interesting to see how this area grows and develops during the next several years with the ever-increasing presence of international tourism. For now, the scene here is very low-key, but it won't be that way forever. Get out and explore this part of Guatemala, where there are relatively few visitors, while you can.

EL PAJAL TO FRAY BARTOLOMÉ DE LAS CASAS

From the El Pajal Junction, the road winds through the mountainous Alta Verapaz terrain north to the small village of **Sebol** (about two hours), which is attractively set on the banks of the Río La Pasiín with waterfalls flowing into it. It might make an attractive stopover someday, though there is no infrastructure to accommodate visitors as of yet. Here the road branches east to Fray Bartolomé de las Casas, referred to simply as "Fray" or "Las Casas." This nondescript town has a few basic accommodations, should you need to stay here. The best of these are **Hotel Diamelas** ($13 d) and **Hotel y Restaurante Bartolo** ($8 d).

You'll find the town is fairly spread out, with the plaza and most visitor services on one end of town and the bus terminal and market on the other, a 10-minute walk away. On or near the plaza, you'll find a post office, police station, Banrural, and the local town hall (*municipalidad*).

There is a bus departing daily for Poptún at 3 A.M. ($4), and hourly buses for Cobán between 4 A.M. and 4 P.M.

Las Conchas Pools

Las Casas's sole nearby attraction is Las Conchas, a series of limestone pools and waterfalls on the Río Chiyú, 50 kilometers east toward Izabal. The pools are rather large and great for swimming, though the water is not of the sweet emerald color found at Semuc Champey. There is a small picnic area.

The falls' remote location means you may find yourself needing to spend the night in the area. Thanks to a recent addition to the local hotel offerings, you can combine a trip to the waterfalls with a stay at a nearby jungle camp. **Oasis Chiyú** (www.naturetoursguatemala .com), a 10-hectare (25-acre) working farm and lodge owned by a transplanted American, is beautifully situated at the confluence of two jungle rivers. The lodge runs on an all-inclusive plan ($30 per person per day with a two-night minimum) and includes three square meals daily, accommodations in the main house or in nearby bungalows, guided hikes, and transportation. The gorgeous views of the surrounding jungle, rivers, and waterfalls alone are worth the price of admission. Meals are prepared on a wood burning stove using fresh ingredients and include vegetarian specialties such as fried rice, pastas, curries, hummus, sandwiches, and salads. Bikes and kayaks are available to explore the surroundings, and guided hikes can take you to nearby waterfalls, mysterious caves, sultry jungles, and cool rivers. This is your chance to really become one with nature: no phones, fax, e-mail, or electricity—truly an oasis of tranquility.

Raxrujá

An alternative base for exploring the Candelaria caves and the nearby ruins of Cancuén is the small town of Raxrujá, a few kilometers east of the "Cruce del Pato" Junction. Among the basic accommodations found here are **Hotel Cancuén** (tel. 7983-0720), on the edge of town, with basic rooms for $10 d or more modern tiled-floor rooms with TV, air-conditioning, and private bath for $12 d. The **Restaurante Tu Casa** next door serves good meals and is well staffed.

Minibuses leave every hour for Chisec with continuing service to Cobán until 4 P.M. Buses and minibuses head north to Sayaxché with similar frequency.

◖ CANCUÉN

The Mayan site of Cancuén (8 A.M.–5 P.M. daily, $8) lies north of Raxrujá, just across the border of the northern Petén department. It is treated in this section because it is actually more accessible from Alta Verapaz. Cancuén's rediscovery dates to the early 1900s, but it is only recently that archaeologists have begun piecing together its rich past and the full extent of its power, along with its corresponding significance in the place of Mayan history. Cancuén was largely overlooked by archaeologists for much of the 20th century because it lacked large temple pyramids and defensive structures like those found elsewhere in the Mayan world. It is thought that Cancuén existed as a mostly secular trading center, which gained much of its prosperity from its enviable position on the Río La Pasíin at a strategic geographic transition zone between the southern highlands and the northern lowlands. Its importance as a trade center is substantiated by large amounts of pyrite (for making mirrors), jade, obsidian, and fine ceramics found here. It has been speculated that the absence of large temple pyramids may be a product of the site's proximity to the Candelaria caves, which certainly held spiritual significance for the Mayans living here in those times, as they still do today.

Adding to Cancuén's splendor is a paved plaza covering two square kilometers. It may have doubled as a marketplace. Among the incredible finds uncovered in recent years by a U.S.-Guatemalan team working under the direction of Vanderbilt University's Arthur Demarest is the largest known Mayan palace. Built in A.D. 770 during the reign of Taj Chan Ahk, the three-story palace covers about 23,000 square meters and has 200 rooms built around 11 courtyards. The archaeologists working here have also recently uncovered the third and final marker from a royal ball court, which has been gradually excavated during the last century. The markers served as goalposts. The first of these markers was unearthed in 1915 and can be seen in Guatemala City's archaeology museum. The second marker was looted from the site in 2001 but recovered two years later thanks to unprecedented collaboration between Guatemalan undercover agents, local villagers, and archaeologists. The third marker is an elaborately carved stone altar uncovered from the stucco surface of the ball court.

A separate, 100-pound stone panel with hieroglyphics and carved images was also found at the ball court, the second such panel to be unearthed here. It depicts Taj Chan Ahk installing a subordinate ruler at the smaller state of Machaquilá. The panel is interesting in that it confirms Taj Chan Ahk's status as a great Mayan king who was able to maintain power over a large area through politics and economic clout, rather than warfare, at a time when most Mayan city-states had begun their decline.

The peaceful prosperity would be short-lived, however, as recent finds reveal a wide-scale massacre of at least 31 nobles and several others at the hands of invading armies from Machaquilá and Ceibal sometime around A.D. 800. This marked the beginning of the end for Cancuén, and the city was abandoned shortly thereafter.

Excavations and restoration work at the site are ongoing, and it is certainly thrilling to walk around the site and see the work in progress. The jungle around the site is thick with vegetation and mosquitoes are there in droves. Bring plenty of bug spray and wear long pants. There is a recently opened visitors center with informative displays and a campground, as well as restrooms and showers.

Accommodations and Food

You can camp at La Unión for $3.50. Meals are available from local families with prior notice ($3.50–5.50). At the Cancuén visitors center, camping and tent rental for two costs $7, or you can camp in your own tent for $3. Meals are also available ($3–5). Book in advance.

Getting There

Pickups leave about every hour from Raxrujá to the village of La Unión, 16 kilometers to the north, where there is a visitors center. From there, boatmen take you on the 30-minute boat ride up the Río La Pasión ($40 for 1–12 people) to the site. You can also book a tour via one of the Cobán travel outfitters.

⟨ CANDELARIA CAVES NATIONAL PARK

From Sebol, the dirt road branches west to Raxrujá, from where a paved road continues west to San Antonio Las Cuevas. The road from Petén also connects to San Antonio Las Cuevas from the "Cruce del Pato" Junction. The main attraction along this corridor is a visit to the fantastic Candelaria caves, recently awarded national park status. The cave system, discovered in 1974 by Frenchman Daniel Dreux, is composed of seven separate caves interconnected by the Río Candelaria and spanning about 22 kilometers. The caves are 20–30 meters wide in places with ceilings typically 10–60 meters high.

Caves were sacred to the Mayans and it is thought that nearby cities such as Cancuén lacked the substantial temple pyramids found elsewhere in the Mayan world because of the proximity of the Candelaria caves, which were used as a center for worship. In Mayan lore, caves are thought to be entrances to the underworld, known as Xibalba. The Candelaria caves are one possible location for the mythical Xibalba; the Chiquibul caves running east-west from the northern Petén department into Belize are another.

In 2002, the Guatemalan government awarded management of the caves to local villagers, though Dreux continues to operate a lodge he built adjacent to one of the cave's entrances. The lodge is staffed by local villagers working for Dreux and there are at least two other options for visiting the caves operated by local tourism initiatives. Among the recreational highlights is the chance to explore the caves via underground rivers on an inner tube or inflatable raft.

the lodge at Complejo Cultural y Ecoturístico Cuevas de Candelaria

Complejo Cultural y Ecoturístico Cuevas de Candelaria

The most convenient gateway for exploring one of Central America's largest cave systems is a stop at the Complejo Cultural y Ecoturístico Cuevas de Candelaria (tel. 7861-2203, www.cuevasdecandelaria.com), at Km. 316.5 of the paved road (RN-5), near San Antonio Las Cuevas. The complex is the brainchild of Daniel Dreux, who quickly set out to map the extensive cave system shortly after discovering it. His growing concern over the long-term survival of this unique natural area led him to establish "Tierra Maya," a conservation and sustainable development organization that aims to protect the forests surrounding the cave system while improving living conditions for local residents.

Entrance to the complex costs $3.50 (two-person minimum), including a guide and two-hour tour of the "Cueva del Mico" section of the caves, featuring large chambers that in places are 20–30 meters wide with ceilings 10–60 meters high. The impressive 200-meter-long "Tzul Tacca" chamber is a standout, with ethereal shafts of light shining from the ceiling onto the rocks below.

For more in-depth explorations, **Maya Expeditions** (tel. 2363-4955, www.mayaexpeditions.com) runs a fantastic three-day/two-night trip to the Candelaria caves ($398) from Guatemala City, allowing the opportunity to journey on inflatable rafts through rarely seen sections of this incredible cavern and its underground rivers.

The Complejo Cultural y Ecoturístico also includes the wonderful ◖ **Candelaria Lodge** (tel. 7861-2203, reservaciones@cuevasdecandelaria.com, $15–20 per person), which serves as the perfect base for exploring the caves and several other local attractions. The comfortable, stylishly decorated cabins (all with shared bath) are set amid the tropical forest. Delectable French and international dishes (including crepes that are to die for) are served in the lodge's main dining room and your gracious host, Arnoldo, will cater to your every need. There are packages, including one night's accommodations and three meals for $50 per person per night. Otherwise, meals range from $5 for breakfast to $15 for lunch or dinner.

If arriving by car, you'll have to park your vehicle at a parking lot across the road from the entrance to the complex. From there, it's a 15-minute walk to the main entrance and another five minutes to the lodge. If staying at the lodge, bring a clean pair of flip-flops, as you'll be required to remove muddy shoes and leave them at the lodge's main door so as not to muddy the wooden walkways crisscrossing the property.

Candelaria Muq'b'il Ha'

Another alternative for visiting the Candelaria caves is via one of the local community tourism organizations at Candelaria Muq'b'il Ha', which you'll find farther west along the Raxrujá–Chisec road (RN-5) at Km. 315. You'll find a marked entrance indicating the turnoff for a two-kilometer dirt road to the parking lot. A 30-minute walk down a trail leads to the visitors center. From here you can take a guided tour of the Venado Seco cave (1.5 hours, $5.50), take a guided cave-tubing tour (1.5 hours, $7), or do both for $10. Food is available and you can stay at the rustic ecolodge **Peña del Tigre** for $7 per person or camp for $3.50 p/p. Overnight parking costs $5, $1.50 for the day.

Candelaria Camposanto

Yet another option is found at Km. 309 along the same road, where there are two dry caves and one river-tubing section available for exploration. The visitors center is right beside the highway. The caves are a 20-minute walk away. You can tour the "Ventana de Seguridad" and "Cúpula de los Murciélagos" caves for $5.50, go cave tubing for $7, or combine all three for $10. Camping costs $3 and there is meal service with prior arrangement ($3–5). Parking is $1.50.

CHISEC AND VICINITY

Chisec lies along the highway (RN-5) connecting Petén and Cobán about 26 kilometers southwest of Raxrujá. The town has grown in the past few years thanks to a ubiquitous infusion of land-hungry peasants seeking to eke out a living on parcels of land in the surrounding wilderness areas. Seeking to provide locals with more ecofriendly economic alternatives, development agencies have masterminded a fairly successful sustainable tourism project to ensure locals benefit from the exploitation of the area's substantial natural and cultural attractions. The community ecotourism projects were developed with financial support from USAID and the help of Guatemala's Ministry of Culture and Sports, the Guatemala Tourist Commission (INGUAT), CONAP, the National Geographic Society, and Vanderbilt University, among others. Local guides can take you to several area attractions, including the Lagunas de Sepalau and Cuevas de B'onb'il Pek. You can find more information online at www.puertamundomaya.com.

Sights

About two kilometers north of town are the "painted caves" of **B'onb'il Pek** ($5.50–8, including equipment rental and guided tour). A community-run guide service (8 A.M.– 3:30 P.M. daily) can be found right beside the highway. You can pay your entrance fee here and grab a flashlight and helmet. Inner tubes are also available for rent ($3) for inner tubing on the cool waters of the **Río San Simón,** another fun nearby activity.

The trip to B'onb'il Pek begins with a 40-minute hike through forest and cornfields. A steep wooden staircase leads you down into the sinkhole. Inside the cave, there are ceramics, and the caves are still used for Mayan religious ceremonies. There is a second, much smaller chamber where there are some faded cave paintings of two monkeys and a jaguar. The community tourism organization offers the option to do the tour with rappelling into the cave for $8. Cobán-based **Aventuras Turísticas** (3a Calle 2-38 Zona 3, tel. 7951-4213/14, www.aventurasturisticas.com) also does rappelling into the sinkhole as well as visits to the Sepalau Lagoons.

The **Lagunas de Sepalau** ($5.50) is a sublime assortment of four turquoise, jungle-shrouded lagoons found nine kilometers east of town. The gateway to these fantastic swimming holes is the small Q'eqchi' village of Sepalau Cataltzul, where another community-run tourism initiative will lead you to the lagoons, a further one kilometer away. The first lagoon you'll find is **Laguna Paraíso,** surrounded by thick jungle. Unfortunately, you can't swim here, as it serves as the source of drinking water for nearby communities. There are, however, boats for rent if you want to paddle across its peaceful waters. The next lagoon is right next to it and is smaller, but you can swim in it. Walking through a jungle path for another kilometer will bring you to the third and fourth lagoons, which are the most spectacular, framed by a background of high limestone cliffs.

At the park entrance, there are showers and restrooms. Camping and tent rental for two costs $7 or you can camp in your own tent for $3. Parking is $1.50. Meals are also available from the local community ($3–5) with prior notice.

Accommodations and Food

Among Chisec's basic accommodations you'll find **Hotel La Estancia de la Virgen** (tel. 7979-7748, $12 d), along the road heading north out of town. Clean, basic rooms with air-conditioning and private bathroom are spread out over two floors. There's a good eatery and a small swimming pool. The other option is the no-frills **Hotel Nopales** ($10 d), just across the road. It's clean. Decent food (and Internet access) can be found in the center of town at **La Huella Café Internet,** serving burgers, Guatemalan favorites, cakes, and coffee. Next to the *municipalidad* (town hall) is **Cafetería El Manantial,** which is a good bet for breakfast. On the southern end of town as you head toward Cobán is the pricier but excellent **Restaurant Bombil Pek.**

Services

There is a Banrural on the plaza where you can change dollars or cash travelers checks, though there are no ATMs in Chisec.

Getting There

Minibuses make the 1.5-hour trip to Cobán every half hour. Heading north, there are hourly minibuses to Candelaria and Raxrujá.

Parque Ecológico Hun Nal Ye

This recently opened eco-amusement park and museum lies along a dirt road turn-off from Km. 259.5 along the road from Chisec to Cobán (RD-09). Hun Nal Ye (tel. 7951-5921, www.parquehunnalye.com, Wed.–Sun. 8 A.M.–6 P.M., $10 adults, $4 children) is a private reserve sprawling across 135 hectares of tropical rainforest with an abundance of plant and animal life and bisected by emerald green rivers and lagoons. Activities include bird-watching (over 200 species of birds have been recorded), fishing, tubing, kayaking, snorkeling, and scuba diving. There's a cave, an eight-meter (26-foot) waterfall, a limestone sinkhole *(cenote),* observation towers, a canopy zipline, and trails for horseback riding, all-terrain vehicles, and mountain bikes. Facilities include a restaurant, archaeology museum, picnic areas, changing rooms, and a swimming pool. You can stay at the comfortable onsite accommodations consisting of five neocolonial tile-roofed cabins ($25 d) with private bath. A family-size cabana sleeping eight goes for $135 a night. You can camp here for $3.50.

Lest Hun Nal Ye strike you as just another theme park, you should know that it lays claim to the very important discovery of an ancient Mayan box dating to Early Classic times and engraved with exquisite hieroglyphs. It was discovered in 2005 by landowner Leonidas Javier and is thought to have once harbored a Maya codex, or book. The box made headlines when it was stolen by looters in 2006 and returned anonymously about a month after it was reported missing from the cave. The item had been purchased on the black market by a collector who, in an apparent attack of conscience, shipped the item to the Ministry of Culture in Guatemala City after realizing the priceless value of his purchase from widespread publicity of the heist. The box is now housed in the park's museum.

To get to the park, take the dirt road turn-off heading east from RD-09 at Km. 259.5. From there, it's about six kilometers to the village of Samanzana, where you'll head south for one kilometer and then continue east another five kilometers to San Vicente Chicatal. From there, follow the signs another 500 meters to the park entrance. If you don't have a car, there are buses and pick-up trucks heading from the Cobán–Chisec road to San Vicente Chicatal.

PLAYA GRANDE (CANTABAL)

This remote outpost in the northwest corner of Alta Verapaz was once the scene of intense fighting during the civil war, with regular military operations in the neighboring Ixcán jungles, where URNG rebels hid out. All that is now in the past, opening some wonderful attractions that were once off-limits. Heading northwest from Chisec, it's a 62-mile journey down a rough dirt road to the town of Playa Grande, also known as Cantabal or Ixcán. There is little to see or do here, but nearby is a remarkable natural attraction.

Laguna Lachuá National Park

This almost perfectly circular turquoise lagoon is its own ecological island, like a square patch of forest floating on a surrounding sea of deforestation. To see it from the air is to get a crash course in tropical forest management and the significance of ecological islands. The razor-sharp park boundaries stand out from the quiltlike fields all around this giant mirror in the middle of nowhere. You'll probably arrive by land, but this description at least gives you some appreciation for the natural beauty of this park and the need to protect it from those who might further encroach upon its boundaries. Already, logging operations have unscrupulously harvested some of the forest's giant mahoganies with reckless disregard for what is, on paper at least, a national park. But I digress.

The 14,500-hectare Laguna Lachuá National Park ($6 admission) is still one of the most beautiful places on earth, despite its challenges. Here you can enjoy the refreshing waters and the dense forest all around in an atmosphere of utter tranquility. From the banks of the lagoon, you can see the forested peaks of El Peyán and La Sultana. There are more than 300 species of birds found here, including mealy parrots and keel-billed toucans. Jaguars still roam the park and you can sometimes see footprints. The lagoon's Caribbean-like waters contain calcium deposits and high levels of sulphur, indicating the probable presence of petroleum beneath its waters. The lake lies partially below sea level, at an altitude of 173 meters above sea level but also 222 meters deep. One of the more exciting theories concerning the lake's formation contends the lakebed is an old meteor crater, with the rest of the meteor that created it having fallen near Cobán in an area known as the Nim Tak'a depression.

There's a visitors center where you'll find cooking facilities, a campground, a shelter with bunk beds ($4 p/p), showers, hiking trails, and canoes for rent ($1).

The park's main entrance is a few kilometers before Playa Grande as you come along the road from the east. From there it's a four-kilometer walk to the lakeside through some very nice forest trails.

Río Ikbolay

This stunning azure river flows through the jungle near Laguna Lachuá. Situated on the banks of this river in the middle of a 600-square-kilometer forest reserve is the community of Rokjá Pomtilá. From this fantastic riverside setting, you can enjoy guided hikes into the surrounding rainforest to view abundant plant and animal life as well as explore lagoons, caves, and waterfalls. **Proyecto Eco-Quetzal** (2a Calle 14-36 Zona 1, tel. 7952-1047, bidaspeq@ hotmail.com, www.ecoquetzal.org; see *Guide Companies* in the *Cobán and Vicinity* section) can arrange homestays with local villagers. A two-night stay at Rokjá Pomtilá costs $45, not including transportation.

PETÉN

Guatemala's northernmost department has always conjured images of a remote wilderness characterized by dense forests and lost Mayan cities inhabited only by loggers and chicle harvesters. Today, that image is only partly true as much of the Ohio-size Petén has been cleared by settlers for subsistence agriculture and cattle ranching. In an attempt to save the remaining forest and the still unexcavated Mayan ruins they harbor, roughly a third of Petén has been protected since 1990 in the form of several national parks collectively known as the Maya Biosphere Reserve. It is one of the largest remaining continuous tracts of tropical forest in Central America. Recreational opportunities inside and outside the reserve are boundless and the region is slowly becoming a magnet for adventure and ecotourism, thanks in large part to the filming of *Survivor Guatemala* here in 2005.

Among the attractions are the enigmatic Mayan ruins of Tikal, one of the largest cities ever populated by the Mayans and certainly a must-see for any visitor to the area. Not only are the restored ruins impressive, to say the least, but the abundant wildlife found in the lush rainforests protected within the adjacent national park make this a prime spot for birders and wildlife enthusiasts. Along the paved road to Tikal, you'll pass the spectacular Lake Petén Itzá, one of Guatemala's largest, surrounded by jungles and characterized by its luminescent turquoise-blue waters. The village of El Remate has sprung up along the highway and is quickly becoming a destination unto itself with a number of very

HIGHLIGHTS

◖ Parque Natural Ixpanpajul: The hanging bridges and nature trail here provide a toucan's-eye view of the Petén forests. There are other fun activities in this private nature reserve just minutes from Flores (page 322).

◖ El Remate: Once a sleepy lakeside fishing village, El Remate's strategic location along the road to Tikal has caused it to grow up and become a destination in its own right. It offers a convenient alternative to staying in Tikal's limited hotel offerings while providing access to beautiful Lake Petén Itzá and a variety of recreational opportunities such as kayaking, swimming, bird-watching, and horseback riding (page 325).

◖ The Ruins of Tikal: No trip to Petén, or Guatemala for that matter, would be complete without a visit to the enigmatic ruins of one of the largest cities ever built and inhabited by the Mayans (page 338).

◖ Yaxhá: Featured in *Survivor Guatemala*, the ruins of Yaxhá enjoy a spectacular location beside the site's namesake lagoon and provide commanding views of the surrounding forests (page 348).

◖ El Mirador: Deep in the northern recesses of the Maya Biosphere Reserve, the ruins of El Mirador offer the opportunity for a world-class adventure encompassing an arduous two-day journey through swampy forests. Marvel at the highest known Mayan structure with a base the size of three football fields (page 349).

◖ Las Guacamayas Biological Research Station: Observe nesting scarlet macaws from observation platforms or forest trails with the knowledge that the money you spend is going directly toward giving them a fighting chance at survival (page 356).

LOOK FOR ◖ TO FIND RECOMMENDED SIGHTS, ACTIVITIES, DINING, AND LODGING.

comfortable accommodations and plenty of activities for the outdoor enthusiast. Many travelers now spend an extra day here after exploring the ruins.

Southeast of Tikal, the remote ruins of Yaxhá, overlooking the site's namesake lagoon, remain a remote jungle outpost despite their prime-time TV fame and you can still have the place all to yourself on a typical afternoon. But that probably won't last too much longer.

Petén is without a doubt the cradle of Mayan civilization, as it lays claim to some of the oldest known Mayan sites along with the earliest evidence of the writing and royal dynastic rule characterizing the civilization that flourished here. At the remote site of El Mirador, on the northern fringes of Petén near the Mexican border, you can gaze in awe at the massive temple pyramids of El Tigre and La Danta, which were erected centuries earlier than most other well-known Mayan sites but nonetheless show much the same level of sophistication. All of these sites are harbored within the Maya Biosphere Reserve and its seemingly interminable expanses of mostly undisturbed tropical forests. Hikers will appreciate the numerous opportunities for trekking to remote Mayan ruins along jungle paths, creating the potential for adventures not unlike those of the early explorers.

HISTORY

During colonial times, Petén remained a backwater, the only Spanish settlement being the island city of Flores, a pleasant town of pastel-colored houses that remains the region's main tourist services hub. In 1840, Guatemalan President Rafael Carrera dispatched a small platoon of soldiers to officially claim the Petén region as part of the country. Mexico decided the territory was not worth the trouble of contesting. The region has been a backwater ever since, officially the poorest of Guatemala's departments, which is especially evident to travelers coming in from Belize along an unpaved highway lined with cattle ranches and simple thatched-roof huts.

Petén harbors 550,000 of Guatemala's inhabitants, making it the country's most sparsely populated region, though its rate of population increase from immigration is the highest in the country. Much of this unprecedented growth is the product of an ill-conceived 1960s government program to colonize Petén, meant as a safety valve to relieve pressures for land reform. A battle is being waged to save this valuable natural and cultural heritage, and visitors to Guatemala's northern parks can derive some satisfaction from the knowledge that their visit lends importance, justification, and the financial means for the continued preservation of what remains.

PLANNING YOUR TIME

Petén is one of Guatemala's most fascinating regions, particularly for lovers of archaeology

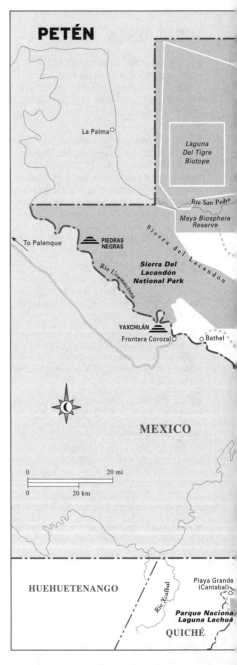

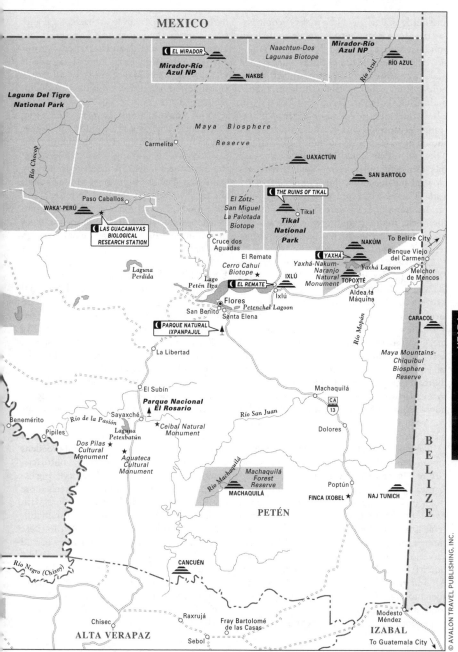

MEXICO

EL MIRADOR

Mirador-Río
Azul NP

Naachtun-Dos
Lagunas Biotope

Mirador-Río
Azul NP

RÍO AZUL

NAKBÉ

Laguna Del Tigre
National Park

Maya   Biosphere

Reserve

Carmelita

Río Chocop

UAXACTÚN

SAN BARTOLO

Paso Caballos

WAKA'-PERÚ

LAS GUACAMAYAS
BIOLOGICAL
RESEARCH STATION

El Zotz-
San Miguel
La Palotada
Biotope

THE RUINS OF TIKAL

Tikal

Tikal
National
Park

NAKÚM

To Belize City

Cruce dos
Aguadas

El Remate

Cerro Cahuí
Biotope

YAXHÁ

Yaxhá-Nakum-
Naranjo
Natural
Monument

Benque Viejo
del Carmen

Melchor
de Mencos

Laguna
Perdida

Lago
Petén Itzá

EL REMATE

IXLÚ

Yaxhá Lagoon

TOPOXTÉ

Flores

Petenchel Lagoon

Ixlú

San Benito

Santa Elena

Aldea la
Máquina

CARACOL

PARQUE NATURAL
IXPANPAJUL

La Libertad

Río Mopán

Maya Mountains-
Chiquibul
Biosphere
Reserve

El Subín

Machaquilá

Parque Nacional
El Rosario

Río San Juan

CA
13

Benemérito

Sayaxché

Río de la Pasión

Ceibal Natural
Monument

Dolores

Pipiles

Dos Pilas
Cultural
Monument

Laguna
Petexbatún

Aguateca
Cultural
Monument

B
E
L
I
Z
E

Machaquilá
Forest
Reserve

MACHAQUILÁ

Poptún

FINCA IXOBEL

NAJ TUNICH

Río Machaquilá

PETÉN

CANCUÉN

Río Negro (Chixoy)

Chisec

Raxrujá

Fray Bartolomé
de las Casas

Modesto
Méndez

ALTA VERAPAZ

Sebol

IZABAL

To Guatemala City

PETÉN

and outdoor activities. The parks encompassing the **Maya Biosphere Reserve** could keep you busy for weeks, in addition to the requisite visit to **Tikal National Park.** Some people make day trips to Tikal, coming across the border from Belize or flying in from Guatemala City. This will certainly serve only to whet your appetite for more Petén explorations. Visitors on one of these short stints should at least consider spending the night at Tikal or nearby **Lake Petén Itzá.** Another increasingly popular destination is the archaeological site of **Yaxhá,** site of *Survivor Guatemala.* There is a comfortable jungle lodge right on the shores of Yaxhá Lagoon where you can spend the night, a good idea if you want to take in all that this site has to offer, given its remote location.

El Mirador, deep in the jungle near the Mexican border, involves an arduous journey of two days from the nearest village but is well worth it for the opportunity to visit one of the largest and earliest Mayan cities in existence. The tallest, and some of the largest, man-made pre-Columbian structures can also be found here in the form of the massive La Danta and El Tigre pyramids, with bases the size of three football fields. A typical round-trip itinerary to El Mirador takes 5–7 days, depending on how long you want to stay at the ruins and if you want to stop at other nearby sites on the way back.

The most natural starting point and hub for any in-depth Petén explorations is the island city of **Flores,** with its pretty pastel-colored houses and quiet streets; it's unlike any other town in Guatemala. Its sister city of Santa Elena, on the mainland shores of Lake Petén Itzá, is an equally logical choice for a base, though it's not nearly as attractive. Many conservation organizations and adventure travel outfitters are based in Flores/Santa Elena. Air and ground service connects Flores/Santa Elena to most of Petén, other parts of Guatemala, and Belize.

In southern Petén, the **Petexbatún** region

harbors many fascinating archaeological sites set alongside the Petexbatún Lagoon. If you have an extra few days after checking out Tikal, Yaxhá, and Lake Petén Itzá, and if you're a big fan of Mayan ruins, by all means continue south and check out the Petexbatún region. Farther east, the area surrounding the town of **Poptún,** along the road connecting Petén and Izabal, lies at a comfortably higher elevation and is an excellent destination for cave tubing, spelunking, hiking, and hanging out at area lodges. A requisite stop along the Petén–Izabal Highway is **Finca Ixobel,** the most popular of the Poptún lodges, and with good reason. If you're heading north into Petén from Izabal, you'll want to spend a night or two in Poptún, assuming you have enough time to visit Tikal.

Exploring the Region

Some of Petén's attractions, Tikal National Park for example, can easily be explored on your own. The remote location and rugged topography characterizing the great majority of Petén's parks and ruins, however, means you will probably find yourself needing the services of an experienced guide sooner or later. Another issue to consider is that hiring a guide provides locals with tangible evidence that the local environment and the Petén forests are worth more standing than cut down for cattle ranching or timber. It also provides a much-needed source of income and broadens cultural horizons. There are several outfitters, based mainly in the city of Flores, offering excellent guided trips to some of Petén's more exotic offerings and all of these work with local communities to ensure the sustainability of their tourism practices. While there is certainly a glut of tour companies in and around Flores, not all of them are reliable, and many of their owners are not in the least socially or environmentally conscious. Try to stick to one of the recommended outfitters. (You'll find details under *Guide Companies* in the *Flores* section.)

Poptún and Vicinity

POPTÚN

Halfway between Río Dulce and Flores, Poptún has always been a favorite stopping point, particularly before the road to Flores was paved and travelers needed to split up the grueling journey on a rutted dirt road. Nestled in the foothills of the Maya Mountains, which extend into neighboring Belize, the area is unlike the rest of Petén in that it is cooler by virtue of its altitude at more than 600 meters (2,000 feet) and features a largely pine-forested, karst landscape. There are many relatively unexplored Mayan sites here as well as some small expanses of tropical forest, which have survived the expansion of the agricultural frontier to which most of southern Peteén has succumbed. A military base once operated in this area, but it has been closed down since the 1996 peace accords, as elsewhere in Guatemala.

NAJ TUNICH

The Naj Tunich caves have long been a local attraction and were even featured in the August 1981 issue of *National Geographic*. The caves, which are more than one kilometer long, are famous for their intricate murals and hieroglyphic text. These were defaced some years ago and the site has been closed to visitors ever since. Naj Tunich appears to have been one of the most highly revered sites in the Mayan world, and it is known that several of the glyphs were painted by scribes from such faraway cities as Calakmul, in present-day Mexico. A replica is slated to open in the near future. Check with the staff at Finca Ixobel for details.

Recreation

Poptún's wonderful setting at a comfortably higher altitude and its pine-studded, karst landscape make exploring this part of Guatemala a delight. You can choose from, among others, treks to remote Mayan sites, jungle hikes, caving, or tubing down lazy stretches of jungle river. All of these activities can be arranged at area lodges, particularly Finca Ixobel (on the road from Río Dulce, tel. 5892-3188, www.fincaixobel.com), which pioneered ecotourism in this neck of the woods and is always on the lookout for new offerings. You can choose from a number of **caves**, which can take two hours, a half day, or a full day of exploring. The full-day trip takes you to **Cueva del Río** ($10), an underground river with rapids and waterfalls where you can swim and leap into the river in total darkness. There are also trips twice a day to **Ixobel Cave** ($5), with its rim stone walls, stalactites, and stalagmites a 45-minute walk from the farm. Just 25 minutes' walk from Finca Ixobel, **Echoing Cave** ($5) offers a fun ad-

venture exploring the cave's hidden chambers and caverns, and it is a good option if you have only two hours' time.

Horseback riding is also available at the Finca Ixobel with trips lasting as little as two hours or as much as two days ($53). A full day of horseback riding costs $23.

Finca Ixobel also runs a number of excellent multiday jungle adventures lasting a minimum of three days and costing $30 per person per day, with a two-person minimum. The treks take you to remote Mayan sites such as **Ixcún,** the caves of **Naj Tunich,** and waterfalls on the **Río Mopán.** All trips are on horseback.

Inner tubing on the **Machaquilá River** from Finca Ixobel ($20, including lunch and transportation) is possible in June and July, when the water is high enough but before the summer rains are in full swing.

Villa de los Castellanos (tel. 7927-7541), another local lodge, is set right beside the river and also offers inner tubing. Trips to the remote ruins and forest reserve of **Machaquilá** are also available from here, as well as to the **Chiquibul Forest Reserve,** farther north.

PETÉN

Accommodations and Food

There is at least one good place to stay in Poptún proper, though you are probably better off staying at one of the local, highly recommended jungle lodges. Should you get stuck in town, **Hotel Posada de los Castellanos** (tel. 7927-7222, corner of 4a Calle and 7a Avenida, $10 d) is your best bet with basic, clean rooms with fan and private hot-water bath. For eating, **La Fonda Ixobel** has tasty baked goods and snacks.

Services

Banrural (5a Calle, 8:30 A.M.–5 P.M. Mon.–Fri., 9 A.M.–1 P.M. Sat.) has a MasterCard ATM and changes U.S. dollars and American Express travelers checks.

Getting There

The Poptún area is accessible via several buses and minivans leaving Flores daily at half-hour intervals during daylight hours. (See *Getting There* in the *Flores* section.) Buses heading north from Guatemala City via Río Dulce also come this way and stop at Finca Ixobel, Poptún, and Machaquilá.

NEAR POPTÚN
Finca Ixobel

Just south of Poptún, on the road from Río Dulce, ◖ **Finca Ixobel** (tel. 5892-3188, www.fincaixobel.com) has long drawn travelers coming overland to Petén for its wonderful accommodations and excellent food at moderate prices in an attractive jungle setting. Its wide-ranging activities allow guests the chance to explore myriad attractions nestled in the surrounding cool pine forests and rolling green hills. There are accommodations to suit every taste and budget, including hammocks ($3), clean, comfortable dorms for $4 p/p, rooms with shared bath for $13 d and rooms with private bath for $26 d. There are more luxurious bungalows and a suite for $30 and $36 d. The latest addition to Finca Ixobel's offerings is a series of tree houses set amid spacious grounds. Some have electricity; others are candlelit. Prices range from $11 d with candlelight to $17 d with electricity. Only one of the so-called tree houses is actually in a tree, but all are attractive, quite comfortable, and set above the ground. A deluxe tree house with its own bath and electricity is popular with honeymooners and goes for $23 d.

The restaurant here serves delicious, inexpensive meals, largely using ingredients grown in the finca's vegetable garden. Breakfast and lunch are à la carte, while dinner is served buffet style ($4–8). Breakfast items include homemade yogurt and granola, pancakes, and eggs, with plenty of vegetarian options for lunch and dinner. There is also a bar set beside a swimming pond where you can chill out in a hammock or play a game of "Twister" with your new friends and fellow travelers.

Any bus traveling the Rio Dulce–Flores Highway will drop you off at the turnoff to Finca Ixobel. From there, it's just a short 15-minute walk to the lodge. You can arrange minibus transport to Flores and book bus tickets to Guatemala City from Finca Ixobel. Minibuses go by every half hour 8 A.M.–5 P.M. and cost $5.50 one-way. Transport to Guatemala City on Linea Dorada bus lines ranges $12.50–20 one-way. If you are arriving at Finca Ixobel after nightfall, your best bet is to go to La Fonda Ixobel in Poptún town and get a cab from there to the farm.

Villa de los Castellanos

In the town of Machaquilá, seven kilometers north of Poptún, Villa de los Castellanos (Aldea Machaquilá, tel. 7927-7541, $25–40 d) is just off the road in a peaceful riverside setting overlooking the Río Machaquilá and set on 12 acres of land encompassing forest and a medicinal plant garden. Its 14 comfortable cabanas all have private bath. There is also a good restaurant and the owners organize trips to local caves, ruins, and forest preserves.

Cocay Camping

Back toward Poptún is Cocay Camping (tel. 7927-7024, $5 per person), set in splendid isolation on the banks of the Río Machaquilá just past the town proper. There are camping spaces, very basic cabins, and a café serving vegetarian fare.

Sayaxché and Vicinity

SAYAXCHÉ

Sayaxché, on the southern shore of Río La Pasión, is the natural gateway for trips to the Mayan sites of **Ceibal** and the archaeological wonders hidden amid the lagoons and forests of the **Petexbatún Wildlife Refuge.** It is a rough-and-tumble kind of town and reports of shootouts in its streets are not uncommon, though security forces were reported to have gotten at least a partial hold on the situation in late 2006. Still, you may want to limit your time here to that required to cross the Río La Pasión on your way south to the Verapaces or to organize a trip to one of the nearby attractions. In addition to serving as an important waterway for trade in Mayan times, the river and surrounding town nowadays serve as a transshipment point for the local cocaine cartels said to operate in this region for some time now. Although they don't tend to get involved with tourists, it certainly adds to the remote lawless frontier atmosphere that seems to permeate this town.

While the Petexbatún region's sites are impressive and the jungle scenery in these parts alluring, you may want to inquire with travel agencies in Flores before heading out here. Robberies were reported for some time at Ceibal, though locals say the group responsible was caught some time ago, and there are no recent robberies to report. If you have plenty of time to explore Petén, it might be worth visiting here. Otherwise, your time might be best spent exploring some equally beautiful but safer sites elsewhere. If it's remote wilderness you seek, there are certainly other areas you can find to explore.

Accommodations and Food
On the north bank of the river, before crossing on the ferry when coming from Flores, is **Café del Río** (tel. 6620-1742, all meals daily). With sweeping views from its perch above the river, it is a great choice for its location away from the considerably busier atmosphere on the other side. Should you need to stay here, your best

bet is **Hotel Guayacán** (tel. 7926-6111) on the southern bank of the river. It has decent rooms with wooden beds and tiled floors going for $17 d with fan on the first floor or $20 d with air-conditioning on the second floor. It also has a good restaurant with a terrace overlooking the Río La Pasión and main dishes costing about $5. One block up the street and three blocks to the right is **Hotel Petexbatún** (tel. 7928-6166), where rooms with fan and TV cost $10 or $15 with private bath. On the second street to the left as you come from the docks, **El Botanero** features a varied menu including shrimp, fish, chicken, and beef in addition to cocktails and has a pleasant atmosphere with decent music.

Getting There
The 62-kilometer road from Flores to Sayaxché is mostly paved, except for the first 20 kilometers or so out of Flores. The road south is now paved all the way to Cobán. Minibuses from Flores leave every half hour between 5 A.M. and 6 P.M., with three daily Pinita buses leaving Flores at 11 A.M., 2 P.M., and 2:30 P.M.

A ferry ($0.25 per person) takes you across the Río La Pasión. A number of boatmen are on hand for trips down the river to Ceibal or up the Arroyo Petexbatún to the other sites. Recommended is **Lanchas Don Pedro** (tel. 7928-6109), on the riverbank, run by the amiable Pedro Méndez. Don Julián Mariona, owner of Posada Caribe, can also help you with boat trips.

If you are going south, there are two daily minibuses to Cobán (3.5 hours) via Chisec at 10 A.M. and 3:30 P.M. You can also catch one of several minibuses to Raxrujá, leaving about every 90 minutes until 4 P.M. Several buses leave from there for Cobán and other Alta Verapaz destinations.

CEIBAL NATURAL MONUMENT
The Mayan site of Ceibal blossomed in the twilight years of the Classic period after being

PETÉN

infused with new life from the invading Putún Mayans' merchant warrior culture from Mexico's Tabasco region. It grew quickly between A.D. 830 and 910, harboring an estimated 10,000 inhabitants at its peak.

There are four main clusters of structures connected via causeways and the ruins here have a distinctly non-Mayan feel to them. Round platforms dot the site and several of the inscribed monuments feature unusual items such as waist-length hair, speech scrolls, and straight noses. There are 57 stelae here, many of them huge and in fairly good condition. Several of these are in the **Central Plaza,** along with its unrestored temples, and in the neighboring **South Plaza.** Another of the site's curiosities is **Structure 79,** a large round stone platform set in a forest clearing used for religious ceremonies and maybe even serving as a platform for astronomical observation.

The protected forest around Ceibal is particularly striking, as it is home to several of the large ceiba trees giving the area its name. It is among the few stands of well-preserved forest remaining in this area.

Getting There

The site is accessible both from land and by river. Boat trips from Sayaxché can be arranged by negotiating with the local *lancheros.* A round-trip boat ride to the ruins with a two-hour wait should cost about $50. The hour-long ride from Sayaxché is a pleasant journey down the Río La Pasión. A short walk up a hill from the river brings you to the site.

Ceibal is only 17 kilometers by road from Sayaxchá and any transport heading south out of town can drop you off at the turnoff for the ruins. From there it's an eight-kilometer walk to the site, but you may get lucky and hitch a ride from someone heading that way. Or you can book a taxi ride from Sayaxchá. Pickup trucks carrying several people might be making the run on any given day and you can inquire at one of the local recommended restaurants or hotels about this possibility.

Several of the Flores tour operators offer Ceibal on their list of itineraries. **Explore** (4a

Calle and 7a Avenida Zona 1 in Santa Elena, tel. 7926-2375, www.exploreguate.com) offers guaranteed daily trips.

PETEXBATÚN WILDLIFE REFUGE

This protected area is set beside the placid waters of Petexbatún Lagoon and harbors the remains of several small Mayan cities along with some nice stretches of forest. Wildlife is abundant and includes several species of fish, freshwater turtles, howler monkeys, crocodiles, and several kinds of birds, including egrets, kingfishers, and herons.

History

The history of this region is fascinating, as it portrays violent struggles between neighboring states concurrent with the widespread abandonment of Petén's Classic Mayan sites, giving us a glimpse into the local state of affairs in various Mayan city-states before the Classic Mayan collapse. The area's largest site, Dos Pilas, was founded sometime around A.D. 640 by a renegade prince from Tikal who fled after Tikal's defeat by Calakmul. Later Dos Pilas defeated Tikal in two wars culminating in the capture of Tikal's ruler Shield Skull in A.D. 679. The event was duly recorded in the stelae at Dos Pilas and launched a reconstruction of the site's plaza.

Subsequent rulers would carry out building programs, including the construction of three hieroglyphic staircases, and wage wars of conquest. Ceibal was defeated in A.D. 735 and several lords from other Mayan cities were captured. Dos Pilas eventually came to dominate most of the lands between the Chixoy and Pasión Rivers.

The same Putún Mayans who came to dominate Ceibal eventually made their way over to Dos Pilas, and in A.D. 761, allied with the vassal state of Tamarindito, they captured and killed the site's fourth ruler. The remaining nobility fled to Aguateca, naturally fortified on a bluff, which had already begun functioning as a second capital. Some of the peasantry stayed behind and continued to farm the area around Dos Pilas, attempting to fortify it against their enemies, but it succumbed to the continuing onslaught of these invaders from the north and was completely abandoned by the 9th century.

Aguateca would suffer a similar fate and was abandoned sometime around A.D. 790, after three defensive moats were built along Petexbatún Lagoon across Punta de Chimino in a vain attempt to keep the invaders at bay.

Aguateca Cultural Monument

This cultural monument protects the site of Aguateca, situated on the banks of the Petexbatún Lagoon, as well as the wonderfully isolated peninsula of **Punta de Chimino.**

Aguateca sits at the southern edge of the lake on a high outcrop. The site is being excavated and restored after its rediscovery in 1957. A dramatic natural chasm splits the site in two and features exuberant vegetation. Two lookout points with wonderful lake views add to the site's sublime atmosphere. The two main groups of ruins being restored include the **Palace Group** and the **Main Plaza,** connected to one another by a causeway. You'll find some wonderful replicas beside the original, fallen over stelae in the Main Plaza.

The rangers here will let you camp for free. It's always a good idea to bring in some extra food as a token of your appreciation. They can also provide walking sticks for the potentially hazardous, slippery trails found throughout the site. A new visitors center and a small eatery might be complete by the time of your visit. **Explore,** (4a Calle and 7a Avenida Zona 1 in Santa Elena, tel. 7926-2375, www.explore guate.com) **Martsam,** and **Tikal Connection** all offer trips to Aguateca and you can camp here with them upon request. (See *Guide Companies* in the *Flores* section for more information on Martsam and Tikal Connection.) **Posada Caribe** and **Chiminos Island Lodge** also offer guided trips. (See *Accommodations and Food* in this section.)

Farther north about four kilometers is **Punta de Chimino,** the peninsula that served as the last stand for the local Mayan population in its attempt to repel its northern invaders. A man-made citadel complete with ramparts and trenches once crossed the peninsula's narrow neck. You won't see any of this in evidence today, but the vegetation and lakeside setting make this a very special place, as Spanish moss graces large trees in a jungle unlike any in Petén. Today, it is the site of the spectacular and highly recommended Chiminos Island Lodge.

Dos Pilas Cultural Monument

In addition to the site of Dos Pilas, you'll find the smaller neighboring sites of **Tamarindito** and **Arroyo de Piedra** within the confines of this protected area. Though the site's well-documented history is almost epic in proportion, its remains are much less astounding, mostly because of the circumstances under which its reign came to an end. Still, there are some well-carved stelae and some rare hieroglyphic staircases surrounding the main plaza. A palace and a temple can also be seen here, with a tomb having been discovered underneath the latter. The jungle vegetation here is also well preserved.

Dos Pilas is accessible by boat from Sayaxché via the Arroyo Petexbatún. A trailhead lies just before the **Posada Caribe** at a place known as **Paso Caribe,** from where it's a three-hour hike down the 12-kilometer trail to the site. You can do the trip for about $26 per person per day including horses and mule skinner. Contact the Posada Caribe (see *Accommodations and Food*) to arrange this option. Along the way, you'll pass the smaller sites of **Arroyo de Piedra,** with a plaza and two stelae, and Tamarindito, the site of another hieroglyphic stairway. Camping is permitted at Dos Pilas and is free. There is also a trail from here to Aguateca, which is about 12 kilometers away.

Thanks to the Guatemalan government's efforts to make remote Mayan sites more accessible, a road also leads to the vicinity of Dos Pilas. Heading south from Sayaxché, the road is paved for the first 34 kilometers to the small community of Las Pozas. From there it's a 21-kilometer dirt road west to El Nacimiento and a further three-kilometer foot trail to Dos Pilas to round out the journey.

PETÉN

Accommodations and Food

All of the area's accommodations are in the vicinity of the Petexbatún Lagoon. Family-owned and operated by the very helpful and friendly Julián Mariona, **Posada Caribe** (tel. 5304-1745, www.posadacaribe.com, $60 d) is the first place you'll come across as you navigate the river network leading from Sayaxché to Petexbatún Lagoon. Comfortable thatched-roof cabanas with private bath are set among tropical landscaping at the river's edge. There are packages for $45 per person including one night's stay and three meals, but you must arrange your own transportation. Packages including transfers from Sayaxché start at $150 and include a guide and one night at the lodge with meals. Whether or not you stay at the lodge, Don Julián can help you with planning and logistics in the Petexbatún area, which he knows quite well. Farther toward the Petexbatún Lagoon, the next place you'll come across is **Petexbatún Lodge** (tel. 7926-0501 or 5806-5860), where the rooms in stucco and wood cottages are slightly nicer and include ceiling fan, mosquito netting, and large private bathrooms with a semioutdoor shower. Rates are $44 d in cabins or $12 p/p in shared-bath dormitory. Breakfast in an attractive open-air dining room costs $5 and lunch/dinner are $12. The Petexbatún area's finest accommodations are at the gorgeous ❰ **Chiminos Island Lodge** (tel. 2335-3506 or 5750-8628, www.chiminosisland.com), where you'll find six comfortable thatched-roof bungalows with lovely views, firm beds, colorful Guatemalan blankets, and wood and tile accents in your private hot-water bathroom. The rooms are made from tropical hardwoods and have beautiful wooden decks overlooking Petexbatún Lagoon. The elegant open-air restaurant serves delicious set meals and is adjacent to a pleasant hammock area overlooking the fantastic lakeside setting. Rates are $110 per person, including one night's accommodations and three meals. Children under 12 are $55 each.

Flores

In the heart of Petén, the twin towns of Flores and Santa Elena are often referred to simply and collectively as "Flores," the latter actually being limited to a small island on Lake Petén Itzá connected to Santa Elena, on the mainland, by a causeway. Flores is a pleasant island town unlike any other in Guatemala with pastel houses and quiet streets. Santa Elena is a bit noisier and more chaotic because of its prominence as Petén's main commercial center. Farther west, Santa Elena runs into the downright ugly town of San Benito.

Flores is the natural starting point for a visit to Petén's wild interior, as it is the region's transportation and services hub. Many NGOs are based here and the quiet streets are lined with a variety of shops, restaurants, and comfortable lodgings. While Flores is excellent from a logistical standpoint and entirely attractive, it has been somewhat displaced in recent years by the emergence of El Remate, a lakeside town on the road to Tikal that is convenient for travelers to and from Belize. Still, there are a number of local attractions that make spending at least one day in the Flores area worthwhile.

HISTORY

Flores started out as the Mayan site of **Tayasal,** home to the Itrzá people and one of the last Mayan strongholds. It is thought that Tayasal was founded by a group of displaced Mayans from Chichen Itzá, in present-day Mexico, sometime between the 13th and 15th centuries. The Itzá held out for quite a while in their remote island outpost deep in the Petén jungle. Spain's relative lack of interest in the hot, steamy lowlands of Petén inevitably allowed

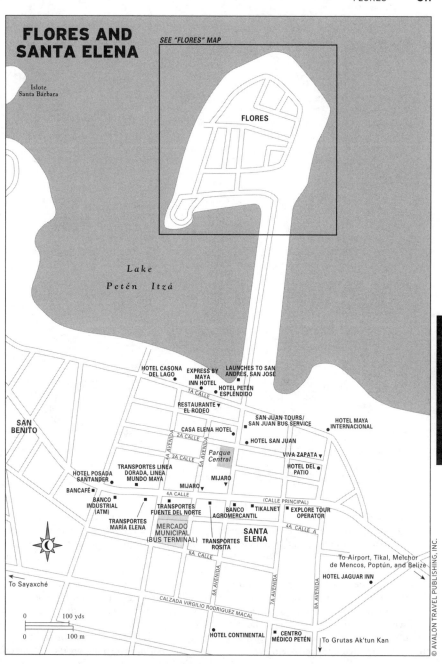

FLORES AND SANTA ELENA

Islote
Santa Bárbara

SEE "FLORES" MAP

FLORES

Lake
Petén Itzá

SAN
BENITO

HOTEL CASONA
DEL LAGO

EXPRESS BY
MAYA
INN HOTEL

LAUNCHES TO SAN
ANDRÉS, SAN JOSÉ

HOTEL PETÉN
ESPLÉNDIDO

1A CALLE

RESTAURANTE ▼
EL RODEO

CASA ELENA HOTEL

SAN JUAN TOURS/
SAN JUAN BUS SERVICE

HOTEL MAYA
INTERNACIONAL

2A CALLE

4A AVENIDA

3A CALLE

5A AVENIDA

Parque
Central

HOTEL SAN JUAN

VIVA ZAPATA ▼

HOTEL DEL
PATIO

TRANSPORTES LINEA
DORADA, LINEA
MUNDO MAYA

MIJARO

MIJARO ▼

HOTEL POSADA
SANTANDER

4A CALLE

BANCAFÉ ■

BANCO
INDUSTRIAL
(ATM)

TRANSPORTES
FUENTE DEL NORTE

BANCO
AGROMERCANTIL

TIKALNET

(CALLE PRINCIPAL)

EXPLORE TOUR
OPERATOR

TRANSPORTES
MARÍA ELENA

MERCADO
MUNICIPAL
(BUS TERMINAL)

TRANSPORTES
ROSITA

SANTA
ELENA

4A CALLE A

5A CALLE

8A AVENIDA

7A AVENIDA

To Airport, Tikal, Melchor
de Mencos, Poptún, and Belize

8A AVENIDA

HOTEL JAGUAR INN

To Sayaxché

0   100 yds

0   100 m

CALZADA VIRGILIO RODRIGUEZ MACAL

HOTEL CONTINENTAL

CENTRO
MÉDICO PETÉN

To Grutas Ak'tun Kan

PETÉN

© AVALON TRAVEL PUBLISHING, INC.

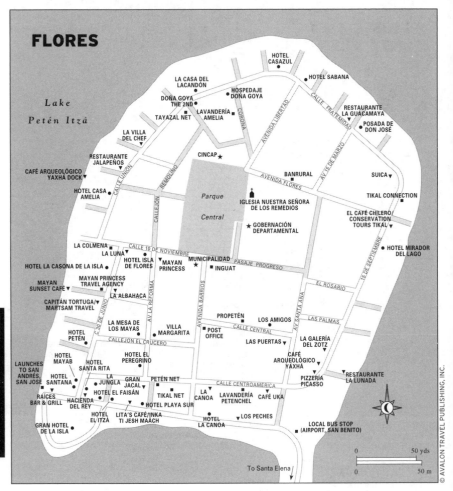

FLORES

Lake
Petén Itzá

HOTEL
CASAZUL

HOTEL SABANA

LA CASA DEL
LACANDÓN

HOSPEDAJE
DOÑA GOYA

CALLE FRATERNIDAD

RESTAURANTE
LA GUACAMAYA

DOÑA GOYA
THE 2ND

AVENIDA LIBERTAD

POSADA DE
DON JOSÉ

TAYAZAL NET

LAVANDERÍA
AMELIA

CORONA

LA VILLA
DEL CHEF

CINCAP

AV. 13 DE MARZO

RESTAURANTE
JALAPEÑOS

BANRURAL

AVENIDA FLORES

SUICA

CAFÉ ARQUEOLÓGICO
YAXHÁ DOCK

TIKAL CONNECTION

HOTEL CASA
AMELIA

CALLE UNIÓN

Parque

IGLESIA NUESTRA SEÑORA
DE LOS REMEDIOS

EL CAFÉ CHILERO/
CONSERVATION
TOURS TIKAL

Central

CALLEJÓN

GOBERNACIÓN
DEPARTAMENTAL

REMOLINO

LA COLMENA

CALLE 10 DE NOVIEMBRE

15 DE SEPTIEMBRE

HOTEL MIRADOR
DEL LAGO

LA LUNA

HOTEL ISLA
DE FLORES

MAYAN
PRINCESS

MUNICIPALIDAD

PASAJE PROGRESO

HOTEL LA CASONA DE LA ISLA

INGUAT

EL ROSARIO

MAYAN
SUNSET CAFÉ

MAYAN PRINCESS
TRAVEL AGENCY

AV. LA REFORMA

LA ALBAHACA

AVENIDA BARRIOS

AV. SANTA ANA

CAPITÁN TORTUGA/
MARTSAM TRAVEL

PROPETÉN

LOS AMIGOS

LAS PALMAS

LA MESA DE
LOS MAYAS

C 30 DE JUNIO

VILLA
MARGARITA

CALLE CENTRAL

HOTEL
PETÉN

POST
OFFICE

LAS PUERTAS

LA GALERÍA
DEL ZOTZ

CALLEJÓN EL CRUCERO

CAFÉ
ARQUEOLÓGICO
YAXHÁ

LAUNCHES
TO SAN
ANDRÉS,
SAN JOSÉ

HOTEL
MAYAB

HOTEL
SANTA RITA

HOTEL EL
PEREGRINO

HOTEL
SANTANA

LA
JUNGLA

GRAN
JACAL

PETÉN NET

CALLE CENTROAMÉRICA

PIZZERÍA
PICASSO

RESTAURANTE
LA LUNADA

RAÍCES
BAR & GRILL

HOTEL EL FAISÁN

TIKAL NET

LA
CANOA

LAVANDERÍA
PETENCHEL

CAFÉ UKA

HACIENDA
DEL REY

HOTEL PLAYA SUR

GRAN HOTEL
DE LA ISLA

HOTEL
EL ITZÁ

LITA'S CAFÉ/INKA
TI JESH MAÁCH

HOTEL
LA CANOA

LOS PECHES

LOCAL BUS STOP
(AIRPORT, SAN BENITO)

0   50 yds
0   50 m

To Santa Elena

© AVALON TRAVEL PUBLISHING, INC.

them to continue life largely unhindered by the Spanish. In 1525, Hernán Cortés stopped by on his way to Honduras and had a peaceful meeting with the Itzá King Canek, also leaving behind a lame horse. A statue of it was made when it died, and Spanish friars visiting the region in 1618 would find it being worshipped by the Itzá. The friars destroyed the idol, which probably explains why the next round of visitors, a military expedition in 1622, was captured and sacrificed.

Tayasal finally came under Spanish rule in 1697 at the command of Martín de Ursúa. As was the custom, the Spanish conquerors destroyed the city's temples, pyramids, and artwork, leaving no trace behind. Today, the small Flores town plaza, church, and government buildings sit on the highest point in the city atop what was once Tayasal's ceremonial plaza.

To the north, across the small finger of Lake Petén Itzá in which Flores lies, are the remains of the Mayan site of Tayazal. It dates to the Classic period, long before the arrival of the Itzá.

SIGHTS

As nothing remains of the original settlement, there is very little to see in terms of sights on the island. The quaint plaza contains a small church and government buildings flanked on one side by a basketball court. Flores itself is very different from any other town in Guatemala and a leisurely stroll around the island will allow you enough time to take in the funky pastel architecture and the quiet streets. While checking out the plaza, stop by **(CINCAP)** (10 A.M.–noon and 2 P.M.–8 P.M. Mon.–Fri.), housed in the Castillo de Arismendi on the north side of the park. CINCAP serves as an information center on *petenero* culture and is run by the environmental group Alianza Verde. There are interesting displays, arts and crafts for sale, and plenty of information on Petén's recreational offerings. (Several attractions outside the town proper are covered in the *Near Flores and Santa Elena* section.)

© AL ARGUETA

Flores has many funky storefronts.

ENTERTAINMENT

Don't get too excited about entertainment in Flores. Like many small towns in Guatemala, Flores tends to shut down after dark. Though the restaurants mentioned here are perfectly fine for stopping in for a drink, you may find yourself drinking alone. Depending on the season, it can get very quiet here and some places may even shut their doors well before their posted 1 A.M. closing time. On weekends, locals like to party and if you are up for it you can certainly mingle with them at any of a number of establishments. Just follow the sound of music.

Aside from being the finest restaurant on the island, **La Luna** (corner of Calle 30 de Junio and Calle 10 de Noviembre, tel. 7926-3346, Mon–Sat. until 1 A.M.) has a pretty swanky bar where you can enjoy the very atmospheric old building in which it's housed under a whirring ceiling fan. **Café-Bar Las Puertas** (corner of Calle Central and Avenida Santa Ana, tel. 7926-1061, 11 A.M.–midnight Mon.–Sat.) is popular with travelers for its margaritas, funky atmosphere and live music on weekends. A house across the street screens movies. Another favorite haunt for movie-watchers is the **Mayan Princess Café** (corner of Calle 10 de Noviembre and Avenida Reforma), showing movies at 4 P.M. and 9 P.M. daily.

Right on the lake, **Raíces Bar and Grill** (tel. 5521-1843, 2 P.M.–10 P.M. Sun.–Thurs., 2 P.M.–1 A.M. Fri./Sat.) is a great place to catch the sunset while you enjoy your favorite cocktail. You'll find the locals in the cantinas on the Playa Sur strip facing the Gran Hotel de la Isla, the best of which is **El Trópico.**

RECREATION

Although Flores's location by the lake would make water sports a logical recreational option, most of the town's recreation is either outside of town and curiously lacks the water-borne focus you would expect to find here. Still, you can rent **kayaks** and **mountain bikes** at La Villa del Chef (tel. 7926-0296, 8 A.M.–11 P.M. Mon.–Sun., 1 P.M.–11 P.M. Tues.–Sun.) for $7 a day.

The other main recreational option involves **lake tours** offered by various boatmen congregating at the embarcaderos opposite Hotel Santana and on Playa Sur. Direct *colectivo* boats ($0.50) can take you across the lake to the town of San Miguel and leave from a dock next to Restaurante Las Guacamayas. The lake tours can be had for $15–20 and include a trip to the lakeshore opposite the island's northwest corner to **Petencito Zoo,** the Mayan ruins of **Tayazal,** and **ARCAS,** a wildlife rescue center. (More details about these attractions can be found in the *Near Flores and Santa Elena* section.)

Guide Companies

The following recommended outfitters can hook you up with one- or multiday adventures to Petén's increasingly popular parks and archaeological sites. Flores makes a natural starting point because of its central location within Petén and its proximity to roads leading from here in all directions. **Tikal Connection** (Calle 15 de Septiembre, tel. 7926-4981, www.tikalcnx.com) works with local communities to involve them in the business of sustainable tourism in and around several of Petén's protected areas. Tikal Connection offers multiday treks from the site of El Zotz to Tikal, rigorous journeys to El Mirador, and the "Scarlet Macaw Trail," in Laguna del Tigre National Park near the Mayan site of Waka'-Perú.

Martsam Tours and Travel (Calle 30 de Junio in the lobby of Capitán Tortuga restaurant, tel. 7926-0346, www.martsam.com) has an excellent reputation and offers a variety of trips throughout Petén. In addition to El Zotz–Tikal, Waka'-Perú, and El Mirador, it offers day trips to Tikal and multiday adventures involving hikes from Tikal to Yaxhá, stopping in Nakum along the way. There are also daily departures from Flores to Yaxhá for $20 per person (minimum of two).

A relatively new venture, **Conservation Tours Tikal** (tel. 7926-0670 or 5592-9509, www.conservationtours.com) is run by locals Nery Medrano and Héctor Aldana. A spinoff of the environmental group Rare (www.rareconservation.org), the company is based out of El Café Chilero (Calle 15 de Septiembre, tel. 5571-9240, 8 A.M.–10 P.M. daily

except Tues.) and offers some unique options, including a jungle survival course, kayaking on Lake Petén Itzá, and mountain biking from Tikal to Uaxactún. Five percent of proceeds go directly toward the protection of the parks they work in. Another newcomer is **Inka Ti Jesh Maâch** (Playa Sur, tel. 7926-3529, www.tikalnaturalhistory.com), owned by the same family that has more than 30 years of experience managing the Tikal Inn. Ricardo Ortiz knows many of the best guides in Petén, depending on where you are going, and can point you in the right direction. Ortiz also claims to have pioneered the popular Tikal sunrise tours.

ACCOMMODATIONS
Under $10

Among the first places you'll come upon after crossing the causeway leading into Flores is **Hotel La Canoa** (tel. 7926-0853), where 10 rooms, all but one with private bath, go for $11 d. The room with shared bath goes for $4 per person. All rooms have firm beds, though the fluorescent lighting can be somewhat dreary. A bar directly underneath the rooms can make things noisy. Farther down the same street is **Hotel Playa Sur** (tel. 7926-0351, $7 d). Its 10 clean rooms feature firm beds, fan, and make a stab at decor. Another option in this part of town is **Hotel El Faisán** (tel. 7926-3438, $11 d), with ceiling fan, cable TV, and acceptably firm beds. The electric hot-water heaters, however, look a bit scary.

Hotel Mirador del Lago (Calle 15 de Septiembre south of Avenida Flores, tel. 7926-4363) is a good value at $11 d in somewhat plain rooms with firm beds and fan. Its 32 rooms are spread between two buildings on opposite sides of the street. Two rooms on the top floor with lake views go for $16. The eight rooms at **Posada de Don José** (Calle Fraternidad, laposadadonjose@hotmail.com, tel. 7926-1371,) offer firm beds, cable TV, air-conditioning ($20 d) or fan ($11 d), electric hot water, and some attempt at decor in a nice family atmosphere. In-room lighting is fluorescent. Guests have free use of the kitchen and there is a tranquil hammock area on the second floor overlooking the lake.

Calle Unión holds a high concentration of lodgings in this budget category. A popular option is **Hospedaje Doña Goya** (tel. 7926-3538), where rooms with shared bath and fan go for $11 and those with private bath cost $13 d. Guests gather at the rooftop terrace with lake views at sunset. An annex just a few houses down, **Doña Goya the 2nd** (tel. 7926-3540), features rooms with slightly more comfortable beds and fan starting at $11 d. Rooms with private bath, air-conditioning, cable TV, and lake views rent for $25 d.

For the best value in town head to Flores's new hostel, **[Los Amigos** (Calle Central next to ProPetén, tel. 5584-8795 or 5521-2873, www.amigoshostel.com). This backpacker's paradise features a restaurant/bar, security lockers, broadband Internet, and laundry service among its well-rounded list of amenities. The friendly Guatemalan and Dutch owners can also help you plan your travels to other parts of Guatemala. For the ultimate in affordable lodging, you can sleep in a hammock for under $3 or in dorm beds costing $3.50. Private rooms with shared bath cost $8 d or $11 d with private bath.

$10-25

There are several good options in this category, including **Hotel La Mesa de Los Mayas** (Avenida La Reforma, tel. 7926-1240, mesamayas@hotmail.com), where clean rooms with reading lamp, cable TV, hot water, and fan cost $20 d. Rooms with air-conditioning are $25. Across the street is the new **Villa Margarita** (tel. 7926-3240, $13 d). Its nine clean but rather plain rooms have firm beds, air-conditioning, cable TV, and private bath with electric hot water. Another good choice on Avenida La Reforma, to the south, is **Hotel El Peregrino** (Calle Reforma Casa #3, tel. 7926-0477, h_peregrino@hotmail.com), a family-run operation in a three-story building where rooms have cable TV and ceiling fan. Rooms with private bath are $17 d; two rooms with shared bath go for $13. **Hotel Posada de la**

Jungla (corner of Calle 30 de Junio and Calle Centroamerica, tel. 7926-0634, www.travel peten.com) offers fan-cooled rooms for $13 d or air-conditioned rooms for $30 d. All have private bath and basic furnishings, including a bedside table and chairs. Internet service is also available.

On Calle 30 de Junio, a good choice in this category is the friendly **[Hotel Mayab** (tel. 7926-3411, $13 d), offering cable TV, hot water, ceiling fan, comfortable beds, and some nice decorative touches. The spotless rooms are painted a pleasant light green, evoking tranquility and space. The reflected fluorescent accent lighting is surprisingly pleasant. Some upstairs rooms have balconies with lake views for the same price. Across the street is the simpler **Hotel Santa Rita** (hotelsanta rita_flores@yahoo.es, tel. 7926-3224), where slightly less attractive rooms with ceiling fan, hot water, and stiffer mattresses cost $11 d. Rounding out the list of possibilities is **La Casa del Lacandón** (Calle Unión, tel. 7926-4359), where pleasant enough rooms with fan and private bathroom (some with lake view and terrace) rent for $13 d.

$25-50

Several Flores hotels fall into this price range. Among them are three belonging to **Corpetur** (www.hotelesdepeten.com), a local hotel chain of excellent repute. The first of these properties is **Casazul** (Calle Unión, tel. 7926-1138, $35–50), where pleasant rooms with air-conditioning, cable TV, private bath, and minibar are housed in a pretty blue house, as its name would indicate. It has a nice balcony with wonderful lake views. **Hotel Petén** (Calle 30 de Junio, tel. 7926-3328, $35–50) is said to be the island's oldest hotel, dating to 1960. You have a choice of air-conditioning and/or ceiling fan in its smallish but comfortable rooms with private bath and cable TV, some of which have balconies overlooking the lake. There are a small swimming pool and dining room on the ground floor just opposite the lobby. Probably the nicest of the three Flores Corpetur properties is the lively **[La Casona de la Isla**

(Calle 30 de Junio, tel. 7926-0593, $40–55), an attractive lakeside house painted in bright yellow and orange hues housing 26 rooms with air-conditioning, cable TV, and private bath. There is a nice outdoor swimming pool, around which the rooms are centered, as well as a whirlpool. The hotel's Isla Bonita restaurant and bar serves three delicious meals a day at reasonable prices.

An excellent value in this price range is **Ⓒ Hotel Casa Amelia** (Calle Unión, tel. 7926-3328). Its attractive, spotless rooms with original decor incorporating burlap bags for curtains, wooden furnishings, firm beds, ceiling fan, air-conditioning, and large hot-water bathroom go for $37 d. Some of the 10 rooms have nice lake views. All have large cable TV. **Hotel Sabana** (Calle Fraternidad, tel. 7926-1248, www.hotelsabana .com, $37) is painted in pretty pastel greens and offers comfortable rooms with air-conditioning, cable TV, in-room phone, reading lamps, and hot water. Some rooms have ceiling fans. There are a swimming pool with deck chairs for lounging and a restaurant, which may or may not be open depending on whether the hotel is hosting tour groups, which fill this usually quiet hotel to capacity. Under the same management as Tikal's Jungle Lodge, the **Hotel Isla de Flores** (corner of Avenida La Reforma and Calle 10 de Noviembre, tel. 2477-0570, $46) is a modern three-story building housing 18 comfortable rooms with ceiling fan, cable TV, firm beds, and air-conditioning. On Calle 30 de Junio, **Hotel Santana** (informacion@ santanapeten.com, tel. 7926-0662, $45 d) has 35 rooms with the usual amenities of its price category as well as firm beds, large mirror, and in-room safe-deposit box. Some rooms have very pleasant balconies with chairs and a hanging lamp. A swimming pool, colonial restaurant, and ice-cream shop are on the ground floor. The hotel caters periodically to large tour groups on package itineraries.

On Playa Sur, facing Santa Elena and the lake, is **Hotel El Itzá** (tel. 7926-3666), where large rooms with cable TV, ceiling fan, air-conditioning, and private bath with on-demand hot water can be had for $30 d.

$50-100

The island's most expensive hotel is near the causeway as you come into town on the shore facing Santa Elena. The multistory **Gran Hotel de la Isla** (tel. 7926-0686, ventas@hotelde laisla.com, www.hoteldelaisla.com, $80) is a large yellow building that seems somewhat out of place in mostly low-rise Flores. Rooms include all the usual comforts of its price range such as private bath, air-conditioning, cable TV, and attractive furnishings. There is a good restaurant/bar and a swimming pool dominated by a wall mural depicting Tikal's Gran Jaguar temple. Internet access is available in the lobby. It's nice enough, but unless you have your heart set on staying on the island, you may want to stay across the lake in Santa Elena in one of several comparable hotels in this price category.

FOOD

Flores has a small supermarket. **La Colmena** (corner Calle 30 de Junio and Avenida 10 de Septiembre, tel. 7926-1268) has a variety of your local and imported favorites. It also takes credit cards.

Coffee Shops and Cafés

Flores has no shortage of coffee shops and cafés, most of which offer something different and equally pleasing, depending on what you're in the mood for. **Café UKA** (Calle Centroamerica, tel. 7926-3493, all meals, closed Sun.) has an excellent assortment of coffees and snacks as well as Internet service. The **Mayan Sunset Café** (Calle 30 de Junio, tel. 7926-4726, 11 A.M.–11 P.M.) has a varied menu, including Thai chicken or beef, pasta, sandwiches, and quesadillas served on an airy deck overlooking the lake's western shore. There are a full bar and good music to chill out to. It also shows movies. Check the daily program to find out what's playing. **Ⓒ Café-Bar Las Puertas** (corner of Calle Central and Avenida Santa Ana, tel. 7926-1061, 11 A.M.–midnight

Mon.–Sat.) serves good espresso beverages and is a popular place, partially on account of its lively atmosphere as a bar with funky decor involving paint-splattered walls. Try one of the many pasta dishes, or if just here for a drink, go with a margarita.

El Café Chilero (Cool Beans Café) (Calle 15 de Septiembre, tel. 5571-9240, 8 A.M.–10 P.M. daily except Tues.) has a wide assortment of hot and cold coffee beverages using gourmet beans from a very well-known coffee farm in Alta Verapaz. It also serves smoothies and light meals in a relaxing jungle garden atmosphere and makes a great place for breakfast.

If you're looking for inspiration before an adventure to one of Petén's numerous archaeological sites, head to ◖ **Café Arqueológico Yaxhá** (Calle 15 de Septiembre, tel. 7926-0367, 7 A.M.–10 P.M. daily), where you can dine in a pleasant atmosphere featuring colorful Guatemalan tablecloths and photo montages of various Mayan sites, including Tikal, Yaxhá, and Nakum. Although it does a variety of dishes, including steak, chicken, seafood, pasta, and even curry, it specializes in what it calls "pre-Columbian" fare (a variety of Petén-Yucatec dishes), which come highly recommended. It is also the local representative for La Casa del Jade, a jade shop based in Antigua, and has a small assortment of jade jewelry on display. A separate dock on the island's western shore is open 5 P.M. to 11 P.M. and is a great place to go for an evening swim or watch the sunset from a hammock while enjoying your favorite drink.

Also on Calle 15 de Septiembre, **La Galería del Zot'z** (tel. 7926-1257, 6 A.M.–10 P.M. daily) serves decent sandwiches, pizzas, and pastas as well as good coffee and espresso drinks in a quaint atmosphere next to the quiet street.

Cheap Eats

On the street facing Playa Sur (South Beach), across from the Gran Hotel de la Isla, is **Lita's** (tel. 7926-3259, all meals daily), serving quality deli sandwiches and smoothies. It opens early and closes late. Plans call for Flores's first ATM to be installed here. It may be a reality by the time of your visit, making the trip

across the causeway to Santa Elena to get cash a thing of the past. Also on Playa Sur and a safe bet for cheap eats is **Los Peches** (5 A.M.–midnight daily), just off the causeway as you enter town, where you can eat from a set menu of chicken, fried fish, burgers, and steaks for about $3.50. It's open early for those crack-of-dawn bus rides to Belize and Tikal. Next door is **Restaurante La Canoa** (tel. 7926-0853) in the hotel of the same name. There are cheap eats here and a decent bar where it is purportedly always happy hour.

Asian

The island's sole Asian food recommendation is **Suica** (Calle Fraternidad, tel. 7926-3790, 1 P.M.–10 P.M. daily), where you can sit on woven mats and dine on sushi, fried rice, and other pan-Asian staples for about $4. It also has books for sale.

Steak Houses

La Hacienda del Rey (corner of Calle Playa Sur and Calle 30 de Junio, tel. 7926-3647, all meals daily) is a South American steak house in the $10 range set in a wooden building with open sides that allow breezes to flow. It serves tacos in addition to sizable *parrilladas* (South American–style barbecued meats). A bar on the second floor, **La Taberna del Rey,** is set in an open-air deck overlooking the street below. Down the street on the island's western shore is ◖ **Raíces Bar and Grill** (tel. 5521-1843, 2 P.M.–10 P.M. Sun.–Thurs., 2 P.M.–1 A.M. Fri./Sat.), serving large portions of grilled steak, chicken, and fish with scrumptious side dishes in a hip semioutdoor setting featuring a deck built over the lake around a hollowed-out fishpond. If you're lucky, you might catch a thunderstorm here during the rainy season for a spectacular lakeside lightning show. Prices are in the $10 range. Order the kebabs and share with a friend. If you're into exotic meats or just want to give them a try, check out **Restaurante El Gran Jacal** (Calle Centroamerica, tel. 7926-3578, 7 A.M.–10 P.M. daily), where the specialty is farm-raised venison, Petén turkey, and *tepescuintle*. For a touch of authentic Petén cuisine, try the Pollo a la Jacal, tasty chicken in a somewhat sweet sauce.

International

Housed in a tastefully decorated old building festooned with overhanging bougainvillea blossoms and painted in bright shades of green and blue, the finest restaurant in Flores is undoubtedly **(La Luna** (corner of Calle 30 de Junio and Calle 10 de Noviembre, tel. 7926-3346, lunch and dinner Mon.–Sat., main dishes $6–12). Culinary highlights include stuffed peppers, steak in a black pepper cream sauce, boneless chicken breast in wine sauce, pastas, and vegetarian dishes, including falafel. Also on Calle 30 de Junio is **(Capitán Tortuga** (tel. 7926-0247, 7 A.M.–10 P.M. daily). There is a spacious dining room housed under a large *palapa* structure and a two-story terrace with lake views where you can enjoy pasta, tacos, sandwiches, chicken quesadillas, grilled meats, and tasty pizzas in addition to a fully stocked bar. For snacks, try the burritos for about $5. Across the street is **(La Albahaca** (tel. 7926-3354 or 7926-0505, 6 P.M.–11 P.M. Tues.–Sun.), a cozy little place with a quiet atmosphere serving delicious beef and chicken recipes as well as scrumptious homemade pasta at reasonable prices. There is a nice assortment of Chilean wines.

For pizza and Italian food, try **Pizzería Picasso** (Calle 15 de Septiembre, tel. 7926-0673, 10:30 A.M.–10:30 P.M. Tues.–Sun.) for reliable pastas and very good pizzas costing around $10 for a large pie. Across the street and on the water's edge is the very pleasant **Restaurante La Lunada** (tel. 5929-3049, 10 A.M.–10 P.M. or later, daily), serving a varied assortment of appetizers and tasty main dishes consisting of pasta, seafood, and steak as well as a full bar. The pleasant dining area is set on a dock over the lake and catches some good breezes because of its location on the eastern shore. There is a live marimba band here almost every night of the week. As you continue around the island, on Calle Fraternidad is **Restaurante La Guacamaya** (tel. 7926-4968, 10 A.M.–11 P.M. daily), where steaks and

Mexican tacos and burritos served in an airy *palapa*-style deck cost about $7.

There are a number of good choices along Calle Unión, on the island's northwest corner. The first of these is **La Villa del Chef** (tel. 7926-0296, 8 A.M.–11 P.M. Mon.–Sun., 1 P.M.–11 P.M. Tues.–Sun.), which theoretically specializes in Arab and Mediterranean food but serves a wide variety of sandwiches, pasta, chicken, and seafood dishes in an attractive lakeside atmosphere atop a small wooden deck. The *parrillada petenera* ($13) is a good option for sharing. Farther along this same street, **Restaurante Jalapeños** (Calle Unión, tel. 5554-3176, 7 A.M.–11 P.M. daily, closed Mon. in May and Sept.) has a decent "economic menu," from which you can choose spaghetti, burgers, soups, and chicken for $2.50–4. The menu here is similar to what you'd find at a U.S. casual dining chain and includes fajitas, ribs, enchiladas, and tasty burgers. Try the ribs in teriyaki sauce ($4). The atmosphere and service here are winners, too, with lake views under a thatched-roof, open-air hut. It is a popular place with travelers.

INFORMATION AND SERVICES
Tourist Information

The friendly folks at the INGUAT office (Central Plaza, tel. 7926-0669, Mon.–Fri. 8 A.M.–4 P.M.) can answer your questions and point you in the right direction. They also have a desk at the airport. Across the park, CINCAP (10 A.M.–noon and 2 P.M.–8 P.M. Mon.–Fri.) serves as an information center on *petenero* culture and has some very informative exhibits.

Communications

Flores's post office is about a block south of the plaza on Avenida Barrios. Calle Centroamerica has several places for access to the Internet. Among the options are Tikal Net and Petén Net, next door to each other and open 8 A.M.–10 P.M. daily. Farther along the same street is Café UKA (tel. 7926-3493, closed Sun.). Another option is Flores Net, just up the way on Avenida Barrios across from the post office. On the north end of town, try Tayazal Net (Calle Unión next to Doña Goya the 2nd, tel. 7926-2052, 8 A.M.–10 P.M. daily). Internet access costs about $1.40 per hour in most places.

Money
The only bank in Flores is Banrural, about a block east of the plaza, but there is no ATM. An ATM was purportedly being installed on Playa Sur across the street from the Gran Hotel de la Isla. Otherwise, you might find yourself crossing the causeway into Santa Elena to get cash at one of the banks there.

Laundry
The Mayan Princess Travel Agency on Calle 30 de Junio does laundry for about $4 a load (wash and dry). There's also Lavandería Petenchel, on Calle Centroamerica, and Lavandería Amelia, behind CINCAP.

Emergency and Medical Services
For the police, dial 7926-1365. The closest hospital is Hospital San Benito (tel. 7926-1459).

Volunteer Work
Volunteer opportunities are available with several of the NGOs working in town. Among the options is the opportunity to volunteer at the Las Guacamayas Biological Station in Laguna del Tigre National Park. (See the listing in *The Maya Biosphere Reserve* section for more information.) Another option is working with the local Wildlife Rescue and Conservation Association, or ARCAS (www.arcasguatemala.com), at its site on the other end of the lake opposite Flores's north shore. San Andrés–based Nueva Juventud Language School has set up a website for volunteers looking to work with it on various projects benefiting the local community. Check out www.volunteerpeten.com or send email at volunteerpeten@hotmail.com.

SANTA ELENA
Accommodations
Santa Elena has several pleasant accommodations along the lakeshore with wonderful views of Flores as well as a variety of less expensive options in the town center. Among the budget accommodations is **Hotel San Juan** (2a Calle between 6a and 7a Avenida, tel. 7924-8358), where you'll find rather plain rooms with saggy mattresses in a large concrete building. Rooms with and without air-conditioning are $20 and $10 d, respectively. A better choice is the **Jaguar Inn** (Calzada Virgilio Rodriguez Macal 8-79, tel. 7926-0002, www.jaguarinn.com, $20), where tastefully decorated rooms are centered around a courtyard and the helpful staff can help you plan your onward travel. Air-conditioning is an extra $5 and there is a small pizzeria on-site. The owners also have a hotel at Tikal National Park by the same name. Another good budget choice is **Hotel Posada Santander** (4a Calle, tel. 7926-0574), where spotless rooms with TV and shared bath go for $10 d. Rooms without TV but with private bath go for the same price. There is no hot water but there is a small restaurant nearby.

Hotel Continental (6a Avenida, south of Calzada Virgilio Rodriguez Macal, tel. 7926-0095, $10–20 d) offers a variety of prices and corresponding levels of comfort in its 51 rooms. The owners and staff are friendly.

Moving up in price range and correspondingly closer to the lakeshore is **Casa Elena** (Calle Principal, Ingreso a Isla de Flores, tel. 7926-2239, www.casaelena.com, $36), where 26 comfortable rooms are set in a pleasant colonial building around a nice swimming pool with palm trees and a garden. A popular repository for tour groups, the **Hotel del Patio** (8a Calle, tel. 7926-0104, www.hoteldelpatio .com.gt, $62) is comfortable and offers many services and amenities but has seen better days. Rooms are in a neocolonial building. Those on the first floor are particularly susceptible to mold. There are better deals elsewhere in this price range.

Along the lakeshore, as you approach town from the airport, is the ◖ **Maya Internacional** (tel. 2334-1818 central reservations or 7926-2083 direct, www.villasdeguatemala.com), with 24 standard rooms and two junior suites ranging in price $70–100. One of the area's first accommodations, the recently remodeled property features tastefully decorated rooms with balconies overlooking the lake, tiled floors, ceiling fans, air-conditioning, and cable TV. The lodge's Vista al Lago Restaurant offers fantastic lake views and a varied menu, including a Sunday brunch. A swimming pool, great service, wireless Internet, and lovely open-air *palapa* lobby round out the list of features making the Maya Internacional an excellent choice.

Farther along the lakeshore near the causeway connecting Santa Elena to Flores are a number of newer options, including the 62-room **Petén Espléndido** (tel. 2360-8140, www.peten esplendido.com), where doubles cost $90 and the feel is that of a U.S. chain hotel with all the usual amenities. Next door is the curiously named **Express by Maya Inn Hotel** (tel. 7926-1817), where 20 comfortable if bland rooms go for $40 d and include air-conditioning, cable TV, and somewhat cheerful furnishings. The in-room lighting is fluorescent.

The standout in this part of town is the 【 **Hotel Casona del Lago** (tel. 7952-8700, www.hotelesdepeten.com, $86–95 d), a beautiful blue house which could just as easily fit into the seaside landscape of Cape May, New Jersey. The large, bright rooms have spacious bathrooms, tasteful decor and the usual comforts, including cable TV. Some have lake views; all are centered around a pretty swimming pool with a whirlpool. The hotel's Restaurante Las Ninfas serves varied international cuisine for breakfast, lunch, and dinner in a pleasant dining room overlooking the pool and lake. The lobby is decorated with classic photos from Petén's past dating to the 1920s, 1930s, and 1940s, along with some more modern scenes.

Food

Although Flores is really where most of the action is, Santa Elena does have a few eateries worthy of mention. A perennial favorite is **Restaurante Mijaro** (Calle Principal, across from the Catholic church, tel. 7926-1615, 7 A.M.–10 P.M. daily), with a varied menu including fish, meats, pastas, and burgers at

very reasonable prices. For Mexican food and a lively atmosphere, head to **Viva Zapata** (8a Calle, across from Hotel del Patio, tel. 7926-4800), which is also a popular dance hall and live music venue. Locals like **Restaurante El Rodeo** (tel. 7924-8045, 10 A.M.–10 P.M. daily), conveniently situated across from Santa Elena's nicer lakefront resorts, for its Western-style decor meshed with tropical architecture and its good chicken, fish, steak, and pasta, mostly under $10. There is also a fully stocked bar. The nicer hotels, including Petén Espléndido and La Casona del Lago, have their own decent restaurants next to swimming pools with lake views. Of these, the best option is La Casona del Lago's **Restaurante Las Ninfas**, with a varied menu, including pastas and grilled meats. The outdoor restaurant at the Hotel Maya Internacional, **Vista al Lago** (tel. 7926-2083, 7 A.M.–9 P.M. daily), serves international dishes and is a fine choice for its Sunday brunch. It offers fantastic lake views from its covered wooden deck.

Money

Three blocks up 6a Avenida from the Flores causeway on the corner of 4a Calle is Banco Agromercantil with a MasterCard ATM. Three blocks west, also on 4a Calle, is Banco Industrial, with a Visa ATM.

GETTING THERE
Air

Flights arrive at **Mundo Maya International Airport** (FRS), a few kilometers outside of Santa Elena east on the road to Tikal. The airport was undergoing a substantial renovation and the facilities should be vastly improved (including badly needed air-conditioning) when the work is completed in late 2007. Most flights to the Flores/Santa Elena airport arrive from Guatemala City, with several daily frequencies on **TACA** (800/400-8222, www.taca.com) and a handful of smaller local carriers. TACA also flies to and from Cancún, Mexico. From Belize City, **Maya Island Air** (www.mayaisland air.com) and Tropic Air (800/422-3435, www .tropicair.com) fly to Flores several times daily.

The only direct service to FRS from the United States, a Saturday-only flight via Houston on Continental Express, was dropped in November 2006 after 18 months in operation.

Within Guatemala, travel agencies in Antigua, Panajachel, Guatemala City, or Quetzaltenango can help you find lower fares from Guatemala City to Flores on the regional carriers. These are in constant flux, with at least one of these airlines having recently gone under. Flights on TACA are usually in the $200 range for a round-trip flight, but you can often save a substantial amount by booking through one of these travel agencies. (See the corresponding sections for recommended travel agencies.)

Bus

Línea Dorada (tel. 7926-1788, www.tikal mayanworld.com, $15–30 one-way) has buses from Guatemala City at 10 A.M. and 9 P.M. daily, stopping in Río Dulce and Poptún along the way. There are also daily buses to and from Belize City ($17 one-way), leaving at 5 A.M. and 7:30 A.M. and returning at 2 P.M. and 5 P.M. Buses arrive and depart from the main bus terminal along 4a Calle in Santa Elena as well as from another office on Playa Sur in Flores (tel. 7926-3649).

You'll find minibuses to Melchor de Mencos, Poptún, and Sayaxché west of the market in Santa Elena on 4a Calle. Buses and minibuses to San José and San Andrés ($1, 40 minutes) leave from 5a Calle, west of the market.

San Juan Travel (2a Calle, Santa Elena, and Playa Sur, Flores, tel. 7926-0041/2) operates service to Belize City ($20), continuing to Chetumal, Mexico, leaving daily at 5 A.M. and 7:30 A.M. from its office on 2a Calle in Santa Elena. The shuttle also picks up passengers at the hotels in Flores and Santa Elena with prior arrangement. Return trips are at 9:30 A.M. and 4:30 P.M.

GETTING AROUND
Taxis and *Tuk-Tuks*

You'll find taxis at the larger hotels in Santa Elena and at the Mundo Maya International Airport. A taxi from the airport to Flores should cost no more than $3. More popular and much less expensive are the *tuk-tuks* (Asian-style motorized rickshaws) you'll find seemingly everywhere. Short trips of about a kilometer or two within the Flores/Santa Elena area on *tuk-tuks* are usually in the range of $0.75.

Shuttle Buses

Shuttle buses and minivans ply the road between Flores and Tikal. **Línea Dorada** (from the market in Santa Elena or Playa Sur in Flores, tel. 7926-1788, www.tikalmayanworld .com) makes the trip from Flores at 5 A.M., 8:30 A.M., and 3:30 P.M., returning at 2 P.M. and 5 P.M. and costing $3 one-way. **San Juan Travel** (2a Calle, Santa Elena, and Playa Sur, Flores, tel. 7926-0041/2) shuttles leave hourly between 5 A.M. and 10 A.M. with a final bus at 2 P.M. *Colectivo* buses also depart the Mundo Maya airport when there are flights coming in, also costing $3 one-way.

Car Rentals

You'll find several options at the airport upon your arrival. Among them are a few local operations I can't bring myself to recommend. **Hertz** (tel. 2470-3700 Guatemala City or 800/654-3001 U.S., www.hertz .com) and **Alamo** (tel. 800/462-5266 U.S., www.alamoguatemala.com) have offices in or near the airport.

NEAR FLORES AND SANTA ELENA

There are a variety of attractions in and around Flores and Santa Elena that work well if you have a day or half a day while awaiting connecting flights or onward travel. Several of these attractions—**ARCAS, Petencito Zoo,** and **Tayazal**—are a five-minute boat ride across the lake from Flores's north shore near the village of San Miguel. A road also goes this way along the shoreline and is useful in this discussion for orientation only, as most visitors find themselves catching a boat when heading out in this direction. You can take in 2–3 of these destinations as part of a lake

PETÉN

tour leaving from Flores, which should cost between $15 and $20. *Colectivo* boats ($0.50) leave from a dock beside Restaurante La Guacamaya, on the north shore of Flores, as they fill up.

◖ Parque Natural Ixpanpajul

Covering an area of nine square kilometers and conveniently just off the highway toward Guatemala City, the main attraction at Parque Natural Ixpanpajul (tel. 7863-1317, www.ixpanpajul.com, 6 A.M.–6 P.M. daily) is a series of six suspension bridges built over the forest canopy, giving you a toucan's-eye view of the forest. The trip along the forest trail takes a little more than an hour and includes a stop at a lookout point to take in the astounding view from the top of the mountain. Other activities include a Tarzan Canopy Tour (zip line), Spot Lighting (nighttime wildlife-viewing), horseback riding, mountain biking, tractor rides, and ATV rentals. You can tour the hanging bridges (Skyway) for $30 per adult or $22 per child. You also have a choice of mountain biking, tractor rides, or horseback riding, ranging from $5 to $25. Packages allow you to combine the Skyway with the Tarzan Canopy Tour and/or the Spot Lighting tour for a full day of adventure. You can combine two activities for $55 or all three for $75.

There is a campsite on the premises ($5) and you can rent tents ($10) and other equipment, but you have to book at least one of the main activities at a cost of $30.

The park can provide transportation from Flores or Tikal if you call in advance. A taxi from Flores should cost about $5.

Ak'tun Kan Caves

If you're really into caves and won't have time to explore the areas of Southern Petén or Las Verapaces, you might want to check out Ak'tun Kan (8 A.M.–5 P.M. daily, $1.50), also known as the *cueva de la serpiente* for the large snake said to inhabit it. To get there, follow 7a Avenida south out of Santa Elena until you get to the power plant, turn left

to get to its east side, and continue south another kilometer.

Hotel Villa Maya

As you head east along the road to Tikal, an unpaved road cuts north toward the Petenchel Lagoon for about four kilometers to the excellent ◖ Hotel Villa Maya (tel. 5410-1592, www.villasdeguatemala.com, $85 d), with its 56 comfortable, tastefully decorated rooms equipped with air-conditioning, hot water, and balcony overlooking the placid lagoon. There are also a swimming pool and an excellent restaurant. It's a bit out of the way, but the exclusive feel of this jungle outpost only adds to its allure.

Petencito Zoo

Farther west along this same road leading to the village of San Miguel is Petencito Zoo (8 A.M.–5 P.M., $3), housing a collection of local wildlife, including jaguars, monkeys, and macaws. The intrepid can ride the concrete water slides here, though their safety is questionable and at least one death has been reported.

ARCAS

Continuing west, the road again connects to the larger Lake Petén Itzá to ARCAS (tel. 7926-0946, www.arcasguatemala.com), the Wildlife Rescue and Conservation Association, where an animal rehabilitation center harbors animals captured from poachers, including jaguars, macaws, monkeys, and coatis. Although the animal rehabilitation area is not open to outsiders, an **Environmental Education and Interpretation Center** caters to the casual visitor. There is a nature trail showcasing a variety of medicinal plants, a beach, a bird observation platform, and an area for observing animals that cannot be reintroduced to the wild.

Although the site is perfectly accessible by road, most visitors come by boat. Tours leave Flores on weekdays at 8:30 A.M. (Spanish) and 3:30 P.M. (English) from the boat dock next to Restaurante La Guacamaya on the north end of the island. A tour costs $7 per person for a group of 1–2 people. Call ahead to confirm availability. You can also take a tour 9 A.M.–3 P.M. for $1.25 but you'll have to arrange your own transportation. Confirmation is not required if you choose to go this route.

Tayazal

Not to be confused with Tayasal, which once occupied the same territory as present-day Flores, the remains of this small site can be found up a hill near the village of San Miguel. Although the ruins themselves are not overly impressive, there is a wonderful lookout, known as a mirador, built into a tree atop a temple mound from where you have an exceptional view of Flores. The lookout is about two kilometers outside of town. Follow the signs for the "mirador."

Chal Tun Ha Lodge

Adding to the charm of this side of the lake is the recently opened 🌑 **Chal Tun Ha Lodge** (tel. 7926-3493, info@chaltunha.com, www .chaltunha.com, $16 d), on a three-acre forest preserve west of San Miguel. Each of the six charming wooden cabins is set on a raised platform and is fully screened with well-ventilated canvas roofing, private hot-water showers, and wonderful lake views from a private balcony. Activities include hiking, canoeing, bird-watching, horseback riding, and mountain biking. A pretty beach known as **La Playita** is also nearby.

Lake Petén Itzá

Once a pit stop for travel between Flores and Tikal, Lake Peten Itzá is quickly becoming a destination in its own right. The area around El Remate is home to Petén's fanciest accommodations, the 72-room Camino Real Tikal and the smaller, more exclusive La Lancha. There are also simpler accommodations, allowing you to take in the serene beauty of this large lake without busting your budget.

On the western shores of the lake, the towns of San Andrés and San José offer pleasant lakeside atmosphere and are an excellent place to learn Spanish. Language instruction here is combined with the opportunity to experience Petén's rich ecology and even contribute to its preservation while helping to meet the needs of local people. The Itzá culture has largely survived the onslaught of modernity and its people are more than willing to share their proud heritage with visitors.

SAN ANDRÉS AND SAN JOSÉ

The road from Flores heads west before cutting north along the lakeside to the small town of San Andés on its shores. You'll find the people here and in neighboring San José extremely friendly and laid-back. Many of the villagers still make their living from

Lake Petén Itzá beckons for a swim.

© AL ARGUETA

PETÉN

harvesting forest products such as chicle, allspice, and *xate* palm. The NGOs have been particularly active here since the creation of the Maya Biosphere Reserve and have found the communities very amenable to their conservation goals. The creation of a Spanish school was done in partnership with Conservation International several years ago, providing a viable alternative for income along the lines of sustainable development. The successful model has been emulated elsewhere, and there are now four Spanish schools operating in this area. They offer a unique alternative to more typical language-school destinations, where a large presence of foreigners sometimes works against the language-immersion experience.

Although the towns are accessible from Flores by boat, the high cost of motorboat fuel and the ease of access from the road have made this a less popular option for getting here. Still, boats sometimes leave from the boat dock near Hotel Santana and this is still the best option if you're staying at the wonderful Ni'tun Lodge near San Andrés.

San Andrés

Most travelers in these parts are almost certainly studying Spanish or helping out with one of the local NGOs in conservation or community development projects. Rates at all the area schools are comparable, somewhere between $150 and $175 per week, including 20 hours of one-on-one instruction and room and board with a local host family. The original San Adrés language school, **Eco-Escuela de Español** (tel. 5498-4539 or 5490-1235, www .ecoescuelaespanol.org), is still going strong and is the area's largest. Also in San Andrés is the newer **Nueva Juventud Spanish School** (tel. 5711-0040, www.volunteerpeten.com), set on a medicinal plant reserve where the focus is largely on volunteer opportunities with various projects benefiting the local community. Recent projects have included the construction of a local library and schools.

For budget accommodations in San Andrés, try the **Hotel Corina,** set atop a hill to the left as you come into town.

A more luxurious option is found three kilometers east of San Andrés along the road from Flores and then a few kilometers down a rugged dirt road accessible only by 4WD vehicle. Charmingly rustic [C] **Ni'tun Lodge** (tel. 5201-0759 or 5414-5780, www.nitun.com, $150 d) is set on the lakeshore with comfortable cabins made from stone, stick, and mortar. Inside you'll find wooden tree-trunk floors and typically Guatemalan accents, including Mayan blankets, rugs, and wooden furniture. All rooms have private hot-water bathroom. Wireless Internet and DirecTV may have been installed by the time you read this. Room rates include breakfast. Gourmet meals, including a choice between 2–3 main courses, cost $20–25 for lunch or dinner. Most of the lodge's high-end clientele arrives by boat from Flores on all-inclusive packages, which you can book directly through the lodge. The lodge's creator and live-in manager, Bernie, has explored Petén extensively and is also the inspiration behind **Monkey Eco Tours,** which can take you to many of Petén's more remote sites in relative comfort and style with accordingly expensive prices. A five-day trek to El Mirador, for example, costs $225 per person per day.

San José

San José is a surprisingly pleasant town complete with a municipal recreation area on the lakeshore. Its somewhat steep streets meander into the surrounding hillside, affording stunning views of the pretty bay below. Adding to the town's intrigue is a Mayan cultural revival of the Itzá people. You'll see signs in this Mayan dialect around town. A community organization, the **Bio Itzá,** has its own language school and also manages a private forest preserve north of town along the fringes of El Zotz-San Miguel La Palotada Biotope.

According to local lore, the Itzá people came to San José from the Yucatán site of Chichén Itzá, led by the mythical figure Taitzá along a pathway known as the Camino Real 100 years before the arrival of the Spanish in the New World. Another unique aspect of the local culture are the town's two main annual **fiestas.** The first of these takes place between

March 10 and 19 and includes a parade and fireworks, capped off by an unusual costumed dance in which a young girl and a horse skip together through the town streets. The second annual festival takes place on October 31 and November 1. It begins with a solemn Mass in the town's Catholic church, which houses three skulls in a glass case thought to belong to Spanish missionaries or the town's founders, depending on whom you believe. One of these skulls is removed from its resting place and is put on the church altar during the service; it is then carried through town on a velvet pillow by black-clad devotees, followed closely by children in traditional village costume and townsfolk. The procession stops along the way in several homes, where cane liquor, along with traditional food, are consumed and prayers and chants are offered. At the end, the skull is returned to its glass case in the town church, where it remains on display throughout the year.

The first of the town's two Spanish schools, **Escuela Bio Itzá** (tel. 7926-1363, bioitza@ guate.net), works with the Bio Itzá's women's cooperative, which runs a botanical garden for the production of natural products such as soap. San José's other language school is the more recently established **Mundo Maya Ecological Spanish School** (tel. 7928-8321, www.mundomayaguatemala.com). For food, there's pleasant **El Búngalo** serving reasonably priced Guatemalan fare right by the lakeside.

For accommodations, there's splendid **◖ Bahía Taitzá** (along the road into town, tel. 7928-8125 or 5402-1961, www.taitza.com, $47 d), set along the lakeshore on one of Lake Petén Itzá's prettiest beaches. Its eight comfortable rooms are housed in a large building. All have high wooden ceilings and come equipped with fan, tiled floors, comfortable beds, and private hot-water bath. A patio out front offers nice views of the manicured lawns toward the lake. There are lakeside hammocks and a restaurant/bar serving good food and wonderful cocktails.

◖ EL REMATE

El Remate starts about one kilometer past the turnoff to Yaxhá and the Belize border on the road from Santa Elena to Tikal. Once considered a stopping point along this road, El Remate has come into its own in recent years and has begun to pull its fair share of the Petén travel market. Its proximity to Tikal, fabulous lakeside setting, and variety of accommodations makes it a wonderful alternative to staying at Tikal or Flores, or better yet, a destination unto itself worthy of at least one night's stay.

Sights

The turnoff for the road heading west toward Belize, about two kilometers south of El Remate, was once known as "El Cruce," though the small settlement here is now known as **Ixlú.** Just off the road, about 200 meters down a signed path, are the ruins of **Ixlú** on the shores of **Laguna Salpetén.** There is a basic campsite where you can rent canoes to take on the lake, but there is otherwise little else to do. A small information center can be found under a thatched-roof shelter by the road, with toilets and a map of the site.

Along the shores of Lake Peten Itzá, three kilometers down a dirt road heading west from the main Tikal-bound branch, is the **Biotopo Cerro Cahuí** (7 A.M.–5 P.M. daily, $4). This 650-hectare mountainside park is particularly good for **bird-watching** and was initially set aside for the protection of Petén's oscillated turkey. It encompasses part of the lake's watershed and ranges in elevation 100–360 meters above sea level. You'll find several lowland rainforest species of birds, including toucans, parrots, and trogons. Two trails (2.75 miles or 3.75 miles long) take you up the hill into the surrounding forest to lookout points where there are wonderful views of the lake below. Maps and information are available at the entrance kiosk. A swimming dock near the entrance juts to a splendidly clear expanse of turquoise water and is a great place for a swim.

Shopping

El Remate is also a great place to pick up local crafts, consisting of some very attractive wood carvings made from fallen logs and providing a sustainable alternative to wide-scale forest

PETÉN

destruction for agriculture. You'll find several handicrafts shops on the main strip along the road to Tikal.

Recreation

Bird-watching tours with knowledgeable, English-speaking local guides can be arranged from La Casa de Don David (tel. 7928-8469 or 5306-2190, www.lacasadedondavid.com) and cost between $40 and $75 for a 3–6 hour tour. In addition to Cerro Cahuí, trips are available across the lake to roosting sites and other birding areas up the Río Ixpop and Río Ixlú.

Most of the area lodges can arrange **horseback riding** to Ixlú and Laguna Salpetén for about $20 per person. Casa Mobego (tel. 5909-6999) does **walking tours** to Laguna Salpetén for $10 per person and rents double **kayaks** for about $4 for one hour or $8 for four. Casa de Doña Tonita (tel. 5701-7114) also rents kayaks for about $2 an hour and **mountain bikes** for $5 a day. Alternatively, La Casa de Don David can arrange almost anything you can think of and also sells discount tickets to area **canopy tours.**

There are some wonderful **swimming** docks around the lake, the best of these at Restaurante El Muelle along the main road, in front of the Cerro Cahui Biotope, and in front of Casa Mobego.

Accommodations

You'll find plenty of accommodations along the town's main drag beside the northbound Tikal road as well as along the dirt road diverting west that hugs the lakeshore.

Under $10: From the northbound Tikal road, the first place you'll come across (on the right) is the **Mirador del Duende** (tel. 5527-0859, miradordelduende@gmail.com), charging $5 for accommodations in seven open-air concrete campsites with thin mattresses and mosquito netting. There's a restaurant serving vegetarian food, a chill-out room, and a place to store valuables. You can also camp or sleep in a hammock for just under $3. The next place down is the colorful, offbeat, and laid-back **Hotel Sak Luk** (tel. 5494-5925,

tikalsakluk@hotmail.com), where four- or five-person dorms with lake views and mosquito netting start at $3 per person. Rooms with private bath, mosquito netting, and lake view are available for $13 d. Hammocks go for $2 and you can camp here for the same price. There is a restaurant serving Italian food and you can have your laundry done here. Guests can also use the kitchen to cook their own meals. Language courses and volunteer opportunities are also available.

Another cheapie along the Tikal road is **Bruno's Place** (tel. 7928-8080, $8 d), with seven shared-bath rooms of acceptable cleanliness with fan and splashes of decor. Entrance is through the host family's living room. Across the street is the friendly **Hotel y Restaurant Sun Breeze** (tel. 7928-8044 or 5898-2665), where clean, simple rooms with mosquito netting and fan go for $10 d in shared-bath accommodations or $13 d with private bathroom. The owner is expanding to include a dormitory. The helpful staff can do your laundry and also arrange reasonably priced transport or guided tours to area attractions such as Tikal and Yaxhá.

On the dirt road running alongside the Lake Petén Itzá shore toward Cerro Cahuí Biotope are a number of very pleasant budget accommodations set far off from the noise of the main highway. **Hostal Casa Mobego** (tel. 5909-6999) is a popular place, also known as Casa Roja. Rooms with shared bath are housed in attractive stone and wood cottages; beds on a concrete base with squishy foam mattress and mosquito netting cost $5 per person. There is a nicely decorated main house where breakfast is served ($5) and dinner ($7) can be arranged with a bit of notice. There's also a book exchange, kayaks for rent, and the staff can arrange minibus transportation anywhere you may need to go. As you continue along the road, a few steps away is **Casa de Doña Tonita** (tel. 5701-7114), offering five simple wooden cabins, all with shared bath and hammocks on balconies affording lovely lake views for $4 per person. A night in the five-bed dorm will set you back a mere $3.50. There is a nice dock out front over the lake with hammocks. **Hotel Don Ernesto** (tel. 5750-8375) is another budget option in this neck of the woods where you have a choice of rooms with shared bath for $4 per person or slightly nicer rooms with private bath, ceiling fan, and deck with hammock for $27 d. A restaurant serves breakfast, lunch, and dinner.

Farther down the road as you approach the entrance to Cerro Cahuí is **Hotel y Restaurante Mom Ami** (tel. 7928-8413 or 7928-8480, www.hotelmonami.com), with a variety of accommodations from a six-bed dormitory with shared bath at $5 per person to bungalows with private hot-water bath costing $16–33 d. The lodge is owned by ecologist Santiago Billy, a pioneer of Peteén's environmental movement who has fought for many years for the preservation of the Maya Biosphere Reserve.

$10-25: There are several excellent values in this price range. Along the main road, you'll find **Posada Ixchel** (tel. 7928-8475), where simple but clean rooms in wooden cabins with shared bath go for $11 d. All have fans; most have mosquito netting and porches with chairs for lounging. Down the street and around the corner you'll find **((Hostal Hermano Pedro** (tel. 2332-4474, hermanopedro12@yahoo .com), a charming little place with a friendly Guatemalan owner. Rustically comfortable wooden bedrooms with high ceilings, hot water, and private bath cost $12 per person, including breakfast. Rooms have patios with chairs and hammocks and there is a small restaurant serving three meals a day. On the ground floor there are several *piletas,* or small pools, for soaking among the tastefully decorated garden festooned with orchids. There is an additional sitting room with hammocks where you can catch the breezes off the lake.

Along the lakeside road, adjacent to the Cerro Cahuí preserve, is the **Hotel Jardín Maya** (tel. 5730-7433), a family-run guesthouse where three rooms with private bath, mosquito netting, and decks with hammocks go for $20 d. There is a small café for guests serving drinks and light meals. The Guatemalan family that owns the lodge is very welcoming and knowledgeable about the area.

$25-50: Along the lakeside road toward Cerro Cahuí, at the junction with the road leading to Tikal, is **((La Casa de Don David** (tel. 7928-8469 or 5306-2190, www.lacasa dedondavid.com), a highly recommended establishment owned by a native Floridian transplanted to Guatemala in the late 1970s. His friendly wife and daughter help run the lodge, consisting of 15 rooms with private hot-water bath set amid nicely landscaped grounds. Eleven of the rooms have air-conditioning; all have fans. Rates range from $32 d for slightly noisier rooms with fan under the restaurant to $52 d for quieter rooms with air-conditioning set farther back from the main house. All prices include one free meal a day. The restaurant serves delicious international dishes ranging $4–8 for lunch or dinner. The friendly staff can help you book transportation to virtually anywhere and can answer your travel questions. You can also snag discounted tickets for area canopy tours at the attractive gift shop in the main lobby. The hotel's very informative website is well worth checking out before visiting Petén.

Charming **((La Mansión del Pájaro Serpiente** (tel. 7928-8498, $44) is another fine choice. Owned by a Guatemalan-American family, the lodge sits along the main road to Tikal at the northbound entrance to El Remate. Set on a hillside overlooking the lake are 11 stylish rooms housed in stone and thatched-roof exteriors with Guatemalan furnishings and stone, tile, and wood accents; they have fan and private hot-water bath inside. It has a restaurant serving three meals a day and a swimming pool amid the tropical landscape.

$50-100: In this price range is the **Hotel Gringo Perdido** (tel. 2334-2305, www.hotel gringoperdido.com, $60–80 d), which started several years ago as a budget accommodation but has gradually worked its way into pricier domains. Rates include a tasty four-course dinner and breakfast. The lodge's setting is right on the lakeshore within the boundaries of the Cerro Cahuí preserve. Rooms have private bath and are semiopen with roll-up blinds.

You can also stay in the shared-bath dormitory for about $10 per person.

$100-200: Lake Petén Itzá is not without a large resort. Enter the **Camino Real Tikal** (tel. 7926-0204/09, www.caminoreal.com.gt, $120 d), a 72-room complex that has been in operation for 15 years. A planned expansion may make it twice as large by the time you read this. The Camino Real has all the comforts you would expect from an international resort chain. The modern rooms are housed in concrete structures topped with thatched-roof exterior. There are two restaurants, a bar, coffee shop, and swimming pool. Recreational activities available to guests include sailing, kayaking, and sailboarding. A large ship does lake tours and transfers from the Mundo Maya International airport can be arranged before arrival via a free shuttle service. Discounted accommodation packages are often available by calling directly or booking via a travel agency.

For Petén's ultimate in style and luxury, head to fabulous **(La Lancha** (tel. 7928-

8331, www.blancaneaux.com), farther west along the lakeshore in the village of Jobompiche. Part of movie director Francis Ford Coppola's impressive portfolio of properties, including two other hotels in Belize, La Lancha is Petén's best-kept secret. Its 10 comfortable rooms are housed in lake-view casitas ($150–210 d) or rainforest casitas ($120–175 d, depending on season). All rooms have exquisite Guatemalan fabrics and Balinese hardwood furniture. The rooms' wooden decks are graced with hammocks where you can lounge the day away watching the sky's reflection on placid lake Petén Itzá or order drinks from the bar via your in-room "shell phone." Rates include a continental breakfast and the restaurant serves gourmet Guatemalan dishes for lunch and dinner for about $20 per person.

There is a swimming pool, but if you wish to cool off in the lake, a short downhill walk leads to the water's edge. Kayaks and mountain bikes are available for exploring at your leisure and you can book day trips to Tikal. Other activities include sightseeing in El Remate and Flores, fishing on the lake, and bird-watching at Cerro Cahuí. Construction of a honeymoon suite and family villa are in the works.

Food

There are a number of more-than-adequate restaurants in El Remate. Along the road to Tikal, the first place you'll come to is **(El Muelle** (tel. 5514-9785, all meals daily), serving daily specials for about $10. The menu is heavy on meat dishes and lake fish, but it also serves pasta, vegetarian fare, and a wide assortment of desserts. The atmosphere is quite pleasant with views of the lake and the establishment's attractive namesake dock from which you can take a refreshing plunge into the turquoise waters. Upstairs, five rooms with air-conditioning and private bath were nearing completion. Expect prices to be in the $50 d range. There is also a small gift shop selling books, wood carvings, and other knick-knacks.

Back on the road toward Tikal, the next place over is **Restaurante Cahuí** (noon–8:30 P.M. daily), a well-established place overlooking

© AL ARGUETA

view of Lake Petén Itzá from a room at La Lancha

the lake under an airy *palapa* roof, where a varied menu of inexpensive dishes is served. Along the road fringing the lake shore, you'll come across **Las Orquídeas** (tel. 5701-9022, lasorquideasremate@yahoo.com, 6 A.M.–10 P.M. Tues.–Sun.), serving decent pizza, pasta, and sandwiches. Just down the road, **Mon Ami** (tel. 7928-8413, all meals daily) serves tasty French and Guatemalan fare.

For a splurge, head to ◖ **La Lancha** (tel. 7928-8331, all meals daily) for gourmet Guatemalan cuisine for about $20 per person for lunch and dinner. You can enjoy an assortment of flavors from the Francis Ford Coppola wineries or your favorite drink from the bar while dining in an airy *palapa*-style building high above the lake. It's housed in its namesake lodge west of El Remate in Jobompiche.

Getting There and Around

El Remate is extremely easy to get to and from, as there is plenty of traffic heading up and down the road between Tikal and Flores. A local transport cooperative also operates minivans for trips to local attractions. Check with **Hotel y Restaurant Sun Breeze** (tel. 7928-8044 or 5898-2665) for availability and prices.

East to Belize

The road heading east to Belize is paved only about halfway despite repeated government announcements to the contrary. It seems the completed, paved road has been inaugurated by several presidents but the truth is that local authorities have inexplicably dragged their heels in getting one of the most important roads in Petén up to snuff.

There are some interesting sites along the way, the most important being the ruins of Yaxhá, 11 kilometers north from the main road. (The ruins are covered in the section on the *Maya Biosphere Reserve,* of which the site is a part.) Encouragingly, some of the lagoons and surrounding forest just north of this road are being opened to ecotourism by forward-thinking entrepreneurs, thus providing an alternative to the ecological destruction that has characterized the traditional northward advance of the agricultural frontier into protected lands.

LAGUNA MACANCHÉ

This lovely lagoon lies seven kilometers east of Ixlú, where there is a small settlement by the same name. A northbound, signed turnoff leads another two kilometers to **El Retiro Lakeside Sanctuary and Eco-Lodge** (tel. 5932-0644, www.retiro-guatemala.com, $40–60 d), a private nature preserve set on the spectacularly wild north shore of the turquoise lagoon. Accommodations are in comfortable thatched-roof bungalows with private hot-water bath and porch or in tents on raised wooden platforms. You can also camp here in your own tent. There are a good restaurant and a dock for swimming as well as a **serpentarium,** featuring 20 species of snakes found in Guatemala; all are professionally housed in secure glass tanks.

The lodge offers guided hikes on jungle trails to remote, jungle-lined lagoons and cenotes (limestone sinkholes) or nighttime crocodile scouting starting at $30 per person.

HOLTÚN

This small, unrestored Mayan site lies 30 kilometers from Ixlú and then a 20-minute walk south from the main road. It features small temple mounds and is really suitable only for the die-hard fan of Mayan ruins.

CANOPY TOUR

As in many tropical regions of Central America, there has been a widespread proliferation of so-called canopy tours, or zip lines between elevated platforms in the jungle. **La Ruta del Mono** (8 A.M.–5 P.M. daily, canopymonoruta@yahoo.com, $30) is one of three canopy tours found in Petén and is conveniently near the

PETÉN

ruins of Yaxhá, about five kilometers along the main road heading west toward Ixlú. It was featured on *Survivor Guatemala*.

MELCHOR DE MENCOS

This small border town sits on the edge of the Río Mopán and is fairly pleasant as far as border towns go. The border crossing with Belize is fairly straightforward, though you'll probably be asked to pay the local equivalent of about $1.50 to exit or arrive in Guatemala, which is technically illegal. Some travelers have asked for a receipt in an attempt to dissuade the collection of the token bribe, but border officials sometimes issue you a deposit stub stamped with an official-looking immigration seal. The account most likely belongs to the bribe's collector.

Many people cross the border from Belize on day trips to Tikal or Yaxhá from one of the Belize jungle lodges. Daily shuttle vans make the trip to the border from Flores continuing to Belize City and there is also public transport to the border from the bus depot in Santa Elena.

On the Belize side, there are buses leaving from the border every half hour. You can also take a taxi ride threee kilometers to **Benque Viejo del Carmen,** the first sizable settlement, from where there are more frequent services. Another 13 kilometers east is **San Ignacio,** a pleasant town with much to see and do.

Accommodations and Food

There is little reason to linger here, as at most border crossings in Guatemala, but there are at least two serviceable hotels should you need to spend the night here. Right at the border overlooking the Río Mopán is the aptly named **Río Mopán Lodge** (tel. 7926-5196, www.tikaltravel.com, $20 d). Its Swiss owner organizes various nature tours to local attractions, including remote archaeological sites such as Holmul, and is a great source for local information. Other activities include canoeing or tubing on the river. The lodge has a restaurant specializing in Mediterranean food. Another option is **Hotel La Cabaña** (Barrio El Centro, tel. 7926-5205, $40 d), with comfortable rooms including air-conditioning, private

hot-water bath, and cable TV. There are also a swimming pool and a restaurant serving local and international dishes. Aside from a few snack and drink stands on the road leading to the border crossing, these two hotels are your best (and really, your only) options for food.

MAYA MOUNTAINS-CHIQUIBUL BIOSPHERE RESERVE

South of Melchor de Mencos and skirting the border between Belize and Guatemala is the Maya Mountains–Chiquibul Biosphere Reserve. Although its name makes it sound rather official, it is really the epitome of a "paper park," as it lacks any real protection and is being lost due to the advance of the agricultural frontier originating around populated areas in southern Petén. Still, there remain some beautiful areas of intact forest and the park is certainly worth saving for the ruggedness of the terrain and its corresponding ecological and biological diversity.

Recreation

National Geographic has put the word out concerning the existence of Central America's longest cave network, the **Chiquibul caves,** which originate in Guatemala but continue for most of their expanse in Belize. The Zactun entrance (Guatemala) is the passageway to the westernmost **Xibalba** cave, harboring one of the cave system's largest chambers, averaging about 80 meters (260 feet) in width and accentuated by spectacular vaulted rooms. The caves are extremely remote and have been explored only by hard-core spelunkers. They are probably more easily accessible from Belize, which is where most scientists studying the caves have focused their efforts. It will be interesting to see if any work is done on the Guatemalan side during the next few years.

Access to the caves begins from the town of Dolores, 24 kilometers north of Poptún (See the *Poptún and Vicinity* section). From there, a gravel road leads to the settlement of Sacul Abajo. A rough dirt road continues to the village of Las Brisas, which is the final jumping-off point for the remaining 3–4-hour hike to the Zactun entrance. Dr. Ric Finch, a retired geology professor, has been leading trips to Guatemala since 1987. In April 2007, together with Antigua resident caver/explorer Mike Shawcross, Finch led a cavers' trip to various sites in Guatemala, including the Chiquibul caves. Finch and Shawcross scouted the access routes and contacted local guides in the village of Las Brisas. The trip may be replicated in the coming years. For more information, contact **Rutahsa Adventures** (299 Allen Hollow Rd., Cookeville, TN 38501, 931/520-7047 U.S., www.rutahsa.com).

The **Río Chiquibul** originates in the hills of Belize and flows westward into Guatemala, going underground in many places through the Chiquibul cave system. It's a cool jungle river perfectly suited for rafting trips. **Maya Expeditions** (tel. 2363-4955, www.mayaexpeditions.com) offers 1–3-day river trips ($85–130) via raft or kayak combining a visit to some little-explored caves along the river's course. Longer trips, including horseback riding to Mayan sites, are also available.

Tikal National Park

Tikal National Park, the oldest and best known of Guatemala's national parks, was created in 1956. It encompasses 575 square kilometers (222 square miles) of primary tropical forest and protects a vast array of wildlife, as well as harboring the remains of one of the Mayan civilization's greatest cities. Tikal is understandably high on the list of priorities for any visitor to Guatemala and shouldn't be missed, as it affords the unique opportunity to combine a visit to a site of mammoth historical importance both in terms of natural and human heritage. Owing to its singular importance in the spheres of natural and human history, UNESCO declared Tikal National Park a World Heritage Site in 1979.

Tikal's towering Temple I dominates the city's Great Plaza and is an icon for Guatemala itself, much like the Eiffel Tower and Paris. Perhaps not as readily apparent, Tikal National Park also represents the ongoing effort to protect what remains of Petén's tropical forest ecosystem. The park is at the edge, geographically speaking, of the Maya Biosphere Reserve, but at the very heart and soul of what conservationists and archaeologists are trying to protect. The conservation of Petén's rich archaeological and natural treasures has the potential to provide a livelihood to a growing population of *peteneros* long after any perceived benefits from clearing the forests for short-term gain.

The lessons learned from Tikal's 50-plus-year existence can help conservationists better manage newer parks deeper inside the forest reserve, which will eventually be open to increasing numbers of visitors. Whatever the approach to managing these newer parks, what is certain is that Petén's vast wealth as the heartland of the Mayan civilization remains largely untapped.

If you are fortunate enough to visit Tikal, go home with the knowledge that you have been afforded a glimpse into the vast wilderness that remains mostly untouched north of this complex. In the forests beyond Tikal are countless other sites, some still undiscovered, which deserve as much protection and require the vigilance of international travelers and activists to ensure their continued preservation.

HISTORY

Tikal was settled somewhere between 900 and 700 B.C. on a site undoubtedly selected because of its position above seasonal swamps that characterize much of the terrain in this part of Petéen, as well as the availability of flint for trade and the manufacture of tools and weapons. It remained little more than a small settlement for at least 200 years. By 500 B.C. the first stone temple was erected and later used as the basis for the large Preclassic pyramid dominating the complex now known as El Mundo Perdido. Tikal continued its steady progress

PETÉN

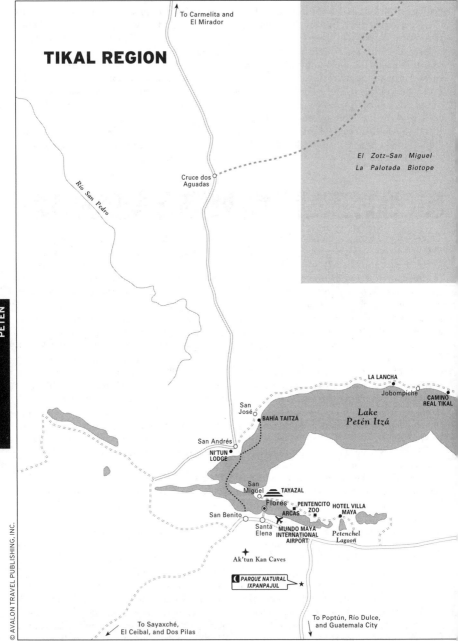

TIKAL REGION

To Carmelita and
El Mirador

Río San Pedro

Cruce dos
Aguadas

El Zotz–San Miguel
La Palotada Biotope

LA LANCHA
Jobompiche
CAMINO
REAL TIKAL

San
José
BAHÍA TAITZÁ

Lake
Petén Itzá

San Andrés
NI'TUN
LODGE

San
Miguel
TAYAZAL

Flores
PENTENCITO
ZOO
HOTEL VILLA
MAYA

San Benito
ARCAS

Santa
Elena
MUNDO MAYA
INTERNATIONAL
AIRPORT

Petenchel
Lagoon

Ak'tun Kan Caves

PARQUE NATURAL
IXPANPAJUL

To Sayaxché,
El Ceibal, and Dos Pilas

To Poptún, Río Dulce,
and Guatemala City

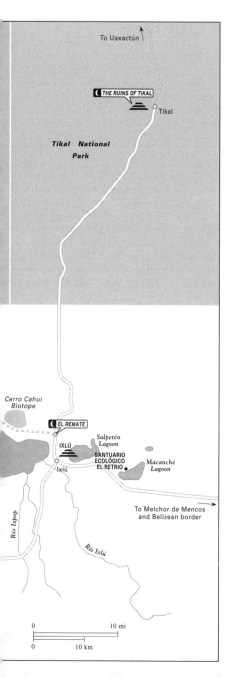

during the late Preclassic period, sometime around 200 B.C., with the construction of ceremonial buildings found in the North Acropolis and the completion of the pyramid at El Mundo Perdido.

Classic Period

By the time of Christ, Tikal's Great Plaza had begun to take shape and by the Early Classic period, around A.D. 250, Tikal was an important religious, commercial, and cultural center with a sprawling population. King Yax Ehb' Xoc established his dynasty at this time, one which was recognized by the 33 subsequent rulers of Tikal until recorded history at the site goes silent in A.D. 869.

The history of Tikal is closely tied to the emergence of Teotihuacán, a powerful city-state to the north in Central Mexico, which it should be noted was completely non-Mayan in origin. Its influence began to be felt during the middle of the 4th century A.D., when Teotihuacán dispatched a warrior by the name of Siyak K'ak' (Born of Fire) to aid Tikal in its war against the neighboring city of Uaxactún. Siyak K'ak' introduced the use of the atlatl, a wooden sling that allowed Tikal's warriors to defeat their enemy by firing arrows without having to engage in hand-to-hand combat. The aid from the north, according to recorded texts chronicling the execution of Tikal's Jaguar Paw I, amounted to a military takeover with the installation of Yax Nuun Ayin I (Curl Nose or First Crocodile), of Teotihuacán royalty, who later married into Tikal's dynasty.

With Teotihuacán hegemony now firmly established, Tikal dominated central Petén for most of the next 500 years. It grew to become one of the richest and most powerful Mayan city-states, aided by its dominance of strategic lowland trade routes. Tikal's influence reached as far south as Copán and as far west as Yaxchilán.

At the same time, the city-state of Calakmul, just north of the Guatemalan border in present-day Mexico, began its assent toward regional dominance. As the power and influence of Teotihuacán waned in the 5th century

A.D., Calakmul emerged as a geopolitical force to be reckoned with, incorporating a number of vassal states surrounding Tikal and contesting its dominion over the Mayan lowlands. A key alliance was forged between Calakmul and Caracol, in present-day Belize. Tikal launched a preemptive strike against Caracol in A.D. 556. With backing from Calakmul, Caracol launched a counterattack on Tikal in A.D. 562; the latter suffered a crushing defeat. Desecration of Tikal's stelae and ritual burials, in addition to the destruction of many of its written records, followed.

After this defeat, Tikal underwent a 130-year hiatus from erecting inscribed monuments, though it has recently been discovered that Temple V was constructed during this period. Mayanists now believe Tikal was never completely broken, despite defeat at the hands of its bitter rival.

Height of Power and Decline

Tikal reemerged as a dominant power beginning in A.D. 682 under the new leadership of Hasaw Chan K'awil (Heavenly Standard Bearer), whose 52-year reign was marked by the definitive defeat of Calakmul in A.D. 695 with reassertion of control over regional satellite cities such as Río Azul and Waka' as well as a frenzy of new temple construction. The six great temples dominating Tikal's ceremonial center were reconstructed between A.D. 670 and 810 by Hasaw Chan K'awil and his successors.

At the height of the Classic period, Tikal covered an area of about 30 square kilometers and had a population of at least 100,000, though some Mayanists believe it may have been much greater.

By the beginning of the 9th century A.D., conditions worsened for many city-states across the Mayan lowlands with the Classic Maya collapse in full swing. Tikal was no exception. The city-state's last inscription is recorded on Stela 24, which dates to A.D. 869. Tikal, like Petén's other Mayan cities, was completely abandoned by the late 10th century A.D. The city would be reclaimed by the jungle and largely forgotten until its rediscovery in the late 17th century.

Rediscovery

The Itzá who occupied the present-day island of Flores probably knew about Tikal and may have worshipped here. Spanish missionary friars passing through Peteén after the conquest mention the existence of cities buried beneath the jungle, but it wasn't until 1848 that the Guatemalan government commissioned explorers Modesto Méndez and Ambrosio Tut to visit the site. The pair brought along an artist, Eusebio Lara, to record their discoveries. In 1877, Swiss explorer Dr. Gustav Bernoulli visited Tikal and removed the carved wooden lintels from Temples I and IV. He shipped them to Basel, where they remain on display at the Museum für Völkerkunde.

Scientific study of the site would begin in 1881 with the arrival of British archaeologist Alfred P. Maudsley. His work was subsequently continued by Teobert Maler, Alfred M. Tozzer, and R. E. Merwin, among others. The inscriptions at Tikal owe their decipherment to the work of Sylvanis G. Morley. In the mid-1950s, an airstrip was built, making access to the site much easier. The University of Pennsylvania carried out excavations between 1956 and 1969, along with Guatemala's Institute of Anthropology and History. With help from Spanish Cooperation, Temples I and V have been restored as part of a project begun in 1991.

A relatively small part of Tikal has been officially discovered and excavated. New discoveries await, along with new information that will undoubtedly continue to shed light on the turbulent history of the Mayan civilization. Among the more recent discoveries are the 1996 unearthing of a stela from A.D. 468 in the Great Plaza and the location of Temple V inscriptions challenging the notion of Tikal's 130-year hiatus after its defeat against Calakmul.

FLORA AND FAUNA

Tikal's abundant wildlife is most active early and late in the day, with birds and forest creatures more easily seen at these times. The summit of Temple IV, Tikal's highest structure, is a particularly popular place at sunrise and sunset. From your position high above the forest

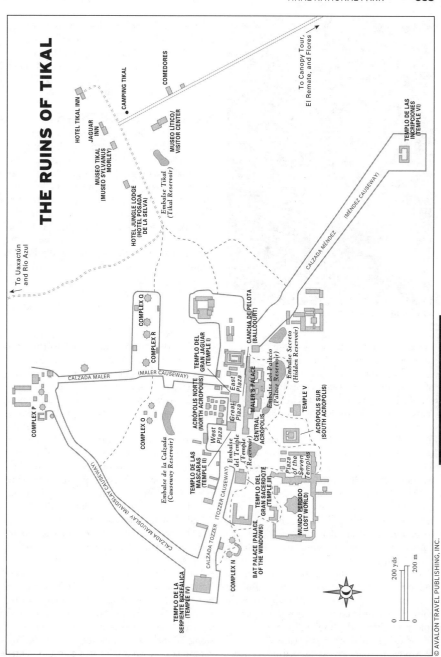

THE RUINS OF TIKAL

To Uaxactún and Río Azul

HOTEL TIKAL INN

JAGUAR INN

MUSEO TIKAL (MUSEO SYLVANUS MORLEY)

HOTEL JUNGLE LODGE (HOTEL POSADA DE LA SELVA)

CAMPING TIKAL

COMEDORES

MUSEO LÍTICO/ VISITOR CENTER

Embalse Tikal (Tikal Reservoir)

To Canopy Tour, El Remate, and Flores

COMPLEX P

COMPLEX Q

COMPLEX R

COMPLEX O

COMPLEX N

CALZADA MALER (MALER CAUSEWAY)

CALZADA MAUDSLAY (MAUDSLAY CAUSEWAY)

CALZADA TOZZER (TOZZER CAUSEWAY)

CALZADA MÉNDEZ

(MÉNDEZ CAUSEWAY)

Embalse de la Calzada (Causeway Reservoir)

TEMPLO DE LA SERPIENTE BICEFÁLICA (TEMPLE IV)

TEMPLO DE LAS MÁSCARAS (TEMPLE III)

ACRÓPOLIS NORTE (NORTH ACROPOLIS)

TEMPLO DEL GRAN JAGUAR (TEMPLE I)

CANCHA DE PELOTA (BALLCOURT)

West Plaza

Great Plaza

East Plaza

Embalse del Temple (Temple Reservoir)

MALER'S PALACE

CENTRAL ACROPOLIS

Embalse del Palacio (Palace Reservoir)

Embalse Secreto (Hidden Reservoir)

TEMPLO DEL GRAN SACERDOTE (TEMPLE III)

TEMPLE V

ACRÓPOLIS SUR (SOUTH ACROPOLIS)

Plaza of the Seven Temples

BAT PALACE (PALACE OF THE WINDOWS)

MUNDO PERDIDO (LOST WORLD)

TEMPLO DE LAS INCRIPCIONES (TEMPLE VI)

0   200 yds

0   200 m

PETÉN

© AVALON TRAVEL PUBLISHING, INC.

© AL ARGUETA

PETÉN

Coatimundis are a common sight in Tikal National Park.

are jaguars. Recent studies done over a two-month span have revealed the confirmed existence of seven of these large spotted cats within the national park's boundaries and it is thought that at least nine roam its 575-square-kilometer (222-square-mile) confines.

EXPLORING THE PARK

Many visitors come to Tikal on day trips from Belize, Flores, and Guatemala City. While a day at the ruins is adequate for seeing some of the archaeological highlights, staying at the park allows you to enjoy its equally splendid natural setting. After the crowds have departed, you'll be free to wander about the ruins unhurried, and at times you may feel as if you have the site all to yourself. The sunset and sunrise from the top of Temple IV are popular activities, undoubtedly facilitated by staying overnight at the park. For movie buffs, the view from Tikal's Temple IV can be appreciated in *Star Wars: Episode IV,* as the site of the rebels' secret base.

Entrance to the park costs $7 and is collected at the gate as you cross into the park on the road from Flores. It's another 17 kilometers to the main entrance and the visitors center. The park is open 6 A.M.–6 P.M. daily. If you arrive after 3 P.M., your ticket should be stamped with the next day's date, allowing you to enter the ruins the next day at no additional cost. Tickets are checked at a booth on the trail between the visitors center and the entrance to the ruins proper, across from an oft-photographed ceiba tree gracing the side of the road. Your best bet for getting in to see the sunrise is to go with a group sunrise tour, usually leaving from the Tikal Inn.

The visitors center is at the main entrance to the park on your left. There are a scale model of the site, the Museo Lítico, an overpriced eatery, and a few small shops selling books, souvenirs, snacks, and sundries, including color print film, bug spray, and sunscreen. Nearby are the park campsite, police substation, and a post office. The other museum is farther along, near the airstrip next to the hotels. You can book licensed guides at the visitors center

canopy, you can watch the sun dip below (or rise above) the horizon of unbroken tropical forest as far as the eye can see, while the chatter of myriad birds and forest creatures permeates the air. The roof combs of the Great Plaza pyramids pop out from the jungle canopy as toucans dart from tree to tree with their curious yellow beaks, like bananas with big black wings. More than 400 species of birds have been recorded at Tikal. *The Birds of Tikal,* by Frank Smythe, is a useful guide in this regard.

Other animals you may come across during your visit include coatis, which you should refrain from feeding. If you spend the night here, don't be afraid if you awake to the raucous of a howling roar emanating from the forest. Sometimes confused with wild cats by first-time visitors, the sounds come from the locally abundant howler monkeys. During your explorations in Tikal, you will probably come across the smaller and ever-more-playful spider monkeys, which swing from tree to tree in the forest surrounding the ruins.

Among the park's most fascinating creatures

BALAM

Among the most beautiful and highly revered rainforest animals both in ancient and modern times is the jaguar *(Panthera onca),* which inhabits Mexico, Central America, and parts of South America. It is one of the big cats, along with the leopard, lion, and tiger, and is the third-largest of these. Jaguars are similar to leopards, though their spots present different arrangements (they are spots within spots, or rosettes, and are larger). Jaguars are also stockier in build. They inhabit mostly forested lands but will also range across grasslands and open terrain. Also notable is their love of water and ability to swim. These gorgeous jungle cats are largely solitary and known for their hunting skills. They will attack cattle on areas fringing jungle zones and have been known to attack jungle camps to stalk human prey, usually children. Their powerful jaws are capable of puncturing tortoise shells.

Perhaps for these reasons, the Mayans had great respect and reverence for the jaguar, which they called *balam.* Jaguars were a symbol of power and strength and were believed to act as mediums for communication between the living and the dead. Kings were often given names incorporating the word *balam,* which they viewed as their companions in the spiritual world and protectors of the royal household. Rulers wearing jaguar pelts and man-jaguar figures frequently appear in pre-Columbian art. The jaguar was the patron deity of Tikal and is featured in a royal burial scene depicted on a human bone fragment found in the burial tomb of Hasaw Chan K'awil (Heavenly Standard Bearer) in which the ruler travels to the underworld in a canoe rowed by mythical animal figures.

Ranges for female jaguars are in the vicinity of 25–40 square kilometers, with the range of males being roughly twice as much and encompassing that of 2–3 females. Male jaguars' ranges do not overlap. For this reason, attempts to conserve existing numbers of jaguars require large expanses of territory such as that found in Guatemala's Maya Biosphere Reserve. The reserve also adjoins reserves in neighboring Mexico and Belize as part of a vast

biological corridor. An estimated 550–650 jaguars remain in the Maya Biosphere Reserve.

Scientists have been studying jaguars in the Maya Biosphere Reserve and are trying to get a more accurate estimate of their remaining numbers in addition to a greater understanding of their behavioral patterns. Within the Laguna del Tigre National Park, biologists have been using radio collars to track five jaguars and a puma in the area surrounding the site of Waka'-Perú in an effort to determine migration patterns along an important biological corridor connecting this area with Mirador Río Azul National Park. It is not uncommon to see jaguar prints on the muddy trails in the vicinity of Waka'-Perú. Ironically, in 2006, a camera crew visiting the park to film a program on scarlet macaws for Guatemalan TV channel Guatevisión was unable to find any macaws but did manage to get a jaguar sighting on tape. Recent video monitoring along 15 stations in the central core of Tikal National Park detected seven jaguars during a two-month period. The Sierra del Lacandón National Park is also believed to harbor large numbers of these jungle cats.

Luckily, you don't need to go traipsing through the jungle with a saucer of milk if you want to see a jaguar, though chances are it will see you first. Guatemala City's excellent zoo has jaguars, as does Petén's ARCAS wildlife-rescue center. A jaguar cub was born in Guatemala City's zoo as recently as 2003. Several zoos in the United States have partnered with facilities in Central America to breed jaguars in captivity. In California, Sacramento's zoo welcomed the arrival of Tina, a Guatemalan jaguar, and Mulac, a male jaguar from Belize, in 2002.

As part of a larger regional initiative along with Mexico and Belize known as Selva Maya, local conservation group Defensores de la Naturaleza and Fundación Monte Carlo Verde launched the **SalvaBalam** campaign in 2006 aimed at increasing public awareness of the jaguar's plight and raising funds for continued study of these fascinating creatures. For more information, visit www.salvabalam.com.

PETÉN

© AL ARGUETA

Watch out for wildlife on the road into Tikal National Park.

for $40 for up to four people, plus $5 for each additional person.

The park website is www.tikalpark.com and has lots of very useful information for planning your visit.

Guided Tours

Guided tours of Tikal are best arranged with one of the recommended Flores travel agencies, though you can also hire the services of a certified freelance guide at the visitors center near the park entrance for $40 for up to four people.

◖ THE RUINS OF TIKAL

There is plenty to explore in this vast Mayan city that once harbored thousands of people and you could easily spend several days here taking it all in. The ruins in evidence today are representative of the latter years of Tikal's existence, as the Mayans built on top of existing temples and palaces. Most of the major structures you'll see were built after the time of Tikal's resurgence in the late 7th century A.D.

The Great Plaza

Most visitors to Tikal head straight from the park entrance to the Great Plaza, and if you are crunched for time this is probably the best

approach. A path from the ticket control booth leads you to the plaza in about 20 minutes. You'll gain an appreciation for the site's elevated setting as you walk uphill toward the heart of the ceremonial center. The view from the back of Temple I as you approach the Great Plaza is always impressive at first sight, as it gives you an idea of the sheer size of the monuments erected by the Mayans. Tourist brochures and posters can never adequately convey just how large and impressive Tikal's temples are.

The path continues alongside the temple and you are at once greeted by the magnificent Temple II, which faces Temple I, as you enter the large, grassy plaza. Also known as "El Gran Jaguar" (The Great Jaguar), Temple I rises to a height of 44 meters (144 feet). The imposing structure was erected to honor Hasaw Chan K'awil (Heavenly Standard Bearer), the ruler who successfully led Tikal to victory against Calakmul. It was built to harbor his remains and was completed shortly after his death in A.D. 721 by son and successor Yik'in Chan K'awil, probably with instructions from his father.

The tomb was situated at the temple's core and contained the ruler's remains surrounded by jade, stingray spines, seashells, and pearls, which were typical of Mayan burials. It was believed the instruments would aid the person in his journey into the underworld. This journey is depicted on a bone fragment, also found in the tomb, showing a royal figure in a canoe rowed by mythical animal figures. Tikal's museum harbors a reconstruction of the tomb, known as Tumba 116. Carried off to a museum in Basel, Switzerland, is the door lintel found at the top of the pyramid depicting a jaguar from which the temple gets its name.

It was once possible to climb Temple I, but this has not been allowed for several years now. The view from the top was truly spectacular, with Temple II in the foreground and the roof combs of Temples III and IV protruding from the jungle behind it. The structure was closed to climbers partly because of damage caused by a chain aiding in this activity, though the death of at least two visitors after tumbling down its steep steps certainly put the final nail in the

PETÉN

coffin. The view from the top was popular in tourism posters and brochures from the early 1980s and you can still sometimes see them in unexpected places.

Across the plaza stands the slightly smaller **Temple II,** built to honor Hasaw Chan K'awil's wife, Lady 12 Macaw. Also known as the Temple of the Masks for the large, severely eroded masks flanking its central staircase, it is thought to predate Temple I by a few years. As recently as five years ago, a staircase was constructed on its side to allow access to the top, though you could once climb directly up its central staircase. The view from the top is still as good as ever, with a frontal view of Temple I and the North Acropolis off to the side. Temple II probably once stood at the same height as its counterpart when its roof comb was intact, though its restored height is 46 meters (125 feet).

The North Acropolis

Occupying the Great Plaza's northern end is the aptly named North Acropolis, its foundations dating as far back as 100 B.C., though the 12 temples sitting atop this large structure are part of a later rebuilding effort dating to A.D. 250. Some of these earlier structures can be seen today thanks to a tunnel excavated by archaeologists that provides a glimpse of two giant masks from Early Classic times guarding the entrance to a still-buried temple. The remains of Yax Nuun Ayin I, the first of Tikal's rulers under Teotihuacán hegemony, were found buried here in 1959 and revealed many details of Teotihuacán influence, including ceramics and the dreaded atlatl.

Some much-eroded stelae line the front of the North Acropolis. These depicted Tikal's ruling elite and many have been subjected to ritual defacement at the hands of invaders from neighboring states such as Calakmul.

The Central Acropolis

Commonly referred to as palaces, this complex of interconnecting rooms and stairways built around courtyards probably housed administrative offices and residences for Tikal's elite,

though their exact use is uncertain. It occupies the south end of the Great Plaza. It is known that the configuration of the various rooms was altered frequently, lending credence to the idea that it served as a royal dwelling place for the ruling elite. One part of the acropolis housed archaeologist Teobert Maler in 1895 and 1904, subsequently coming to be known as **Maler's Palace.**

The West Plaza and Temple III

The West Plaza, or Plaza Oeste, lies north of Temple II. Its main features include the presence of a large Late Classic temple on its north end and the unrestored **Temple III,** across the Tozzer Causeway, to the southwest. Temple III, which is 60 meters high, gives you a good idea of what Tikal's temples looked like to the early explorers when they were still covered in jungle vegetation. That's about all you'll be able to admire of it, as it is closed to visitors.

Some believe Temple III was built to honor the last of Tikal's great rulers, Dark Sun, and he may in fact be the figure depicted in the structure's badly eroded lintels. Behind the temple is a large palace complex. One of them, known as the **Bat Palace,** has been restored. It is also known as Palacio de las Ventanas.

Temple IV and Complex N

Continuing along the Tozzer Causeway, which is one of the original elevated walkways connecting various parts of the city, you'll come across Complex N on the left. Complex N is a twin-temple complex of the variety frequently constructed by Tikal's Late Classic rulers, supposedly to commemorate the passing of a *katun,* or 20-year cycle in the Mayan calendar. Found here is the beautifully carved **Stela 16,** showing Hasaw Chan K'awil in a plumed headdress. The complex was built in A.D. 711 to mark the 14th *katun* of *baktun* 9, a *baktun* being 400 years. **Altar 5,** also found here, depicts Hasaw victoriously presiding over sacrificial skull and bones with a lord from one of Calakmul's former vassal states. The corresponding text also mentions the death of Lady 12 Macaw, Hasaw's wife.

© AL ARGUETA

Tikal's Temple IV

Farther along, you'll come to the colossal Temple IV, the tallest of Tikal's temples at 65 meters (212 feet). Like the Great Plaza's temples, it was completed in A.D. 741 by Yik'in Chan K'awil and may have served as his burial monument, though there is no concrete evidence as of yet. In addition to offering the best views of the site from its summit, it is also known as the origin of some excellent lintels depicting a victorious king surrounded by glyphs. As in the case of the lintels from Temple I, you'll now have to travel to Basel if you want to see the originals. A replica of Lintel 3 is in Guatemala City's archaeology museum.

The climb to the top of the temple up a series of wooden ladders attached to its side can be described as simply breathtaking, both for the effort required and for the spectacular views of the forest on all sides.

Temple V and the South Acropolis

The South Acropolis, due south of the Great Plaza, is the site of some excavations that are just beginning to unravel its significance. Its top layers are from Late Classic times, much like elsewhere in Tikal. Temple V lies just east of the South Acropolis. Standing to a height of 58 meters, it may be the original of Tikal's six temples dating to A.D. 600. A wooden staircase provides access to the somewhat cramped area below the roof comb, from which an interesting side view of the Great Plaza can be had.

Plaza of the Seven Temples

This small plaza can be found to the west of the South Acropolis and contains a series of seven temples arranged in a straight line dating to Preclassic times. There is a triple ball court on the plaza's north side similar to a larger one just south of Temple I.

The Lost World Complex

Known in Spanish as El Mundo Perdido, this complex is strikingly different from the rest of the site owing to its Preclassic origins, which may help to shed light on Tikal's early history. The area is dominated by the presence of a 32-

meter pyramid, its foundation dating as far back as 500 B.C., when it served as an astronomical observatory similar to the one found at Uaxactún. The structure now in evidence marks the top of four layers of construction. There are fabulous views of the Great Plaza and Temple IV from the top, though the stone central staircase on the temple's steep face can be slippery after it rains. Exercise due caution.

Temple of the Inscriptions (Temple VI)

The most remote of Tikal's temples, Temple VI lies about one kilometer southeast of the Central Acropolis along the **Mendez Causeway,** where it stands all by itself. Rediscovered in 1957, this temple is unique because it contains inscriptions much like the temples found at Quiriguá and Copán but unlike Tikal's other temples. On the back side of the temple's 12-meter roof comb are a series of 180 glyphs, barely visible today, charting the history of Tikal's ruling dynasty A.D. 200–766. They also chart Tikal's early history as far back as 1139 B.C., which the Mayans probably guessed at. Still, ceramic evidence at Tikal has corroborated other dates found at the site. The temple is most likely the work of Yik'in Chan K'awil. Stela 21 and Altar 9 adorn the front of the temple at its base and date to A.D. 736.

The temple's relative isolation makes it an excellent location for spotting wildlife. Robberies, none of them recent, have been reported here. You should probably not wander off to these parts unaccompanied.

Complexes Q and R

Two other areas deserve mention in this discussion of Tikal's archaeological highlights. You'll find them shortly after entering the park, on a path bearing right after passing the ticket control booth. Complex Q and Complex R comprise two sets of Tikal's twin-temple complexes built by Yax Ain II to commemorate the passing of a *katun*. One of the pyramids at Complex Q has been restored with its corresponding stelae repositioned in front of it. The best of these, **Stela 22,** can be seen at the **Museo Lítico** and

depicts Yax Ain II's ascension to the throne. The temple here dates to A.D. 771.

Farther west, as you approach the Maler Causeway, is Complex R, another twin-pyramid complex dating to A.D. 790.

MUSEUMS

Tikal's two museums are oddly in different parts of the park. The first of these is the **Museo Lítico** (9 A.M.–noon and 1 P.M.–4:30 P.M.Mon.–Fri., 9 A.M.–4 P.M. Sat. and Sun., free admission), housing stelae and carved stones from the archaeological site with a scale model outside showing what the city probably looked like around A.D. 800. There are some interesting photos taken by explorers Alfred Maudslay and Teobert Maler showing Tikal's temples overgrown by a tangle of jungle vines and branches as they looked when they were first discovered.

The **Museo Tikal** (9 A.M.–5 P.M. Mon.–Fri., 9 A.M.–4 P.M. Sat. and Sun., $1.35), across the way next to the Jaguar Inn, has some interesting exhibits, including the burial tomb of Hasaw Chan K'awil found inside Temple I. It may have been renovated by the time you read this.

RECREATION

In addition to exploring the ruins, there are a variety of recreational opportunities in and around Tikal National Park.

Canopy Tour

You have a choice of two zip-line trajectories between raised platforms in the jungle at **Tikal Canopy Tour** (tel. 5819-7766, www.canopy tikal.com, 7 A.M.–5 P.M. daily, $30, at the national park entrance). The first of these includes 11 platforms with zip lines ranging in length 75–150 meters while you dangle 25 meters over the forest floor. The second, more adrenaline-inducing option, includes zip lines up to 200 meters long hovering 40 meters above the safety of ground level. Pick your poison.

Bird-Watching

Specialty tours for bird-watchers can be

PETÉN

arranged by contacting **La Casa de Don David** (tel. 7928-8469 or 5306-2190, www.lacasade dondavid.com) in El Remate. The lodge's knowledgeable staff can connect you with good English-speaking local guides who know the park and its birds. Another recommended outfitter is Guatemala City–based **Cayaya Birding** (tel. 5308-5160, www .cayaya-birding.com).

ACCOMMODATIONS

Lodging at Tikal National Park is limited by law to three lodges and a campground. An increasing amount of competition from accommodations at nearby El Remate has spurred the Tikal hotels toward higher standards while keeping prices relatively reasonable. There are few places in the world where you can stay in a comfortable jungle lodge inside a national park just minutes away from a UNESCO World Heritage Site.

Electricity at the park is sporadic, with accommodations and other facilities having to limit the hours during which this convenience is available. Power is usually turned on in the morning for 2–3 hours and then again in the evening shortly after sunset for another three hours. If you need to use a computer provided by one of these facilities for checking email or need to recharge digital/video camera batteries or cell phones, you should plan accordingly. If you absolutely need a fan to cool your room while you sleep overnight in the humid Petén jungle, you may want to stay outside the park, as ceiling fans go silent once the electricity turns off. It can get very hot here, even at night. None of the lodges have air-conditioning.

Coming from the ruins, the first place you'll come across is the **Jungle Lodge** (tel. 2476-8775, www.junglelodge.guate.com, $40–80 d), offering decent bungalows with private hot-water bath, ceiling fan, and two double beds as well as a few very basic, less expensive rooms with shared bath. All are set amid a pleasant tropical garden atmosphere and there is a swimming pool. The restaurant here serves breakfast ($5), lunch, and dinner ($8–10). Tour groups often lunch here. Be advised the lodge is closed every year during September. As you head toward the old airstrip just past the museums, you'll reach the friendly **Jaguar Inn** (tel. 7926-0002, www.jaguartikal.com), where you can choose from nine comfortable bungalows with small front patios with hammock ($53 d), a dormitory ($10 p/p), hammocks with mosquito netting ($5), or camping ($3.50). You can rent a tent for $7. The restaurant here is a safe bet, serving adequate portions of good food three meals a day. Dinner is about $8. There are laptops available for Internet surfing and checking email ($5/hour), but the electricity shuts off at 9 P.M. Next door, **Tikal Inn** (hoteltikal inn@itelgua.com, $60–100 d), gets consistent praise for its large, comfortable rooms centered around the swimming pool just behind the hotel's restaurant. You can choose from standard rooms or pricier, more private bungalows; all have ceiling fan and private bath. The restaurant serves three meals a day.

Tikal's **campground** is opposite the visitors center with a spacious grassy area for tents as well as *palapa* structures for stringing hammocks. There are showering stalls among the bathroom facilities. Hammocks and mosquito netting are available for rent and there are tiny, two-person basic cabanas for $6.50 p/p. It costs $4 p/p to camp here.

FOOD

Your best bet for food is at one of the three lodges on-site, but there are a number of *comedores* here serving basic yet passable fare in adequate portions for about $5 for a full meal and a drink. The menus are virtually indistinguishable from one another and are heavy on local staples such as beans, eggs, and tortillas. The restaurant at the visitors center, **Restaurant Café Tikal,** is fancier but a bit overpriced and you are probably better off eating at one of the lodges if you're not on a small budget. It serves pasta, steaks, chicken, and sandwiches and is open until 6 P.M. daily. The other *comedores* are across from the visitors center on the right-hand side as you enter the park from the main road. They include **Comedor Corazón de Jesús, Comedor Tikal, Restaurant Imperio Maya,** and **Comedor Ixim Kúa,** all of which open early for breakfast and close at 9 P.M. daily.

As for the hotel restaurants, the large dining room at the **Jungle Lodge** is a popular stop for lunch with tour groups. As such, it tends to offer dependable set-menu lunches of meat or chicken dishes accompanied by rice and salad for about $8. Dinner options include a varied assortment of meat dishes, pasta, and sandwiches. The **Jaguar Inn** caters largely to the international backpacker crowd and makes a particularly decent place for good-value dinners, including tasty pastas and desserts.

The **Tikal Inn** gets props for its hearty breakfasts with good, strong coffee, but there are better options for lunch and dinner.

GETTING THERE

Most people arrive here from Flores, El Remate, or Belize. See the corresponding sections for information on how to get here. Minibuses leave Tikal from the airstrip fairly frequently, particularly after about noon, heading south toward El Remate, Ixlú, and Flores. Change buses at Ixlú if you're heading east to Belize. If all else fails, a taxi to Flores should cost about $40.

The Maya Biosphere Reserve

The largest protected tropical forest in North America, this 1.7 million-hectare (4.3 million-acre) reserve is Guatemala's last chance for preserving a significant part of the forests that once covered all of Petén. It is gradually gaining notoriety among international travelers for its vast expanses of tropical forest and the remote Mayan ruins that lie buried within. It is hoped that ecotourism here will take hold as a major industry, providing jobs and a viable alternative to ecological destruction, as in neighboring protected areas in Belize and Costa Rica. A cursory glance at a map of Guatemala reveals that the northern third of Petén is a sparsely populated region harboring an unusually high concentration of Mayan sites, remote jungle wetlands, rivers, and lagoons. Those with a strong sense of adventure will find plenty to see and do in one of Central America's last ecological frontiers.

Although the biosphere reserve has been in existence since 1990, many of the parks that compose it remain little more than "paper parks," as the government entities charged with enforcing protection of these areas are woefully underfunded and understaffed. Several of the parks are now being administered jointly between Guatemala's National Protected Areas Council (CONAP) and local conservation or-

ganizations. Foreign NGOs have also joined the battle to preserve the Maya Biosphere for future generations against seemingly insurmountable odds. Threatening the continued existence of this unique area are traditional factors common to tropical forests in Third World countries, including the expansion of the agricultural frontier by land-hungry peasants and changes in land use such as cattle grazing. But there are also more sinister forces at work here, and the reserve is under serious assault by wildlife and timber poachers, both from within Guatemala and neighboring Mexico, as well as from the activities of drug smugglers occupying large extensions of the park to move their product.

Guatemalan authorities have stepped up their efforts to regain control of this vast wilderness area and it should be noted that not all of the above-mentioned forces are in operation throughout the park. There are many areas within this vast biosphere reserve that are easily and safely explored, combining the splendors of some of the Mayan civilization's most spectacular ruins with the wonders of a largely intact tropical forest all around. In some cases, these are not so easily accessible, but the rewards for those putting forth the effort to reach some of Guatemala's least-visited attractions are well worth it.

PETÉN

THE MURALS OF SAN BARTOLO

Recent, fascinating discoveries at the newly famous site of San Bartolo have rocked the world of Mayan scholars, completely shattering long-held beliefs about the origin of elaborate Mayan art and writing that narrates the stories of ruling monarchies. It is now clear that Preclassic Mayan societies had achieved a degree of sophistication in art, writing, and government once thought to have been attained only several centuries later. San Bartolo, deep in the jungle near Río Azul, has yielded the earliest known Mayan mural and the oldest known Mayan burial tomb. The murals are impressive not only for their early date (A.D. 100-200), but also for their quality. The best-known Mayan murals, at the site of Bonampak (Mexico), date to the late 8th century A.D. San Bartolo's location, while no longer secret, is known only to a few in the archaeological community. Visitors are not welcome, but there are plans to make a replica of the murals available to tourists in the future. The Mayan site of San Bartolo encompasses more than 100 structures, among them temple pyramids (at least two of which are more than 25 meters high), a palace, and ball court, and is still being excavated.

The mural was discovered in 2001 by Harvard University's William Saturno when he ducked into a trench hacked by looters under an unexcavated pyramid in search of shade from the midday sun. After two years of planning the painstaking excavation, the mural depicting creation mythology was reclaimed from the soil beneath the temple structure. It is similar to one found in the *Dresden Codex*, one of three Mayan books to survive the wide-scale destruction of ancient Mayan texts by Spanish priests in the 16th century (the other two are the Madrid Codex and the Paris Codex).

Among the themes depicted are the establishment of order to the world, the latter portrayed as held up by trees with roots leading to the underworld and branches holding up the sky. Stationed at each tree are four deities providing a blood sacrifice and an offering.

In another section, the mural shows the maize god setting up the tree at the center of the world and crowning himself king. This section of the panel traces the maize god's birth, death, and resurrection. In the final scene, a historic coronation of an actual Mayan king is depicted with his name and title written in hieroglyphics.

Project iconographer Karl Taube believes the writing style differs from that evidenced in later periods of Mayan history, but it is nonetheless sophisticated. He also points to the appearance of similar scenes in the *Dresden Codex*. Saturno speculates the king depicted in the mural likely claimed the right to rule from the gods themselves and not merely from lineage, as did kings in later times.

The second major discovery is the tomb of an early Mayan king dating to 150 B.C. found about a mile away from the mural, also under a small temple pyramid, by Guatemalan archaeologist Mónica Pellecer Alecio, in 2005. The find provides further evidence of early monarchic rule.

A full-length feature on these amazing discoveries can be found in the January 2006 edition of *National Geographic* magazine and online at www.sanbartolo.org.

Among the highlights of the reserve are the **Mirador-Rio Azul National Park,** which is home to the largest man-made pre-Columbian structures in the Americas, found at **El Mirador,** and at least 25 other smaller Mayan sites. Some, such as Wakná, have been discovered only as recently as 1998 and many more undoubtedly await discovery. Even more recently, at the site of **San Bartolo,** archaeologists have uncovered the earliest evidence of Mayan writing in a wall mural discovered in 2001. The area is also home to the last remaining undisturbed tropical forests in Guatemala and is being considered for special protection as the **Mirador Basin National Park.**

Much of the western part of the reserve, particularly **Laguna del Tigre National Park,** has unfortunately been lost due to population pressures. Still, the area around the Mayan site of **Waka'** (also known as El Perú or Waka'-Perú), remains well preserved and is the home of a biological research station and a project to help conserve Petén's last remaining populations of scarlet macaws.

In 2006, The Nature Conservancy helped local conservation organization Defensores de la Naturaleza secure the purchase of 31,000 hectares (77,000 acres) of privately held land to help ensure the preservation of **Sierra del Lacandón National Park,** an area of incredible biological diversity due to the ruggedness of the terrain, which includes mountains, freshwater lakes, savannas, and rainforests running along the magnificent Usumacinta River. Squatters were evicted from the park soon after (not without much difficulty), and how this area will be managed and opened to low-impact tourism is yet unknown. Nestled in the jungles of Sierra del Lacandón are at least two sites worthy of mention and exploration—Piedras Negras and, across the Usumacinta and upstream in Mexico, Yaxchilán.

The Maya Biosphere was also featured on U.S. television with the filming of *Survivor Guatemala* at the Mayan ruins of Yaxhá. The spectacular ruined city is rivaled in magnificence only by Tikal and El Mirador, and its splendid setting next to a tropical lagoon complete with hungry crocodiles is second to none.

Survivor Guatemala certainly catapulted Guatemala and Yaxhá into the collective consciousness, and many people believe it is just a matter of time before the treasures hidden in the Peteén forest gain greater notoriety and become an engine for the preservation of this incredible but often-overlooked adventure-travel destination.

UAXACTÚN

The remote site of Uaxactún lies just 23 kilometers north of Tikal on an unpaved road through the jungle passable by 4WD vehicle. The Wrigley Company once had a busy chicle extraction operation here, complete with an airstrip. Today the airstrip lies in disuse, with the ruins and small community built around it. Many of Uax-

actún's residents make their living from gathering forest products such as chicle, allspice and *xate* palm leaves. In 2000, Guatemala's Protected Areas Council (CONAP) granted the community a sustainable forestry concession to selectively harvest timber from surrounding multiple-use zones of the Maya Biosphere Reserve. While it's yet to be seen how sustainable it is in practice, the logging concession has already been partially nullified in areas approaching the subsequently created Mirador Basin archaeological zone and could be completely eliminated with the eventual creation of a proposed Mirador Basin National Park. Locals also guide visits from here to remote sites such as Río Azul and El Zotz, which may be their best hope for earning income without harming the fragile tropical forest ecosystem they inhabit.

The ruins themselves might seem a bit unimpressive after a visit to their better-known neighbor to the south, as they are smaller and not nearly as well preserved, though Uaxactún's main claim to fame is the presence of a fairly elaborate astronomical observatory. Sylvanus G. Morley is credited with rediscovering Uaxactún in 1916. Its original name has subsequently been deciphered as Siaan K'aan (Born in Heaven), though Morley is said to have chosen the name Uaxatún (Eight Stone) as a reference to a stone dating to the 8th *baktun* in the Mayan calendar, then the earliest-known Mayan inscription. It is also speculated that his choice of name was a play on words for "Washington," the U.S. capital and home of the Carnegie Institute that funded his explorations. Morley's initial investigations focused on the site's inscriptions. Uaxatún's structures would have to await being mapped and more closely inspected until the arrival of Frans Blom in 1924. The Carnegie Institution excavated the site between 1926 and 1937.

History

Uaxactún is a Middle Preclassic site dating to about 600 B.C. that came into its own in the Late Preclassic sometime between 350 B.C. and A.D. 250 with the appearance of its first ceremonial plazas in the areas now known

PETÉN

as Groups A and E. Its earliest stelae date to around A.D. 328. More complex architecture and several other plazas also make their appearance at this time.

After the decline of El Mirador in the 2nd century A.D., Uaxactún and Tikal became embroiled in a great political and military rivalry for local supremacy until the site was conquered by Tikal in A.D. 378. Tikal was aided in its takeover of Uaxactún by its newly formed alliance with Teotihuacán and the introduction of a spear-throwing apparatus imported from the Central Mexican city-state. Uaxactún remained a subordinate state for the remainder of its history.

The Ruins

The most impressive set of ruins lies a 15-minute walk southeast of the airstrip and is called **Group E.** A series of small, partially restored temples, Structures E-I, E-II, and E-III, are arranged side by side, going north to south, and designed as an astronomical observatory. The structures are arranged in such a manner as to coincide with the sunrise on key dates. When viewed from the top of nearby Temple E-VII-Sub, the sun rises over E-1 on the summer solstice and over the southernmost E-III on the winter solstice. Temple E-VII-Sub's foundations date to about 2,000 B.C. and there are some much-deteriorated jaguar and snake heads flanking the temple's side.

Northeast of the airstrip are Groups A and B, which were less carefully excavated but include several altars and stelae found mostly fallen among the remains of the larger temple palaces.

Accommodations and Food

Lodging and dining options in Uaxactún are extremely basic, as it is a remote forest community literally in the middle of nowhere. The settlement's best accommodations are at **Campamento El Chiclero** (tel. 7926-1095) on the north end of the airstrip with 10 basic rooms with shared bath and mosquito-netted windows for $7 per person. You can also camp or string a hammock here for $3. The restau-

temple pyramid at Uaxactún

© AL ARGUETA

rant here serves large portions of good, basic food ($5 per meal) and there is a small on-site museum (free admission) with local artifacts. The friendly owners can arrange trips to some of the more remote places in the biosphere reserve, including El Zotz, Río Azul, Naachtun, and El Mirador. A less expensive alternative is **Aldana's Lodge,** just off the street leading to Groups A and B, where simple thatched-roof cabanas are $4 per person, or you can camp for $2 per person. Aldana's can also arrange visits to area sites.

You can eat at your choice of three simple *comedores* in town: **Comedor Uaxactún, Comedor La Bendición,** and **Comedor Imperial Okanarin.**

Getting There

A Pinita bus leaves Santa Elena at 1 P.M. daily, stopping in Tikal at about 3 P.M. From there it's about 1.5 hours to Uaxactún. These times are not set in stone, as with most schedules in Guatemala, and the bus can arrive in Uaxactún as late as 6 P.M. sometimes. The return trip to Santa Elena leaves Uaxactún at 6 A.M.

If you're driving, be aware that the road is passable only in a 4WD vehicle at any time of year. If you're unable to full your gas tank in Flores, the last gas station en route is at Ixlú, south of El Remate.

BIOTOPO EL ZOTZ-SAN MIGUEL LA PALOTADA

"Zotz" means "bat" in Mayan, and this CECON biotope, predictably, is set up for the protection of the thousands of bats that emerge from the mouth of a large cave at dusk. It's quite an impressive sight to see, the sky darkening with myriad winged creatures making their way out in search of insects and fruit. The biotope also protects an archaeological site that has been severely plundered and remains unexcavated. You can climb to the top of the tallest mound, the **El Diablo Temple,** from which you can make out the roof combs of Tikal's pyramids 23 kilometers to the west. The forest here remains well preserved and there is a small biological station with guards patrolling the

park stationed here. You can camp for free and there is no park admission fee, as in most of the remote jungle parks of the Maya Biosphere Reserve. The biotope abuts Tikal National Park to the east, which partially explains why it remains mostly intact. It is part of an important biological corridor ensuring the survival of many of Petén's most threatened species.

Several Flores travel agencies arrange trips to the biotope. Highly recommended is **Martsam Tours and Travel,** offering an excellent three-day/two-night trek from El Zotz to Tikal for about $175 per person for two people. It begins in Flores with a private vehicle transfer to the village of Cruce dos Aguadas, west of the park. From there, you hike five hours to El Zotz, see the bat cave, and spend the night. The second day is spent exploring the site's temple mounds before hiking to a campsite midway between El Zotz and Tikal, where you bed down for the night before the final 18-kilometer march to Tikal the next day. You explore Tikal on the last day, and the trip concludes with a chance to see the sunset from Temple IV. **Tikal Connection** also runs a similar trip for the same price. Both use local community guides.

Another option is to book a trip from Uaxactún. **Campamento El Chiclero** can arrange pack horses, guides, and equipment. The trip from Uaxactún affords the opportunity to see a little more of the forest, as the forests along the western approach from Paso Caballos have been somewhat disturbed.

YAXHÁ-NAKUM-NARANJO NATURAL MONUMENT

This park encompasses the Mayan sites of Yaxhá, Topoxté, Nakum, and El Naranjo. Most prominent of these is Yaxhá, which gained international fame in 2005 with the filming of *Survivor Guatemala*. The park was closed for two months, during which time contestants lived among the ruins eating corn, plotting ways not to get voted off, and fighting off mosquitoes. Only El Mirador and Tikal are bigger than Yaxhá (8 A.M.–5 P.M. daily, $10 admission includes entrance to Nakum), and its isolated setting on a limestone ridge overlooking the lagoons of Yaxhá and Sacnab is simply splendid. Despite its TV fame, you can still wander the site with nary another visitor in sight. Don't even think of swimming in the lakes here, as they have a healthy population of rather large crocodiles.

◖ Yaxhá

The relative lack of inscribed monuments found at Yaxhá has made tracking its history a bit of a challenge, though it appears it was a major player during the Classic period. It is believed Yaxhá was locked into an ongoing power struggle during much of this time with its smaller neighbor, Naranjo, about 20 kilometers northeast. Yaxhá's sphere of influence was almost certainly limited by the proximity of Tikal and the architecture here shows many similarities to that of the latter site. Naranjo eventually overran Yaxhá in A.D. 799. Spanish friars passed through here in 1618, and Austrian explorer Teobert Maler visited in 1904. Much of the site remained unexcavated until recently. A German-Guatemalan effort is conducting the site's ongoing excavation and restoration.

Yaxhá's highest structure is **Structure 216,** offering wonderful views of the lagoons and forests from its summit. Watchers of *Survivor Guatemala* will probably recognize the temple from numerous aerial shots shown during the program's run. It features a broad central staircase and rises to a height of about 100 feet. Access is via a wooden staircase built into the temple's side.

The temples at Yaxhá appear constructed from a very light-colored limestone markedly different from the stones used elsewhere in the Mayan world, giving the ruins a very different feel. You'll find the ruins spread out over nine plazas with 500 mapped structures, including temples, ball courts, and palaces. Other highlights include the recently restored **North Acropolis,** surrounded by three temples, two of which are fairly large. A path known as **Calzada Blom** leads almost one kilometer north from here to the **Maler Group,** a com-

plex featuring twin temples facing each other across a plaza similar to the setup at Tikal. A number of weathered stelae and the broken remains of a large circular altar further adorn the complex. Another great location affording wonderful views closer to the heart of the ruined city is the top of an unnamed astronomical observation pyramid between Plaza F and Structure 116.

The parking lot and restrooms are on the east side of the park near Plaza C, along with a small museum. There are two boat docks here, one below the parking lot and one at the western end of the site.

You can camp for free at **Campamento Yaxhá,** a designated lakeside campsite below the ruins proper. A more comfortable option is the friendly **Campamento Ecológico El Sombrero** (tel. 7861-1687/8, www.eco sombrero.com), about 200 meters from the main road before you come to the park entry post. Its 13 comfortable rooms are housed in thatched-roof bungalows fronting the lake. There's a dock, but it's not recommended for swimming because of the crocodiles. A restaurant serves adequate food, with the variety of menu items on offer heavily dependent on whether or not there's a group staying at the lodge. If you're just stopping by, you'll probably end up eating pasta, which actually seems a delicacy when you're in the middle of the jungle. The lodge arranges boat trips to **Topoxté** and guided tours of Yaxhá.

A series of roads leads to Yaxhá. About 31 kilometers east of Ixlú, on the road toward the Belize border, a well-marked turnoff leads a further 11 kilometers north to the Yaxhá guardpost, where you pay admission and sign in to the park. It's another three kilometers from here to the actual ruins of Yaxhá. The road is in good condition, even during the rainy season. If traveling by bus, you can get off at the junction to Yaxhá and hitch a ride with an occasional passing pickup truck or fellow travelers. There is some traffic along this route because of the presence of the small village of La Máquina, about two kilometers from the park guardpost.

Several of the Flores tour operators now do Yaxhá with certain frequency. You can also get a minivan from El Remate to the site, but expect to pay about $60 round-trip. Try to find people to share the ride.

Reserva Natural Privada Yaxhá

Reserva Natural Privada Yaxhá (tel. 2360-4415/20, www.yaxhanatural.org) is a private, 407-hectare nature reserve on the southwest corner of Yaxhá Lagoon. Established as a site for scientific investigation, it has a newly completed biological station with dorms for up to 20 people. The reserve is most easily accessible by boat from the Yaxhá archaeological site, though you can also get here via roads traversing neighboring properties. In addition to providing opportunities for scientific study in its biological station, there are nature trails for hiking as well as kayaks and mountain bikes. The project is still in its early stages, so your best bet is to contact the reserve if you are planning a visit or simply want more information.

Topoxté

This smaller site is situated on an island close to the southwest shore of Yaxhá Lagoon near the Reserva Natural Privada Yaxhá and dates to Preclassic times, though the structures in evidence are mostly from the Late Postclassic period. Plazas and temples are being restored, though nothing is of the scale found at Yaxhá. Topoxté was one of the last strongholds of the Itzá people.

The site was surveyed on several different occasions throughout the 20th century starting in 1904, though restoration and preservation would have to wait until the early 1990s. The most notable structure here is **Temple Pyramid C,** the only Postclassic building remaining in Petén. Similar to structures in the Yucatán and Guatemala's highlands, it has three levels crowned by a portal supported by two pillars.

The only feasible way of getting here is to catch a boat ride from Campamento Ecologico El Sombrero.

Nakum

North of Yaxhá on a road suitable only for dry-season driving is the Late Classic site of Nakum, now being excavated. Near the site lies the marshy swampland of **Bajo La Justa,** which was under intense cultivation during Mayan times. You'll pass through it on your way there. Nakum features the usual assortment of pyramids, plazas, and temples, though there are some unique arches found here along with stelae dating from A.D. 771–849. Noted archaeologist Alfred Tozzer passed though here in 1909–1910, working for the Peabody Museum; he recorded his findings in a work titled, *A Preliminary Study of the Prehistoric Ruins of Nakum, Guatemala.*

MIRADOR-RÍO AZUL NATIONAL PARK

This vast wilderness area encompasses the ruins of El Mirador, one of the earliest and largest Mayan cities to emerge from Petén's jungles, as well as several other Preclassic Mayan sites. It abuts Mexico's Calakmul Biosphere Reserve to the north, which protects another important archaeological site and a large tract of forest in its vicinity. The protected status along the southern border of Guatemala's northern neighbor, and the lack of road access, have allowed this park to remain a largely untrammeled wilderness. Access is difficult and best attempted during the dry season, as seasonal flooding of swamps known as *bajos* turns forest paths into knee-deep mud for much of the year. The other major Mayan site giving its name to this park is Río Azul, which lies deep in the jungle near the western border with Belize.

Archaeologists and environmentalists are lobbying for the creation of the **Mirador Basin National Park** (see sidebar *The Mirador Basin Project*) and the Guatemalan government has shown interest in preserving this wilderness area harboring Mayan ruins of at least equal importance to that of Tikal.

◖ El Mirador

This massive city, rediscovered in 1926 and photographed from the air in 1930, but only

THE MIRADOR BASIN PROJECT

Deep in the untouched forests of northern Petén in what archaeologists call the Mirador Basin, far from the throngs of tourists at other Mayan sites, lie the overgrown remains of the most fascinating cities ever built in Preclassic times. The Mirador Basin, as defined by its geographical characteristics, is an elevated basin dominated by low-lying swamps known as *bajos* and surrounded by karst limestone hills to the south, east, and west, forming a triangular trench covering roughly 2,120 square kilometers (820 square miles). Some of its sites, including El Mirador and Nakbé, are being excavated and have yielded many clues concerning the advanced nature of early Mayan civilization. As the excavations continue to yield fascinating new discoveries, archaeologists, conservationists, and local residents remain at odds about how best to preserve the remaining Petén forests and the important monuments they harbor.

At the heart of the controversy is the proposal for a Mirador Basin National Park, spearheaded by UCLA's Dr. Richard Hansen, who heads the excavation project at El Mirador. The park would stretch clear to the Mexican border at its northernmost points, encompassing parts of Mirador-Río Azul National Park. At its southern tip, it would stretch all the way down to El Zotz-San Miguel La Palotada Biotope. The area is home to Petén's last remaining expanses of well-preserved forests.

Hansen envisions a large national park guarded by armed rangers similar to those of the U.S. National Park Service. There would be several luxurious ecolodges, visitors centers, an airstrip, a narrow-gauge railroad, and hiking trails linking the various restored Mayan sites within the basin. The proposed park would be roughly four times the size of Tikal National Park and would be largely based upon the same management model. Hansen sees the potential to accommodate up to 80,000 visitors per year.

Against the odds, Hansen has made some incredible headway toward achieving his ambitious goals. In 2002, President Alfonso Portillo agreed to create the Regional System for the Special Protection of Cultural Heritage as a means of protecting archaeological sites in Petén and declared 600,000 acres of the Maya Biosphere as a "special archaeological zone." Its official name became the Mirador Basin. The agreement nullified community forestry concessions permitting sustainable logging and forest-product extraction in multiple-use zones near the Mirador Basin archaeological sites, much to the dismay of the local communities benefited by the concessions.

More recently, Hansen also found the support of President Oscar Berger and important government officials in the departments of archaeology, forestry, and tourism. He also has representatives lobbying the Inter-American Development Bank for funding and has rallied wealthy investors inside and outside of Guatemala to his cause. All of this is being coordinated through The Foundation for Anthropological Research and Environmental Studies (FARES), established by Hansen in 1996.

In 2003, the California-based Global Heritage Fund and several other organizations donated $880,000 toward the restoration of four temples at Nakbé. Hansen says he needs $35 million by 2020 to excavate and protect the area while developers build tourist infra-

recently the focus of ongoing excavations, holds great promise both as a tourism destination rivaling the magnitude of Tikal and as an important piece in the puzzle concerning the advancements of Preclassic Maya society. El Mirador flourished between 200 B.C. and A.D. 150, much earlier than Tikal, and has revealed a greater level of sophistication than once thought concerning early Mayan society. It is thought to have been home to 80,000 people at the height of its occupation.

The site sits on a series of limestone hills at an altitude of just over 240 meters (800 feet) and occupies about 16 square kilometers. El Mirador's dominating feature is the presence of two large pyramid complexes, El Tigre and

structure. FARES now provides the funding for year-round protection of the Mirador Basin sites from looters. In the long run, Hansen believes increased tourism could fund the preservation and protection of the sites, making the project self-sufficient while providing new economic opportunities for residents.

Hansen's plans, if a bit grandiose, seem well intentioned. But they have met substantial opposition from local communities and Petén's powerful environmental groups, who have spent many years and millions of dollars developing relationships with local communities to encourage the sustainable extraction of forest products. The sustainable forestry programs have received support from The Nature Conservancy and the U.S. Agency for International Development, among others.

Some believe the communities could receive greater economic benefit from sustainable forestry than from working as staff in tourist hotels and restaurants. The community of Uaxactún, for example, was awarded a sustainable forestry concession in 2000 by CONAP and villagers there have made a living from collecting forest products for decades.

Although the park itself will supposedly be without roads, new infrastructure would have to be built to make the region more accessible to visitors, raising the specter of a much-talked-about road connecting Tikal to Mexico's Calakmul. Along these lines, Mexico has been insisting on the construction of a road from Chetumal to Tikal in an attempt to integrate the two countries' archaeological sites as part of the Plan Puebla-Panama, an idea vehemently opposed by local conservationists because it would bisect some of the best-conserved areas of the Maya Biosphere Reserve. Representatives from various NGOs working in Petén cite a recent study predicting the loss of 60 percent of the forest in Mirador-Rio Azul National Park within 15 years if the road is constructed. A valuable wildlife corridor would also be severed in half. As demonstrated in other parts of the biosphere reserve, most notably Laguna del Tigre, roads bring in settlers, looters, drug traffickers, and clandestine loggers. Others believe the airstrips and luxurious accommodations would allow high-end tourists to fly in and out of the Mirador Basin without contributing much to the local communities.

Because the forestry concessions are still relatively young, it remains to be seen whether or not they are indeed sustainable. Scientific studies to answer this question have determined it is too early to decide, though it should be noted that the seasonal fires affecting much of the western half of the Maya Biosphere Reserve have been almost absent from the Mirador Basin, Uaxactún, and surrounding areas. Supporters of the concessions believe the vested interest the communities have in protecting the very resources from which they derive their livelihoods will prevent them from destroying the forests.

What is certain is that something must be done soon to prevent the Mirador Basin's forests from disappearing and to protect its rich cultural heritage from looting. Time is of the essence, as conservationists, archaeologists, and local communities run the risk of not knowing what they've truly lost until it's gone.

For more information on the Mirador basin project, check out the FARES website at www.miradorbasin.com.

La Danta, running east to west and facing each other. The architecture is characterized by triadic structures composed of one large temple pyramid flanked on either side by two smaller pyramids, a pattern that is repeated elsewhere in the Preclassic sites of the Mirador basin.

The base of the **El Tigre Complex** is as large as three football fields, while the large temple dominating the structure reaches 55 meters (180 feet) in height. The lower flanking pyramids contain gigantic stucco jaguar masks.

The city's **Central Acropolis** takes the form of a narrow plaza bordered on one side by a series of small buildings. Moving south from the El Tigre Complex, you come to the **Monos Complex,** another triadic structure named after the howler monkeys tending to congregate in this area.

The colossal **La Danta Complex** lies to the east of the main plaza and Central Acropolis. Although technically lower than El Tigre, it rises to a height of 70 meters (230 feet) thanks to its elevated location on a hillside, making it the tallest structure in the Mayan world. Its base is equally impressive. There are jaguar and vulture heads built into the sides of the smaller temples here and the spectacular views from the top of the pyramid afford views of nearby Mayan sites, including Nakbé and Calakmul.

Other interesting site features include the León Pyramid, at the northern edge of the city, and Structure 34—a Preclassic building with the oldest known Mayan standing wall.

Excavations are being done under the direction of UCLA's Dr. Richard Hansen, who has led a larger project aiming to protect the entire Mirador basin as an ecoarchaeological preserve. (See sidebar *The Mirador Basin Project.)* The preservation of its delicate monuments is being aided by technological advances, including housing structures under polycarbonate roofs designed by Hansen and his associates, so as to protect them from rain and ultraviolet light.

Getting to El Mirador

Getting to El Mirador is not an easy task, though you wouldn't know it judging by the readiness of certain Flores tour operators to book you on a trip even at the height of the rainy season. The trek to El Mirador is not for the faint of heart and should not be attempted July–November, when the mud is knee-deep throughout most of the trail. In the worst of places, a rope is tied to the end of a tree and trekkers must pull themselves through shoulder-deep mud. This is, after all, a tropical forest and the terrain is characterized by swamplands. Add to this the incessant buzz of hungry mosquitos, extreme heat and humidity, and you start to realize why so few people make it to this remote site. Your best bet is to attempt the trek at the height of the dry season between February and April. Mel Gibson is rumored to have visited in 2005. He came in by helicopter.

Treks begin in the village of **Carmelita,** inside the biosphere reserve at the end of the line for the road from Flores. Carmelita is a small cluster of houses grouped alongside the road with a few basic services such as a *comedor,* a small general store, and simple accommodations. The journey usually lasts five days. The first night is spent at El Tintal and the next day is a grueling hike that puts you at El Mirador close to nightfall. You spend two nights at the ruins before the two-day hike back to Carmelita. Trip prices vary, but expect to pay about $250 per person for two people. Some outfitters do the trip in seven days, allowing more time at El Mirador and stopping en route at Nakbé and Wakná. Mules carry the supplies, but you can also rent additional mules or horses for riding. This is particularly recommended if you make the journey in the wet season. Expect to pay an extra $10 per day for riding horses.

Be very careful in your selection of an outfitter to get you to El Mirador. The community of Carmelita, with help from NGOs, has trained and licensed guides to take visitors on the hike as part of a sustainable tourism initiative contributing to the ecologically friendly livelihood of local residents. While it's a nice idea in theory, it may not always be the best way to go. Not all of the local guides have the same skills or experience in running the trek and you run the risk of getting one of these lesser-experienced guides if you book your trip directly through the community. The task invariably falls on whoever is available to take you at that particular time. Further complicating the scenario is the presence of "gypsy" guides claiming to be part of the local tourism committee but indeed not.

That being said, you can save some money by taking public transport to Carmelita and then hooking up with the local **Comité de Turismo** (tel. 7861-1809, Spanish-only, ask for Brenda Zapata). The trip should cost about $235 per person for two people. Book at least a few days in advance, as the supplies and food must be brought in from Flores and the guides must go into town to get them. If you do go this route, make sure the guide buys adequate amounts of food for the duration of the trip. A common complaint is that food runs low halfway through the trek. You should also verify that there is enough water. Have the guide unpack all the supplies and show you exactly what you're taking. Don't hesitate to tell the guide if the food supply is inadequate for the trip's duration. In the worst of cases, you might buy a chicken to eat from the guards at the site, though it won't be cheap and there's no guarantee they'll have one to sell to you.

A final consideration if booking directly through the community is that the guide will want the money up front so as to buy food and supplies. This may or may not be an inconvenience to you, but it bears mentioning nonetheless. The more established Flores tour operators take credit cards and arrange everything for you in advance.

This leads us to your second option, that of booking the trip from Flores through one of several recommended outfitters (see *Guide Companies* in the *Flores* section). Although any Flores travel agency will claim to offer the trip, the quality of the service is not the same and you run the risk of getting set up with an inferior guide at premium prices. These outfitters may or may not contract the services of the local Carmelita guides. Matthias, one of the friendly owners of **Los Amigos Hostel** in Flores (tel. 5584-8795 or 5521-2873, www .amigoshostel.com), organizes trips using local guides for $200 per person for two people and says he is happy with his current selection of guides after much trial and error.

Nakbé, El Tintal, and Wakná

Also part of the proposed Mirador Basin park, the smaller sites of Nakbé, El Tintal, and Wakná are important links in the chain unveiling the mysteries of early Mayan civilization. **Nakbé** is thought to be the earliest of Petén's Mayan cities with settlement as early as 1,000 B.C. and several thousand inhabitants by 400 B.C. Its layout is much like that of El Mirador, with triadic temple structures in two groups separated by a causeway. Its tallest structure, the Western Temple, reaches a height of just under 46 me-

ters (150 feet), making it about as tall as Tikal's Temple I. It was completed in 500 B.C. A large stucco mask has also been unearthed here, on the side of one of the temples, much like at El Mirador. The excavations here, under the direction of Richard Hansen, are still in their early stages but more finds are sure to follow.

On the trek to El Mirador, 21 kilometers south, you'll pass by the site of **El Tintal,** which is also similar in construction to the larger city to the north. It has been badly looted and the temples here remain unrestored. There are excellent views of the surrounding forest from the top of its highest temple, including a glimpse of El Mirador far off in the distance. It's sure to motivate you to continue the second leg of the journey. Trekkers usually camp here the first night en route to El Mirador.

Rediscovered by Landsat imagery as recently as 1998, **Wakná,** is another Preclassic site buried under the forest cover of the Mirador Basin. A ground crew led by Dr. Hansen confirmed the site's existence but unfortunately also found evidence of looting. A deep trench had been dug into a tomb allowing looters to cart off the priceless artifacts found therein. Richard Hansen's plans to restore and protect the Mirador Basin's sites may prevent further plunder of Wakná and other sites within the proposed park.

Río Azul

Occupying a remote corner of Guatemala near a border shared with Mexico and Belize, the Middle Preclassic site of Río Azul was rediscovered in 1962. The population reached its zenith sometime between A.D. 410 and 530, coinciding with the installation of the new Teotihuacán rulership at Tikal, with which it also shares a similar city layout. The population is believed to have reached 5,000 inhabitants occupying an area of about 300 hectares (750 acres).

Río Azul played an important part in the expansion of Tikal's dominance of the Petén area, likely as a vital trading post linking Tikal to sites on the Caribbean coast and farther north to Central Mexico. It also served as an important

PETÉN

ally against Tikal's archrival, Calakmul. By A.D. 530, however, the tables had turned and Calakmul invaded Río Azul, forcibly allying it. After Tikal regained its former splendor in the Late Classic period, Río Azul's population once again soared and new monuments were built, further reflecting the city's status as a subservient outpost to the area's more powerful cities. It rounded out the Classic period invaded by Puuc Mayans from the Yucatán in A.D. 830.

Río Azul's claim to fame is the discovery of several tombs with bright red paintings on white plaster. Many of the burial scenes contain elements of Teotihuacán culture, providing further evidence of strong influence on Tikal and its satellite cities. Unfortunately, Río Azul fell prey to some of the most severe looting ever seen in the Mayan world in the 1960s and '70s. A minor section of these murals lining royal burial tombs remains intact, as most were chiseled out and taken away. There are some more recent discoveries, though not nearly as elaborate, pertaining to burial chambers of noblemen. It is hoped Peteén's newer discoveries can avoid the same fate through better protection. Many of Río Azul's treasures are in private collections, though you can see several pieces on display in Guatemala City's archaeology museum.

Getting to Río Azul

Río Azul is connected by road to Uaxactún at a distance of about 95 kilometers. The road is passable only in the dry season via 4WD. About halfway, you'll pass the **Naachtun-Dos Lagunas Biotope**. It is also possible to hike or ride horseback to this remote outpost, taking about five days each way. Trips can be arranged at **Campamento El Chiclero** in Uaxactún. Once at the site, you'll need to cross the Río Ixcán to the guards' campsite on the other side, where you can stay the night. The archaeological site proper is another six kilometers away, along a good road.

The road continues north another 12 kilometers to the intersection of the Belize, Guatemala, and Mexico borders, a place known as **Tres Banderas.** There are plans to improve the road from Uaxactún clear to the border at Tres Banderas under the auspices of a regional initiative known as *Plan Puebla Panamá.* So far, conservationists have been able to get the project shelved, arguing that the new road would bring in settlers, much as in Laguna del Tigre to the west, with devastating consequences for this well-preserved swath of forest.

NAACHTUN-DOS LAGUNAS BIOTOPE

This biotope is managed by Guatemala's University of San Carlos Center for Conservation Studies (CECON) and was established for the protection of white-tailed deer. The biotope forms a corridor connecting the area around El Mirador to that surrounding Río Azul within the larger **Mirador-Río Azul National Park.** It also protects the Mayan ruins of Naachtun.

Naachtun lies 25 kilometers east of El Mirador and about one kilometer from the Mexican border in a remote pocket of jungle. A Late Classic site, its architecture bears strong influence from Tikal and Calakmul, probably owing to its being caught in the tug-of-war between these two great rivals. At least 45 stelae have been found here.

The biotope is in fairly good shape because of its remote location and the absence of roads, with abundant wildlife, including many of Guatemala's endangered species—jaguars and other jungle cats, such as margays and ocelots, brocket deer, crocodiles, river turtles, monkeys, tapirs, peregrine falcons, and mealy parrots. The plant diversity here and within the Mirador-Río Azul National Park is said to be the highest in the Maya Biosphere Reserve with a particularly high concentration of mahogany trees. Little has been done to promote tourism to the reserve and it remains a delightfully remote natural oasis off the beaten tourist trail.

Access to the biotope is along the road connecting Uaxactún to Río Azul, a little more than halfway. The road is passable only in the dry season, and then only via 4WD. You can also hike or ride on horseback to the site from Uaxactún in about two days. Trips can be arranged through **Campamento El Chiclero.**

Park facilities are rudimentary and only about 40 visitors make it here every year, mostly foreigners. The park rangers have an encampment on the shore of one of the lagoons and will allow you to stay and cook there. Basic shelters for setting up a tent or stringing up a hammock are available, as are showers.

LAGUNA DEL TIGRE NATIONAL PARK

This vast park on the northwestern corner of Petén encompasses important wetlands, the largest in Central America. It also contains the only remaining populations of scarlet macaws in Guatemala, which are being protected via ongoing conservation efforts at a biological research station. Oil drilling, present before the park's creation, continues in the western part of the reserve, despite protests from environmental groups and their having been declared a violation of the park's intended use. In 2006, the Guatemalan government granted further oil exploration concessions in the park's multiple-use zone.

Visitors to this park should limit their activities to those centered around the Scarlet Macaw Biological Research Station and the site of Waka'-Perú, as the security conditions and the loss of much of the local habitat prevent me from recommending more in-depth explorations of this wild frontier. (For more on this topic, see the *Background* chapter.)

Within the larger national park is the **Biotopo Laguna del Tigre Río-Escondido,** which has two biological stations open to researchers. It has been badly fragmented by seasonal forest fires and the encroachment of communities illegally settled inside park boundaries.

Sights

Unlike other parts of Petén, Laguna del Tigre has not been widely explored for the presence of archaeological sites or in terms of its biological diversity. Among the few archaeological

PETÉN

LOST AND FOUND: THE MYSTERY OF SITE Q

For much of the 20th century, looters worked Petén's remote sites undisturbed, raiding tombs and extracting precious artifacts before archaeologists had a chance to study and document them. At the height of the looting, in the 1960s, archaeologists marveled at a series of magnificent glyphs making their way into a number of private collections and museums from an unknown site. Archaeologists dubbed the pieces' origin "site Q" and the search to find the mysterious producer of the wonderful glyphs was on.

The glyphs made repeated references to a place deciphered as *kan,* or "snake head," which was eventually deduced to be Calakmul, and recorded several events in its history. It was once thought that this might be Site Q, but the badly eroded stelae at Calakmul were not of the same high-quality limestone.

The identity of Site Q would remain a mystery for more than four decades. It first began to unravel in 1997 when an expedition headed by Ian Graham of Harvard University and David Stuart, now at the University of Texas at Austin, found evidence at remote La Corona leading them to suggest the possibility that it was Site Q. Then, in 2005, a one- by half-meter limestone panel containing 144 hieroglyphs was unearthed when an anthropologist working at the site followed a looter's trench into a small chamber.

Marcello A. Canuto, of Yale University, made the amazing discovery, which matches the Site Q pieces geologically. The translated text of the La Corona glyph panel, meanwhile, is consistent with the writings on the other Site Q pieces.

Although archaeologists are satisfied with finally putting to rest one of the longest-running searches for a lost Mayan city, they still have some unanswered questions. Among the Site Q glyph panels in private collections is one known as the "Dallas panel," which archaeologists believe was cut from a throne room. No such room has yet been found at La Corona.

discoveries is the site of **Waka'-Perú,** now being excavated by archaeologists from Southern Methodist University under the direction of David Freidel and Héctor Escobedo. Waka'-Perú has yielded some amazing finds, including the 2004 discovery of the royal burial tomb of a queen dating to about A.D. 620. The find is especially significant because there are only a handful of known tombs pertaining to women in the entire Mayan World. The location of yet another royal tomb was announced in May 2006.

Waka'-Perú is thought to have been an important commercial and political center because of its location on a tributary of the Río San Pedro, giving it direct access to the sites of Central Petén, the Southern Highlands, and Mexico. It flourished between A.D. 400 and 800, apparently coming under the dominion of Calakmul in its protracted power struggle with Tikal. It was later invaded by a resurgent Tikal in A.D. 743. There are several well-preserved stelae here, including Stela 16, which tells of the visit of a Tikal-bound Teotihuacán warrior in A.D. 378.

Nearby, the rediscovery of **La Corona** has solved the 45-year mystery of the location of a long-sought Mayan city. (See sidebar *Lost And Found: The Mystery Of Site Q.*) The limited amount of exploration in this part of Petén inevitably leads you to wonder what else may be lying undiscovered in this vast park of wetlands and jungle.

The park enjoys on-site protection by armed guards that are part of a joint task force involving the Civilian National Police (PNC) and SEPRONA, a specially trained unit of the military created to guard and protect nature preserves. You will see the guards at the site's ranger station, about a 25-minute walk from the riverbank. You are welcome to camp here.

◖ Las Guacamayas Biological Research Station

Las Guacamayas Biological Research Station (tel. 7926-1370, www.propeten.org) is owned

---

SAVING GUATEMALA'S SCARLET MACAWS

Among Petén's most beautiful creatures are the brightly colored scarlet macaws that once roamed freely throughout Petén. You'll probably run into these large parrots throughout your travels in Guatemala, as they are popular pets in hotel courtyards on account of their colorful red, blue, and yellow plumage, including two beautiful red tail feathers, in addition to their boisterous squawking and ability to mimic human speech. Unfortunately, their populations have been decimated by wildlife poaching for the international pet trade and habitat loss. Still, there remain pockets where macaws continue to nest, and local scientists have taken it upon themselves to help protect what's left of Guatemala's dwindling numbers of these exotic birds.

In the dense forests that still surround the site of Waka'-Perú, biologists from several agencies working in Petén, including ProPetén and Wildlife Conservation Society, have established protected nesting grounds. There are 21 nests in hollow forest trees and additional "artificial" nests are being created. The latter involve creating hollowed-out tree trunks which are then placed high in the treetops. Biologists report success with this new method. Like most parrots, scarlet macaws lay 2-4 white eggs in a tree cavity, with their young hatching after about 25 days. They fly about 105 days later and leave their parents as late as one year.

The nests at Waka'-Perú enjoy year-round protection by a newly created joint military-police force charged with safeguarding Guatemala's natural resources.

Volunteers are welcome at the site, giving visitors an exciting opportunity to help out in the conservation of Guatemala's exotic creatures while helping to fund the biological station's efforts.

by ProPetén and welcomes visitors. The biological station sits amid verdant jungle on the shores of the Río San Pedro, a 20-minute boat ride from the village of Paso Caballos. It is one of the best places in Petén to combine wildlife-viewing and rainforest trekking while staying in relative comfort, offering easy access to the ruins of Waka'-Perú and the surrounding forests. The current facility is the second incarnation of the biological station; the first was burned to the ground by angry villagers from Paso Caballos in the 1990s. ProPetén has since worked on strengthening ties to local communities and educating them about conservation.

You may contact ProPetén directly if you wish to stay here, as you don't need to be on an organized trip (Scarlet Macaw Trail) to book a room. It's recommended that you stay at least one night, as the station's remote location doesn't make for a reasonable day trip. A stay here can be arranged with or without meals, and you are free to use the kitchen to cook your own. There are basic dorm rooms with stiff mattresses, shared bath, mosquito netting, and screened-in rooms accommodating up to 20 people. For extended stays, try packing a sleeping pad for extra cushioning.

Nice views of the river and a series of nature trails round out the list of amenities. The shortest trail leads to an observation tower, where you have a sweeping view of the Río San Pedro and the wetlands of Laguna del Tigre National Park west to the foothills of the Sierra del Lacandón. There is a six-kilometer-long network of trails but it was awaiting repair because of a series of forest fires affecting areas near the station in 2003. Much of the forest traversed by the trail was burned to the ground.

In the evening, you can go out on the river in search of crocodiles with the station's staff. Bird-watching is available in the mornings. There are observation platforms inside the site of Waka'-Perú where the scarlet macaw project operates. The staff may offer photo safaris whereby you can watch and photograph macaws from a platform sometime in the near future. The best time to visit for a glimpse at

nesting macaws is during February and March, though the macaws can usually be seen between November and April.

A two-day, three-night package including meals, accommodation, round-trip transport from Flores, bird-watching, and a tour of El Perú costs $300 each for two people, but better deals can probably be found through one of the Flores travel agencies.

Volunteers are also welcome at the biological station. During my last visit, two Spanish women were busy on a two-week tour of duty recollecting animal droppings for scientific investigation as to the health of local populations of certain species. Volunteers provide their own food and pay an average of $7 per day. The station prefers a two-week minimum commitment. Other activities you may be asked to assist with include wildlife monitoring and trail building/maintenance.

Recreation

Many travelers visit Waka'-Perú as part of a tour known as the **Scarlet Macaw Trail,** which can be booked from a number of travel agencies in Flores and costs anywhere between $200 and $300 per person. The duration of the trip, as well as the places to visit, can be adjusted to suit your preferences. Most visitors combine the site of Waka'-Perú with hikes into the surrounding pristine forests to see the nesting sites of scarlet macaws, which local scientists here are working to protect. A nearby biological station offers comfortable accommodations on a nice stretch of jungle river. Some travelers extend their stay to include a hike to the impressive cliffs of **Buena Vista,** which stand out from the surrounding jungle and afford wonderful views from the top.

Getting There

Access to the park and, more specifically, Waka'-Perú, is via a dirt road heading northwest from Flores to the village of Paso Caballos (two hours). From there, it's a 20-minute motorboat ride up the Río Sacluc to the biological station and another five minutes to the entrance of Waka'-Perú.

PETÉN

SIERRA DEL LACANDÓN NATIONAL PARK

Ironically, Guatemala's civil war helped protect many pristine areas from invasion and environmental degradation. This was especially the case in Sierra del Lacandón, a mountain chain in the western part of Petén along the Usumacinta River, where guerrillas and so-called Permanent Communities in Resistance (CPR) hid out in the jungle along the Guatemalan shore. Their presence discouraged illegal logging, poaching, and looting, as well as the surveying activities of dam engineers. The subsequent absence of the expelled CPRs after the end of the civil war left the area open to invasion, illegal logging, and smuggling of immigrants, arms, Mayan relics, and drugs.

The 1996 Guatemala peace accords and the Zapatista Rebellion across the border in Mexico reshaped the nature of things in the Usumacinta watershed. Bandits began robbing rafting trips, including the author and eight others while camping on the Mexican bank in April 2004. Wilderness travel on the river north of Yaxchilán (Mexican bank) has pretty much ended since then, putting a monkey wrench into one option for low-impact, economically beneficial activities contributing to the conservation of this beautiful area.

That said, the park is extremely important as a biological corridor and is believed to hold one of the largest populations of jaguars in all of Central America as well as an incredible degree of biodiversity, qualities enhanced by the rugged terrain of this jungle mountain park. Hidden in the forests are the remains of several Mayan sites, the most important of which is Piedras Negras, deep inside the park along the Usumacinta River. The only other way to reach the site is by air.

The park is privately administered by Fundación Defensores de la Naturaleza. In June 2006, together with The Nature Conservancy, it completed the purchase of 77,000 acres of privately owned land in the core zone of Sierra del Lacandón. Soon thereafter, a number of ranger stations inside the park were burned to the ground by squatters invading parklands.

As in other cases, the squatters are said to have ties to drug traffickers and smugglers of illegal immigrants who find these remote areas very attractive. An attempt to evict squatters from an area known as Arroyo Macabilero in June 2006 ended with a gunfight between heavily armed men and park rangers. Four park rangers were taken captive but were released a few days later unharmed.

In the summer of 2006, authorities were attempting to regain control of the area in a joint venture between Defensores de la Naturaleza and governmental security forces. Shortly thereafter, in October 2006, the press widely reported the retaking of Sierra del Lacanón by large numbers of Guatemalan security forces, who ousted about 80 families living at Arroyo Macabilero in a peaceful expropriation overseen and verified by human rights organizations. It remains to be seen if control of this wild frontier can be retained and if ranger stations or other tourist infrastructure will be rebuilt. For now, it is advisable to stay out of this park, with the possible exception of visits to Yaxchilán, across the Usumacinta River in Mexico, or via motorboat to Piedras Negras. In any case, check on the situation with one of the recommended Flores outfitters before heading out to these parts, as the situation can vastly improve or degenerate in a matter of weeks.

If the security situation is ever cleared up, Sierra del Lacandón promises to be one of the Maya Biosphere's most exquisite offerings because of the diversity of the terrain and corresponding biological significance. It is an absolutely beautiful park despite its current woes. Piedras Negras is a fascinating Mayan city and the jungle-lined banks of the Usumacinta offer an incredible river adventure. Having flown over much of the reserve, I can personally attest to the relatively well-preserved state of its mountain rainforests.

El Naranjo

This rough-and-tumble frontier town, accessible by bus from Santa Elena, is a jumping-off point for those heading west to Mexico via an unreliable boat transport down the Río San

Pedro to La Palma. A better option into Mexico is to cross the Río Usumacinta via Bethel, arriving in Frontera Corozal.

Bethel

This small, pleasant settlement serves as a much better option for onward travel to Mexico or down the Río Usumacinta. There is an immigration office here, lodging, and several simple *comedores*. The best place to stay is at the community-run **Posada Maya** (tel. 7861-1799 or 7861-1800, $20 d) with simple rooms in thatched-roof bungalows. The restaurant here serves decent meals in a pleasant *palapa* building.

There is a small Mayan site here about 1.5 kilometers from the village, though its most impressive feature is probably the view of the river from a lookout about 20 minutes' walk from the site's core.

Boats leave Bethel downstream for Frontera Corozal, Yaxchilán, and Piedras Negras. Five daily buses and three daily minibuses leave the Santa Elena bus depot for the 3–4 hour ride to Bethel. The last of these departs at 1:30 P.M.

Río Usumacinta

This mighty river is Central America's longest and harbors the remains of at least two important Mayan cities along its banks. Ten-day rafting trips once made their way down this waterway starting at Yaxchilán and putting out at the Mexican town of Tenosique, but these have been suspended for the time being because of robberies. The robberies seem to occur downstream from Yaxchilán on a very remote stretch of the river on the way to Piedras Negras. It's really a shame, as the stretch harbors some truly spectacular banks of riverside rainforest on the Guatemalan side protected as the Sierra del Lacandón National Park. On the Mexican side, there are a variety of communities and some bad deforestation, though there are some beautiful waterfalls downstream from Piedras Negras. All is not lost, however, as you can still reach **Busiljá Falls** from Mexico. Willy Fonseca, the friendly owner of **Restaurante Vallescondido** (Km. 61 on the Palenque–Comitán Road, 01 916-348-0721), can get you there and also offers trips to Piedras Negras.

© AL ARGUETA

PETÉN

aerial view of the Río Usumacinta

Farther downstream, the river leaves Guatemala behind and narrows into the impressive **Cañón de San José,** where there are Class III rapids flanked by 1,000-foot canyons.

While it is entirely possible to do part of the trip by motorboat, as opposed to slow-moving inflatable rafts, it seems even these vessels are occasionally shot at from the riverbank in an attempt to make them stop. Much of the boat traffic here pertains to the transport of illegal immigrants crossing international borders on their way north, and thieves are only too eager to rid them of their money. Drug smugglers also use the river as a highway for transporting their merchandise. It really makes you long for the "good old days" when the Guatemalan ORPA guerrillas patrolled the banks, at worst flagging you down from the shore for a lecture on the justice of their cause. If the Mexicans can get their security issues straightened out, white-water rafting trips may once again be a viable recreational option here. But don't hold your breath.

Yaxchilán

This beautiful Mayan site enjoys a spectacular setting on the Mexican shore of the Río Usumacinta, on a densely forested horseshoe-shaped bend on the river. It was unquestionably the most important Usumacinta site in Mayan times. At the height of its power, in the late 7th century A.D., it came to dominate much of the river's trade and formed powerful alliances with neighboring sites as far away as Tikal and Palenque. Sprawled throughout the site's raised banks are several temples, plazas, and ball courts. Several palaces can be found along lower parts of the city.

Among the site's most impressive features is the presence of superb artwork adorning several structures, including door lintels and stucco carvings on roof combs. Many of these have been removed to museums around the world. A long staircase leads from the plaza to **Temple 33,** Yaxchilán's most impressive structure, featuring impressive carved lintels under its doorways.

The ruins are open 8 A.M. to 5 P.M. daily.

Admission costs $3. You can pitch a tent at a campground overlooking the river if you wish to spend the night. The easiest way to get here is from the community of Bethel. The **Posada Maya Bethel** can arrange trips to Yaxchilán for about $100 round-trip. A cheaper option is to book a trip on one of several boats heading downstream to **Frontera Corozal.** You can hire a boat from Frontera Corozal to the ruins for about $60 round-trip for up to four people. It's about a 45-minute trip downstream to the site and an hour upstream on the return.

Piedras Negras

About 40 kilometers downstream amid the dense rainforests of Sierra del Lacandón lie the exotic ruins of Piedras Negras. The site is exquisite both because of its location on a lonely stretch of river and for the quality of its carved monuments, which are considered some of the best in the Mayan world. Its remoteness gives you the privileged sensation of being one of a very select number of visitors and, along with El Mirador, most closely mirrors what the early explorers must have felt upon first rediscovering some of the great Mayan cities.

Piedras Negras was founded sometime around A.D. 300 and fought Yaxchilán for much of its history in a struggle for supreme control over the Usumacinta's trade routes. It would form strategic alliances both with Tikal and Calakmul in this pursuit. This large city is thought to have housed 10,000 inhabitants at its peak population.

Among Piedras Negras's excellent carvings are several stelae, hieroglyphic panels, and even a royal hieroglyphic throne. Several of these are on display in Guatemala City's archaeology museum.

The site gets its Spanish name from the black rocks lining the riverbank here. Among them is a giant stone near the entrance to the site with several eroded hieroglyphs and a depiction of two seated figures. From here, you head up the hill to the ruins. Several structures remain well preserved, among them the **Acropolis,** containing a large twin-palace complex, as well as several Mayan saunas used by the elite and scattered throughout the site. The remains of a giant **stairway** reaching down to the riverbank can also be found here.

Famed Russian epigrapher Tatiana Proskouriakoff, who deciphered many of the Mayan glyphs here and at Yaxchilán, is buried among the ruins. Proskouriakoff first postulated the idea that many of the events described in Mayan hieroglyphs corresponded to events in a ruler's life span, a theory initially discarded by Mayanists but subsequently proven correct.

Since 1997, after the departure of the guerrillas formerly occupying Piedras Negras, excavations have once again been carried out under the leadership of Héctor Escobedo. The site is among the World Monuments Fund's list of "100 Most Threatened Places" because of a hydroelectric project tossed around by the Mexican government for decades, threatening to flood Piedras Negras and several smaller, recently discovered nearby sites. Only about 200 visitors make the trip to Piedras Negras every year.

The best way to visit Piedras Negras is on an organized tour. Though her company no longer offers rafting trips to the site, Tammy Ridenour of **Maya Expeditions** (www.maya expeditions.com) can answer your questions about current security issues and access to the site. Folks at the **Posada Maya** in Bethel can

© AL ARGUETA

superbly carved glyphs from Piedras Negras

PETÉN

do the same and help arrange transport if you choose to go. There is an excellent riverside campsite with a wide sandy beach a few hundred meters downstream from Piedras Negras at El Porvenir, where there is a CONAP guard station.

BACKGROUND

The Land

GEOGRAPHY

Guatemala is the third-largest country in Central America. It occupies 42,042 square miles, making it about the size of Tennessee. The country shares borders with Mexico, Belize, Honduras, and El Salvador. Within Guatemala's relatively small area are 14 distinct ecosystems found at elevations varying from sea level to higher than 4,200 meters (14,000 feet). Many people think of Guatemala as a sweltering tropical country, which is only partially true. While it does feature warm tropical coastal environments and hot lowland jungles, a rugged spine of mountains and volcanoes runs through the country's center. In the tropics, elevation mostly determines climate and this is certainly the case in Guatemala. Temperatures drop dramatically the higher you go in elevation and precipitation varies greatly depending on what side of a mountain chain you're on. All of this translates into a dizzying array of landscapes, making Guatemala a delight to explore.

The country divides rather neatly into various geographical zones. The volcanic highlands run through the country's center going west to east from Mexico to El Salvador. Elevation tends to get lower closer to the Salvadoran border. The eastern areas of Alta and Baja Verapaz are largely mountainous but also

© AL ARGUETA

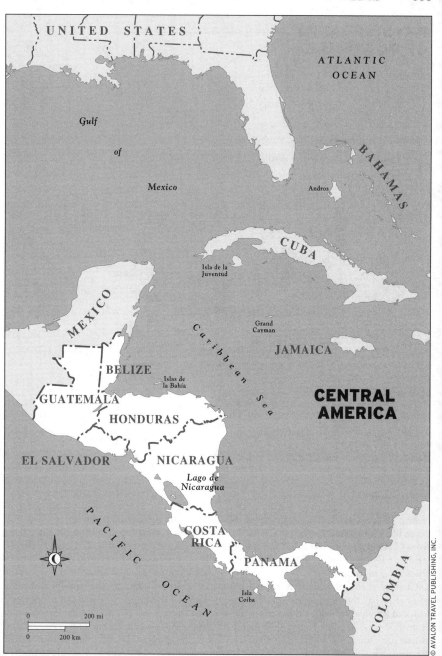

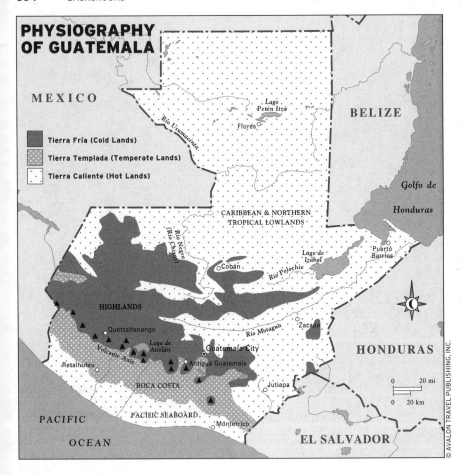

PHYSIOGRAPHY OF GUATEMALA

MEXICO

BELIZE

- Tierra Fría (Cold Lands)
- Tierra Templada (Temperate Lands)
- Tierra Caliente (Hot Lands)

Lago Petén Itzá

Flores

Golfo de

Honduras

Río Usumacinta

CARIBBEAN & NORTHERN
TROPICAL LOWLANDS

*Río Negro
(Río Chixoy)*

Cobán

*Lago de
Izabal*

Puerto
Barrios

Río Polochic

HIGHLANDS

Quetzaltenango

Río Motagua

Zacapa

*Lago de
Atitlán*

Guatemala City

Volcanic Axis

Retalhuleu

Antigua Guatemala

HONDURAS

BOCA COSTA

Jutiapa

PACIFIC

PACIFIC SEABOARD

OCEAN

Monterrico

EL SALVADOR

0   20 mi
0   20 km

© AVALON TRAVEL PUBLISHING, INC.

largely composed of limestone. A curious feature of this area, found in its northern limits, is the presence of small, forested limestone hills much like those found in parts of China. East from Guatemala City toward Honduras, the terrain is largely dominated by semiarid flatlands covered with cactus.

Closer to the Caribbean coast in the department of Izabal, the terrain once again becomes lush and largely filled with banana plantations. A small sliver of Caribbean coastline runs between the Honduran border and Belize but features white-sand beaches, swamplands, and some impressive tropical rainforests. Small mountains are interspersed throughout parts of the Caribbean coastal region.

Running roughly parallel to the highlands, to the south, are the Pacific Coast flatlands. This is a rich agricultural area once covered in tropical forest but now home to vast sugarcane and coffee plantations, the latter being on the slopes of the highland zones as they descend into the coastal plain. The Pacific Coast is also home to wetlands, mangrove swamps, and beaches of curiously dark color because of their proximity to the country's volcanic chain.

The northern third of Guatemala is a vast Ohio-size limestone flatland known as Petén. Once covered entirely in tropical forests, it has increasingly become deforested in its southern parts with only the northern third retaining large unbroken swaths of forest.

Here is a brief discussion of some of Guatemala's outstanding geographic features and why they might be of interest to the visitor.

Mountains

The highest of Guatemala's mountains are actually volcanic peaks. There are 33 of them in total with a handful now active. Volcán Tajumulco, at 4,220 meters (13,845 feet), is the highest point in all of Central America, followed closely by nearby Volcán Tacaná, at 4,110 meters (13,484 feet). The most frequently climbed volcanoes include the active Pacaya, near Guatemala City, the three volcanoes on the shores of Lake Atitlán, and Agua and Acatenango near Antigua. Some volcanoes, such as Chicabal and Ipala, feature turquoise lagoons, which fill their craters. Other active volcanoes include Fuego and Santiaguito.

Among the nonvolcanic mountains, the Sierra de los Cuchumatanes, near the border with Mexico, is Guatemala's, and Central America's, highest mountain chain. It stands 3,837 meters (12,588 feet) at its highest point. Its smooth, rounded peaks attest to years of erosion from being glaciated thousands of years ago. Other noteworthy mountain chains include the Sierra de Las Minas, in the eastern part of the country. Protected as a private forest reserve, it still contains large stands of virgin cloud forest. Farther east near the Caribbean Coast are the Cerro San Gil and Montañas del Mico, which are still covered in dense tropical rainforest. Petén has relatively few mountains, but the foothills of the Maya Mountains of neighboring Belize run into the department's southeastern corner with an elevation of over 1000 meters (3,300 feet) at Petén's highest point. Petén's other noteworthy mountain range is the remote and mostly forested Sierra del Lacandón, at the far western edge of the department

© AL ARGUETA

Atitlán and Tolimán Volcanoes

bordering Mexico and exceeding 600 meters (2,000 feet) at its highest point.

Guatemala's mountain scenery comes largely as a product of its geographic location at the intersection of the North American, Cocos, and Caribbean plates, making it one of the most seismically and volcanically active places in the world. Indeed, Guatemala is no stranger to earthquakes. Among the many fault lines running through the country are the parallel Chixoy-Polochic and Motagua faults. The latter is responsible for the most recent major earthquake to rock Guatemala, a magnitude-7.5 whopper in February 1976 killing thousands and wiping entire villages off the face of the map. A series of massive earthquakes in 1776 resulted in the relocation of the Guatemalan capital from the Panchoy Valley (Antigua Guatemala) to the Valley of the Hermitage, where it remains today, better known as Guatemala City.

Rivers

Guatemala has several rivers worthy of mention. The greatest of these is the Usumacinta, which is formed by the confluence of the Chixoy and Pasión Rivers, making it Central America's most voluminous river. Guatemalan author Virgilio Rodríguez Macal, in his novel *Guayacán,* calls it the "father and lord of the Central American rivers." The Usumacinta forms much of Guatemala's border with Mexico and continues its northwesterly flow all the way to the Gulf of Mexico. On the Guatemalan side, the Usumacinta borders the relatively untouched Sierra del Lacandón National Park, which harbors dense tropical rainforests. Rafting trips once made their way down the Usumacinta, visiting Yaxchilán (Mexico) and the Guatemalan site of Piedras Negras, but an increase in violent armed robberies has meant their indefinite suspension. The Usumacinta is indeed a wild frontier and is an active waterway for drug smuggling, contraband logging,, and boats carrying illegal immigrants on their journey north. An on-again, off-again Mexican dam project has been vehemently opposed by en-

vironmentalists and, until 1996, Guatemalan rebels camped out in the jungle. The project would reportedly flood Piedras Negras, Yaxchilán, and several smaller sites along the Usumacinta. The project appears to have been called off, for the time being.

The Pasión, an Usumacinta tributary, meanders through southern Petén. Much like the larger Usumacinta, its watershed was extremely important in Mayan times. Several Mayan sites lie near the river. In the arid southeastern part of the country, the Río Motagua connects the highlands to the Caribbean Sea and forms a dry river valley of agricultural importance since Mayan times. Other notable rivers include the Río San Pedro, also in Petén;the Verapaces-area Río Cahabon, which has excellent whitewater runs year-round; and the Río Dulce, a lazy tropical river connecting Lake Izabal to the Caribbean.

Lakes and Lagoons

Guatemala has several lakes noteworthy for their size, recreational opportunities, and sheer natural beauty. Foremost among these is highland Lake Atitlán, called "the most beautiful lake in the world" by author Aldous Huxley during his travels through the region. The lake's spectacular mountain scenery is punctuated by the sentinel presence of three towering volcanoes along its southern shores. Near Guatemala City, Lake Amatitlán has been a weekend getaway for city dwellers since time immemorial but industrial pollution has spoiled the once-clear waters. Still, Guatemalans have taken on the ominous task of rescuing its waters with foreign help and the lake may soon be safe again for swimming. An aerial tram operating on surrounding hillsides has recently reopened the area to visitors, making a side trip to this tranquil spot increasingly alluring for wonderful views of the rugged mountain terrain. The largest of Guatemala's lakes, Lake Izabal, is a tropical lake connected to the Caribbean by the Río Dulce. The Río Polochic delta, on Izabal's southwestern shore, is becoming increasingly popular as a bird-watcher's paradise. Petén's Lake

© AL ARGUETA

Lake Petén Itzá

Petén Itzá is also a tropical flatland lake with the added bonus of tropical forests, crystal-clear waters, and a variety of accommodations from which to enjoy all of these. As much of Petén is limestone, the lake's waters have a distinct turquoise color near the lakeshores and from the air look very much like those of the Mexican Caribbean. Farther east toward Belize is Yaxhá Lagoon, near the ruins of the same name. The lagoon, and its aggressive crocodiles, was made famous by the *Survivor Guatemala* television series filmed here in the summer of 2005.

There are many beautiful lagoons in the Guatemalan highlands. Some, atop volcanoes such as Ipala and Chicabal, are believed by the Mayans to harbor mystical powers and are the site of rituals. Laguna Lachuá is a beautiful, almost perfectly round lagoon in the Ixcán jungle region just north of the highlands. The surrounding rainforest has been preserved, but unfortunately it is an ecological island, a green square in a surrounding ocean of deforestation.

The Coasts

Guatemala has a significant amount of coastline along the Pacific Ocean, though there are few beaches to speak of. Still, there are a few places with surf-worthy waves and the Pacific Coast beaches are exotic because of their dark sands, which are due to the proximity of active volcanoes. Among the best places to hit the beach are Monterrico and Las Lisas. Guatemala is gaining international fame among anglers for the quality of its deep-sea fishing. On the Caribbean side, there are a few pleasant white-sand beaches on the remote peninsula of Punta de Manabique as well as closer to the towns of Puerto Barrios and Lívingston. There is excellent scuba diving in the outlying Belize cayes and around Punta de Manabique.

CLIMATE

Guatemala has a tropical climate, though temperatures vary greatly between regions because of differences in altitude. The coastal plains and lowlands have an average yearly temperature of about 27°C (80°F), with little seasonal change. Mountain valleys 1,200–1,800 meters (4,000–6,000 feet) high are usually comfortably mild. Major cities such as Guatemala City, Antigua, and Quetzaltenango all lie at these altitudes, meaning they have mostly pleasant year-round springlike temperatures of 16°C–21°C (60°F–70°F). Higher mountain peaks and valleys sometimes have frost and average 4°C (40°F). Keep in mind that these are averages and certain times of year are markedly warmer than others. The North American winter solstice often brings the arrival of cold fronts, which make temperatures in the highlands dip below freezing on mountain summits but also in highland cities such as Quetzaltenango. If you're traveling to Guatemala November–February, bring a warm sweater or two for the chilly highlands and a heavy jacket if you plan to climb some volcanoes. At the other extreme, March and April, coinciding with the spring equinox, is the warmest time of year. Temperatures in the Petén lowlands, Izabal, and Pacific Coast plain routinely hover around 38°C (100°F) during these months. Guatemala City and Antigua hover at around 29°C (85°F).

There are distinct dry and rainy seasons in Guatemala. The dry season runs from November to the beginning of May. If you are a photographer interested in capturing images of Guatemala's fantastic mountain scenery, you may want to avoid visiting during March and April, when haze from dust and agricultural burning tends to obliterate any views of surrounding scenery. The volcanoes around Antigua and Lake Atitlán become extremely difficult to spot during this time of year.

The rainy season generally lasts May–November with daily showers during most of this period, usually in the afternoon. Mornings are usually sunny and clear, with a gradual buildup of giant rain clouds throughout the day, culminating in a torrential downpour. The latter months tend to be the rainiest with deluges sometimes lasting entire days. The rainy season is sometimes referred to as *invierno,* meaning winter, though it is officially summer in the Northern Hemisphere, where Guatemala lies. *Verano,* or summer, refers to the tail end of the dry season.

The Pacific coastal plain and Western Highlands receive 76–150 centimeters (30–60 inches) of rain a year, and the Eastern Highlands average 51–76 centimeters (20–30 inches). Again, these figures will vary greatly from place to place depending on factors such as altitude and what side of the mountain chain you're on. An example of this is the presence of ample rainfall and lush cloud forests on the forested slopes of the Sierra de las Minas in contrast to semiarid plains in the mountain's rain shadow along the neighboring Motagua Valley. Petén receives 200–381 centimeters (80–150 inches) of rain annually, which falls throughout most of the year. The rainiest place in Guatemala is said to be the Cerro San Gil rainforest, on the Caribbean Coast, where warm, moist air rises from the ocean and dumps precipitation on this small mountain chain. There is really no dry season to speak of in this area.

There are sometimes breaks in the rainfall, known as *canícula,* for a week or two in July and/or August. Rainfall can vary substantially from year to year, which is due to factors such as the presence of El Niño or La Niña. El Niño often means a prolonged dry season, which can lead to intense wildfires in forested areas such as Petén.

Hurricanes and tropical storms sometimes hit Guatemala during the latter months of the rainy season, causing widespread damage. Much of this is due to soil saturation on deforested and waterlogged hillsides, which give way to devastating mudslides, as occurred in parts of the Lake Atitlán basin after Hurricane Stan in 2005. Hurricane Mitch also left a trail of devastation along the Caribbean Coast in 1998, obliterating much of the banana harvest and destroying thousands of homes.

ENVIRONMENTAL ISSUES

Guatemala's environmental issues, particularly in regard to tropical deforestation, can seem daunting at times. The country and its people seem to be caught in a vicious cycle that will end only when the environmental degradation reaches its peak and the consequences are fully reaped. It seems greed, apathy, poverty, corruption, ignorance, and neglect have all conspired against Guatemala's precious natural resources. I do not mean to sound pessimistic in my introduction to this subject. I just think I've had the opportunity to see what's at stake, having explored much of Guatemala during my teenage years and seeing firsthand the gradual encroachment of the agricultural frontier into what was once virgin forest. It is hoped that visitors to Guatemala, much like those to Belize and Costa Rica, will play a pivotal role in getting Guatemalans to fully appreciate the abundant natural heritage with which their country has been blessed, enabling the conservation of these resources to become a source of economic and moral value.

There is a long way to go to make environmental awareness a matter of national consciousness, as demonstrated by the frequency one sees garbage by the roadside or car and bus passengers casually throwing refuse out their windows. The problem of raising this consciousness is exacerbated when one takes into account the overwhelming lack of education of the general populace, with its alarming levels of illiteracy, and the fact that environmental protection always takes a back seat when it comes down to a question of preserving the forest or cutting it down to plant subsistence crops.

At the same time, there is much to be hopeful about, particularly in the past 20 years since Guatemala's democratic opening, when the country finally had a civilian president interested in environmental matters. In addition to establishing the Maya Biosphere Reserve, Vinicio Cerezo Arévalo pushed through Congress much of the legislation serving as a basis for the protection of Guatemala's natural heritage. Many valiant Guatemalans have likewise done their part to establish a genuine environmental movement in their country. Their courage is underscored by the fact that, in Guatemala, environmental activism necessarily entails standing firm in the face of death threats and intimidations. Environmental protection often conflicts with the interests of the still-powerful agricultural elites, among these lumber barons, drug cartels using remote parks for illicit activities, cattle ranchers, some of whom have military ties, and land-hungry peasants. Environmental martyrs are many in Guatemala, much the same as the legacy of those campaigning for greater respect for human rights and better socioeconomic conditions. In these ways, environmental issues in Guatemala are largely circumscribed within the larger social issues of endemic poverty, power politics, and the rule of law.

Deforestation

In 2005, about 37 percent of Guatemala was still forested, down from 40 percent in 2001. Most of the country was at one time covered by forests, a fact attested to by Guatemala's ancient Mayan-Toltec name meaning "land of the trees." The once-forested Pacific plains have given way largely to sugarcane and coffee plantations while the forests of the Caribbean slope

tropical deforestation in the Maya Biosphere Reserve

have been turned largely over to banana plantations. The highlands, for their part, have been under intense cultivation since preconquest times, though there are still substantial forests left in remote corners of Quiche and Huehuetenango. Most of the loss of forest cover in the past 40 years has been due to government incentives aimed at colonizing the northern department of Petén in an attempt to ease pressure for land by an ever-increasing population. The Petén thus became an escape valve from pressures for land reform historically thwarted by Guatemala's agricultural elites. It is here that a modern-day battle is being waged over Guatemala's remaining forests.

It is hoped that history will not repeat itself, as the ancient Mayans have a valuable lesson to teach about what happens when the forests are cut down. It is speculated that among the reasons for the Classic Mayan collapse is widespread drought caused by the overwhelming deforestation of the tropical lowlands the Mayans inhabited. This may have, in turn, led to widespread warfare among Mayan city-states as populations scrambled to assert dominance over dwindling resources. The southern and central sections of Petén have been almost completely deforested, leading to local declines in annual rainfall marked by prolonged and warmer dry seasons. The northern third of Petén remains mostly intact, for now, protected as the Maya Biosphere Reserve. Pressures against the reserve continue to mount, however, with illegal land grabs and clandestine logging continuing to make inroads. There is no guarantee that the reserve's borders will remain inviolate or that they will stave off the advance of the agricultural frontier.

It bears discussing here the process by which seemingly endless tracts of forest become tropical wastelands resembling the dustbowl-era plains of Kansas. While the lowland Mayans practiced advanced farming techniques, including terracing and irrigation canals, what survives today is a simplified form of subsistence farming known as slash-and-burn agriculture. An area of forest will be felled and burned to the ground, with nutrient-rich ashes allowing crops to grow, though generally for a period of only two years. After that, a new plot of forest must be destroyed to grow crops again. The problem lies in that the soil of tropical forests is notoriously lacking in nutrients; the vast part of the ecosystem's biomass is in the trees themselves, with forest topsoil only reaching about two inches in depth. The old plot is abandoned, with the soil having been compacted, and sold to cattle ranchers. And so, each year more and more land is deforested and turned into a jungle wasteland. The forests are particularly at risk at the tail end of the dry season, when slash-and-burn agriculture can get out of hand and burn uncontrolled into protected areas. Many times fires are set purposely inside park lands.

In addition to the activities of peasant farmers steadily encroaching on virgin forests, the activities of contraband loggers, looters of unexcavated archaeological sites, and wildlife poachers inside park boundaries constitute an additional threat to the forests. Adding insult to injury, contraband loggers, wildlife poachers, and peasants from neighboring Mexico have been scuttling the border separating their country from Guatemala to burn forest, kill wildlife, and plant crops in cleared lands. A now-famous Landsat image appearing in the October 1989 issue of *National Geographic* shows the once razor-sharp border between Mexico and Guatemala's Laguna del Tigre National Park. The border is now dotted with burned-out land parcels along much of this boundary marker as a curious extension of the wide-scale deforestation in Mexico.

A recent development is the clearing of forest to build clandestine landing strips for drug-laden aircraft coming in from South America. With the virtual absence of local law enforcement and the aid of poor peasants eager for extra income, drug lords have found a haven for their illicit activities in Guatemala's remote parks. They have even gone so far as to acquire property by buying lands from settlers and then registering them illegally in their own names. Whether through bribes or the falsification of documents, *narcos* have infiltrated Guatemala's protected lands to suit their illicit operations. The existence of these "narco-farms" was brought to the attention of Guatemalan authorities after eight park guards were kidnapped and held hostage by armed men in June 2005 in Sierra del Lacandón National Park. The guards and members of a conservation group had decided to verify reports of clandestine logging inside the park. They were later released unharmed. The Public Ministry began a long process of expropriating the illegally titled lands while lawyers and land surveyors working the case faced intimidations and death threats. Meanwhile, the narcos reportedly moved their operations south to the Petexbatún region after a new military-trained environmental protection unit was created to destroy many of the clandestine landing strips and prevent further illicit activity.

Water Resources

Access to safe drinking water is a widespread problem throughout most of Guatemala. According to figures from the United Nations Development Program, roughly a quarter of Guatemalans still lack this basic necessity. This figure becomes even more dramatic in rural areas, where it is actually closer to 50 percent. The lack of potable water in turn leads to many illnesses, including intestinal parasites and amoebic dysentery, among others. Although most cities have sewer systems, wastewater treatment is virtually nonexistent with raw sewage often flowing into rivers, lakes, and oceans. Guatemala City's sewage, for example, is responsible for polluting the nearby Motagua River with human excrement, solvents, and metallic waste. Adding to Guatemala's water woes is pollution from petroleum-based fertilizers used in commercial coffee, banana, and sugar plantations, which openly dump wastewater into nearby rivers and streams.

Air Quality

Guatemala City is notoriously polluted by old, recycled U.S. school buses, the basis of its public transportation network, which belch out

© AL ARGUETA

Air quality is a growing concern in Guatemala City.

diesel fumes in the form of black clouds. A promising recent development is a revamping of the city's public transportation system to include newer vehicles and stop older buses from circulating in the city center. In addition to auto exhaust, pollution from industrial facilities and burning garbage from the city dump combine to form a thick haze often hanging over the city. The worst days occur when thermal inversions cause the haze to hang in a low-altitude pollution gulag, much like a pineapple-upside-down cake. Concentrations of particulates, ozone, and nitrogen dioxide often exceed World Health Organization safety standards, particularly on these days. During the rainy season, the haze is washed away by the afternoon rains, after which the atmosphere is amazingly free of pollutants.

Elsewhere, smoke and ash from occasional volcanic eruptions can make the atmosphere somewhat hazy, though the worst pollution comes from dry-season agricultural burning and forest fires. When one considers that more than half of all energy consumption comes from burning firewood, the reasons behind the thick haze hanging over much of the country during March and April begin to emerge.

Resource Extraction (Mining and Oil Drilling)

Mining activities have made Guatemalan newspaper headlines in recent years, as mining interests have cast an interested eye upon Guatemalan lands. Although environmental-impact studies are required by law, these often fall prey to government corruption in the form of payoffs in exchange for a favorable assessment. Threats and intimidation against environmental groups often attempt to quell any opposition to these projects.

Residents of the Western Highlands town of Sipacapa have demonstrated vehement opposition to the opening of a strip mine in the vicinity of their town, bringing the case directly to the president of the World Bank and officials of the International Finance Corporation (IFC), the World Bank's private-sector lending arm. Among the arguments against the installation of mining activities is the conflict of an open-pit mine with Mayan belief in the sacredness of the Earth.

Residents of Sipacapa held a referendum overwhelmingly rejecting the presence of a mine on community lands. In early 2005, protests against the mine's establishment, including roadblocks, were broken up by military forces, resulting in 11 people's being injured and one killed.

More than 550 mining concessions now cover 10 percent of the country. Almost 20 percent of these are for open-pit mining of minerals such as gold, silver, nickel, and copper.

Petroleum extraction continues in the northern Petén lowlands and parts of Alta Verapaz, including the Laguna del Tigre National Park, although ecological organizations have long denounced its negative effects upon the environment. Oil exploration and extraction were present before the creation of the Maya Biosphere Reserve and have thus been allowed to continue, mostly in parts of the buffer and multiple-use zones. During the civil war, oil pipelines became a frequent target for guerrillas sabotaging the activities of multinationals involved in resource extraction. Occupations of oil-drilling facilities were also frequent. In addition to creating roads through sparsely populated areas, the oil extraction activities have come under fire because of oil spills in protected lands.

In 2005, the Guatemalan government opened new concessions in an area along the Petén-Alta Verapaz border said to harbor an estimated 200 million barrels of oil. Guatemala's total estimated reserves amount to about 2 billion barrels. Guatemalan oil's high sulfur content prevents it from being used in the production of diesel or gasoline, relegating it to use in the production of asphalt.

Soil Erosion

Unbridled deforestation on steep hillsides is responsible for much of the erosion of Guatemala's soil. Already about one-third of all land cover is considered eroded or seriously degraded, a significant amount when one considers the high degree of susceptibility to erosion of Guatemala's soil, which is composed largely of unconsolidated volcanic ash. Deforestation and soil erosion work hand in hand and are responsible for many of the tragic mudslides in the aftermath of tropical storms such as Hurricanes Mitch and Stan. Soil erosion has also contributed to greatly shortening the useful life of Chixoy Dam, which supplies about 15 percent of Guatemala's electricity, through siltation of the dam's reservoir.

Conservation Groups

Many grassroots environmental organizations operate in Guatemala in partnership with international conservation organizations. Among the best-known groups is **Fundación Defensores de la Naturaleza** (7a Avenida 7-09 Zona 13, Guatemala City, tel. 2440-8138 or 2471-7942, www.defensores.org.gt), which administers Sierra del Lacandón National Park, Sierra de Las Minas Biosphere Reserve, Bocas del Polochic Wildlife Refuge, and the United Nations National Park just outside of Guatemala City. Through private land purchases, Defensores has been able to acquire large tracts of land in Sierra de las Minas and Sierra del Lacandón with help from The Nature Conservancy.

The Nature Conservancy also works locally with the Fundación para el Desarrollo y la Conservación (Foundation for Development and Conservation), or **FUNDAECO** (7a Calle "A" 20-53 Zona 11, Colonia Mirador, Guatemala City, tel. 2474-3645). Together, they have bought more than 9,000 acres of tropical rainforest in the Caribbean coastal mountain chain of Cerro San Gil.

Another organization working to protect local ecosystems is **FUNDARY** (Diagonal 6, 17-19 Zona 10, Guatemala City, tel. 2333-4957, 2366-7539, or 2367-0171, www.guate.net/fundarymanabique/index.htm), named after the late Mario Dary Rivera, creator of the CECON biotopes. FUNDARY has centered its efforts on the protection of coastal environments, particularly the Punta de Manabique peninsula, on Guatemala's Caribbean Coast.

The forests of Petén are understandably the center of much attention from local and international organizations. **ProPetén** (Calle Central, Flores, Petén, tel. 7926-1370, www.propeten.org), an offshoot of Conservation International, began operating shortly after the creation of the Maya Biosphere Reserve and is credited with implementing innovative approaches to bridge the gap between the need for environmental conservation and the needs of communities living in or near the reserve. Among its successful programs are the establishment of a research station for the protection of scarlet macaws, forestry concessions with local communities in the Maya Biosphere Reserve's buffer zone, and two Spanish-language schools owned and operated by local villagers.

Alianza Verde (Parque Central, Flores, Petén, www.alianzaverde.org), for its part, has done an excellent job of promoting low-impact tourism in Petén as part of its mandate to aid in the protection and conservation of the region's precious natural resources. In addition to marketing efforts, Alianza Verde certifies ecotourism operations and aids in the training of tourism staff to improve Petén's tourism offerings and visitor experience. It functions as an association of businesses, organizations, and individuals who make their livelihood from Petén's valuable tourism industry.

Another important organization is the Asociacion de Rescate y Conservacion de Vida Silvestre (Wildlife Rescue and Conservation Association), or **ARCAS** (4 Ave. 2-47, Sector B5, Zona 8 Mixco, San Cristóbal, Guatemala, tel. 2476-6001, www.arcasguatemala.com). It works to protect and rehabilitate wildlife, including sea turtles on the Pacific Coast and animals falling prey to poaching for the lucrative pet trade in Petén, including cats, monkeys, and birds.

Several organizations operate in Guatemala's eastern Verapaces and Izabal regions. Working to preserve the endangered quetzal, **Proyecto Ecoquetzal** (2a Calle 14-36 Zona 1, Coban, Alta Verapaz, tel. 7952-1047, www.ecoquetzal.org) works with local communities to provide alternative income sources such as ecotourism and promote sustainable agriculture in the remaining cloud forests of northern Alta Verapaz. **Asociacion Ak' Tenamit** (11 Avenida "A" 9-39 Zona 2, Guatemala City, tel. 2254-1560 Guatemala City, tel. 7908-3392 Lívingston, www.aktenamit.org) is a grassroots, Mayan-run development organization focusing its efforts on education, health care, the creation of alternative income sources and sustainable agriculture.

Finally, **Tropico Verde** (Vía 6 4-25 Zona 4, Edificio Castañeda, Oficina 41, Guatemala City tel. 2339-4225 www.tropicoverde .org) is a watchdog organization monitoring the state of Guatemala's parks via field studies. In addition to local monitoring, it helps bring awareness of local repercussions of international environmental issues such as Guatemala's participation in international conventions on whaling, to name just one example.

Flora and Fauna

Guatemala harbors an astounding degree of biodiversity due greatly to the variety of ecosystems found within its borders. Its location in the Central American land bridge between North and South America means it is the southernmost range for certain North American species as well as the northernmost range for certain Southern Hemisphere species. Fourteen of the 38 Holdridge Life Zones are represented in Guatemala.

FLORA

Among the cornucopia of plant life are 8,000 varieties of plants, including more than 600 types of orchids. Of these, nearly 200 are unique to Guatemala. The rugged cloud forests of Sierra de las Minas, meanwhile, boast the presence of 17 distinct species of pine trees found nowhere else on earth. Endemic orchid species include Guatemala's national flower, the rare *monja blanca*, or "white nun." It is found in the cloud forests of the Verapaces region.

Guatemala means "land of the trees" in the ancient Mayan-Toltec language. According to 2005 figures, 37 percent of Guatemala remained covered in forest in 2005, down from 40 percent in 2001. Among the different types of forest present in Guatemala's varied climate zones are tropical rainforest, tropical dry forests, evergreen forests, and cloud forests. In some cold, mountainous parts of Guatemala there are temperate forests whose broadleaf

trees' leaves briefly change color before falling to the ground, though not at all to the extent of the displays of fall foliage present in parts of North America.

The forests of Petén are officially classified mostly as tropical moist and tropical wet forests. Guatemala's only true rainforests, strictly speaking, are found in the Cerro San Gil along the Caribbean Coast.

Most of Guatemala's remaining forest cover is found in Petén, especially the northern third of the department in a huge park known as the Maya Biosphere Reserve. The Verapaces, Izabal, Quiché, and Huehuetenango also have significant amounts of forest cover remaining. Many of these forests are on remote mountains that have remained inaccessible and have therefore escaped the ravages of the advance of the agricultural frontier. Significant wetlands, including four of international importance, are found in Petén, Izabal, and the western section of the Pacific Coast plains near the Mexican border. Mangrove forests are found on the Pacific and Caribbean Coasts.

Among the plants you'll find in Guatemala's tropical forests is the towering ceiba *(Ceiba pentandra)*, which is Guatemala's national tree and was considered sacred by the Mayans. It has a wide trunk and buttressed roots with branches found only at the very top. The ceiba can reach heights of 60 meters. You will often find them in cleared fields—one of only a few trees left standing amid grazing cattle. The most famous example is along the footpath at the entrance to Tikal National Park, where visitors are often photographed standing next to the tree's colossal trunk.

Another common tropical forest tree is the *chicozapote,* from which chicle is extracted for use in the manufacture of chewing gum. *Chicleros* cut V-shaped notches in the tree's trunk, allowing the sap to drip down the tree to a receptacle placed there for its collection. These days chicle goes to Japan, which still favors the traditional base for making gum. During the early 20th century, most of Guatemala's chicle went to the Wrigley Company.

The *ramón,* or breadnut tree, is found throughout the tropical flatlands and was widely used during Mayan times for making tortillas and drinks, among other things. Archaeologists have linked the increasing consumption of ramón seeds to decreasing food-production cycles during Mayan times, speculating that it served as a replacement to more traditional staples during periods of drought.

One of the most curious plants found in the tropical forests is the strangler fig, or *mata palo (Ficus obtusifolia),* which wraps itself around its host, eventually killing it. It has thick roots and looks much like a wooden rope wrapped around a tree. It's easy to spot and you'll recognize it when you see it.

Guatemala's forests contain excellent hardwoods, the most prominent of these being cedar *(Cedrela angustifolia)* and mahogany *(Swientenia alicastrum).* Much of the Petén forest has been logged, legally and illegally. Peasant forestry cooperatives operate in the multiple-use zone of the Maya Biosphere Reserve sustainably harvesting ecocertified hardwoods. Guatemalan mahogany is highly prized in the making of furniture. The cabinets of the Four Seasons resort on Costa Rica's Pacific Coast, for example, are made from Guatemalan mahogany. Also important as a forest product is *xate* palm *(Chamaedorea spp),* which is harvested in the forests using sustainable methods, though overcutting is entirely possible. The bright green palm leaves are used in floral arrangements throughout the United States and Europe.

FAUNA
Birds

Guatemala's abundant birdlife includes more than 700 different species. Although not nearly as popular a bird-watching destination as Belize or Costa Rica, Guatemala has become increasingly well known among birders now that pristine areas conducive to the activity are no longer the site of skirmishes between army and guerrilla forces, as was the case during the civil war. This has opened new areas to bird-watching and Guatemalans are quickly taking steps to gain some ground in catering to this very lucrative tourism market.

Among the highlights of a visit to Guatemala is the opportunity to spot its rare, endangered national emblem, the resplendent quetzal *(Pharomacrus mocino).* The quetzal gives its name to the national currency and was revered by the Mayans for its long green tail feathers

Numerous species of parrots dwell in Guatemala's forests.

used in ceremonial headdresses. Quetzals have become increasingly rare because of the loss of their cloud forest habitat, but they still survive on the slopes of the Lake Atitlán volcanoes, parts of the Sierra de los Cuchumatanes, and particularly in the Sierra de las Minas. A forest preserve in Baja Verapaz, known as the Quetzal Biotope, has been set aside specifically to protect the quetzal. It can often be seen on the grounds of one of the area lodges feeding on the *aguacatillo* trees. The larger, nearby Sierra de Las Minas Biosphere Reserve is also a safe bet. Some grassroots organizations such as Proyecto Eco-Quetzal are working with local communities in Alta Verapaz to promote sustainable tourism in the hopes they will see the economic value of preserving the forest instead of destroying it for slash-and-burn agriculture. (This and other such projects are covered in the *Las Verapaces* chapter.)

Among endemic species is the flightless Atitlán grebe *(Podilymbus gigas),* commonly known as *poc,* which was officially declared extinct in 1989. The introduction of nonnative large- and smallmouth bass into the lake seems to have precipitated its drastic decline in numbers from about 200 in 1960 to only 32 in 1983. The bass ate the young grebes as well as the crabs and fish species on which *poc* fed.

Endemic to the northern Petén region is the Petén ocellated turkey *(Meleagris ocellata),* readily seen strutting around Tikal. It is smaller but much more colorful than its northern relatives, somewhat resembling a peacock. Other interesting birds found in Guatemala's tropical forests include the keel-billed toucan *(Ramphastos sulfuratus),* a perennial jungle favorite because of its large, colorful, bananalike beak. Many of these can be seen at Tikal around sunrise and sunset flying among the temples peeking from the forest canopy. A large variety of parrots also inhabit the Petén forests. The most impressive of these is the scarlet macaw *(Ara macao),* which once inhabited large parts of Petén as well as the Pacific coastal plain. It now inhabits only very remote parts of the Petén forests. Conservationists are fighting to save the birds from local extinction and protected nesting sites

have been established in the Maya Biosphere Reserve, specifically in Laguna del Tigre National Park. Rounding out the list of noteworthy birds is the harpy eagle *(Harpia harpyja),* a large, powerful raptor that also enjoys healthy populations at Tikal National Park.

Land Mammals

Guatemala's list of native land mammals is impressive, with a large variety of exotic cats, primates, and other furry creatures. The largest of Guatemala's cats is the jaguar *(Felis onca),* found in lowland parts of Petén, Izabal, and the Verapaces. Referred to as *tigre* by locals, it is known to sometimes wander into *chiclero* camps as well as kill livestock in remote cattle ranches that have encroached on remote areas. Sightings of this beautiful spotted cat are rare, so consider yourself lucky if you are able to spot one in the wild. Its tracks are more likely to be seen on travels to the remote forests of the Maya Biosphere Reserve, which can be exciting enough. Other cats include the jaguarundi *(Herpailurus yaguarondi),* puma *(Puma concolor),* and their smaller relatives the margay *(Leopardus wiedii)* and ocelot *(Leopardus pardalis).*

Among the most widely seen mammals are monkeys. You are likely to hear the roar of howler monkeys *(Alouatta pigra)* during the early morning hours if camping overnight in Petén. Less aggressive, smaller, and ever more playful, are spider monkeys *(Ateles geoffroyi).* The gray fox *(Urocyon cinereoargenteus)* can often be seen in the early morning and evening among Tikal's temples. More exotic forest dwellers include the piglike collared peccary *(Tayassu tajacu)* and white-lipped peccary *(Tayasu pecari)* as well as the hefty baird's tair *(Tapirus bairdii),* and the tamandua anteater *(Tamandua mexicana).*

Also easy to spot are some of the smaller mammals, particularly in parks such as Tikal and Yaxhá. Among these are the raccoonlike white-nosed coati *(Nasua narica),* which practically walk up to you at Tikal; mouselike agoutis *(Dasyprocta punctata),* and kinkajous *(Potos flavus).*

If you happen to like bats, you'll be pleased

to know Guatemala harbors more than 100 species of the flying critters. Many of these are found in the limestone caves of Petén and the Verapaces. Most of these are harmless to humans, feeding on fruits and insects. There are blood-sucking vampire bats *(Desmodus rotundus)* flying about, though these feed mostly on cattle.

Sealife

Five species of sea turtles can be seen on Guatemala's Atlantic and Pacific Coasts, where they also come ashore to lay their eggs. These are olive ridley, hawksbill, leatherback, green, and loggerhead. Of these, olive ridley, leatherback, and hawksbill turtles nest on the Pacific shores and can be seen at the Monterrico-Hawaii Biotope. Between September and January, visitors to this park have the rare opportunity to hold baby sea turtles in their hands before releasing them to begin their mad dash across the sand and a lifetime at sea. If they survive to adulthood, the females will return to very same beach to lay their eggs and begin a new life cycle. All of these turtle species are endangered because of the harvesting of their eggs by poor coastal dwellers in search of food and a means to supplement their incomes.

Guatemala's Pacific sailfish have become the object of widespread praise in the angling circuit with blue marlin, Pacific sailfish, and yellowfin tuna just waiting to be caught. Humpback whales can also be seen breaching in the Pacific waters. As for the Caribbean Coast, Guatemala just missed out on the Belize Barrier Reef, as it ends right at the doorstep of the Punta de Manabique peninsula. The barrier reef is easily accessible, however, along with the wonders of its corals and exotic fish. Although lacking the barrier reef per se, the waters off Guatemala's Atlantic Coast are certainly not devoid of exotic sea life. Bottle-nosed dolphins readily follow motorboats as they make their way along the Caribbean coast. The endangered manatee *(Trichechus manatus),* or sea cow, has become increasingly rare as the large, slow, sea grass–eating mammal has fallen prey to hunting, motorboats, and drowning in fish-ing nets. A small reserve in Izabal's El Golfete is attempting to protect the few that remain in Guatemalan waters.

Amphibians

There are 112 species of amphibians represented in Guatemala. Guatemala is out of range for some of the colorful miniature frogs, such as poison arrow frogs, found farther south in Costa Rica and Panama, but there are still some interesting frogs to be found in Guatemala's tropical forests; among these are the red-eyed tree frog *(Agalychnis callidryas)* and the similar Morelet's tree frog *(Agalychnis moreletti).* Fleischmann's glass frog *(Hyalinobatrachium fleischmanni)* is translucent and lime green with small yellow spots and yellowish hands. Its organs and bones are visible through the abdominal skin. All three of these prefer vegetation near rivers and streams.

Reptiles

With 214 species of reptiles, Guatemala has no shortage of snakes. Among the little critters to watch out for are the fer-de-lance *(Bothrops asper),* known locally as *barba amarilla.* The aggressive pit viper is found in abundant quantities in the tropical forests of Petén, Izabal, and the Verapaces, though you are not likely to see one. Baby fer-de-lance can be especially dangerous as they are yet unable to control the amount of poison they inject into a bite.

Other snakes include tropical rattlesnakes *(Crotalus durissus),* several species of colorful coral snakes, and nonvenomous boa constrictors.

If you watched the *Survivor* TV series, you probably noticed there are crocodiles in Guatemala, particularly in and around Lake Yaxhá. The crocodiles seen on *Survivor* are Morelet's crocodiles *(crocodylus moreleti).* The larger American crocodile *(crocodylus acutus)* can be found in coastal areas, swamps, and larger rivers in Petén and Izabal. Many species of river turtles inhabit the tropical lowlands. Basilisk lizards and at least two species of iguana round out the highlighted list of Guatemala's reptiles.

Insects and Small Creatures

This subject might give some readers "the itchies" but in addition to the myriad species of arachnids, such as tarantulas and scorpions, or plentiful amounts of mosquitoes in some places, Guatemalan lands are host to many other and more beautiful creatures. Among these are thousands of species of butterflies, including the beautiful blue morpho, which you might see flitting about the forest in an iridescent flash of blue. While hiking Guatemala's forests, keep an eye out for the industrious leaf-cutter ants, which cut pathways through the forest and carry small pieces of bright green leaves to their nests, where they are used as compost for underground fungus farms. Butterflies and leaf-cutters are virtually guaranteed favorites among younger travelers to these parts.

History

Guatemala's history is complicated and fascinating, an understanding of which is a crucial element for the well-informed traveler hoping to get the most out of a visit to this mystifying land of culture and contrasts. This section discusses the basics of Guatemala's past and what it means in relation to its present. A basic understanding of what makes the country tick will aid you in your travels and allow you to get the most out of this destination. (Those wishing to delve deeper are invited to check out the *Suggested Reading.*)

PREHISTORY

It is generally accepted that the first inhabitants of the American continent came in waves by way of a land bridge across the Bering Strait connecting Siberia to Alaska about 25,000 years ago. The migrants continued to make their way southward, possibly using boats, and eventually came to populate, albeit thinly, large sections of the Americas occupying a diverse range of climates. It is believed passage via the Bering Strait was intermittently open until about 10,000 years ago, when the last Ice Age ended, submerging the land bridge with rising sea levels.

A recognizable culture known as Clovis emerged by 11,000 B.C., demonstrating the use of stone tools such as spear points, blades, and scrapers. Many of these have been found by archaeologists in the Guatemalan highlands dating to 9,000 B.C.

A warming climate and, with it, the disappearance of the big game these hunter-gatherers depended on resulted in a gradual transition to agriculture in which beans, squash, peppers, and a distant relative of maize, *teosinte,* became staple crops. By 3000 B.C. this new system of agriculture began to support the beginnings of settled population patterns, which would eventually become the great Mesoamerican civilizations. Interestingly, research in northern Guatemala's Petén region suggests this area was covered at the time in broadleaf forest and savanna, with dense tropical forests not making an appearance until well into the days of the Mayan civilization.

EARLY MAYAN CIVILIZATION (PRECLASSIC MAYA)

Archaeologists have made various designations to describe the Mayan culture's development along the path from nascent agricultural societies to increasing sophistication and thriving civilization. The Preclassic period officially occupies the time span between 1800 B.C and 250 A.D. This period is further subdivided into Middle Preclassic (1000–300 B.C.) and Late Preclassic (300 B.C.–A.D. 250). The Preclassic period then gives way to the Classic period (A.D. 250–900) with its respective Early (A.D. 250–600) and Late (A.D. 600–900) subperiods. The Terminal Classic involves the period between A.D. 800 and 910, when Mayan city-states were widely abandoned after wars, regional drought, and overpopulation took their toll. Finally, the Postclassic period comprises the years between A.D. 910 and 1530, shortly after the arrival of the Spanish conquerors.

Of particular note is what is sometimes referred to as the Classic Maya collapse, giving the impression that the civilization collapsed and vanished into thin air. This is certainly not the case. The Mayan civilization proper indeed came crashing down for reasons that are becoming increasingly evident, but the Mayans themselves simply dispersed into other parts of present-day Mexico, Guatemala, Belize, and Honduras while falling prey to increasing cultural and military dominance from invading Central Mexican Toltecs.

The Preclassic Mayan era began somewhere between 2000 and 1500 B.C. A large part of the puzzle in the development of Mayan culture and civilization is the existence of the Olmec culture in Mexico, to the northwest. The Olmecs are often referred to as a "mother culture," characterized among other things by the construction of pyramidal ceremonial structures and giant stone heads. Their influence on early Mayan culture can be seen along Guatemala's Pacific Coast, in El Salvador, and Copán, Honduras. Olmec artistic, political, and religious influence on Mayan lands included the later adoption by the Mayans of a calendar known as the "Long Count." The Olmecs also introduced the early forms of a writing system.

The developing civilization also made a clear transition from hillside swidden agriculture to more intensive forms of cultivation, including terrace farming, the construction of drainage ditches, and the development of fertilizers, which in turn produced large food surpluses. With greater food security, members of the population were gradually able to become more specialized in their individual occupations, paving the way for advances in writing, art, architecture, mathematics, and astronomy, which would later come to full fruition.

The Mayan population continued to thrive during the Middle Preclassic period (1000–300 B.C.). By 500 B.C., the Petén site of Nakbé had grown to become one of the first Mayan

Tikal's Great Plaza

© AL ARGUETA

cities with temples and stucco sculptures. Also in Petén, Tikal and El Mirador began building their first ceremonial structures. A common language and universal belief system is thought to have existed throughout the Mayan region, providing the needed social cohesion that served as a catalyst for the development of a larger civilization.

In the Late Preclassic period (300 B.C.–A.D. 250) Nakbé continued to thrive and was the dominant city until prominence shifted sometime around 100 B.C. to the nearby site of El Mirador, about 12 kilometers away. To this day, it has the honor of housing the tallest known pre-Columbian structure, which rises to a height of 70 meters. El Mirador sprawled to encompass an area of more than 20 square kilometers with a population of about 100,000.

The site of modern-day Guatemala City was occupied at this time by Kaminaljuyú, whose commercial dominance was established largely on the strength of its strategic location for the trading of obsidian and jade. Meanwhile, at Tikal, Uaxactúnn and other sites throughout the Mayan lowlands, pyramids and temple platforms began to emerge from about A.D. 1. Mayan society also became increasingly stratified, with astronomical and calendrical events led by rulers and shamanic priests dominating the direction of individual population centers. Local architects, craftsmen, tradesmen, scribes, and farmers became increasingly specialized in their individual occupations. Irrigation using vast reservoirs and far-reaching canal networks allowed the continued expansion of agriculture.

Toward the end of the Preclassic period comes a foreshadowing of the later Classic Mayan collapse with the advent of significant natural disasters and, possibly, widespread warfare. El Mirador was abruptly abandoned in A.D. 150 after a prolonged drought severely affected agricultural production. In the southern Mayan highlands, the eruption of Ilopango Volcano, in present-day El Salvador, smothered a large part of the region in volcanic ash, resulting in the subsequent abandonment of Kaminaljuyú sometime around A.D. 250. Trade routes between the Pacific lowlands and Mexico became disrupted and trade with the Mayan region subsequently shifted to the northern lowlands, with its accompanying Mexican influence.

THE CLASSIC MAYA

This period marks the phase of greatest Mayan achievement, including the adoption of the Long Count calendar and the distinctive Mayan writing style encompassing glyphs. The Mayan cities now lying in ruins in northern Guatemala came to full fruition at this time—trading, stargazing, and fighting wars before being abandoned and disappearing into obscurity to be later reclaimed by the surrounding jungle. The Mayans constructed the temples and palaces seen today atop previous constructions so that what we see now is literally the pinnacle of their progress.

Knowledge of the Classic Mayans comes largely from the erection of large carved monuments, or stelae, which documented the lives of the individual city-states' rulers and historical events associated with their reigns, such as battles, marriage alliances, successions, and so forth. Part of this evidence points to increasing dominance in the early Classic period from northern powerhouse Teotihuacán, a city-state in Central Mexico boasting a population of 250,000. Teotihuacán dispatched armed merchants known as *pochteca,* who spread the city-state's authority to the far reaches of the Mayan lands in present-day Petén, Yucatán, and Honduras. Teotihuacán was not a part of the Mayan culture but a separate civilization. Teotihuacán is credited with establishing new dynasties at Tikal and Copán in A.D. 378 and 426, bringing with them new religious beliefs, architectural, and artistic styles. Many of these are depicted in temples and stelae from this period at these sites. Also around A.D. 400, the Mayan highland site of Kaminaljuyú was rebuilt in Teotihuacán style.

After Teotihuacán influence faded in the 6th century A.D., Tikal and Calakmul emerged as the regional powerhouses, each controlling a sophisticated trade network and struggling against each other for ultimate control. The power struggle took a definitive turn against Tikal when Calakmul forged an alliance with Caracol (in present-day Belize) and defeated the city-state in A.D. 562. A 130-year construction hiatus at Tikal and the cities under its influence followed this event.

Tikal reemerged as a dominant power beginning in A.D. 682 under the new leadership of Hasaw Chan K'awil (Heavenly Standard Bearer), whose 52-year reign was marked by the definitive defeat of Calakmul in A.D. 695 with reassertion of control over regional satellite cities such as Rio Azul and Waká as well as a frenzy of new temple construction. The six great temples dominating Tikal's ceremonial center were reconstructed between A.D. 670 and 810.

Also flourishing during this Late Classic (A.D. 600–850) period were the lowland sites of Piedras Negras, Yaxchilán, Yaxhá, Dos Pilas, Bonampak, Palenque, Uxmal, Altun Ha, Copán, and Quiriguá. Mayan architecture, astronomy, and art reached unprecedented lev-

© AL ARGUETA

a finely carved hieroglyphic bench from Piedras Negras

els of sophistication to a degree never before achieved by any of the pre-Columbian societies. Trade prospered and an exploding population across the Mayan region is thought to have numbered around 10 million.

MAYAN DECLINE AND COLLAPSE

By A.D. 750, however, change was in the air and Mayan civilization began its sudden decline. Changes in politics and society, including the breakdown of alliances and trade links, brought increased warfare among various city-states. Cities gradually became depopulated and the carving of stelae became less frequent. The Mayan decline is thought to be a product of many factors, not the least of which is environmental. By the late 9th century A.D., the Mayan lowlands were already suffering heavily from deforestation, which in turn probably led to a severe drought felt throughout the region at this time. Food production declined and was unable to sustain dense population levels, which were further taxed by an onslaught of

epidemics. In a classic variation of the timeless chicken-or-egg–first quandary, it remains unclear whether warfare led to ecological collapse or if the environmental stress of overpopulation and soil depletion led to warfare.

It is speculated that an increasingly disenfranchised peasantry may have revolted against the rule of what they began to view as an unproductive and incompetent elite. Widespread warfare among rival city-states also appears to have engulfed the entire region at this time. There is ample evidence of protracted warfare at Dos Pilas and the cities in and around the Petexbatún region, including the construction of defensive walls to guard against enemy attack. There is evidence at Dos Pilas of resettlement by the peasantry into the city's ceremonial center, where they may have hunkered down for protection. Farther south, at Cancuén, archaeologists have recently uncovered evidence of a mass killing of the city's elites. During this aptly named Terminal Classic period, widespread strife and disorder appear to have dominated throughout Mesoamerica.

Settlements across the Yucatán Peninsula seemed to have avoided the worst of the depopulation but came under control from invading Central Mexican Toltecs in A.D. 987, resulting in a Toltec-Mayan hybridization. As the exodus from the Mayan heartland region in present-day Petén continued, the populations of neighboring Yucatán, Belize, and southern Guatemala undoubtedly increased. By the end of the Classic period, small settlements began to appear throughout the Southern Highlands, supporting populations with terrace farming and irrigation under a basic village structure.

THE PRECONQUEST PICTURE

The Toltec-Mayan Yucatán cities such as Chichén Itzá and Uxmal finally gave out sometime in the late 13th century and were abruptly abandoned. At about the same time, the Guatemalan highlands were invaded by groups of Toltec-Mayans, though it is uncertain whether they are the product of a mass exodus from the Yucatán cities or a new group from the Toltec heartland in the Gulf of Mexico. In any case, their arrival in the Guatemalan highlands signaled a transition from the existence of relatively peaceful, religious village societies to ones increasingly secular and warlike.

Quickly establishing themselves as a ruling elite, the Toltec invaders founded a series of competing empires, including the K'iche', Kaqchikel, Tzutujíl, Mam, Ixil, Achi', and Q'eqchi', among others. Interestingly, these and other tribes encompassing the highland indigenous groups continue to form the basis for today's cultural landscape with differentiation based on their individual dialects.

Among these tribes, the K'iche' and Kaqchikel emerged as dominant forces, a rivalry the conquering Spanish would later use to their advantage. Before the arrival of the Spanish, the highland region was engulfed in a widespread power struggle between rival groups for cultivable land to feed an increasing population.

THE SPANISH CONQUEST

After the Spanish conquered the Aztec empire and captured its capital at Tenochtitlán in 1521, the K'iche' sent ambassadors north to Mexico informing Hernán Cortés of their desire to be vassals of the newly established power structure. In 1523 Cortés dispatched Pedro de Alvarado to Guatemala on a fact-finding mission meant to verify the veracity of the Indians' claims. If indeed Cortes's intentions were limited to fact finding, he could have done better than to choose Alvarado for the job.

From accounts of the Spanish conquest, a picture of Alvarado emerges. He is described as handsome, athletic, distinguished, eloquent, and graceful, among other things. When the Aztec king Moctezuma's spies were asked to describe the approaching Spanish invaders before their initial contact, they cited Alvarado as the finest specimen of the foreign army, calling him "Tonatio," or Child of the Sun. What these early fact-finders couldn't have known was that Alvarado was also extremely cruel, a fact that became evident when Cortées left Alvarado in command of the conquered Aztec territory during a temporary absence. Alvarado massacred Aztecs with unbridled zeal and was later chastised for his actions.

Alvarado arrived in Guatemala along the Pacific Coast flatlands accompanied by 120 horsemen, 173 horses, 300 soldiers, and 200 Mexican warriors from the allied Tlaxcalan armies. He made his way up to the highlands where he met the K'iche' in battle near present-day Quetzaltenango, also known as Xelajú. An estimated 30,000 K'iche' were unable to forge alliances with neighboring tribes to repel the Spanish invasion and faced the Spanish alone. Legend has it Alvarado met Tecún Umán, grandson of the K'iche' ruler, dressed in a quetzal-feather headdress, in hand-to-hand combat, cutting him down.

After these events, the K'iche' invited the Spanish to their capital at Utatlán for the signing of a formal surrender but secretly planned to ambush them from the safety of their mountain fortress. Alvarado, noticing the single access to the city via a causeway, narrow streets in which his horses would be unable to maneuver, and the conspicuous absence of women and children, grew suspicious of the K'iche's intentions. He withdrew to the outskirts, followed by the K'iche' rulers, whom he seized and later had burned at the stake. Eight days of fighting followed, with the Spanish enlisting the help of the rival Kaqchikels to finally gain the upper hand against the K'iche'. Utatlán was then burnt to the ground.

The Kaqchikel alliance with the Spanish stuck for a time with the Spanish establishing the first capital of Guatemala alongside the Kaqchikel capital of Iximché, from which they launched raids to conquer Guatemala's remaining highland tribal groups. The campaign would last several years and was made increasingly difficult when the Kaqchikel severed their alliance with the Spanish in 1526 in response to demands for tribute. They abandoned their capital at Iximché and took refuge in the mountains, launching a guerrilla war. The Spanish then moved the Guatemalan capital, establishing the city of Santiago de Los Caballeros on November 22, 1527. Now known as Ciudad Vieja, it lies near present-day Antigua.

Alvarado was unable to subdue the Q'eqchi' and Achi' tribes in the present-day Verapaces, eventually giving up all hope of their conquest. Years later, in 1537, Catholic friar Fray Bartolomé de Las Casas would travel to the region in an attempt to bring acceptance of both Christianity and the Spanish crown. Surprisingly, de Las Casas succeeded, bringing the last of the highland tribes under Spanish authority in 1540. Part of his success was due to his taking a radically different approach in getting the Spanish crown to accept the Indians as vassals to the king. De las Casas saw the Indians as spiritual infants needing guidance into the ways of Christianity and worthy of special care under the Spanish crown.

Indigenous uprisings and resistance, however, would continue throughout Guatemala's history into the present day as the various groups have responded to repressive policies imposed by those in power. The recently ended civil war has been likened by scholars, human rights activists, and journalists to a kind of "second conquest" aimed at eliminating the indigenous population through genocidal extermination attempts.

A final aspect of the conquest that bears mentioning is the work of European diseases and their hand in greatly reducing the population of the indigenous peoples, who had no resistance to smallpox, plague, typhus, or measles. These diseases were responsible for the loss of more than three-quarters of Guatemala's two million inhabitants in the first 30 years after contact with the Spanish. It is thought that a third of the population died before Alvarado's invading army even set foot in the indigenous peoples' Guatemalan homeland.

COLONIAL GUATEMALA

The Guatemalan capital required 10 years from its founding to complete and included a cathedral, town hall, and Alvarado's palace. Alvarado died in 1541 while in Mexico attempting to subdue an uprising but left behind a widow by the name of Beatriz de la Cueva, who declared an extended period of mourning in the Guatemalan capital. She may have tempted fate when she painted the inside and outside of the palace black as a symbol of mourning, calling herself "La Sinventura" (Unlucky One)—probably not a wise thing to do when your city is built on the slopes of a volcano. The city was destroyed shortly thereafter by a mudslide, which rolled down Agua Volcano after an earthquake and heavy rains combined to unleash the contents of the flooded crater. De la Cueva died in the mudslide, along with several other members of the city's ruling elite.

The Guatemalan capital was then moved a few miles away to present-day Antigua. It would serve as the administrative headquarters of the newly established Audiencia de Guatemala, which included the provinces of San Salvador, Nicaragua, Honduras, Costa Rica, Chiapas, and Guatemala. The city of Santiago de los Caballeros, as it was officially known, would grow to become the third-largest city in Spanish Colonial America, surpassed only by Mexico City and Lima. In 1776, a series of devastating earthquakes destroyed most of the city's buildings and churches, leading to a final move of the Guatemalan capital to the Valley of the Hermitage, just over a mountain to the east, where it has been ever since.

The colonial period is significant in that it completely transformed Guatemala's physical and cultural landscape, establishing new cities and institutionalizing new economic and religious systems that would come to form the basis for a racist hierarchy persisting largely unaltered to this day. Guatemala's history displays a striking symmetry throughout the years. The key to understanding many of the more recent tragedies to befall its people lies in understanding the significance of earlier events dating back to just before the conquest.

At the center of Guatemala's new power structure was the Catholic Church, which arrived with the conquistadors and included various sects such as Franciscans, Mercedarians, Dominicans, and Jesuits. These were granted large concessions of land and indigenous peoples, allowing them to amass huge fortunes from the cultivation of cash crops, including sugar, indigo, and wheat. This power structure was held in place by institutions established by the Spanish Crown, namely the *encomienda* and *repartimiento.*

The *encomienda* was a grant of Indian labor and tribute, though not necessarily of land, over a geographical area. The *encomenderos* holding such a grant were allowed to tax the indigenous peoples under their care and to conscript them for labor in exchange for their promise to maintain order and educate the indigenous populace in the Spanish language and Catholicism. With the Spanish governing authorities thousands of miles away, enforcement of these policies was anything but stringent. *Encomenderos* ruthlessly exploited the indigenous peoples under their care using their influence and power as well as downright trickery to seize more lands from the natives, increase taxes, and ultimately force the natives into debt bondage.

The *encomienda* system came under increasing scrutiny from the Catholic Church. Indigenous rights advocates, led by Fray Bartolomé de las Casas, eventually succeeded in convincing the Spanish Crown to pass the New Laws in 1842, which brought reform to the system, albeit superficially. The changes included prohibition of the enslavement of the Indians and provisions for the gradual abolition of the *encomienda* system. It required fair taxation on the Indians, prohibited them from being unnecessarily conscripted for work, and ordered their fair treatment. It also ordered public officials and clergy with *encomienda* grants to immediately return them to the Crown and stated that *encomienda* grants would expire at the death of the individual *encomendero,* so as not to be passed down as an inheritance.

The *repartimiento,* which is essentially indistinguishable from its predecessor, is a reformed version of the *encomienda* system, at least on paper. It put control of the distribution of workers into the hands of local magistrates and called for the donation of a percentage of laborers from populations close to Spanish settlements, between 2 and 4 percent of the indigenous population. It is interesting to note that a variation of this system still exists in the form of a seasonal migration of indigenous workers from the Guatemalan highlands involved in the coffee and sugarcane harvests on the Pacific plains. The institutionalization of this labor force throughout the country's history would take many forms in years to come.

Further adding to the transformation of community organization in the conquered territories was the establishment of *reducciones,* part of the larger process of *congregación,* consisting of towns founded in the Spanish vein with the purpose of congregating indigenous populations into manageable settlements and assimilating them into the dominant culture and religion. They would also serve handily as a nearby source from which to pool labor. Remarkably, this system also finds equivalents in Guatemala's recent history in the Guatemalan military's civil war-era policy of grouping survivors of destroyed Mayan villages into strategic hamlets known as "model villages." The system allowed the military to keep a close watch on the peasantry while further contributing to the suppression of their culture and paving the way for assimilation into Western ways.

INDEPENDENCE

Guatemalan, and indeed Central American, independence came more as a result of pressures from without than from a genuine internal uprising demanding freedom from Spanish rule. This is not to say that all was well with Spanish colonial rule, as there were policies and social stratifications in place contributing to unrest among the lower strata of society. Spanish policies kept wealth and power in the hands of Spanish-born elites *(chapetones)*. Creoles, or those born in the New World of Spanish descent, were the next rung down the ladder, with the lowest standings reserved for mixed-blood *mestizos* and full-blooded Indians.

Napoleon's invasion of Spain in 1808 led to the imposition of a liberal constitution on Spain in 1812. When Mexican General Agustín Iturbide declared his own country's independence from Spain, Guatemala followed suit. The reigning Captain General Gabino Gaínza bowed to demands for independence but hoped to maintain the existent power structure with the support of the church and landowning elites. The declaration of independence essentially maintained the old power structure under new management. Mexico quickly dispatched troops to annex Guatemala, and all of Central America, to Iturbide's new empire.

Iturbide was dethroned in 1823 and Central America, minus the state of Chiapas, declared its independence from Mexico. This second declaration joined the remaining states in a loose federation and adopted many U.S.-modeled liberal reforms such as the abolition of slavery. A power struggle between liberals advocating a secular, more egalitarian state and conservatives wanting to maintain the church-dominated political and economic structures marked the early years of independence. The Central American Federation was weakened not only by inner power struggles within individual member states, but also by a struggle to determine regional leadership over neighboring states.

The liberals of Guatemala, Honduras, and El Salvador united under the leadership of Honduran General Francisco Morazán in a bid to unite all of Central America under liberal government. In Guatemala, chief of state Mariano Gálvez (1831–1838) instituted liberal reforms, including the abolition of the death penalty, educational reform, trial by jury, and civil marriage. A cholera epidemic and widespread discontent in rural Guatemala translated into indigenous uprisings and support for the overthrow of the liberal government by Rafael Carrera, who seized power at 23 years of age and ruled from 1844 to 1865. Charismatic, but also naive and illiterate, Carrera reversed the reforms instituted under Morazán and Gálvez and practically handed the territory of Belize to Great Britain in exchange for a road that was never built. The territorial dispute still exists, with Guatemala claiming sovereignty over its eastern neighbor alluding to the broken terms of the agreement that allowed the British temporary control of Belize for logging.

Carrera also fought a war with Morazán and his federation and was finally able to free Guatemala from federation rule in 1847. Meanwhile, an area encompassing much of the Western Highlands and known as "Los Altos" declared itself an independent republic but was soon brought back into the fray.

After Carrera's death at the age of 50, he was succeeded by conservative Vicente Cerna, who would rule during the next six years. Liberal unrest grew during this time with various unsuccessful uprisings aiming to take power back from the conservatives.

JUSTO RUFINO BARRIOS AND THE LIBERAL REFORMS

The liberals would finally succeed in 1871 under the leadership of General Justo Rufino Barrios, who, along with Miguel García Granados, set out from Mexico with a force of just 45 men, gaining numbers as their approach to the capital grew closer. The capital was taken on June 30, 1871, and Granados was installed as the leader of the new liberal government. Granados made only limited reforms and by

1872 a frustrated Barrios marched to the capital with his troops and demanded elections, which he won overwhelmingly.

Among the reforms quickly instituted by Barrios, who would go down in Guatemalan history as "The Reformer," were educational reform and separation of church and state. Barrios was the first of the *caudillos,* or military strongmen who ruled the country with an iron fist and sense of absolute omnipotence, mostly uninterrupted, until the revolution of 1944. He masterfully strengthened his power over the entire country with links to local strongmen in rural areas who wielded power on his behalf but who were unable to challenge his hold because of the restricted development of secondary market centers and the overwhelming economic dominance of Guatemala City.

To further exercise his dominion, Barrios professionalized the military, creating a military academy, the Escuela Politecnica, still in existence today. The addition of rural militia further strengthened national control over the rural hinterlands. Barrios was decidedly pro-Western and sought to impose a European worldview to the suppression of what he saw as a vastly inferior Indian culture. Liberal economic policies ensured minimal protection of village lands, Indian culture, or the welfare of peasant villages.

During this time, coffee came to dominate the Guatemalan economy and Barrios's economic policies ensured the availability of a peasant workforce to supply the labor-intensive coffee harvest with its share of needed workers. Furthermore, the increasingly racist attitudes of Guatemala's coffee elites toward the Indians served to justify the coercive means used to secure this labor force. The Indians were seen as lazy, making forced labor and the submission of the indigenous masses both necessary and morally justified. In this regard, the *mandamiento,* which came to replace the *repartimiento,* was increasingly enforced in the last two decades of the 19th century and required villages to supply a specified number of laborers per year.

Increasingly, however, elites found more coercive ways to exact labor from the Indians by way of debt peonage. Rural workers were required to carry a *libreto,* a record containing an individual's labor and debt figures. *Habilitadores,* or labor contractors, were charged with advancing money to peasants in exchange for labor contracts. The contractors often used alcohol as an added incentive and took advantage of widespread peasant illiteracy to ensure that many of them contracted debts they would never be able to repay. In this way, depressed rural wages from debt peonage and low-cost labor increased the wealth of agricultural elites while making the rural peasantry even poorer.

MANUEL ESTRADA CABRERA

Justo Rufino Barrios died in battle in 1885 while fighting to create a reunified Central America under Guatemalan leadership. He was succeeded by a string of short-lived caudillo presidents. The next to hold power for any significant time was Manuel Estrada Cabrera, whose legacy included undivided support for big business and crackdowns on labor organization. He ruled from 1898 until his overthrow in 1920, having been declared mentally insane. Among Cabrera's many peculiarities was the construction of several temples to honor Minerva, the Roman goddess of wisdom. Cabrera's legacy includes gross corruption, a beefed-up military, and a neglected educational system.

Export agriculture continued its unprecedented growth under Cabrera, thus paving the way for the dominance of two foreign groups that would come to control much of Guatemala's economy in later years. The first of these were German coffee planters who settled in the region of Las Verapaces. By 1913 this German enclave owned 170 of the country's coffee plantations, with about half of them in the vicinity of Cobán. The other significant foreign presence in Guatemala during this time was the U.S.-owned United Fruit Company (UFCo), aptly nicknamed El Pulpo (the octopus), with its tentacles consisting of International Railways of Central America (IRCA) and the UFCo Steamship Lines. Its vast control of land, rail, and steamship transportation, in addition to

Guatemala's sole Caribbean port, Puerto Barrios, made it a political and economic powerhouse. Its political clout would be seen in the mid-20th century when, together with the CIA, it would be directly responsible for the ousting from power of Guatemala's president Arbenz when land-reform policies interfered with the company's vast land holdings. Cabrera is credited with courting UFCo to set up shop in Guatemala in 1901.

JORGE UBICO

After the overthrow of Estrada Cabrera in 1920, the country entered a period of instability and power struggles culminating in the rise to power of Jorge Ubico. Continuing in the now well-established pattern of megalomaniacal, heavy-handed leadership that would come to characterize many of Guatemala's presidents, Ubico continued the unconditional support for U.S. agribusiness and the local oligarchy. By 1940 90 percent of Guatemala's exports were sold to the United States. Ubico caved in to U.S demands for the expulsion of the German coffee planters from Guatemala during World War II, evidencing the increasing U.S. hold on Guatemalan domestic policy.

Within Guatemala, Ubico embarked on various reforms, including ambitious road-building projects, as well as improvements in health care and social welfare. Debt peonage was also outlawed but was replaced by a vagrancy law enforcing compulsory labor contributions of 150 days upon landless peasants in either rural plantations or in the government road-building programs. Ubico's reforms always had in mind the modernization of the state economy. Far from an attempt to free the indigenous peoples from coercive labor practices, the vagrancy law asserted centralized control over the national labor force while keeping the political power of the oligarchy firmly in check.

Ubico was also obsessed with internal security. He saw himself as a reincarnated Napoleon and became increasingly paranoid, creating a network of spies and informers used to repress opposition to his increasingly tyrannical rule. Much of this opposition came from the indigenous peasant population, whom Ubico ignored and regarded as retrograde and inferior. This led to numerous Indian revolts in the late 1930s and early 1940s. The discovery of an assassination plot in 1934 led to the execution of 300 suspected conspirators within 48 hours.

THE OCTOBER REVOLUTION OF 1944

Opposition finally reached a head in June 1944, when widespread discontent erupted in violent street protests by a large share of the urban middle class demanding democratic opportunities and new economic policies. Ubico was forced to resign after 14 years in office. When his interim replacement signaled to be more of the same, young students, professionals, and forward-thinking military officers orchestrated a widespread social movement culminating in his overthrow in what has been dubbed "The October Revolution." Elections were called for in December of that same year. In a radio address, then-front-running presidential candidate Juan José Arévalo, an exiled professor living in Argentina, described the transcendental nature of the recent events: "What has occurred in Guatemala is not a *golpe de estado* (coup d'etat); it is something more profound and beneficial; it is a revolution…It is a revolution that will go to the roots of the political system…In a word: It is a revolution called to wash, to purify our political life, to quiet everyone, and to honor Guatemala."

Arévalo would go on to win the election with an overwhelming majority and take office on March 1, 1945.

A DECADE OF "SPIRITUAL SOCIALISM"

Guatemala made much progress under Arévalo, who quickly set out on the road of badly needed structural reform. Prominence was given to education and health care with the construction of new schools and hospitals, immunization programs, and literacy campaigns. A new national budget allowed for a third of government spending to go into these programs, which were further facilitated by a new constitution drafted before Arévalo's taking office. Ubico's hated vagrancy laws were abolished and in their place a labor code was instituted establishing union representation and granting workers the right to strike. Many of the farms expropriated from German planters during World War II, now in state hands, were transformed into peasant cooperatives. Government policies provided technical assistance and credit for peasant farmers and protected their lands from usurpation by agricultural elites and foreign agribusiness.

The gains in social justice ruffled the feathers of many of Guatemala's traditional power elites, including the Church, urban business elites, the landed aristocracy, and the politicians who defended their interests. They increasingly opposed much of the reformist legislation passed by Arévalo in Congress. A divided military also became the source of much opposition, with Arévalo surviving 25 coup attempts originating from conservative sectors of the armed forces. Meanwhile, U.S. business interests became increasingly unsettled by the reforms. At the top of this list was the United Fruit Company. As opposition stiffened, Arévalo was unable to fully implement the social transformation of the country he had intended and passed on to his successor an increasingly polarized political landscape.

His successor, Jacobo Arbenz Guzmán, continued along the path of reform, concentrating on fomenting economic development and independence from foreign intervention in politics and the economy. At the core of his economic development program was the Agrarian Reform Law of 1952, which was intended to redistribute land ownership by breaking up large plantations and promoting high productivity on smaller, individually owned farms. The urgent need for land reform was historically evident in the nature and function of institutions which, through time, had placed Guatemalan land in the hands of a wealthy few to the detriment of indigenous peasants. It is estimated that 2 percent of the country's population controlled 72 percent of all arable land in 1945, but only 12 percent of it was being used.

Central to the law were stipulations limiting expropriation to lands lying fallow. Arbenz himself was not immune from land expropriation, giving up 1,700 acres of his own land in the process. Also among the lands to be expropriated were extensive holdings by United Fruit ceded to the company under Estrada Cabrera and Ubico, which had made United Fruit Guatemala's largest landowner. Fully 85 percent of its holdings remained uncultivated. The Agrarian Reform Law allowed for the compensation of expropriated lands based on values declared for tax purposes, which United Fruit had, of course, grossly underreported.

Unfortunately for Arbenz and his reformist policies, UFCo had strong ties to the U.S. government and, more specifically, the CIA. Among United Fruit's shareholders were U.S. Secretary of State John Foster Dulles and his brother, CIA Director Allen Dulles. Eisenhower's Undersecretary of State Walter Bedell Smith had equally close ties to the company, having once sought employment there. United Fruit had been lobbying the CIA to oust reform governments in Guatemala since Arévalo's time but it wasn't until the Eisenhower administration that it found a willing supporter in the White House.

On the home front, it was clear that Arbenz had incurred the wrath of the oligarchy and conservative military sectors. He faced increasing political fragmentation despite attempts to forge a functional revolutionary coalition of political parties to further his goals, and he looked to several dedicated, competent individuals for support in implementing the agrarian reform and labor organization. Many inside and outside of Guatemala conveniently labeled Arbenz and his supporters Communist, though how much influence the Communists actually had in Guatemala is still hotly debated. In 1952 Guatemala's official Communist Party, the Guatemalan Labor Party (PGT), was legalized. Communists subsequently gained considerable minority influence over important peasant organizations and labor unions, but not over the governing political body, winning only four of 58 seats.

In any case, the country became increasingly unstable. This instability, combined with Arbenz's tolerance of the PGT and other Communist and labor influences, caused Washington to grow increasingly alarmed. The CIA finally orchestrated the overthrow of Arbenz in 1954 in the form of a military invasion from Honduras dubbed "Operation Success" and led by two exiled Guatemalan military officers. The invading forces established Colonel Carlos Castillo Armas, who had previously led a failed coup against Arbenz, as chief of state. A series of military governments supported by the nascent military-oligarchy partnership and conservative elements of Guatemalan society followed. Thus began one of the most tragic chapters in Guatemala's already turbulent history.

THE CIVIL WAR (1960-1996)

With the professionalization of Guatemala's army now in place thanks to the policies of Barrios and Ubico, the military was now poised to become the country's dominating political force and would do so for the next 30 years. Further paving the way for military dominance over Guatemalan politics was the Cold War climate and the fight against Communism. United States policy and military aid would assist the dictators' rise to power and facilitate their increasingly repressive nature, all in the name of defeating Communist insurrection.

Among the new regime's first moves was the revocation of the 1945 constitution and the consequent reversal of the reforms of the previous years. The rule of the oligarchy was firmly reestablished and a wave of repression against peasants, labor unions, and agrarian reformers was unleashed.

Castillo Armas would be in power only until 1957, when he was shot by one of his own palace guards. Political turmoil ensued, followed by the rise to power of Miguel Ydígoras Fuentes, an army officer from the Ubico years now representing the National Democratic Renovation Party. His five years in office were characterized by incompetence, corruption, nepotism, patronage, and economic decline. Opposition to Ydígoras grew, with young army officers led by Marco Yon Sosa and Turcios Lima attempting an unsuccessful coup in 1960. Ydígoras was finally ousted by a military coup in 1963 with approval from Washington after Arévalo threatened to return to Guatemala to run in the next election, firmly putting the establishment in both Guatemala and Washington on edge.

During the subsequent military government of Alfredo Enrique Peralta Azurdia, Turcios Lima and Yon Sosa launched a guerrilla offensive from the Eastern Highlands, which marked the beginning of a protracted armed conflict between leftist rebels and the Guatemalan government. Ironically, both had received U.S. military training while serving in the Guatemalan forces and now used their skills to attack local army garrisons. The battle was soon joined by another armed rebel group, the Fuerzas Armadas Rebeldes (FAR). The PGT, meanwhile, formed an alliance with the rebels while advocating the return of Arévalo.

A self-proclaimed "third government of the revolution" came to power in 1966 under Julio Cesar Montenegro of the center-left Partido Revolucionario, who tried to continue in the vein of Arévalo and Arbenz. It was clear, however, that his hands were tied and power was in the hands of the military. Political violence escalated during his administration with death squads killing hundreds of students, unionists, academics, and peasant leaders.

By the end of the decade the guerrilla movement had been virtually eliminated from the Eastern Highlands. FAR shifted its focus to Guatemala City, where it kidnapped and murdered the U.S. ambassador, John Gordon Mein, in 1968.

Electoral fraud and political violence, accompanied by economic decline, would mark much of Guatemala's history between 1970 and 1990. A reign of terror became firmly entrenched, with successive governments each going to greater lengths to contain the guerrilla threat and repress an increasingly unsatisfied populace from which the movement drew its support. At the heart of the matter was a

CHRONICLE OF A FORCED DISAPPEARANCE

Among the most horrific aspects of Guatemala's civil war was the kidnapping, torture, and murder of at least 50,000 citizens by an army bent on brutal counterinsurgency and the elimination of any and all political opposition, whether real or imagined. Parallel to the oppression at the hands of the military, death squads such as "White Hand" and "Eye for Eye" began operating independently of government forces but with their full knowledge and acquiescence. The kidnappings targeted people from all walks of life but especially journalists, union leaders, intellectuals, opposition party leaders, university students, laborers, teachers, and clergy.

In the 1970s the Inter-American Commission on Human Rights (IACHR), a branch of the Organization of American States, began issuing a series of annual human-rights reports on countries around the world. In 1985, it issued a scathing report on the human-rights situation in Guatemala, just before the country's return to democratic rule. As the stories of the tortured and disappeared are probably best told by the victims themselves, the 1985 report is significant in that it includes testimony from an actual kidnapping victim and torture survivor.

Following is an excerpt from a transcript of a testimony corresponding to a kidnapping victim during the government of General Oscar Humberto Mejía Víctores. The report states that the capture was denied by security forces, as was always the case, and the victim classified as "missing." Incredibly, the victim managed to escape from the hands of his captors and took refuge in a Guatemala City embassy, where he interned himself by hurdling over a gate before being severely wounded by machine-gun fire.

CASE 9303 ALVARO RENÉ SOSA RAMOS

On June 24, 1985 the IACHR received the following communication: On Sunday March 11, at 9:00 A.M., Alvaro René Sosa Ramos was captured while walking near Avenida Roosevelt on a soccer field in Guatemala City's Zone 11. In his testimony he relates: "As I walked that way, a man off to the side called me and, as I turned around to see who it was, aimed a gun at me. I thought about running, but I saw eight men getting out of three vehicles with dark polarized windows. They captured me and put a jacket over my face, violently pushing me into a van. They then took me to a house. The men left me seated for more than two hours, during which time I could hear the screams of people coming from other rooms.

With my hands in cuffs, they forced me to take off my clothes, then tied my feet and hung me upside-down. Moments later, they beat me with the butt of a machete, accusing me of being a member of the Guatemalan Revolutionary Organization. I remember that a 'kaibil' (special forces) struck my face with the butt of his rifle. One of these blows opened my eyebrow completely. When they weren't beating me, I could hear the beatings and screams of the other victims. I lost all track of time while being tortured. Afterwards, they lowered me and threw me to the ground. A few hours later they hung me upside-down by my feet again and a kaibil would arrive periodically just to kick me in the face. After receiving these blows, they would lower me so that I could see them doing the same thing to another man.

They asked me if I knew that man, who was very deformed from the tortures he had endured. I recognized him as SILVIO MATRICARDI SALAM. I knew him when he was President of the National Front of Professors and I was a union leader of the Diana Products factory. I was impressed upon seeing his body so deformed by the many blows he received. I immediately told them that I did not know the man. When we returned to the first room, they hung me up again, this time applying electrical currents to my body.

It is incredible how violently the body reacts to electrical shocks, even hitting the wall at times. There were times that I would let my head hit the wall, hoping to lose consciousness, but I was never able to. After the electrical shocks my body burned with fever. I was thirsty and asked for water, but they gave me none. They said that I was crazy, that what I heard was air. I could hear the other victims also requesting water, but the torturers denied that there was any.

After the application of electrical shocks, they always asked me if I would talk and identify people. The fact that I had remained conscious helped me to think what I could do to escape. On one occasion when they asked me, I said that perhaps there would be people I knew on Montúfar Street in Zone 9. I had remembered there was an embassy on that street. I told the torturers that if they continued striking me, I would have no energy left to walk. In addition, it became nearly impossible for me to see because my eyes were very swollen from all of the blows. After that, the kidnappers stopped hitting me.

Sosa was able to escape the next day while his captors were temporarily distracted with executing another kidnapping operation. He managed to open the door of the van he was in and flung himself onto the pavement. Running straight to the Belgian embassy, he somehow jumped over the main gate before running across the grounds to find the entrance to the building. His kidnappers, meanwhile, shot into the embassy without any regard for innocent staffers housed inside the compound, managing to inflict multiple gunshot wounds upon Sosa. He eventually reached safety and was taken to a nearby hospital, where he was operated on.

The Belgian and Venezuelan embassies provided protective custody, and Canada agreed to grant him asylum. Still, Sosa feared greatly for his life during the few days leading to his departure from Guatemala on March 21, knowing full well that survivors are often killed while recovering in their hospital beds, as was the case with a peasant surviving the 1980 firebombing of the Spanish embassy. The body of the man Sosa recognized while in captivity, Silvio Matricardi Salam, was found on March 14 on the outskirts of the coastal city of Escuintla.

In addition to shedding light on the heinous crimes perpetrated against thousands of Guatemalans, Sosa's testimony is significant in that it demonstrates the kidnappings and torture were carried out with surgical precision using methods undeniably linked to the training of counterinsurgency forces throughout Latin America by the United States's very own CIA. This and other documented cases of abuse by military and paramilitary forces, some involving U.S. citizens, offer irrefutable evidence of U.S. involvement in perpetuating widespread oppression and human-rights abuses via military aid and training to repressive regimes. This fact was acknowledged during President Clinton's visit to Guatemala in 1999, when he officially apologized for U.S. involvement in Guatemala's civil war.

Clinton's apology came shortly before the official release of a secret Guatemalan military document smuggled out by human-rights organizations that revealed the fate of more than 180 victims of forced disappearance between August 1983 and March 1985. The document's release provided the first news many of the victims' families had concerning the fate of their loved ones. After years of getting nowhere with Guatemalan authorities in the pursuit of justice against perpetrators of torture, murder, and forced disappearance, the relatives of 20 of the victims filed a suit against the Guatemalan government for denial of justice with the Inter-American Commission on Human Rights.

system of government that ensured the continued prosperity of a wealthy minority to the detriment of a poor, landless, illiterate peasant class forced to work the elites' land. The demands of a growing urban middle class, meanwhile, were repressed with the help of the armed forces and right-wing death squads.

The United States, meanwhile, continued to pour money and logistical support into the increasingly bloody repression. Three years after the election in 1970 of Carlos Arana Osorio, nicknamed "the butcher of Zacapa," 15,000 Guatemalans had been killed or disappeared. The United States did its share by training 32,000 Guatemalan policemen through the Agency for International Development (AID) via its public-safety program. Guatemala's Policía Nacional was notoriously linked to the paramilitary death squads operating with impunity in the cities and countryside. Many off-duty policemen filled the ranks of these right-wing extremist groups working parallel to, but with unofficial sanction from, the more traditional forms of counterinsurgency.

Subsequent governments would open the Petén province as an escape valve to ease much of the tension caused by land-hungry peasants and demands for reform would periodically appear. The army continued on its path of power consolidation, spreading its influence across a broader spectrum of businesses and commercial interests and even coming to own a bank in the process.

In 1971, another guerrilla unit, the Revolutionary Organization of the People in Arms (ORPA), was formed. The unit was led by Rodrigo Asturias, the son of Nobel Peace Prize-winning novelist Miguel Angel Asturias. It operated in the vicinity of Lake Atitlán, Quetzaltenango, San Marcos, and Suchitepéquez, setting up operations in a strategically important corridor between the highlands and the agriculturally rich coastal lowlands. ORPA spent eight years recruiting local combatants, and then training and indoctrinating them into its ranks. Believed to be the most disciplined of the rebel organizations, it launched its first offensive in 1979 with the occupation of a coffee farm near Quetzaltenango.

Yet another guerrilla organization, the Guerrilla Army of the Poor (EGP), exploded onto the scene in 1975 with the much-publicized execution of a notoriously ruthless Ixcán landlord. It had spent three years developing political consciousness among the peasantry in the remote Ixcán jungle where it operated before launching its first assault. The Guatemalan military began increasingly violent reprisals against the peasantry living in remote jungle outposts, some of whom kept the guerrillas fed and supplied. In Ixcán, as well as throughout Guatemala, peasants would become increasingly caught in the cross fire between the military and the rebel groups, often serving as a scapegoat for the army's wrath.

On February 4, 1976, a massive earthquake struck the Guatemalan highlands, leaving 23,000 dead, 77,000 injured, and about a million homeless. The reconstruction efforts saw a renewed push to reform the inherent injustices of Guatemalan society with increased activity on behalf of the trade unions. In 1977 President Jimmy Carter, citing increasingly gross human rights violations, cut off military aid to Guatemala.

The 1978 elections were rigged to the benefit of Romeo Lucas García, who unleashed a fresh wave of repression against the usual victims but now also added academics, journalists, and trade unionists to the mix. The guerrilla war grew increasingly strong in rural Guatemala, with the number of total combatants estimated at 6,000 distributed among the four guerrilla groups, along with about 250,000 collaborators. The guerrillas actively recruited from a historically disenfranchised peasant base, particularly in the Ixil and Ixcán regions, which only strengthened the army's resolve to do away with the insurgency and intensified punitive measures against real and perceived collaborators. Peasants, priests, politicians, and anyone perceived to have ties to the guerrillas were massacred in the thousands. It is estimated that 25,000 Guatemalans were killed during the four-year Lucas regime.

Among the many atrocities committed by the Lucas regime, in a spiral of violence making the Spanish conquest look increasingly benign by comparison, were an army massacre in the village of Panzós, Alta Verapaz, and the firebombing of the Spanish embassy in Guatemala City during a peaceful occupation by peasant leaders. The first of these events occurred when approximately 500–700 villagers arrived in Panzós to formally present a letter to the mayor announcing the arrival of a union delegation dispatched from Guatemala City to give ear to long-standing peasant grievances against local planters. Eyewitness accounts differ as to the particular action/reaction to blame for the atrocity, but what is undeniable is that by the end of the day at least 35 peasants, including some children, lay murdered in the town square with dozens more injured or killed as they tried to make their escape. Author Greg Grandin has called the massacre at Panzós, "The Last Colonial Massacre," arguing that the 1978 killing of indigenous peasants heralded the official transition from now-obsolete patterns of protest and reaction to more carefully orchestrated counterinsurgent tactics on behalf of the Guatemalan military and eventually leading to all-out genocide.

The second of these events involved the peaceful occupation of the Spanish Embassy in Guatemala City by Ixil peasants on January 31, 1980. Without regard for embassy staff or the Spanish ambassador, the National Police forces stormed the embassy and firebombed it. The sole survivor was the Spanish ambassador. The victims included the father of Nobel Peace Prize winner Rigoberta Menchú, who recounts this and other atrocities in her book, *I Rigoberta Menchú*. Spain severed diplomatic relations with Guatemala in the aftermath of the massacre, not restoring them until several years later.

Besides the ambassador, it should be noted that one of the peasant activists also survived the tragedy, only to be murdered a few days later by a paramilitary death squad while recovering in a local hospital.

In 1982, Guatemala's armed rebel groups, FAR, EGP, ORPA, and PGT-FAR consolidated to form the Guatemalan National Revolutionary Unity (URNG), which would go on to fight for its ideals as a political force, while continuing armed resistance, and negotiate a peace treaty with the government in 1996.

Ríos Montt

The 1982 elections were again manipulated by the extreme right, this time to the benefit of Aníbal Guevara, but a coup on March 23 orchestrated by young military officers installed General Efraín Ríos Montt as the head of a three-member junta. The coup leaders cited the rigging of elections three times in eight years as justification for their actions, which were supported by most of the opposition parties. It was hoped Guatemala could be somehow steered once again on the path of peace, law, and order and that the terror would stop.

Ríos Montt was an evangelical Christian with ties to Iglesia del Verbo, one of several U.S.-based churches gaining ground in Guatemala after the 1976 earthquake. Among his many eccentricities was the delivery of weekly Sunday night sermons in which he expressed his desire to restore law and order, eliminate corruption, and defeat the guerrilla insurgency, allowing for the establishment of a true democracy.

On the surface things did seem to get better, particularly in the cities, thanks to an odd mix of heavy-handed discipline and strict moral guidelines governing all facets of government operations, from activities at the immigration office to the conduct of military officers. Montt purged Guatemala's government and security forces from corrupt elements and made a show of routinely executing criminals to show that disorder would not be tolerated. He also offered amnesty to the guerrillas during the month of June 1982, but only a handful of these accepted. Some later accounts of the Guatemalan civil war attribute this to communities' being either held hostage by guerrilla occupation and unable to make the trip down from the mountains or simply too frightened and distrustful of the military.

Whatever the reason, the cool response to

Montt's amnesty offer unleashed a new wave of counterinsurgency terror against the guerrillas and the indigenous peoples believed to be aiding and abetting them. Under a scorched-earth campaign, entire villages were destroyed, with survivors being resettled into a series of so-called "model villages" that allowed the army to keep a close watch on the peasantry while indoctrinating them with anticommunist rhetoric. The repression was made worse by a new system of conscripted labor in the form of civil defense patrols (PAC) composed of rural peasants controlled by the army. PACs were forced to make routine night patrols and report any suspicious activities. Failure to do so would result in their own suspicion in the army's eyes, meaning further reprisals on their villages. In this way, two modern-day variants of important colonial structures survived well into Guatemala's recent history, the *congregacion* and the *encomienda*.

An estimated 100,000 of Guatemala's indigenous Mayan descendants fled the violence, flooding refugee camps in neighboring Mexico or migrating farther north to the United States during the reign of Lucas García and Ríos Montt.

Cerezo and the Democratic Opening

Ríos Montt was eventually overthrown in August 1983 after just over a year in power by a military coup with U.S. backing. The underlying ideal was to get Guatemala firmly on the road back to democracy. Elections were called to take place in 1985 and General Mejía Víctores was installed as an interim chief of state. Repression in the countryside continued to escalate under the military's tireless scorched-earth campaign. The Ixil Triangle alone saw the displacement of 72 percent of its population and the destruction of 49 villages. Totals for Guatemala at this time included the destruction of 440 villages and more than 100,000 dead. In this context, the first free election in more than three decades took place. A new constitution was also drawn up.

Vinicio Cerezo Arévalo, a Christian Democrat, won the election with an overwhelming majority of the vote and widespread hope for change in Guatemala with the country firmly on the road to democracy. It was clear that the military still held the cards, however, and kept Cerezo under a tight leash via the Estado Mayor Presidencial, a notorious military security force officially charged with presidential protection but in reality designed to keep presidential power in check. Cerezo candidly admitted that the military still held 75 percent of the power.

Cerezo would seek to give the democratic opening a chance, knowing that the military's power could not be broken in the five years his term in office would last, by taking a nonconfrontational approach to the demands of Guatemala's various societal sectors. He kept a happy courtship with the powerful business interests, landowners, and generals. Among the latter was his defense minister, General Héctor Alejandro Gramajo, who curtailed much of the violence in the countryside and allowed Cerezo to survive numerous coup attempts.

In September of 1987, the Central American heads of state convened in the Eastern Highland town of Esquipulas, where they signed a treaty aimed at bringing the pacification and democratization of the region. Costa Rica's Oscar Arias Sánchez would later win the Nobel Peace Prize for his role in bringing the peace plan to fruition. Esquipulas II, as it was called, would open the doors for peace negotiations between the Guatemalan government and the URNG.

Although the levels of repression and violence dropped, they by no means disappeared. The armed struggle continued in remote corners of the highlands and Petén while death squads continued their reign of terror. Among the victims were an American nun, Sister Dianna Ortiz, abducted and tortured in 1989 by a paramilitary death squad, and the 1990 murders of U.S. citizen Michael Devine, who lived and worked his farm in Petén, and Guatemalan anthropologist Myrna Mack Chang. Ortiz escaped from her captors and lived to tell her harrowing story on ABC's *20/20*. CIA involvement was later found to have been involved in the Devine murder, as his assailants were CIA-trained Guatemalan military officers. In December 1990, the army massacred villagers in Santiago Atitlán, leading to the eventual closing of the town's military base.

Formal labor organization was once again given the official go-ahead and widespread protests marked much of Cerezo's later years as the average Guatemalan saw little economic improvement. Adding to the mix of societal sectors demanding justice was the Mutual Support Group (GAM), which demanded answers concerning disappeared family members and friends. Despite death threats and the disappearance of many of its members, GAM fought on, paving the way for future victories in securing official recognition of atrocities committed during the height of the civil war.

Jorge Serrano Elías

Barred from running for a second term under the 1985 Constitution, Cerezo yielded power to his successor, Jorge Serrano Elías, in 1991. Also barred from running under the new constitution was Efraín Ríos Montt, though there was much speculation as to his role behind the scenes because Serrano had served in his government. The new constitution wisely prohibited anyone's rising to power as the result of a military coup from running for president, a decision Montt has repeatedly tried unsuccessfully to have rescinded.

Indigenous-rights advocates, already enjoying greater freedom since the democratic opening, received a huge bolster from the awarding of the Nobel Peace Prize in 1992 to Indian rights activist Rigoberta Menchú Tum for her efforts in bringing worldwide attention to the genocidal civil war still raging in the countryside. The Guatemalan military issued an official protest to what it saw as disgraceful approval for an advocate of Communist insurrection, but it removed its opposition on the wave of worldwide fanfare for the awarding of the prize to Menchú.

Guatemala's historical problems continued to plague the nation and Serrano's incompe-

tence at the helm soon became evident. The peace process stalled with the Catholic Church mediator accusing both sides of intransigence. Popular protests against Serrano's government, bolstered by corruption charges involving his suspected links with Colombian drug cartels, forced him to declare an autocoup in May 1993. He assumed dictatorial powers, citing the country's purported spiral into anarchy and also dissolved Congress, citing the gross corruption of the legislative body while calling for the election of a new one.

Widespread protests and the withdrawl of U.S. support for Serrano's government resulted in his removal from office just two days later. Congress met and voted on the appointment of Ramiro de León Carpio, the country's human-rights ombudsman, to succeed Serrano and finish out his term.

De León quickly set about rearranging the military high command in an attempt to purge some of the more radical elements and achieve a measure of political stability. The URNG declared a cease-fire as a measure of goodwill toward the new administration. The guerrillas made some progress with the new administration, eventually signing an accord on indigenous rights and identity as well as a human rights accord establishing the creation of UN-mandated MINUGUA to oversee the implementation of the peace accords once the final agreement was reached. Although optimistic at first, Guatemalans soon lost hope in the De León administration when they saw he was incapable of addressing crime, constitutional reform, land, and tax issues.

Alvaro Arzú Irigoyen

Former Guatemala City Mayor Alvaro Arzú won the 1996 presidential elections thanks to a strong showing in the capital despite widespread electoral abstention elsewhere. Arzú, a businessman, represented the National Advancement Party (PAN), with deep roots in the oligarchy and a commitment to economic growth fostered by the development of the private sector under a free market. He quickly appointed new defense, foreign, and economic ministers and set out to sign a final peace accord with the URNG.

The agreement for a "Firm and Lasting Peace" was signed on December 29, 1996, in the Palacio Nacional de la Cultura, which once served as the presidential palace. After years of bloodshed, the final death toll stood at 200,000 with about 50,000 being cases of forced disappearance. A subsequent UN report by the Historical Clarification Commission (CEH) squarely placed blame for most of the violence in the hands of the military and the civil-defense patrols, with 80 percent of the victims said to be of Mayan origin. "The majority of human rights violations occurred with the knowledge or by order of the highest authorities of the state," the report declared. It further stated that, "State terror was applied to make it clear that those who attempted to assert their rights, and even their relatives, ran the risk of death by the most hideous means. The objective was to intimidate and silence society as a whole, in order to destroy the will for transformation, both in the short and long term."

The ambitious peace accords marked the culmination of years of negotiations between the government and guerrillas, which, if properly implemented, would serve as the basis for the construction of a completely different Guatemala. Unfortunately, the provisions set forth in the accord have yet to be fully adopted. One example of this disappointing trend was the failure to amend the constitution via a May 1999 referendum to officially redefine the country as "multiethnic, multilingual, and pluricultural," as stipulated in the accord on indigenous rights and identity. Voters stayed away from the polls in droves and the few who did vote decided against the reforms.

The Catholic Church issued its own report on the violence during the country's civil war; it also placed the blame for the majority of the atrocities in the hands of the military. Two days after issuing his report, Bishop Juan Gerardi Conedera was murdered in his garage, much to the outrage of the general populace. By this time, most political killings had all but ceased and the murder sent shock waves of indignation throughout Guatemalan society, which clamored for justice against Gerardi's killers. It soon became clear the act was a reprisal from the military intent on demonstrating its continued hold on the country's power structure.

Subsequent investigations and attempts to bring the guilty parties to justice ended in frustration as key witnesses, prosecutors, and judges fled the country in the face of death threats. While political kidnappings and disappearances became mostly a thing of the past, the country's security situation drastically worsened in the aftermath of the civil war. Bank robberies, murders, extortionary kidnappings, and armed robbery were at an all-time high. Using many of the same methods as in the "disappearance" of thousands of Guatemalans, kidnappers unleashed a wave of terror in which 1,000 people were abducted in 1997 alone. The country, at the time, had the fourth-highest kidnapping rate in the world.

U.S. President Bill Clinton visited Guatemala in March 1999 for a summit meeting with the Central American presidents. In a surprising declaration, he expressed regret on behalf of the United States government for its role in the atrocities committed during the country's civil war, saying that U.S. support for military forces that "engaged in violent and widespread repression" in Guatemala "was wrong."

The crime spree was largely blamed on a power vacuum created during the departure of Guatemala's Policía Nacional and its subsequent replacement by the new Policía Nacional Civil, in accordance with the peace accords. The new police force was trained by experts from Spain, Chile, and the United States. It was hoped that a more professional police force would help bring greater security once fully established, but it quickly became evident that this was not the case. Meanwhile, political murders such as the Gerardi and Myrna Mack Chang murders remained unresolved, shedding light on the lackluster state of Guatemala's judicial system, a situation exacerbated by widespread lynching of supposed criminals in remote areas where the rule of law was merely a vague concept.

Security issues aside, Arzú was a gifted administrator and government corruption remained at low levels, for Guatemala. Arzú's strengths as Guatemala City's mayor had always been infrastructure and public works. His time as president was no different in this regard, with various infrastructural projects being completed during his term in office. Guatemalans widely recognize his hard work, backed by a concrete list of accomplishments, and he is still popular in opinion polls. If Guatemala were to ever allow former presidents to run in elections, it is speculated that Arzú might give opponents a run for their money.

Arzú also privatized many state entities, including the notoriously inefficient telephone company, as part of a neoliberal economic approach to state participation in the economy. Guatemala's telecommunications laws have subsequently been heralded for their contributions to vast improvements in service coverage, increased competition, and lowered prices. At the end of Arzú's presidency, however, many critics pointed to a perceived affinity for serving the interests of Guatemala's wealthy elite, a criticism his successor would play largely to his advantage at the polls in the 1999 election campaign.

POSTWAR GUATEMALA
Alfonso Portillo and the "Corporate Mafia State"

During the 1999 elections, Alfonso Portillo ran on a populist ticket hoping to lure the lower classes away from his main opponent, who was fashioned after Arzú. He promised to cut poverty by ending corruption and tax evasion. His party, the Guatemalan Republican Front (FRG), was actually the brainchild of Ríos Montt, the mastermind behind some of the worst atrocities against Guatemala's indigenous peoples during the army's scorched-earth campaign of the early 1980s. He was forbidden, once again, from running in the election. It never stopped him from trying.

Another important campaign issue, and one Portillo played masterfully to his advantage, was citizen safety in the face of skyrocketing crime rates. A long-past incident in Mexico, whereby Portillo killed two men in self-defense before fleeing the country, was dug up during the campaign but actually worked in his favor in machismo-dominated Guatemalan society. Portillo played off the incident as evidence that he was willing and able to take a hard stance on crime.

History has not been kind in its assessment of the Portillo administration. It can be confidently stated without fear of exaggeration that the Portillo administration was one of the worst, if not *the* worst, of Guatemala's governments to date. Among the elements of his atrocious legacy was the solidifying of what analysts have called the "Corporate Mafia State," defined in a February 2002 Amnesty International report as, "The 'unholy alliance' between traditional sectors of the oligarchy, some 'new entrepreneurs,' elements of the police and military, and common criminals."

The report eloquently describes Guatemala under the Portillo government:

> Members of all these sectors collude to control lucrative "black," "dirty" or illegal industries, including drugs and arms trafficking, money laundering, car theft rings, the adoption racket, kidnapping for ransom, illegal logging and other proscribed use of state protected lands. They also conspire to ensure monopoly control of legal industries such as the oil industry. Such crimes were always current, but are more visible and prevalent in post-conflict Guatemala. Those involved use their connections – political and with the military and police – to reap profits and intimidate or even eliminate those who get in their way, know too much, offer competition, or try to investigate their activities. The victims are not targeted for "classic" human rights reasons, such as reasons of conscience or opposition to the government. They are victimized because they threaten the financial interests of Guatemala's powerful economic elite and those in the security forces who protect them or share the spoils.

THE 1996 PEACE ACCORDS

In addition to officially marking the end of hostilities between leftist insurgents and the Guatemalan government, the UN-brokered 1996 peace accords established a starting point from which to address historical grievances leading to the conflict and begin the construction of a more equitable society. From the start, the agreements established a fact-finding mission known as the **Historical Clarification Commission** (CEH) to investigate culpability for wartime atrocities committed largely against the country's Mayan population. The CEH and an independent wartime inquiries body created by Guatemala's Catholic Church, the **Recuperation of the Historical Memory Project** (REMHI), blamed the vast majority of atrocities on the army, with some violations also committed on the part of the guerrillas. Since the findings, many family members of victims of the civil war have sought to bring to justice those responsible for crimes against humanity, including genocide, torture, and illegal arrest. Because of the inadequacies of the Guatemalan judiciary, many have been forced to seek recourse in international courts, as in the case of the suit filed in a Spanish court under universal jurisdiction by the Rigoberta Menchú Foundation against eight government officials accused of crimes against humanity.

The accords also created an ambitious framework for reestablishing the rule of law as the country returned to peacetime while also seeking to address the war's underlying causes. In this regard, agreements were reached in the following areas: human rights, socioeconomic and agrarian issues, the strengthening of civil society and the role of the army in a democratic society, and rights and identity of indigenous peoples. Interestingly, these were negotiated by the establishment of a consensus among various sectors of society working with the Guatemalan government to have their interests and demands addressed at the negotiating table.

The first accord in the long process of negotiations dating to 1991 was the **Human Rights Accord,** signed in March 1994. While human rights were already guaranteed on paper in the 1986 Constitution, the accord was significant in that it created a new mechanism for ending their systematic violation via a UN verification mission known as **MINUGUA.**

The **Accord on Socioeconomic and Agrarian Issues** officially recognizes poverty as a problem and hints at government responsibility to ensure the well-being of the general populace. It committed the government to increasing the tax base as a percentage of GDP from 8 percent (the lowest in the hemisphere) to 12 percent within the next four years. A glaring omission was the ubiquitous issue of land reform. The government's conservative economic policies and the need to get Guatemala's wealthy elites to support the peace process were undoubtedly behind the relative weakness of this accord's reach.

In contrast, a relatively far-reaching accord, if fully implemented, is the **Accord on Strengthening of Civilian Power and the Role of the Army in a Democratic Society,** signed in September 1996. It covers the demilitarization of Guatemalan society, in which the military has long had its tentacles, requiring far-reaching constitutional reforms to be fully implemented. The accord limits the role of the military to the defense of Guatemala's territorial integrity. It eliminated the much-hated Civil Defense Patrols and counterinsurgency security units while reducing the size and budget of the military by a third. It also created a new civilian police force to replace the notoriously corrupt Policia Nacional with a mandate to guarantee citizen safety. Last, it mandates necessary reforms of the judicial system to eliminate pervasive impunity. The importance of this last point cannot be understated, as the state of the judiciary serves as a type of barometer in the progress report for Guatemala's democratization. As the CEH described in its final report:

> The justice system, non-existent in large areas of the country before the armed confrontation, was further weakened when the judicial branch submitted to the requirements of the dominant national security model...by tolerating or participating directly in impunity, which concealed the most fundamental violations of human rights, the judiciary

became functionally inoperative with respect to its role of protecting the individual from the State, and lost all credibility as guarantor of an effective legal system. This allowed impunity to become one of the most important mechanisms for generating and maintaining a climate of terror.

The **1995 Accord on Identity and Rights of Indigenous Peoples** issues a groundbreaking call to amend the 1985 Constitution to redefine Guatemala as "multiethnic, multilingual and pluricultural." Its full implementation requires deep reforms in the country's educational, judicial, and political systems, laying the foundation for a new entitlement of Guatemala's indigenous majority to make claims upon the state and creating a new context for social interactions. It thus goes beyond mere antidiscrimination protections for Guatemala's indigenous majority.

The far-reaching accords offer hope for the construction of a brand-new Guatemala among more equitable lines. The implementation of the reforms called for in the accords, however, has been a daunting task. A major blow to the implementation of the peace accords came in 1999 after a constitutional referendum defeated 50 proposed reforms. Although the peace accords called for only 12 such changes, it is believed that many Guatemalans voted against the package of 50 reforms because they simply felt uninformed about what they were voting to approve. The government did little to explain the nature of the numerous complex reforms or to promote their approval. Voter apathy was widespread with just 18 percent of eligible voters participating in the referendum. In areas where voters were mostly in favor of the reforms, mainly the rural areas most affected by the civil war, voter turnout was generally less than in the capital, which voted overwhelmingly against them.

Whatever the reasons, failure to implement the key changes to Guatemala's legal framework to allow full implementation of the accords meant change would have to come via the legislature. In Guatemala, this is easier said than done. The Portillo administration, in office from 2001 to 2004, was particularly reluctant to implement the main elements of the accords or to use them as a basis for the elaboration of government policy. Observers pointed out that the peace process stalled, and in many cases receded, under Portillo. Among the most critical areas requiring immediate attention were human rights, justice, and security.

The peace accords were officially taken up again by the Berger administration as government policy with concrete plans for new legislation to address many of the pending elements of the agreements. Many laws associated with the accords had trouble making their way through Congress, however, in a legislative assembly that was notorious for its inability to reach consensus on many issues. On a positive note, the reduction of the military by one-third was completed, as stipulated in the accords, and a plan for its modernization is in the works. Its official mandate now includes protecting the country's borders and combating drug traffic, environmental depredation, and smuggling of illegal immigrants.

In the end it can be said that the peace accords have brought some degree of benefit to Guatemalan society. Some of the agreements have been fully complied with, state repression ended, and some opening for political participation has been opened up in recent years. There are still, however, many lingering issues, including lack of security, poverty, socioeconomic exclusion, and a high degree of confrontation between varying sectors of society. Structural problems also persist, a case in point being the glaring deficiencies in the judiciary, leaving it open to manipulation and corruption while preventing it from being truly at the service of the country's citizenry. In essence, what we are seeing is a reflection of the peace accords' intimate connection to the process of Guatemala's continued democratization. Ironically, it is this very process of democratization that opened the door for the ending of the civil war via negotiations in the first place and that will ensure that the spirit and the letter of the accords are eventually fulfilled.

The report goes on to declare that "state agents are accomplices in the crimes or help cover them up."

Indeed, the whole country under Portillo seemed immersed in a crime wave of epic proportions. Punctuating the state of siege was a June 2001 prison break involving 78 high-profile criminals, including numerous bank robbers, kidnappers, and murderers from some of the most notorious organized crime groups.

Among the few achievements under the Portillo administration was the 2001 conviction of three people involved in the Gerardi murder. Although two military officers and a priest were tried and convicted of the murder, the general consensus was that the intellectual authors of the crime were still at large. Progress was also made in the case of the long-running saga of the murder of anthropologist Myrna Mack Chang. The material author of the crime, Noel de Jesús Beteta, is serving a 25-year prison sentence. The intellectual author, Colonel Juan Valencia Osorio, was sentenced to 30 years in prison in 2002 but an appeals court granted his release the next year. Shortly after an order for his rearrest and return to prison, Valencia escaped while under military custody under nebulous circumstances.

Meanwhile, Efraín Ríos Montt, the dictator who presided over some of the worst atrocities during the army's scorched-earth campaign of the early 1980s, got himself elected president of Congress. From his position, he and the military interests were said to run the show via the creation of a parallel power structure while Portillo remained a convenient government front man. Corruption, always a problem plaguing Guatemala's governments, ballooned to unparalleled proportions. Scandals involved embezzlement by the interior minister as well as a highly publicized coverup involving Ríos Montt himself.

Subsequently labeled "Guategate" by the local press, Ríos Montt and 19 other FRG congressmen were accused of secretly altering a liquor tax law, which had already been passed by Congress, at the behest of powerful liquor interests. The altered rate lowered the tariffs by as much as 50 percent. When opposition parties denounced the illegal changes to the law, congressional records from the meeting disappeared, while other documents were falsified. Although a popular outcry arose to have Montt and the other congressmen stripped of their diplomatic immunity to stand trial for their actions, the crime remained in impunity, as is so often the case in Guatemala.

In May 2003, the FRG nominated Ríos Montt as its presidential candidate in the elections to be held in November of that year. Once again, his candidacy was rejected by the electoral authorities and by two lower courts, in accordance with the constitutional ban on coup participants' running for presidential office. In July 2003 the Constitutional Court, with several judges appointed by the FRG, approved his candidacy for president, ostensibly ignoring the constitutional ban that had prevented him from running in previous elections. Adding insult to injury, Ríos Montt had publicly (and correctly) predicted the margin by which he would win the decision before its announcement. Days later, the Supreme Court suspended his campaign for the presidency and agreed to hear a complaint presented by two opposition parties.

Ríos Montt denounced the ruling as tampering with the judicial hierarchy and issued veiled threats concerning possible agitation by supporters of his candidacy. Days later, on July 24, a day known as Black Thursday, thousands of ski-masked and hooded FRG supporters invaded the Guatemala City streets armed with machetes, guns, and clubs. They had been bused in from the interior by the FRG and were led in organized fashion by well-known FRG militants, including several congressmen, who were photographed by the press while coordinating the actions.

The demonstrators quickly targeted the offices of outspoken media opposing Ríos Montt's candidacy, holding an entire building hostage for several hours after trying to occupy it. They also marched on the courts and opposition party headquarters, shooting out windows and burning tires in city streets. Journalists were attacked, including a TV cameraman who died of a heart attack while running away from an angry mob. The rioters finally disbanded after the second day of riots when Ríos Montt publicly called on them to return to their homes.

Afater the unrest, the Constitutional Court, laden with allies of Ríos Montt and Portillo, overturned the Supreme Court decision and cleared the way for Ríos Montt to run for president. A majority of Guatemalans were disgusted with his actions and the corrupt legacy of his party. They expressed their discontent at the polls, where Ríos Montt finished a distant third in the presidential race.

Óscar Berger

The winner after a second, runoff election between the top two candidates was Óscar Berger Perdomo of the GANA party, a former Guatemala City mayor who represented the interests of the economic elites but surrounded himself with a diverse cabinet. Among them was Rigoberta Menchú, who was named as governmental goodwill ambassador for the peace accords, which the government promised to take up again.

The new government's first priority quickly became cleaning up the mess left behind by the FRG. The National Treasury had been ransacked by corruption on an unprecedented scale involving theft, money laundering, monetary transfers to the army, and creation of secret bank accounts in Panama, Mexico, and the United States by members of Portillo's staff and totaling more than $1 billion. Berger promised to bring corrupt officials from the FRG government to justice. Remarkably, he was able to make good on his promises and many corrupt officials are now behind bars awaiting trial, although some have managed to escape prosecution by way of inefficiency and corruption still rampant in the country's judicial system. Portillo, meanwhile, quietly fled the country by slipping into El Salvador in the early morning of February 18, 2004, before flying from there to Mexico, where he still lives. Guatemalan authorities are actively seeking his extradition on several charges.

Among the other messes left behind were agreements for compensation to the civil defense patrols operating during the civil war and disbanded in its aftermath. An agreement was finally reached whereby ex-civil defense patrollers would be involved in community reforestation projects in exchange for the monetary compensation they had demanded.

Crime and insecurity continued to be problems affecting a wide spectrum of the population. Gang violence plagued Guatemala City and numerous other cities and towns. The police forces increasingly came under fire for corruption, initiating a long process of cleansing out its corrupt elements in the hopes of making it more effective. In the face of the police force's inability to abate the continuing upswing in violent crime, which included 16 daily homicides, Berger was forced to integrate joint police-military patrols. These came under fire as evidence of increasing militarization, contrary to the 1996 peace accords.

The economic picture was severely disrupted when thousands of rural peasant farmers had their crops annihilated and their villages destroyed by Hurricane Stan in October 2005. Government reconstruction efforts in the storm's aftermath were slow in making it to affected communities.

Despite some public opposition, Berger was able to implement many of his neoliberal economic policies, including laws governing the concession of government services and construction projects to private entities, securing mining rights for multinational mining conglomerates, and the ratification of DR-CAFTA, the Central American Free Trade Agreement.

The judicial and legislative branches continued to come under fire for gross inefficiency and corruption charges. The existence of clandestine groups, a legacy of the corporate mafia state with links to state agents and organized crime, continued to plague the government. Meanwhile, the creation of a UN-sponsored Commission for the Investigation of Illegal Groups and Clandestine Security Organizations (CICIACS) was blocked by Constitutional Court rulings. A second, reworked version of the proposal, known as the International Commission Against Impunity in Guatemala (CICIG) was the product of an agreement signed between the United Nations and Guatemalan government in December 2006, though it was still pending final approval by the Guatemalan legislature. The United States and other foreign governments offered financial support for the program, which will be composed of expert international detectives who will give material support to the Public Ministry in its investigations of parallel power structures.

In February 2007, the urgent need to get CICIG up and running was demonstrated by a heinous crime perpetrated against three visiting Salvadoran diplomats and their chauffeur, who were found dead, shot execution-style and burned in their car on the outskirts of Guatemala City. After an unprecedented investigation fueled by outrage from Salvadoran authorities, much to everyone's surprise the perpetrators turned out to be high-ranking police officers from the Department of Criminal Investigations (DINC) operating as contract killers. Things really came to a head when the captured policemen were executed by a death squad while awaiting questioning in a high-security prison just days later. Initial government statements and doublespeak had pinned the blame for the executions on fellow prison inmates, including gang members. The incident opened a can of worms in which high-ranking government officials have been implicated in the continued operation of death squads and ties to organized crime. The reconstruction of the Civilian National Police (PNC), already a matter of national concern, came to the forefront after these incidents.

As Berger's presidency drew to a close, the general consensus was that his time as president was marked by mostly good intentions but also some modest gains, particularly in terms of a redress of Guatemala's historical ills requiring deep structural reforms of the state apparatus. Among the glaring omissions was a long-term, inclusive strategy to develop rural areas, where the majority of Guatemala's indigenous peoples live. Delays in the reconstruction process after Hurricane Stan were continually cited as symptoms of weak leadership and an inability to coordinate efforts to reach a common goal. Among the positive aspects of his presidency were infrastructural projects, or *megaproyectos,* including new roads and airports to make Guatemala more attractive to investors. The creation of so-called *gabinetes móviles* was also a welcome aspect of Berger's administration, allowing those in rural areas the opportunity to have their demands personally addressed by the president and his cabinet members during visits to their towns and cities. Continued economic growth and a more favorable investment climate were duly recognized by international financial organizations. The full effect of DR-CAFTA, which officially took effect on July 1, 2006, remains to be seen.

Guatemala's arrival on the international scene and its newfound attractiveness to investors were showcased in a single week in March 2007 in which Guatemala City hosted visits from President George W. Bush, an international sculpture festival, and 5,000 delegates in town for a yearly assembly of the Inter-American Development Bank. Guatemala also hosted a meeting of the International Olympic Committee in June 2007. Bush's visit to Guatemala, part of a larger trip through Latin America, was limited to what seemed a cultural sightseeing tour through the highlands. He and the first lady visited Chirijuyú, site of a Mayan agricultural collective exporting vegetables to neighboring Central American countries with irrigation projects financed by USAID. They also visited Santa Cruz Balanyá, another highland village where U.S. doctors are helping the local population. Their final stop was the ruins of Iximché, where they were treated to marimba music and traditional Mayan folklore, including the Dance of the Deer, performed by local children. Guatemalans had hoped Bush would declare an end to deportations of Guatemalan nationals pending legislative reform of immigration laws in U.S. Congress, to no avail.

As this book went to press, the presidential

hopefuls for the September 2007 election were still being decided, though among the early candidates were Nobel Peace Prize winner and Indian rights activist Rigoberta Menchú as the candidate for the Encuentro Por Guatemala (EG) party. Other notables included Rafael Espada, a well-respected surgeon who has lived in Houston for several years, as a vice presidential candidate with UNE (National Unity for Hope). The party has come under close scrutiny for alleged ties to drug trafficking and organized crime and was the subject of a scandal that involved siphoning millions of dollars of campaign funds from the National Treasury during the 2003 election campaign. In a classic case of Guatemalan voter amnesia from one election to the next, UNE was ahead in the polls at last check. The former pastor of one of Guatemala City's largest churches with a popular nationwide radio ministry was another presidential hopeful.

Government

ORGANIZATION

Guatemala is a constitutional democracy. The president is the chief of state, assisted by a vice president, both of whom are elected to office for a single four-year term. The president is constitutionally barred from a second term, but the vice president may run for office after a four-year hiatus from office. The Congreso de la República is the national (unicameral) legislative body, now consisting of 158 members. Congress members serve four-year terms running concurrently with the presidential term. Guatemala has 22 administrative subdivisions (departments) headed by governors appointed by the president. Popularly elected mayors or councils govern Guatemala City and 331 other municipalities.

JUDICIAL SYSTEM

The judicial branch is independent of the executive and the legislature branches and consists of a Constitutional Court and a Supreme Court of Justice. The Constitutional Court is the highest court in the land and consists of five judges elected for five-year terms, with each judge serving one year as president of the court. One judge each is elected by Congress, the Supreme Court of Justice, the Superior Council of the Universidad de San Carlos de Guatemala, and the bar association (Colegio de Abogados), and appointed by the president. The Supreme Court of Justice consists of 13 magistrates who serve five-year terms and elect a president of the court each year from among their members. The judiciary suffers from a poor public image because of suspicions that it has become porous to influence from drug traffickers as well as being corrupt and inefficient.

ELECTIONS

The current power balance is a product of the 1985 Constitution, formulated before the country's official return to democracy in 1986. A series of reforms in 1993 shortened terms of office for president, vice president, and members of congress from five years to four; for Supreme Court justices from six years to five; and increased terms for mayors and city councils from 2.5 years to four.

Between 1954 and 1986, Guatemala was ruled primarily by a military-oligarchy alliance that installed presidents periodically via widely fraudulent elections or military coups. In the few elections considered free and fair during this period, the military quickly stepped in to assert its dominant role while ensuring that the president remained a figurehead. All of the elections from 1985 onward have been considered free and fair, though the military still holds much power in Guatemala, probably more so than in any other Latin American country. Much of Guatemala's democratic process has consisted of a gradual strengthening of the state while trying to limit the power of the

POLITICAL GEOGRAPHY OF GUATEMALA

MEXICO

BELIZE

⊛ Belmopan

Flores ⊙

PETÉN

HUEHUE-
TENANGO

ALTA VERAPAZ

IZABAL

Puerto
⊙ Barrios

QUICHÉ

⊙ Cobán

Huehuetenango ⊙

SAN
MARCOS

TOTO-
NICAPÁN

Santa Cruz
del Quiché

BAJA
VERAPAZ

Salamá ⊙

ZACAPA

San Marcos ⊙

⊙ Totonicapán

EL
PROGRESO

⊙ Zacapa

HONDURAS

Quetzaltenango ⊙

QUEZAL-
TENANGO

Sololá ⊙

GUATEMALA

El Progreso ⊙

Chiquimula ⊙

Chimaltenango ⊙

⊛ Guatemala
City

Jalapa ⊙

CHIQUIMULA

Antigua ⊙
Guatemala

JALAPA

Retalhuleu ⊙

⊙ Mazatenango

RETALHULEU

JUTIAPA

Escuintla ⊙

Cuilapa ⊙

Jutiapa ⊙

SUCHITEPÉQUEZ

ESCUINTLA

SANTA
ROSA

EL SALVADOR

SOLOLÁ

SACATEPÉQUEZ

San Salvador ⊛

CHIMALTENANGO

PACIFIC   OCEAN

0   40 mi

0   40 km

military. Other general characteristics of the democratic process have been the growth of citizen participation from all sectors of society in an atmosphere of greater freedom concurrent with the gradual strengthening of institutions having extremely limited experience with governance under a democratic system.

POLITICAL PARTIES

Guatemala's political parties constitute a veritable alphabet soup and change from year to year depending on the capricious nature of alliances between different factions. The ruling party from 2004 to 2007 was the Gran Alianza Nacional, or GANA (Great National Alliance), originally consisting of the Patriot Party, Reform Movement, and National Solidarity Party. Some of the other parties, in order of their percentage of congressional seats, are the Guatemalan Republican Front (FRG), National Unity of Hope (UNE), National Advancement Party (PAN), Unionist Party (PU), New Nation Alliance (ANN), and the Guatemalan National Revolutionary Unity (URNG). The latter is the political party formed by the guerrilla movement that fought against the government for 36 years in the country's civil war.

BUREAUCRACY

There is still a long way to go in the consolidation of a genuine functioning democracy in Guatemala. The judiciary and legislative branches are badly in need of reform and have lost virtually all credibility with their constituents. The current situation is still very much like that described in 2000 by the Guatemalan Institute of Political, Economic and Social Studies, an NGO:

In our society, agents or former agents of the State have woven a secret, behind-the-scenes network dedicated to obstructing justice. They have created a virtual alternative government that functions clandestinely with its own standardized and consistent modus operandi. In such a context, crimes are not clarified, and those responsible are not identified.

Society finally forgets the cases and becomes resigned.

If the actual material authors left evidence at the scene of their crimes, they then decide who to implicate as scapegoats. If there are actually any inquiries and if these eventually lead to any arrests, these are always of low-ranking members of the army, or at best, an official not in active service.

When they can't pin the crime on some scapegoat, the scene of the crime is contaminated and legal proceedings are obstructed and proceed at a snail's pace. If nonetheless, investigations still continue, these powerful forces hidden behind the scenes destroy the evidence. And of course it cannot be forgotten that pressure, threats, attacks and corruption are all part of the efforts to undermine and demoralize the judiciary, who, knowing they are not able to count on a security apparatus that will guarantee that the law is enforced, feel obliged to cede in the face of this parallel power.

The powerlessness of the Guatemalan judiciary has forced some people to seek remedies for their grievances in international courts under universal jurisdiction established by the United Nations concerning crimes against humanity. One example is the suit filed before the Spanish National Court in 1999 by the Rigoberta Menchú Foundation against eight former Guatemalan officials, including General Efraín Ríos Montt, for murder, genocide, torture, terrorism, and illegal arrest. The case seeks to try those responsible for wartime abuses and centers around the 1980 attack on the Spanish Embassy in Guatemala City that claimed the lives of 37 peasant activists, among them Menchú's father, and embassy staff. The Spanish court has heard other cases involving genocide and established a precedent for universal jurisdiction in the 1998 arrest of Chile's General Augusto Pinochét in the United Kingdom.

He remained in custody for 14 months until British authorities ruled Pinochet was unfit for trial and let him return to Chile.

In July 2006, a Spanish judge ordered the detention of all eight accused after an unfruitful visit to Guatemala with the intention of gathering testimonies from plaintiffs and questioning the accused. Ríos Montt and General Mejía Víctores effectively paralyzed the process with a series of appeals upheld by the Constitutional Court. Menchú admitted the difficulty of getting Guatemalan officials to execute the arrest orders, calling it "a test of the Guatemalan justice system" and adding, "We will see if we have advanced."

As for the legislature, there is talk of reducing the number of members of congress, elected partly by proportional representation. The Guatemalan Congress has suffered in recent years from a gradual erosion of confidence on the part of its constituents because of gross inefficiency, corruption, and growing suspicion of widespread links to drug trafficking. In essence, a majority of Guatemalans view their congressional body as practically useless and expensive to maintain.

Political parties, likewise, have suffered a gradual decline in credibility. As 2007 is an election year, it remains to be seen what new options, if any, will be offered to a populace increasingly tired of the same faces and the same options for leadership. The general pattern since 1986 has been one of great expectation for change before elections and the installation of a new government, followed by disappointment with the new government's failure to deliver on its promises, ending in frustration and renewed hope for change with the next round of elections. Opinion polls point to a growing desire to see the emergence of better leadership and an authentic political class, something Guatemala still lacks.

Economy

Guatemala's gross domestic product in 2005 was $27.5 billion, an increase of 3 percent over the previous year, with a per capita GDP of about $2,000. Inflation was about 9 percent for the same year. Although it is the largest economy in Central America, large sectors of the population remain only marginally active in the economy. Guatemala is also the region's most populous country. The economy has been growing steadily since the 1996 peace accords and has demonstrated macroeconomic stability.

AGRICULTURE, TRADE, AND INDUSTRY

Agriculture accounts for 23 percent of GDP, with agricultural exports of coffee, sugar, bananas, cardamom, vegetables, flowers and plants, timber, rice, and rubber being the chief products. Guatemala exported $3.8 billion worth of goods in 2005, with 75 percent of these being agricultural products. Light industry contributes to 19 percent of the GDP and manufactures include prepared food, clothing and textiles, construction materials, tires, and pharmaceuticals. The service sector accounts for 58 percent of Guatemala's GDP. The United States is Guatemala's biggest trading partner, accounting for more than half of the country's exports and a third of its imports. Other important trading partners include the neighboring Central American countries, Mexico, South Korea, China, and Japan.

In terms of employment, agriculture is the largest employer, with half of the population employed by this sector. Services, bolstered by tourism, employ 35 percent of the population and industry employs the remaining 15 percent. Unemployment in 2003 was 7.5 percent.

After the signing of the 1996 peace accords, Guatemala appeared poised for rapid economic growth, but a financial crisis in 1998 disrupted the expected pace. Despite gains in industry,

Guatemala's economy is still very much based on agriculture.

the country's economy still showed much of its historical susceptibility to world commodity prices, specifically coffee. A collapse in coffee prices severely affected rural incomes and brought the industry into a serious recession, though exports of this commodity have bounced back since then.

Foreign investment has remained weak, with Guatemala unable to capitalize on foreign investment to the same degree as its neighbors. A notable exception is the privatization of utilities. Potential investors cite corruption, crime and security issues, and a climate of confrontation between the government and private sector as the principal barriers to new business. A project announced by the Berger government in 2004 aims to make Guatemala more competitive, among other things. Concrete results remain to be seen, as Guatemala's powerful agricultural, financial, and industrial elites will need to cooperate with the government's agenda in any attempt to make the country more attractive to investors.

Guatemala's economy is dominated by the private sector, which generates about 85 percent of GDP. The government's involvement is small, with its business activities limited to public utilities, many of which have been privatized under a neoliberal economic model, the operation of ports and airports, and several development-oriented financial institutions. The Berger administration passed legislation allowing the government to concession more of these services to the private sector in 2006.

The U.S.-Dominican Republic-Central America Free Trade Agreement (DR-CAFTA) was ratified by Guatemala on March 10, 2005. Priorities within DR-CAFTA include the elimination of customs tariffs on as many categories of goods as possible, opening services sectors, and creating clear and easily enforceable rules in areas such as investment, customs procedures, government procurement, electronic commerce, intellectual property protection, the use of sanitary measures for the protection of public health, and resolution of business disputes. Import tariffs were lowered as part of Guatemala's membership in the Central

American Common Market, with most now below 15 percent.

Other priorities include increasing transparency and accountability in Guatemala's public finances, broadening the tax base as part of the peace accords, and completing implementation of reforms of the finance sector. The implementation of these changes involved reforming Guatemalan laws and a long, involved process in the national legislature. The process finally ended in June 2006, with DR-CAFTA officially taking effect on July 1, 2006, after the U.S. Department of Commerce officially certified the country in compliance with the trade agreement.

The ratification of DR-CAFTA was met with protests in Guatemala City. Its detractors feared the loss of jobs, increased dependence on food imports, and a broadening of the deep gap between Guatemala's rich and poor. Peasant organizations and at least one NGO calculated the loss of up to 100,000 jobs in the agricultural sector. The government has offered to counteract perceived imbalances through a series of credits supporting small and medium-size businesses, which employ more than 70 percent of the population and are the engine of the rural economy. Nontraditional export sectors were quick to point out the treaty will create an estimated 50,000 jobs in nontraditional agriculture in the first two years of its implementation. Whatever the result, the implementation of DR-CAFTA will certainly require major adjustments requiring the strengthening of agroindustry, and small farms in particular, via expansion to new markets and the application of new technologies, among other things.

Another major contributor to Guatemala's economy is the money sent home by 1.2 million expatriate Guatemalans living and working in the United States. In 2006, this amounted to $3.4 billion, which Guatemalans on the receiving end used to supplement their incomes, start businesses, and put into savings. This phenomenon has helped to widely ameliorate the country's endemic poverty and accounts for 11 percent of the GDP.

DISTRIBUTION OF WEALTH

It remains to be seen whether the treaty will aggravate or alleviate Guatemala's skewed wealth- and land-distribution patterns, which are already some of the most unequal in the world. The wealthiest 10 percent of the population receives almost one-half of all income and the top 20 percent receives two-thirds. About 80 percent of the population lives in poverty, with two-thirds of that number living in extreme poverty and surviving on less than $2 a day. Belying these patterns of wealth and income distribution are Guatemala's social-development indicators, such as infant mortality and illiteracy, which are among the worst in the hemisphere. Chronic malnutrition among the rural poor worsened with the onset of the late-'90s coffee crisis and devastation wrought by Hurricane Stan in 2005. The United States has provided disaster assistance and food aid in response to the tragedy.

TOURISM

On a much more positive note, tourism has had a great impact on the economy in recent years, particularly since the end of the civil war in 1996. In 2004, Guatemala received one million visitors for the first time and increased visitor numbers have continued in the years since. In 2006, Guatemala registered 1.5 million foreign arrivals, with a total tourism expenditure totaling just over $1 billion. According to the World Tourism Organization, between 2003 and 2004 Guatemala had the largest increase of international arrivals of any country in the Americas, with a growth of 34.3 percent. Between 2003 and 2006, Guatemala's tourist arrivals increased by a whopping 70 percent. In Central America, only Costa Rica receives more visitors.

About 30 percent of Guatemala's visitor arrivals come from North America, with another 34 percent coming from Central America, particularly El Salvador. United States visitors may be closing the gap, however, as statistics from the peak Easter travel season of 2006 show more Americans arriving in Guatemala than Salvadorans. Approximately 18 percent of Guatemala's tourists come from Europe and another 18 percent come from various other countries.

Much of the money generated by tourism stays in local hands, as many communities have been able to capitalize on their proximity to area attractions by catering to the demands of an increasing number of visitors. Foreign tourism investment is limited mostly to main tourist areas and local entrepreneurs have done an excellent job of filling in the void created by the lack of foreign investment.

The government, meanwhile, is actively promoting tourism abroad via ad campaigns sponsored by the state tourism agency, INGUAT,

and investing in much-needed infrastructural improvements to the country's airports. The industry also got a boost from the filming of the CBS television series *Survivor* in the rainforests of Petén, which aired in 2005.

The main obstacle to the continued growth of Guatemala's tourism industry is security and the Guatemalan government is actively working to make travel safer for visitors to Guatemala. Among the improvements in visitor security is the establishment of a tourism police in the main tourist destinations. In many places, their presence has resulted in fewer occurrences of robbery and assault.

People and Culture

DEMOGRAPHICS

Guatemala's population is one of the fastest growing in Latin America, with 2004 census figures (the last available) placing the population at just over 14 million. The annual growth rate was 2.61 percent and 43 percent of the population is under the age of 15. The country's population density is 301 people per square mile, with an urban-to-rural ratio of 38.7 percent to 61.3 percent. Population density is much less in the northern Petén department, comprising a third of Guatemala's total land area but harboring only about 5 percent of the population. Urbanization is greatest in the Western Highlands region centered around Guatemala City and Quetzaltenango.

ETHNIC DIVERSITY

Guatemala has an incredible wealth of ethnic diversity, as attested to by the as-of-yet-unfulfilled push to amend the national constitution to officially describe the country as "pluri-cultural, multilingual and multi-ethnic." The country is divided about evenly between indigenous Mayan descendants, comprising 21 different linguistic groups, and ladinos, who are of Mayan descent but have adopted European culture and dress

in addition to the Spanish language. A sizable percentage of the population is a mixture of Mayan and European, also known as mestizo. A much smaller percentage of the population is of purely European descent, primarily from Spanish and German families, and control a disproportionate share of the country's wealth. Many of these are direct descendants of the criollo (New World Spanish–born elite) families dominating the country's economy since colonial times. Indigenous Mayan descendants are found in greatest numbers in the Western Highlands, with Guatemala City, the Pacific, Caribbean, and Petén lowlands being largely ladino.

Additionally, there are two non-Mayan ethnicities thrown into the mix, Xinca and Garífuna. Only about 100–250 Xinca speakers remain, confined to a small area near the Salvadoran border. The Garinagu (plural of Garífuna), a mixture of Amerindian and African peoples, arrived from St. Vincent via Roatán, Honduras, in the early 1800s and settled in the Guatemalan Caribbean coastal town of Lívingston. Their culture is more similar to that of the Western Caribbean, with whom they identify more readily, than to that of the rest of Guatemala.

Mayan Groups

Ethnicity and language are intertwined when it comes to Guatemala's principal Mayan groups, which include K'iche', Kaqchikel, Tz'utujil, Mam, Ixil, Q'eqchi', Poqomchi', Poqomam, and Q'anjob'al. (For a more in-depth look at Guatemala's Mayan languages and where they are spoken, see the sidebar *Mayan Ethnolinguistic Groups in Guatemala*.) By far the most numerous group is K'iche', with nearly one million speakers. Just more than 400,000 people speak Kaqchikel and there are about 686,000 Mam speakers.

RELIGION

Religion in Guatemala is fairly complex, with traditional Mayan spirituality still very much a presence, particularly in the highlands, along with Catholicism and the more recent incursions of Evangelical Christianity. In much smaller numbers, Guatemala's Jewish population is centered in Guatemala City. There is also a small Muslim population with at least one mosque in Guatemala City.

Mayan Spirituality

Mayan spirituality has its origins in pre-Columbian religious practices and a cosmology that venerated natural phenomena, including rivers, mountains, and caves. The soaring temples built by the Mayan and other Mesoamerican civilizations were built to mimic mountains and were usually built in alignment with the cardinal directions. The solstices were very important in this regard and many of their temple pyramids and observatories were built in precise fashion so as to mark these events. Caves were also sacred to the Mayans and believed to be passages to the underworld, a belief that persists to this day. Archaeologists speculate that at least one powerful economic center, Cancuén, lacked buildings of strictly religious significance because of its proximity to the massive Candelaria cave network nearby.

The Mayan calendar is still in use in parts of Guatemala today, particularly the Western Highlands, and is pegged closely to the agricultural cycle. Maize is a sacred crop and is believed to have been the basis for the modern formation of man by the gods, as told in the K'iche' book of myths and legends, the *Popol Vuh*, discovered by a Spanish priest in Chichicastenango in the 18th century. (For more, see the sidebar *The* Popul Vuh in the *Chichicastenango* section.) Although the vast majority of the Mayans' sacred writings were burned by Bishop Diego de Landa in a 16th-century Yucatán bonfire, three Mayan texts, known as codices, survive in European museums. The *Chilam Balam* is another sacred book based on partially salvaged Yucatecan documents from the 17th and 18th centuries.

Modern-day Mayan religious practices, also known as *costumbre*, often take place in caves, archaeological sites, and volcanic summits. They often include offerings of candles, flowers, and liquor with the sacrifice of a chicken or other small animal thrown in for good measure.

Another curiosity of the Western Highlands is the veneration of a folk saint known alternatively as Maximón or San Simón with a particularly persistent following in Santiago Atitlán and Zunil. The cigar-smoking, liquor-drinking idol is a thorn in the side of many Catholic and Evangelical groups, whose followers sometimes profess conversion to Christianity but often still hold allegiance to Maximón, who is thought to represent Judas and/or Pedro de Alvarado. Syncretism, combining Mayan religious beliefs and Catholicism, is a major player in highland Mayan spirituality.

The cult following of folk saints is also tied to the presence of *cofradías,* a form of Mayan community leadership with roots in Catholic lay brotherhoods wielding religious and political influences. The *cofradías* are responsible for organizing religious festivities in relation to particular folk saints and a different member of the *cofradía* harbors the Maximón idol in his home every year.

The Catholic Church

Catholicism has played an important role in Guatemala ever since colonial times, though the state increasingly took measures to limit its

MAYAN ETHNOLINGUISTIC GROUPS IN GUATEMALA

Achi': Spoken in western Baja Verapaz, including Cubulco, Rabinal, San Miguel Chicaj, San Jerónimo, and Salamá.

Akateko: Spoken in San Miguel Acatán and San Rafael La Independencia (Huehuetenango).

Awakateko: Spoken in Aguacatán, Huehuetenango.

Ch'orti: Spoken in La Unión (Zacapa) and Jocotán, Camotán, Olopa, and Quetzaltepeque (Chiquimula).

Chuj: Spoken in San Mateo Ixtatán and parts of Nentón.

Itzá: Spoken in Flores, San José, San Andrés, San Benito, La Libertad, and Sayaxché.

Ixil: Spoken in Chajul, Cotzal, and Nebaj (El Quiché department).

Kaqchikel: Spoken in 47 municipalities in seven departments, including Guatemala, Sacatepéquez, Chimaltenango, Escuintla, Sololá (Panajachel, Santa Catarina Palopó, San Antonio Palopó, Santa Cruz La Laguna, and San Marcos La Laguna), Suchitepéquez, and Baja Verapaz.

K'iche': Guatemala's most widely spoken Mayan dialect, with speakers in 75 municipalities spanning six departments, including Sololá, Totonicapán, Quetzaltenango, El Quiché, Suchitepéquez, and Retalhuleu.

Mam: Spoken in 55 municipalities in three departments, including Quetzaltenango, San Marcos, and Huehuetenango (Todos Santos, San Juan Atitán, among others).

Mopán: Spoken in San Luis, Dolores, parts of Melchor de Mencos, and Poptún (Petén).

Popti (Jakalteko): Spoken in parts of western Huehuetenango, including Jacaltenango, La Democracia, Concepción Huista, San Antonio Huista, Santa Ana Huista, and Nentón.

Poqomam: Spoken in Mixco and Chinautla (Guatemala department), Palín (Escuintla), and Jalapa department.

Poqomchi': Widely spoken in Alta and Baja Verapaz, including San Cristóbal Verapaz, Tactic, Tamahú, Tucurú, and Purulhá.

Q'anjob'al: Spoken in Soloma, San Juan Ixcoy, Santa Eulalia, and Barillas (Huehuetenango).

Q'eqchi: Most widely spoken in Alta Verapaz, including Cobán, Panzós, Senahú, San Pedro Carchá, San Juan Chamelco, Lanquín, Chisec, and Cahabón. Other locales include Uspantán (El Quiché department) and parts of Petén and Izabal.

Sakapulteko: Spoken in parts of Sacapulas, El Quiché.

Sipakapense: Spoken in Sipacapa, San Marcos.

Tektiteko: Spoken in parts of Cuilco and Tectitán (Huehuetenango).

Tz'utujil: Spoken in several of the Lake Atitlán villages, including San Lucas Tolimán, San Pablo La Laguna, San Juan La Laguna, San Pedro La Laguna, and Santiago Atitlán.

Uspanteko: Spoken in Uspantán, El Quiché.

power starting in the late 19th century, when liberal reformers confiscated church property and secularized education. More recently, the church wrestled with its official mandate of saving souls and its moral obligation to alleviate the misery and injustice experienced by many of its subjects, particularly the Mayans. Many parish priests, faced with the atrocities and injustices of the civil war, adopted the tenets of Liberation Theology, seeking a more just life in the here and now and officially opposing the military's scorched-earth campaign throughout the highlands. Many clergy paid for their beliefs with their lives or were forced into exile. Even after the civil war ended, Bishop Juan Gerardi was murdered in the days after his issuance of a scathing report on civil war atrocities perpetrated mostly by the military. The church remains a watchdog and defender of the poor, which is evident in the ongoing work of the Archbishop's Human Rights Office.

Although there are many churches throughout the country, the Catholic Church often has trouble finding priests to fill them, a factor that has contributed to the explosive growth of Evangelical Christianity. Pope John Paul II visited Guatemala three times during his term at the helm of the Vatican; the last visit was for the purpose of canonizing Antigua's beloved Hermano Pedro de San José Betancur.

Catholicism can still draw a big crowd, though, most noticeably during Holy Week, with its elaborate processions reenacting Christ's crucifixion, and the annual pilgrimage to Esquipulas on January 16 to pay homage to the Black Christ in the town's basilica.

Evangelical Christianity

According to some estimates, a third of Guatemala now claims adherence to Protestantism and, more specifically, Evangelical Christianity. The growth of this sect will become obvious as you travel around the country and hear the sounds of loud evening worship services, known as *cultos,* emanating from numerous churches, particularly in the highlands. The trend toward Evangelical Christianity dates

to the aftermath of the 1975 earthquake, which destroyed several villages throughout the highlands. International aid agencies, several of them overtly Christian, rushed in to Guatemala at a time of great need and gained many grateful converts in the process. During the worst of the civil war violence of the 1980s, many Guatemalans sought comfort in the belief of a better life despite the hardships of the present. Other factors making Evangelical Christianity attractive to Guatemalans include the tendency toward vibrant expressions of faith, spontaneity, and the lack of a hierarchy, which makes spiritual leaders more accessible to common people.

A notorious legacy of Guatemala's trend toward Protestanism was the dictatorship of Efraín Ríos Montt, a prominent member of Guatemala City's Iglesia El Verbo (Church of the Word), who sermonized Guatemalans on subjects including morality, Christian virtues, and the evils of Communism via weekly TV broadcasts. Meanwhile, a scorched-earth campaign aimed at exterminating the guerrilla presence raged in the highlands, though violence in the cities was widely curtailed and order somewhat restored. He faces charges of genocide in a Spanish court, though it's doubtful he will ever be brought to justice. Also disturbing was the brief presidency of Jorge Serrano Elías, another self-proclaimed Evangelical now exiled in Panama after he dissolved Congress in a failed autocoup, which ended in his ouster a few days later. His government faced widespread corruption charges.

On a more promising note, it is a well-documented fact that some Guatemalan villages have converted to Evangelical Christianity almost in their entirety with astounding results. The town of Almolonga, near Quetzaltenango, is a particular case in point. Alcoholism, which once ran rampant (as in other parts of the highlands), is now virtually unheard of and the city jail has been closed for years. It is hailed as a "miracle city" by Evangelical leaders, who like to point out that it was once a hotbed of cult worship for the folk idol Maximón. The town exports its fantastic fruits and vegetables to El Salvador, including carrots the size of a human arm, making it very prosperous.

Evangelicals these days, while still adhering to the belief in a better afterlife, are also very much focused on making things better in the here and now. There is a growing movement toward producing a generation of morally grounded political leaders with a vision to develop the country along inclusive lines that address Guatemala's substantial needs and challenges, though it remains to be seen if they can overcome the unfortunate legacy handed to them by the substandard Christian leadership experienced by Guatemalans thus far.

LANGUAGE

Guatemala's official language is Spanish, though as mentioned there are 23 other ethnolinguistic groups in this very diverse nation. Guatemalan Spanish is fairly clean and tends to avoid the dropping off of the last syllables in words, a common occurrence in Caribbean Spanish–speaking countries. This makes Guatemalan Spanish particularly easy to learn and understand for foreigners, a fact attested to by the overwhelming number of Spanish-language schools present in many parts of the country, but especially in Antigua and Quetzaltenango. Spanish schools are also present in Cobán, Huehuetenango, Todos Santos, San Andrés, San José (Petén), and Panajachel, to name a few. It's also possible to learn the Mayan languages in many of these schools.

ARTS
Literature

Guatemala's first literary figure was Jesuit priest and poet Rafael Landívar (1731–1793). A native of Antigua, his most well-known work is *Rusticatio Mexicano,* a poem describing rural customs of the times. Landívar was forced to leave Guatemala in 1767 when his order was expelled from the Americas by the Spanish Crown. The country's best-known writer is Miguel Ángel Asturias (1899–1974), winner of the 1967 Nobel Prize in literature. His most famous works include *El Señor Presidente* (1946), about the maniacal dictator Manuel Estrada Cabrera, and *Hombres de*

A FEW *CHAPINISMOS*

A full glossary is found at the end of this book. The following is a listing of a few more commonly used Guatemalan expressions and slang terms.

aguas!: watch out!

a todo mecate: full-speed ahead

babosadas: lies or nonsense

cachito: a little bit

canche: blond or fair-skinned; also was a term used of guerrilla fighters during the civil war

capearse: to play hooky

caquero: arrogant or stuck-up, usually someone of wealth

casaca: tall tales or embellishments

clavos: problems

(tener) conectes: to have influence because of important or powerful friends

cuates: buddies

chapparro: person of short stature

chupar: to drink alcoholic beverages

goma (estar de): to be hungover

güiro: a child

jalón: a lift or ride (in a vehicle)

mango: a handsome man

mordida: bribe

muco: a person of low social class, usually used disdainfully by upper-class Guatemalans in reference to lower classes

pisto: money

salsa: to (mistakenly) think oneself cool and hip

sho (hacer): to be quiet (shut up)

shuco: dirty

shute: nosy

virgo: cool, hip

vonós: "let's go," a shortened version of "vámonos"

Maíz (1949, translated as *Men of Maize*), about the Mayan peasantry. One of the characters in the latter is a guerrilla warrior by the name of Gaspar Ilom, a name that Asturias's son Rodrigo, influenced by his father's writings, would appropriate as a pseudonym while leading one of the guerrilla factions comprising the Guatemalan National Revolutionary Unity (URNG). Other of his well-known works include *El Papa Verde (The Green Pope),* 1954, about the United Fruit Company) and *Weekend en Guatemala* (1968, about the 1954 coup that ousted Jacobo Arbenz Guzmán).

Modern Guatemalan authors of note include Francisco Goldman, author of several novels, including *The Long Night of White Chickens,* which takes place mostly in Guatemala, *The Ordinary Seaman* (1997), and *The Divine Husband* (2004). Arturo Arias is another modern-day author known for having written the screenplay for the movie *El Norte* and the book *After the Bombs,* chronicling the Arbenz period and the aftermath of his overthrow. Víctor Perera has written several excellent books on Guatemalan culture and history, including *Unfinished Conquest* (1993) and *Rites: A Guatemalan Boyhood* (1986).

Visual Arts

Guatemala's rich history in the visual arts dates to pre-Columbian times, with the painting of exquisite murals and the carving of stelae by the Mayans. The colonial period also left a substantial artistic legacy, mostly by anonymous artists. An exception is the work of Thomas de Merlo (1694–1739), whose paintings can still be seen in Antigua's Museo de Arte Colonial. Sculptor Quirio Cataño carved the Black Christ of Esquipulas in 1595, now an object of much veneration for pilgrims from all over Central America.

More recently, Kaqchikel painter Andrés Curruchich (1891–1969) pioneered the "primitivist" style of painting from his hometown in Comalapa, Chimaltenango. The currents of *indigenismo* ran strongly throughout the 20th century and were marked by an often-romanticized portrayal of indigenous culture,

as evidenced by the murals found in Guatemala City's Palacio Nacional de la Cultura, which are the work of Alfredo Gálvez Suárez (1899–1946). Also in this vein was sculptor Ricardo Galeotti Torres (1912–1988), whose works include the giant marimba sculpture found in Quetzaltenango and the Tecún Umán statue in the plaza of Santa Cruz del Quiché.

Perhaps Guatemala's best-known visual artist, Carlos Mérida (1891–1984) was a contemporary of Pablo Picasso, whom he met while studying painting in Paris between 1908 and 1914. His *indigenista* art predates the work of Mexican muralists the likes of Diego Rivera by about seven years and sought to unify European modernism with themes more specific to the Americas. Mérida's work exhibits three major stylistic shifts throughout the years: a figurative period from 1907 to 1926, a surrealist phase from the late 1920s to the mid-1940s, and a geometric period from 1950 until his death in 1984. Mérida. Many of his works can be seen in Guatemala City's Museum of Modern Art, which bears his name. Mérida's murals also grace the walls of several Guatemala City public buildings.

Another artist whose work adorns Guatemala City architecture is sculptor and engineer Efraín Recinos, designer of the city's Centro Cultural Miguel Ángel Asturias. A large Recinos mural composed of blue and green tiles was formerly housed inside La Aurora International Airport but was recently demolished as part of the airport renovation project. The large, white sculptures lining the airport's exterior facade were also created by Recinos and have been restored and incorporated into the terminal's new design.

In March 2007, Guatemala City hosted a sculpture festival with the participation of 12 internationally acclaimed artists working during a two-week period to create unique art pieces from blocks of marble. It's the first event of its kind held in Central America and the finished works will have become part of the city's artistic legacy by the time you read this.

Architecture

In addition to the well-documented architectural legacy of the Mayans, Guatemala is also known for its baroque architecture, found mostly in Antigua and Guatemala City cathedrals and government buildings. This style of architecture is a Spanish adaptation to local conditions, marked by the prevalence of earthquakes, with squat, thick-walled structures designed to weather numerous tremors throughout the years. Architecture in rural towns and villages tends to be rather functional, with a recent trend toward grotesque multistory concrete buildings replacing more traditional construction. Classic forms of rural architecture consist (or consisted) largely of whitewashed adobe houses with red-tile roofs.

Guatemala City has its fair share of assembly-line high-rise condominiums, though it also has some noteworthy modern architecture. If you have an interest in this topic, a recommended book is *Six Architects* (Ange Bourda, 2002), filled with wonderful color photographs chronicling the work of six Guatemala City architects who merged into a single firm and are responsible for several of the city's nicest buildings.

In April 2007 the Parisian Grande Arche de la Défense played host to a fascinating 48-image exhibit by photographer Ange Bourda, which chronicled the rich history of Guatemalan architecture from pre-Columbian times to the present.

Music

Guatemala's national instrument is the marimba, a huge wooden xylophone with probable African origins. You'll often hear marimba in popular tourist regions such as Antigua, where its cheerful notes can be heard emanating from garden courtyards housed in the city's larger hotels. Pre-Columbian musical instruments consisted largely of drums, wooden flutes, whistles, and bone rasps. An excellent place to check out the history and origins of Guatemala's highland Mayan musical traditions is Casa K'ojom, just outside Antigua in Jocotenango.

It's also not uncommon to hear music with Mexican influence in Guatemala, with the occasional mariachi band contracted to liven up a birthday party. Tejano and *ranchera* music can often be heard. You'll also hear American rock bands here and there, sometimes on bus rides, though the sounds favored by bus drivers seem to have gotten stuck somewhere around 1984.

On the Caribbean Coast, the Garífuna population tends to favor the mesmerizing beats of *punta* and reggae, with variations including *punta rock* and *reggaeton,* English-Spanish rap laid over slowed-down Caribbean-style techno and reggae beats.

Grammy award–winning rock musician Ricardo Arjona is Guatemala's best-known international recording artist. He lives in Mexico City. Spanish-language pop and rock are, of course, also widely heard throughout Guatemala.

TV and Cinema

Guatemala has its very own cable TV channel, Guatevisión, which can be seen in the United States. It features a morning show based in Guatemala City as well as some fairly humorous entertainment programs that provide a glimpse of the nightlife and outdoor recreation scene throughout the country. Guatemala even has a celebrity newscaster of sorts, CNN's Mexico City–based Harris Whitbeck, who reports events around the world in English and Spanish. One of his more recent projects is a local TV show, *Entrémosle a Guate* (Let's Get in on Guate), with profiles of everyday Guatemalans who make the country a special place.

As for movies about Guatemala, *El Norte* (1983, directed by Gregory Nava) is a classic tale of Guatemalan immigrants fleeing the civil war during the 1980s. More recently, in the summer of 2006, Antigua was the scene for on-location shooting for *Looking for Palladin,* a film about a young Hollywood go-getter who finds himself in Guatemala. Many folks in Antigua are hoping the film will open doors for more movies to be filmed in Guatemala.

CRAFTS

Guatemala is world famous for the artistic quality and variety of its crafts, with weaving at the top of the list. Each village has its unique style and you can recognize villagers from a particular location based solely on their traditional attire. Among the most fascinating handwoven pieces are *huipiles,* embroidered blouses worn by highland Mayan women that feature colorful motifs that often include plants, animals, and lightning bolts in a dizzying array of colors. While you are certainly welcome to buy village attire, it's never a good idea to wear it around while in Guatemala, as indigenous peoples will find this highly offensive (or downright hilarious, at best). Many people buy *huipiles* to frame and hang as home decor, laying the blouse flat with the large head opening at its center or hanging it from a wooden rod. You can see examples where this has been tastefully done in numerous Antigua boutique hotels.

Jade jewelry mined from local quarries is a popular item in upscale shops in Antigua. "Primitivist" paintings are popular in the villages of San Pedro and Santiago, on the shores of Lake Atitlán. For wool blankets, check out Momostenango, though you can also find them in markets throughout the country. The best wood carvings are found in the village of El Remate, in the northern Petén department, though traditional wooden ceremonial masks are still an item found exclusively in the Western Highlands.

ESSENTIALS

Getting There

Most international travelers to Guatemala arrive by plane. Several factors are working together to make Guatemala more easily, though not always cheaply, accessible in this regard. First, Guatemala has become increasingly popular as a travel destination. Tourism statistics show the country has been welcoming more than a million visitors per year since 2004. The Guatemalan government has recognized this and has invested millions of dollars into remodeling the country's two international airports while developing local airports for the creation of a domestic route network. Carriers from the United States have stepped up their presence in Guatemala in recent years and are expected to continue this trend, particularly with the vastly improved infrastructure at Guatemala City's La Aurora International Airport and the Mundo Maya Airport in Flores/Tikal.

The media have reported interest on the part of several Asian carriers considering the possibility of flying into Guatemala. These flights may be in effect by the time you read this, after the unveiling of the new La Aurora Airport. Flights from Europe have also become somewhat easier thanks in part to U.S. laws post-9/11 making Iberia's Miami minihub for flights to Latin America a major headache. After the United States started requiring in-transit passengers from Europe to come off

© AL ARGUETA

the plane, Iberia finally opted to fly nonstop from Madrid to Guatemala City three times per week, with more frequency reportedly in the works.

In addition to increased tourism, more and more Guatemalans have family living in the United States, which means this is easily one of the fastest-growing markets on U.S. carriers' radar screens. As for cost, the market is very elastic. The arrival of a new carrier into Guatemala often signals an all-out pricing war, as seen with service start-ups by Delta in 1998 and US Airways in 2005, when flights from the United States to Guatemala hovered around $300 round-trip. Demand quickly catches up with supply, however, and prices double as carriers see little reason to discount flights in a market where planes are already flying full.

Still, deals can be had if you know where to look and are willing to give up some comforts such as advance seat selection and ticket changeability. Internet sites offering discounted tickets and air-ticket consolidators are worth checking out if this describes you.

Some visitors choose to drive to Guatemala, traveling through Mexico en route, and entering the country at one of several border crossings. Guatemala also has border crossings on roads connecting it to Belize, Honduras, and El Salvador. (See the *By Land* section.)

BY AIR

Guatemala has an open-skies agreement with the United States, meaning that any carrier from either country can fly to any point in the other. Guatemala once had an official flag-carrier, Aviateca, but Salvadoran-owned TACA has since absorbed it. Domestic flights between Flores and Guatemala City are officially operated by Aviateca, but this appears to be a mere formality, as the aircraft livery, ticket jackets, and related travel documents all clearly make it known that you are flying TACA. That being said, TACA operates the majority of flights into and out of Guatemala, flying nonstop from a handful of gateway cities in the United States as well as via its hubs in San Salvador and San José, Costa Rica. The U.S. carriers

also have a strong presence here, one that is likely to increase. Several Latin American carriers, some of them noteworthy, operate here as well. The only European airline serving Guatemala is Iberia, the Spanish flag-carrier.

Flights to Guatemala City

Most international travelers flying to Guatemala arrive via Guatemala City's **La Aurora International Airport (GUA).** La Aurora could not be any more convenient for the city's residents, though its location very much within the confines of this large urban area is both a blessing and a curse. Its short runway is flanked on one end by the city's business district and by a ravine at its other extreme. Runway overruns, some fatal, have occurred. Among the notable mishaps was a nonfatal TACA Boeing 767 crash in 1993, which happened when the plane skidded off the runway during a rainstorm. The worst was a Cubana Airlines DC-10 crash involving another runway overrun in 1999 that killed 26.

While plans call for a new airport to be built outside the city limits sometime in the future, an ambitious renovation and expansion project, due for completion in 2007, has brought the once-obsolete La Aurora into the 21st century. New gates, a new arrivals hall featuring more immigration kiosks for quicker processing, a new baggage claim area, and greatly reduced chaos upon exiting the terminal will pleasantly surprise arriving passengers.

The majority of nonstop flights come from a handful of North American hub cities, including Miami, Fort Lauderdale, New York/Newark, Chicago, Houston, Atlanta, Charlotte, Dallas/Fort Worth, and Los Angeles. San Salvador and Panama City are becoming increasingly important as connecting points for flights from South America on TACA and Copa Airlines, respectively. Madrid holds the distinction of being the sole European city with direct service to Guatemala City.

Among the U.S. carriers, **American Airlines** (tel. 800/433-7300 U.S., www.aa.com) flies twice daily to Guatemala City nonstop from Miami and daily nonstop from Dallas/Fort Worth. It code-shares with British Airways on flights from the United Kingdom as well as offering excellent European connections of its own. **Continental Airlines** (tel. 800/231-0856 U.S., www.continental.com) has twice-daily nonstop service to Guatemala City from Houston Intercontinental (IAH) as well as a Saturday-only nonstop flight from New York/Newark. **Delta Airlines** (tel. 800/221-1212 U.S., www.delta.com) expanded its Guatemala City service to include daily nonstop flights from Los Angeles, complementing an existing daily nonstop flight from its Atlanta hub. During high seasons, it uses comfortable and spacious Boeing 767-300 aircraft on the Atlanta route. At press time, Delta also planned to add three nonstop flights per week to Guatemala City from New York's JFK airport. **United** (tel. 800/538-2929 U.S., www.united.com) bought out Pan Am's routes to Latin America back in the early 1990s but has cut back considerably on its predecessor's service into the region. The airline operates daily nonstop service to Guatemala City from Los Angeles. It reportedly had intentions of opening a new flight to Guatemala City from Washington Dulles sometime in 2008. **US Airways** (tel. 800/622-1015 U.S., www.usairways.com) began service to Guatemala in February 2005 from Fort Lauderdale. After dropping some less successful Central American start-ups, it rerouted its service and now flies daily nonstop to Guatemala City from its hub in Charlotte. In May 2007, low-fare carrier **Spirit Airlines** (tel. 800/772-7117 U.S., www.spiritair.com) became the latest U.S. airline to enter this market, with daily non-stop service to Guatemala City from Fort Lauderdale and Los Angeles.

Among the foreign carriers, **Copa Airlines** (tel. 800/359-2672 U.S., www.copaair.com), the Panamanian flag-carrier, is partially controlled by Continental Airlines. Its corporate branding readily attests to this fact, with the two aircraft liveries being virtually indistinguishable from each other. The airline offers twice-daily nonstop and direct service (stopping in Managua) to Guatemala City from its hub in Panama City, with excellent connections to/from South America and the Caribbean. It is affiliated with Continental's OnePass frequent-flier program.

Cuba's national airline, **Cubana** (www.cubana.cu), flies nonstop to Guatemala City several times a week from Havana. If you're flying to Guatemala from Europe, you'll be happy to know that **Iberia** (www.iberia.com) offers nonstop service to Guatemala City three times per week (Tues., Thurs., Sat.) from its hub in Madrid with excellent connections to the rest of the continent. **Mexicana** (tel. 800/531-7921 U.S., www.mexicana.com) offers three daily nonstops to Guatemala City from Mexico City. Salvadoran conglomerate Transportes Aereos del Continente Americano, or **TACA** (tel. 800/400-8222 U.S., www.taca.com), flies daily nonstop to Guatemala City from Miami and Los Angeles with three or four weekly nonstops each from Chicago, New York JFK, and Washington, D.C. Other nonstops include flights from Mexico City, Cancún, and San Pedro Sula. There are numerous daily flights from TACA's hubs in San Salvador and San José, Costa Rica, with onward connections to/from South America.

Flights to Flores/Tikal

Flores/Tikal (FRS), officially known as **Mundo Maya International Airport,** serves the northern department of Petén and the ruins of Tikal. It was also being remodeled and will have been transformed by the time you read this into a modern open-air terminal with Mayan temple motifs, a bit reminiscent of Kailua-Kona's airport on Hawaii's Big Island.

Flights to Flores/Tikal arrive primarily from Guatemala City, Belize City, and Cancún. Continental Airlines operated weekly service to Flores from its hub in Houston for just more than a year, but the flights were discontinued in November 2006. It may have been an idea ahead of its time. **Maya Island Air** (www.mayaislandair.com) is a Belizean carrier flying to Flores/Tikal from Belize City. **Tropic Air** (tel. 800/422-3435, www.tropicair.com), also a Belizean airline, flies to Flores/Tikal from Belize City twice daily. The list of domestic carriers flying from Guatemala City to Flores seems to be getting smaller every year, with now-absconded Tikal Jets becoming the latest carrier to have been pushed out of the market by powerhouse TACA. (See the *Getting Around* section for remaining options for domestic air transport.)

BY SEA

Cruise ships dock at Puerto Quetzal, on the Pacific Coast, and Puerto Santo Tomás de Castilla, on the Caribbean side. Cruise lines offer a variety of activities for those wishing to disembark and explore Guatemalan shores, including visits to local resorts and beaches near Santo Tomás and inland trips to Antigua, Tikal, and Lake Atitlán or deep-sea fishing in the Pacific. For those wishing not to travel inland, there is not much to see and do in either port of call, although the pier is usually packed with vendors selling everything from bags of Guatemalan coffee to colorful textiles and clothing. The one land-based activity close to a port of call worth mentioning is hiking in the Cerro San Gil forest preserve near Santo Tomás de Castilla.

Ferry and water-taxi services connect the Guatemalan town of Lívingston with Punta Gorda, Belize (2.5 hours, $35), and Omoa, Honduras (1.25 hours, $16), both offered by **Exotic Travel** (tel. 7947-0449 Lívingston) on Tuesdays and Fridays. **Transportes El Chato** (tel. 7948-5525 Puerto Barrios) has a daily boat to and from Punta Gorda costing $16 and taking roughly an hour to make the trip. A $10 departure tax applies when leaving Guatemala by sea.

BY RIVER

The most popular route into Guatemala by river is via the Usumacinta River, which divides Mexico and Guatemala. Boats travel from the Mexican town of Frontera Corozal to La Técnica and Bethel, in Guatemala's northern Petén department. This is the route of choice for travelers wanting to combine visits to the Mexican sites of Palenque and Yaxchilán with trips to the various Petén ruins. Yaxchilán lies on the Mexican bank of the Usumacinta and is highly recommended. Buses from Palenque to the Mexican border are available via **Transportes Montebello** (Calle Velasco Suarez, Palenque) and **Autotransportes Rio**

Chancala (5 de Mayo 120, Palenque). From La Técnica, buses leave for the Petén departmental capital of Flores at 4 A.M. and 11 A.M. (five hours, $4). Buses leave Bethel for Flores at 5 A.M., noon, 2 P.M., and 4 P.M., take four hours to make the trip, and cost $4. Package trips encompassing this bus and boat transportation are available from various travel agencies in Palenque and Flores for travel in either direction for about $35.

It is also possible to travel from Benemérito, south of Frontera Corozal, up the Río La Pasión to Sayaxché, Guatemala, and via the Río San Pedro between La Palma and El Naranjo. These routes lack scheduled passenger service and are not recommended as they are increasingly being used as transshipment points by the growing drug and illegal immigrant trade between Petén and Mexico.

BY LAND

Many travelers enter Guatemala by bus, as part of larger explorations encompassing neighboring countries. If traveling by car or bus, try to make the border crossing as early in the day as possible, as there are few serviceable hotels and restaurants in border towns and they are notorious for their seedy atmosphere. Onward bus service tends to wind down further into the day, so try to get a move on while you can. (More details on specific border towns are available in the corresponding geographical chapter listings.)

Driving

Should you decide to bring a car into Guatemala, the following documents are required:

Current, valid registration.

Current, valid driver's license or International Driving Permit (IDP) issued by AAA or your home country's automobile association.

Proof of vehicle ownership or notarized letter from its owner allowing its possession by you.

Temporary import permit available free at the border. Maximum validity is 30 days.

Guatemala does not recognize foreign insurance, forcing drivers to buy a policy locally. This can usually be done at the border post. As a final caveat, Guatemalan law requires exiting the country using the same vehicle used to enter it. Beware of being listed as the designated driver if you don't own the car, as you and the vehicle will need to leave the country together. Selling the car locally involves a mountain of tedious paperwork purposely designed to discourage foreigners from selling cars in Guatemala.

Be sure to ask for receipts for all fees. A proper receipt will have the Guatemalan country emblem on it. Don't be fooled by shady border officials who issue a deposit slip stub (probably from their personal bank account) with an Immigration Office stamp, which they attempt to pass off as a receipt for bogus fees.

From Mexico

The main border crossings on the Pacific flatlands are Ciudad Hidalgo/Tecún Umán and Talismán/El Carmen, near Tapachula, Mexico. On the Pan-American Highway, the border crossing is at Ciudad Cuauhtemoc/La Mesilla between Comitán, Mexico, and Huehuetenango, Guatemala. All of these border towns have frequent bus service to nearby cities within both countries. There is direct bus service to Flores from Chetumal on **Linea Dorada** (tel. 7926-1788, Flores) and **San Juan Travel** (tel. 7926-0041, Flores). Both services stop in Belize City en route with a total trip duration of about eight hours.

From Belize

The Belize border crossing into Guatemala is at Benque Viejo del Carmen/Melchor de Mencos. There is twice-daily bus service from Belize City to Flores via **Linea Dorada** (tel. 7926-1788, Flores). The trip lasts 4–5 hours and costs $15. **San Juan Travel** (tel. 7926-0041, Flores) also has a daily bus covering the route.

A less expensive option is to take Novelo's or Batty's buses from Belize City to the border and make onward connections to other points in Guatemala on frequent buses and minibuses from Melchor de Mencos.

From Honduras

The main border crossings are at El Florido (between Copán Ruinas, Honduras, and Chiquimula, Guatemala), Agua Caliente (between Nueva Ocotepeque, Honduras, and Esquipulas, Guatemala), and Corinto (between Omoa, Honduras, and Puerto Barrios, Guatemala). There are shuttle minibuses running between Copán, Guatemala City, and Antigua, as well as first-class bus service to Guatemala City from the main Honduran cities. **Hedman Alas** (tel. 237-7143 Tegucigalpa, 441-5347 La Ceiba, 557-3477 San Pedro Sula, 651-4037 Copán Ruinas, www.hedmanalas.com) has daily service to Guatemala City via the El Florido border from Copán, San Pedro Sula, Tegucigalpa, and La Ceiba.

From El Salvador

El Salvador's numerous borders with Guatemala are at Las Chinamas/Valle Nuevo (Highway CA-8), La Hachadura/Ciudad Pedro de Alvarado on Pacific Coast Highway (CA-2), San Cristóbal/San Cristóbal on the Pan-American Highway (CA-1), and Anguiatu/Anguiatu (Highway CA-10). Several bus lines operate service between Guatemala City and San Salvador, mostly via Las Chinamas, including **Pullmantur** (www.pullmantur.com). **Moon-Ray Tours** (tel. 7832-0198 Antigua) offers direct bus service between Antigua and San Salvador on comfortable, brand-new buses.

From Points South

Ticabus (www.ticabus.com) connects Guatemala City to San Salvador, Managua, San José, and Panama City, taking several days to make the trip and stopping in the listed capitals along the way. A one-way ticket from Guatemala City to San José, Costa Rica, costs $50.

TRAVEL COMPANIES

A cursory inspection of popular travel magazines reveals the relative absence of package tours from the United States to Guatemala, particularly when compared to Belize and Costa Rica. Still, there are a few good companies to recommend for travelers wanting to visit

Guatemala on a package tour or needing the services of an established tour operator. This is certainly not an exhaustive list, but the following come highly recommended for the quality of service and established experience.

Adventure Life Journeys

A Montana-based company specializing in Central and South America, Adventure Life Journeys (800/344-6118 U.S., www.adventure-life.com) offers several options for exploring Guatemala. Among its itineraries is an eight-day Mayan Multisport, which includes trekking to mountain villages, kayaking on Lake Atitlán, and mountain biking. Other, more traditional itineraries are also available.

Maya Expeditions

Rated one of the top ecooutfitters in the world by *Condé Nast Traveler,* Maya Expeditions (www.mayaexpeditions.com) is a Guatemala-based adventure-travel outfitter and comes highly recommended for its adventurous itineraries, particularly white-water rafting. Company founder Tammy Ridenour, a Colorado native, started the company in 1987 and is credited with pioneering ecotourism in Guatemala. Among the company's various offerings, which also include archaeology and cultural tourism, is a trip retracing the steps of the wildly popular *Survivor Guatemala* television series.

Clark Tours

Highly recommended is Clark Tours (800/707-5275 U.S., www.saca.com/guat/intro.html), represented in the United States by Massachusetts-based SACA Tours. The company, established by an American living in Guatemala, has been around for 80 years. You will probably come across the company's large, luxurious tour buses more than once during your travels in Guatemala. Clark Tours has a variety of established itineraries and can also tailor custom itineraries to suit the needs of the most discriminating travelers. Clark Tours is also the local representative for American Express Travel Services and has offices in many of the Guatemala City luxury hotels, including the Marriott, Westin Camino Real, and Holiday Inn.

Cayaya Birding

Bird-watchers will want to contact German-owned Cayaya Birding (tel. 5308-5160 Guatemala City, www.cayaya-birding.com) for information on Guatemala's birding hot spots and to arrange trip details, including full itineraries. Knut Eisermann, an ornithologist living in Guatemala since 1997, runs the company.

STA Travel

Guatemala is a popular destination for student travelers, so it comes as no surprise that established, full-service student travel agency STA Travel (800/781-4040 U.S., www.statravel.com) would have offices here. Among its more than 300 offices around the world is a location in Antigua at 6a Calle Poniente, #21. STA offers special student and youth discounted airfares as well as travel-planning services. Special student fares require the purchase of an International Student Identity Card (ISIC) available to bona fide students. Alternatively, those under 26 years of age can buy an International Youth Travel Identity Card providing essentially the same benefits as the ISIC. In addition to discounted airfares, many of these tickets are valid for stays of up to one year and allow changes without penalty.

Getting Around

BY AIR

The only scheduled domestic service within Guatemala is between Guatemala City and Flores, although ongoing improvements to local infrastructure at many smaller airports may mean a small network of local flights may soon be up and running. Some of the flights to and from Flores operate using smaller aircraft, so unless you enjoy the cramped space and longer flight time of a ride in an ATR-42, pay careful attention to the equipment being used on the flight. Airfares for this domestic service have recently skyrocketed and are surprisingly expensive, particularly when taking into account the short distance involved in flying within Guatemala.

All of the domestic carriers flying out of Guatemala City operate from their private hangers, on the east side of the runway, opposite the main terminal building. The only airline operating its domestic service from the main terminal at La Aurora airport is TACA.

Airlines

TACA (tel. 800/400-8222 U.S., www.taca .com) operates two daily flights between Guatemala City and Flores using Airbus A319 aircraft. Additional flights on certain days of the week make the trip on an ATR-42. **TAG** (tel. 2332-1897 Guatemala or 800/528-8216 U.S.) has a daily flight to Flores from Guatemala City leaving at 6:30 A.M. The return trip from Flores is at 5 P.M.

BY LAND

Most travelers get around Guatemala by **bus** or **shuttle bus.** (Bus schedules are covered in the individual geographical chapter sections.) The majority of buses are "chicken buses," as travelers have dubbed them, recycled U.S. school buses painted in lively colors. Cargo and carry-on baggage often consists of live animals, hence the name. Please be aware that robberies, including pickpocketing and hijacking, are increasingly common on these inexpensive public

© AL ARGUETA

The chicken bus can get you almost anywhere you may want to go.

buses serving the interior. They are also frequently involved in traffic accidents in which the bus plunges into a ravine or makes a blind pass into a head-on collision. Tourist shuttle buses plying the main tourist routes, though more expensive, have become increasingly popular for safety reasons and are highly recommended. For the intrepid, the chicken bus is still a great way to see Guatemala and get to virtually any part of the country cheaply. Another common form of getting around, particularly in remote rural areas with infrequent bus service, is via (roughly) scheduled service aboard **pickup trucks.** (Where available, these are also covered in the relevant geographical chapter sections.) **Minivans** have also replaced cumbersome chicken buses in many rural areas with poor roads.

Roads in Guatemala are surprisingly good in some places, particularly on well-trodden paths such as the Pan-American Highway. They are much better, overall, than the roads in neighboring Belize and Costa Rica. Roads in and around tourist areas are generally well marked, some courtesy of the Guatemala Tourist Commission (INGUAT). If, while driving, you come across a large tree branch in the middle of the road, be prepared to stop. This is Guatemalans' way of officially signaling that danger lies ahead, usually in the form of an accident. At night, or during the day around a blind curve, ignoring this very informal warning sign might land the front of your car into the rear end of another vehicle.

Whether it be by bus or by car, do not travel on rural highways in Guatemala after dark.

Highway Overview

Guatemala has several main highways with which it might be useful to get acquainted. The Pan-American Highway (CA-1), also known as the Interamericana, runs from the Mexican border at La Mesilla through much of the Western Highlands, to Guatemala City, and east to El Salvador at the San Cristóbal border. This is the road taken (at least for much of the journey) to many of the main travel destinations, including Antigua, Lake Atitlán, Quetzaltenango, and Huehuetenango.

The Pacific Coast Highway (CA-2) crosses the Pacific slope from the Mexican border at Tecún Umán all the way to Ciudad Pedro de Alvarado and El Salvador. A new, wider Pacific Highway is in the planning stages.

Highway CA-9 runs from the Pacific Coast to Guatemala City, encompassing the country's only toll road, a good, fast *autopista,* or freeway. From Guatemala City it heads east to Puerto Barrios and is being widened to four lanes from the capital to El Rancho Junction. CA-14 branches north from El Rancho into the departments of Baja and Alta Verapaz.

If you continue east along CA-9, the next junction is at Río Hondo, where CA-10 branches southeast to Zacapa and Chiquimula before linking up with eastbound CA-11 for Copán, Honduras. Back on the main branch of CA-9, CA-13 is the designation given to the road branching off at La Ruidosa Junction, just before Puerto Barrios, heading north to Rio Dulce and continuing to Petén. It arrives in Flores and then branches eastward to the Belize border at Melchor de Mencos.

A road crossing the country from Izabal department west all the way to Huehuetenango is also planned for the near future and will be called the Franja Transversal del Norte. Also in the works is a Guatemala City Ring Road project circumscribing the city's metro area and allowing heavy cargo traffic between Pacific and Atlantic Coast ports to bypass the already traffic-congested capital.

Rental Cars

Rental cars are plentiful in Guatemala and can be rented in Guatemala City, Panajachel, Antigua, Quetzaltenango, Cobán, and Flores. (Some local agencies are also available and will be listed in the individual chapters. See the sidebar *Rental Cars* for Guatemala City agency listings.)

Shuttle Buses

Shuttle buses have become an increasingly popular option with visitors because they offer better safety than public transport and, sometimes, door-to-door service. Recommended

RENTAL CARS

The following U.S. car-rental agencies are represented in Guatemala and have kiosks at La Aurora International Airport:

Advantage (tel. 2332-7525 Guatemala City or 800/777-5500 toll-free U.S., www.advantagerentacar.com)
Alamo (tel. 5219-7469 Guatemala City or 800/462-5266 toll-free U.S., www.alamo.com)
Avis (tel. 2331-0017 Guatemala City or 800/331-1212 toll-free U.S., www.avis.com)
Dollar (tel. 2331-7185 Guatemala City or 800/800-4000 toll-free U.S., www.dollar.com)
Budget (tel. 2332-7744 Guatemala City or 800/472-3325 toll-free U.S., www.budget.com or www.budgetguatemala.com.gt)
Hertz (tel. 2470-3800 Guatemala City or 800/654-3001 toll-free U.S., www.hertz.com)
Thrifty (tel. 2379-8747 Guatemala City or 800/847-4389 toll-free U.S., www.thrifty.com)

shuttle buses (covered in relevant chapters) include **Atitrans** (tel. 7832-3371 Antigua, www.atitrans.com), **Turansa** (tel. 2437-8182 Guatemala City or 5651-2284 after business hours, www.turansa.com), and **Grayline Tours** (tel. 5511-9052, 24 hours, www.graylineguatemala.com).

Taxi

Taxicabs are available in almost any town or city. When in smaller towns, the best way to find a taxi is in the central square, or *parque central.* In Guatemala City, taxis are available at the Zona 10 hotels, shopping malls, or (as a last resort) can be hailed from street corners. Sometimes, it's a good idea to call a cab, depending on what part of town you're in, as certain city zones get more taxi traffic and not all companies are reliable. The following taxicab companies are recommended for getting around the capital. **Amarillo Express** (tel. 2332-1515 Guatemala City) requires you to call for a cab and will need an exact address to pick you up. Another option is **Taxis Blanco y Azul** (tel. 2360-0903 Guatemala City). As a final word of caution, the U.S. embassy discourages travelers from hailing cabs off the street in Guatemala City.

Hitchhiking

Though hitchhiking in its traditional form is not widely practiced in Guatemala, a local adaptation exists in remote rural areas where there is limited or nonexistent bus service. People with pickup trucks will often give you a ride in the back of their trucks. The fee is usually nominal.

Visas and Officialdom

TOURIST REQUIREMENTS

Citizens of the United States traveling to Guatemala will need a U.S. passport valid for at least three months beyond their intended length of stay and ticket documents for onward or return travel. Stays of up to 90 days are permitted without a visa. The United States now requires passports as the sole travel document for all travelers returning to the United States by air.

Requirements for other countries, including Australia, Canada, The European Union, Israel, Japan, New Zealand, and Switzerland include a passport valid for at least three months beyond their intended length of stay and ticket documents for onward or return travel. Entry is limited to 30 days. Extensions are allowed by going through the local Migración (Immigration) office.

Foreigners are required to carry their

passport (or a clear photocopy) with them at all times. If you are driving a rental car and happen to be stopped, the police officer will ask for your passport in addition to your driver's license.

In June 2006, Guatemala entered into an agreement with El Salvador, Honduras, and Nicaragua known as the **CA-4 Border Control Agreement.** Under its terms, citizens of these four countries may travel freely across each other's land borders without completing entry and exit formalities at Immigration checkpoints. United States citizens and other eligible foreign nationals who legally enter any of the four member countries may also travel within the CA-4 without obtaining additional visas or tourist entry permits for the other three countries. Immigration officials at the first port of entry determine the length of stay, up to a maximum of 90 days. Foreign tourists who wish to remain in the four-country region beyond the length of stay initially granted for their visit will need to request a one-time extension from local Immigration authorities or travel to a country outside the CA-4 region and then reenter.

For visa extensions, head to the Departamento de Extranjería (7a Avenida 1-17 Zona 4, INGUAT Building, Guatemala City, tel. 2361-8476, 8 A.M.–2 P.M. Mon.–Fri.). You'll need to show evidence of financial solvency as well as an onward ticket.

CUSTOMS

Foreign travelers to Guatemala may import the following items duty free: personal effects, including clothing, jewelry, medicine, photography and video equipment, sports equipment, a personal computer, a wheelchair if the traveler has disabilities, 500 grams of tobacco, and three liters of alcoholic beverages. INGUAT can provide assistance to professional photographers and videographers needing to bring in large amounts of equipment.

FOREIGN CONSULATES

A list of foreign consulates can be found in the *Guatemala City* chapter.

Recreation

PARKS AND PROTECTED AREAS

Guatemala has more than 90 protected areas encompassing about 28 percent of the country's total land area. Among the different types of protected areas are biosphere reserves, national parks, biotopes, natural monuments, wildlife refuges, and private nature reserves. Several of these are encompassed within larger areas, as is the case with the national parks and biotopes making up the larger Maya Biosphere Reserve. Most of Guatemala's protected areas, including the biosphere reserves, have been created since 1990. All of Guatemala's volcanoes are protected areas. There are also laws in effect to protect endangered wildlife species; among these are Guatemala's big cats and parrots.

The National Protected Areas Council (CONAP) is the entity charged with administering Guatemala's protected areas. It was created in 1990, along with the National Environmental Commission (CONAMA), which oversees broader environmental matters and was replaced in 2000 by the Ministry of the Environment and Natural Resources (MARN). CONAP has been historically underfunded and understaffed, leaving few resources with which to protect vast areas of land from invasion. Private conservation groups have stepped in to assist CONAP in its mandate and there are now several parks coadministered or primarily administered by private organizations. A specially trained police force began operating in Guatemala's protected areas in 2005, particularly in the Maya Biosphere Reserve, aided by M-16s and AK-47s

PROTECTED AREAS OF GUATEMALA

Mirador–Río Azul National Park

El Zotz–San Miguel La Palotada Biotope

Laguna Del Tigre National Park

Tikal National Park

Belmopan

Sierra del Lacandón National Park

Yaxhá–Nakum–Naranjo Natural Monument

MEXICO

Cerro Cahuí Biotope

Lake Petén Itzá

BELIZE

Maya Mountains–Chiquibul National Park

Parque Nacional El Rosario

Ceibal Natural ★ Monument

Dos Pilas Cultural Monument

Petexbatún Wildlife Refuge

Aguateca Cultural Monument ★

Laguna Lachuá National Park

Punta de Manabique Wildlife Refuge

Lanquín Caves National Park

Biotopo Chocón Machacas

P.N. Río Dulce

Parque Nacional Las Victorias

Lake Izabal

Reserva Protectora de Manantiales Cerro San Gil

Semuc Champey Natural Monument

Bocas del Polochic Wildlife Refuge

Biotopo Mario Dary Rivera

Sierra de las Minas Biosphere Resere

Parque Nacional Riscos De Momostenango

★ Monumento Cultural Quiriguá

Zona de Usos Múltiples Cuenca de Atitlán

Monumento Cultural ★ Iximché

HONDURAS

Parque Regional Laguna de Chicabal ★

Lake Atitlán

Guatemala City

Reserva Natural Privada Manchón Guamuchal

Parque Nacional Naciones Unidas

Área de Protección Especial Takalik Abaj

Pacaya Volcano National Park

Biotopo Monterrico–Hawaii

EL SALVADOR

San Salvador

PACIFIC OCEAN

0   40 mi

0   40 km

to combat well-armed timber and wildlife poachers. All the parks have at least rudimentary ranger stations. In an ongoing effort to attract more park visitation, many have excellent facilities for guest accommodations and well-marked trails.

Biosphere Reserves

Privately managed by conservation group Defensores de la Naturaleza, **Sierra de las Minas Biosphere Reserve** is a vast, 583,000-acre mountain park encompassing a diverse variety of ecosystems, including cloud forests harboring several species of endemic conifers, as well as tropical moist and rainforests. The peaks of Sierra de las Minas surpass 3,000 meters (9,800 feet) in elevation and are home to healthy populations of quetzals and jaguars, among other exotic animals. Sixty-two permanent streams have their source in the upper slopes of the biosphere reserve, making it an important watershed supplying the Motagua and Polochic Rivers. Together with the adjacent Bocas del

Polochic Wildlife Refuge, the parks account for 80 percent of Guatemala's biodiversity.

The four-million-acre **Maya Biosphere Reserve** is composed of Tikal National Park, Laguna del Tigre National Park, Mirador-Dos Lagunas-Rio Azul National Park, Sierra del Lacandón National Park, Biotopo El Zotz-San Miguel La Palotada, Yaxhá-Nakum-Naranjo Natural Monument, and multiple-use and buffer zones. This large swath of land encompasses roughly a third of the Petén department and is Guatemala's last hope for preserving a sizable part of the Petén forests. Contiguous with large parks in neighboring Mexico and Belize, it is part of the largest protected tropical forest in Mesoamerica. The various parks are protected, on paper at least, from all human activity, though a sizable multiple-use zone exists in large areas of the park, permitting sustainable extraction of forest products such as *xate* palm and chicle, oil drilling (present before the park's creation), and community forestry concessions. Standing between the core zones and the deforestation characterizing much of the rest of Petén is an ever-shrinking buffer zone increasingly porous to the advance of the agricultural frontier. The individual parks making up the biosphere reserve are covered here in their respective sections. (For more detailed information, see the *Maya Biosphere Reserve* section in the *Petén* chapter.)

National Parks

Tikal National Park, the oldest and best known of Guatemala's national parks, was created in 1956 and declared a UNESCO World Heritage Site in 1979. It encompasses 222 square miles of primary tropical forest and protects a vast array of wildlife, as well as harboring the remains of one of the Mayan civilization's greatest cities. Tikal is understandably high on the list of priorities for any visitor to Guatemala and shouldn't be missed.

Laguna del Tigre National Park is a vast park on the northwestern corner of Petén encompassing important wetlands, the largest

---

SAFETY IN THE MAYA BIOSPHERE RESERVE

Potential travelers to Guatemala's Maya Biosphere Reserve are urged to contact one of the conservation groups managing the individual parks before planning a visit, so as to ascertain current safety conditions. As conservationists and archaeologists working in the field can attest, there are too many illegal activities perpetrated by heavily armed men, and far too many stories of run-ins with them, to be out running around in these parts oblivious to the potential dangers. That said, some well-established parks such as Tikal and Yaxhá can be considered generally safe, along with some well-established ecotourism circuits in the Maya Biosphere Reserve, including the Scarlet Macaw Trail, trips to El Zotz-San Miguel La Palotada, and treks to El Mirador.

Tikal National Park, a UNESCO World Heritage Site, combines ancient Mayan ruins and spectacular tropical rainforests.

in Central America. It also contains the only remaining populations of scarlet macaws in Guatemala, which are being protected via ongoing conservation efforts at a biological research station. Oil drilling, present before the park's creation, continues inside the reserve, despite protests from environmental groups and its having been declared a violation of the park's intended use. Also going on inside the park are the clandestine activities of loggers, wildlife poachers, drug traffickers, and smugglers of illegal immigrants across the border to Mexico. The western border with Mexico running along the park's boundaries has also become permeable to incursions from Mexican peasants, who have made a once razor-sharp border between the two countries look more like patchwork. Archaeologists working in these parts enter under the escort of heavily armed guards. Visitors to this park should limit their activities to those centered around the Scarlet Macaw Biological Research Station, as the current lawless conditions prevent my recommending more in-depth explorations of this wild frontier.

Sierra del Lacandón National Park is a densely forested, rugged mountain park said to harbor one of the largest populations of jaguars in all of Central America as well as an incredible degree of biodiversity. Hidden in the forests are the remains of several Mayan sites, the most important of which is Piedras Negras, deep inside the park along the Usumacinta River, which marks the western border with Mexico. The park is privately administered by Fundación Defensores de la Naturaleza. In June 2006, together with The Nature Conservancy, it completed the purchase of 31,000 hectares (77,000 acres) of privately owned land in the core zone of Sierra del Lacandón. There are a number of ranger stations inside the park, the most prominent of which is at Piedras Negras.

A large park in the northern section of the Maya Biosphere Reserve near the Mexican border, **Mirador-Dos Lagunas-Río Azul**

National Park protects vast expanses of tropical forests and the remains of several Mayan cities. Among the most impressive ruins are those at El Mirador, including El Tigre temple, which is 18 stories high with a base the size of three football fields. Other sites inside the park include Río Azul and Nakbé, visible from the top of El Mirador's massive temples. Access to the park is by foot, a full day's walk from the village of Carmelita, or helicopter.

Laguna Lachuá National Park consists of a circular lagoon in the Ixcán jungle west of Cobán surrounded by 14,500 hectares of tropical forest and several miles of hiking trails. The karst limestone nature of this placid pool makes it a very attractive turquoise. A high concentration of mahogany trees in the surrounding forests has made it vulnerable to clandestine logging.

One of Guatemala's oldest protected areas encompassing the watershed of its namesake river connecting Lake Izabal with the Caribbean Sea, **Río Dulce National Park** covers 7,200 hectares along its 30-kilometer-long course. In many places, the banks of the river are shrouded in dense tropical forest punctuated at one point by a large canyon with high rock faces.

Natural Monuments

TV reality-show aficionados might recall **Yaxhá-Nakum-Naranjo Natural Monument** as the setting for *Survivor Guatemala*, filmed here during the summer of 2005. The park encompasses the ruins of three Mayan cities set amid dense tropical forest adjacent to Tikal National Park. Also in the park is Yaxhá Lagoon, with its healthy numbers of crocodiles.

The site of **Semuc Champey Natural Monument** is high in the Alta Verapaz mountains, where the Rio Cahabón flows into a giant cave before reemerging a few hundred feet downstream. Atop the churning turmoil is a natural bridge holding a splendid series of turquoise limestone pools surrounded by tropical forest. It is probably Guatemala's finest swimming hole.

Biotopes

Guatemala's biotopes are administered by **CECON** (Avenida La Reforma 0-63 Zona 10, Guatemala City, tel. 2361-5450 or 2331-0904), the Center for Conservation Studies of Guatemala's San Carlos University (USAC). The biotopes are the brainchild of former USAC Dean Mario Dary Rivera, who was murdered when the establishment of the Quetzal Biotope in Alta Verapaz conflicted with local lumber interests. The biotopes were created with the protection and study of a particular animal species in mind. Biotopes protect sea turtles on the Pacific Coast, manatees in the Izabal region, and bats in the Petén forests, among others.

Biotopo Mario Dary Rivera, also known as the *Biotopo del Quetzal* (Quetzal Biotope), is a cloud forest preserve conveniently situated along the road to Cobán near the village of Purulhá, in Baja Verapaz department. It covers 1,022 hectares with ranges in elevation up to 2,300 meters (7,500 feet). In the early morning, it is easily one of the best places to see Guatemala's national bird, the resplendent quetzal. The cloud forest vegetation consists largely of conifers, broadleaf trees, orchids, mosses, ferns, and bromeliads. There is an excellent network of nature trails, some of which lead to waterfalls and excellent views of the surrounding areas. Other amenities include information and visitor centers, a store, a cafeteria, showers, and cooking facilities. A variety of accommodations are found nearby.

On Guatemala's Pacific Coast, **Biotopo Monterrico-Hawaii** was designated for the protection of Guatemala's endangered sea turtles, which come to lay their eggs on its black sandy beaches. Between May and September, local residents are actively involved in collecting eggs for hatching at a local nursery in exchange for being allowed to keep part of the booty. After incubation, the hatchlings are released with the help of tourists, who jump at the opportunity to hold one of the tiny hatchlings in hand before sending them on their journey across the sand and into the sea. Monterrico is a popular beach with Guatemalans and foreigners alike. Nearby Hawaii is substantially quieter. The park also protects important mangrove forests and marshes in addition to several species of plants and animals. There is also an iguana-breeding program at the site.

Chocón Machacas Biotope, within Río Dulce National Park, encompasses 7,600 hectares and was created with the protection of the manatee in mind, though studies suggest very few of these creatures remain anywhere in Guatemala. The park is in an area known as El Golfete and features old-growth forests, flooded forests, mangrove swamps, canals, and lagoons. In addition to manatees, the park also harbors important populations of crocodiles, otters, and jungle cats.

"Zotz" means "bat" in Mayan dialects, and the multitude of furry little creatures emanating from one of **El Zotz-San Miguel La Palotada Biotope**'s caves at sunset is a dead giveaway for the park's nomenclature. Adjacent to Tikal National Park, 34,934-hectare El Zotz covers substantial areas of tropical forest and wetlands with unexcavated Mayan temple mounds breaking the landscape here and there. It is possible to hike from the park to Tikal and vice versa. The Tikal temples, about 23 kilometers away, can be seen far off in the distance from Devil's Pyramid, the tallest of the unexcavated mounds at El Zotz.

Also in Petén, on the shores of Lake Petén Itzá, **Cerro Cahuí Biotope** covers 650 hectares and consists of a small hill varying in altitude 200–300 meters (650–985 feet). The preserve was created to protect the Petén oscillated turkey and consists mostly of secondary-growth forest. There are several lookouts with excellent views of the lake along the park's well-marked trails. It is a popular spot for bird-watching, with a good range of nearby accommodations.

Wildlife Refuges

Punta de Manabique Wildlife Refuge encompasses a remote peninsula on Guatemala's Caribbean Coast and is unique for its combination of aquatic, coastal, and terrestrial habitats. The coastline is sparsely populated

© AL ARGUETA

Birds abound in the wetlands of Bocas del Polochic Wildlife Refuge.

and includes some very attractive white-sand beaches. Logging, wildlife poaching, and the activities of drug traffickers pose the greatest threats to the park. A small biological station at the peninsula's northwestern tip houses visitors and scientists.

Petexbatún Wildlife Refuge is a wetland and tropical forest park in southern Petén encompassing a variety of lakes abounding in flora, fauna, and Mayan sites. It is one of the few areas in southern Petén where dense forests are still found. The archaeological sites of Ceibal, Aguateca, Dos Pilas, and Tamarindito are also in this area.

The Río Polochic delta, protected as **Bocas del Polochic Wildlife Refuge,** harbors important Lake Izabal wetlands and offers some of Guatemala's finest bird-watching. The park's wetlands and freshwater rivers and lagoons are crucial to the lake's ecological balance and water quality. The ecosystem is also vital to many migratory bird species and provides refuge to a variety of animals, including crocodiles, howler monkeys, and manatees. Together with the adjacent Sierra de las Minas Biosphere Reserve, it accounts for about 80 percent of Guatemala's biodiversity.

HIKING

Guatemala's terrain, featuring mountains, volcanoes, and vast forested flatlands, is a hiker's dream. Adding to the allure of hiking in Guatemala is the opportunity to interact with locals along the way. Many hiking circuits in Guatemala, particularly in the Verapaz cloud forests and the plateaus of the Western Highlands region, are operated via local community tourism initiatives. In addition to providing the opportunity to see the environment and culture through the eyes of local inhabitants, hiring the services of community guides also provides locals with a much-needed source of income and instills a sense of pride in their home. It also speaks loudly to the value (both economic and moral) of conserving precious ecosystems when tourists come from faraway lands to enjoy them. (Community tourism operations, where available, are covered in the relevant geographical chapters.)

Among the most popular hikes are the summits of several of Guatemala's 33 volcanoes (some active), including Agua, Acatenango, Pacaya, San Pedro, Santa María, and Tajumulco. (These are also covered in their relevant geographical chapters.)

Many tourism circuits operated by local community tourism initiatives include adequate visitors centers and there are often campsites. The same is true for the government-run system of parks and protected areas.

BIKING

Road biking is a fairly popular sport in Guatemala, particularly in the highlands, where mountain roads offer unique challenges to strength and endurance. The country even has its own version of the Tour de France, known as La Vuelta Ciclística a Guatemala (The Biking Circuit of Guatemala). The event takes place yearly sometime in August.

More popular with visitors, **mountain biking** is increasingly popular in the hills around Antigua and Lake Atitlán thanks in part to a number of excellent local outfitters.

ROCK CLIMBING

Rock climbing is a relatively new phenomenon in Guatemala, though there are now at least two outfitters specializing in this activity. The rock faces fronting Lake Amatitlán, near Guatemala City, and an area known as "La Muela" (The Molar, also known as "Cerro Quemado"), near Quetzaltenango, are the prime climbing spots. Difficulty ratings of the various routes range from 5.8 to 5.13. It's also possible to rappel inside a waterfall, also known as canyoning, in Jalapa and other areas. (The outfitters covered in the *Guatemala City* chapter and *Quetzaltenango (Xela) and Vicinity* section of *The Western Highlands* chapter also offer instruction in rock climbing.)

BEACHES

While Guatemala is not as well known for its beaches as some of its Central American neighbors, it nonetheless boasts some nice stretches on both the Pacific and Caribbean Coasts. On the Pacific, the wild black-sand beaches found along the coast near the **Manchón Guamuchal** wetlands are one of the region's best-kept secrets. If you're escaping the chilly highlands from Quetzaltenango for some sand and surf, other good bets include **Tilapa, Tilapita,** and **Playa El Tulate.** The closest beach to Guatemala City is **Puerto San José,** reached in about 90 minutes by a four-lane highway, though it's certainly not the most pleasant of the country's beaches. Just west of San José is **Chulamar,** with at least one recommended resort hotel.

Farther east, there are also some lovely stretches between **Iztapa** and **Monterrico.** The 25-kilometer road connecting both towns is experiencing a modest construction boom of stylish resort hotels, with land speculators quickly snapping up the remaining parcels of oceanfront property. East of Monterrico, **Hawaii** also has pretty stretches of nearly deserted beaches, though there are increasing numbers of Guatemala's elite building vacation homes here. The end of the line is **Las Lisas,** another attractive, though very remote, beach close to the Salvadoran border.

On the Caribbean Coast, Guatemala has some fairly decent white-sand beaches on the **Punta de Manabique** promontory. Along the coastline between Lívingston and the Belize border, the nicest beaches are at palm-fringed **Playa Blanca.** For talcum-powder white-sand beaches lapped by turquoise waters, head off the coast to the Belize Barrier Reef, where you'll find the **Zapotillo cayes.**

FISHING
Sailfishing

The Pacific Ocean waters off the port of Iztapa are hailed as the "Sailfish Capital of the World," with world records for single-day catch-and-release firmly supporting these claims. Apparently, a unique pattern of swirling ocean currents between Mexico and El Salvador creates an eddy unusually rich in pelagic fish, such as herring and mackerel, right on Guatemala's doorstep. Sailfish and marlin gather to feed on this bait, along with large concentrations of dorado, yellow-fin tuna, and wahoo. The result is some of the world's best sailfishing.

Numerous outfitters have set up shop in Iztapa offering sailfishing year-round, though the most active season is between November and May because of the colder weather prevalent in the North American region from which most anglers hail. The Presidential Challenge, a yearly sportfishing event that has been held since 1997, usually takes place here in January.

Lake Fishing

Thanks to grand plans for recreational options to be offered on behalf of now-absconded Pan American Airways, Lake Atitlán saw the introduction of largemouth bass in the late 1950s. The lake's extreme depths make catching the larger fish said to inhabit the deeper waters quite a challenge, which only adds to the allure of fishing these waters. Your best bet for catching "the big one" is during the annual spring spawning season, between March and May.

WATER SPORTS
White-Water Rafting and Kayaking

Guatemala has a number of white-water rivers with rapids ranging from Class II–VI (Class VI being unpassable waterfalls). The most popular river for rafting and kayaking is the **Río Cahabón,** found in the region of Las Verapaces. It features some of Central America's finest stretches of white water complemented by jungles, caves, hot springs, and waterfalls. Also in the Verapaces region, the **Río Candelaria** winds its way through its namesake cave system and is a great place for river tubing and kayaking, allowing the chance to explore these fascinating caves to their full potential. Another worthy white-water excursion is Petén's **Río Chiquibul,** at the eastern end of the department near the Belize border. Although the rapids are not quite as exhilarating as those on the Cahabón, it's highly attractive

canoeing on the Río Usumacinta

for its jungle-lined riverbanks and proximity to Mayan sites such as Tikal and Yaxhá.

For more sedate kayaking on ocean kayaks, Lakes Petén Itzá and Atitlán are good bets.

Scuba Diving and Snorkeling

It's possible to scuba dive off the Caribbean Coast near **Punta de Manabique,** though you're probably better off heading just a bit farther north to the exquisite **Zapotillo cayes,** part of the Belize Barrier Reef. Several outfitters arrange trips from Lívingston. Scuba diving is also a popular activity in **Lake Atitlán,** where you might even be able to feel the heat emanating from underwater lava flows in this still-active volcanic region. Another peculiarity of diving here is that the lake is at a rather high altitude just over 1,500 meters (5,000 feet), adding another variable to the mix.

Surfing

An emerging surfing scene is centered around the Pacific Coast village of **Sipacate,** which enjoys excellent breaks. **Iztapa** also reportedly has good breaks, as does **Monterrico.** A useful website for checking out Guatemala's surf scene is www.surfinguatemala.com.

Boating

Boaters will find marinas on both Guatemalan coasts. On the Pacific, a new marina was being planned with partial backing from Dutch interests near the aging port facilities of **Champerico.** Farther east, the **Marina Pez Vela** caters to sportfishing boats and is adjacent to the **Puerto Quetzal Cruise Ship Terminal.** It has restaurants and good tourism infrastructure. On the Caribbean Coast, you'll find many boats traveling up the **Río Dulce** from the Caribbean Coast and docking at any of a number of marinas in the river's namesake town.

GOLF

Guatemala has some excellent golf courses, all in or around Guatemala City, housed in private clubs open to foreign visitors. Some afford

surfing on the Pacific Coast

excellent views of the city and all enjoy spectacular locations in the mountains flanking the urban area. New golf courses were in the planning stages on the Pacific Coast adjacent to IRTRA's theme parks at Xocomil and Xetulul, near Retalhuleu, and along the coastal corridor between Iztapa and Monterrico.

SPECTATOR SPORTS
Fútbol

Guatemalans love their soccer, known as *fútbol*. It is by far the most widely played sport in the country, with every town or village having at least something that resembles a soccer field. Almost everywhere you go, you'll find games being played on Sunday afternoons. As for professional soccer playing, the two most popular teams in the country's four-team national soccer league, denoted by the colors of their jerseys, are the Rojos (Municipales) and Cremas (Comunicaciones). The two usually end up going head to head at the end of the season for the championship title.

Games can be seen at Guatemala City's Estadio Mateo Flores, but be advised it can get quite rowdy. In 1996, things got so out of hand that a stampede ensued when stands collapsed, killing 100 people. The soccer stadium has been remodeled in the aftermath. If you've always wanted to see a Latin American soccer match, you might want to check it out. Guatemala also has a few star players in U.S. Major League Soccer and on some European teams.

International games played by the national squad are a big event, as Guatemala has never been to a World Cup. Guatemala is part of CONCACAF, the Caribbean, North, and Central American Confederation. CONCACAF gets three slots for the World Cup, which usually end up going to the United States, Mexico, and Costa Rica. In 2004–2005, the national squad (also known as *la bicolor*) got closer than it's ever been, advancing into the Final Round of the World Cup qualifiers tied in points with Costa Rica after beating Honduras 1–0. Postgame celebrations spilled into the streets and lasted into the wee hours of the morning. Unfortunately, the high hopes ended in bitter disappointment. Things got off to a great start with a 5–1 routing of Trinidad and Tobago, but Guatemala then lost 2–0 to the United States and never fully recovered.

Baseball

Known locally as *béisbol,* games can be seen at Parque Minerva's ballpark. The game has become increasingly popular in recent years and you'll often see league games going on at area ballparks, usually on Saturday mornings.

Accommodations

Options for accommodations in Guatemala vary from the backpacker's basic $3-a-night room in cheap, blue-light hotels or hostels to ultraswanky boutique hotels and five-star international chain hotels and resorts. It's possible to tour the country entirely on either end of the budget spectrum. There are certainly plenty of options in between, as well as the more recent development of attractive ecolodges in areas adjacent to pristine natural areas. Camping is also another fairly common alternative, particularly at the national parks, though RV hookups are still virtually nonexistent. The government levies a 12 percent sales tax in addition to a 10 percent tax that goes to INGUAT (Guatemala Tourist Commission), bringing the total to a whopping 22 percent. Most of the budget and many of the midrange hotels include these taxes in the prices they'll quote you, but this is not the case in higher-end accommodations.

In popular tourist areas, you'll often be approached by *comisionistas* offering to find you a place to stay. These people work with local hotels and are paid commissions for each person they bring to a particular property. Usually, the places they work with aren't the best deals in town since they have to pay these people, an expense that simply gets added to the room rates. Also, more reputable hotels with good clientele and favorable word of mouth are rarely the kinds of places that would need the services of these freelancers.

HOSPEDAJES, HOSTELS, AND CHEAP HOTELS

Guatemala is a major stop along the Central American backpacking circuit, so it's no surprise that there are a plethora of low-budget hotels to choose from. Many of these are *hospedajes* or *pensiones* with very basic rooms run by local families. The rooms at the most basic places may all be on a shared-bath *(baño compartido)* basis. This is particularly the case in some of the very remote mountain villages in the Western Highlands region. The next-highest level in comfort consists of rooms with private bath *(baño privado).* A recent trend in areas with heavy tourist presence is the establishment of excellent *hostales* (hostels), where several travelers share dormitory-type bedrooms and bathrooms. Antigua, Copán, Guatemala City, Flores, and Cobán, to name a few, have some excellent hostels.

The key thing to look for when scoping out hotels with bargain-basement prices is cleanliness. All of the hotels recommended in this guidebook pass the cleanliness standard, as there are some budget hotels that are truly filthy. I'm all about making my dollar go as far as possible, but I draw the line here. If you do end up staying in a hotel room of questionable cleanliness, break out the sleeping bag. It's always a good idea to pack one along if you're traveling on a budget. Rooms in the highlands tend to suffer from mold problems, so keep this in mind if you're susceptible to this. For rooms in tropical areas, make sure there is a fan, preferably a ceiling fan, as this will make for a much more restful night's sleep.

Another consideration in budget hotels is the quality of the mattresses. Definitely check this out, as the quality of beds

© AL ARGUETA

Guatemala has accommodations for every taste and budget.

varies widely. In some tropical areas beds might consist of a thin mattress atop a concrete block. This peculiar arrangement has been called to attention in hotel descriptions where applicable.

The cheapest of the cheap hotels may not offer hot water or may not have it on during the whole day. Always inquire about this. In many budget hotels, the hot water comes from an electric hot-water heater attached to the showerhead. These can often look scary, with wires jutting out all over the place. It's a good idea to check out your water-heater situation before taking a room. Be very careful not to touch the showerhead while in the shower, unless, of course, you enjoy being mildly electrocuted. As a final note, bring flip-flops or some other type of shower shoe to avoid catching a nasty fungus in shared bathrooms.

MIDRANGE HOTELS

There are a number of good-value, moderately priced hotels throughout Guatemala charging somewhere in the vicinity of $25–

50 per night. Spending $50–100 a night in Guatemala gets you a very nice spread indeed. Despite its newfound popularity, you can still get some very good travel deals in Guatemala. You'll certainly get more bang for your buck than in Belize or Costa Rica, but it's anyone's guess as to how much longer this will last. In the $25–50 range, you'll be surprised at what you'll find. Many rooms in this category come with private bathroom and almost all moderately priced rooms have cable TV (with channels in English), so you can catch up on the news back home or keep up with your favorite sports team while on the road. Decent mattresses and air-conditioning are also available in some of the better-value accommodations in this category.

Spending $50–100 on a hotel room in Guatemala City will land you in the chic Zona Viva district very close to the airport and near the best restaurants and nightlife venues. In Antigua, you can book a decent boutique property or even stay in a resort. Ditto for the coasts, Petén, and Lake Atitlán.

HIGH-END HOTELS AND RESORTS
Luxury Hotels

Guatemala City boasts the presence of many luxury chains, including Marriott, Westin, and InterContinental, among others. You'll also find luxury hotels in Antigua, Lake Atitlán, and the vicinity of Tikal and Flores, in Petén. Antigua has some of the nicest boutique hotels anywhere in the world, and plenty of them. Rates at Guatemala's nicer hotels can range $100–900 a night. Many Guatemala City luxury hotels cater to business travelers and deals might be available for weekend stays. These are usually advertised on their websites. Near Retalhuleu, the Hostales del IRTRA seem like a bit of a misnomer, as the complex is less like a hostel and more like a large resort complex with some truly luxurious suites with all the look and feel of a Four Seasons. There are plans in the works for a convention center and golf resort.

Beach Resorts

This category has gained relevance only in recent years as the Pacific Coast's long-neglected beaches have become the target of tourism development. Most of the Pacific Coast's resorts are along the Iztapa–Monterrico corridor or in either of these towns, including brand-new Cayman Suites and Dos Mundos Pacific Resort. West of Puerto San José, Chulamar features the sprawling Villas del Pacífico, a sizable all-inclusive resort fronting black-sand beaches. It's popular on weekends, but you may have the place all to yourself during the week if a cruise ship isn't docked at nearby Puerto Quetzal.

On the Caribbean Coast near Puerto Barrios, Amatique Bay Resort is a sizable complex fronting an artificial white-sand beach with its own marina and three restaurants. Across the bay near Puerto Santo Tomás de Castilla and its new cruise-ship terminal, Green Bay Hotel also fronts an artificial beach along a lagoon and provides easy access to nearby nature preserves. It is rumored that international hotel chains have expressed interest in developing the remote beaches on the Punta de Manabique promontory, though it seems to contradict its status as a wildlife refuge. But then again, that's never stopped tourism development before.

Ecolodges

Another recent trend is the development of ecolodges springing up seemingly everywhere. These vary from somewhat simple community-run ecolodges to downright stylish, with Francis Ford Coppola's La Lancha (on Lake Petén Itzá) at the forefront of the latter category. Most ecolodges are found in Petén department and in the regions of Izabal and Las Verapaces.

Food

WHAT TO EAT

Guatemalan food may at first seem a bit odd to gringo palates, though the freshness and pungency of local ingredients, including a bounty of tropical fruits and vegetables, soon has many people enticed by the local flavors. Guatemalan dishes are based largely on corn, a staple crop with Guatemala's indigenous population. Corn is ground and made into a dough, which in turn is used to make tortillas, cooked over an open fire on a *comal*. Tortillas are a staple with Indians and ladinos alike and the average Guatemalan family consumes several dozen tortillas per week. In the countryside, tortillas with a dash of lemon and salt, along with beans, form the basis of meals in many low-income households. Even in the cities, tortillas are bought from the local *tortillería* or, in many cases, delivered fresh daily. Unlike revenge, tortillas are not a dish best served cold. Guatemalans like them piping hot and they usually arrive in a basket wrapped in traditional cloth to keep them warm. Many restaurants will have a *tortillería* at the front of the restaurant, where you can watch the tortillas being made, attesting to their freshness.

Other Guatemalan dishes include *tamales,* made from corn meal, pork or turkey, tomato sauce, and olives wrapped in a banana leaf and boiled. Traditionally, Guatemalans will eat a *tamal* at midnight on Christmas morning. *Chuchitos* are a delicious combination of cornmeal with turkey and tomato sauce wrapped in a cornhusk. *Paches* are similar to *tamales,* but they are made from potato-based dough instead of corn. Guatemalans are no strangers to tacos, though the local version is a corn tortilla filled with pork or chicken, rolled up, fried, and covered with tomato sauce and traditional cheese bits. Tostadas are flat, fried corn tortillas topped with tomato sauce or bean paste, shredded parsley, and cheese bits.

Among Guatemala's dishes are also a variety of spicy stews found regionally. Found in the northern region of Las Verapaces, *kakik* is a turkey stew requiring 24 ingredients. Served along the Caribbean Coast of Izabal, *tapado* is a seafood stew made with plantains and coconut milk. Spicy meat dishes include *pollo en jocón* (chicken in a tomatillo-cilantro sauce) and *pollo en pepián* (chicken in a tomato-pumpkin seed sauce).

In addition to three meals a day, Guatemalans are also big fans of the *refacción,* a midafternoon snack consisting of a light sandwich or pastry and coffee. The prominence of bakeries and cake shops throughout the country attests to the popularity of this extra half meal. Not all Guatemalans can afford to eat three square meals a day, as a large part of the population subsists on less than $2 daily. In many places, meat is a luxury few can afford. Dinner is usually late for North American tastes and is usually eaten sometime around 8 P.M.

Besides traditional food, heavy European influences on Guatemalan culture throughout the years have resulted in a wide array of culinary tastes. You"ll see plenty of evidence of this in Guatemala City and Antigua, where there are numerous options for dining in addition to some very interesting fusions of Guatemalan and international flavors. In food and culture, Guatemalans love to emulate the consumption patterns of their North American neighbors. You'll see plenty of fast-food franchises, mostly in Guatemala City, but also with surprising frequency in other urban areas. Guatemala City also has its fair share of U.S. casual dining franchises the likes of T.G.I. Friday's, Chili's, and Applebee's. But, since you didn't come all this way to eat the same food you'd have back home you'll need a few tips on where to eat locally.

WHERE TO EAT

You can expect to find table service and menus in *restaurantes. Comedores* are much simpler eateries, sometimes with a menu but other times with a set dish for the day. The best *comedores* are easy to spot: They'll have the greatest number of locals eating there. You'll find Guatemalans often eat at streetside stalls serving greasy tacos, fried chicken, and the like. These places are often referred to in jest as *shucos* (dirties) and are best avoided by international travelers unless you have a very strong stomach or have developed resistance to intestinal critters through continued exposure to food of questionable cleanliness south of the border.

ORDERING AND PAYING

The menu is known as *la carta* or *el menú.* To request the check, order *la cuenta* or ask, *"¿cuánto le debo?"* ("How much do I owe you?"). Tips are not required at simple eateries and may already be included on your bill in many midrange restaurants. Check to see. If not, an average tip in Guatemala is 10 percent.

BUYING GROCERIES

Corner stores known as *tiendas* carrying basic food items are common in cities and towns throughout the country. Larger grocery stores are found in Guatemala City and some of the larger cities. Major grocery chains include Paiz (recently acquired by Wal-Mart) and La Torre.

Every town and village has a *mercado* (market), where folks go to buy fruits and vegetables as well as meats. Try to avoid the butcher section if you don't take well to displays of raw flesh covered with flies. Inquire about the price per pound of any required items instead of just picking up an odd-numbered assortment and then asking how much it is, as that's the best way to get ripped off.

BEVERAGES
Non-Alcoholic Drinks

Although Guatemala produces some of the world's finest coffee, most of it is set aside for export. Still, you can find an excellent cup of java in Antigua, Guatemala City, Cobán, and other tourist places, though the coffee served at many less expensive restaurants is not usually the greatest. There's almost always at least one decent place in town for coffee and these have been indicated in the appropriate chapter sections.

With the wide variety of fruits available in Guatemala's myriad vegetation zones, fruit smoothies (often made with milk and called *licuados*) are common beverages. At simpler smoothie stands, you should always be careful to make sure the water used in making your drink is purified. Also, try to get fruit smoothies made from produce that requires peeling, rather than from fruits that are found on or close to the ground. Good, safe bets are pineapple or cantaloupe (or, even better, mixed together). Strawberries sold locally are notorious for carrying amoebas and other parasites, so unless you plan on disinfecting them yourself or are in a place where you have assurance that this has been done, stick to fruits with peels. Orange juice served in Guatemala is often freshly squeezed and delicious, a delightful surprise for North American palates that have become all too accustomed to the taste of juice made from concentrate.

Sodas and carbonated beverages are widely available, as you'll guess from the ubiquitous advertising on town walls. Although plastic soda bottles and cans have become more widely available in recent years, you'll still see plenty of glass bottles in use. If you plan on buying a soda and taking the glass bottle with you, you'll have to fork over a few extra bills for the glass deposit. Otherwise, you can have it put in a sandwich bag with a straw, which is a bit unnerving for first-time visitors but perfectly normal and hygienic.

Alcoholic Beverages

Guatemala's eastern region produces Zacapa Centenario, a highly acclaimed rum that has won numerous international awards. It makes a great gift for folks back home. If you're not heading to the eastern lowlands of Zacapa or don't want to lug your purchase around the country during the rest of your travels, keep in mind the Guatemala City airport has a Zacapa Centenario Duty Free shop where you can buy a bottle or two on your way out of the country. In the Mayan highland towns and villages, the liquor of choice is *aguardiente*, locally made moonshine also known as *guaro*. Popular brands include *Quezalteca Especial* and *Venado*. *Rompopo* and *caldo de frutas* are two types of alcoholic beverages made in the town of Salcajá, near Quetzaltenango. The first is essentially a spiked eggnog and the latter is made from fermented fruits.

Cervecería Centroamericana produces most of Guatemala's beers from its brewery in Guatemala City, including Gallo, a lager that is Guatemala's national brew. You can find it in the United States under the name Famosa, as Ernest and Julio Gallo Wines holds the rights to the use of the Gallo name in North America. "Gallo" means rooster in Spanish and the beer is easily identifiable by the stylized cock on its label. Other beers brewed by Cervecería Centroamericana include Dorada Draft, smooth export pilsner Monte Carlo, and dark beer Moza. Brewed by Cervecería Nacional and available only in and around Quetzaltenango, Cabro is another good beer. Cervecería Centroamericana once enjoyed uncontested dominion of the Guatemalan beer market but has seen competition in recent years with the arrival of competing brands, most notably Brazilian Brahva.

Conduct and Customs

You'll find most Guatemalans are warm and friendly. In many instances, they will be very curious about you as a foreigner, particularly in areas that are still getting accustomed to a growing presence of gringo travelers. Urban and rural settings have varying degrees of formality, though politeness and good manners are appreciated by Guatemalans from all walks of life and will get you far.

DRESS AND APPEARANCE

Guatemala, true to its roots as Central America's aristocratic colonial capital, is rather formal and conservative in many ways. It's a very class-conscious society and neat dress, good grooming, and cleanliness are held in high regard. In many instances, the way you look is the way you'll be treated. You'll notice this the first time you go to a Guatemala City shopping mall (especially on weekends) and see well-dressed urbanites going for a cup of coffee or to a movie. Sneakers and shorts are considered much too casual for many events foreigners would find perfectly acceptable. This is starting to change, however, and you'll also see younger Guatemalans wearing shorts, T-shirts, and flip-flops typical of the Abercrombie and Fitch look that is also wildly popular with Guatemalan youth from wealthy families. If you plan on going out to dance clubs, be sure to bring a good pair of shoes, as you won't make it past the front door wearing sneakers. As everywhere else, dress is much more relaxed at the beach or in the countryside.

For business travelers, suits are still very much the norm for men. Women tend to dress very elegantly here, which is attested to by the relative abundance of upscale shops (some of international fame) doing a brisk business in this country. Men do not lag far behind, as the middle-to-upper class Guatemalan metrosexual is very much alive and well as a species. The less affluent will pay careful attention to dress as neatly as possible, especially for trips to the capital or other urban centers.

Backpackers, known as *mochileros,* are sometimes looked down upon by local tourism operators and well-to-do locals as an unsophisticated, rag-tag bunch creating more problems than contributions to the tourism market. This is generally manifested as a form of marked distrust, though this is usually not the case in places, such as budget hostels, that cater to these types of travelers as their main clientele.

ETIQUETTE

Guatemalans are also very formal in their etiquette and take titles seriously (including *Doctor* or *Doctora* for doctors and *Licenciado(a)* for an attorney or holder of a bachelor's degree). When known, try to use these when addressing someone in-person or via mail. Women usually greet men and each other with air kisses. Men will greet friends with a handshake different from the standard business handshake. Grips tend to be firm. When meeting someone for the first time, it's customary to say, "*mucho gusto*" (a shortened version of "nice to meet you"). Simply saying "*hola*" is considered too casual. Other greetings include "*Buenos días*" (good morning), "*Buenas tardes*" (good afternoon), and "*Buenas noches*" (good evening). Particularly in rural areas, people will greet each other with one of these as they pass each other along the trail, road, or street. In urban settings, you'll often hear one of these greetings when someone walks into a place of business, such as a doctor's office waiting room, for example. Another formality is the use of "*Buen provecho*" when walking into a restaurant where people are eating and "*muchas gracias*" upon getting up from the table after a meal.

Guatemalans tend to use the *vos* form of *tú* (you), a derivative of the archaic *vosotros* now used only in Spain. This is particularly the case with two men of the same age or similar social standing. It shouldn't be used to address a person of perceived lesser social stature, as it's somewhat demeaning when used in this way, though upper-class Guatemalans tend to do it anyhow. Stick to the formal *usted* unless the other person switches to the informal *tú* or *vos*.

PHOTOGRAPHIC ETIQUETTE

It's never a good idea to photograph Mayan people without their permission, as they consider it highly offensive and it intrudes upon their spiritual beliefs. The old photographers' rule contending that it's easier to apologize (for taking a candid photo) than to ask permission doesn't really apply in Guatemala. This is especially true concerning photographs of children, and you should be careful not to show them undue interest and attention, as persistent rumors of foreigners involved in child-snatching of Guatemalan children for organ transplant abroad have led to mob incidents on at least

two occasions, with two people killed and one seriously injured. (The last incident was in 2000 in the village of Todos Santos). In both cases, the foreigners were trying to photograph a child. This scenario is most plausible in the highlands, though not exclusively so.

It can be understandably difficult at times to refrain from taking photographs because Mayan children (and Mayan people in general) are photogenic and can provide some wonderful opportunities for portraiture or candid shots. On the up side, the situation forces you to interact with the locals and get to know them. You'll soon find that many are willing to let you photograph them (often for the promise of sending them a photo) and your photographs will be better because of the rapport you've established with the subject.

Tips for Travelers

OPPORTUNITIES FOR STUDY AND VOLUNTEER WORK
Language Study
Guatemala is a popular place for Spanish-language study, particularly Antigua and Quetzaltenango. (Details on individual language schools are provided in the appropriate geographical chapters.) Here are a few basic things to look out for when deciding where to study Spanish in Guatemala. First of all, you'll want to decide what sort of environment you're looking for to choose a location. Antigua and Quetzaltenango offer some fine institutions in addition to the chance to combine your language instruction with time spent in interesting urban locales. Both towns have a lively nightlife scene and a fairly substantial presence of foreign travelers. This might be a pro or a con, depending on how you look at it. If you're looking to make new friends and traveling companions after your courses are finished, then this will certainly suit you. But if you're looking for a total language-immersion experience, you might find yourself

speaking English outside of classroom time more often than not.

There are a few highland towns and villages with language schools that offer good instruction with (for now) a relatively small foreign presence. These include the language schools in Nebaj, Cobán, and Huehuetenango. San Pedro La Laguna, on the shores of Lake Atitlán, also has decent language schools and a slightly less substantial gringo presence compared to Antigua and Quetzaltenango. It's certainly a winner for its location on the shores of this magnificent lake. Monterrico is the place to go if you want to combine fairly decent language instruction with some serious time at the beach. The northern Petén region's language schools are found in the Itzá Maya towns of San Andrés and San José, on the shores of Lake Petén Itzá, and they are a good place to learn Spanish with little foreigner presence and a more ecological focus thanks to the proximity of the Maya Biosphere Reserve.

For the altruistic, Quetzaltenango offers the chance for language instruction in an environment oozing with fellow travelers, volunteers, and NGO workers plugged into a variety of projects hoping to make life better for people in Guatemala's impoverished Western Highlands.

Virtually all of Guatemala's language schools offer one-on-one instruction, and your choice of an instructor is particularly important to your progress. You should never feel locked into a deal with a particular instructor. If you find that you and the instructor just aren't jiving, don't hesitate to ask for a new one. All of the recommended schools get their strength from the quality of their individual instructors, so finding one that's right for you shouldn't be too difficult if you know where to look.

In terms of cost, you'll find it fairly accessible. The bulk of Guatemala's schools charge somewhere between $150 and $225 per week, including at least 20 hours of instruction per week and room and board with a local host family. Some schools, particularly in Antigua and Quetzaltenango, provide the option of staying in on- or off-campus housing or apartments.

As a final note, Guatemalan Spanish is relatively clear of the accents found in Caribbean, Mexican, and even Costa Rican Spanish. Guatemalans also tend to speak more slowly than Caribbean Spanish speakers. It's actually a very melodic Spanish and you'll soon recognize its singsong sound. In terms of value for the money you spend and variety of locales in which to learn, you really can't beat Spanish-language instruction in Guatemala.

Volunteer Opportunities

The country is also the focus of many relief and development projects on the part of NGOs, some of which are almost always looking for volunteers. (Information on volunteer opportunities is also provided in the individual geographical sections.) Many of these are linked to local language schools. Areas with a particularly heavy concentration of NGOs include Quetzaltenango, the Ixil Triangle, and Petén.

Foreign Study Programs

For college students seeking a study-abroad opportunity, **The University of Arizona** (www.studyabroad.arizona.edu), in partnership with the Center for Mesoamerican Research (CIRMA), offers semester- and yearlong programs in Antigua focusing on intensive Spanish-language instruction in addition to Central American history, politics and culture.

TRAVELING WITH CHILDREN

Guatemalans love children and traveling with them will often be all that you need to break the ice with locals. Guatemala's cultural and natural wealth can also form the basis for a very educational trip allowing children to see and experience what they might only read about in textbooks and classrooms. (See the sidebar *Kid-Friendly Guatemala* for a list of kid-friendly attractions.)

Guatemala is also a popular place for adoptions and on almost any given flight leaving Guatemala City you'll see at least one couple bringing home an adopted baby. Several Guatemala City hotels, particularly the Radisson, have special accommodations for travelers visiting Guatemala to adopt a child, including rooms with stuffed animals and cribs, among other amenities. The U.S. government was discouraging adoptions from Guatemala because of deficient legal parameters ensuring the protection of adopting parents and adopted children in line with international standards. Guatemala had not (at last check) ratified the international Treaty of The Hague, which governs inter-country adoptions.

ACCESS FOR TRAVELERS WITH DISABILITIES

Guatemala is a somewhat challenging country for people with disabilities, as there is little in the way of public infrastructure specifically catering to the needs of travelers with disabilities. Antigua might be a bit cumbersome for travelers in wheelchairs because of its cobblestone streets but nonetheless it has ramps for wheelchair access on every street corner. There are a few exceptions to the general lack of access for

KID-FRIENDLY GUATEMALA

Latin Americans are very family oriented and Guatemalans are no exception. There is plenty to see and do in Guatemala for families traveling with children of all ages. The following is a list of kid- and family-friendly attractions throughout the country.

GUATEMALA CITY

Among the city's museums, none is more kid friendly than the **Museo del Niño** (Children's Museum), in Zona 13 near the airport. There are a number of interactive displays as well as opportunities for play. Just across the street, you'll find the city's excellent **La Aurora Zoo,** harboring a good collection of animals from Guatemala and around the world. Cages are being gradually phased out. If you want to see the city's sights but have kids in tow who might not want to walk, opt for a **trolley tour.**

LAKE ATITLÁN

On the lake's beautiful shores, there are plenty of places to stay for families traveling with children. Among the best are the family-size villas at **San Buenaventura de Atitlán,** equipped with a kitchen and several rooms. Nearby, kids (and outdoor-loving parents) will enjoy the **Reserva Natural Atitlán,** where they can see monkeys and coatimundis along the nature trails leading to waterfalls. There are also a butterfly farm and private lake beach in addition to an excellent visitors center.

PACIFIC COAST

The Pacific Coast is extremely family friendly, primarily thanks to the presence of the twin theme parks of **Xocomil and Xetulul,** near Retalhuleu. Xocomil is a water park on par with the finest in the United States and Xetulul includes re-creations of famous Spanish, French, Italian, and Guatemalan landmarks along with an exhilarating roller-coaster and assorted other rides. After the parks close, the fun continues across the street at the excellent accommodations of **Hostales del IRTRA,** with numerous swimming pools, restaurants, and activities. For some seaside fun, head to **Monterrico,** where (in season) you can participate in a race involving newly hatched sea turtles making their maiden voyage across the sandy beach to their ocean home. Kids will also get a kick out of the **Auto-Safari Chapín,** in Taxisco about 90 minutes from Guatemala City. It's a drive-through safari experience, in which you can see several of kids' favorite animals, including lions, zebras, and parrots.

PETÉN

Children will certainly be impressed by the Mayan ruins at **Tikal,** along with the abundant wildlife found along the various nature trails criss-crossing the park or swinging from the trees. At the entrance to Tikal, older kids and adults will enjoy the **Tikal Canopy Tour,** allowing them to zip across the forest canopy along metallic cables while strapped to a harness. If you want to see more of the forest canopy on slightly less adrenaline-inducing conditions, head to **Parque Natural Ixpanpajul,** where there are plenty of outdoor activities, including walks along hanging bridges connecting forested jungle canyons.

---

those with disabilities. Guatemala City's new public transportation system, the Transmetro, was said to offer wheelchair access as part of its innovative infrastructure. The international airport now also features several elevators as part of its recent renovation. Modern Guatemala City hotels housed in high-rise buildings also have these amenities. For intercity travel, the best option for travelers with disabilities is to take shuttle buses.

WOMEN TRAVELING ALONE

As elsewhere in Latin America, men in Guatemala tend to be chauvinistic, particularly the country's ladinos. Women traveling alone might find themselves the object of unwanted attention. Guatemalan women are accustomed to fairly constant harassment by men on the street, including catcalls, whistling, and horn honking, which they tend to ignore. This is usually the best tactic, though it's somewhat difficult to put into practice. Take a deep breath and count to 10. Your best bet as a preventive measure in this regard is to dress demurely, particularly in urban areas. Although much less likely, there's also the possibility of having your butt or breasts groped by a passing stranger. It usually happens in an instant, with nary a second glance from the perpetrator. If it should come to a case of a lingering pervert, some Guatemalan women will scream at the perpetrator, something along the lines of "*cerdo*" (pig), which usually scares them off. The last thing they want is to be confronted in public and they certainly wouldn't expect it. Blonds and brunets tend to be the most common targets of dudes who just can't keep their hands to themselves.

Solo female travelers should try to stick to the main tourist destinations in Guatemala and not venture too far off the beaten path. There's really no reason to travel alone for too long unless you really want to, as you'll probably make friends along the way thanks to an abundance of foreign visitors. After dark, take a cab, but try to find someone to share it with.

GAY AND LESBIAN TRAVELERS

The same machismo (male-dominated culture) that sometimes makes travel unpleasant for solo women travelers can also make things difficult, if not downright dangerous, for gay and lesbian couples choosing to express mutual affection publicly. Gay travelers should try to keep a low profile while in Guatemala. As in any other international city, there's a growing gay movement in Guatemala City, where there are a number of gay bars and nightclubs, mostly in Zona 1. For information on gay venues, log on to www.gayguatemala.com.

Health and Safety

Guatemala's status as a poor, developing nation translates into a variety of health and safety risks for the foreign traveler. Many of these are directly related to poor hygiene. When it comes to safety and law enforcement, the **Policía Nacional Civil** (created by the 1996 peace accords) has not lived up to its expectations as an efficient, incorruptible, and professional police force. On a positive note, the **Tourism Police** have demonstrated proficiency in helping travelers as well as making areas somewhat safer with patrols and group escorts. Private initiatives, as they almost always do in Guatemala, have stepped in to fill the gaps, also providing some measure of protection for foreign visitors.

Travelers might want to consider buying traveler's insurance before heading to Guatemala. Several different types of insurance with varying degrees of coverage are available in the United States, Canada, and Europe. A relatively new Guatemalan initiative offering assistance to foreign travelers is **Asistur** (www.asisturcard .com), which provides services via the purchase of its Asistur Card. You can buy policies for one day, 15 days, 30 days, or one year costing just $1 per day. Included in the coverage is round-the-clock telephone assistance for issues including legal and medical situations. Security escorts, roadside assistance, helicopter evacuation from remote areas such as volcanic summits or jungles, and special assistance in case of robbery, including provision of hotel room and meals, are also provided to those insured by Asistur. Other coverage options (extra cost) include life insurance, coverage of medical expenses, and theft insurance. The card is available at the INGUAT kiosks at the Guatemala City and Flores/Tikal Airports. Asistur can be reached from anywhere in Guatemala by dialing 1500 or 1-801-ASIST (1-8012-7478). As this is a new venture, you could probably call if you find yourself in a bind, even if you haven't bought coverage. An Asistur agent might be nearby. Crimes against tourists are a great concern to Guatemalans in general and their gracious hospitality dictates their desire to help out a traveler in need. That being said, for $1 a day, the coverage and peace of mind are certainly worth it.

BEFORE YOU GO

Officially, no vaccinations are required for entry into Guatemala, though it's a good idea to be up to date on rabies, typhoid, measles-mumps-rubella (MMR), yellow fever, and tetanus shots. A hepatitis vaccine is now widely available and is probably also a good idea. If you plan on taking preventive medications against malaria, you'll need to start taking them a few weeks before potential exposure to the disease. The Centers for Disease Control and Prevention (CDC) maintains an international travelers' hot line, which can be reached at 888/232-3228, and a travel health home page found at www.cdc.gov/travel.

PREVENTIVE MAINTENANCE

As the saying goes, "An ounce of prevention is worth a pound of cure." This is certainly the case for travel in Guatemala, as there are certain measures you can take to avoid succumbing to many of the most common ailments. Washing hands frequently and drinking only bottled water will help keep you free of stomach ailments as will consuming only cooked foods or peeled fruits such as bananas and oranges. Lettuce and strawberries are two common culprits, often leading to severe gastrointestinal distress. Likewise, stay away from ice cubes unless you have complete assurance that they come from purified water. By law, all ice cubes served in Guatemalan restaurants must come from purified water, a good idea in theory but certainly not always the case. I've often had my doubts even about supposedly purified ice cubes in restaurants after falling ill. When in doubt, leave the ice out. Be careful not only with what you eat, but where you eat. Stay away from street stalls selling cheap food, referred to jokingly by locals as *shucos* (literally, "dirties"). While Guatemalan stomachs have developed immunity through the years

to nasty food-borne bugs, the average gringo traveler's has not.

FOOD OR WATER-BORNE DISEASES

Despite these precautions, many travelers to Guatemala might find themselves experiencing a classic case of "the runs" as their digestive tracts adjust to new flora. This usually lasts only a day or two. If the problem persists, it may be a sign of more serious issues. In some cases, it may be food poisoning, which can occur just as easily back home. If this is the case, drink plenty of water and get some rest. You'll probably end up just having to ride it out for a few days and may want to take an anti-diarrhea medicine such as Pepto Bismol or Lomotil.

Travelers' Diarrhea

In addition to diarrhea, symptoms of this often-acquired malady include nausea, vomiting, bloating, and weakness. The usual culprit is *E. coli* bacteria from contaminated food or water. It's important to stay hydrated. Drink plenty of water and clear fluids and keep your strength up by eating bland foods such as crackers or steamed rice. As with food poisoning, you may want to take some over-the-counter anti-diarrhea medication.

Dysentery

Characterized by many of the same symptoms as described above, along with the possibility of bloody stools and generally prolonged malaise, dysentery comes in two flavors: bacillic (bacterial) and amoebic (parasitic). The onset of bacillic dysentery is usually sudden, characterized by vomiting, diarrhea, and fever. Treatment is via antibiotics, to which it responds well. Amoebic dysentery, on the other hand, has an incubation period and symptoms may not show up for several days. It's also harder to get rid of. It is usually treated with a weeklong course of Flagyl (Metronidazole), an extremely potent drug that will wipe out all intestinal flora—good and bad. It also has some marked side effects, such as a bitter taste in the mouth, irritability, and dizziness. You should avoid alcohol while taking this drug, as the combination can make you violently ill.

As with all gastrointestinal issues, it's very important to stay hydrated. Also, see a doctor to get an exact diagnosis. Because of the prevalence of gastrointestinal diseases among Guatemalans, most cities have at least one clinic that can take a stool sample and diagnose the exact nature of the problem.

Cholera

Not entirely unheard of in Guatemala, cholera can be an issue in poorer neighborhoods lacking adequate sanitation, which are usually not visited by foreign travelers. Today's cholera strains are not nearly as deadly as those of the past, though there have been outbreaks in Guatemala in years past. It's best to avoid raw fish and ceviche, a marinated raw-seafood salad popular throughout Latin America.

INSECT-BORNE DISEASES

Mosquitoes are the main carriers of insect-borne illnesses common throughout tropical areas around the world. The best approach to avoiding malaria and other mosquito-borne illnesses is to avoid being bitten by mosquitoes in the first place. Mosquitoes are most abundant during the rainy season, so take special care to protect against mosquito bites during this time of year. Some travelers favor liberal application of bug spray with DEET as the active ingredient, which seems to be the most effective at keeping the critters at bay. Plant-based bug sprays seem to be less effective. It's also possible to buy clothing treated with permethrin, a bug-repellent chemical. It's also possible to buy it separately and treat your clothing with it. Treated garments are scentless in addition to being highly insect repellent. You can find these products in camping and outdoor stores.

Malaria

Malaria is transmitted by the female *Anopheles* mosquito and is prevalent in the Caribbean lowlands and Petén jungles, though not in the highlands. Anopheles mosquitoes tend to bite at night. Flulike symptoms of malaria include high fever, chills, headaches, muscle pain, and fatigue. It can be fatal if left untreated.

Some travelers also opt to take antimalarial drugs, available locally without a prescription (and quite cheaply). The most widely used is chloroquine, known by its brand name Aralen. Although chloroquine-resistant strains of malaria are found in other parts of the world, including South America, this is not the case in Guatemala. You'll need to start taking the drug (500 mg) a week before arriving in malarial zones, weekly while there, and continue to take it once a week for at least four weeks after you've left the malarial zone. Other travelers opt to take two 500 mg doses with them to use if and only if the disease strikes.

Some people experience marked side effects while taking chloroquine, including nausea, headaches, fever, rashes, and nightmares. A newer antimalarial drug, malarone, was approved by the FDA in 2000, supposedly with fewer side effects than traditional drugs and which does not need to be taken for as long. It is not yet widely available in Guatemala.

Dengue

Dengue is also transmitted by mosquitoes and is prevalent in lowland areas, though it is far less common than malaria and only rarely fatal. Although there is no treatment, most people recover from its debilitating symptoms, which include a fever that can last 5–7 days, headache, severe joint pain, and skin rashes. The disease may last up to another week after the fever has lifted. Tylenol can help reduce the fever and counteract the headaches. Dengue is transmitted by a mosquito that bites during the daytime, the *Aëdes aegypti*. A far less common, though potentially fatal, form of dengue is hemorrhagic dengue. It needs to be treated within a few days of the appearance of symptoms, which are a carbon copy of regular dengue symptoms until severe hemorrhaging sets in, making medical treatment well advised at the first sign of dengue.

Chagas' Disease

Spread by the bites of the conenose and assassin bugs living in adobe structures and feeding at night, Chagas' disease is most common in Brazil but also affects millions of people between Mexico and Argentina. Curiously, Panama and Costa Rica are Chagas-free, probably because of the absence in local construction styles of adobe structures. Chickens, dogs, and rodents are thought to carry the disease. Avoid sleeping near the walls of an adobe structure and wear DEET-containing bug spray to bed. The only time this may be a consideration for the average traveler is if trekking across areas of the Western Highlands and staying with local families, who tend to live in adobe structures. Chagas-carrying bugs also tend to be found in dried palm leaves, which makes mosquito netting a must for the traveler sleeping under thatched-roof structures that are not insulated by wire mesh.

The disease usually starts off as a swollen bite accompanied by fever, which eventually subsides. Chagas' disease may eventually cause heart damage leading to sudden death and there is no cure for this disease. Only about 2 percent of those bitten ever develop Chagas' disease.

BITES AND STINGS
Sand Fleas and Sand Flies

Among the more annoying *bichos* (bugs) are sand fleas, which are virtually imperceptible but can leave a trail of welts on feet and ankles. The best way to avoid bites is by washing off after walking on sandy areas. Annoying and also extremely painful are the bites of sand flies known as *tábanos* inhabiting coastal areas, mostly on the Caribbean Coast. They look like a cross between a bee and housefly. You may not feel them on you until it's too late, as they have a knack for landing gently on their victims. Tábano infestations are worst during the dry months, when breezes off the ocean are greatly reduced. If traveling to remote beaches, go prepared with pants, long sleeves, bandana, hat, and bug spray. It may seem silly going to the beach with pants and long sleeves, but it sure beats the very unpleasant experience of being bitten and pursued by these persistent critters (I speak from experience).

Snakes

Lowland Guatemala is home to some of the world's deadliest snakes, including the aggressive fer-de-lance, a pit viper also known as *barba amarilla* for the yellow coloring under its mouth. It's easily distinguishable by its diamond-shaped head and intricate diamond patterns on its skin. It is fairly common in Petén, Izabal, and the Verapaces. Bites are usually fatal unless the victim receives medical attention within a few hours. Other poisonous snakes include rattlesnakes, the red, black, and yellow-banded coral snake, and the eyelash viper, which you should be particularly wary of, as it tends to blend in to vegetation, especially palm trees.

Wear high boots and long pants for hiking in the jungle. Always watch where you step and be particularly careful of woodpiles and rocks. Snakes tend to hang out near jungle watering holes and gaps created by fallen trees. For extended trips into the jungle, it's a good idea to go with a guide. Let guides lead the way, as their eyes are keenly attuned to the presence of snakes and they are usually armed with a machete.

HIV/AIDS

AIDS is a growing concern in Guatemala, particularly because of the wide-spread use of prostitutes in a society ruled by *machismo*. Certainly not making things any better is the economic need of infected prostitutes who continue working after being infected. If you plan on sleeping with a stranger or friend met in your travels, be sure to use a condom, available almost anywhere and known as *preservativos* or *condones*.

MEDICAL ATTENTION
Doctors and Hospitals

Medical services in Guatemala City are generally top-notch, particularly in many private hospitals. Outside the capital, there are several private hospitals providing quality medical care in urban areas. Public facilities such as the Instituto Guatemalteco de Seguridad Social (IGSS) should be avoided, as they are set up to cater to low-income people with no other alternative and are notoriously understaffed and underfunded. Rural areas are extremely lacking in health care, which has resulted in the presence of Cuban doctors in parts of the highlands who have arrived to help bridge the health-care gap. Asistur can help you find excellent English-speaking doctors for those under its coverage.

Pharmacies

In many cases pharmacists sometimes serve as de facto doctors, as prescriptions are not necessary for medications in Guatemala. Patients will often describe symptoms and take something on the pharmacist's recommendations. Still, it's always best to see a doctor. Many drugs can be found more cheaply in Guatemala, as they are produced locally by a handful of pharmaceutical companies.

In almost every town, at least one pharmacy will be open all night thanks to a system known as *farmacia de turno* (on-call pharmacy), in which the local pharmacies stay open on a rotating basis. Local newspapers publish a listing of these pharmacies and sometimes the outlets themselves have a neon sign stating as such.

SAFETY
Crime

Crime has been a problem throughout Guatemala in the aftermath of the civil war, though statistics show most foreign travelers enjoy their visit to the country without any problems. As many veteran travelers to Guatemala like to point out, you're still safer here than in many large U.S. cities.

Among Guatemala's urban areas, Guatemala City has by far the greatest prevalence of crime. Much of this consisted of groups perpetrating robberies against arriving passengers heading into the city from La Aurora International Airport. Private vehicles, taxis, and shuttle buses have been targeted indiscriminately. Authorities were investigating suspected groups while simultaneously opening security checkpoints

and police kiosks to provide greater police presence along this route. It remains to be seen whether large-scale infrastructural improvements involving roads adjacent to the airport (as part of the airport renovation project) will make things safer for arriving passengers.

A related issue is that of highway holdups on rural roads, a very unpleasant topic that I must nonetheless cover here. Sometimes, groups will use bends in the road and speed bumps to their advantage, stopping vehicles as they slow down and robbing passengers of valuables. In the most spectacular cases of highway banditry, pickup trucks carrying armed men will pursue a vehicle and then pass it. Another car might come alongside the victim's vehicle while the car in front shoots at it in an attempt to make the driver stop the car. In addition to taking the passengers' possessions, perpetrators occasionally drag the car's occupants out of the vehicle, tie them up, and steal the car.

Guatemalans who sniff out an impending carjacking have been known to speed up as would-be perpetrators signal them to slow down, not without significant risk of being harmed by the bullets that are often landed on the car by frustrated assailants. If you are stopped and robbed, it's best to remain calm and give them what they want. Opposing a robbery will only make things worse, as the thieves will see this as an invitation to use greater force. (I speak from a personal experience in Mexico). It's hard to predict where robberies may occur, though certain areas do seem more prone to this type of crime than others. Among these areas are RN-11, along the southeastern side of Lake Atitlán, the road to El Salvador outside the Guatemala City area (Salvadorans are a favorite target), and some rural Petén roads.

For more on this topic, read the U.S. government's Consular Information Sheet, found online at www.travel.state.gov. Another useful site is that concerning recent incidents of crime against foreigners in Guatemala, available at http://guatemala.usembassy.gov/recent_incidents.html. It will give you an idea of what can happen, but try not to let it alarm you.

Gang violence is also a growing concern. The groups, known as *maras,* operate in parts of Guatemala City not usually frequented by international travelers as well as in some urban areas throughout the country.

Kidnappings reached an all-time high after the civil war, usually involving prominent citizens held for ransom and sometimes returned to their families, depending on whether or not the ransom money was collected. They seem to have subsided in more recent years and rarely, if ever, involve foreigners.

During your trip to Guatemala, there are a number of common-sense measures you can take to avoid being becoming the victim of street crime. Don't walk around wearing flashy jewelry and carry only the amount of cash you need for the day in a concealed place. Use safety-deposit boxes for important documents such as passports and plane tickets. In crowded cities, carry your backpack in front of you and be aware of your surroundings at all times. Always keep an eye on your luggage at the airport, bus terminals, and hotels. At night, take a cab and don't go walking out and about after dark. At the beach, be sure not to bring too many things that might tempt thieves while you're in the water. Also, be careful not to walk along isolated stretches of beach, particularly around the Caribbean city of Lívingston. It's never a good idea to climb volcanic summits without a guide, particularly those around Antigua and Lake Atitlán, as these are especially prone to robberies. (Some volcanoes are more infamous than others and these are clearly pointed out in the appropriate chapter headings.)

That being said, there are still many areas of the country that are beautiful for backcountry hiking and remain crime-free, particularly the Western Highlands region of the Ixil Triangle, where you can still explore freely. Before embarking on a backcountry hike or volcano climb, always inform someone who is not going with you of your plans and when you plan to return.

Police

The Policía Nacional Civil (PNC) was created after the civil war with help from Chil-

Guatemala's tourist police

© AL ARGUETA

ean and Spanish security forces but has not been the efficient security force it was hoped it would be. In addition to widespread allegations of corruption, it is perceived as being grossly inefficient. Corrupt agents are suspected of involvement with drug trafficking and the highway holdups, as many robberies occur shortly after travelers are stopped at police checkpoints and perpetrators are often described as wearing police uniforms. Despite these conditions, if you are stopped by police it is best not to offer a bribe, as straight cops will not hesitate to throw you in jail. It's best to go through the usual mechanisms and pay the fine (if applicable). After being stopped, be particularly mindful of your surroundings and especially on the lookout for vehicles that might be following you a little too closely. If you have hired the services of Asistur, you may want to call and see if there is an agent in the vicinity to accompany you the rest of the way to your destination.

The Guatemalan military sometimes jointly patrols areas with police forces because of the latter's demonstrated inability to provide a security presence that dissuades criminal activity. This has led to criticism because the joint patrols (as they're called) run counter to the peace accords allowing for the creation of a professional civilian security force. The involvement of high-ranking police officers in the assassination of three Salvadoran diplomats and their driver in February 2007, in addition to denunciations that police forces harbor death squads within their ranks, may have served as the needed impetus for a systematic purge and revamping of the police forces (once again) from the ground up. It was a hot topic leading up to the election campaign.

In contrast, Tourist Police (Politur) are generally helpful and have been dispatched to patrol tourist areas. They have been particularly effective at curbing robberies in areas where criminal activity was once getting out of hand, including Tikal National Park and areas in the vicinity of Antigua.

Drugs

Guatemala is a major transshipment point for cocaine coming into the United States from South America, as evidenced by the many clandestine landing strips found in isolated areas of Petén department. Marijuana is grown in remote lowland areas of Guatemala and poppy (the basis for heroin) is grown in the Western Highlands, particularly in the department of San Marcos.

High-ranking military officials have been implicated in drug smuggling, working with local cartels linked to Colombia's powerful Cali cartel. United States drug officials have begun referring to Guatemala as *la bodega* (the warehouse), as it houses a large share of the cocaine continuing north to Mexico, from where it makes its final entry into the United States. Among the local cartels, the most prominent are based in the eastern lowlands near Zacapa (not an area frequented by foreign tourists), Izabal department, and the southern part of Petén department near Sayaxché. Some travelers have reported run-ins with local drug traffickers on private lands, but you're unlikely to be harmed as long as you adopt a live-and-let-live attitude.

Cocaine consumption is an increasing problem among affluent Guatemalans, particularly in Guatemala City night clubs. Drug use is strictly forbidden by law and you will be thrown in jail without hesitation for violations. If you are arriving in Guatemala by air from elsewhere in Latin America, drug-sniffing dogs will probably be on hand to greet your flight and you may be questioned by authorities after clearing immigration procedures.

Information and Services

MONEY

Guatemala's currency is the quetzal, which is pegged to the U.S. dollar and denoted by Q. The exchange rate was about Q7.68 to 1 US$ and it has remained at about the same rate for several years now. Bills come in denominations of 5, 10, 20, 50, and 100 quetzales, though at last report the Central Bank was planning to issue new Q1 bills printed on a polymer hybrid form of paper in addition to Q200 and Q500 quetzal notes that might be in use by the time of your visit. Coins come in denominations of 1, 5, 10, 25, 50 *centavos* (Q0.01, Q0.05, Q0.10, Q0.25, Q.50) and Q1, though other than the one-quetzal coin they are more of a nuisance than anything else. Often, if your change is a few centavos, the merchant will keep it.

In smaller towns and villages, you might have trouble breaking Q100 (or larger) notes, so bring smaller bills with you if possible.

Exchange

Travelers have the option of getting around with cash U.S. dollars (which you will need to at least partially exchange for local currency), travelers checks (American Express being the most widely recognized and accepted), wire transfers (most expensive option), Visa or MasterCard cash advances (watch those interest rates), or through ATMs linked to international networks (recommended).

Banks

Banks in Guatemala tend to keep long hours, typically 9 A.M.–6 P.M. Monday–Friday and 9 A.M.–1 P.M. on Saturday. Changing money and travelers checks at banks is relatively painless and routine, though you'll probably be asked to show your passport or at least a photocopy of it for identification. You'll also notice that banks, like convenience stores and other businesses, are heavily guarded by armed watchmen.

In border areas, you'll typically be approached by money changers offering slightly better rates than local banks. It's perfectly safe to change your money with them, though it's probably a good idea to exchange only what you might need for the first day or two in the new country. Try not to pull out a wad of bills for all to see.

Travelers Checks

This is still the safest way to carry money during your travels, though you'll be able to exchange them only in urban areas and tourist destinations with full-service banks. There's also a bit more bureaucracy involved in exchanging travelers checks and you might be asked to show your original purchase receipt. American Express is by far the most widely accepted type of travelers check. The local American Express representative is Clark Tours (7a Avenida 14-76, Plaza Clark, Zona 9, Guatemala City, tel. 2412-4700, www .clarktours.com).

Wire Transfers

Because of the widespread phenomenon of remittances sent home by Guatemalan nationals living abroad, several companies have set up shop all over Guatemala. This may be your best bet if you happen to run short of cash during your travels. Many local banks and businesses are Western Union affiliates. For a list of these affiliates in Guatemala, visit the website at www.westernunion.com. You can also send money via American Express Money-Gram. Keep in mind these companies make their money off exorbitant fees charged for their services in addition to a poor exchange rate for the money, which you'll end up getting in local currency.

Credit Cards and ATMs

Credit cards have become more and more commonplace in Guatemala, though they are still accepted mainly in urban centers, major tourist attractions, and luxury hotels or expensive restaurants and shops. Some smaller merchants may charge a fee, usually 7 to 10 percent of the transaction amount, the justification being that they are charged this amount by the credit card companies and can't afford to absorb the cost because of their smaller sales volume. Visa and MasterCard are the most widely accepted.

ATMs in Guatemala are hooked up to international networks and most travelers have no problems accessing their bank accounts in this way. It's always a good idea to keep an eye on transactions online while you're on the road if you're able to and report any inconsistencies immediately. You will never be required to enter your pin number on a pad to enter an ATM kiosk, a common scam to steal card and PIN numbers that has fooled some travelers. Always be aware of your surroundings and try not to visit the ATM at night or unaccompanied.

You can search for Visa ATM locations in Guatemala online at http://visa.via.info now.net/locator/global/jsp/SearchPage.jsp and MasterCard ATMs at www.mastercard .com/atm. A useful listing of Banco Industrial Visa ATMs throughout Guatemala can be found at www.bi.com.gt/Cajeros-BI_ body.htm. This will give you an idea of the availability of ATMs along your planned travel route.

COMMUNICATIONS AND MEDIA

Postal Services

Guatemala's postal service, known as El Correo, was privatized a few years back and placed in the very capable hands of a Canadian company, making it much more reliable than it once was. It's also fairly inexpensive, though a letter to the United States might take three weeks to arrive at its destination. International couriers such as Federal Express, UPS, and DHL also have a sizable presence here, along with several local companies used largely by Guatemalan expats living in the United States. The latter are substantially more affordable.

Telephone Service

Guatemala's country code is 502. There are no separate area or city codes. All phone numbers, save a few emergency numbers, are eight digits long. There are also a few toll-free numbers belonging to airlines and services that begin with 1-801. The national telephone service was privatized in 1999 and is now known as Telgua. A number of other phone companies, including Spanish Telefónica also operate here, providing some welcome competition. Each of the local phone companies have its own dialing codes for calling the United States from a land line, which will save you money. Most travelers, however, end up using any of the numerous phone centers in major tourist cities, from where you can call fairly cheaply to anywhere in the world. (These are covered in the appropriate geographical sections and are almost always housed in the same places offering Internet services.) Telgua also has call centers in major cities.

The most convenient and cheapest way to call home (and be able to call hotels and make reservations while on the road) is to have a cell phone. The most popular phone network is Tigo, which likewise has the widest coverage and charges by the second, saving you money in the long run. Rates for domestic calls are about $0.16 a minute and you can call the United States for about $0.12 a minute. You can buy a phone locally, with the cheapest somewhere around $45, or bring one with you and use it in Guatemala if it's a GSM phone. The Tigo frequency is 850 MHZ. Your phone's SIM card will need to be replaced with a Tigo SIM card, available for about $7. If your phone is locked, you will need to have a technician perform a *flasheo* to unlock it, costing about another $7. Most places selling cell phones can do this for you. You can buy talk time almost everywhere, available by buying cards in various denominations, which you then call in and have credited to your account. After your trip, you can put your original SIM card back in your phone.

Internet

Internet access is widely available in most cities and tourist destinations throughout the country. You'll have no trouble finding places to check your email or surf the web. Hourly rates are usually in the $1–2 range.

Newspapers and Magazines

Prensa Libre is Guatemala's most widely circulated newspaper and is highly respected. You can find the online version at www.prensa libre.com.gt. Other excellent newspapers include *Siglo XXI* (www.sigloxxi.com) and *elPeriódico* (www.elperiodico.com.gt). All of these are tabloid, rather than broadsheet, in format. A tabloid in the sense of being filled with plenty of yellow journalism, scandal, and not much else of use is *Nuestro Diario,* which nonetheless seems to be somewhat popular in the country's interior. Guatemala's respectable newspapers are an excellent source of information and make a great way to practice reading Spanish. They have a long tradition of investigative reporting and have done a wonderful job of uncovering numerous scandals Guatemala's corrupt politicians would probably get away with (at least without public knowledge) were it not for the work of these intrepid journalists. Journalism can still be a dangerous occupation in Guatemala, though press freedom has come a long way since the dark times of the civil war.

Published in Antigua, the monthly *Revue* magazine has tons of helpful tips and contact information for hotels, restaurants, and businesses in Guatemala as well as parts of Honduras and El Salvador. There are also well-written stories on topics of interest to locals and visitors alike. It's available in tourist shops, hotels, and restaurants free of charge.

TV

Guatemala has a handful of local channels, though cable TV with channels beamed in from the United States is also widely available. The country also has its own cable network, Guatevisión, with a morning show and some entertaining programs covering recreational options throughout the country.

MAPS AND TOURIST INFORMATION
Maps

Recently introduced, Mapas de Guatemala (www.mapasdeguatemala.com) makes an excellent series of beautifully illustrated full-color maps of Guatemala's main tourist regions, which also include helpful information on local businesses. The free maps are available at INGUAT as well as tourist gift shops and restaurants throughout the country. If you need a good map before leaving for Guatemala, ITMB Publishing (530 W. Broadway, Vancouver, BC, Canada, 604/879-3621, www.itmb.com) publishes an excellent *International Travel Map of Guatemala* ($10.95), which is weatherproof and can be found at well-known bookstores in the United States.

Tourist Information

The Guatemala Tourist Commission (INGUAT) provides tourist information from its offices in major tourist areas and the country's two international airports. It is also in charge of promoting Guatemala internationally and you may see ads for Guatemala in travel magazines from time to time. Unfortunately, it's not the catchiest advertising, and chances are you missed it. Still, INGUAT deserves credit for its attractive country logo developed with information gleaned from marketing studies and unveiled

Guatemala *soul of the earth*

© INGUAT

Guatemala country logo

in 2005. It consists of a dark oval embedded inside a multicolored ring and the slogan, "Soul of the earth," which pretty much describes Guatemala.

INGUAT does a fairly good job with its mandate and has been instrumental in the organization of community-based tourism providers. It also participates in international tourism fairs promoting Guatemala, provides logistical support for travel journalists covering the country for international publications, keeps tabs on hotel pricing standards, and is credited with wooing airlines to begin service to Guatemala.

INGUAT's central office is in Guatemala City's Zona 4 at 7a Avenida 1-17 and its website is www.visitguatemala.com.

WEIGHTS AND MEASURES
Time
Guatemala is six hours behind GMT and in the same time zone as U.S. Central Standard Time. Hours of daylight do not vary greatly between seasons, but daylight saving time is sometimes observed, depending on the whims of individual governments. It was observed in the summer of 2006 but not in 2007. Check locally for the latest.

Electricity
Nearly all outlets are 110 volts, 60 cycles with outlets for plugs consisting of parallel flat blades just like the ones found in the United States, Canada, and Mexico. Power outages and electrical surges are common in rural areas, especially during unusually arid dry seasons or very wet rainy seasons in thunderstorms. Be extra careful with sensitive equipment such as laptop computers.

Measurements
Like the American and European influences on its culture, Guatemala uses a sometimes confusing mixture of weights and measures from both the metric and old English systems. Fruits and vegetables are weighed by the pound, but folks weigh themselves in kilos; gas is dispensed in gallons but distances are computed in kilometers, and so on and so forth.

Another commonly used distance measurement is the *vara,* equivalent to 0.84 meters or a little less than a yard. For measuring land areas, the *manzana* equals about 0.7 hectare or 1.7 acres and the *caballería* covers a little more than 45 hectares or 111.5 acres. The *quintal* is widely used for weighing coffee and is the equivalent of 46 kilos.

RESOURCES

Glossary

aduana customs

agua literally "water" but also used in reference to soda pop

agua pura bottled water

aguas termales hot springs

aguardiente cane alcohol or moonshine

alcalde mayor

alfombra a colorful carpet made of sawdust and flowers central to Holy Week celebrations in Antigua and elsewhere in Guatemala

altense a resident of Quetzaltenango

al tiempo referring to drinks at room temperature

altiplano the highlands

artesanías handicrafts

avenida avenue

ayudante in cheap public buses, the man who helps the driver in collecting fares and helping passengers with baggage

bajo lowland swampy areas of the Petén lowlands

balneario a bathing or swimming hole

baño compartido/general shared bath (in reference to accommodations)

baño privado private bathroom

barranco a ravine

baule a leatherback turtle

billares pool or billiards

billete a banknote or bill

bistec beef steak

bolo drunk; also *borracho*

brujo a male witch or sorcerer

cajero automático automated teller machine (ATM)

calle street

camioneta a second-class bus

campesino peasant farmer

canícula a brief one- or two-week dry spell during the rainy summer months of July/August

cantina a seedy bar

caoba mahogany

casa de huéspedes a guesthouse

cayuco canoe

cerveza beer

champa thatched-roof, wall-less structure

chapín/chapina what Guatemalans call themselves

chichicaste a stinging plant somewhat like poison ivy

chiclero a tapper of chewing-gum resin of the jungle Petén region

coche a pig, not a car, as in other parts of Latin America

cofradía traditional political-religious organization present in some highland Mayan communities

comedor a simple eatery

corte traditional wraparound skirt worn by Mayan women

costumbre traditional Mayan religious practices that include offerings of flowers, candles, and sometimes animal sacrifices

coyote a smuggler of undocumented immigrants across Mexico and into the United States

criollo Guatemalan of Spanish heritage

cucurucho costumed carriers of procession parade floats during Semana Santa celebrations

curandero traditional healer or shaman

edificio a building; used in street addresses in urban areas

encomienda a colonial system enabling landholders to exact tribute and labor from the local indigenous population

farmacia de turno a pharmacy that remains open all night on a rotating basis

finca a farm of any type but usually referring to a coffee farm

hospedaje inexpensive family-run accommodations

ingenio a sugar mill

invierno literally "winter" but used to describe the May–October rainy season

IVA short for *impuesto al valor agregado* (value added tax) VAT; in Guatemala it's 12 percent

ladino a person of indigenous descent who has adopted European ways

lancha small motorboat

latifundia large landholding in the form of a plantation or hacienda

lavandería laundry

machista a male chauvanist

maquiladora an industrial plant where clothes are assembled for reexport by cheap local labor; more commonly known in the United States as a "sweat shop"

mara a gang but also used to describe a "gang" in the manner referring to an agglomeration of people or a crowd

mestizo person of mixed Spanish-Indian descent

milpa a maize or corn plant; also sometimes used in reference to a cornfield

minifundia small landholdings, usually in the hands of Mayan peasantry

morería small crafts shop producing costumes and masks for traditional dancing

palapa a high-ceilinged thatched-roof structure commonly used in restaurant or hotel architecture

parlama green sea turtle

parque nacional national park

pensión inexpensive accommodations

petate a reed mat

picop pickup truck

Pullman a first-class bus, though to varying degrees of newness and quality

rancho a simple thatched structure; also sometimes referred to in its diminutive *ranchito.*

recargo a surcharge; usually associated with credit card transactions

refacción snack time between lunch and dinner; also on menus as *refacciones* consisting of pastries and sandwiches

repatriado returned civil war refugee, usually from Mexico

reserva natural privada a privately owned nature preserve

reserva protectora de manantiales a watershed protection preserve

retablo an altarpiece in a colonial church

revueltos scrambled (eggs)

ron rum

sacbe once-paved Mayan causeways present in the modern-day lowlands of Petén and still used as footpaths

stela (stelae) pre-Columbian stone monuments, usually carved

timbre a type of stamp sold in banks used in paying fees such as visa renewals

traje traditional Mayan costume worn by inhabitants of individual highland villages

túmulo a speed bump

verano literally "summer," but usually in reference to the height of the dry season between March and the beginning of the rainy season in May

zafra sugarcane harvest in the Pacific lowlands

zancudo mosquito

zona a city zone into which Guatemala's principal urban areas are divided

Spanish Phrasebook

Your Guatemalan adventure will be more fun if you use a little Spanish. Though Guatemalans may smile at your funny accent, they will certainly appreciate your halting efforts to break the ice and transform yourself from a foreigner into a potential friend.

Spanish commonly uses 30 letters—the familiar English 26, plus four straightforward additions: ch, ll, ñ, and rr, which are explained in *Consonants*.

PRONUNCIATION

Spanish pronunciation rules are straightforward and easy to learn, because—in contrast to English—they don't change. Spanish vowels generally sound softer than in English. (Note: The capitalized syllables below receive stronger accents.)

Vowels

a like ah, as in "hah": *agua* AH-gooah (water), *pan* PAHN (bread), and *casa* CAH-sah (house)

e like ay, as in "may:" *mesa* MAY-sah (table), *tela* TAY-lah (cloth), and *de* DAY (of, from)

i like ee, as in "need": *diez* dee-AYZ (10), *comida* ko-MEE-dah (meal), and *fin* FEEN (end)

o like oh, as in "go": *peso* PAY-soh (weight), *ocho* OH-choh (eight), and *poco* POH-koh (a bit)

u like oo, as in "cool": *uno* OO-noh (one), *cuarto* KOOAHR-toh (room), and *usted* oos-TAYD (you); when it follows a "q" the **u** is silent; when it follows an "h" or has an umlaut, it's pronounced like "w"

Consonants

b, ch, d, f, k, l, m, n, p, q, s, t, v, w, x, y, z pronounced almost as in English; h occurs, but is silent – not pronounced at all.

c like k as in "keep": *cuarto* KOOAR-toh (room), *corazón* kor-a-SOHN (heart); when it precedes "e" or "i," pronounce **c** like s, as in "sit": *cerveza* sayr-VAY-sah (beer), *encima* ayn-SEE-mah (atop).

g like g as in "gift" when it precedes "a," "o," "u," or a consonant: *gato* GAH-toh (cat), *hago* AH-goh (I do, make); otherwise, pronounce **g** like h as in "hat": *giro* HEE-roh (money order), *gente* HAYN-tay (people)

j like h, as in "has": *jueves* HOOAY-vays (Thursday), *mejor* may-HOR (better)

ll like y, as in "yes": *toalla* toh-AH-yah (towel), *ellos* AY-yohs (they, them)

ñ like ny, as in "canyon": *año* AH-nyo (year), *señor* SAY-nyor (Mr., sir)

r is lightly trilled, with tongue at the roof of your mouth like a very light English r, as in "ready": *pero* PAY-roh (but), *tres* TRAYS (three), *cuatro* KOOAH-troh (four).

rr like a Spanish r, but with much more emphasis and trill. Let your tongue flap. Practice with *burro* (donkey), *carretera* (highway), and Carrillo (proper name), then really let go with *ferrocarril* (railroad).

Note: The single small but common exception to all of the above is the pronunciation of Spanish **y** when it's being used as the Spanish word for "and," as in "Ron y Kathy." In such case, pronounce it like the English ee, as in "keep": Ron "ee" Kathy (Ron and Kathy).

Accent

Native English speakers often make errors of pronunciation by ignoring accented, or stressed, syllables. All Spanish vowels—a, e, i, o, and u—may carry accents determining which syllable of a word is emphasized.

The rule for accent, the relative stress given to syllables within a given word, is straightforward. If a word ends in a vowel, an n, or an s, accent the next-to-last syllable; if not, accent the last syllable.

Pronounce **gracias** GRAH-seeahs (thank you), **orden** OHR-dayn (order), and **carretera** kah-ray-TAY-rah (highway) with stress on the next-to-last syllable.

Otherwise, accent the last syllable: **venir**

vay-NEER (to come), **ferrocarril** fay-roh-cah-REEL (railroad), and **edad** ay-DAHD (age).

Exceptions to the accent rule are always marked with an accent sign: (á, é, í, ó, or ú), such as **teléfono** tay-LAY-foh-noh (telephone), **jabón** hah-BON (soap), and **rápido** RAH-pee-doh (rapid).

NUMBERS

zero cero
one uno
two dos
three tres
four cuatro
five cinco
six seis
seven siete
eight ocho
nine nueve
10 diez
11 once
12 doce
13 trece
14 catorce
15 quince
16 dieciseis
17 diecisiete
18 dieciocho
19 diecinueve
20 veinte
21 veinte y uno or veintiuno
30 treinta
40 cuarenta
50 cincuenta
60 sesenta
70 setenta
80 ochenta
90 noventa
100 cien
101 ciento y uno
200 doscientos
500 quinientos
1,000 mil
10,000 diez mil
100,000 cien mil
1,000,000 millón
one-half medio
one-third un tercio
one-fourth un cuarto

TIME

What time is it? ¿Qué hora es?
It's one o'clock. Es la una.
It's three in the afternoon. Son las tres de la tarde.
It's 4 A.M. Son las cuatro de la mañana.
six-thirty seis y media
a quarter till eleven un cuarto para las once
a quarter past five las cinco y cuarto
an hour una hora
today hoy
tomorrow mañana
yesterday ayer
a week una semana
a month un mes
a year un año
after después
before antes
last night anoche
the next day el día siguiente

DAYS OF THE WEEK

Monday lunes
Tuesday martes
Wednesday miércoles
Thursday jueves
Friday viernes
Saturday sábado
Sunday domingo

MONTHS

January enero
February febrero
March marzo
April abril
May mayo
June junio
July julio
August agosto
September septiembre
October octubre
November noviembre
December diciembre

BASIC AND COURTEOUS EXPRESSIONS

Most Spanish-speaking people consider formalities important. Whenever approaching anyone for information or some other reason, do not forget the appropriate salutation—good morning, good evening, and so forth. Standing alone, the greeting *hola* (hello) can sound brusque.

Hello. *Hola.*
Good morning. *Buenos días.*
Good afternoon. *Buenas tardes.*
Good evening. *Buenas noches.*
How are you? *¿Cómo está usted?*
Very well, thank you. *Muy bien, gracias.*
Okay; good. *Bien.*
Not okay; bad. *Mal or feo.*
So-so. *Más o menos.*
And you? *¿Y usted?*
Thank you. *Gracias.*
Thank you very much. *Muchas gracias.*
You're very kind. *Muy amable.*
You're welcome. *De nada.*
Good-bye. *Adios.*
See you later. *Hasta luego.*
please *por favor*
yes *sí*
no *no*
I don't know. *No sé.*
Just a moment, please. *Momentito, por favor.*
Excuse me, please (when you're trying to get attention). *Disculpe or Con permiso.*
Excuse me (when you've made a boo-boo). *Lo siento.*
Pleased to meet you. *Mucho gusto.*
What is your name? *¿Cómo se llama usted?*
Do you speak English? *¿Habla usted inglés?*
Is English spoken here? (Does anyone here speak English?) *¿Se habla inglés?*
I don't speak Spanish well. *No hablo bien el español.*
I don't understand. *No entiendo.*
How do you say . . . in Spanish? *¿Cómo se dice . . . en español?*
My name is . . . *Me llamo . . .*
Would you like . . . *¿Quisiera usted . . .*
Let's go to . . . *Vamos a . . .*

TERMS OF ADDRESS

When in doubt, use the formal *usted* (you) as a form of address.

I *yo*
you (formal) *usted*
you (familiar) *tu*
he/him *él*
she/her *ella*
we/us *nosotros*
you (plural) *ustedes*
they/them *ellos* (all males or mixed gender); *ellas* (all females)
Mr., sir *señor*
Mrs., madam *señora*
miss, young lady *señorita*
wife *esposa*
husband *esposo*
friend *amigo* (male); *amiga* (female)
sweetheart *novio* (male); *novia* (female)
son; daughter *hijo; hija*
brother; sister *hermano; hermana*
father; mother *padre; madre*
grandfather; grandmother *abuelo; abuela*

TRANSPORTATION

Where is . . . ? *¿Dónde está . . . ?*
How far is it to . . . ? *¿A cuánto está . . . ?*
from . . . to . . . *de . . . a . . .*
How many blocks? *¿Cuántas cuadras?*
Where (Which) is the way to . . . ? *¿Dónde está el camino a . . . ?*
the bus station *la terminal de autobuses*
the bus stop *la parada de autobuses*
Where is this bus going? *¿Adónde va este autobús?*
the taxi stand *la parada de taxis*
the train station *la estación de ferrocarril*
the boat *el barco*
the airport *el aeropuerto*
I'd like a ticket to . . . *Quisiera un boleto a . . .*
first (second) class *primera (segunda) clase*
round-trip *ida y vuelta*
reservation *reservación*
baggage *equipaje*
Stop here, please. *Pare aquí, por favor.*
the entrance *la entrada*

the exit *la salida*
the ticket office *la oficina de boletos*
(very) near; far *(muy) cerca; lejos*
to; toward *a*
by; through *por*
from *de*
the right *la derecha*
the left *la izquierda*
straight ahead *recto*
in front *en frente*
beside *al lado*
behind *atrás*
the corner *la esquina*
the stoplight *el semáforo*
a turn *una vuelta*
right here *aquí*
somewhere around here *por acá*
right there *allí*
somewhere around there *por allá*
street; boulevard *calle; bulevar*
highway *carretera*
bridge; toll *puente; peaje*
address *dirección*
north; south *norte; sur*
east; west *oriente (este); poniente (oeste)*

ACCOMMODATIONS

hotel *hotel*
Is there a room? *¿Hay cuarto?*
May I (may we) see it? *¿Puedo (podemos) verlo?*
What is the rate? *¿Cuál es el precio?*
Is that your best rate? *¿Es su mejor precio?*
Is there something cheaper? *¿Hay algo más económico?*
a single room *un cuarto sencillo*
a double room *un cuarto doble*
double bed *cama matrimonial*
twin beds *camas gemelas*
with private bath *con baño*
hot water *agua caliente*
shower *ducha*
towels *toallas*
soap *jabón*
toilet paper *papel higiénico*
blanket *frazada; chamarra*
sheets *sábanas*
air-conditioned *aire acondicionado*

fan *ventilador*
key *llave*
manager *gerente*

FOOD

I'm hungry *Tengo hambre.*
I'm thirsty. *Tengo sed.*
menu *lista; menú*
order *orden*
glass *vaso*
fork *tenedor*
knife *cuchillo*
spoon *cuchara*
napkin *servilleta*
soft drink *refresco*
coffee *café*
tea *té*
drinking water *agua pura; agua potable*
bottled carbonated water *agua mineral*
bottled uncarbonated water *agua sin gas*
beer *cerveza*
wine *vino*
milk *leche*
juice *jugo*
cream *crema*
sugar *azúcar*
cheese *queso*
snack *refacción*
breakfast *desayuno*
lunch *almuerzo*
daily lunch special *el menú del día*
dinner *cena*
the check *la cuenta*
eggs *huevos*
bread *pan*
salad *ensalada*
fruit *fruta*
mango *mango*
watermelon *sandía*
papaya *papaya*
banana *banano*
apple *manzana*
orange *naranja*
plantain *plátano*
lime *limón*
fish *pescado*
shellfish *mariscos*
shrimp *camarones*

meat (without) *(sin) carne*
chicken *pollo*
pork *puerco*
beef; steak *res; bistec*
bacon; ham *tocino; jamón*
fried *frito*
roasted *asada*
barbecue; barbecued *barbacoa; al carbón*

SHOPPING
money *dinero*
money-exchange bureau *casa de cambio*
I would like to exchange travelers checks. *Quisiera cambiar cheques de viajero.*
What is the exchange rate? *¿Cuál es el tipo de cambio?*
How much is the commission? *¿Cuánto cuesta la comisión?*
Do you accept credit cards? *¿Aceptan tarjetas de crédito?*
money order *giro*
How much does it cost? *¿Cuánto cuesta?*
What is your final price? *¿Cuál es su último precio?*
expensive *caro*
cheap *barato; económico*
more *más*
less *menos*
a little *un poco*
too much *demasiado*

HEALTH
Help me please. *Ayúdeme por favor.*
I am ill. *Estoy enfermo.*
Call a doctor. *Llame un doctor.*
Take me to . . . *Lléveme a . . .*
hospital *hospital; sanatorio*
drugstore *farmacia*
pain *dolor*
fever *fiebre*
headache *dolor de cabeza*
stomach ache *dolor de estómago*
burn *quemadura*
cramp *calambre*
nausea *náusea*
vomiting *vomitar*
medicine *medicina*

antibiotic *antibiótico*
pill; tablet *pastilla*
aspirin *aspirina*
ointment; cream *pomada; crema*
bandage *venda*
cotton *algodón*
sanitary napkins use brand name, e.g., Kotex
birth control pills *pastillas anticonceptivas*
contraceptive foam *espuma anticonceptiva*
condoms *preservativos; condones*
toothbrush *cepillo dental*
dental floss *hilo dental*
toothpaste *crema dental*
dentist *dentista*
toothache *dolor de muelas*

POST OFFICE AND COMMUNICATIONS
long-distance telephone *teléfono de larga distancia*
I would like to call . . . *Quisiera llamar a . . .*
collect *a cobrar*
station to station *a quien contesta*
person to person *persona a persona*
credit card *tarjeta de crédito*
post office *correo*
general delivery *lista de correo*
letter *carta*
stamp *estampilla, timbre*
postcard *postal*
air mail *correo aéreo*
registered *registrado*
money order *giro*
package; box *paquete; caja*
string; tape *cuerda; cinta*

AT THE BORDER
border *frontera*
customs *aduana*
immigration *migración*
tourist card *tarjeta de turista*
inspection *inspección; revisión*
passport *pasaporte*
profession *profesión*
marital status *estado civil*

single *soltero*
married; divorced *casado; divorciado*
widowed *enviudado*
insurance *seguros*
title *título*
driver's license *licencia de conducir*
gas station *gasolinera*
car *carro*
gasoline *gasolina*
unleaded *sin plomo*
full, please *lleno, por favor*
tire *llanta*
tire repair shop *vulcanizadora* or *pinchazo*
air *aire*
water *agua*
oil (change) *(cambio de) aceite*
grease *grasa*
My . . . doesn't work. *Mi . . . no sirve.*
battery *batería*
radiator *radiador*
alternator *alternador*
generator *generador*
tow truck *grúa*
repair shop *taller mecánico*
tune-up *afinación* or *tune-up*

VERBS

Verbs are the key to getting along in Spanish. They employ mostly predictable forms and come in three classes, which end in *ar*, *er*, and *ir*, respectively:

to buy *comprar*
I buy, you (he, she, it) buys *compro, compra*
we buy, you (they) buy *compramos, compran*
to eat *comer*
I eat, you (he, she, it) eats *como, come*
we eat, you (they) eat *comemos, comen*
to climb *subir*
I climb, you (he, she, it) climbs *subo, sube*
we climb, you (they) climb *subimos, suben*

Here are more (with irregularities indicated).

to do or make *hacer* (regular except for *hago*, I do or make)
to go *ir* (very irregular: *voy, va, vamos, van*)
to go (walk) *andar*
to love *amar*
to work *trabajar*
to want *desear, querer*
to need *necesitar*
to read *leer*
to write *escribir*
to repair *reparar*
to stop *parar*
to get off (the bus) *bajar*
to arrive *llegar*
to stay (remain) *quedar*
to stay (lodge) *hospedar*
to leave *salir* (regular except for *salgo*, I leave)
to look at *mirar*
to look for *buscar*
to give *dar* (regular except for *doy*, I give)
to carry *llevar*
to have *tener* (irregular but important: *tengo, tiene, tenemos, tienen*)
to come *venir* (similarly irregular: *vengo, viene, venimos, vienen*)

Spanish has two forms of "to be:"

to be *estar* (regular except for *estoy*, I am)
to be *ser* (very irregular: *soy, es, somos, son*)

Use *estar* when speaking of location or a temporary state of being: "I am at home." *"Estoy en casa." "*I'm sick." *"Estoy enfermo."* Use *ser* for a permanent state of being: "I am a doctor." *"Soy doctora."*

Suggested Reading

HISTORY AND POLITICS
Pre-Columbian History

Coe, Michael D. *Breaking the Maya Code.* New York: Thames and Hudson, 1999. Chronicles the work of several scolars involved in the eventual decipherment of the meaning behind the Mayan glyphs.

Coe, Michael D. *The Maya,* 7th edition. New York: Thames and Hudson, 2005. A classic reference manual on the Mayans and essential guide for the traveler that includes useful color plates.

Demarest, Arthur. *Ancient Maya: The Rise and Fall of a Rainforest Civilization.* Cambridge: Cambridge University Press, 2005. Written by a prominent archaeologist who has worked on numerous projects in Guatemala, this book explores the ecological aspects of the rise of Mayan civilization and the role of internecine warfare in its demise.

Harrison, Peter. *The Lords of Tikal: Rulers of an Ancient Maya City.* New York: Thames and Hudson, 2000. Traces the history of Tikal from its humble beginning to its apogee in the late 9th century A.D.

Montgomery, John. *Tikal: An Illustrated History of the Ancient Maya Capital.* New York: Hippocrene Books, 2000. Wonderfully illustrated with photos, maps, and drawings, this is a good introduction to Tikal for the visitor and casual Mayanist.

Colonial Era

Lovell, W. George. *Conquest and Survival in Colonial Guatemala: A Historical Geography of the Cuchumatán Highlands,* 3rd edition. Kingston, Ontario: McGill-Queen's University Press, 2004. Quickly becoming a classic, this landmark work covers the Spanish conquest and the survival of the local indigenous culture despite the ravages of colonial legacies while linking the roots of the past in more recent sociopolitical conditions.

Civil War

Arnson, Cynthia J., editor. *Comparative Peace Processes in Latin America.* Washington, D.C.: Woodrow Wilson Center Press, 1999. Provides a good analysis of the peace process that led to a negotiated settlement of the civil war in Guatemala and other countries as well as issues concerning the roles of truth-telling reports, the search for justice, and reconciliation.

Burgos-Debray, Elizabeth, editor. *I, Rigoberta Menchú: An Indian Woman in Guatemala.* London: Verso, 1984. The classic autobiography of Nobel Peace Prize winner Rigoberta Menchú.

Grandin, Greg. *The Last Colonial Massacre: Latin America in the Cold War.* Chicago: The University of Chicago Press, 2004. This thought-provoking book argues that the Latin American Cold War was actually a struggle between two differing notions of democracy, with its main achievement being the elimination of grassroots attempts at building social democracy. It uses Guatemala as a case study and concludes, somewhat convincingly, that the version of democracy now being extolled as the best option in the war against terror is itself a product of the same.

Handy, Jim. *Revolution in the Countryside: Rural Conflict and Agrarian Reform in Guatemala, 1944–1954.* Chapel Hill: The University of North Carolina Press, 1994. A good in-depth look at the Agrarian Reform Law and the Guatemalan political scene during the Arévalo and Arbenz years.

Manz, Beatriz. *Paradise in Ashes: A Guatemalan Journey of Courage, Terror, and Hope.* Berkeley: University of California Press, 2004.

Written by an anthropologist, this book centers around the Ixcán village of Santa María Tzejá, whose inhabitants were caught in the violence between the guerrillas and military during the civil war.

Perera, Víctor. *Unfinished Conquest: The Guatemalan Tragedy.* Berkeley: University of California Press, 1993. A must-read for travelers to Guatemala, covering sociopolitical aspects of the Guatemalan civil war as well as environmental issues in a well-written travel narrative style.

Sanford, Victoria. *Buried Secrets: Truth and Human Rights in Guatemala.* New York: Palgrave Macmillan, 2004. A highly recommended read with well-researched information from a number of different sources, including eyewitness testimonies from massacre survivors, interviews with members of forensic teams, human rights workers, high-ranking military officers, guerrillas, and government officials. It is an instrumental book for understanding the full scale of the genocidal civil war and the attempt to rebuild society in its aftermath.

Schlesinger, Stephen C., and Stephen Kinzer. *Bitter Fruit: The Story of the American Coup in Guatemala.* Cambridge: Harvard University Press, 2005. This is a classic book on Guatemala and its historical relationship with the United States. First published in 1982, it covers in much detail the 1954 CIA-orchestrated coup ousting Jacobo Arbenz.

Stoll, David. *Between Two Armies in the Ixil Towns of Guatemala.* New York: Columbia University Press, 1993. A controversial book postulating the theory that the Ixil Mayans of Nebaj, Chajul, and Cotzal were not so much enamored with revolutionary possibilities for social change as much as simply caught between the opposing fires of the military and guerrilla forces with widely differing sociopolitical agendas.

Stoll, David. *Rigoberta Menchú and the Story of All Poor Guatemalans.* Boulder, Colorado:

Westview Press, 1999. Also quite controversial, this work directly challenges much of the testimony presented by Rigoberta Menchú in her autobiography as embellishments or fabrications while granting that the atrocities described therein were accurate depictions of events during the civil war.

Wilkinson, Daniel. *Silence on the Mountain: Stories of Terror, Betrayal, and Forgetting in Guatemala.* New York: Houghton Mifflin, 2002. Part travelogue and part history book, this is a fascinating, well-written account of the American author's experience in Guatemala; it manages to uncover many of the issues relating to the origins and unfolding of Guatemala's civil war as told by those who survived the violence.

Central America

LaFeber, Walter. *Inevitable Revolutions: The United States in Central America.* New York: W. W. Norton, 1993. Traces the historical roots of Central America's armed conflicts along with the role of U.S. hegemony in perpetuating them.

TRAVELOGUES AND LITERATURE
Travelogues

Benz, Stephen Connely. *Guatemalan Journey.* Austin: University of Texas Press, 1996. A humorous, insightful, and well-written account of an American traveler's experiences living in Guatemala during the late 1980s.

Huxley, Aldous. *Beyond the Mexique Bay.* New York: Harper and Brothers Publishers, 1934. A classic take on early 20th-century travel in Guatemala by a well-known author.

Shaw, Christopher. *Sacred Monkey River: A Canoe Trip with the Gods.* New York: W. W. Norton, 2000. A superbly written adventure-travel narrative packed with historical and natural history anecdotes about the mighty

Usumacinta River, which flows along the Mexico-Guatemala border.

Stephens, John Lloyd. *Incidents of Travel in Central America, Chiapas and Yucatán.* New York: Dover Publications, 1969. A classic book and a must-read for the traveler to Guatemala, also featuring the fantastic illustrations of Stephens's friend and traveling companion Frederick Catherwood. It created quite an interest in the region, particularly its Mayan sites, when it was first published in 1841.

Wright, Ronald. *Time Among the Maya: Travels in Belize, Guatemala and Mexico.* New York: Grove/Atlantic, 2000. Another good read with insights on culture, history, adventure, and anthropology by a writer with an evident love for the modern-day Mayan people.

Fiction

Goldman, Francisco. *The Long Night of White Chickens.* New York: Grove/Atlantic, 1998. This well-written novel is a tale of intrigue set in 1980s Guatemala governed by military dictatorships. It's an entertaining read and does a nice job of bridging the gap between the seemingly parallel worlds of the United States and Guatemala.

ART

Gieseman, Peter, and Ange Bourda. *Six Architects.* Bogotá: Villegas Editores, 2003. An art-photography book documenting the architecture of the Guatemala City *Seis Arquitectos* firm.

Moller, Jonathan. *Our Culture Is Our Resistance: Repression, Refuge and Healing in Guatemala.* New York: PowerHouse Books, 2004. A beautiful photographic collection of highland Mayan culture in the aftermath of the civil war with wonderful guest commentaries from Rigoberta Menchú, Francisco Goldman, and various other authors of books on Guatemala.

NATURAL HISTORY

Beletsky, Les. *Traveller's Wildlife Guides: Belize and Northern Guatemala.* Northampton: Interlink Books, 2005.

Lee, Julian C. *Field Guide to the Amphibians and Reptiles of the Maya World: The Lowlands of Mexico, Northern Guatemala and Belize.* Ithaca: Cornell University Press, 2000.

Peterson, Roger Tory, and Edward L. Chalif. *A Field Guide to Mexican Birds: Mexico, Guatemala, Belize, El Salvador.* New York: Houghton Mifflin, 1999. Describes and illustrates 1,038 species.

Primack, Richard B., et al., eds. *Timber, Tourists, and Temples: Conservation and Development in the Maya Forest of Belize, Guatemala, and Mexico.* Washington, D.C.: Island Press, 1998. Covers the delicate political and social issues implicated in conserving the region's remaining rainforests as told from the perspective of social scientists, conservationists, and biologists working in the field.

Internet Resources

GENERAL INFORMATION

www.prensalibre.com.gt
www.sigloxxi.com
www.elperiodico.com.gt

If you can read Spanish (or want to use them to practice reading Spanish), Guatemala's main newspapers all have decent web pages.

http://guatemalapost.com

An English-language wrap-up of news on Guatemala from various sources.

http://lanic.utexas.edu/la/ca/guatemala

The University of Texas has compounded a comprehensive list of links on everything pertaining to Guatemala.

www.revuemag.com

The highly recommended *Revue* magazine (in English) can be downloaded online in PDF format.

TRAVEL AND ENVIRONMENT

www.planeta.com

An excellent website with plenty of information on ecotravel in Guatemala and elsewhere in Latin America.

www.visitguatemala.com

The Guatemala Tourist Commission (INGUAT) website with a variety of information on Guatemala.

http://senderonatural.com

A Guatemalan-run website dedicated to sustainable tourism in Guatemala with a variety of good recreational options and recommended accommodations.

LEARNING SPANISH

www.123teachme.com
www.guatemala365.com

Both sites have reviews and rankings made by former students in the recommended language schools.

VOLUNTEERING

www.idealist.org

International volunteer website listing several opportunities in Guatemala.

www.volunteeradventures.com

Features a few Guatemala projects looking for international volunteers, mainly in the areas of wildlife conservation and opportunities to teach English.

www.entremundos.org

Quetzaltenango-based organization with tons of information on volunteer opportunities in the Western Highlands.

DESTINATION-SPECIFIC SITES

Chisec
www.puertamundomaya.com

Cobán
www.cobanav.net

Guatemala City
www.muniguate.com

Lívingston
www.livingston.com.gt

Nebaj
www.nebaj.com

Pachalum
www.pachalum.com

Quetzaltenango
www.xelawho.com
www.xelapages.com
www.xelapages.net

Uspantán
www.uspantan.com

Semuc Champey
www.semucchampey.com

Index

N

OP

Acknowledgments

This guidebook would not have been possible without the help and inspiration of several folks to whom I owe my gratitude. First, I'd like to thank my Creator for his omnipresent love and inspiration, which are always available to help, comfort, strengthen, and encourage. I'd also like to thank my parents for their support, for planting in me a love for both Guatemala and the United States, and allowing me to experience the best of both worlds.

In Austin, I'd like to thank Shanna Offutt for providing some needed encouragement, and lots of love, along the way. My friends and housemates Ryan Bowers and Micah Behrens I'd like to thank for providing me with meals when I had barely enough time to eat, let alone cook, and for putting up with my crazy antics induced from long days staring at the computer screen. Jared Cullison put together a variety of set props to create my author picture, which I'm thrilled with. Thanks, buddy. Props also go to Jack Johnson for the inspiration. Jared also made a great traveling companion on a previous trip.

Justin Brown made a great traveling companion in Petén and I enjoyed checking out the Mayan sites, restaurants, and accommodations with him. I'm up for trying the El Mirador trip again—in the dry season. You in?

At INGUAT my thanks go to Marlene de Sterkel and Migdalia de Barillas for providing logistical support and to my drivers Damián and Noé. I'd like to thank my family in Guatemala City and Huehuetenango for putting me up and providing a home away from home.

In Antigua, thanks go to Martha Hettich for several key recommendations, her excellent walking tour, and being my eyes and ears with some needed postvisit follow-ups. John Heaton and Catherine Docter I'd like to thank for their gracious hospitality. In Copán, I'd like to thank Flavia Cueva and the staff at Hacienda San Lucas for their hospitality and excellent service. I also enjoyed my visit to Carlos Castejón's coffee farm and made a new friend along the way. Thanks also to the folks at the Via Via.

In Guatemala City, I'd like to thank Axel Ramírez for his help with all things concerning the very important airport improvements. And though I wasn't able to hang out with my longtime pal Tammy Ridenour during my latest visit, thanks go out to her for allowing me to tag along on many of her adventurous trips through the years.

Finally, I'd like to thank the staff at Avalon Travel Publishing, especially my editor, Cinnamon Hearst, for all their hard work and help in making this book read and look its best. I'd like to thank my production coordinator, Nicole Schultz, for going the extra mile to make this book look its best. I'd like to thank Acquisitions Editor Rebecca Browning for believing in my talents as a guidebook writer and recognizing my love and enthusiasm for Guatemala.

www.moon.com

For helpful advice on planning a trip, visit www.moon.com for the **TRAVEL PLANNER** and get access to useful travel strategies and valuable information about great places to visit. When you travel with Moon, expect an experience that is uncommon and truly unique.

MAP SYMBOLS

▨ Expressway	◖ Highlight	✗ Airfield	⚲ Golf Course
▨ Primary Road	○ City/Town	✈ Airport	℗ Parking Area
▨ Secondary Road	◉ State Capital	▲ Mountain	⛰ Archaeological Site
▫ Unpaved Road	⊛ National Capital	✚ Unique Natural Feature	⛪ Church
▫ Trail	★ Point of Interest		⛽ Gas Station
⋯ Ferry	● Accommodation	🖏 Waterfall	Glacier
⊢⊢⊢ Railroad	▼ Restaurant/Bar	▲ Park	Mangrove
▨ Pedestrian Walkway	▪ Other Location	⊡ Trailhead	Reef
▨ Stairs	Λ Campground	⛷ Skiing Area	Swamp

CONVERSION TABLES

°C = (°F - 32) / 1.8
°F = (°C x 1.8) + 32
1 inch = 2.54 centimeters (cm)
1 foot = 0.304 meters (m)
1 yard = 0.914 meters
1 mile = 1.6093 kilometers (km)
1 km = 0.6214 miles
1 fathom = 1.8288 m
1 chain = 20.1168 m
1 furlong = 201.168 m
1 acre = 0.4047 hectares
1 sq km = 100 hectares
1 sq mile = 2.59 square km
1 ounce = 28.35 grams
1 pound = 0.4536 kilograms
1 short ton = 0.90718 metric ton
1 short ton = 2,000 pounds
1 long ton = 1.016 metric tons
1 long ton = 2,240 pounds
1 metric ton = 1,000 kilograms
1 quart = 0.94635 liters
1 US gallon = 3.7854 liters
1 Imperial gallon = 4.5459 liters
1 nautical mile = 1.852 km

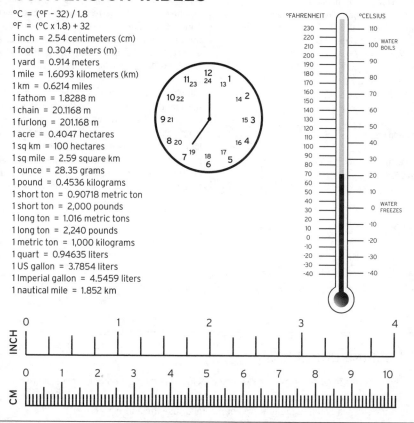

MOON GUATEMALA

Avalon Travel Publishing
a member of the Perseus Books Group
1400 65th Street, Suite 250
Emeryville, CA 94608, USA
www.moon.com

Editor: Cinnamon Hearst
Series Manager: Kathryn Ettinger
Acquisitions Manager: Rebecca K. Browning
Copy Editor: Karen Gaynor Bleske
Graphics Coordinator: Nicole Schultz
Production Coordinators: Nicole Schultz,
  Darren Alessi
Cover Designer: Nicole Schutz
Map Editor: Albert Angulo
Cartographers: Chris Markiewicz, Landis Bennett,
  and Kat Bennett
Cartography Director: Mike Morgenfeld
Indexer: Judy Hunt

ISBN-10: 1-59880-057-4
ISBN-13: 978-1-59880-057-9
ISSN: 1533-4201

Printing History
1st Edition – 2001
2nd Edition – October 2007
5 4 3 2 1

KEEPING CURRENT

If you have a favorite gem you'd like to see included in the next edition, or see anything that needs updating, clarification, or correction, please drop us a line. Send your comments via email to feedback@moon.com, or use the address above.